D1554232

# McGraw-Hill's
# Spanish and English Legal Dictionary

# Diccionario Jurídico Inglés-Español

## Dahl's Abridged Law Dictionary
## Diccionario Jurídico Abreviado Dahl

### Henry Saint Dahl

Attorney and Law Professor • Attorney in Washington, D.C., Texas, and New York; Abogado en Madrid y Buenos Aires • LL.M. (London, England), Stazhor (St. Petersburg, Russia) • Sworn Translator (English, French); Traductor Público Nacional (Buenos Aires, Argentina) • Visiting Law Professor Conservatoire National des Arts et Métiers (Paris, France) • Associate Director of the SMU NAFTA Law Center • Vice Presidente de la Cámara de Comercio Panamericana • Special Counsel to Jones, Walker, Waechter, Poitevent, Carrère & Denègre

With the collaboration of Tamera Boudreau
Member of the Texas Bar

## McGraw·Hill

New York   Chicago   San Francisco   Lisbon   London   Madrid   Mexico City
Milan   New Delhi   San Juan   Seoul   Singapore   Sydney   Toronto

1 2 3 4 5 6 7 8 9 0   AGM/AGM   2 1 0 9 8 7 6 5 4 3

ISBN 0-07-141529-7

Interior design by Terry Stone

McGraw-Hill books are available at special quantity discounts to use as premiums and sales promotions, or for use in corporate training programs. For more information, please write to the Director of Special Sales, Professional Publishing, McGraw-Hill, Two Penn Plaza, New York, NY 10121-2298. Or contact your local bookstore.

This book is printed on acid-free paper.

*For Tammy, Wills, and Olivia,
three stars shining on my life*

## Other books by the author

*Dahl's Law Dictionary / Dictionnaire Juridique Dahl*
(New York, Paris, 2001)

*Dahl's Law Dictionary / Diccionario Jurídico Dahl*
(New York, 1999)

*Costa Rican Family Law*
(The Hague, 2003)

*West's Law & Commercial Dictionary in Five Languages*
(St. Paul, 1985)

*Multinational Corporations*
(Lanham/London, 1986)

*Derecho Privado Soviético*
(Buenos Aires, 1981)

*Legal Accountability for Human Rights Violations in Argentina*
(Kelhm am Rhein/Strasbourg/Arlington, 1987)

# Contents

# Índice

# Introduction

*McGraw-Hill's Spanish and English Legal Dictionary* is designed to help communication between people from different cultures. To this end, two important features characterize this dictionary. One is an extensive use of authoritative sources, like codes and legal writing, to provide definitions. The other is a thematic index, at the end, which allows a search by topic. This second feature is helpful when the reader knows what area he or she is interested in, but is not aware of the exact word being searched. The possibility of researching by topic allows the dictionary to be used in non-conventional ways. For instance, a person who has a meeting to discuss a certain issue can go to the index, find entries related to that topic, and build up vocabulary by reading them.

In addition to traditional bilingual definitions, the English-speaking reader will find terms in Latin American and Spanish law that are explained in English, while concepts in American and English law are explained in Spanish in the Inglés-Español half of the dictionary. Care has been placed in choosing the most basic and representative legal texts, such as constitutions, codes, statutes and legal writing to illustrate some of the definitions. An effort was made to include all branches of law, covering the wide fields of business transactions, constitutional issues, criminal law, family relations, procedural matters, etc. No area was emphasized more than others. To the contrary, we tried to be as generally inclusive as possible.

I hope that the reader will find in this dictionary a dynamic and practical tool for communication between different legal systems and languages. Those interested in researching deeper are referred to *Dahl's Law Dictionary / Diccionario Jurídico Dahl* (3rd edition, NY, 1999) where lengthier definitions can be found.

# Table of Abbreviations, Sources, and Copyright Acknowledgments

## Spanish-English

### 1. STATUTORY, CODIFIED, AND CASE LAW

Bust. C., Bustamante Code.

C.R. C. of Civ. P., Costa Rican Code of Civil Procedure.

Conv. on Checks, Inter-American Convention on Conflicts of Laws Concerning Checks.

Conv. on Intl. Comm. Arb., Inter-American Convention on International Commercial Arbitration.

Conv. on Power of Att., Inter-American Convention on the Legal Regime of Powers of Attorney to be Used Abroad.

Conv. on Prev. Meas., Inter-American Convention on Execution of Preventive Measures.

FLL., Ley Federal del trabajo (Mexico), Federal Labor Law.

Incoterms. INCOTERMS, 1990, Spanish and English Edition, by the International Chamber of Commerce.

LPRA., Laws of Puerto Rico Annotated. The Spanish version is called *Leyes de Puerto Rico Anotadas.*

Lou. Civ. C., Louisiana Civil Code.

Mex. Civ. C., Mexican Civil Code.

Mex. Com. C., Mexican Commercial Code.

PR Mort. Law 1979, Puerto Rican Mortgage Law, 1979.

PRR., Puerto Rico Reports. The Spanish version is called *Decisiones de Puerto Rico.*

Sp. Civ. C., Spanish Civil Code, originally *Código Civil Español.* Official translation published in *Revised Statutes and Codes of Porto Rico*, published by authority of the Legislative Assembly (1901).

Sp. Com. C., Spanish Commercial Code, originally *Código de Comercio Español*. Official translation published in *Revised Statutes and Codes of Porto Rico*, published by authority of the Legislative Assembly (1901).

Sp. L. Civ. P., Spanish Law of Civil Procedure, originally *Ley Española de Enjuiciamiento Civil*. Official translation published in *Revised Statutes and Codes of Porto Rico*, published by authority of the Legislative Assembly (1901). There is another English version published by the U.S. War Department, Division of Insular Affairs (1901).

Sp. L. Crim. P., Spanish Law of Criminal Procedure, originally *Ley Española de Procedimiento Criminal*. Official translation published in *Revised Statutes and Codes of Porto Rico*, published by authority of the Legislative Assembly (1901). There is another English version published by the U.S. War Department, Division of Insular Afffairs (1901).

St. P.C. for LA., Standard Penal Code for Latin America, originally *Código Penal Tipo Para América Latina*. A full English translation with a related article is published in (17) 3 *American Journal of Criminal Law 235-285* (1990), by José M. Canales and Henry Dahl.

Unidroit, Princ., *Principles for International Commercial Contracts*, Study L-Doc. 40 Rev. 13. Rome 1994. Spanish version under the direction of Alejandro M. Garro.


## 2. LEGAL WRITING

Alonso Penã, A., from an essay on Argentine law (1996).

Amado, J. *Recognition and Enforcement of Foreign Judgments in Latin American Countries: An Overview and Update*, by José Daniel Amado, in *Virginia Journal of International Law*, Vol 31:99, 1990, pp. 99-304.

Mex. Labor Law. *A Primer on Mexican Labor Law*. U.S. Department of Labor, Bureau of International Labor Affairs, 1991. Translation from English to Spanish of *Regimen jurídico de protección de los Trabajadores en México*, by Nestor de Buen Lozano y de Carlos E. Buen Unna.

Barrios-Mannucci, J. E. *Contractual Responsibility and Torts in Latin America*, in Texas Transnational Law Quarterly, Vol. 12, May 96, Nr. 1, pp. 34-54.

Bell, *Bell's Dictionary and Digest of the Law of Scotland*, 7th ed.

Comparison of Labor Law. *A Comparison of Labor Law in the United States and Mexico: An Overview*, by the Secretaría del Trabajo y Previsión Social (Mexico) and the United States of America Department of Labor, 1992.

Escriche, *Diccionario de Legislación y Jurisprudencia.*

LA Laws & Inst. *Latin American Laws and Institutions,* by A.S. Golbert and Y. Nun, Praeger, 1982. Reprinted with permission of Greenwood Publishing Group, Inc., Westport, Connecticut.

L & D in LA. Law and Development in Latin America. *Law and Development in Latin America: A Casebook.* By Kenneth Karst and Keith Rosenn, University of California Press, 1975.

Orihuela, S. *Latin America: A New Era for Mining Investment,* in *The International Lawyer,* Spring 1996, Vol. 30, Nr. 1, pp. 31-56.

Pratter, J. *Mexican Law in English,* by Jonathan Pratter, in *Texas Transnational Law Quarterly,* Vol. II, July 95, Nr. 2, pp. 26-29.

Rosenn, K. *Federalism in the Americas in Comparative Perspective,* by Keith S. Rosenn, *Inter-American Law Review,* Fall 1994, Volume 26, Number 1, pp. 1-50.

Vargas, J. A. *Conflict of Laws in Mexico: The New Rules Introduced by the 1988 Amendments,* in *The International Lawyer,* Fall 1994, Vol. 28, Nr. 3, pp. 692-694.

W. Eur. & LA Leg. Sys. Western European and Latin American Legal Systems. *Comparative Law: Western European and Latin American Legal Systems,* by J. H. Merryman and D. S. Clark. The Michie Company, 1978.

# English-Spanish

## 1. STATUTORY, CODIFIED, AND CASE LAW

C.C.U. Código de Comercio Uniforme, originally *Uniform Commercial Code.* Copyright 1987 by the American Law Institute and the National Conference of Commissioners on Uniform State Laws. Reprinted with the permission of the Permanent Editorial Board for the Uniform Commercial Code.

Cód. Pen. Mod. *Comentarios al Código Penal Modelo para los E.E. U.U.,* by Ernesto Chiesa Aponte, Jaime E. Granados Peña and Antonio José Cancino M., Editorial Jurídica Futuro, Bogotá, 1993.

D.P.R. Decisiones de Puerto Rico. The English version is called *Puerto Rico Reports.*

Incoterms. INCOTERMS, 1990. Spanish and English Edition, by the International Chamber of Commerce.

LPRA. Leyes de Puerto Rico Anotadas. The English version is called *Laws of Puerto Rico Annotated.*

R. Fed. Evid. Reglas Federales de Evidencia.

R. Fed. P. Civ. Reglas Federales de Procedimiento Civil, originally *Federal Rules of Civil Procedure*, Spanish version published in Práctica Forense Federal, Equity Publishing Corporation.

R. Fed. P. Crim. Reglas Federales de Procedimiento Criminal, originally *Federal Rules of Criminal Procedure*, Spanish version published in Práctica Forense Federal, Equity Publishing Corporation.

Rstmnt, 2nd, Conflict. Restatement of the Law, 2d., Conflict of Laws. No previous translations exist. Copyright by The American Law Institute. Translated and published with the permission of The American Law Institute.

Rstmnt, 2nd, Con. Restatement of the Law, 2d., Contracts. No previous translations exist. Copyright by The American Law Institute. Translated and published with the permission of The American Law Institute.

Rstmnt, 2nd, Judg. Restatement of the Law, 2d., Judgments. No previous translations exist. Copyright by The American Law Institute. Translated and published with the permission of The American Law Institute.

Rstmnt, 2nd, Torts. Restatement of the Law, 2d., Torts. No previous translations exist. Copyright by The American Law Institute. Translated and published with the permission of The American Law Institute.

R. Fed. P. Civ. Reglas Federales de Procedimiento Civil, originally *Federal Rules of Civil Procedure*, Spanish version published in Práctica Forense Federal, Equity Publishing Corporation.

Unidroit, Pric. *Principios para los Contratos Mercantiles Internacionales.* Translation into Spanish, under the direction of Alejandro M. Garro, from the English text published as Study L-Doc. 40 Rev. 13 (Rome, 1994).

## 2. Legal Writing

Carl, B. (Prof. Beverly May Carl), originally in the article *El Derecho Internacional Privado en los Estados Unidos y la Creación de un Puente entre los Diversos Sistemas Jurídicos de las Américas.*

Morales Lebrón, M. (Prof. Mariano Morales Lebrón) originally in *Diccionario Jurídico Según la Jurisprudencia del Tribunal Supremo* (San Juan, 1977).

Intro al USA. Introducción al Sistema Legal de USA. E. Allan Farnsworth, *Introducción al Sistema Legal de los Estados Unidos*, Editorial Zavalía

(1990, Buenos Aires), translated by Horacio Abeledo. Published originally in English as *Introduction to the Legal System of the United States.*
Stuchiner, T. B. (Theresa Berlin Stuchiner, LL.B.), originally in *Delitos y Penas en los Estados Unidos*, translated into Spanish and introduction written by Fernando Diaz Palos, Barcelona, Editorial Bosch, 1ra Edición.

# Other Abbreviations Used

## GEOGRAPHIC

| | |
|---|---|
| AR | Argentina |
| CA | Central America |
| CH | Chile |
| CO | Colombia |
| CR | Costa Rica |
| GB | Great Britain |
| GU | Guatemala |
| HO | Honduras |
| ME | Mexico |
| NI | Nicaragua |
| PR | Puerto Rico |
| SP | Spain |
| UR | Uruguay |

## NONGEOGRAPHIC

| | |
|---|---|
| Crim. | Criminal |
| (L) | Latin |
| Mar. | Maritime |
| (s) | noun |
| (v) | verb |

# Introducción

El *Diccionario Jurídico Inglés y Español McGraw-Hill* está diseñado para facilitar la comunicación entre gente de culturas distintas. Para ello, dos importantes elementos caraterizan esta obra. Uno es el uso extenso de fuentes fehacientes, como códigos y doctrina para brindar definiciones. Otro es un índice temático, al final, que permite una búsqueda por tópico. Este segundo elemento es util cuando el lector conoce el área de su interés, pero no sabe que término específico está buscando. La posibilidad de una búsqueda temática permite usar el diccionario en formas no-convencionales. Por ejemplo, una persona que tuviese una entrevista para discutir cierto tema, podría ir al índice, hallar entradas relativas a tal tema y mejorar su vocabulario leyendo tales definiciones.

Además de las tradicionales definiciones bilingües, el lector hispanohablante encontrará términos del derecho estadounidense e inglés explicados en español, en la sección English-Spanish del diccionario, y también conceptos del derecho latinoamericano y español explicados en inglés. Hemos elegido cuidadosamente los textos jurídicos más representativos, como constituciones, códigos, leyes y doctrina para ilustrar algunas de las definiciones. Pusimos empeño en incluir todas las ramas jurídicas, cubriendo el vasto campo de transacciones comerciales, temas constitucionales, derecho penal, relaciones familiares, cuestiones procesales, etc. Ninguna área se enfatizó más que otras. Al contrario, tratamos de ser tan inclusivos como era posible.

Esperamos que el lector halle aquí un diccionario dinámico así como una herramienta práctica de comunicación entre sistemas jurídicos y lenguas diferentes. Se refiere a aquéllos interesados en una investigación más profunda al Dahl's Law Dictionary / Diccionario Jurídico Dahl (3ra edición, NY, 1999), donde podrán encontrar definiciones más extensas.

# Tabla de Abreviaciones, Fuentes y Propiedad Intelectual

## Español-Ingles

### 1. Leyes, Codificaciones y Fallos

Bust. C., Código Bustamante.

C.R. C. of Civ. P., Costa Rican Code of Civil Procedure, *Código Procesal Civil de Costa Rica.*

Conv. on Checks, Inter-American Convention on Conflicts of Laws Concerning Checks, Convención Interamericana sobre Conflicto de Leyes en Materia de Cheques.

Conv. on Intl. Comm. Arb., Inter-American Convention on International Commercial Arbitration, Convención Interamericana sobre Derecho Comercial Internacional.

Conv. on Power of Att., Inter-American Convention on the Legal Regime of Powers of Attorney to be Used Abroad, Convención Interamericana sobre el Regimen Legal de Poderes para ser Utilizados en el Extranjero.

Conv. on Prev. Meas., Inter-American Convention on Execution of Preventive Measures, Convención Interamericana sobre Cumplimiento de Medidas Cautelares.

FLL., Ley Federal del Trabajo (México).

Incoterms., INCOTERMS, 1990. Edición Inglesa y Española, por la Cámara de Comercio Internacional.

LPRA., Laws of Puerto Rico Annotated. La versión Española es *Leyes de Puerto Rico Anotadas.*

Lou. Civ. C., Louisiana Civil Code, *Código Civil de Luisiana.*

Mex. Civ. C., *Código Civil Mexicano.*

Mex. Com. C., *Código de Comericio Mexicano.*

PR Mort. Law 1979, Puerto Rican Mortgage Law, 1979, *Ley Hipotecaria de Puerto Rico,* 1979.

PRR., Puerto Rico Reports. La versión española es *Decisiones de Puerto Rico.*

Sp. Civ. C., Spanish Civil Code, originalmente *Código Civil Español.* Traducción oficial publicada en *Revised Statutes and Codes of Porto Rico*, publicada por orden de la Asamblea Legislativa (1901).

Sp. Com. C., Spanish Commercial Code, originalmente *Código de Comercio Español.* Traducción oficial publicada en *Revised Statutes and Codes of Porto Rico*, publicada por orden de la Asamblea Legislativa (1901).

Sp. L. of Civ. P., Spanish Law of Civil Procedure, originalmente *Ley Española de Enjuiciamiento Civil.* Traducción oficial publicada en *Revised Statutes and Codes of Porto Rico*, publicada por orden de la Asamblea Legislativa (1901). Existe otra versión inglesa, publicada por el U.S. War Department, Division of Insular Affairs (1901).

Sp. L. of Crim. P., Spanish Law of Criminal Procedure, originalmente *Ley Española de Procedimiento Criminal.* Traducción oficial publicada en *Revised Statutes and Codes of Porto Rico*, publicada por orden de la Asamblea Legislativa (1901). Existe otra versión inglesa, publicada por el U.S. War Department, Division of Insular Affairs (1901).

St. P.C. for LA., Standard Penal Code for Latin America, originalmente *Código Penal Tipo para América Latina.* Una traducción completa, con un artículo explicativo aparece en (17) 3 *American Journal of Criminal Law* 235-285 (1990), por José M. Canales y Henry Dahl.

Unidroit, Princ., *Principles for International Commercial Contracts*, Study L-Doc. 40 Rev. 13. Rome 1994. Versión española bajo la dirección de Alejandro M. Garro.

## 2. DOCTRINA

Alonso Peña, A., de un ensayo sobre derecho argentino (1996).

Amado, J. *Recognition and Enforcement of Foreign Judgments in Latin American Countries: An Overview and Update*, por José Daniel Amado, en *Virginia Journal of International Law*, Vol 31:99, 1990, pp. 99-304.

Mex. Labor Law. *A Primer on Mexican Labor Law.* U.S. Department of Labor, Bureau of International Labor Affairs, 1991. Traducción del inglés al español de *Régimen Jurídico de Protección de los Trabajadores en México*, por Nestor de Buen Lozano y de Carlos E. Buen Unna.

Barrios-Mannucci, J. E. *Contractual Responsibility and Torts in Latin America*, en Texas Transnational Law Quarterly, Vol. 12, Mayo 96, Nr. 1, pp. 34-54.

Bell, *Bell's Dictionary and Digest of the Law of Scotland*, 7th ed.

Comparison of Labor Law. *A Comparison of Labor Law in the United States and Mexico: An Overview*, por la Secretaría del Trabajo y Previsión Social (Mexico) y por el United States of America Department of Labor, 1992.

Escriche, *Diccionario de Legislación y Jurisprudencia*.

LA Laws & Inst. *Latin American Laws and Institutions*, por A.S. Golbert e Y. Nun, Praeger, 1982. Reimpreso con permiso de Greenwood Publishing Group, Inc., Westport, Connecticut.

L & D in LA. Law and Development in Latin America. *Law and Development in Latin America: A Casebook*. Por Kenneth Karst y Keith Rosenn, University of California Press, 1975.

Orihuela, S. *Latin America: A New Era for Mining Investment*, en *The International Lawyer*, Spring 1996, Vol. 30, Nr. 1, pp. 31-56.

Pratter, J. *Mexican Law in English*, por Jonathan Pratter, en *Texas Transnational Law Quarterly*, Vol. II, Julio 95, Nr. 2, pp. 26-29.

Rosenn, K. *Federalism in the Americas in Comparative Perspective*, por Keith S. Rosenn, *Inter-American Law Review*, Fall 1994, Vol. 26, Nr. 1, pp. 1-50.

Vargas, J. A. *Conflict of Laws in Mexico: The New Rules Introduced by the 1988 Amendments*, en *The International Lawyer*, Fall 1994, Vol. 28, Nr. 3, pp. 692-694.

W. Eur. & LA Leg. Sys. Western European and Latin American Legal Systems. *Comparative Law: Western European and Latin American Legal Systems*, por J. H. Merryman y D. S. Clark. The Michie Company, 1978.

# Ingles-Español

## 1. Leyes, Codificaciones y Fallos

C.C.U., (Código de Comercio Uniforme), originalmente *Uniform Commercial Code*. Copyright 1987 de The American Law Institute and the National Conference of Commissioners on Uniform State Laws. Reproducido con permiso del Permanent Editorial Board for the Uniform Commercial Code.

Cód. Pen. Mod., *Comentarios al Código Penal Modelo para los E.E. U.U.*, por Ernesto Chiesa Aponte, Jaime E. Granados Peña y Antonio José Cancino M., Editorial Jurídica Futuro, Bogotá, 1993.

D.P.R., (Decisiones de Puerto Rico). La versión inglesa se llama *Puerto Rico Reports*.

Incoterms., INCOTERMS, 1990. Edición Inglesa y Española, por la Cámara Internacional de Comercio.

LPRA., Leyes de Puerto Rico Anotadas. La versión inglesa se llama *Laws of Puerto Rico Annotated*.

R. Fed. Evid., Reglas Federales de Evidencia.

R. Fed. P. Civ., Reglas Federales de Procedimiento Civil, originalmente *Federal Rules of Civil Procedure*, versión española publicada en Práctica Forense Federal, Equity Publishing Corporation.

R. Fed. P. Crim., Reglas Federales de Procedimiento Criminal, originalmente *Federal Rules of Criminal Procedure*, versión española publicada en Práctica Forense Federal, Equity Publishing Corporation.

Rstmnt, 2nd, Conflict., Restatement of the Law, 2d., Conflict of Laws. Restatement, Conflicto de Leyes. No existe una traducción anterior. Copyright de The American Law Institute. Traducido y publicado con permiso de The American Law Institute.

Rstmnt, 2nd, Con., Restatement of the Law, 2d., Contracts. Restatement, Contratos. No existe una traducción anterior. Copyright de The American Law Institute. Traducido y publicado con permiso de The American Law Institute.

Rstmnt, 2nd, Judg., Restatement of the Law, 2d., Judgments. Restatement, Sentencias. No existe una traducción anterior. Copyright de The American Law Institute. Traducido y publicado con permiso de The American Law Institute.

Rstmnt, 2nd, Torts., Restatement of the Law, 2d., Torts. Restatement, Cuasidelitos. No existe una traducción anterior. Copyright de The American Law Institute. Traducido y publicado con permiso de The American Law Institute.

Unidroit, Prin., *Principios para los Contratos Mercantiles Internacionales*. Traducción al español, bajo la dirección de Alejandro M. Garro, del texto inglés publicado como Study L-Doc. 40 Rev. 13 (Roma, 1994).

## 2. DOCTRINA

Carl, B. (Prof. Beverly May Carl), originalmente en el artículo *El Derecho Internacional Privado en los Estados Unidos y la Creación de un Puente entre los Diversos Sistemas Jurídicos de las Américas*.

Morales Lebrón, M. (Prof. Mariano Morales Lebrón) originalmente en *Diccionario Jurídico Según la Jurisprudencia del Tribunal Supremo* (San Juan, 1977).

Intro al USA., Introducción al Sistema Legal de USA. E. Allan Farnsworth, *Introducción al Sistema Legal de los Estados Unidos*, Editorial Zavalía (1990, Buenos Aires), traducido por Horacio Abeledo. Publicado originalmente en inglés como *Introduction to the Legal System of the United States.*

Stuchiner, T. B. (Theresa Berlin Stuchiner, LL.B.), originalmente en *Delitos y Penas en los Estados Unidos*, traducido al Español, y la introducción escrita por Fernando Diaz Palos, Barcelona, Editorial Bosch, 1ra Edición.

# Otras Abreviaciones Usadas

### GEOGRÁFICAS

| | |
|---|---|
| AR | Argentina |
| CA | America Central |
| CH | Chile |
| CO | Colombia |
| CR | Costa Rica |
| GB | Gran Bretaña |
| GU | Guatemala |
| HO | Honduras |
| ME | México |
| NI | Nicaragua |
| PR | Puerto Rico |
| SP | España |
| UR | Uruguay |

### NO GEOGRÁFICAS

| | |
|---|---|
| Crim. | Criminal |
| (L) | Latín |
| Mar. | Maritime |
| (s) | sustantivo |
| (v) | verbo |

# Spanish-English

# A

**A buen recaudo.** In a safe place. In a secure position.

**A cargo de.** Under the responsibility of. In charge of.

**A cargo y riesgo.** At one's cost and risk.

**A continuación.** Hereinafter, following.

**A _contrario sensu_ (L).** By contrary logic or meaning. A construction device or technique expressed in terms like: "if the statute says that X and Z are banned, it is implicitly stating that Y is allowed."

**A corto plazo.** Short term.

**A costa de.** At the expense of.

**A cuenta.** On one's account.

**A destajo.** Payment by each piece or unit.

**A días vista.** The number of days in which payment of a debt becomes due after a specific event has happened, e.g. the protest (_protesto_) of a promissory note (_pagaré_).

**A granel.** Bulk, without wrapping or packaging.

**A instancia de parte.** On motion.

**A jornal.** Payment by the day.

**A la orden.** To order.

**A la par.** Par value.

**A la vista.** On sight. Note payable on demand.

**A mano.** At hand, available, close. Even.

**A mano armada.** Using fire arms.

**A nombre propio.** In his (her) own name.

**A _non domino_ (L).** The fact of buying property from a person whom is not the owner. Usually this situation does not result in the transfer of ownership. The party who paid the price only has a personal action for reimbursement against the one who said to be the owner.

**A petición.** On demand.

**A puerta cerrada.** Behind closed doors, in chambers. Hearing, deliberation or other proceeding where the public is generally excluded.

**A quemarropa.** Shot fired from such a short distance that it is impossible to miss.

**A _quo_ (L).** From which, the court from where the case has been sent. A companion Latin expression is _ad quem_, or to whom, meaning the court where the case has been sent. Normally the District Court would be the _a quo_ while the Court of Appeals would be the ad quem. In motions it is customary to capitalize the phrase.

**A ruego.** By request. Term usually employed to indicate that a person unable to sign requests another to sign on his behalf. The expression is _firma a ruego_, signature by request.

**A sabiendas.** Knowingly, consciously.

**A salvamano.** In a very safe way.

**A sangre fría.** In cold blood.

**A sangre y fuego.** Causing great death and destruction.

**A sobrehora.** Unduly late.

**A tenor de.** In conformity with, according to. E.g. _a tenor del artículo 33_ ... in conformity with article 33.

**A una voz.** Unanimously.

**Ab _intestato_ (L).** Intestate probate proceedings.

**Abanderado.** Flag bearer, valedictorian. Champion of a cause.

**Abandonar.** To abandon, desert, forsake, relinquish, renounce, waive.

**Abandono.** Abandon, abandonment, desertion, relinquishment, renunciation.

**Abandono del servicio.** Dereliction of service. Dereliction of service—which justifies the suspension or dismissal of a State employee—is not any kind of absence of the employee, but the unauthorized absences of a vicious nature and without a reasonable justification. (Lebron v. Personnel Board, 100 PRR-163).

**Abaratamiento.** Reduction in price.

**Abarcar.** To embrace, entail, comprehend, contain, cover, include, involve.

**Abastecer.** To supply, furnish, provide.

**Abastecimiento.** Supply.

**Abdicación.** Abdication.

**Abdicar.** To abdicate, renounce, resign, surrender, yield.

**Aberración.** Aberration, abnormality, anomaly.

**Aberrante.** Aberrant, abnormal, sick.

**Abigeato.** Stealing of cattle.

**Abigeo.** Cattle thief, rustler.

**Abintestato.** Intestate proceedings. In order to be able to institute intestate proceedings, it is necessary: 1) That there is information of the recent death of the principal. 2) That the existence of a testamentary disposition is not known. (Sp. L. Civ. P. sec 959).

**Abjurar.** To abjure, disavow, forsake, relinquish, repudiate, retract.

**Abofetear.** To slap, spank, whack.

**Abogacía.** Legal profession, lawyering.

**Abogado.** Lawyer, attorney, advocate, barrister (GB), counsel, counselor, defender, solicitor (GB).

**Abogado de empresa.** In-house counsel, corporate attorney, transactional attorney.

**Abogado interviniente.** Attorney of record.

**Abogar.** To advocate, plead, support.

**Abolición.** Abolition, abolishment, banning, eradication.

**Abolicionismo.** Abolitionism, abolishment, elimination, eradication.

**Abolir.** To abolish, abrogate, annul, cancel, revoke.

**Abonar.** To pay.

**Abordaje (mar.)** Collision (mar.). If a vessel should collide with another through the fault, negligence, or lack of skill of the captain, sailing master, or any other member of the complement, the owner of the vessel at fault shall pay indemnity for the loss and damage suffered, after an expert appraisal. (Sp. Com. C., sec. 826/28, 830).

**Abortar.** To abort, to have a miscarriage, to thwart.

**Aborto.** Abortion, miscarriage.

**Abrevadero.** Trough.

**Abrir.** To open, release, unlock.

**Abrir a viva fuerza.** Break open.

**Abrogación.** Abrogation, annulment, cancellation, repeal.

**Abrogar.** To abrogate, annul, invalidate, void.

**Absentismo.** Absenteeism.

**Absolución.** Absolution, acquittal, exculpation, dismissal, pardon.

**Absolución de posiciones.** Answering of interrogatories by a party.

**Absolución de preguntas.** Answering of questions by a witness.

**Absoluto.** Absolute, complete, total.

**Absolutorio.** Absolutory.

**Absolvente.** Deposing party.

**Absolver.** To absolve, acquit, clear, exculpate.

**Absorción de empresas.** Merger, acquisition, takeover.

**Abstención de sentencia.** Arrest judgment.

**Abstenerse de.** To abstain, refrain from.

**Abstinencia.** Abstinence, continence, self restraint.

**Absurdo.** Absurd, absurdity, nonsense.

**Abuela.** Grandmother/ascendant.

**Abuelo.** Grandfather/ascendant.

**Abulia.** Lethargy, apathy, disinterest, indolence, passivity.

**Abusivo.** Abusive, disparaging.

**Abuso.** Abuse, misuse.

**Abuso de confianza.** Abuse of trust.

**Abuso de derecho.** Abuse of rights. Rights must be exercised in conformity with principles of good faith. The law does not protect the abusive or the antisocial use of a right. Abuse of a law is to rely on a legal provision, on a law closing the eyes to the reality of the facts, to the course of the world, and to act as if only that provision were a reality, even though trailing off the roads of justice and of equity. (Berrios v. International Gen. Electric, 88 PRR 106 (1963)).

**Acaparador.** Person who stashes away.

**Acaparar.** To stash, cache, hoard, monopolize, store.

**Acápite.** Paragraph, section in a page.

**Acarreador.** Carrier.

**Acatamiento.** Respect and obedience to a legal system, a contract, a court or any other institution.

**Acatar.** To obey, comply with, conform, follow an order.

**Acceder.** To express consent or agreement. To have access to.

**Accesión.** Accession. The ownership of a thing by accession includes the ownership of everything that it produces or is united with it, either naturally or artificially. (Louisiana Civ. Code art. 482).

**Accesión, derechos.** Accession, rights. In virtue of accession the following belong to the owner:
I. Natural fruits;
II. Industrial fruits;
III. Legal gains. (Mex. Civ. C., art. 887).

**Accesión sobre y bajo la superficie.** Accession above and below the surface. Unless otherwise provided by law, the ownership of a tract of land carries with it the ownership of everything that is directly above or under it. (Louisiana Civ. Code art. 490).

**Acceso.** Admission, admittance, entrance.

**Acceso carnal.** Sexual intercourse, penetration.

**Accesorio.** Accessory, ancillary, appendage, supplement.

**Accidental.** Accidental, unintentional, coincidental, by chance.

**Accidente.** Accident. In the field of insurance, the term accident means an unforeseen, sudden, or unexpected happening from the point of view of the one sustaining the damage and not of the tort-feasor. (Barrietos v. Gov. of the Capital, 97 PRR 539 (1969)). Casualty, misfortune, mishap.

**Accidente compensable.** Compensable accident. For the purposes of the Workmen's Accident Compensation Act, the accident suffered by a workman or employee is a compensable accident, if it is the result of an act or function inherent to his work or employment and occurs in the course thereof or as a consequence of same. (B.C.R. Co., Inc. v. Superior Court, 100 PRR 753 (1971)).

**Accidente de trabajo.** Labor accident.

**Accidente inevitable.** Unavoidable accident.

**Acción.** Action, lawsuit, suit, case, proceedings. Share, stock certificate. Motion, movement.

**Acción accesoria.** An accessory action.

**Acción cambiaria.** An action filed for the collection of a check, a note or some other commercial paper. This type of lawsuit allows only limited defenses, such as that of forgery or payment.

**Acción civil por un delito.** Civil action based on a crime. A criminal action arises from every crime or misdemeanor for the punishment of the culprit, and a civil action may also arise for the restitution of the thing, the repair of the damage, and the indemnity of the losses caused by the punishable act. (Sp. L. Crim. P., art. 100).

**Acción contractual.** Contractual remedy, action in contract.

**Acción de jactancia.** Action in jactitation. Originally used in Spain when someone claimed to possess certain rights, e.g. to a future inheritance—which someone else wanted to contest. Historically, this type of action is the origin of *sentencias declarativas* (declaratory judgments).

**Acción de reducción.** Action for reduction of excessive donations. Any disposal of property, whether *inter vivos* or *mortis causa*, exceeding the quantum of which a person may legally dispose to the prejudice of the forced heirs, is not null, but only reducible to that quantum. (Louisiana Civ. Code art. 1502).

**Acción declarativa.** Declaratory action.

**Acción diferida.** Deferred stock.

**Acción negatoria de paternidad.** Action in disavowal of paternity. The husband can disavow paternity of a child if he proves by a preponderance of the evidence any facts which reasonably indicate that he is not the father. (Louisiana Civ. Code art 187).

**Acción oblicua.** Oblique action. If an obligor causes or increases his insolvency by failing to exercise a right, the obligee may exercise it himself, unless the right is strictly personal to the obligor. (Louisiana Civ. Code art 2044).

**Acción ordinaria.** Common stock.

**Acción para recobrar propiedad mueble.** Replevin.

**Acción para resolver reclamaciones opuestas.** Action to quiet title.

**Acción pauliana.** See *acción oblicua* and *acción revocatoria.*

**Acción penal.** Criminal action. A criminal action arises from every crime or misdemeanor for the punishment of the culprit, and a civil action may also arise for the restitution of the thing, the repair of the damage, and the indemnity of the losses caused by the punishable act. (Sp. L. Crim. P., sec 100, 101).

**Acción penal, preclusión.** Criminal action, preclusion. The following persons cannot bring criminal actions against each other: 1) spouses, except for a crime or misdemeanor committed by one against the person of the other or that of his or her children, and for the crimes of adultery, concubinage and bigamy; 2) the ascendants, descendants, the uterine brothers or sisters, or relatives by consanguinity or affinity, unless for a crime or misdemeanor by either against the persons of the other. (Sp. L. Crim. P., sec 103).

**Acción penal, renuncia.** A criminal action for a crime or misdemeanor which gives rise to proceedings *ex officio* is not extinguished by the withdrawal of the complaint by the person offended. (Sp. L. Crim. P., sec 106).

**Acción popular.** By 1910 the Colombian system created an institution known as the "popular action" (*acción popular*), which permits any citizen to challenge the constitutionality of any law on its face. Any citizen (defined loosely by the case law to include corporations and even aliens), irrespective of any personal stake in the outcome or the exhaustion of administrative remedies, may bring an action at any time directly before the Colombian Supreme Court by filing a simple written statement setting forth the asserted conflict between the law and the constitution. The Court is not limited to the complainant's theory of the case; if it believes the law unconstitutional for reasons other than those set out in the complaint, the Court has the duty to invalidate the law. If the law is declared unconstitutional, the Court's decision has an *erga omnes* effect. (L & D in LA).

**Acción popular, otros países.** Popular action, other countries. With slight modifications, the popular action has spread to Panama, Venezuela, and El Salvador. From 1931 until 1959 Cuba permitted the popular action, but required a petition signed by 25 citizens instead of an individual complaint. (L & D in LA).

**Acción por enriquecimiento indebido, o sin causa.** Restitution. Action for enrichment without cause or for unjust enrichment.

**Acción posesoria.** Possessory action. One where only the right of possession is the issue, ownership being immaterial.

**Acción preferida.** Preferred stock.

**Acción redhibitoria.** Redhibitory action. A claim for the hidden defects of something that was purchased.

**Acción reivindicatoria.** Vindicatory action. The owner of a thing is entitled to recover it from anyone who possesses or detains it without right and to obtain judgment recognizing his ownership and ordering delivery of the thing to him.

In all civil law systems, the owner of a thing may bring a vindicatory action (*acción en reivindicación*) for the recognition of his ownership and for the recovery of the thing from anyone who possesses or detains it without right. (Louisiana Civ. Code art. 526 and note).

**Acción revocatoria. Acción Pauliana.** Revocatory action. Paulian action. An obligee has a right to annul an act of the obligor, or the result of a failure to act of the obligor, made or effected after the right of the obligee arose, that causes or increases the obligor's insolvency.

The revocatory or Paulian action, an institution derived from Roman law, is the civil-law analogue to the common law suit to set aside a fraudulent conveyance. (Louisiana Civ. Code art. 2036 and note).

**Acción subrogatoria.** Action for subrogation.

**Accionante.** Plaintiff, claimant, petitioner, relator.

**Accionar.** To file a lawsuit.

**Acciones.** Acts, shares, stock certificates.

**Acciones con derecho a voto.** Voting stock.

**Acciones nominativas.** Shares payable to order. The shares payable to bearer shall be numbered, and shall be recorded in stub books. (Sp. Com. C., sec. 163).

**Acciones, nuevas series.** Shares, new series. No new series of stock can be issued before the total of the series previously issued has been fully paid. (Sp. Com. C., sec. 165).

**Acciones ordinarias.** Common stock.

**Acciones parcialmente pagadas.** Partly paid shares.

**Acciones preferidas.** Preferred stock.

**Acciones sin valor a la par.** No-par value stock.

**Acciones sin valor nominal.** No-par stock.

**Accionista.** Shareholder, stockholder.

**Acefalía.** Acephalia. Absence of a leader.

**Aceptación dentro de un plazo fijo.** Acceptance within a fixed period of time. A period of time for acceptance fixed by the offeror in a telegram or a letter begins to run from the moment the telegram is handed in for dispatch of from the date shown on the letter or, if no such date is shown, from the date shown on the envelope. A period of time for acceptance fixed by the offeror by means of instantaneous communication begins to run from the moment that the offer reaches the offeree. (Unidroit, Prin., art. 2.8).

**Aceptación disconforme.** Modified acceptance. A reply to an offer which purports to be an acceptance but contains additional or different terms which do not materially alter the terms of the offer constitutes an acceptance, unless the offeror, without undue delay, objects to the discrepancy. (Unidroit, Prin., art. 2.11).

**Aceptación mediante silencio.** Acceptance by silence. When, because of special circumstances, the offeree's silence leads the offeror reasonably to believe that a contract has been formed, the offer is deemed accepted. (Louisiana Civ. Code art. 1942).

**Aceptación no en acuerdo con la oferta.** Acceptance not in accordance with offer. An acceptance not in accordance with the terms of the offer is deemed to be a counteroffer. (Louisiana Civ. Code art. 1943).

**Aceptación por cumplimiento.** Acceptance by performance. When an offeror invites an offeree to accept by performance and, according to usage or the nature or the terms of the contract, it is contemplated that the performance will be completed if commenced, a contract is formed when the offeree begins the requested performance. (Louisiana Civ. Code art. 1939).

**Aceptación por intervención.** Acceptance for honor.

**Aceptación sólo por cumlimiento total.** Acceptance only by completed performance. When, according to usage or the nature of the contract, or its own terms, an offer made to a particular offeree can be accepted only by rendering a completed performance, the offeror cannot revoke the offer, once the offeree has begun to perform, for the reasonable time necessary to complete the performance. (Louisiana Civ. Code art. 1940).

**Aceptación tardía. Demora en la transmisón.** Late acceptance. Delay in transmission. A late acceptance is nevertheless effective as an acceptance if without undue delay the offeror so informs the offeree or gives notice to that effect. (Unidroit, Prin., art. 2.9).

**Aceptación, tiempo.** Time of acceptance. An offer must be accepted within the time the offeror has fixed or, if no time is fixed, within a reasonable time having regard to the circumstances, including the rapidity of the means of communication employed by the offeror. (Unidroit, Prin., art. 2.7).

**Aceptante.** Acceptor.

**Aceptar.** To accept, admit, adopt, acquiesce, concede.

**Acequia.** Drain.

**Acervo.** Assets, belongings, capital, patrimony, possessions.

**Acervo hereditario.** Estate of a deceased. The estate of a deceased means the property, rights, and obligations that a person leaves after his death, whether the property exceeds the charges or the charges exceed the property, or whether he has only left charges without any property. (Louisiana Civ. Code art. 872).

**Aclaración.** Clarification, elucidation, explanation.

**Aclaración y adición de una sentencia.** Clarification and addition of a judgment. The clarification of or addition to a judgment is only possible concerning its dispositive part. (C.R. C. of Civ. P., art. 158).

**Acometedor.** Attacker, aggressor.

**Acometer.** To assault, attack, assail.

**Acometimiento.** Assault, attack, assailment.

**Acomodación.** Accommodation, adaptation, adjustment, arrangement.

**Aconchabamiento.** Employment, job, occupation, work.

**Aconsejar.** To counsel, advise, recommend, suggest.

**Acontecer.** To happen, occur.

**Acontecimiento.** Event, happening, incident, occasion, occurrence.

**Acordada.** Procedural rule, or set of rules, issued by the Supreme Court.

**Acordar.** To agree, accord, concur.

**Acorde.** Corresponding, in agreement, in harmony.

**Acosamiento.** Harassment.

**Acosamiento sexual.** Sexual harassement.

**Acostumbrado.** Customary, accustomed, habitual, normal, routine, usual.

**Acotación.** Remark, comment, commentary, gloss, note, observation.

**Acrecentamiento.** Increase, augmentation, enlargement, growth, rise.

**Acrecentar.** To increase, augment, boost, enlarge, raise.

**Acrecer, derecho de.** Right to increase one's share when other heirs or legatees fail to take their portion.

**Acreditar.** To ascertain, determine, confirm, prove, verify.

**Acreedor.** Creditor, obligee. Obligee or creditor is the person in favor of whom some obligation is contracted. (Louisiana Civ. Code art. 3556).

**Acreedor con gravamen.** Lien creditor.

**Acreedor solidario.** Joint creditor.

**Acreedores privilegiados.** Preferred creditors.

**Acreedores singularmente privilegiados.** Specially preferred credtors.

**Acta de defunción.** Death record, death certificate. No interment or cremation will be done without authorization given by the judge of the Civil Registry, who will make sure of the death, with a certificate issued by a physician legally authorized. (Mex. Civ. C., art. 117).

**Acta de defunción, contenido.** Death record, contents. The death record shall contain:
I. The name, last name, age, occupation, and address of the defunct;
II. The civil status of the defunct, and if he or she was married or widowed, and the name and last name of the spouse;
III. The names, last names, ages, occupations, and addresses of the witnesses, and if they were relatives, their relationship to the defunct;
IV. The name of the parents of the defunct, if known;
V. The type of disease that caused the death, and specifically the place where the body was buried;
VI. The time of death, if known, and all the information available in case of a violent death. (Mex. Civ. C., art. 119).

**Actas.** Records, minutes, report.

**Actividades de alto riesgo.** Abnormally dangerous activities.

**Activo.** Assets, holdings, net worth. Active.

**Activo fijo.** Fixed assets.

**Activo líquido.** Liquid assets.

**Acto.** Act, action, judicial proceeding.

**Acto auténtico.** Authentic act. An authentic act is a writing executed before a notary public or other officer authorized to perform that function, in the presence of two witnesses, and signed by each party who executed it, by each witness, and by each notary public before whom it was executed. (Louisiana Civ. Code art. 1833, 1834).

**Acto bajo signo privado.** Act under private signature. An act under private signature need not be written by the parties, but must be signed by them. An act under private signature is regarded *prima facie* as the true and genuine act of a party executing it when his signature has been acknowledged, and the act shall be admitted in evidence without further proof. (Louisiana Civ. Code art. 1837, 1836).

**Acto cometido en ocasión del trabajo.** Conduct within scope of employment.

7

**Acto de comercio.** Commercial transactions shall be considered those enumerated in this Code and any others of a similar character. (Sp. Com. C., sec. 2 (2)).

**Acto entre vivos.** Transaction *inter vivos.*

**Acto jurídico.** Legal act, juridical act.

**Acto voluntario.** Wilful act. A wilful act is the act which is born of the will and not by force or necessity extraneous to the former. (Ppl. v. Sanchez Lugo, 96 PRR 480 (1968)).

**Actor/a.** Plaintiff, claimant, petitioner, relator.

**Actos de comercio.** Commercial acts. The law considers the following to be commercial transactions:

I. All purchases, sales, and rentals entered into for the purpose of commercial speculation, of maintenance, articles, chattels, or articles, be it in a natural state, after improvement or manufactured;

II. The purchases and sales of real estate, when done with the purpose of commercial speculation;

III. The purchases and sales of portions, shares, and obligations of mercantile associations;

IV. The contracts relating to obligations from state bonds and other certificates of obligations which are in the flow of commerce;

V. Companies that deal with provisions and supply;

VI. Companies that deal with construction and public and private works;

VII. Companies that are factories and manufacturers;

VIII. Companies that deal with transportation or people and goods, by land or by water; and tourist companies;

IX. Bookstores, as well as printing shops, and publishing companies;

X. Companies that deal with brokerage, agencies commercial enterprises and auctioneering outfits to the public;

XI. Companies that deal with public entertainment;

XII. Transactions by commercial agencies;

XIII. Brokerage operations in mercantile dealings;

XIV. Banking operations;

XV. All the contracts dealing with marital commerce and interior and exterior navigation;

XVI. Insurance contracts of all types, as long as they are created by companies;

XVII. Commercial deposits;

XVIII. Deposits made in general stores and all operations with certificates of deposit and pledge documents issued by them;

XIX. Checks, drafts or transfer of moneys from one place to another between all types of individuals;

XX. Commercial paper and other instruments payable to order or bearer, unless proven unrelated to a commercial transaction;

XXI. Obligations between merchants and bankers, except if they are of a civil nature;

XXII. The contracts and obligations of the employees of the merchants in regards to the business;

XXIII. The disposition and transfer of crops by the owner or grower, from his estate or parcel;

XXIV. Any other activity similar to the ones expressed in this Code.

In case of doubt, the commercial nature of the act will be determined by a judge. (Mex. Com. C., art. 75).

**Actos de conciliación.** Proceedings to avoid litigation.

**Actuación.** Proceeding, lawsuit, suit, step in litigation.

**Actuar.** To act, appear, litigate.

**Actuario.** Court clerk, secretary, actuary.

**Acudir.** To apply, request.

**Acudir a la vía judicial.** File a suit, bring a lawsuit

**Acueducto.** Aqueduct.

**Acuerdo.** Accord, agreement, arrangement, contract, deal, pact.

**Acuerdo de rescisión.** Agreement of rescision.

**Acuerdo de voluntades.** Meeting of the minds.

**Acuerdo en finiquito.** Accord and satisfaction.

**Acuerdo pre-nupcial.** Pre-nuptial agreement. A community property marriage will be governed by the pre-nuptial agreement, and any matter not expressly stipulated will be governed by the provisions applicable to civil associations. (Mex. Civ. C., art. 183).

**Acumulación.** Joinder, accumulation.

**Acumulación de acciones.** Consolidation of actions. The plaintiff may consolidate in his complaint as many causes of action as he may have against the defendant, even though they proceed from different titles, provided that said actions are not incompatible with each other. (Sp. L. Civ. P., sec. 153, 154).

**Acumulación de acusados.** Joinder of defendants.

**Acumulación de autos.** Consolidation of records of proceedings.

The consolidation may be ordered in the following cases: 1) When the judgment to be rendered in one of the actions, the consolidation of which is requested, would raise the exception of *res judicata* in the other. 2) When an action is pending before the competent court on the same matter which is the object of that instituted subsequently. 3) When bankruptcy or insolvency proceedings are pending and the property of the insolvent or bankrupt is the subject of the action instituted. 4) When testamentary or intestate proceedings are pending and the property of the estate is the subject of the action instituted and said action is declared to be subject to consolidation with said proceedings. 5) When the unit of the action would be destroyed if the actions should be prosecuted separately. (Sp. L. Civ. P., sec. 160, 161).

**Acumulación de delitos.** Joinder of offenses.

**Acumulación de reclamaciones.** Joinder of claims.

**Acumulación indebida o no acumulación de partes.** Misjoinder or non-joinder of parties.

**Acumular.** To join, accrue.

**Acumulativo.** Cumulative.

**Acuñación.** Minting.

**Acusación del fiscal.** Information. Indictment.

**Acusado.** Accused, defendant.

**Acusador.** Accuser, prosecutor, prosecution, district attorney.

**Acusar.** To accuse, arraign, charge, impeach, indict, prosecute, blame.

**Ad effectum videndi (L).** Literally "to the effect of seeing." Phrase used by one court to request a file from a lower court, to study it and to decide if a particular appeal should or should not be granted.

**Adagio.** Adage, aphorism, maxim, proverb.

**Adelantar.** Advance, forward, further, place in front.

**Adaptación del contrato en caso de error.** Loss of right to avoid.

If a party is entitled to avoid the contract for mistake but the other party declares itself willing to perform or performs the contract as it was understood by the party entitled to avoidance, the contract is considered to have been concluded as the latter party understood it. The other party must make such a declaration or render such performance promptly after having been informed of the manner in which the party entitled to avoidance had understood the contract and before that party has acted in reliance on a notice of avoidance. (Unidroit, Prin., art. 3.13).

**Adeudar.** To owe, be in debt.

**Adhesión.** Adhesion, adherence.

**Adición.** Addition, increase summation, totaling.

**Adicional.** Additional, added, supplemental, supplementary.

**Adiestramiento.** Training, apprenticeship, pupilage.

**Adjudicación.** Adjudication, award.

**Adjudicar.** To adjudicate, adjudge, arbitrate, award, rule, sentence.

**Adjunto** Attached, enclosed, herewith. Adjunct.

**Administración.** Administration, direction, management, supervision.

**Administrador.** Manager, administrator, director, trustee.

**Administrar.** To administer, manage, direct, oversee, supervise.

**Administrativo.** Administrative, executive, managerial, supervisory.

**Admisibilidad limitada.** Limited admissibility.

**Admisible.** Admissible, acceptable, permissible.

**Admisión.** Admission. An admission on the part of the defendant refers to some specific fact which tends to establish the guilt of the defendant or some element of the crime charged against him. (Ppl. v. Barreto, 85 PRR 753 (1962)).
  Acknowledgment, confession. Admittance.

**Admisiones tácitas de un acusado.** Tacit admissions of a defendant. By tacit admissions of a defendant, it is meant the inculpatory statements not contradicted or denied by the defendant in the course of the investigation of the offense. (Ppl. v. Alvarez, 86 PRR 596 (1962)).

**Admitir.** To admit, acknowledge, concede, confess.

**Admonición.** Admonition, warning, advice.

**Adolecencia.** Adolescence, youth.

**Adopción.** Adoption.

**Adopción, capacidad.** Adoption, capacity. The capacity to adopt and to be adopted and the conditions and limitations of adoption are subject to the personal law of each of the interested persons. (Bust. C., art. 73).

**Adopción, efectos.** Adoption, effects. The effects of adoption are regulated by the personal law of the adopting party inso far as his estate is concerned, and by that of the adopted one in respect to the name, the rights and duties which he retains regarding his natural family, as well as to his estate in regard to the adopting person. (Bust. C., art. 74).

**Adopción, repudio.** Adoption, repudiation. Either one of the interested persons may repudiate the adoption in accordance with the provisions of his personal law. (Bust. C., art. 75).

**Adoptado.** Adopted.

**Adoptante.** Adopter.

**Adoptivo.** Adopted.

**Adornar.** To adorn, decorate, dress up, embellish, ornate.

**Adquirente.** Acquirer, buyer, purchaser.

**Adquirir.** To acquire, buy, procure, purchase.

**Adquisición.** Acquisition, property, procurement, purchase.

**Adscribir.** To ascribe, assign, attribute, impute.

**Adscripto.** Attached, placed under.

**Aduana.** Customs, customhouse.

**Aduanero.** Relating to customs, as in customs duty.

**Aducir.** Adduce, affirm, declare, inform, narrate, relate, state.

**Adulteración.** Adulteration, forgery.

**Adulterar.** To adulterate, forge, pervert.

**Adulterino.** Adulterine.

**Adulterio.** Adultery.

**Adulterio con cónyuge ajeno.** Criminal conversation with someone else's spouse.

**Adúltero.** Party to an adultery.

**Adulto.** Adult, of age, mature.

**Advenimiento.** Happening, existence, occurrence.

**Adversario.** Adversary, antagonist, contrary party, opponent, rival.

**Advertencia.** Warning, admonition, advice.

**Advertir.** To warn, alert, caution.

**Adyacente.** Adjacent, adjoining, contiguous, bordering.

**Afección, afecto.** Affection, fondness, love.

**Afectación.** Burden, charge, encumbrance. Simulation.

***Affectio societatis* (L).** The intention of forming and belonging to an enterprise. This is the subjective element that distinguishes a partner from another type of investor.

**Afianzar.** To bail, give bond, guarantee, warrant.

**Afiazamiento, fianza mercantil.** Commercial guaranty. All guaranties the purpose of which is to insure the fulfillment of a commercial contract shall be considered commercial, even though the guarantor is not a merchant. (Sp. Com. C., sec. 439, 440).

**Afiliación.** Affiliation, association, belonging, connection.

**Afiliado.** Affiliated, member.

**Afincamiento.** Firm rooting.

**Afinidad.** Affinity, family relationship.

**Afirmación.** Affirmation, affirmance, averment, assertion, avowal.

**Afirmante.** Affirmant, declarant.

**Afirmar.** To affirm, assert aver, avow, declare.

**Afirmativo.** Affirmative, positive.

**Aforar.** To appraise, assess, evaluate.

**Aforismo.** Aphorism, adage, maxim, saying. Particularly in a foreign language.

**Aforo.** Appraisal, assessment, evaluation.

**Agencia.** Agency, bureau, department, office.

**Agencia de financiamiento.** Financing agency.

**Agenciar.** To obtain.

**Agente.** Agent, attorney-in-fact, delegate, proxy, representative.

**Agente viajero.** Travelling agent.

**Agentes de cambio y bolsa.** Money and stock brokers. Money and stock brokers shall be authorized: 1) To take part privately in negotiations and transfers of all kinds of public instruments or securities which can be quoted, 2) To take part, in concurrence with commercial agents, in all other exchange transactions and contracts, subject to the liabilities appertaining to these transactions. (Sp. Com. C., sec. 100).

**Agentes mediadores del comercio.** Commercial agents.

**Agio.** Usury. Overcharging.

**Agiotaje.** Agiotage, overcharging, overreaching.

**Agiotista.** Profiteer.

**Agotamiento.** Depletion. Exhaustion.

**Agravante.** Aggravating circumstance.

**Agravar.** To aggravate, worsen.

**Agravatorio.** Aggravating, rendering worse.

**Agraviado.** Aggrieved.

**Agravio.** Damage, harm, injury, offense, tort.

**Agravioso.** Damaging, harmful, injurious, tortious.

**Agredir.** Assault, attack, assail, strike.

**Agregado.** Added, appended. Combination, composite. Attache.

**Agregar.** Add, affix, annex, incorporate, supplement.

**Agremiado.** Union member.

**Agremiar.** To unionize.

**Agresión.** Aggression, assault, attack, battery, hostility.

**Agresor.** Aggressor, assailant.

**Agrimensor.** Land surveyor.

**Agrimensura.** Measuring and marking land.

**Agrupación.** Grouping, group, association.

**Agrupamiento.** Grouping, group, gathering.

**Agua, uso en ganado.** Water, livestock use. The utilization of national water for the raising and fattening of livestock, poultry and animals, and their preparation for initial transfer, provided that industrial processing is not included.

**Agua, uso industrial.** Water, industrial use. The utilization of national water in plants or undertakings that carry out the extraction, preservation, or processing of raw materials or minerals, the finishing of products or the manufacture of satisfactory products, and the utilization of national water in industrial parks, boilers, cooling and cleaning devices, and bathing and other services within the undertaking, the brines used for the extraction of any type substances and water, including when in gaseous state, used for electric power generation or any other processing use or development.

**Aguas alumbradas.** Artesian waters. Artesian waters belong to the person discovering them. When the owner of artesian waters abandons the same to their natural course, they shall become public domain. (Sp. Civ. C., sec. 425, 426).

**Aguas de dominio privado.** Waters of private ownership. To private dominion belong: 1) Waters, either continuous or intermittent, rising on private tenements, as far as they run through the same. 2) Lakes and marshes, and their beds, when formed by nature on the said tenements. 3) Subterranean waters found on the same. 4) Rain water falling on private tenements, as long as they remain within the boundaries of the same. 5) The beds of flowing waters, continuous or intermittent, formed by rain water, and those of brooks crossing tenements which do not belong to the public domain. (Sp. Civ. C., sec. 415).

**Aguas de dominio privado, aprove chamiento.** Waters of private ownership, use. The owner of a tenement in which a spring or brook rises, be it continuous or intermittent, may use its waters as far as they run through the said tenement; but after the said water leaves the tenement it shall become public and its use is governed by special legislation. (Sp. Civ. C., sec. 419, 423).

**Aguas de dominio público.** Water of public domain. To the public domain belong: 1) Rivers and their natural beds. 2) Continuous or intermittent waters from sources or brooks running in their natural beds, and the beds themselves. 3) Waters rising continuously or intermittently in lands, within the same public domain. 4) Lakes and marshes formed by nature on public lands, and also their beds. 5) Rain water running through ravines or sandy beaches, the beds of which may also belong to the public domain. 6) Subterranean waters existing on public lands. 7) Waters found within the zone of operation of public works, even when they are executed by a grantee. 8) Waters flowing continuously or intermittently from tenements belonging to private parties. (Sp. Civ. C., sec. 414).

**Aguas, obras defensivas.** Water, defensive works.

**Aguas pluviales.** Rain water.

**Aguas públicas, aprovechamiento.** The use of public waters is acquired: 1) By administrative concession. 2) By prescription after twenty years. The limits of the rights and obligations of these uses shall be those shown, in the first case, by the terms of the concession; and in the second case, by the manner in which the waters have been used. (Sp. Civ. C., sec. 416, 417).

**Aguas subterrraneas.** Subterranean water. Only the owner of a tenement or another person with his permission, may search for subterranean waters thereon. (Sp. Civ. C., sec. 424).

**Aguas vivas.** Running water.

**Aguinaldo.** Annual bonus. A Christmas bonus, consisting of at least 15 days' salary, is considered as part of the salary and should be paid each year. (FLL, Article 87).

**Ahijado/a.** Godchild.

**Ahorcar.** To hang, execute, lynch.

**Ahorrado.** Saved, kept, put aside.

**Ahorro.** Savings, economy.

**Aislado.** Isolated, alone, ostracized, protected, separate.

**Ajustado a derecho.** Lawful, complying with the law, legal.

**Ajustador.** Adjuster.

**Ajustador de seguros.** Claims adjustor.

**Ajustar.** To adjust, settle, compensate. Accommodate, regulate, rectify.

**Ajuste alzado.** System providing payment in only one installment or lump sum.

**Ajustes por modernización.** Adjustments due to modernization. The law also regulates those cases where there are some workers become redundant due to the introduction of machinery or new production processes. (FLL, Article 439).

**Al amparo de.** Under the protection of.

**Al calce.** At the foot, at the end.

**Al frente.** At the head, in front.

**Al pie, al final.** At the foot, at the end.

**Al pie de la letra.** Literally, undeviantly, rigorously.

**Alimentante.** Person in charge of providing support, e.g. to his spouse or to his children.

**Alimentos, cese.** Support, termination. The obligation to pay support terminates:

I. When the supporting party is unable to do so;

II. When the person receiving the support does not need it anymore;

III. When the person receiving the support injures or causes serious damage against the supporting party;

IV. If the need of support is caused by the misconduct or improper work attitude of the person being supported. The suspension of the obligation shall be for as long as this condition lasts;

V. If the person receiving support abandons the house of the supporting party without consent and without justified cause. (Mex. Civ. C., art. 320).

**Al por mayor.** Wholesale.

**Al por menor.** Retail.

**Al portador.** To bearer.

**Alargar.** Enlarge, extend, lengthen, prolong.

**Albacea.** Executor. Executors may be universal or special. In any case executors may be appointed either severally, successively, or jointly. (Sp. Civ. C., sec. 868). In case of a women, she is called the executrix.

**Albaceazgo.** Executorship. Executorship is but an administration accompanied by a right of representation to perform specific functions relating to the conservation of the hereditary estate until the inheritance is accepted by the heirs. (Paine v. Sec. of the Treas., 85 PRR 787 (1962)).

**Albedrío, libre.** Autonomy, free choice, power to decide freely.

**Albergar.** To lodge, cover, guard, shelter.

**Albergue.** Hosted, shelter.

**Alborotar.** To agitate, disturb, upset.

**Alboroto.** Brawl, confusion, tumult, revolt, riot.

**Alcahuete.** Pimp.

**Alcahuetería.** Pandering, procuring.

**Alcaide.** Warden of a prison.

**Alcalde.** Mayor.

**Alcaldía.** City hall.

**Alcance.** Scope, amplitude, breadth, expanse, reach, span.

**Alcohol.** Alcohol, liquor, spirits.

**Alcoholismo.** Alcoholism, drunkenness.

**Alcurnia.** Ancestry, descendance, genealogy line, lineage, progeny.

**Aleatorio.** Aleatory, depending on chance.

**Alegable.** Pleadable.

**Alegación.** Plea, argument, affirmation, allegation, averment, contention, hypothesis.

**Alegación de admisión.** Plea of *nolo contendere*.

**Alegación preacordada.** Plea agreement, plea bargaining.

**Alegaciones.** Pleadings.

**Alegar.** To plead, argue, advocate, advance a theory or idea.

**Alegato.** Plea, brief, allegation, legal opinion.

**Alerta.** Alert, attentive, vigilant. Alarm, warning.

**Alevosía.** Cruelty, reckless disregard.

**Alfonso el Sabio.** Alfonso, the Wise.

**Alguacil.** Bailiff.

**Alianza.** Alliance, coalition, compact, league.

**Alias.** Alias, A.K.A. (also known as), nickname, otherwise known as.

**Alienable.** Saleable.

**Alienación.** Alienation, transfer of ownership, sale.

**Alienado.** Alienated.

**Alienar.** To alienate, transfer, sale.

**Alijo.** Lighten the vessel, jettison.

**Alimentos.** Alimony. By alimony we understand what is necessary for the nourishment, lodging and support of the person who claims it. It includes the education, when the person to whom the alimony is due is a minor. (Louisiana Civ. Code art. 230).

**Alimentos del cónyuge.** Spousal support. In the case of a contested divorce, the judge, taking into account the circumstances of the case and the ability of the spouses to work and their economic situation, will direct the spouse at fault to pay alimony in favor of the innocent spouse. (Mex. Civ. C., art. 288).

**Alistar.** To enlist, enroll, recruit, volunteer. To prepare.

**Allanamiento.** Acceptance, admission. Judicial search of a building, usually conducted by the police.

**Almacenes de adeudo.** Bonded warehouses.

**Almirantazgo.** Admiralty.

**Almirante.** Admiral.

**Alquiler.** Rent, rental, lease.

**Alta mar.** High seas.

**Alta traición.** High treason, rebellion, sedition.

**Alterar.** Alter, change.

**Altura.** Hight.

**Alucinación.** Hallucination, mirage, vision.

**Alucinógeno.** Hallucinatory.

**Alumbrado.** Illumination, light. Bright.

**Aluvión.** Alluvion. Alluvion, in its most strict and common meaning, is defined as the increase of land which is successively and imperceptibly formed on the banks or shores of the rivers. (Vachier v. MacCormick, Alcaide & Co., 86 PRR 677 (1962)).

**Aluvión, derelicción.** Alluvion, dereliction. Accretion formed successively and imperceptibly on the bank of a river or stream, whether navigable or not, is called alluvion.

The alluvion belongs to the owner of the bank, who is bound to leave public that portion of the bank which is required for the public use. The same rule applies to dereliction formed by water receding imperceptibly from a bank of a river or stream. The owner of the land situated at the edge of the bank left dry owns the dereliction. (Louisiana Civ. Code art. 499).

**Alzada.** Court of a higher rank, court with overseeing jurisdiction. Appeal.

**Ama de casa.** Housewife, homemaker.

**Ambiente.** Environment, ambience, climate, milieu.

**Ambiguo.** Ambiguous, confusing.

**Amenaza.** Threat, danger, warning.

**Amenaza de huelga.** Threatened strike.

**Amenaza, fuerza o intimidación.** Threat.
A party may avoid the contract when it has been led to conclude the contract by the other party's unjustified threat which, having regard to the circumstances, is so imminent and serious as to leave the first party no reasonable alternative. (Unidroit, Prin., art. 3.9).

**Amigable componedor.** Amicable compounder. Amicable compounders shall decide the questions submitted to their decision according to their knowledge and belief without being subject to legal forms. (Sp. L. Civ. P. sec. 832).

**Amnistía.** Amnesty. Amnesty extinguishes the penal action and the punishment, together with all its ancillary effects. Security measures will not be annulled for reason of amnesty or pardon. (St. P.C. for LA, sec. 99 and 62).

**Amo.** Master, lord, owner, proprietor, ruler.

**Amojonamiento.** Fencing, placing boundaries, demarcation.

**Amojonar.** To fix boundaries, to outline a perimeter.

**Amparo.** Amparo. The amparo applies to violations of the numerous guarantees of individual freedoms, whether by government agencies or by the judiciary. From Mexico the amparo procedure very rapidly spread to other countries such as Argentina, Guatemala, Honduras, Nicaragua, El Salvador, and Costa Rica, although it is not used as widely. (W. Eur. & LA Leg. Sys.).

**Anatocismo.** Anatocism. Compounding of interest.

**Anclaje.** Anchorage, mooring.

**Anejo.** Enclosed, included, herewith.

**Anexar.** To annex, merge, join, unify.

**Anexo.** Annex, appendix, in a schedule.

**Angaria.** Angary.

**Angustia mental.** Emotional distress.

**Angustias mentales intencionales.** Emotional distress intended, intentional infliction of emotional distress.

**Angustias mentales no intencionales.** Emotional distress unintended.

**Animal doméstico.** Domestic animal.

**Animal salvaje.** Wild animal.

**Animales fieros.** Wild animals.

**Animo de lucro.** With the intent to make a profit.

**Animus domini (L).** Believing that one is the owner and acting accordingly. The expression is used mainly in the area of real property law, particularly when talking of adverse possession.

**Año civil.** Calendar year, from January 1 to December 31.

**Anotación.** Annotation.

**Anotación de embargo.** Record of attachment.

**Anotación marginal.** Notation on margin.

**Anotación preventiva.** Recordation, cautionary notice.

**Anotar.** To record, annotate, register.

**Ante mí.** Before me.

**Antecedentes del acusado.** Defendant's prior record.

**Antedatado.** Antedated.

**Antejuicio.** Preliminary proceedings.

**Antepasado.** Ancestor, ascendant, forefather, precursor.

**Anteproyecto.** Preliminary design.

**Anteproyecto de ley.** Proposed law or bill.

**Anterior.** Foregoing, mentioned above, previous.

**Anticipación.** Anticipation, expectation.

**Anticipado.** Anticipatory, ahead of time.

**Anticipo.** Advance payment, earnest money, deposit.

**Anticresis.** Antichresis. By antichresis a creditor acquires a right to receive the fruits of real property of his debtor, with the obligation to apply them to the payment of interest, if due, and afterwards to the principal of his credit.

**Antigüedad.** Antique, ancient. Archaic. Seniority. Antiquity.

**Antijurídico.** Illegal, illicit, unlawful, lawless.

**Anualidad.** Annuity, rent.

**Anuencia.** Acceptance, tacit approval, lack of opposition.
Consent, acquiescence, acceptance, assent.

**Anulable.** Subject to an action for nullity.

**Anulación parcial.** Partial avoidance.
Where a ground of avoidance affects only individual terms of the contract, the effect of avoidance is limited to those terms unless, having regard to the circumstances, it is unreasonable to uphold the remaining contract. (Unidroit, Prin., art. 3.16).

**Anunciar.** To announce, advertise.

**Anuncio.** Announcement, declaration, publication. Advert.

**Año básico.** Base year.

**Año del Señor.** Year of our Lord. A.D.

**Año fiscal.** Fiscal year.

**Año natural.** Calendar year.

**Aparcería de tierras de labor.** Lease for partnership of arable lands.

**Aparcero agrícola.** Sharecropper.

**Aparejar.** Trigger certain consequences.

**Aparejo.** Rigging.

**Apariencia jurídica.** Juridical appearance. In the relations between the purchaser and the vendor of a real property, juridical appearance is defined as the appearance of a burden or encumbrance derived from the publicity of registries, that by legal presumption is considered known by all those who make contracts on the property. (Miralli v. Fullana Corp., 98 PRR 323 (1970)).

**Apartado.** Paragraph, section, subsection.

**Apátrida.** Stateless, person with no citizenship.

**Apatridia.** Statelessness.

**Apelación.** Appeal.

**Apelación en ambos efectos.** Appeal for review and stay of proceedings. If the appeal be admitted both for review and stay of proceedings, the original record shall be ordered transmitted to the audience, if the latter is to take cognizance of the appeal, and the parties shall be summoned for appearance before the same within a period of ten days. (Sp. L. Crim. P., art. 224).

**Apelación en un sólo efecto.** Appeal for a review of proceedings only. If the appeal be admissible for a review of the proceedings only, a certified copy of the decision appealed from shall be ordered made, as well as of the other matters which the appellant may request and which can be given him, taking into consideration, in a proper case, the secret character of the sumario, and such other matters as the judge may order *ex officio*. (Sp. L. Crim. P., art. 225).

**Apelado.** Appellee.

**Apelante.** Appellant.

**Apellido.** Surname, family name.

**Apéndice.** Appendix, addendum, rider, supplement.

**Apercibido.** Under warning, on notice.

**Apercibimiento.** Warning, notice.

**Apercibir.** To put on notice, to warn.

**Apertura.** Opening, beginning.

**Apertura de crédito.** Opening a line of credit or a letter of credit.

**Apertura de la sesión.** Opening of a meeting.

**Apertura de propuestas.** Opening bids. Opening of the bids.

**Apertura de testamento.** Act of opening before the court of a closed will.

**Aplazamiento del cumplimiento.** Withholding performance.
Where the parties are to perform simultaneously, either party may withhold performance until the other party tenders its performance. (Unidroit, Prin., art. 7.1.3).

**Aplicación de leyes laborales.** Enforcement of labor law.

**Aplicación del derecho extranjero.**
Application of foreign law. The following is to be observed in the application of foreign law:

I. It shall be applied as the corresponding foreign judge would do it; to that end, the judge may obtain the necessary information about the text, validity, meaning, and legal scope of said law.

II. The substantive foreign law should be applied, save when given the special circumstances of the case, the conflict-of-law rules of said foreign law should be taken into account, as an exception, making applicable the local substantive rules of those of a third country.

III. It will not be an impediment for the application of foreign law that the local law does not provide institutions or procedures essential to the applicable foreign institutions, if analogous institutions do exist.

IV. Previous, preliminary, or incidental questions that may arise from a principal issue, should not necessarily be resolved with the law that governs said issue; and

V. When different aspects of the same juridical relationship are governed by different [foreign] laws, these shall be applied harmoniously endeavoring to attain the purposes pursued by each of said laws. The difficulties caused by the simultaneous application of said [foreign] laws shall be resolved taking into account the requirements of equity in the specific case. (J.A. Vargas).

**Aplicación indebida.** Misapplication.

**Apoderado.** Attorney, agent, proxy, attorney in fact, assignee.

**Apoderado especial.** Special agent.

**Apoderado constituido.** Attorney-in-fact. If a person has been absent from his domicile and he has appointed an attorney-in-fact before or after his departure, the attorney-in-fact shall be reputed to be present for all the civil effects, and his affairs can be handled through him up to the authority vested in him. (Mex. Civ. C., art. 648).

**Apoderado general.** General agent, managing partner.

**Apoderamiento indebido de bienes muebles.** Trespass to chattel.

**Apodo.** Alias, also known as, nickname.

**Apología.** Apology, defense, justification.

**Aportar.** To contribute. To arrive in port.

**Aportar prueba.** To produce evidence.

**Apostilla.** Catchline. Apostille.

**Apremio.** Court order, decree, legal proceedings for collection.

**Apremio real.** Sale of attached property.

**Aprendiz.** Apprentice. Apprentices, that is, those who engage to serve any one, in order to learn some art, trade or profession. (Lou. Civ. C., art. 164).

**Aprendizaje.** Apprenticeship.

**Apresamiento.** Capture.

**Aprisionamiento indebido.** False imprisonment.

**Aprobación de proyectos legislativos.** Passage of bills.

**Aprobación de una ley.** Passage of a law, enactment.

**Aprobar.** Approve, adopt, agree, assent, consent.

**Apropiación.** Appropriation.

**Apropiación de nombre o parecidos físicos.** Appropriation of name or likeness.

**Apropriación por el gobierno.** Taking by the government.

**Apropiación temporaria.** Temporary appropriation. In the crime of robbery it is sufficient to prove the appropriation of the personal property stolen, even though the appropriation by defendant be for a few moments—temporary appropriation doctrine. (Ppl. v. Torres Rosario, 89 PRR 142 (1963)).

**Apropiar.** To appropriate for oneself.

**Aptitud legal.** Situation where it is legally permissible to perform an act with all its normal consequences. The phrase is many times used to indicate that a person is of age and without any incapacity.

**Apto.** Apt. Fully competent to appear in court, enter into a contract and acquire any type of right or obligation.

**Aquí me remito.** Expression denoting a remission to another text.

**Aquiescencia.** Consent, acceptance, acquiescence, assent.

**Arancel.** Tariff, price list, rate, schedule of fees.

**Arbitrable.** Subject to be arbitrated.

**Arbitrador.** Arbitrator.

**Arbitraje, acuerdo.** Arbitration, agreement. An agreement in which the parties undertake to submit to arbitral decision any differences that may arise or have arisen between them with respect to a commercial transaction is valid. The agreement shall be set forth in an instrument signed by the parties, or in the form of an exchange of letters, telegrams, or telex communications. (Conv. on Intl. Comm. Arb., art. 1).

**Arbitraje, arbitración.** Arbitration, arbitrage, reference.

**Arbitraje, finalidad.** Arbitration, finality. An arbitral decision or award that is not appealable under the applicable law or procedural rules shall have the force of a final judicial judgement. (Conv. on Intl. Comm. Arb., art. 4).

**Arbitraje, reglas de procedimiento.** Arbitration, rules of procedure.

**Arbitraje, viabilidad.** Arbitration, viability. Disputes may be submitted to the decision of one or more arbitrators of uneven number, before or during judicial proceedings, provided they do not concern matters of civil status, divorce or separation of husband and wife, or other matters not susceptible to a settlement. (Amado).

**Arbitrar.** To arbitrate.

**Arbitrariedad.** An unreasonable situation tainted by illegality and unfairness.

**Arbitrio.** Free choice, power of decision, discretion.

**Árbitro.** Arbitrator, mediator, referee, umpire.

**Arbitro, nombramiento.** Arbitrator, appointment. Arbitrators shall be appointed in the manner agreed upon by the parties. Their appointment may be delegated to a third party, whether a natural or juridical person. (Conv. on Intl. Comm. Arb., art. 2).

**Archivar.** To file.

**Archivo.** Archive.

**Argüir.** To argue, to plead, to represent.

**Argumento.** Argument, pleading, legal theory.

**Armada.** Armada, navy, fleet.

**Armador.** Charterer, owner of a ship.

**Armisticio.** Armistice, cease-fire, truce.

**Arraigo.** Belonging to or having roots in one place. Bond to pay for legal costs that plaintiff has to post when not a resident of the forum.

**Arras.** Down payment.

**Arrebatar.** Snatch, grab, seize, wrest, wring.

**Arrebato.** Seizure, tantrum. Order given with a bugle (military).

**Arreglo.** Arrangement, settlement.

**Arrendable.** Suitable to be leased.

**Arrendador y arrendatario.** Lessor and lessee. A person who binds himself to grant the use of a thing, to execute a work, or to render a service is a lessor; and a person who acquires the use of the thing or a right to the work or service, for which he binds himself to pay, is a lessee. (Sp. Civ. C., sec. 1449).

**Arrendamiento.** Lease, rent.

**Arrepentimiento.** Repentance, remorse.

**Arrestar.** To arrest.

**Arresto civil.** Civilian arrest. Any person may place under arrest: 1) he who shall attempt to commit a crime, at the moment he is about to commit it; 2) a criminal captured *in fragranti*; 3) he who shall escape from a penal institution in which he may be serving a sentence; 4) he who shall escape from a prison in which he may be awaiting his transfer to a penal institution or place in which he is to serve the sentence which may have been imposed upon him by a final sentence; 5) he who shall escape while being conducted to the institution or place mentioned in the foregoing number; 6) he who shall escape while under arrest or detention awaiting trial; 7) a person accused or convicted who may be in default. (Sp. L. Crim. P., sec. 490).

**Arribada forzosa.** Arrival under stress.

**Arriendo.** Lease, rent.

**Arrimo y arrastre.** Hauling and transportation.

**Arrogarse.** To bestow on oneself, e.g., a title.

**Arroyo.** Brook.

**Arsenal.** Arsenal, armory.

**Artesano.** Artisan.

**Articulado.** Way of referring to part of a code or a statute.

**Artículo.** Article, section in a statute.

**Artículo corriente.** Routine, common, predictable, unremarkable.

**Artículo mortis.** On the verge of death, when death is imminent.

**Artículos de previo pronunciamiento.** Preliminary exceptions. The following questions or pleas shall be the subject of preliminary exceptions: 1) A declinatory plea. 2) A plea of *res judicata*. 3) The prescription of the crime. 4) The plea of amnesty or pardon. 5) The lack of administrative authority to conduct proceedings, in cases in which it is necessary in accordance with the constitution and special laws. (Sp. L. Crim. P., art. 666, 668).

**Artillería de campaña.** Field artillery.

**Asalariado.** Worker, jobber, wage earner. Salaried.

**Asalto.** Assault, battery. Robbery. Storming of a fortified place.

**Asamblea.** Assembly, committee.

**Asamblea general de accionistas.** General shareholders' meeting.

**Ascendiente.** Ascendant.

**Ascenso.** Promotion, advancement, raise. Ascent, climbing.

**Asediar.** To storm, assail, attack. To inconvenience.

**Asedio.** Siege, taking by storm. Cornering.

**Asegurable.** Insurable.

**Asegurado.** Insured.

**Asegurador.** Insurer, insurance company.

**Asegurar.** To insure.

**Aserción.** Assertion, averment, declaration, statement.

**Asertar.** To assert, aver, avow, declare, state.

**Asesinar.** To murder.

**Asesinato.** Murder, assassination, homicide.

**Asesino.** Assassin, murderer.

**Asesor.** Counselor, adviser, advisor.

**Asfixia.** Asphyxia, choking, smothering, suffocation.

**Asfixiar.** To asphyxiate, choke, smother, strangle, suffocate.

**Asiento.** Entry. The following kinds of entries shall be made in the registry books: presentation, registrations, cautionary. notices, cancellations and notations. (PR Mort. Law 1979 sec. 80).

Annotation, inscription, registration, recordation.

**Asignación.** Appropriation, allocation, allotment, attribution, allowance.

**Asilado.** Person who enjoys political asylum.

**Asilar.** To grant political asylum.

**Asilo.** Asylum. Safe harbor. Hospital for the mentally unbalanced and indigent.

**Asistencia.** Attendance, appearance.

**Asociación.** Association.

**Asociación con fines no pecuniarios.** Non-profit association.

**Asociación cooperativa de crédito.** Credit union.

**Asociación sindical voluntaria.** Free membership to unions.

**Astillero.** Dockyard.

**Asunción del riesgo.** Assumption of risk.

**Asunción expresa del riesgo.** Express assumption of risk.

**Asunción implícita del riesgo.** Implied assumption of risk.

**Ataque epiléptico.** Epileptic seizure.

**Atentado.** An attack, usually of a terrorist nature.

**Atentado contra la libertad de comercio.** Restraint of trade.

**Atentar contra.** To impair, attempt against, jeopardize.

**Atenuación del daño.** The nonperforming party is not liable for harm suffered by the aggrieved party to the extent that the harm could have been reduced by the latter party's taking reasonable steps. (Unidroit, Prin., art. 7.4.8).

**Atenuante.** Extenuating circumstance.

**Aterrizaje.** Landing, descent, touch down.

**Aterrizar.** To land, alight, descend, touch down.

**Atestación.** Attestation, testimony.

**Atestado.** What has been testified.

**Atestar.** To testify.

**Atestiguar.** To testify.

**Atraco.** Robbery.

**Atraer.** To attract, appeal, beguile, draw, entice, lure, seduce.

**Atraque.** Mooring. The term mooring is defined as a fee charged to the vessel for being moored to a dock to unload or load or to do any operation. (San Miguel Fertil Corp. v. P.R. Drydock, 94 PRR 403 (1967)).

**Atrasado.** Delinquent, backward, in arrears, overdue, unpaid.

**Atribución.** Attribution, attribute, characteristic.

**Atribuciones.** Powers, authority, faculty.

**Atropello.** Gross abuse.

**Audiencia.** Hearing, audience, appointment, session, sitting.

**Auditor.** Person who performs a financial audit. An attorney in the armed forces (AR).

**Aun cuando.** Notwithstanding, regardless.

**Ausencia.** Absence. If a person shall not have appeared either in person or through an attorney in fact at his place of domicile or habitual residence after five years have elapsed from the time of his departure, or if no news concerning him has been received in the same period of time, his presumptive heirs may by producing proof of the fact, solicit and obtain from the court an order placing them in provisional possession of the estate belonging to the absentee at the time of his departure or the last news receive of him, on condition that they give sufficient security for their administration.

**Ausente.** Absentee. An absentee is a person who has resided in the State, and has departed without leaving anyone to represent him. It means also the person, who never was domiciliated in the State and resides abroad. In matters of succession, the heir whose residence is not known is deemed an absentee. (Louisiana Civ. Code art. 3556).

**Auténtica.** The certification, proof or attestation that a document is authentic.

**Autenticación.** Authentication, acknowledgment, certification.

**Autenticación *prima facie*.** Self-authentication.

**Autenticar.** To certify, to give authenticity, to legalize.

**Auténtico.** Authentic. That cannot be rebutted (for documents).

**Auto.** Writ, decree, order, ruling.

**Auto de ejecución.** Writ of execution.

**Auto de entrada y registro en domcilio particular.** Warrant for entry and search in a private home. The warrant for the entry and search of the domicile of a private party shall always set forth the reasons therefor, and the judge shall state therein concisely the building or closed space to be entered and searched, whether it is to take place in the daytime only, and the authority or official to perform the service. (Sp. L. Crim. P., art. 558).

**Auto de prisión.** Indictment. Arraignment.

**Auto defensa mediante fuerza.** Self-defense by force.

**Auto inhibitorio.** Writ of prohibition.

**Auto inicial.** First ruling.

**Auto resolutorio.** Ruling of the court.

**Autoincriminación.** Self incrimination.

**Autonomía.** Autonomy, freedom, home rule, self-government.

**Autonomía de la voluntad.** Choice of law. In general, Latin American nations favor the ample party's autonomy in the choice of governing law. The Bustamante Code lists a series of rules for choosing the law of certain contracts: agreements relating to marriage, purchases and sales, leases, loans, aleatory contracts, pledges, and mortgages. A contract must comply with the law of the place where it is entered into. (LA Laws & Inst.).

**Autónomo.** Autonomous, independent.

**Autopsia.** Autopsy.

**Autor de un delito, penalidad.** Author of a crime, penalty. Whoever commits a criminal act by his own conduct or by the conduct of another person, and those who commit it jointly, will be sentenced to the penalty provided for the corresponding crime. (St. P.C. for LA, sec. 33).

**Autoridad.** Authority. Authorities.

**Autoridad aparente.** Apparent authority.

**Autorización.** Authorization, permission.

**Autorización denegada.** Permission refused. The refusal of a permission affecting the validity of the contract renders the contract void. If the refusal affects the validity of some terms only, only such terms are void if, having regard to the circumstances, it is reasonable to uphold the remaining contract. (Unidroit, Prin., art. 6.1.17).

**Autorización judicial.** Court approval.

**Autorización que no ha sido otorgada ni denegada.** Permission neither granted nor refused. (1) If, notwithstanding the fact that the party responsible has taken all measures required, permission is neither granted nor refused within an agreed period or, where no period has been agreed, within a reasonable time from the conclusion of the contract, either party is entitled to terminate the contract. (2) Where the permission affects some terms only, paragraph (1) does not apply if, having regard to the circumstances, it is reasonable to uphold the remaining contract even if the permission is refused. (Unidroit, Prin., art. 6.1.16).

**Autos.** Rulings. Rulings are those deciding incidental issues or essential points which affect in a direct manner the accused, the private complainants, or parties to the civil actions; when they decide the jurisdiction of the superior or inferior court, the sustaining or overruling of challenges, the reversal of some order, the refusal to reverse an order, imprisonment or liberation, the admission or rejection of evidence, or of the benefits of poverty, and, finally, all others which according to law must set forth the reasons therefor. (Sp. L. Crim. P., art. 141).

**Autos y legajos.** Records and files.

**Auxiliar.** Deputy, assistant, auxiliary, representative.

**Auxilio.** Assistance, aid, attendance, help, support.

**Auxilio necesario o indispensable.** Necessary or indispensable help. Whoever renders to the principal or principals aid of such nature that without it the criminal act could not have been committed, will also be sentenced with the penalty provided for the corresponding crime. (St. P.C. for LA, sec. 35).

**Aval.** Aval. Special guarantee endorsement.

**Avalar.** To back, support, vouch for, to endorse.

**Avalista.** Endorser who guarantees payment.

**Avalúo de bienes.** Appraisement, appraisal of property.

**Avenimiento.** Conciliation, when it is common to both parties. Acceptance by one party of the position taken by the other party.

**Avería (Mar.).** Average. For the purposes of this code the following shall be considered averages: 1) All extraordinary or accidental expenses which may be incurred during the navigation for the preservation of the vessel or cargo, or both. 2) All damages or deterioration the vessel may suffer from the time she puts to sea from the port of departure until she casts anchor in the port of destination, and those suffered by the merchandise from the time it is loaded in the port of shipment until it is unloaded in the port of consignment. (Sp. Com. C., sec. 806/7).

**Avería gruesa o común.** General or gross average. General or gross averages shall be, as a general rule, all the damages and expenses which are directly caused in order to save the vessel, her cargo, or both at the same time, from a real and known risk.

**Avería simple o particular.** Simple or particular average. Simple or particular averages shall be, as a general rule, all the expenses and damages caused to the vessel or to her cargo which have not redounded to the benefit and common profit of all the persons interested in the vessel and her cargo. (Sp. Com. C., sec. 809/10).

The owner of the goods which gave rise to the expense or suffered the damage shall bear the simple or particular averages.

**Aviso.** Notice.

**Avocarse al conocimiento.** The act by which one court accepts a case under its jurisdiction.

**Avulsión.** Avulsion.

**Axioma.** Axiom, assumption, premise.

**Ayuda impedida intencionalmente.** Intentionally preventing assistance.

**Ayuda impedida negligentemente.** Negligently preventing assistance.

**Ayuntamiento.** City hall, city council, township, town council.

**Azar.** Fate, chance, destiny, luck.

# B

**Baja.** Discharge, cancellation.

**Bajeza.** Low action, dishonor, shame.

**Bajo.** Under, below, beneath.

**Bajo el poder.** Under the control.

**Bajo juramento solemne.** Under oath.

**Bajo libertad condicional.** On parole. System by which a prisoner who has discharged a substantial part of the sentence and has observed good behavior while in jail is released. Certain conditions are imposed, like the duty to report periodically to the authorities who monitor the person's conduct. Should the conditions be broken, or a new crime be committed, the person in question could be sent back to serve the remainder of the prison term.

**Bala.** Bullet, ammunition, projectile, shell.

**Balance.** Balance, equilibrium, stability. Excess, remnant, surplus. Financial sheet .

**Balanza.** Scale.

**Baldío.** Unoccupied land.

**Balística.** The study of bullets and of their trajectories.

**Balotaje.** Election that can be decided on a second round if there is not a clear majority.

**Banca.** Banking.

**Bancario.** Banker. Related to banks.

**Bancarrota.** Bankruptcy, insolvency. Case of merchant unable to meet his debts.

**Banco.** Bank. Cache, reserve. Bench.

**Bancos de emisión y descuento.** Banks of issue and discount. The following is the principal business of these institutions: Discounts, deposits, current accounts, collections, loans, drafts, and contracts with the government or public corporations. (Sp. Com. C., sec. 177).

**Bancos y sociedades agrícolas.** Agricultural banks and associations.

**Banda.** Gang. Group of criminals acting jointly.

**Bandera.** Flag, banner, emblem, ensign.

**Bandido.** Bandit, brigand, burglar, crook, robber, thief.

**Bando.** Edict, decree, order, proclamation, ruling. Band, clique, gang.

**Bandolero.** Bandit, brigand, burglar, crook, robber, thief.

**Banquillo.** Bench, stool.

**Barbitúricos.** Barbituric drugs.

**Barco.** Ship, boat, vessel, seacraft.

**Barra.** Bar. College of advocates.

**Barraganería.** Concubinage, cohabitation without marriage.

**Barrio.** Neighborhood.

**Basado en.** Based upon.

**Base.** Base, headquarters. Basis, essence, root.

**Bases.** Bases, cornerstone, foundation. Terms and conditions, requirements.

**Bastardía.** Bastardy.

**Bastardo.** Bastard, born out of wedlock, illegitimate child. Scoundrel, villain. Adulterated, forged.

**Batalla.** Battle. Combat, war. Conflict, dispute.

**Batirse.** To fight. To fight a duel.

**Bautizmo, bautizo.** Christening, naming.

**Beca.** Scholarship, endowment, grant, financial support.

**Bedel.** Caretaker, guard, janitor.

**Beligerancia.** Belligerency, aggression, hostility. Battle, war.

**Beligerante.** Belligerent, aggressive, bellicose, hostile.

**Beneficencia.** Charitable activity, work or gifts for the poor.

**Beneficiado.** Beneficiary, recipient.

**Beneficiar.** To benefit, aid, help. To gain, profit from.

**Beneficiario.** Beneficiary, recipient.

**Beneficio.** Benefit, advantage.

**Beneficio de la excusión.** Benefit of a levy against the principal.

**Beneficio de litigar sin gastos. *In forma pauperis.*** Right to receive *pro bono* assistance.

**Beneficio, minería.** Benefaction, mining. Works for the preparation, treatment, first hand smelting and refining of mineral products, at any of their stages, with the purpose of recovering or obtaining minerals or substances, as well as to increase the concentration and purity of their contents.

**Beneficios.** Proceeds, benefit, earning, gain, income, profit.

**Beneficioso.** Beneficial, advantageous, fruitful, gainful, profitable.

**Beodez.** Alcoholism, drunkenness, intoxication.

**Beodo.** Alcoholic, drunk, drunkard.

**Bestialidad.** Bestiality.

**Bien común.** Common good.

**Bien mueble peligroso para su uso específico.** Chattel dangerous for intended use.

**Bienes.** Assets, chattels, estate, goods, holdings, net worth, property.

**Bienes, clases.** Things, kinds. Things or property are either common or public. (Sp. Civ. C., sec. 325).

**Bienes comunes.** Common things. Common things are those the ownership of which belongs to no one in particular and which all men may freely use, in conformity with their innate nature; such as air, rainwater, the sea and its shores. (Sp. Civ. C., sec. 326).

**Bienes, cosas.** Things, property. The word "property" is applicable in general to anything of which riches or fortune may consist. This word is likewise relative to the word "things," which is the second object of jurisprudence, the rules of which refer to persons, things and actions. (Sp. Civ. C., sec. 324).

**Bienes de dominio público.** Things of public domain. The following are things of public domain: Those intended for public use, as roads, canals, rivers, streams, and others of a like nature. (Sp. Civ. C., sec. 327).

**Bienes de uso público.** Things of public use. The property of public use comprises the insular and local roads, the squares, streets, fountains and public waters, walks, and public works for general use paid for by the towns or from the state Treasury. (Sp. Civ. C., sec. 328).

**Bienes fungibles y no fungibles.** Fungible and non-fungible, consumable and non-consumable. Movables are either consumable or nonconsumable. To the first class belong those which cannot be used in a manner appropriate to their nature, without their being consumed; all others belong to the second class. (Sp. Civ. C., sec. 329).

**Bienes inmuebles.** Immovables, real property. Immovable are, in general, those which cannot move themselves or be removed from one place to another. This definition, strictly speaking, is applicable only to such things as are immovable by their own nature, and not to such as are so only by the disposition of the law. (Sp. Civ. C., sec. 346).

**Bienes muebles.** Movables, chattels, personal property. Movables are considered such things as are susceptible of appropriation and not defined as immovables and, in general, all of those which can be carried from place to place without impairing the movable to which they may be attached. (Sp. Civ. C., sec. 337, 339, 343).

**Bienes no susceptibles de apropiación.** Thing not susceptible of ownership. Among the things which are not susceptible of ownership are comprised those which cannot become private property by reason of the object for which they are intended, such as things in common, or those the use and enjoyment of which belongs to all men. (Sp. Civ. C., sec. 349).

**Bienes ocultos.** Concealed property.

**Bienes raíces.** Real property, realty.

**Bienes semovientes.** Cattle, animals.

**Bienes susceptibles de apropiación.** Things susceptible of ownership. Things susceptible of being owned are those which may be the object of private ownership and which may be alienated by sale, exchange, donation, prescription, or in any other manner. (Sp. Civ. C., sec. 350).

**Bienes y derechos hipotecables.** Real estate and rights which may be mortgaged.

**Bienes, y derechos no hipotecables.** Property and right which may not be mortgaged.

**Bienestar.** Welfare, comfort, prosperity, well-being.

**Bigamia.** Bigamy.

**Bígamo.** Bigamist.

**Bilateral.** Bilateral.

**Bimetalismo.** Bimetallism.

**Bisabuelo, bisabuela.** Great-grandfather, great-grandmother.

**Blanqueo de capital.** Money laundering.

**Blasfemia.** Blasphemy, cursing, profanity.

**Bloquear.** To block, bar, hinder, prevent. To set a blockade.

**Bloqueo.** Blockade, barrier.

**Boda.** Wedding, marriage, matrimony, nuptials.

**Bodega.** Cargo hold.

**Boicot.** Boycott, ban, embargo. Block list.

**Boicotear.** To boycott, ban. To plot against.

**Boleta.** Ticket, ballot, certificate, slip, stub.

**Boletín.** Bulletin, announcement, dispatch, report.

**Boletín oficial.** Official bulletin, official gazette. Federal Register.

**Boleto de compraventa.** Bill of sale, deed.

**Bolsa.** Stock exchange, stock market.

**Bolsa de comercio.** Commercial exchange, stock exchange. Legally authorized public establishments in which merchants and licensed intermediary agents usually assemble to agree upon or carry out commercial transactions. (Sp. Com. C., sec. 64).

**Bolsa de comercio, contrato de bolsa.** Commercial exchange, transaction on exchange. The following shall be the subjects of transactions on exchange: 1) Public bonds and securities. 2) Industrial and commercial securities issued by private parties or associations or enterprises legally constituted. 3) Bills of exchange, drafts, promissory notes, and any other commercial paper. 4) The sale of precious metals, in coin or bullion. 5) Merchandise of all kinds and warehouse receipts. 6) The insurance of commercial effects against land or marine risks. 7) Transportation and freightage, bills of lading, and waybills. 8) Any other transactions similar to those mentioned in the foregoing subdivisions, provided they are lawful. (Sp. Com. C., sec. 67).

**Bolsa de comercio, efectos emitidos por particulares.** Commercial exchange, private securities.

**Bolsa de comercio, efectos públicos.** Commercial exchange, public securities.

**Bolsa de comercio, operaciones al contado.** Commercial exchange, cash transactions. Transactions for cash made on exchange must be consummated on the same day of their execution, or at the utmost, in the time intervening until the next meeting of the exchange. The seller shall be under the obligation to deliver, without further delay, the instruments or securities sold and the purchaser to receive them, satisfying their price immediately. (Sp. Com. C., sec. 76).

**Bonificación.** Bonus.

**Bono.** Bond, debenture, debt certificate, voucher.

**Borrachera.** Drunkenness, intoxication.

**Borracho.** Alcoholic, drunk, drunkard.

**Borrador.** Draft, rough draft, outline, sketch.

**Borradura, borrón.** Blotch, deletion, erasure, spot, stain.

**Botín.** Booty, loot, spoils. Prize, reward.

**Bracero.** Journeyman.

**Brigada.** Brigade, battalion, division, regiment, squadron.

**Buena conducta.** Good conduct.

**Buena fe.** Good faith means to act honestly, without fraud, collusion or deceit, or the cleanliness of purpose which satisfies the moral conscience of another judge. (Martinez v. Llavat, 86 PRR 23 (1962)).

**Buena fe y lealtad negocial.** Good faith and fair dealing.
   Each part must act in accordance with good faith and fair dealing in international trade.

**Buenos oficios.** Good offices, mediation.

**Bufete.** Law office, law firm.

**Buhonero.** Person who sells trinkets door to door or on the street. (C.A.)

**Bulto.** Package, parcel, lot.

**Buques mercantes.** Merchant vessels. Merchant vessels constitute property which may be acquired and transferred by any of the means recognized by law.

**Buques mercantes, ataque por un corsario.** Merchant vessels, attack by a privateer.

**Buques mercantes, constructores.** Merchant vessels, builders.

**Buques mercantes, contramaestre.** Merchant vessels, first mate. The mate shall take command of the vessel in case of the impossibility or disability of the captain and sailing master, assuming in such case his powers and responsibilities. (Sp. Com. C., sec. 633).

**Buques mercantes, dotación.** Merchant vessels, complement. By the complement of a vessel shall be understood all the persons embarked, from the captain to the cabin boy, necessary for her management, evolutions, and service, and there shall, therefore, be understood in the complement the crew, sailing master, engineers, stokers, and other persons not having a specific name; but there shall not be included the passengers nor the persons whom the vessel is merely transporting.

**Buques mercantes, embargo y venta.** Merchant vessels, attachment and sale. For all purposes of law, vessels shall be considered as personal property. (Sp. Com. C., sec. 585).

**Buques mercantes, partícipe en la propiedad.** Merchant vessels, part owner. Part owners of vessels shall enjoy the right of option of purchase and withdrawal in sales made to strangers.

**Buques mercantes, piloto.** Merchant vessels, sailing master. The sailing master, as the second chief of the vessel, shall take the place of the captain in cases of absence, sickness, or death, and shall then assume all his powers, obligations, and liabilities. (Sp. Com. C., sec. 627).

**Buques mercantes, propietario y naviero.** Merchant vessel, owner and agent. The owner of a vessel and the agent shall be civilly liable for the acts of the captain and for the obligations contracted by the latter to repair, equip, and provision the vessel, provided the creditor proves that the amount claimed was invested therein. (Sp. Com. C., sec. 586, 587).

**Buques mercantes, venta.** Merchant vessels, sales. The rigging, tackle, stores, and engine of a vessel, if a steamer, shall always be understood as included in the sale thereof if they are in the possession of the vendor at the time of the sale. The arms, munitions of war, provisions, and fuel shall not be considered as included in the sale. (Sp. Com. C., sec. 576, 577).

**Burdel.** Brothel, bordello, whorehouse.

**Burgués.** Bourgeois, middle class.

**Burgesía.** Bourgeoisie, middle class.

**Burlar la ley.** To flout the law.

**Burocracia colonial.** Colonial bureaucracy. The manner in which Spain and Portugal administered their New World colonies also indelibly stamped the legal institutions of Latin America. Despite the new constitutions and codes which followed independence, general responses and attitudes towards law continue to be conditioned by this colonial heritage. The diversity of means for transmitting the royal will to the colonists was nearly matched by the diversity of means for colonial administrators to frustrate that will. The result was bureaucratic confusion, administrative delay, mistrust of government officials, and disrespect for law. This legacy from the colonial era has impeded a great many attempts at administrative reform in Latin American nations. (L & D in LA.)

**Bursátil.** Related to the stock exchange or to quoted commodities.

**Buscapleitos.** Person who sues without a serious reason. Ambulance chaser.

**Buzón.** Letter box, letter drop.

# C

**Cabal juicio.** Sane of mind, able to think clearly.

**Cábala.** Intrigue, machination plot.

**Caballero.** Gentleman. Knight, warrior.

**Cabecera.** Head, peak, top.

**Cabecilla.** Chieftain, head, leader of a group, ringleader.

**Cabeza de familia.** Family head, householder.

**Cabida.** Capacity, space, volume.

**Cabildear.** To deliberate, to consider in a group, to confer.

**Cabildeo.** Deliberation, conference, pondering.

**Cabildo.** City hall.
  Congress, assembly. The name was used more currently during the Spanish rule and in the early days of independence. It has now been replaced by expressions such as *Congreso* (Congress), *Asamblea Nacional* (National Assembly), etc.

**Cabotaje.** Coastal trade or navigation.

**Cacheo.** Frisking.

**Cachiporra.** Truncheon, blundgeon.

**Caciquismo.** From "*cacique*," indian chief. Political system or situation where one person has all the power and little or no accountabilty.

**Caco.** Thief, burglar, robber.

**Cadalso.** Scaffold, execution platform.

**Cadaver.** Body, cadaver, corpus delicti, remains.

**Cadena.** Chain. Sequence, series.

**Cadena perpetua.** Life imprisonment.

**Caducar.** To lapse, expire, forfeit, lose. To cease, terminate.

**Caducidad.** Lapsing, expiration.

**Caducidad de instancia.** Dismissal for want of prosecution, extinction of actions. All actions shall be considered abandoned and he extinguished by law, even if minors or incapacitated persons are parties thereto, if, after having been instituted, they are not prosecuted. 1) Within four years when the cause is at first instance. 2) Within two if it is at second instance. 3) Within one year if on appeal for annulment of judgment. (Sp. L. Civ. P. sec. 410-11).

**Caduco.** Lapsed, expired.

**Caer.** To fall, collapse, drop, decline.

**Caer en cuenta.** To realize, dawn on someone, find out.

**Caer en desgracia.** To fall in disgrace

**Caer en desuso.** To discontinue, forget, stop using.

**Caída.** Fall, drop. Decline, defeat, min.

**Caja.** Box, cash, safe.

**Caja común.** Common capital.

**Cajero.** Cashier.

**Calabozo.** Jail, cell dungeon, prison.

**Cálculo.** Calculation, assessment, computation, evaluation.

**Calendario.** Calendar.

**Calificación.** Characterization.

**Calificación de documentos.** Judgment on documents. Registrars shall have the responsibility of passing judgment on the legality of all kinds of documents by virtue of which an entry is requested. Said judgment shall include the extrinsic forms of the documents presented, the competence of the grantors and the validity of the transactions and contracts contained in these documents. (PR Mort. Law 1979, sec. 64).

**Calificaciones.** Qualification. Grade.

**Calificado.** In criminal law, a crime that is aggravated.
  Competent or well qualified for a job.

**Calificar.** To qualify, grade.

**Caligrafía.** Calligraphy, handwriting, penmanship.

**Calígrafo.** Handwriting expert.

**Callar.** To remain silent, to keep silent.

**Calumnia.** Calumny, defamation, false accusation, libel.

**Calumniador.** Slanderer.

**Calumniar.** To slander, defame.

**Calumnioso.** Slanderous, calumnious, defamatory.

**Cámara.** Chamber.

**Cámara de apelaciones.** Court of appeals.

**Cámara de diputados.** Chamber of Deputies, House of Representatives, House of Commons (G.B.).

**Cámara de representantes.** House of representatives.

**Camarilla.** Gang, band, group. Assembly.

**Camarista.** Appellate judge.

**Cambial.** Negotiable instrument, bill of exchange.

**Cambiario.** Pertaining to negotiable instruments.

**Cambio de circunstancias.** Changed conditions.

**Cambio de pretensión.** Change of remedy. An aggrieved party who has required performance of a non-monetary obligation and who has not received performance within a period fixed or otherwise within a reasonable period of time may invoke any other remedy. (Unidroit, Prin., art. 7.2.5).

**Cambista.** Money trader.

**Camino de sirga.** Towpath.

**Camorra.** Brawl, melee, fight, scuffle, tussle. Provocation.

**Campo.** Countryside, meadow, pasture. Field, area, domain, sphere.

**Cancelable.** That can be cancelled. Repealable, retractable, revocable, voidable.

**Cancelación.** Cancellation, annulment, invalidation, rescission, retraction, revocation. Deletion.

**Cancelar.** To cancel, annual invalidate, rescind, retract, revoke. Delete.

**Canciller.** Chancellor. Minister of foreign affairs, Secretary of state.

**Cancillería.** Chancellery. Ministry of Foreign Affairs. State Department.

**Canje.** Exchange, barter, change, swap. Exchange of foreign currency.

**Canjeable.** That can be exchanged. Convertible.

**Canjear.** To exchange, barter, change, swap. To convert from one currency into another.

**Canon.** Rental, rent, royalty.

**Capa.** Primage.

**Capacidad.** Capacity, ability, competence, qualification.

**Capacidad contractual.** Contractual capacity. All people are able to contract but those precluded by the law. (Mex. Civ. C., art.1798).

**Capacidad legal de las personas físicas.** Legal capacity of individual persons. The legal capacity of individual persons is acquired at birth and lost at death; but since the moment a person is born, he is under the protection of the law. (Mex. Civ. C., art. 22).

**Capacidad nupcial.** Matrimonial capacity. The parties thereto shall be subject to their personal law in so far as it relates to their capacity to celebrate the marriage, the parent's consent or advice, the impediments and their dispensation. (Bust. C., art. 36).

**Capacidad remunerativa.** Earning capacity.

**Capacidad sucesoria.** Standing to inherit.

**Capacitar.** To train, instruct, teach, prepare. To empower, enable. To render capable.

**Capa de ozono.** Ozone layer.

**Capataz.** Foreman.

**Capaz.** Capable, able, competent, proficient, talented.

**Capitación.** Capitation.

**Capital.** Capital, seat of government. Assets, funds, wealth.

**Capital emitido.** Shares already issued by the corporation.

**Capital en giro.** Turnover, capital that the corporation uses to trade; not including concepts such as reserves, secured investments, etc.

**Capital líquido.** Capital in cash.

**Capital mobiliario.** Capital formed by assets other than real property.

**Capital no desembolsado.** Shares that the corporation may issue.

**Capital realizado.** Capital formed by shares already issued and paid by the shareholders.

**Capital social.** Capital of an enterprise.

**Capitalizar.** To capitalize, to increase liquid resources. To take advantage from something.

**Capitán.** Captain. Chief, leader.

**Capitulación.** Surrender. Agreement. When used in its contractual sense it is normally to indicate a prenuptial agreement (*capitulación matrimonial*).

**Capítulo.** Chapter, division, heading, part, section.

**Captador.** Captator.

**Captura.** Capture, apprehension, arrest, seizure. Appropriation, confiscation.

**Carabinero.** Border guard. Police.

**Carácter.** Character, integrity, mature, personality, traits. Letter, symbol.

**Cárcel.** Jail, gaol, penitentiary, prison.

**Carear.** To confront two witnesses who contradict each other.

**Carecer de fundamento.** Unfounded, lacking substance or merit, ungrounded.

**Carencia.** Lack of, deficiency, need, shortage.

**Careo.** Confrontation of witnesses.

**Careo de testigos y procesados.** Confrontation between witnesses and the accused. When the witnesses or the accused disagree among themselves, or the former with the latter, as to some fact or some circumstance of moment in the sumario, the judge may cause those disagreeing to confront each other; but this proceeding, as a general rule, must take place only between two persons at the same time. (Sp. L. Crim. P., art. 451, 452, 455).

**Carga.** Load, cargo, freight. Burden, charge. Encumbrance.

**Carga procesal.** Burden of proof.

**Cargador.** Shipper.

**Cargo.** Post, position. Accusation, charge.

**Cargo judicial.** Judicial appointment. File-mark or date stamp placed on a motion.

**Carnal.** Carnal. Pertaining to the flesh.

**Carrera.** Race, competition, chase. Profession, pursuit, vocation.

**Carta de pago.** Acknowledgment of payment.

**Carta de porte.** Bill of lading.

**Carta orgánica.** Organic act.

**Carta patente.** Letter patent.

**Cartas-órdenes de crédito.** Letters of credit. Letters of credit are those issued by one merchant to another, of for the purpose of attending to a commercial transaction.

**Cartas testamentarias.** Letters testamentary.

**Cartel.** Cartel, monopoly, syndicate. Announcement, bill, sign.

**Cartera.** Briefcase, billfold, handbag. Area of a cabinet minister.

**Carterista.** Pickpocket.

**Cartilla.** Booklet. Letter-size piece of paper.

**Cartografía minera.** Mining cartography. An official title record of the legal status of the lots subject to mining concession or assignments. The cartography is open to the public and it includes a layout of the location and the perimeters of the lands covered by the mining concessions, assignments and reserves, as well as those applications for mining concessions, assignments and reserves that are pending.

**Cartular.** Related to a negotiable instrument.

**Casa de expósitos.** Foundling home, foster house.

**Casa, vivienda, morada.** House, dwelling. A house or dwelling is a place where people live or may live. (Ppl. v. Cosme Vargas, 96 PRR 815 (1969)).

**Casación.** Cassation, annulment, quashing, reversal, revocation.

**Casadera.** Spinster, nubile.

**Casamiento.** Marriage, matrimony, wedding, wedlock.

**Casar.** To marry. To annul, quash, reverse, revoke.

**Casco del buque.** Hull of the vessel.

**Caso de autos.** Case at bar, instant case.

**Caso fortuito.** A fortuitous event is one that, at the time the contract was made, could not have been reasonably foreseen. (Louisiana Civ. Code art. 1875).

**Caso fortuito o fuerza mayor.** Fortuitous event on vis major. The concept of fortuitous event or *vis major*—occurrence which exempts from liability because it cannot be foreseen or if foreseen cannot be prevented —is defined as that occurrence not chargeable to the debtor which prevents the performance of the obligation. (Riviera v. Caribbean Home Const. Corp., 100 PRR 105 (1971)).

**Castigable.** Punishable.

**Castigo.** Punishment, castigation, correction, penalty, penance.

**Castigo cruel e inusitado.** Cruel and unusual punishment.

**Castrar.** To castrate, to neuter an animal.

**Casual.** Accidental, by chance, fortuitous, unexpected. Casual, informal.

**Casualidad.** Coincidence, by chance.

**Catástrofe.** Catastrophe, calamity, disaster.

**Categoría.** Category, class, division, group, rank.

**Cauce.** River bed.

**Caucionable.** Subject to bail.

**Caucionar.** To post a bond, to bail, guarantee, secure.

**Caudal.** Fund, capital, estate, patrimony.

**Causa.** Cause, consideration. Contracts without a cause, or with an illegal cause, do not produce any effect. A cause is illegal when it contravenes the law or good morals. (Sp. Civ. C., sec. 1275).

An obligation cannot exist without a lawful cause. Cause is the reason why a party obligates himself. A party may be obligated by a promise when he knew or should have known that the promise would induce the other party to rely on it to his detriment and the other party was reasonable in so relying. Recovery may be limited to the expenses incurred or the damages suffered as a result of the promisee's reliance on the promise. Reliance on a gratuitous promise made without required formalities is not reasonable. (Louisiana Civ. Code art. 1966-67).

Consideration. In contracts, involving a valuable consideration, the prestation or promise of a thing or services by the other party is understood as a consideration for each contracting party; in remuneratory contracts, the service or benefits remunerated, and in those of pure beneficence, the mere liberality of the benefactor.

Even though the consideration should not be expressed in the contract, it is presumed that it exists and that it is licit, unless the debtor proves the contrary. (Sp. Civ. C., sec. 1241, 1244).

Case, lawsuit.

*Causa contrahendi.* Reason why an obligation is entered into.

**Causa ilícita.** Unlawful cause. The cause of an obligation is unlawful when the enforcement of the obligation would produce a result prohibited by law or against public policy. (Louisiana Civ. Code art. 1968).

**Causa interventora, interviniente.** Intervening cause. An intervening cause—in an accident in which damages are claimed—is one which comes into active operation in producing the result after the actor's negligent act or omission has occurred. (Gines v. Aqueduct and Sewer Authority, 86 PRR 490 (1962)).

**Causa justificada de rescisión de trabajo.** Just cause for firing a worker. Under labor law, integrity at work is mandatory behavior for the employee. A worker is deemed to act with integrity when the work is carried out with intense effort, care, and attention, in the agreed upon time, place, and manner. Lack of integrity is a generic cause for dismissal. (Mex. Labor Law).

**Causahabiente.** Heir, assign, successor.

**Causal.** Ground or requirement for something.

**Causalidad.** Causation. Causation is the nexus between the breach of the legal or contractual duty and the damage, without which the result would have occurred. In other words, it is the nexus between the proximate cause and the proximate result or consequence. Hence, causation is what determines whether there is indirect or direct consequence of an act. (Barrios-Mannucci).

**Causante.** Decedent, deceased. Originator, responsible party.

**Causar.** To cause, generate, produce, provoke.

**Cautelar.** Preventive, precautionary. Normally used as preventive measure (*medida cautelar*).

**Cautio.** Security, bond, lien.

**Cautiverio, captividad.** Captivity, confinement, imprisonment, incarceration.

**Cautivo.** Captive, convict, hostage, inmate, prisoner.

**Cedente.** Assignor, grantor, transferor.

**Ceder.** To assign, convey, transfer. To yield, give up, relinquish.

**Cedible, cesible.** Assignable, transferable.

**Cedido.** Transferred. Assigned. Assignee.

**Cédula.** Notice. Summons. Bond.

**Cédula de citación.** Summons. Service of process.

**Cédula de emplazamiento.** Summons. Service of process.

**Cédula de notificación.** Writ for notification. When the residence is known of the person upon whom service is to be made and at the first attempt he should not be found, whatever be the cause or the time of absence, service shall be made by writ (*cédula*) at the same time and without the necessity of a judicial mandate therefore. (Sp. L. Civ. P. sec. 266, 267).

**Celador.** Jail keeper, guard.

**Celda.** Cell, jail, prison.

**Célibe.** Celibate, nubile, single, unmarried. Bachelor, spinster.

**Celebración.** Celebration, carrying something out. The making of a contract (*celebración de un contrato*) the act of getting married (*la celebración de un matrimonio*).

**Celebrar.** To celebrate, to make as in "*celebrar un contrato*," to make or to get into a contract.

**Célibe.** Celibate, unmarried.

**Celular.** Pertaining to a cell.

**Censario.** Lessor in a contract of censo.

**Censatario.** Lessee in a contract of censo.

**Censo.** Annuity. An annuity is constituted when any real property is subjected to the payment of a pension or annual income in compensation for a capital which is received in cash or for the full or partial ownership of the property which is conveyed. The nature of the annuity requires that the transfer of the principal or of the estate should be perpetual or for an unlimited time; however, the person paying the annuity may redeem it at his will, even though the contrary should be stipulated this provision being applicable to annuities actually existing. (Sp. Civ. C., sec. 1507, 1511).

**Censo, Código Bustamante**. Annuity, Bustamante Code. The territorial law is applied to the determination of the concept and classes of annuities, the redeemable character and prescription thereof, and the real action arising therefrom. (Bust. C., art. 200).

**Censo consignatario.** Transferable or consignative annuity. An annuity is transferable or consignative (*censo consignativo*) when the owner of land imposes upon an estate belonging to him the charge of an income or pension which he binds himself to pay to the lender for a sum in cash which he has received from the latter. (Sp. Civ. C., sec. 1509).

**Censo enfiteútico.** Emphyteutic annuity. An annuity is called emphyteutic when a person transfers to another the beneficial ownership of an estate reserving to himself the legal ownership and a right to receive from the emphyteuticary an annual income in recognition of such ownership. (Sp. Civ. C., sec. 1508, 1531).

**Censo reservativo.** Reservative or set-apart annuity. An annuity is reservative or set apart when a person transfers to another the full ownership of an estate, reserving to himself the right to receive from said estate an annual pension which is to be paid by the owner of the land. (Sp. Civ. C., sec. 1510, 1563).

**Censualista.** Annuitant.

**Censuario.** Annuitant in a contract of censo.

**Centralización y descentralización del poder.** Centralization and decentralization of power. A major difference between the United States and Latin American countries is that the latter, whether federalist or unitary, are civil law countries with a completely or relatively unified national juridical system. Private law as well as penal or business law is codified, and in the few countries where unification is not complete (for example, in Mexico) the federation's member states have no other recourse than to adapt national standards to local needs. In this respect, too, the system is closer to the former Soviet system than to the United States. Latin American countries may have state courts in addition to federal courts. Although both categories of jurisdictions may have different competence in *ratione materiae and ratione personae,* they apply the same national law. This judicial unity has spared the Latin American federal countries a great deal of the usurpations of power that United States jurists have had to justify in order to permit the federation to pursue one national economic and social policy. (West-

29

**Cepo.** Trap, block.

**Cercas.** Fences, enclosures, live hedges.

**Cerciorarse.** Ascertain, check, corroborate, find out, verify.

**Ceremonial.** Ceremonial, formalities, rite, ritual.

**Cerramiento.** Confined space, enclosure.

**Cerramiento de fincas rústicas.** Enclosing of agricultural lands. Every owner may enclose or fence his tenements by means of walls, ditches, live or dead hedges, or in any other manner without injury to the servitudes existing thereon. (Sp. Civ. C., sec. 395).

**Certeza del daño.** Certainty of harm.
Compensation is due only for harm, including future harm, that is established with a reasonable degree of certainty. Compensation may be due for loss of a chance in proportion to the probability of its occurrence. (Unidroit, Prin., art. 7.4.3).

**Certificación.** Certification. Statement as to the truthfulness of a document.

**Certificado.** Certificate, affiant, attestation, document.

**Certificar.** To certify, attest, authenticate, verify, vouch.

**Certificatorio.** Relating to a certificate. Certifying.

**Cesación.** Cessation, ceasing, coming to an end. Completion, conclusion, discontinuance.

**Cesantía.** Ending of labor relationship. Firing, lay off.

**Cesibilidad.** Assignability, transferability.

**Cesión.** Cession, assignment, conveyance, transfer. Delivery. Capitulation.

**Cesión de derechos.** Assignment of rights.

**Cesionario.** Transferee.

**Cesiones a granel.** Bulk transfers.

**Cesionista.** Assignor, grantor, transferor.

**CFR. Coste y Flete (...puerto de destino convenido).** CFR. Cost and Freight (...named port of destination). "Cost and Freight" means that the seller must pay the costs and freight necessary to bring the goods to the named port of destination but the risk of loss of or damage to the goods, as well as any additional costs due to events occurring after the time the goods have been delivered on board the vessel, is transferred from the seller to the buyer when the goods pass the ship's rail in the port of shipment. (Incoterms).

**Chaleco.** Jacket, coat, waist coat.

**Chaleco a prueba de balas.** Bullet-proof jacket.

**Chaleco de fuerza.** Straight jacket.

**Chanchullo.** Subterfuge, graft, trick.

**Chantaje.** Blackmail.

**Chantajear.** To blackmail.

**Chantajista.** Blackmailer.

**Chapa.** Shingle. License number. Plate. Badge.

**Charlatán.** Chatter box, talkative. Charlatan, hoax, fraud.

**Chauvinismo.** Excessive and undiscerning patriotism.

**Cheque.** Check, cheque (G.B.). An order to pay, known in commerce by the name of check, is an instrument which permits the maker to withdraw for his benefit or for that of a third person the whole or part of the funds he may have at his disposal in the hands of the depositary. (Sp. Com. C., sec. 534).

**Cheque cancelado.** Cancelled check.

**Cheque cruzado.** Crossed check.

**Cheque de caja o gerencia.** Cashier's check.

**Cheque de viajero.** Traveler's check.

**Cheques, derecho internacional privado.** Checks, conflicts of laws. The law of the place in which a check is to be paid shall determine: a. Its nature; b. Its form and the effects thereof; c. The time of presentation; d. The persons against whom the check may be drawn; e. Whether it may be drawn for deposit only, crossed, or be certified or confirmed, and the effects of these acts; f. The rights of the holder in regard to the provision of funds and the nature of such rights; g. Whether the holder may demand, or is obliged to accept, partial payment; h. The rights of the drawer to cancel the check or oppose payment; i. The necessity of protest or other equivalent act for the preservation of rights against the endorser, the drawer, or other obligated parties; j. The measures to be taken in case of robbery, theft, forgery, loss, destruction, or of the instrument deteriorating to the point of being useless; k. In general, all matters relating to the payment of a check. (Conv. on Checks, art. 7).

**Cheques, derecho internacional privado, capacidad.** Checks, conflict of laws, capacity. Capacity to enter into an obligation by means of a check shall be governed by the law of the place in which the obligation was contracted. However, if such obligation was contracted by a person who was incompetent according to the law, such incompetency shall not be valid in the territory of any other State Party to this Convention if the obligation is valid under the law of that State. (Conv. on Checks, art. 1).

**Cheques, forma.** Checks, form. The forms of legal checks such as the drawing, endorsement, guaranty, protest and the like that may appear on a check shall be governed by the law of the place in which each one of those acts is performed. (Conv. on Checks, art. 2).

**Cheques, obligaciones.** Checks, obligations. All obligations arising from a check shall be governed by the law of the place in which they are constructed.

**Cheques, protesta.** Checks, protest. The procedures and time limits for the protest of a check or other equivalent act for the preservation of rights against endorsers, the drawer, or other obligated parties shall be governed by the law of the place where the protest or other equivalent act is or should be performed. (Conv. on Checks, art. 6).

**Cheque en descubierto.** Check not covered by funds.

**Chicana, chicanería.** Chicanery, deception, graft, ruse, subterfuge, trick.

**Chicanero.** Attorney who resorts to deceit. Shyster.

**Chicanear.** To trick. To prolong legal proceedings unnecessarily.

**Chivato.** Detective, informant. Spy.

**Choque.** Collision, accident, crash, impact.

**Chorizo.** Petty thief, pickpocket, purse snatcher (slang).

**Cierre.** Closing, closure. Conclusion, end. Lockout.

**Cierto, incierto.** Certain, uncertain. In matters of obligations, a thing is certain, when its essence, quality and quantity, are suffi-

ciently described; such as one hundred dollars, such a house, or such a horse. It is uncertain, when the description is not that of an individual object, but designates only the kind; such as some corn, some wine, a horse. (Louisiana Civ. Code art. 3556).

**Ciencias jurídicas.** Juridical science, the study of law.

**CIF. Coste, Seguro y Flete (...puerto de destino convenido).** CIF. Cost, Insurance, and Freight. "Cost, Insurance, and Freight" means that the seller has the same obligations as under CFR but with the addition that he has to procure marine insurance against the buyer's risk of loss of or damage to the goods during the carriage. The seller contracts for insurance and pays the insurance premium. The buyer should note that under the CIF term the seller is only required to obtain insurance on minimum coverage. The CIF term requires the seller to clear the goods for export. This term can only be used for sea and inland waterway transport. When the ship's rail serves no practical purposes such as in the case of roll-on/roll-off or container traffic, the CIP term is more appropriate to use. (Incoterms).

**CIP. Transporte y Seguro Pagados Hasta (...lugar de destino convenido).** CIP. Carriage and Insurance Paid to (...named place of destination). "Carriage and insurance paid to..." means that the seller has the same obligations as under CPT but with the addition that the seller has to procure cargo insurance against the buyer's risk of loss of or damage to the goods during the carriage. The seller contracts for insurance and pays the insurance premium. The buyer should note that under the CIP term the seller is only required to obtain insurance on minimum coverage. The CIP term requires the seller to clear the goods for export. This term may be used for any mode of transport including multimodal transport. (Incoterms).

**Circuito.** Circuit.

**Circunscripción.** District, area, region, sector. Electoral precinct.

**Circunstancia.** Circumstance, event.

**Circunstancia atenuante.** Mitigating circumstance.

**Circunstancial.** Circumstantial, conjectural, implied, incidental, presumed, speculative.

**Circunstancias relevantes.** Relevant circumstances.

In applying Articles 4.1 and 4.2, regard shall be had to all the circumstances, including (a) preliminary negotiations between the parties; (b) practices which the parties have established between themselves; (c) the conduct of the parties subsequent to the conclusion of the contract; (d) the nature and purpose of the contract; (e) the meaning commonly given to terms and expressions in the trade concerned; (f) usages. (Unidroit, Prin., art. 4.3).

**Cita.** Citation, summons. Appointment. Quotation.

**Citación.** Citation. A person charged with a punishable act must be cited only for the purpose of being heard, unless the law shall provide otherwise or unless his immediate detention should be proper. (Sp. L. Crim. P., art 486 and 487).

Summons.

**Citación en garantía.** Call in warranty. The purchaser threatened with eviction, who wishes to preserve his right of warranty against his vendor, should notify the latter in time of the interference which he has experienced. (Louisiana Civ. Code art. 2517).

**Citación por cédula.** Citation by summons.

**Citación por edictos.** Citation by publication.

**Citar.** To cite, summon. To make an appointment. To quote.

**Ciudadanía.** Citizenship, nationality.

**Ciudadano.** Citizen, inhabitant, national, resident. Civilian.

**Civil.** Civil, civilian. Personal.

**Civilista.** Civilian. Specialized in civil systems or in civil law.

**Civismo.** Civisim.

**Clandestinidad.** Clandestinity, furtiveness, secrecy, surreptitiousness.

**Clandestino.** Clandestine, hidden, secret, undercover.

**Clase.** Class, classification, category, kind, nature.

**Clasificar.** To classify, arrange, categorize, sort, systematize.

**Cláusula.** Clause, article, section.

**Cláusula de indemnización líquida.** Liquidated damages clause. When the contract provides that the party who breaches will have to pay a certain sum as damages (liquidated damages or penalty clauses),the other party can recover neither a larger nor a smaller sum. The court may, however, increase such contractual penalty when it is obviously inadequate or decrease it when it is manifestly excessive. The presence of this clause does not indicate waiver of other damages (*damnum emergens, lucrum cessans*, moral damages) unless they expressly provide for it. (Barrios-Mannucci).

**Cláusula derogatoria.** Repealing clause.

**Cláusula inicial.** Enacting clause.

**Cláusula penal.** Liquidated damages, penal clause.

The nullity of the penal clause does not carry with it that of the principal obligation. The nullity of the principal obligation carries with it that of the penal clause. (Sp. Civ. C., sec. 1120, 1123).

**Cláusulas de exoneración.** Exemption clauses.

A clause which limits or excludes one party's liability for nonperformance or which permits one party to render performance substantially different from what the other party reasonably expected may not be invoked if it would be grossly unfair to do so, having regard to the purpose of the contract. (Unidroit, Prin., art. 7.1.6).

**Cláusulas de restricción probatoria.** Merger clauses.

A contract in writing which contains a clause indicating that the writing completely embodies the terms on which the parties have agreed cannot be contradicted or supplemented by evidence of prior statements or agreements. (Unidroit, Prin., art. 2.17).

**Cláusulas limitativas de responsabilidad.** Clauses limiting liability. Legal writing and case law deny the validity of the exonerative, limitative and indemnity clauses when the damage is due to willful misconduct or gross negligence. (Barrios-Mannucci).

**Cláusulas que exigen que la modificación o extinción del contrato sea por escrito.** Written modification clauses. A contract in writing which contains a clause requiring any modification or termination by agreement to be in writing may not be otherwise modified or terminated. (Unidroit, Prin., art. 2.18).

**Clausura.** Closing, closure.

**Clemencia.** Clemency, compassion, forgiveness, leniency, mercy, pardon.

**Cleptomanía.** Kleptomania.

**Cleptómano.** Kleptomaniac.

**Clérigo.** Priest, clergyman.

**Cliente.** Client, customer, patron.

**Clientela.** Clientele, clients, customers, goodwill.

**Clonación.** Cloning.

**Co-autores de un cuasidelito.** Contributing tortfeasors.

**Co-empleado.** Fellow servant.

**Co-partícipe.** Person who acts jointly, or in agreement with, another. Accessory, accomplice.

**Coacción.** Duress. No criminal liability attaches to whoever acts under duress or threatened by a clear, present and serious harm, caused or not by a third party; provided that a different conduct cannot be reasonably expected. (St. P.C. for LA, sec. 31).

**Coaccionar.** To coerce, compel, constrain, force.

**Coalición.** Coalition, alliance, confederation, league, syndicate.

**Coartada.** Alibi.

**Cobertura.** Cover, roof.

**Cobrabilidad.** Collectibility.

**Cobrable.** Collectible.

**Cobrador.** Collector.

**Cobranza.** Collection. Request for payment.

**Cobrar.** To collect, earn, make.

**Cobro.** Collection.

**Cobro de lo indebido.** Collection of what is not due. If a thing is received when there was no right to claim it and which, through an error, has been unduly delivered, there arises an obligation to restore the same. (Sp. Civ. C., sec. 1796, 1798).

**Cobro mediante procedimiento de apremio.** Collection by constraint.

**Cocaína.** Cocaine.

**Cocainómano.** Cocaine addict.

**Codicilo.** Codicil. Amendment to a will.

**Codificación.** Codification.

**Codificación comercial.** Commercial codification. The forces that led to codification of the civil law were also operating in the commercial arena. Here too the French codification (1807) served as an influential model, though not so influential as the more comprehensive Spanish Code of Commerce of 1829. The latter was copied almost verbatim by Ecuador, Paraguay, Peru, Costa Rica, and Colombia, while the former was copied by Haiti, the Dominican Republic, and Venezuela (1867 code). The most influential of the Latin American commercial codes were those of Brazil(1850), Argentina(1859), and Chile (1867). (L & D in LA).

**Codificación visigótica.** Visigothic codification.

**Codificaciones latinoamericanas.** Latin American codifications. There were three great Latin American codifications: (1) Andrés Bello's Chilean Code (drafted 1846-1855); (2) Vélez Sársfield's Argentine Code (drafted 1863-69); and (3) Teixeira de Freitas' draft code for Brazil (1856-65). The three have served as models for the civil codes of most Latin American countries. (L & D in LA).

**Codificador.** Codifier. Legislator.

**Codificar.** To codify. To encode.

**Código.** Code.

**Código Bustamante.** Bustamante Code. The most important document in the field of Latin American private international law is the Bustamante Code, approved at the Sixth International Conference of American States in Havana in 1928. The code was signed by all American states except the United States and has been ratified by Bolivia, Brazil, Chile, Costa Rica, Cuba, the Dominican Republic, Ecuador, El Salvador, Guatemala, Haiti, Honduras, Nicaragua, Panama, Peru, and Venezuela. (LA Laws & Inst.).

**Código civil.** Civil code. In Latin America, as in other civil-law countries, the heart of private law is expressed in the civil code. In theory a civil code is a systematic and harmonious set of general principles and specific rules governing legal relations among private persons. The code contains the rules governing contracts, domestic relations, damages, restitution, inheritance, legal personality and torts. Even when no provision appears to be specifically applicable, the civil code is frequently consulted as a source of general principle, serving to fill in gaps in other legislation in much the same way as the common law serves in Anglo-American jurisdictions. (L & D in LA).

**Código civil, influencia francesa.** Civil code, French influene. The model that most appealed to the jurists designated to draft Latin American codes during the middle of the 19th century was the French Civil Code (*Code Napoléon*) enacted in 1804. The Code's newness, rationality, and clarity of style all recommended it to these new nations. (L & D in LA).

**Código comercial, obsolencia.** Commercial code, obsolescence. The experience of Latin American countries with their commercial codes has generally been far less felicitous than with their civil codes. Though most countries have traded in their commercial codes several times, complaints about obsolescence are continually heard. (L & D in LA).

**Códigos laborales.** Labor codes. Since 1931 almost all Latin American nations have enacted elaborate, comprehensive codes of labor law. The typical labor code confers a great many modern benefits upon the worker, such as minimum wages, paid vacations, profit sharing, maternity benefits, bonuses, family allowances, free medical services, death and retirement benefits, job security, and special protection for women and children. Most of these benefits have been paternalistically bestowed by legislators eager to co-opt working-class political support by imitating the more advanced European nations; seldom have they reflected the economic power of the working class. (L & D in LA).

**Códigos penales.** Criminal codes. Like the commercial codes, criminal codes have generally been short-lived in Latin America. No sooner is a code of criminal law enacted than drafts of a reform project begin to circulate. Most of the countries have gone

through at least half a dozen penal codes since independence. Moreover, a great many criminal offenses are found elsewhere than in the criminal code, and are subject to frequent amendment. The substantive provisions of a typical Latin American penal code do not differ greatly from those of a typical Anglo-American jurisdiction. (L & D in LA).

**Coeficiente.** Coefficient, fraction.

**Coercible.** Coercible. Subject to pressures.

**Coerción.** Coercion, compulsion, constraint, duress, intimidation, irresistible force.

**Coercitivo.** Coercive, compelling, intimidating, irresistible.

**Coexistencia pacífica.** Peaceful co-existence.

**Cognación.** Cognation, parentage by blood.

**Cognado.** Cognate.

**Cognición.** Cognition, knowledge, understanding. Cognizance.

**Cognitivo.** Cognitive.

**Cohabitación.** Cohabitation, living together as husband and wife. Coexistence.

**Cohechador.** One who offers a bribe.

**Cohechar.** To bribe, pay off, suborn.

**Coima.** Payola.

**Coimear.** To pay off, bribe.

**Coincidencia.** Coincidence, concurrence.

**Coito.** Coitus.

**Colaborador.** Collaborator, associate, partner.

**Colación.** Collation.

The collation of goods is the supposed or real return to the mass of the succession which an heir makes of property which he received in advance of his share or otherwise, in order that such property may be divided together with the other effects of the succession. (Louisiana Civ. Code art. 1227).

**Colación de descendientes.** Collation by descendants. Children or grandchildren, coming to the succession of their fathers, mothers or other ascendants, must collate what they have received from them by donation *inter vivos*, directly or indirectly, and they can not claim the legacies made to them by such ascendants unless the donations and legacies have been made to them expressly as an advantage over their coheirs, and besides their portion. (Louisiana Civ. Code art. 1228).

**Colación en especie.** Collation in kind. The collation is made in kind, when the thing which has been given, is delivered up by the donee to be united to the mass of the succession. (Louisiana Civ. Code art 1252).

**Colación por toma reducida.** Collation by taking less. The collation is made by taking less, when the donee diminishes the portion he inherits, in proportion to the value of the object he has received. (Louisiana Civ. Code art. 1253).

**Colacionar.** To classify, collate. To send a telegram.

**Colateral.** Collateral, bond, pledge, security. Relative by marriage, in an indirect line.

**Colección.** Collection, aggregate, assortment, compilation.

**Colecta.** Collection, gathering of contributions.

**Colectable.** Suitable for a collection.

**Colectar.** To collect.

**Colectivismo.** Collectivism.

**Colector.** Collector.

**Colectoría.** Revenue service, tax office.

**Colegiado.** Admitted to the bar, or to a profession.

**Colegiarse.** To join a professional organization.

**Colegiatura.** Bar. Professional organization.

**Colegio.** Bar. Professional organization.

**Colegio de abogados.** Bar. College of advocates.

**Colegio de corredores.** Association of brokers.

**Cólera.** Anger, fury, ire, wrath.

**Colisión.** Collision, accident, crash. Collision.

**Colocar a interés.** Place upon interest.

**Colonia.** Colony.

**Colonia penitenciaria.** Penal colony.

**Colono.** Settler, farmer.

**Color, (so color).** Color, pigment, tint, tinge. Intention, mood, true meaning. Under the color of.

**Colusión.** Collusion, complicity, conspiracy.

**Colusorio.** Collusive, conspiratorial.

**Comandante en jefe.** Commander in chief.

**Comandita.** Type of commercial partnership.

**Comanditado.** Managing partner.

**Comanditar.** To manage a partnership.

**Comanditario.** Sleeping partner, or silent partner, partner who only provides capital.

**Comando.** Command, authority, control, mastery. Order, decree. Commando.

**Combate.** Combat, battle, fighting, war, warfare.

**Combinación.** Combination, alliance, amalgamation, cartel, coalition, consolidation, merger, pool.

**Combinar.** To combine, amalgamate, consolidate, merge, pool.

**Comentador, comentarista.** Commentator, critic, observer.

**Comentario.** Comment, commentary, criticism, explanation, observation, remark, suggestion.

**Comerciable.** Marketable, saleable.

**Comercial.** Commercial, business related, mercantile.

**Comercializar.** To market, sale, trade.

**Comerciante.** Merchant. Practically all the Latin-American codes have followed the French system as to the essential qualifications of a merchant. Usually a merchant is described as one who: (1) performs acts of commerce, (2) in his own name, (3) as a profession. (W. Eur. & LA Leg. Sys.). Merchant, business man, dealer, distributor, retailer, salesman, trader, wholesale dealer. Marchand.

**Comerciar.** To trade, deal, market, sale.

**Comercio.** Commerce, business, industry, shop, store, trade, traffic.

**Comercio al por mayor.** Wholesale.

**Comercio de cabotaje.** Coastwise trade.

**Comercio interestatal.** Interstate commerce.

**Cometer.** To commit, perform, perpetrate. To promise, swear. To confine, institutionalize.

**Cometido.** Committed, performed. Duty, job.

**Comicio.** Election, poll, vote.

**Comida y habitación.** Board and lodging.

**Comisar.** To confiscate, impound, forfeit, seize.

**Comisaría.** Police station.

**Comisario.** Chief inspector, police officer. Commissary.

**Comisión.** Commission, performance, perpetration. Board, committee, council. Fee, percentage.

**Comisión mercantil.** Commercial agency.

**Comisión mercantil, factores, dependientes y mancebos.** Commercial agency, factor, employees and shop clerks.

The acts of these special employees or agents shall only bind the principal with regard to transactions which are usual to the branch of business which has been intrusted to them.

**Comisión mercantil, rescición.** Commercial agency, rescission. A Contract shall be rescinded by the death of the agent or by his incapacity; but it shall not be rescinded by the death or incapacity of the principal, although it may be revoked by his representatives. (Sp. Com. C., sec. 280).

**Comisión mercantil, responsabilidad del comisionista y comitente.** Commercial agency, liability of principal and agent. When the agent transacts business in his own name, it shall not be necessary for him to state who is the principal. (Sp. Com. C., sec. 246).

**Comisión mercantil, responsabilidad del comitente.** Commercial agency, principal's liability. After a contract has been made by the agent with all the legal formalities, the principal must accept all the consequences of the commission, reserving the right of action against the agent by reason of error or omission committed in its fulfillment. (Sp. Com. C., sec. 253, 254).

**Comisión mercantil, revelación del nombre del comitente.** Commercial agency, disclosure of principal's name. If the agent transacts business in the name of the principal, he must state that fact. (Sp. Com. C., sec. 247).

**Comisión mercantil, revocación.** Commercial agency, revocation. The principal may revoke the commission intrusted to an agent at any stage of the transaction. (Sp. Com. C., sec. 279).

**Comisionado.** Commissioner.

**Comisionista.** Agent.

**Comiso de instrumentos delictivos.** Forfeiture of instruments used for a crime. Instruments used to commit crimes, or the assets or money from their sale, or things that imply a gain for the perpetrator and originate from the crime itself, will be forfeited to the State, except for the better right that the victim or third parties might have. (St. P.C. for LA, sec. 97).

**Comiso, decomiso.** Forfeiture, seizure.

**Comité.** Committee, board, commission, council.

**Comité asesor.** Advisory committee.

**Comité de supervisión.** Supervisory committee.

**Comitente.** Shipper of goods, principal, seller.

**Comitir.** To commit. To institutionalize.

**Como.** Such as. These are words employed to give some example of a rule, and are never exclusive of other cases which that rule is made to embrace. (Louisiana Civ. Code art. 3556).

**Comodante.** Bailor.

**Comodato.** Commodatum. The bailor retains the ownership of the thing loaned. The bailee acquires the use thereof but not its fruits; if any compensation is involved, to be paid by the person requiring the use, the agreement ceases to be a commodatum. (Sp. Civ. C., sec. 1643, 1644).

**Comodatario.** Bailee.

**Compañero.** Fellow worker. Originally, someone with whom one shares the bread. Friend, mate, pal.

**Compañero/a de vida.** Common law spouse. In several Latin American countries consensual or informal marriages are given full legal effect. Such is, for instance, the case of El Salvador. Literally this expression means "companion for life."

**Compañía.** Company. Association, business concern, enterprise, corporation, firm. Assembly, gathering, group.

**Compañía colectiva.** General copartnership.

All the members of the general copartnership, be they or be they not managing partners of the same, are personally and jointly liable with all their property for the results of the transactions consummated in the name and for the account of the partnership, under the signature of the latter, and by a person authorized to make use thereof. (Sp. Com. C., sec. 126).

**Compañías en comandita.** Limited copartnership.

The liability of special partners for the obligations and losses of the copartnership shall be limited to the funds which they contributed or bound themselves to contribute to the limited copartnership. Special partners can not take any part whatsoever in the management of the business of the copartnership, not even in the capacity of special agents of the managing partners. (Sp. Com. C., sec. 148).

**Compañías mercantiles.** Commercial enterprises. Articles of association by which two or more persons obligate themselves to place in a common fund any property, industry, or any of these things, in order to obtain profit, shall be commercial, no matter what its class may be, provided it has been established in accordance with the law. (Sp. Com. C., sec. 116).

**Compañías o bancos de crédito territorial o hipotecario.** Mortgage loan association or banks.

**Comparecencia.** Appearance.

**Comparecencia al solo efecto de alegar incompetencia.** Special appearance.

**Comparecencia del demandado.** Dendant's appearance. The defendant may appear at any time during the proceedings; but the appearance will not operate retroactively in any case. (Panamanian Judicial Code, art. 674.)

**Comparecer.** To appear, to make an appearance, to stand trial. To participate in proceedings.

**Compareciente.** Party who appears in court. One who participates in proceedings.

**Comparendo.** Citation. Summons.

**Comparición.** Appearance in court. Participation in proceedings.

**Compartimiento.** Compartment, booth, cubicle.

**Compatible.** Compatible, cogent, congruous, consistent, harmonious.

**Compeler.** Compel.

**Compendiar.** To abridge, condense, summarize, outline, recapitulate. To compile.

**Compendio.** Abridgment, condensation, summary, outline, recapitulation. Compilation, collection.

**Compensable.** Suitable for compensation, for settlement. Accruing a salary.

**Compensación.** Compensation, offset, salary, payment for damages, settlement. Compensation takes place by operation of law when two persons owe to each other sums of money or quantities of fungible things identical in kind, and these sums or quantities are liquidated and presently due. In such a case, compensation extinguishes both obligations to the extent of the lesser amount. (Louisiana Civ. Code art. 1893).

**Compensatorio.** Compensatory. Equalizing. Countervailing.

**Compentencia.** Competence. Jurisdiction. Venue. Legal capacity, legal ability. Skill, expertise. Competition.

**Competencia, determinación.** Jurisdiction, determination. Jurisdiction is determined in reference to the state of facts existing at the time when the petition was filed, or when the respective right is enforced. Later changes in the state of said facts is irrelevant, unless the law states differently. (Panamanian Judicial Code, art. 232).

**Competencia en causas penales.** Venue for criminal cases.

**Competencia internacional.** International jurisdiction.

**Competencia negativa.** Negative jurisdiction. If the question of jurisdiction raised between two or more judges or courts be negative by all refusing to take cognizance of the cause, the superior judge or court, or, in a proper case, the supreme court shall decide it, observing therein the procedure prescribed for other questions of jurisdiction. (Sp. L. Crim. P., art. 46 and 47).

**Competencia para embargar.** Attachment jurisdiction.

**Competencia preventiva.** Exclusionary jurisdiction. Exclusionary jurisdiction is the one that belongs to one or more courts, so that the first one that takes cognizance of the case prevents or impedes the other courts from adjudicating in the matter. (Panamanian Judicial Code, art. 237).

**Competencia sobre la persona.** Jurisdiction *in personam.*

**Competente.** Competent, able, appropriate, capable, entitled, qualified.

**Compilación.** Compilation, digest.

**Compilador.** Compiler, chronicler, collector.

**Complacencia.** Complaisance.

**Complejo.** Complex, complicated, difficult. Group, system. Obsession.

**Complemento.** Complement, companion, counterpart, supplement.

**Completo.** Complete, entire, full, whole. Total, thorough.

**Cómplice.** Accomplice. Whoever in any other way renders aid for the commission of a criminal act, even by promising aid after the fact, will be sentenced to no less than half of the minimum, nor more than half of the maximum provided for the crime in question. (St. P.C. for LA, sec. 36).

**Complicidad.** Complicity, collusion, connivance, understanding.

**Complot.** Plot, conspiracy, intrigue, machination, scheme, plan.

**Complotar.** To plot, conspire, scheme, plan.

**Componedor.** Arbitrator. Person who solves a dispute informally.

**Componenda.** Arrangement, agreement, compromise, settlement, understanding.

**Comportamiento.** Behavior, conduct, way of acting.

**Composición.** Settlement. Retaliation. Adjustment. Under the provisions of the Spanish administrative law the term adjustment—the transformation of a default in a substantial performance—means the proceeding by which a citizen who had received from the State a conditional grant of unappropriated land, could consolidate its dominion title thereon by establishing that he had substantially complied with the conditions imposed by the State in granting him said land. (Commonwealth v. Superior Court, 95 PRR 328 (1967)).

**Compostura.** Repair, adjustment.

**Compra y venta.** Sale. By a contract of purchase and sale one of the contracting parties binds himself to deliver a specified thing and the other to pay a certain price therefore in money or in something representing the same.

**Comprador.** Buyer, acquirer, purchaser, vendee.

**Comprador de buena fe.** Innocent purchaser.

**Comprador en el curso ordinario del negocio.** Buyer in ordinary course of business.

**Compraventa comercial, daño y menoscabo a las mercaderías.** Commercial sale, damages and impairment to goods. The damages and impairment suffered by merchandise after the contract has been consummated and the vendor has the goods at the disposal of the purchaser in the place and at the time agreed upon, shall be suffered by the purchaser, except in cases of carelessness or negligence on the part of the vendor.

**Compraventa comercial, entrega parcial.** Commercial sale, partial delivery. In contracts in which the delivery of a certain amount of merchandise is stipulated within a certain time, the purchaser shall not be obliged to receive part of said amount even on the promise of delivering the balance: but if he accepts the partial delivery the sale shall be consummated with regard to the goods received, reserving the right of the purchaser to demand for the rest the fulfillment of the contract or its rescission. (Sp. Com. C., sec. 330).

**Compraventa comercial, evicción y saneamiento.** Commercial sale, warranty of title. In all commercial sales the vendor shall be obliged to legally defend the title to the articles sold to the purchaser, and to indemnify him for any loss he may suffer by being disturbed in his possession of the same. (Sp. Com. C., sec. 345).

**Compraventa comercial, gastos de entrega.** Commercial sale, delivery expenses. The expenses of the delivery of merchandise in commercial sales shall be defrayed by the vendor until the merchandise is placed at the disposal of the purchaser, weighted or measured, unless there is an agreement to the contrary. (Sp. Com. C., sec. 338).

**Compraventa comercial, negativa del comprador.** Commercial sale, purchaser's refusal. In the purchaser refuses without just cause to receive the goods bought, the vendor may demand the fulfillment or rescission of the contract, depositing the merchandise in court in the first case. (Sp. Com. C., sec. 332).

**Compraventa comercial, vicios de calidad y cantidad.** Commercial sale, quality and quantity defects. A purchaser who, at the time of receiving the merchandise carefully examines the same, shall have no right of action against the vendor, alleging a defect in the quantity or quality of the merchandise. (Sp. Com. C., sec. 336).

**Compraventa mercantil.** Commercial sale. A purchase and sale of personal property for the purpose of resale, either in the form purchased or in a different form, for the purpose of deriving profit in the resale, shall be considered commercial. (Sp. Com. C., sec. 325).

**Compraventa mercantil sobre muestras.** Commercial sale by samples. If the sales takes place by samples or by a fixed quality known in commerce, the purchaser can not refuse to receive the articles contracted for if they conform to the samples or quality mentioned in the contract. (Sp. Com. C., sec. 327).

**Compraventa no mercantil.** Non-commercial sale. The following cannot be considered commercial: 1) The purchase of goods destined for the consumption of the purchaser or of the person for whom they are bought. 2) Sales made by owners and by farmers or cattlemen of the fruits or products of their crops or cattle, or of the goods in which their rents are paid them. 3) Sales made by artisans in their workshops of the articles constructed or manufactured by them. 4) The resale made by any person who is not a merchant, of the remainder of the stock laid in for his own consumption. (Sp. Com. C., sec. 326).

**Comprendido.** Comprised.

**Comprobación.** Control, check, confirmation, corroboration, validation, verification.

**Comprobante.** Voucher, receipt, stub.

**Comprobar.** To control, check, confirm, corroborate, validate, verify.

**Comprobatorio.** Proving, demonstrating, showing. Validating.

**Comprometedor.** Compromising, blaming, implicating, incriminating.

**Comprometer.** To compromise, implicate. To bind, engage, obligate.

**Compromiso.** Commitment, compromise. Duty, engagement, obligation. Settlement.

**Compulsa.** Audit, check, inspection. Poll.

**Compulsar.** To audit, check, inspect. To poll.

**Compulsión.** Compulsion, obsession.

**Compulsivo, compulsorio.** Compulsive, obsessive.

**Cómputo del tiempo.** Computation of time.

**Común.** Common, ordinary, routine, usual. Collective, communal, belonging to the community.

**Comunero.** Owner in common, joint owner.

**Comunicabilidad de circunstancias.** Transferability of personal circumstances. Whenever a particular requirement of status, personal relationship, and other individual circumstances incorporated in the statutory description of the criminal act is fulfilled by one of the perpetrators, all other principals and accessories who were aware of it will be dealt with as if they too fulfilled the requirement. (St. P.C. for LA, sec. 38).

**Comunicación.** Notice.
  Where notice is required it may be given by any means appropriate to the circumstances. A notice is effective when it reaches the person to whom it is given. (Unidroit, Prin., art. 1.9).
  Communication, connection, link. Message.

**Comunicado.** Communicated, connected, linked. Communiqué. Announcement, declaration, proclamation.

**Comunicar.** To communicate, connect, link. To announce, declare, proclaim. To inform, appraise, notify. To warn.

**Comunidad.** Community. Commune, district. Population, citizency. Commonwealth. Association.

**Comunidad de bienes.** Ownership in common. When the ownership of a thing or of a right belongs undividedly to different persons, it is held to be owned in common. In default of contracts or of special provisions, the common ownership of property shall be governed by the provisions of this title. (Sp. Civ. C., sec. 399-401).

**Comunidad de pastos.** Pasturage in common.

**Comuníquese.** Let it be known.

**Comunismo.** Communism. Marxism-Leninism.

**Comunista.** Communist. Marxist.

**Con abuso de función pública.** Under color of law.

**Con arreglo a.** Pursuant to, in pursuance to.

**Con citatión.** After summoning.

**Con intervención de.** With the participation of, upon the recommendation of.

**Conato.** Attempt. Beginning, commencement.

**Concedente.** Assignor. Grantor. Licensor. Transferor.

**Conceder.** To concede. To acknowledge, acquiesce, recognize. To allow, permit. To surrender, yield. To grant, convey. To admit, confess.

**Concejal.** Alderman.

**Concentración.** Concentration. Convergence.

**Concepción.** Conception. Understanding. Birth, genesis.

**Concernir.** Behoove.

**Concertar.** To agree, accord, concur. To plan, scheme.

**Concesión.** Concession, franchise, license, permit, privilege. Allowance.

**Concesión minera.** Mining concession. A typical mining project in Latin America requires a governmental concession that grants its holder the right to exploit and explore the mineral resources conferred by the concession. Prospecting and sampling, however, generally do not require a concession and may be conducted freely. Concession holders may transfer or mortgage their interests in the concession, as well as pledge the extracted or treated minerals to a third party. These transactions may be beneficial to the mining investor because the mining rights can serve as security for loans or other financing, a practice recognized by almost all Latin American countries. However, unlike in the United States, in Latin America a concession grant does not allow the concessionaire to freely alienate its property.

The state may not convey, along within the concession, the right to free transferability of the concessionaire's interest in the mining property, and prior government approval may be required for any transfer to be effective. (Orihuela).

**Concesionario.** Concessionaire. Beneficiary of a concession.

**Conciencia.** Conscience. Ethics. Equity.

**Conciliación, reconciliación.** Conciliation, reconciliation.

**Conciliador.** Conciliator.

**Conciliativo.** Conciliating.

**Conclusión.** Conclusion, completion, termination. Inference.

**Conclusión de hecho.** Finding of fact.

**Conclusivo, concluyente.** Conclusive, concluding. Categorical, convincing. Irrefutable. Decisive.

**Concomitante.** Concomitant, concurrent. Simultaneous.

**Concordancia.** Concordance.

**Concordar.** To accord, agree, concur.

**Concordato.** Concordat. Settlement between bankrupt and creditors.

**Concubinato.** Concubinage.

**Concubinos.** Concubines.

**Conculcador.** Infringer, intruder, invader, trespasser. Tortfeasor.

**Conculcar.** To infringe, intrude, invade, trespass. To violate.

**Concurrencia.** Concurrence, accord, agreement. Attendance, appearance, presence. Competition.

**Concurrencia desleal.** Unfair trade practices.

**Concurrente.** Party in agreement. Person who attends or is present.

**Concurrir.** To attend, appear. To concur, agree. To compete.

**Concursado.** Bankrupt. Insolvent.

**Concursal.** Related to a state of bankruptcy.

**Concursante.** Creditor of a bankrupt debtor.

**Concursar.** To file for bankruptcy. To compete.

**Concurso.** Competition, contest. Bankruptcy proceedings. Agreement.

**Concurso aparente, criterio de especialidad.** False double jeopardy, specialty theory. The criminal act will only be ruled by a statute that is not, expressly or by implication, subordinated to another one. (St. P.C. for LA, sec. 64).

**Concurso formal o ideal.** Subjective double jeopardy. When a single act constitutes two or more crimes, the penalty will be not less than the maximum provided for the more serious crime, reduced up to one third, nor greater than said maximum increased by one third. (St. P.C. for LA, sec. 65).

**Concurso por oposición.** Contest in the form of an exam.

**Concurso preventivo.** Bankruptcy proceedings.

**Concurso real o material.** Objective double jeopardy. Whenever more than one crime is punished with penalties of the same nature, the minimum will be the highest penalty for the crimes in question, and the maximum will be two thirds of addition of the maximum established for each crime. (St. P.C. for LA, sec. 66).

**Concurso, unidad de acción.** Double jeopardy, single action. Prosecution for multiple offenses. Except for cases of subjective double jeopardy (*Concurso formal o ideal*), the law can take a criminal act into account only once in order to impose a penalty. (St. P.C. for LA, sec. 63).

**Concusión.** Concussion, collusion. Injury.

**Condado.** County.

**Condecoración.** Decoration, distinction, medal.

**Condena.** Sentence, conviction, penalty, punishment.

**Condena de ejecución condicional.** Suspended sentence. In a judgment of conviction the court may, stating the reasons, suspend the execution of a sentence of imprisonment of two years, or less, provided that: a) The convict is not a repeat offender. b) He has shown good conduct before and after the criminal act. c) Based on the circumstances and characteristics of the crime, the predominant motivations and a complete study of the convict's personality, he is not expected to commit new crimes. (St. P.C. for LA, sec. 74).

**Condena de ejecución condicional, restricciones.** Suspended sentence, restric-

tions. The beneficiary of a suspended sentence will be duty bound to: a) Comply with the security measures established for him; b) Reside, or abstain from residing, in a certain area and to report any change of domicile. c) Start working, within a specified time, in a lawful profession, occupation or trade; d) Refrain from using narcotics, hallucinatory substances or others of an addictive nature. e) Refrain from consuming alcoholic beverages. f) Comply with the agreement to pay damages within the established time and formalities. (St. P.C. for LA, art. 75 and 76).

**Condena de ejecución condicional, revocación.** Suspended sentence, revocation. A suspended sentence will be automatically revoked whenever the beneficiary commits a new intentional crime before the end of the trial period. A suspended sentence can be revoked by judicial decree of the court that granted it, in the following cases: a) When the beneficiary breaches one or more of the conditions imposed; b) When he commits a new intentional crime and the suspended sentence was entered for a crime of the same nature. (St. P.C. for LA, sec. 77 and 78).

**Condenación.** Condemnation, punishment.

**Condenado.** Convict, convicted, inmate, prisoner, sentenced.

**Condenar.** To sentence, condemn, convict.

**Condenar en costas.** Tax for costs.

**Condenatorio.** Condemnatory, of conviction.

**Condición.** Condition. Caveat, clause, prerequisite, requirement, requisite. Proviso, stipulation. State, status, situation.

**Condicionado.** Conditioned, qualified.

**Condicional.** Conditional, contingent. Dependent on a condition.

**Condicionar.** To make dependent on a condition.

**Condiciones de trabajo.** Working conditions. In general, it may be said that working conditions constitute the specific rights and obligations of the parties in a given work relationship. (Comparison of Labor Law).

**Condominio.** Co-ownership, condominium, joint ownership, tenancy in common.

**Condómino.** Co-owner, joint owner, tenants in common.

**Condonación de deuda.** Remission of a debt. A remission may be made either expressly or by implication. (Sp. Civ. C., sec. 1155).

**Condonador.** Person who condones, pardons.

**Conducente.** Conducive to. Fitting, pertinent, related, relevant.

**Conducta.** Conduct, bearing, behavior, demeanor.

**Conducta anterior.** Course of dealing.

**Conducta cuasidelictiva.** Tortious conduct.

**Conductor.** Carrier.

**Confabulación.** Collusion, complicity, conspiracy, intrigue, plot, scheme.

**Confabular.** To connive, conspire, contrive, plan, scheme.

**Confederación.** Confederation, federation.

**Conferencia.** Conference, consultation, deliberation, discussion, interview, meeting. Assembly, colloquium, convention, symposium.

**Conferencia con antelación al juicio.** Pretrial conference.

**Conferenciar.** To confer, consult, deliberate. To exchange views.

**Conferir.** To confer, accord, award, bestow. To convey, grant, transfer.

**Confesante.** Party who makes a confession.

**Confesar.** To confess, acknowledge, admit, avow. To disclose, reveal.

**Confesión.** Confession, admission, acknowledgement, avowal.

Confession may be made either judicially or extrajudicially. In either case it shall be an indispensable condition for the validity of the confession that it should relate to personal acts of the confessor and that he should have legal capacity to make it. (Sp. Civ. C., sec. 1199).

**Confesión del procesado.** Confession of the accused. The confession of the accused shall not excuse the judge from taking all the steps necessary in order to be convinced of the truth of the confession and the existence of the crime. (Sp. L. Crim. P., art. 406).

**Confesión en juicio.** Confession in court. Confession in court made with all necessary requisites constitutes full proof against him

who makes the same. (Decision of November 18, 1886, Spain).

**Confesión judicial.** Judicial confession. A judicial confession is a declaration made by a party in a judicial proceeding. (Louisiana Civ. Code art. 1853).

**Confeso.** Party who has confessed.

**Confiable.** Trustworthy, dependable, reliable. Credible, reputable. Stable, steady. Faithful, loyal.

**Confiar.** To rely on, count on, depend on. To trust, entrust.

**Confidencial.** Confidential, private, restricted.

**Confidente, informante.** Informer. A mere informer is the one who furnishes information to the authorities but plays no part in the transaction object of the offense. (Ppl. v. López Rivera, 91 PRR 672 (1965)).

**Confinado.** Prisoner, captive, convict.

**Confinamiento.** Confinement, jailing. Isolation.

**Confirmación.** Confirmation.

If the party entitled to avoid the contract expressly or impliedly confirms the contract after the period of time for giving notice of avoidance has begun to run, avoidance of the contract is excluded.

**Confirmación contractual.** Confirmation of a contract. Confirmation is a declaration whereby a person cures the relative nullity of an obligation. An express act of confirmation must contain or identify the substance of the obligation and evidence the intention to cure its relative nullity. Tacit confirmation may result from voluntary performance of the obligation. (Louisiana Civ. Code art. 1842).

**Confirmación por escrito.** Writings in confirmation.

If a writing which is sent within a reasonable time after the conclusion of the contract and which purports to be a confirmation of the contract contains additional of different terms, such terms become part of the contract, unless they materially alter the contract or the recipient, without undue delay, objects to the discrepancy. (Unidroit, Prin., art. 2.12).

**Confirmación, ratificación.** Confirmation, ratification. The unilateral juridical act by which validity is given to a voidable act executed by the interested person personally is called confirmation. (Madera v. Metropolitan Const. Corp., 95 PRR 625 (1967)). Acknowledgement. Certification, corroboration, verification.

**Confirmar.** To confirm, affirm. To authenticate, certify, corroborate, ratify, verify.

**Confiscable.** That can be confiscated or expropriated.

**Confiscación.** Forfeiture, condemnation, expropriation. The means by which the State deprives the owner of his property without compensation by the due process of law of being notified and heard. (Ppl. v. Gonzalez Cortes, 95 PRR 161 (1967)).

**Confiscador.** Confiscatory.

**Confiscar.** To confiscate, expropriate. To commandeer, seize. To impound.

**Confiscatorio.** Too onerous. Excessively burdensome.

**Conflicto.** Conflict, clash, confrontation, controversy, friction, struggle.

**Conflicto entre tribunales eclesiásticos y seculares.** Conflict between ecclesiastical and secular courts.

When ecclesiastical judges or tribunals shall consider that they have jurisdiction of a cause of which a secular judge or court is taking cognizance, they may interpose an inhibitory plea, and if it should be overruled they may complain to the proper court, which, after hearing the public prosecutor, shall decide without further remedy what it may deem proper. (Sp. L. Crim. P., art 48 and 49).

**Conformarse.** To content oneself with. To accept.

**Conforme.** Satisfied in agreement with. According to.

**Conformidad.** Conformity. Acquiescence, approval, compliance, consent. Agreement, concurrence. Authorization, permission.

**Confronta.** Audit, check, investigation.

**Confrontar.** To face, challenge, encounter. To check, compare.

**Confusión.** Confusion. Chaos, commotion, disorder. Merger of ideas or theories. When the qualities of obligee and obligor are united in the same person, the obligation is extinguished by confusion. (Louisiana Civ. Code art. 1903).

**Confusión de derechos.** Confusion of rights. Whenever the characters of creditor and debtor are merged in the same person the obligation is extinguished. The case in which this confusion take place by virtue of inheritance is excepted, if said inheritance should have been accepted under benefit of inventory. (Sp. Civ. C., sec. 1160).

**Congresista, congresal.** Congressman, congress person.

**Congreso.** Congress. Assembly, conclave, convention, synod. Legislature, parliament.

**Congruencia.** Congruity. Compatibility, correspondence, harmony.

**Conjetura.** Conjecture. Assumption, estimation, presumption. Hypothesis. Inference. Speculation.

**Conjuez.** Associate justice.

**Conjunto.** Joint, common, in common. Collective, shared. Set, group.

**Conjura, conjuración.** Conspiracy. Collusion, complicity, connivance. Machination, plot, scheme.

**Conjurador.** Conspirator, cohort, confederate. Partner in crime.

**Conjurar.** To conspire, connive, contrive, plot, scheme.

**Conminación.** Summons. Subpoena. Citation. Admonition.

**Conminar.** To order a certain conduct under a threat in case of refusal.

**Conminatorio.** Comminatory.

**Conmoción.** Commotion, disturbance, turmoil.

**Conmorientes.** People dying simultaneously in a common disaster.

**Conmutación.** Commutation. Pardon, absolution, grace.

**Conmutar.** To commute. To pardon. To exchange, barter.

**Conmutativo.** Commutative.

**Connivencia.** Connivance, collusion, conspiracy, intrigue, plot, scheme.

**Conocedor.** Party who knows or is aware of something.

**Conocimiento.** Invoice or manifest of the cargo. Cognizance.

**Conocimiento de embarque.** Bill of lading.

**Conocimiento judicial.** Judicial notice.

**Conocimiento real.** Actual knowledge.

**Consanguíneo.** Of the same blood. Directly related.

**Consanguinidad.** Consanguinity, kinship.

**Consecuente.** Ensuing, following, successive. Congruent, congruous, consistent. Logical.

**Consecutivo.** Consecutive, ensuing, successive.

**Consejero.** Adviser, advisor, counselor, confidant, counsel.

**Consejo.** Council, assembly, cabinet, chamber, committee, meeting. Advice, instruction, opinion, recommendation, suggestion.

**Consejo de incautación.** Board of receivers

**Consejo de Indias.** Council of the Indies. Directly subordinate to the king in the governance of the Spanish colonies was the Council of the Indies (*Real y Supremo Consejo de las Indias*). (L & D in LA).

**Consejo ejecutivo.** Executive council.

**Consenso.** Consensus, accord, concurrence, harmony, unanimity, understanding.

**Consensual.** Consensual, agreed.

**Consentido.** Consented, approved, assented, authorized, permitted.

**Consentimiento.** Consent. Consent is shown by the concurrence of the offer and the acceptance of the thing and the cause which are to constitute the contract. (Sp. Civ. C., sec. 1229, 1233).

**Consentimiento expreso.** Express consent.

**Consentir.** To consent, approve, authorize, consent, permit.

**Conservación.** Preservation.

**Conservación de artículos y bienes.** Conservation of articles and goods. An agent who has in his possession articles and goods of a third party shall be responsible for their conservation in the same state as he received them. (Mex. Com. C., art.295).

**Conservador.** Conservator, trustee. Conservative (adj.).

**Considerando, los considerandos.** Whereas, introductory part to a judgment.

**Considerar.** Consider, think, ponder, reflect on something with.

**Consigna.** Pass word. Motto.

**Consignación.** Consignment, shipment.

**Consignación en pago.** Tender and deposit. When the object of the performance is the delivery of a thing or a sum of money and the obligee, without justification, fails to accept the performance tendered by the obligor, the tender, followed by deposit to the order of the court, produces all the effects of a performance from the time the tender was made if declared valid by the court. (Louisiana Civ. Code art. 1869).

**Consignador.** Consignor, person who commits or entrusts something to another.

**Consignar.** To consign, commit, entrust. To make a judicial deposit.

**Consignatario.** Consignee, custodian, depositary, receiver, trustee.

**Consolidable.** Cumulative, that may be merged.

**Consolidación.** Consolidation, merge, unification.

**Consolidar.** To consolidate, combine, merge, unify.

**Consorcial.** Relating to a collective body or entity.

**Consorcio.** Consortium, association, group with a common objective acting in an organized way.

**Consorte.** Co-defendants or co-plaintiffs. Spouses.

**Conspiración.** Conspiracy, collusion, connivance, complicity, intrigue, machination, plot.

**Conspirar.** To conspire, connive, contrive, plot, scheme.

**Constancia.** Record, entry, evidence, indication, inscription, proof.

**Constar, hacer constar.** To record, to cause an entry, to enter in the record, to establish.

**Constatar.** To confirm, authenticate, certify, corroborate, ratify, verify.

**Constitución.** Constitution, charter, magna carta, supreme law. Composition, formation, structure. Foundation, founding, creation, settlement.

**Constitución en mora.** Putting in default. When a term for the performance of an obligation is either fixed, or is clearly determinable by the circumstances, the obligor is put in default by the mere arrival of that term. In other cases, the obligor must be put in default by the obligee, but not before performance is due. (Louisiana Civ. Code art. 1990 and notes).

**Constitucional.** Constitutional.

**Constitucionalidad.** Constitutionality.

**Constitucionalismo.** Constitutionalism. After the Latin American countries became independent, they all adopted rigid written constitutions. English political empiricism does not seem to have held great sway over countries of Latin culture. Under the twofold influence of the codifying trend of the French revolution and the prototype of rigid constitutions embodied in the 1789 United States Constitution, Latin America has never stopped drawing up solemn declarations of rights and stubbornly adding new legal guarantees to the constitutions each time they are violated. (W. Eur. & LA Leg. Sys.).

**Constituir.** To constitute, build, construct create, fashion, form, make, mold.

**Constituir en mora.** Place in default, put in default.

**Constituirse en.** Become, assume the quality of.

**Constitutivo.** Composing part, essencial element. Part of a forming process.

**Constituyente.** Constituent. Party to or part of a constitutional process.

**Construcción defectuosa.** Defective construction. Defective construction—in a construction contract—means all such kinds of vices that exceed the measure of imperfection expected in a construction. (Pereira v. I.B.E.C., 95 PRR 28 (1967)).

**Consuetudinario.** Customary, habitual. Routine, systematic.

**Consul.** Consul.

**Consulado.** Consulate.

**Consular.** Consular.

**Consulta.** Consultation. Doubt, enquiry, query, question.

**Consultante.** Consultant. Advisor. Advising.

**Consultar.** To consult, to request an opinion, to ask for advice.

**Consultivo.** Consultative, consulting, counseling, advisory, instructional. Not binding.

**Consultorio.** Legal or medical office. Place where professional advice is dispensed.

**Consultorio jurídico.** Law office, law firm.

**Consumación.** Consummation, completion, culmination, fulfillment, termination.

**Consumo.** Consumption. Ingestion. Depletion, waste.

**Contabilidad.** Accounting, accountancy, bookkeeping.

**Contado (al).** Cash, currency, money. Legal tender.

**Contador.** Accountant, auditor, bookkeeper. Chartered public accountant, CPA.

**Contaduría.** Accounting department, auditor's office.

**Contaminación.** Contamination. Adulteration, pollution.

**Contaminación del aire.** Air pollution.

**Contaminación del ambiente.** Environmental pollution.

**Contaminante.** Contaminant, pollutant. A harmful, irritant or nuisance material that is foreign to the normal atmosphere. Any material or energy in any of its physical states and forms, which upon being incorporated or acting in air, water, soil, flora, fauna, or any natural element, alters or modifies its natural composition and condition.

**Contaminantes del ambiente del trabajo.** Work environment contaminants. Physical biological or chemical agents, elements or compounds capable of altering workplace environmental conditions and that, due to their properties, concentration level and action time, may harm worker health.

**Contante.** Cash, currency, money. Legal tender. That can be counted.

**Contención.** Contention, conflicting position, contested opinion. Clash, dissension. Continence.

**Contencioso.** Subject to adversarial legal proceedings. Contested, challenged, disputed. Of a litigious nature.

**Contencioso-administrativo.** Adversarial legal proceedings where the state is a party.

Special jurisdiction where a governmental entity is involved.

**Contenedor.** Container, holder, receptacle, repository.

**Contestabilidad.** Contestability, that can be argued or challenged.

**Contestable.** Contestable, arguable, subject to dispute. Not clear, clouded, uncertain.

**Contestación.** Answer.

In the answer to the complaint, the defendant must plead all the peremptory exceptions which may be proper and the dilatory ones which were not taken within the period prescribed by law. In the same answer may also be included the counter-claim in cases in which it may be proper. (Sp. L. Civ. P. sec. 540, 541).

**Contestación de demanda.** Answer. Once the case is assigned to a particular Court, the defendant may file an answer even if not served, in which case service will be deemed accomplished. (Panamanian Judicial Code, art. 671).

**Contestar.** To contest, challenge, confront. To answer, replicate, reply, respond, retort.

**Contexto.** Context, background, framework. With a common point of reference.

**Contextual.** Within context. In harmony with the rest.

**Contienda.** Controversy, altercation, argument, conflict, polemic, quarrel.

**Contigüedad.** In the same area or locality. Envirous, vicinity.

**Contiguo.** Contiguous. Abutting, adjacent, adjoining, bordering. Next to.

**Contingencia.** Contingency, eventuality, possibility. Uncertain event. Possible occurrence.

**Contingencia ambiental.** Environmental risk. A risk situation deriving from human activities or natural phenomena which could place the integrity of one or more ecosystems in danger.

**Contingente.** Contingent. Group or squad of soldiers or workers.

**Continuación.** Continuation, continuance, progression, succession. Sequence.

**Continuar.** To continue, carry on, persist, prolong, renew, resume.

**Contra.** Against, contra, counter, facing, opposite. Guerrilla or opponent to the government (n).

**Contra el orden público.** Against public policy.

**Contrabandear.** To smuggle, to sneak in.

**Contrabandista.** Smuggler.

**Contrabando.** Smuggling, contraband.

**Contractual.** Contractual, by agreement, by consent of the parties.

**Contradicción.** Contradiction, difference, discrepancy, disparity, inconsistency, variance.

**Contradictorio.** Contradictory, conflicting, discrepant, inconsistent, irreconcilable.

**Contradocumento.** Counterdocument, proof that another document is a simulation.

**Contraer.** To contract. To agree, covenant, to make or to enter an agreement. To acquire, catch. To abridge, compress, condense.

**Contraescritura.** Counter document.

**Contraespionaje.** Counterespionage.

**Contrainterrogar.** To cross examine.

**Contrainterrogatorio.** Cross examination.

**Contralor.** Controller, inspector (n). Control, inspect.

**Contraoferta.** Counter-offer.

**Contraorden.** Counterorder.

**Contraparte.** Counterpart. Adversary or opposing party in litigation.

**Contrapartida.** On the other side. By the same token. *Quid pro quo.*

**Contraprueba.** Proof that contradicts previous evidence offered by the opposing party. Counterevidence, rebutting evidence, rebuttal.

**Contrapunto.** Point where two parties have a divergence or are in conflict. Note of contrast.

**Contrareferencia.** Cross reference.

**Contrariamente.** To the contrary. In an adversarial position.

**Contrariar.** To counter, disobey, disregard. To infringe or transgress.

**Contrario.** Contrary. Adversary party.

**Contrario a las buenas costumbres.** Contrary to morality.

**Contrarréplica.** Rebuttal, rejoinder. Answer to a refutation.

**Contrarrestar.** To counter, balance, compensate, countervail, offset.

**Contrasentido.** Absurdity, nonsense. Logical contradiction.

**Contraste.** Contrast. Comparison.

**Contratable.** Contractable in the sense of a contract.

**Contratación, contrato.** Contract, agreement, bargain, covenant, deal, pact.

**Contratante.** Contracting party.

**Contratar.** To make or enter into a contract. To hire personnel.

**Contratiempo.** Obstacle, hurdle. Accident. Misfortune.

**Contratista independiente.** Independent contractor.

**Contrato.** Contract, agreement, covenant. A contract exists from the moment one or more persons consent to bind himself or themselves, with regard to bind another or others, to give something or to render some service. (Sp. Civ. C., sec. 1221, 1226).

**Contrato accesorio.** Accessory contract. A contract is accessory when it is made to provide security for the performance of an obligation. Suretyship, mortgage, and pledge are examples of such a contract. (Louisiana Civ. Code art. 1913).

**Contrato aleatorio.** Aleatory contract. By an aleatory contract one of the parties binds himself, or both mutually bind themselves, to give or do something as an equivalent for what the other party is to give or do in case of the occurrence of an event which is uncertain or may happen at an undetermined time. (Sp. Civ. C., sec. 1692).

**Contrato bilateral o signalagmático.** Bilateral or synallagmatic contract. A contract is bilateral, or synallagmatic, when the parties obligate themselves reciprocally, so that the obligation of each party is correlative to the obligation of the other. (Louisiana Civ. Code art. 1908).

**Contrato colectivo de trabajo.** Collective bargaining agreement. The agreement executed between one or more workers' unions and one or more employers or one or more employers' associations, for the purpose of establishing the conditions according to which work is to be performed in one or more enterprises or establishments. (Mex. Labor Law).

**Contrato colectivo de trabajo, extensión.** Collective bargaining agreement, scope. The provisions of the collective bargaining agreement cover all the employees of the enterprise or establishment, even if they are not members of the union (FLL, Article 396).

**Contrato colectivo de trabajo, revisión.** Collective bargaining agreement, revision. Either of the parties may request revision of a collective barganing agreement, although normally a union takes the initiative. (Comparison of Labor Law).

**Contrato colectivo de trabajo, terminación.** Collective barganing agreement, termination. A collective barganing agreement can be terminated by mutual consent; at the conclusion of the job for which it was agreed; or by the shut down of the enterprise or establishment, provided it applied only to the establishment which was shut down (FLL, Article 401). (Comparison of Labor Law).

**Contrato con estipulaciones dejadas deliberadamente pendientes.** Contract with terms deliberately left open. If the parties intend to conclude a contract, the fact that they intentionally leave a term to be agreed upon in further negotiations or to be determined by a third person does not prevent a contract from coming into existence. (Unidroit, Prin., art. 2.14).

**Contrato conmutativo.** Commutative contract. A contract is commutative when the performance of the obligation of each party is correlative to the performance of the other. (Louisiana Civ. Code art. 1911).

**Contrato de adhesión.** Contract of adhesion, adhesion contract. An adhesion contract is one in which the economically strongest party imposes specific conditions or the full scheme of the contracts to his advantage and in detriment to the other contracting party who, being economically weaker, has no freedom of choice other than to accept those conditions or scheme or refuse to enter into the contract. (Maryland Cas. Co. v. S.J. Racing Ass'n., 83 PRR, 538 (1961)).

**Contrato de dación en prenda de un pagaré hipotecario.** Contract of pledge to secure a mortgage note. A contract of pledge securing a mortgage note constitutes a juridical business and by its nature the pledgee acquires a special interest in the note itself. (Vendrell v. Torres, 85 PRR 842 (1962)).

**Contrato de entregas parciales.** Installment contract.

**Contrato de estacionamiento.** Parking contract. A parking contract is of an atypical nature which, depending on the surrounding circumstances, may be classified as a lease contract or bailment for hire. (Rivera v. San Juan Racing Assoc.; Ins., 90 PRR 405 (1964)).

**Contrato de fletamento.** Charter party. A charter party must be drawn in duplicate and signed by the contracting parties. (Sp. Com. C., sec. 652).

**Contrato de fletamento, abandono de mercancías.** Charter party, abandonment of damaged merchandise. The charterers and freighters cannot abandon merchandise damaged on account of the character of the goods or by reason of an accidental case, for the payment of the freight and other expenses.

**Contrato de fletamento, aumento natural.** Charter party, natural increase. The natural increase in weight or size of the merchandise loaded on the vessel shall accrue to the benefit of the owner, and shall pay the proper freight fixed in the contract for the same. (Sp. Com. C., sec. 664).

**Contrato de fletamento, conocimiento.** Charter party, bill of lading. The bill of lading may be issued to bearer, to order, or in the name of a specific person, and must be signed within twenty-four hours after the cargo has been received on board, the freighter being allowed to demand the unloading thereof at the expense of the captain should he not sign it, and in every case indemnity for the loss and damage suffered thereby. (Sp. Com. C., sec. 706).

**Contrato de fletamento, derecho a subrogar.** Charter party, right to subcharter. The charterer of an entire vessel may subcharter the whole or part thereof for the amounts he may consider most convenient, the captain not being allowed to refuse to receive on board the freight delivered by the second charterers, provided the conditions of the first charter are not changed, and that the person from whom the vessel is chartered be paid the full price agreed upon even though the full cargo is not embarked, with the limitation established in the following article. (Sp. Com. C., sec. 679).

**Contrato de fletamento, guerra o bloqueo.** Charter party, war or blockade. In such case the captain shall be obliged to make the nearest safe and neutral port, and request and await orders from the freighter; and the expenses incurred and salaries earned during the detention shall be paid as general average. (Sp. Com. C., sec. 677).

**Contrato de fletamento, malas condiciones para navegar.** Charter party, unseaworthiness. The captain shall lose the freight and shall indemnify the freighters if the latter should proved, even against the certificate of inspection, should one have taken place at the port of departure, that the vessel was unseaworthy as the time of receiving the cargo. (Sp. Com. C., sec. 676).

**Contrato de fletamento, mercaderías arrojadas al mar.** Charter party, jettison. Merchandise jettisoned for the common safety shall not pay freight; but its value shall be considered as general average, and shall be computed in proportion to the distance covered when it was jettisoned. (Sp. Com. C., sec. 660).

**Contrato de fletamento, pago de flete y capa.** Charter party, payment of freight and primage. After the vessel has been unloaded and the cargo placed at the disposal of the consignee, the latter must immediately pay the captain the freight due and the other expenses incurred by reason of the cargo. (Sp. Com. C., sec. 686).

**Contrato de no demandar.** Contract not to sue.

**Contrato de opción.** Option contract.

An option is a contract whereby the parties agree that the offeror is bound by his offer for a specified period of time and that the offeree may accept within that time. (Louisiana Civ. Code art. 1933).

**Contrato de refacción agrícola.** Contract of advances for agricultural purposes. A contract of advances for agricultural purposes is one under which one of the parties thereto turns over an the other party receives, subject to reimbursement, a certain amount of money in cash or specie, whether in a lump sum or in different installments, with which to meet the expenses of administration, maintenance, cultivation and improvement of rural properties, or for the construction, conservation, repair and operation of buildings and machinery devoted to agricultural or industrial purposes in connection with the cultivation or the manufacture of any agricultural product, the products of said properties being answerable and encumbered for the repayment of the amounts received with such interest as may have been agreed upon. (P.R. Act Nr. 66 of 8/1/25).

**Contrato de seguro.** Insurance contract.
An insurance contract is one by which the underwriter is liable for the fortuitous damages which may occur to the insured personal or real property, in consideration of a certain price, which may be unrestrictedly fixed by the parties. (Sp. Civ. C., sec. 1693).

**Contrato de seguro contra incendio.** Fire insurance. All personal or real property which is liable to be destroyed or injured by fire may be the subject of an insurance contract against fire. (Sp. Com. C., sec. 386, 387).

**Contrato de seguro contra incendio, extensión.** Fire insurance, coverage. The insurance against fire shall include the repair or indemnity for all the loss and material damage caused by the direct action of the fire and by the inevitable consequences of the fire. (Sp. Com. C., sec. 393).

**Contrato de seguro contra incendio, valuación del daño.** Fire insurance, appraisal of damage. The appraisement of the damage caused by the fire shall be made by experts in the manner established in the policy, by an agreement between the parties, in the absence of which, said appraisement shall be made in accordance with the provisions of the Law of Civil Procedure. (Sp. Com. C., sec. 406).

**Contrato de seguro de transporte terrestre.** Transportation insurance. All goods which can be transported by the usual means of land locomotion may be the subject of an insurance contract against the risks of transportation. (Sp. Com. C., sec. 432, 437).

**Contrato de seguro de vida.** Contract for life insurance. Life insurance shall include all the combinations which can be made, making agreements with regard to the payment of premiums or of capital in exchange for the enjoyment of a life annuity or up to a certain age, or the receipt of capital on the death of a certain person, in favor of the insured, his legal representative, or of a third person, or any other similar or analogous combination. (Sp. Com. C., sec. 416, 418).

**Contrato de seguro de vida, beneficiarios.** Life insurance, beneficiaries. The insurance may be made in favor of a third person, stating in the policy the name, surname, and status of the donor or person insured, or identifying said person in some other unquestionable manner. (Sp. Com. C., sec. 419).

**Contrato de seguro de vida, pólizas endosables.** Contract for life insurance, negotiable policies. Life insurance policies, after the premiums or installments which the insured bound himself to pay have been satisfied, shall be negotiable. (Sp. Com. C., sec. 430).

**Contrato de seguro marítimo.** Contract for marine insurance. In order that a marine insurance contract may be valid, it must be reduced to writing in a policy signed by the contracting parties. This policy shall be drawn and signed in duplicate, one copy being kept by each of the contracting parties. (Sp. Com. C., sec. 737, 743).

**Contrato de seguro marítimo, represamiento.** Contract for marine insurance, recapture of vessel. If by reason of the recapture of the vessel the insured should regain possession of his goods, all the costs and damages caused by the loss shall be considered average, and shall be suffered by the underwriter. (Sp. Com. C., sec. 802).

**Contrato de seguro contra incendio.** Fire insurance contract. The contract of fire insurance is governed by the law of the place where the thing insured is located at the time of its execution. All other contracts of insurance follow the general rule, being regulated by the personal law common to the parties, or in the absence thereof, by the law of the place where the contract of insurance was executed.

**Contrato de seguro marítimo, rescate de mercadería.** Contract for marine insurance, redemption of foods insured. In case of the capture of the vessel, and should the insured not have time to act in concurrence with the underwriter, nor to await instructions from him, he in person, or the captain, in his absence, may redeem the goods insured, informing the underwriter at the first opportunity. (Sp. Com. C., sec. 801).

**Contrato de seguro, riesgos varios.** Insurance contract, various risks. Any other risks may be the subject of a commercial insurance contract, which arises from accidental cases or natural accidents and the agreements and the agreements made must be compiled with provided they are lawful. (Sp. Com. C., sec. 438).

**Contrato de sociedad.** Civil association agreement. In a civil association agreement, members mutually bind themselves to combine their assets and their efforts for the realization of a common goal. (Mex. Civ. C., art.2688).

**Contrato de trabajo.** Labor contract.

**Contrato de transporte terrestre.** Contract for overland transportation. A contract for all kinds of transportation overland or by river shall be considered commercial: 1) When it involves merchandise or any commercial goods. 2) When, no matter what his object may be, the carrier is a merchant or is customarily engaged in transporting goods for the public. (Sp. Com. C., sec. 349).

**Contrato de transporte terrestre, carta de porte.** Contract for overland transportation, bill of lading. The shipper as well as the carrier of merchandise and goods may mutually demand of each other the issuance of a bill of lading. (Sp. Com. C., sec. 350, 354).

**Contrato de transporte terrestre, derecho de retención.** Contract for overland transportation, lien over goods. The goods transported shall be specially obligated to answer for the transportation charges and for the expenses and fees caused by the same during their transportation, or until the time of their delivery. (Sp. Com. C., sec. 375).

**Contrato de transporte terrestre, entrega al consignatario.** Contract for overland transportation, delivery to consignee. The carrier must deliver to the consignee without any delay or difficulty the merchandise received by him, by reason of the mere fact of being designated in the bill of lading to receive it; and should the carrier not do so he shall be liable for the damages which may arise therefrom. (Sp. Com. C., sec. 368).

**Contrato de transporte terrestre, riesgos.** Contract for overland transportation, risk. Merchandise shall be transported at the risk of the shipper, unless the contrary was expressly stipulated. (Sp. Com. C., sec. 361).

**Contrato de transporte terrestre, ruta.** Contract for overland transportation, route. If there should be an agreement between the shipper and the carrier with regard to the road over which the transportation is to be made, the carrier can not change the route, unless obliged to do so by *force majeure*.

When on account of *force majeure* the carrier is obliged to take another route, causing an increase in the transportation charges, he shall be reimbursed for such increase after presenting the formal proof thereof. (Sp. Com. C. sec. 359).

**Contrato en favor de tercero.** Contract in favor of a third party. In the field of contracts, a contract which having been validly executed between two persons, is intended, nevertheless, to attribute a right to a third person who has not intervened at all, either directly or indirectly in its execution. (A.L. Arsuaga v. La Hood Const., Inc., 90 PRR 101 (1964)).

**Contrato innominado.** Innominate contract. Innominate contracts are those with no special designation. (Louisiana Civ. Code art. 1914).

**Contrato integrado.** Integrated agreement.

**Contrato, invalidación.** Contract, invalidation. A contract can be invalidated:
I. For legal incapacity by one or all parties;
II. Because of a vice of consent;

III. Because the objective of the contract may be illegal;

IV. Because consent was not given as legally required. (Mex. Civ. C., art.1795).

**Contrato nominativo.** Nominate contract. Nominate contracts are those given a special designation such as sale, lease, loan, or insurance. (Louisiana Civ. Code art. 1914 and 1916).

**Contrato oneroso.** Onerous contract. A contract is onerous when each of the parties obtains an advantage in exchange for his obligation. (Louisiana Civ. Code art. 1909).

**Contrato por tiempo indefinido.** Contract for an indefinite period.

A contract for an indefinite period may be ended by either party by giving notice a reasonable time in advance. (Unidroit, Prin., art. 5.8).

**Contrato principal.** Principal contract. When the secured obligation arises from a contract, either between the same or other parties, that contract is the principal contract. (Louisiana Civ. Code art. 1913).

**Contrato sustituto.** Substituted contract.

**Contrato unilateral.** Unilateral contract. A contract is unilateral when the party who accepts the obligation of the other does not assume a reciprocal obligation. (Louisiana Civ. Code art. 1907).

**Contrato, venta de cosas futuras.** Contracts, sale of future things. A sale is sometimes made of a thing to come: as of what shall accrue from an estate, of animals yet unborn, or such like other things, although not yet existing. (Louisiana Civ. Code art. 2450).

**Contrato-ley.** Contract-law. An agreement executed by one or several workers' unions and several employers, or one or several employers' associations, for the purpose of establishing the conditions according to which work in a particular industrial activity should be rendered. From this definition it follows that the contrato-ley, as compared to the contrato colectivo de trabajo (collective barganing agreement): a) requires the participation of one or more employers; b) covers an industrial activity in a certain geographic area; and c) is mandatory for that whole industry, including enterprises and establishments that have not entered into it. (Mex. Labor Law).

**Contrato leonino.** Unconscionable contract.

**Contratos, arrendamiento.** Contracts, lease. A lease may be of things, works, or services. Perishable things, which are consumed by use, cannot be the object of this contract. (Sp. Civ. C., sec. 1445, 1448).

**Contratos, Chile.** Contracts, Chile. Chilean private international law makes a distinction between the three main aspects of contracts: formalities, intrinsic validity, and effects. If a contract takes place in Chile, Article 14 of the Civil Code provides that the formalities are governed by Chilean law. There is no general rule covering the formalities of a contract entered into abroad. Nevertheless, the locus regit actum principle is applied to some contracts and specific juridical acts effected abroad, such as formalities of marriage, execution of wills, and public deeds. Therefore, judicial decisions have repeatedly held that the extrinsic validity of acts juridical must be ascertained in accordance with the law of the place of performance. (LA Laws & Inst.).

**Contratos comerciales, claúsula penal.** Commercial contracts, liquidated damages. In a commercial contract containing an indemnification clause against the person who fails to comply therewith, the party aggrieved may take legal steps to demand the fulfillment of the contract or the indemnification stipulated; but in resorting to either of these two actions the other one shall be annulled unless there is an agreement to the contrary. (Sp. Com. C., sec. 56).

**Contratos comerciales, efectos de la morosidad.** Commercial contracts, effects of delay. The effects of delay in compliance with commercial obligations shall begin: 1) In contracts in which a day is fixed for compliance therewith by the will of the parties or by law, on the day following the one on which they fall due. 2) In contracts in which no such day is fixed, from the day on which the creditor legally makes demand upon the debtor or notifies him of the declaration of loss and damage made against him before a justice, notary, or other public official authorized to admit the same. (Sp. Com. C., sec. 63).

**Contratos comerciales, ejecución, cumplimiento.** Commercial contracts, performance. Commercial contracts shall be executed and complied with in good faith according to the terms in which they were made and drafted, without evading the honest, proper, and usual meaning of written or spoken words with arbitrary interpretations, nor limiting the effects which are naturally derived from the manner in which the parties may have explained their wishes and contracted their obligations. (Sp. Com. C., sec. 57).

**Contratos comerciales, por correspondencia.** Commercial contracts, by mail. Contracts executed through correspondence shall be perfected from the time an answer is made accepting the proposition or the conditions by which the latter may be modified. (Sp. Com. C., sec. 54).

**Contratos comerciales, términos de gracia.** Commercial contracts, effects of delay. Days of grace, courtesy, and others, which under any designation whatsoever defer the fulfillment of commercial obligations, shall not be recognized, but only those which the parties may have previously fixed in the contract, or which are founded on a definite provision of law. (Sp. Com. C., sec. 61).

**Contratos comerciales, validez.** Commercial contracts, validity. Commercial contracts shall be valid and serve as the basis of an obligation and cause of action in suits, whatever may be the form or in whatever foreign language they may be executed, the class to which they correspond, and the amount involved, provided their existence is proven by some of the means established by the civil law. (Sp. Com. C., sec. 51, 52).

**Contratos en documento público.** Contracts in public instrument. The following must appear in a public instrument: 1) Acts and contracts the object of which is the creation, modification, or extinction of property rights on real property. 2) Leases of the same property for six or more years, provided they are to the prejudice of third persons. 3) Marriage contracts, and the creation and increase of dowries, whenever it is intended to enforce them against third persons. 4) The assignment, repudiation, and renunciation of hereditary rights or of those of the conjugal partnership. 5) The general power for lawsuits and the special ones to be presented in suits; the power to administer property and any other, the object of which is an act drafted or which is to be drafted in a public instrument, or which may prejudice a third person. 6) The assignment of actions or rights arising from an act contained in a public instrument. All other contracts, in which the amount of the prestations of one of the two contracting parties exceeds a certain minimum amount, must be reduced to writing even though it be private. (Sp. Civ. C., sec. 1247).

**Contratos innominados.** Innominate contract. Contract that is not specifically treated by statute, e.g. the civil code or the commercial code, and it is ruled by principles of general contractual law.

**Contratos matrimoniales.** Contracts by reason of marriage. Persons who may be joined in matrimony may, before celebrating it, execute contracts, stipulating the conditions for the conjugal partnership with regard to present and future property. In the absence of contracts relating to property it shall be understood that the marriage has been contracted under the system of legal conjugal partnership. (Sp. Civ. C., sec. 1282).

**Contratos mercantiles.** Business contracts. Business contracts, concerning all that relates to their requirements, amendments, exceptions, interpretation, and cancellation and to the capacity of the parties, shall be controlled by the general rules of common law in all that is not expressly established in this Code or in special laws. (Sp. Civ. C., sec. 50).

**Contratos, permuta.** Contracts, exchange or barter. Exchange is a contract by which each of the contracting parties binds himself to give a thing in order to receive another. (Sp. Civ. C., sec. 1441).

**Contratos por correspondencia.** Mail contracts.

**Contratos, requisitos.** Contracts, requirement. There is no contract unless the following requisites exist: 1) The consent of the contracting parties. 2) A defined object which may be the subject of the contract. 3) The cause for the obligation which may be established. (Sp. Civ. C., sec. 1228).

**Contratos, transmisión de créditos y demás derechos.** Contracts, assignment of credits and other incorporeal rights. The assignment of a credit, right, or action shall produce no effect against a third person but from the time the date is considered fixed. If said assignment involves real property, from the date of its entry in the registry. (Sp. Civ. C., sec. 1429).

**Contravención.** Misdemeanor. Traffic violation. Breach, infringement, violation.

**Contravenir.** To contravene, encroach, invade someone else's rights. To infringe, transgress, trespass.

**Contraventor.** Offender, infringer, tortfeasor, transgressor. Defendant.

**Contrayente.** Contracting party.

**Contribución.** Contribution, donation, endowment, subsidy. Tax, assessment, duty, excise.

**Contribuyente.** Tax payer. Donor. Person or factor that contributes towards something.

**Control entrelazado.** Interlocking control.

**Controlar.** To control, command, direct. To regulate. To contain, restrain.

**Controversia.** Controversy, altercation, argument, conflict, disagreement, dispute.

**Controversia obrero-patronal.** Labor-management controversy.

**Controvertible.** Arguable, disputable, doubtful, questionable.

**Controvertir.** To challenge, contest, dispute, face. To attack an established order or theory.

**Contubernio.** Cohabitation without marriage. Secret understanding between two or more parties. Common plot or scheme.

**Contumacia.** Default, disobedience to a judicial summons.

**Contumaz.** Party in default, contemnor.

**Contundente.** Convincing. Solid, strong.

**Convalecer.** To recover from an illness.

**Convalidación.** Validation, acquiescence, approval, ratification.

**Convalidar.** To validate, approve, authenticate, authorize, certify, confirm, verify.

**Convencimiento.** Conviction, assurance, certainty, firm belief.

**Convención.** Convention. Assembly, conclave, meeting. Agreement, contract, deal.

**Convencional.** Conventional. Customary, standard, traditional. Derived from an agreement or contract.

**Convenciones ilícitas.** Unlawful agreements.

**Convenido.** Agreed. Party who has been summoned.

**Conveniencia.** Convenience.

**Convenio.** Agreement. An agreement is the agreement between two or mor people to create, transfer, modify or extinguish obligations. (Mex. Civ. C., art.1792).

Settlement, pact.

**Convenio colectivo.** Collective bargaining agreement.

**Convenio del quebrado con acreedores.** Settlement of bankrupt with creditors. At any stage of the proceedings, after the examination of the credits and after the classification of the bankruptcy has been made, the bankrupt and his creditors may make any settlements they may deem proper. Fraudulent bankrupts shall not enjoy this right, nor those who flee during the bankruptcy proceedings. (Sp. Com. C., sec. 898).

**Convenir.** To convene. To call, invite, summon. To agree, contract, covenant.

**Conversión.** Conversion, change, modification, interchange.

**Conversión de sanciones penales.** Fine instead of imprisonment. The court may substitute, in favor of a first offender, a prison term not exceeding six months by a fine or forced labor for the benefit of the State. The judgment will substantiate this decision assessing the convict's personal background, the motives behind his conduct and the factual circumstances of the act. (St. P.C. for LA, sec. 80).

**Convertible.** Convertible.

**Convicción.** Conviction, assurance, certainty, firm belief. Dogmatic assumption.

**Convicto.** Convict. Inmate, prisoner. Convicted. The term convicted, in its strict legal sense, means that judgment has been rendered against a defendant on a verdict of guilty returned by a jury or by the judge, or when the defendant has pleaded guilty.

(Castro v. Delgado, Warden, 87 D.P.R. 503 (1963)).

**Convincente.** Convincing, believable, credible, tenable, reliable, trustworthy.

**Convivencia.** Coexistence, cohabitation.

**Convocar.** To convene, call, invite, summon. To request attendance.

**Convocatoria.** Convention, assembly, gathering, meeting. Summons to a meeting.

**Conyugal.** Conjugal, belonging to the spouses.

**Cónyuge.** Spouse, husband or wife.

**Conyugicida.** Person who murders his or her spouse.

**Conyugicidio.** Murder of one's spouse.

**Coobligado.** Joint obligor, co-debtor, co-obligor.

**Cooperación entre las partes.** Cooperation between the parties.

Each party shall cooperate with the other party when such cooperation may reasonably be expected for the performance of that party's obligations. (Unidroit, Prin., art. 5.3).

**Cooperación judicial.** Judicial cooperation. Judges and courts shall mutually aid each other in the execution of all proceedings necessary for the hearing and decision of criminal causes. (Sp. L. Crim. P., art. 183).

**Cooperativa.** Cooperative society.

**Cooperativa de ahorro y crédito.** Savings and credit union.

**Cooperativista.** Relating to a cooperative society or movement.

**Copar.** To monopolize, assail, storm. To take over.

**Coparticipación.** Taking part in a common venture or activity. Co-participation.

**Copia.** Copy, duplicate, facsimile, transcript. Replica, reproduction. Counterfeit, fake, imitation. Any one issue or print of a given publication.

**Copia certificada.** Conformed copy, certified copy.

**Copiador de cartas.** Copybook.

**Coposesión.** Joint possession. Possession held in common by two or more persons.

**Copropiedad.** Co-ownership, tenancy in common, joint ownership. Two or more persons may own the same thing in indivision,

each having an undivided share. (Louisiana Civ. Code art. 480).

**Cópula.** Copulation, carnal knowledge, coitus, sexual penetration.

**Corchete.** Curly bracket, bracket.

**Corolario.** Corollary.

**Coronel.** Colonel

**Corporación.** Corporation. Guild, professional association.

**Corporación, capacidad.** Corporation, capacity. The civil capacity of corporations is governed by the law which has created or recognized them. (Bustamante C., art. 33).

**Corporativo.** Corporate, corporative.

**Corporeo, corporal.** Corporeal. Bodily.

**Corre en autos.** Matter of record, part of the record.

**Corrección monetaria.** Monetary adjustment, usually due to inflation.

**Correccional.** Correctional, corrective. Relating to misdemeanor. Penitentiary.

**Correcciones disciplinarias.** Disciplinary sanctions. The disciplinary corrections which may be imposed upon the officials of juridical persons shall be: 1) Admonition. 2) Warning or advice. 3) Reprehension. 4) A fine. 5) Partial or total retention of the fees or of the charges pertaining to the instruments or acts in which the offence was committed. 6) Suspension from the exercise of the profession or employment with the deprivation of salary and emoluments, which can not exceed three months, but may be extended to six months if a second offence be committed. (Sp. L. Civ. P. sec. 448, 449).

**Correctivo.** Penalty (n). Corrective (adj).

**Correcto.** Correct. Accurate. Appropriate, apt.

**Corrector.** Person who corrects.

**Corredor.** Broker, agent, intermediary, middleman, traveling salesman.

**Corredores de comercio.** Commercial brokers.

**Corregidor.** Magistrate.

**Corregir.** To correct. To alter, amend, change, modify.

**Correlacionar.** Correlate.

**Correo.** Mail, post office. Courier. Carrier, emissary, envoy. Correspondence.

**Correspondencia.** Correspondence, dialogue, letters, mail. Counterpart.

**Corresponder.** To correspond, affect, concern, pertain. To communicate, write. To agree, concur.

**Correspondiente.** Corresponding, conforming, matching. Counterpart.

**Corretaje.** Brokerage, agency, mediation.

**Corriente.** Current, common, habitual, ordinary, standard, usual.

**Corroborar.** To corroborate, ascertain, authenticate, certify, confirm, validate, verify.

**Corroborativo.** Corroborating, corroborative, certifying, validating.

**Corromper.** To corrupt, abuse, bribe, defile, deprave, pervert.

**Corrompido, corrupto.** Corrupt, crooked, degenerate, dishonest, dissolute.

**Corrupción.** Corruption, debauchery, depravity, sin. Decline, deterioration.

**Corruptela.** Corrupted practice. Way of bending or stretching the law.

**Corruptibilidad.** Corruptibility, vulnerability.

**Corruptible.** Corruptible. That lends it self to being corrupted.

**Corsario.** Corsair, buccaneer, pirate, privateer.

**Corte.** Court, bench, judiciary, tribunal. Entourage.

**Corte abierta y órdenes en cámara.** Open court and orders in chamber.

**Corte Suprema.** Supreme Court. Latin American supreme courts have not been as daring in their use of power as has the United States Supreme Court. They are very careful to disqualify themselves whenever a question is of a political nature. They find in such a case that it is not for them to judge the constitutionality of the legislator's action, and they hesitate to acknowledge that a president is acting unconstitutionally. They tend to find that his action is based on his discretionary power. Thus the courts condone delegations of power by the legislative branch which contradict the constitutions. Similarly they tolerate very broad interpretations of the president's ordinance power. In Mexico, Argentina, and even in Brazil the courts have been very accommodating in suspending constitutional guarantees. They have been too lenient in recognizing provisional governments. They have accepted too easily improper interventions of the federal government in the affairs of the member states. (W. Eur. & LA Leg. Sys.).

**Cortes.** Legislative power, congress (SP).

**Cortesía.** Clemency, favor, forgiveness, mercy. Courtesy, courteousness, politeness.

**Cosa.** Thing, chose. Article, commodity, object.

**Cosa donada.** Thing bestowed.

**Cosa juzgada.** *Res judicata.* Thing adjudged. Thing adjudged is said of that which has been decidedby a final judgment from which there can be no appeal, either because the appeal did not lie, or because the time fixed by law for appealing is elapsed, or because it has been confirmed on the appeal. (Louisiana Civ. Code art. 3556).

**Cosa raíz.** Real estate, land, immovable.

**Cosas.** Things. Things are divided into common, public, and private; corporeals and incorporeals; and movables and immovables. (Louisiana Civ. Code art. 448).

**Cosas comunes.** Common things. Common things may not be owned by anyone. They are such as the air and the high seas that may be freely used by everyone conformably with the use for which nature has intended them. (Louisiana Civ. Code art. 449).

**Cosas consumibles.** Consumable things. Consumable things are those that cannot be used without being expended or consumed, or without their substance being changed, such as money, harvested agricultural products. stocks of merchandise, foodstuffs, and beverages. (Louisiana Civ. Code art. 536).

**Cosas corporales.** Corporeal things. Corporeals are things that have a body, whethere animate or inanimate and can be felt or touched. (Louisiana Civ. Code art. 461).

**Cosas incorporales.** Incorporeal things. Incorporeals are things that have no body, but are comprehend by the understanding. (Louisiana Civ. Code art. 461).

**Cosas no consumibles.** Nonconsumable things. Nonconsumable things are those that may be enjoyed without alteration of their substance, although their substance may be diminished or deteriorated naturally by time or by the use to which they are applied, such as lands, houses, shares of stock, animals, furniture, and vehicles. (Louisiana Civ. Code art. 537).

**Cosas principales y accesorias.** Principal and accessory things. Things are divided into principal and accessory. For purposes of accession as between movables, and accessory is a corporeal movable that serves the use, ornament, or complement of the principal thing. (Louisiana Civ. Code art. 508).

**Cosas privadas.** Private things. Private things are owned by individuals, other private persons, and by the state or its political subdivisions in their capacity as private persons. (Louisiana Civ. Code art. 453).

**Cosas privadas de uso público.** Private things subject to public use.

The banks of navigable rivers or streams are private things that are subject to public use. The bank of a navigable river or stream is the land lying between the ordinary low and the ordinary high stage of the water. Nevertheless, when there is a levee in proximity to the water, established according to law, the levee shall form the bank. (Louisiana Civ. Code art. 455 and art. 456).

**Cosas públicas.** Public things. Public things are owned by the state or its political subdivisions in their capacity as public persons. Public things that belong to the state are such as running waters, the waters and bottoms of natural navigable water bodies, the territorial sea, and the seashore. Public things that may belong to political subdivisions of the state are such as streets and public squares. (Louisiana Civ. Code art. 450 and note).

**Cosas públicas y comunes de uso público.** Public and common things subject to public use. Public things and common things are subject to public use in accordance with applicable laws and regulations. Everyone has the right to fish in the rivers, ports, roadsteads, and harbors, and the right to land on the seashore, to fish, to shelter himself, to moor ships, to dry nets, and the like, provided that he does not cause injury to the property of adjoining owners. (Louisiana Civ. Code art. 452).

**Cosecha.** Crop, harvest, produce, yield. Vintage.

**Costas.** Legal costs, costs. Charge, expenditure, expense.

**Costas legales.** Law charges. Law charges are such as are occasioned by the prosecution of a suit before the courts. But this name applies more particularly to the costs, which the defeated party has to pay to the party gaining the cause. (Louisiana Civ. Code art. 3195).

**Costas penales.** Criminal costs. All parties to a cause, if not declared indigent, shall be obliged to pay the fees of the solicitors who represent them, of the attorneys who defend them, of the experts testifying in their behalf, and of the witnesses which they present, if the experts and witnesses at the time of testifying shall have filed their claim and the judge or court shall have allowed it. (Sp. L. Crim. P., art. 121).

**Costas procesales, concepto.** Legal costs, extent. The costs shall consist of: 1) The cost of the stamped paper used in the cause. 2) The payment of the court fees according to schedule. 3) The payment of the fees of attorneys and experts. 4) The payment of the indemnities pertaining to the witnesses who may have demanded them, and the other expenses which may have arisen in connection with the hearing of the cause. (Sp. L. Crim. P., art. 241).

**Costas procesales, pago.** Legal costs, payment. A ruling or decision which terminates a cause or any of the issues therein must contain a decision as to the payment of costs in the proceedings. (Sp. L. Crim. P., art. 239 and 240).

**Costear.** To pay, disburse, expend. Finance, refund.

**Costo.** Cost, amount, charge, expense, price. Effort.

**Costo en el punto de origen.** Cost at the point of origin. Price which prevails at the time of remittance of the merchandise to the consignee. (Power Electric Co. v. Sec. of the Treasury, 88 PRR 536 (1963)).

**Costumbre.** Custom, convention, habit, practice, usage. Custom results from practice repeated for a long time and generally accepted as having acquired the force of law.

Custom may not abrogate legislation. According to civilian theory, the two elements of custom are a long practice (*longa consuetudo*) and the conviction that the practice has the force of law (*opinio necessitatis* or *opinio juris*). (Lou. Civ. C., art. 3 and note).

**Cotejo de letras, de escritura.** Comparison of handwriting. Comparison of handwriting may always be requested whenever its genuineness is denied by the person prejudiced thereby, or when a doubt is raised as to the authenticity of any private or public document, an original of which does not exist and which can not be verified by the official who issued the same. (Sp. L. Civ. P. sec. 605-608).

**Cotización.** Listing, financial quotation.

**CPT. Transporte Pagado Hasta (...lugar de destino convenido).** CPT. Carriage Paid to (...named place of destination). "Carriage paid to..." means that the seller pays the freight for the carriage of the goods to the named destination. (Incoterms).

**Crear una falsa impresión sobre alguien.** Placing a person in false light.

**Crecimiento.** Growth, development, enlargement, expansion, increase.

**Credencial.** Credential, accreditation, certificate, document.

**Credibilidad.** Credibility, dependability, believability, reliability, trustworthiness.

**Crédito.** Credit.

**Crédito incobrable.** Bad debt, uncollectible.

**Creible.** Credible, believable, conceivable, plausible. Reliable, trustworthy.

**Cretinismo.** Cretinism.

**Cretino.** Cretin, ignoramus, imbecile.

**Criado doméstico.** Domestic servant.

**Crimen.** Crime, felony, misdeanor. Malfeasance, misconduct, misdeed. Outrage, villainy. Offense, tort, wrong.

**Criminal.** Criminal, felon. Convict, culprit, offender. Lawbreaker, tortfeasor, transgressor.

**Criminal reincidente.** Recidivist, repeat offender.

**Criminalidad.** Criminality.

**Criminalista.** Criminalist, criminologist, penalist.

**Criminología.** Criminology.

**Criminologística.** Criminology.

**Criterios para determinar el tipo de obligación.** Determination of kind of duty involved. In determining the extent to which an obligation of a party involves a duty of best efforts in the performance of an activity or a duty to achieve a specific result, regard shall be had, among other factors, to (a) the way in which the obligation is expressed in the contract; (b) the contractual price and other terms of the contract; (c) the degree of risk normally involved in achieving the expected result; (d) the ability of the other party to influence the performance of the obligation. (Unidroit, Prin., art. 5.5).

**Crítica injuriosa.** Unseemly criticism.

**Cruce.** Cross, crossing, interchange, intersection, juncture.

**Crueldad.** Cruelty, brutality, evilness, malignity.

**Crueldad mental.** Mental cruelty

**Cruz.** Cross, crucifix. Burden, misfortune.

**Cuaderno de bitácora.** Binnacle book.

**Cuadrilla.** Group, party, squad. Band, gang.

**Cuadro.** Table, chart, diagram, graph, index, list. Picture, portrait. Scene, sight, spectacle.

**Cualidad.** Qualification, ability.

**Cualquiera.** Whatsoever

**Cuantía.** Amount, import.

**Cuarentena.** Quarantine.

**Cuartel.** Garrison, headquarters, stronghold. Barrack.

**Cuasicontractual.** Quasi-contractual, of a tortious nature.

**Cuasicontrato.** Quasi-contract. Quasi contracts are licit and purely voluntary acts by which the author thereof becomes obligated with regard to a third person, and, sometimes, by which there results a reciprocal obligation between the parties concerned. (Sp. Civ. C., sec. 1788).

**Cuasicontratos, Chile.** Quasicontracts, Chile. Three types of quasicontracts are dealt with and regulated by Chilean domestic law. These include management of another's business by one who is not his agent or legal representative (*Gestión de negocios*), mistaken payment of a sum that is not owed, and common ownership of property not originating in a contract. There is no specific conflicts provision regulating quasicontracts in Chilean domestic law. (LA Laws & Inst.).

**Cuasidelito.** Tort, offense, wrong.

**Cuasidelito, obligación que nace de culpa o negligencia.** Tort, obligation arising from fault or negligence. A person who by an act or omission causes damage to another when there is fault or negligence shall be obliged to repair the damage so done. (Sp. Civ. C., sec. 1803, 1811).

**Cuasidelitos, Chile.** Torts, Chile. In tort actions, Chilean law is applied when the facts allegedly constituting the wrong have taken place in Chile (Article 14, Civil or Commercial Code). If an action for damages is brought in a Chilean court upon a tort committed abroad, the Bustamante Code should be used. (LA Laws & Inst.).

**Cuasipúblico.** Quasipublic.

**Cuatrerismo.** Cattle stealing or rustling.

**Cuatrero.** Cattle rustler.

**Cubiletear.** To obtain advantages through deceit or subterfuge.

**Cuchillada.** Stab, knife wound.

**Cuenta.** Account. Bill, invoice.

**Cuenta convenida.** Account stated.

**Cuenta corriente.** Open account, current account.

**Cuenta de ahorro.** Savings account.

**Cuenta en participación.** Joint accounts. Merchants may have an interest in the transactions of other merchants, contributing thereto the amount of capital they may agree upon, and participating in the favorable or unfavorable results of such transactions in the proportion which may be fixed. (Sp. Com. C., sec. 239, 240).

**Cuerda floja, por.** Documents attached to a judicial record, usually for evidentiary purposes only.

**Cuerda separada, por.** Dealt with in a separate or independent way.

**Cuerpo.** Body. Cadaver, corpse. Build, frame. Association, group.

**Cuerpo del delito.** *Corpus delicti. Corpus delicti* is the body and substance of the crime and with respect to specific crimes it means the actual commission by some of the particular crime charged, which may be established by prima facie evidence from which the commission of the offense may be logically inferred, said evidence not having to be complete, direct, nor positive, it being sufficient that there be circumstantial evidence from which it may be reasonably inferred that a crime has been committed. (Ppl. v. Castro Cruz, 90 PRR, 201 (1964)).

**Cuestión.** Question, affair, situation. Issue, matter, problem.

**Cuestión de derecho.** Matter of law.

**Cuestión de hecho.** Matter of fact.

**Cuestionar.** To question, challenge, dispute. To ask, interrogate, inquire.

**Cuestionario.** Questionnaire, form.

**Cuestor.** Burser, treasurer.

**Cuidado.** Care, attention, caution, diligence, prudence. Charge, custody, supervision.

**Culpa, clasificación.** Culpability, classification. Culpa or fault is also divided in *Culpa in Faciendo* (positive action) which is called "imprudence," or *Culpa In Omittendo* (omission) called "negligence." Thus, in Civil Law negligence only has a negative sense, it is used to denote lack of action, or omission of care that should otherwise be given to matters. (Barrios-Mannucci).

**Culpa Criminal.** Criminal negligence or recklessness. A person acts negligently or recklessly when he performs a criminal act by failing to maintain the duty of care imposed by the surrounding circumstances and his personal conditions and—if the consequences of the act were foreseen at all—he trusted to be able to avoid them. (St. P.C. for LA, sec. 26).

**Culpa, culpabilidad.** Guilt, blame, culpability, fault, negligence, liability. For the purpose of the Civil Code, guilt means any fault, willful or not, of a person which produces a wrong or damage, in which case guilt is equivalent to cause. (Reyes v. Heirs of Sánchez Soto, 98 PRR 299 (1970)).

**Culpa, dolo.** Culpability, *dolus.*
*Culpa* is to be distinguished from the Civil Law term *dolus,* fraud or willful misconduct in Common Law, meaning all intentional acts or omissions involving the breach of a legal or contractual duty and

resulting to damage to another. In other words, *dolus* is any malicious failure to fulfill obligations. (Barrios-Mannucci).

**Culpa, grados.** Fault degrees. There are in law three degrees of faults: the gross, the slight, and the very slight fault. The gross fault is that which proceeds from inexcusable negligence or ignorance; it is considered as nearly equal to fraud. The slight fault is that want of care which a prudent man usually takes of his business. The very slight fault is that which is excusable, and for which no responsibility is incurred. (Louisiana Civ. Code art. 3556).

**Culpa, graduación.** Culpability, degrees. In general, Latin American countries follow the French model of fault which has three degrees of culpability: a) *lata culpa*, gross fault or negligence in Common Law, meaning lack of the most basic due diligence of a careful person to avoid harm; b) *levis culpa*, ordinary fault or neglect in Common Law, meaning lack of attention or care of an ordinary reasonable person; and c) *levissima culpa*, slight fault or neglect in Common Law, meaning lack of diligence resulting in a omission of an ordinary reasonable person. (Barrios-Mannucci).

*Culpa in contrahendo* **(L).** Liability generated by a breach of contract.

*Culpa in eligendo* **(L).** Theory of culpa in eligendo. The diligence exercised by the principal in choosing the person who is going to perform certain functions in connection with the disposition of a thing—property of the principal—which may cause damages to third persons, is known as the theory of *culpa in eligendo*. (Ortiz v. Heirs of J. Serrallés, 89 PRR 410 (1964)).

**Culpa o negligencia.** Fault or negligence. The fault or negligence is the failure to exercise due care, which also consist essentially in not anticipating and foreseeing the rational consequences of an act, or of the failure to perform an act which a prudent person could have foreseen under the same circumstances. (Ramos v. Carlo, 86 PRR 337 (1962)).

**Culpabilidad.** Liability. Nobody can be punished for an act legally classified as a crime, if it was not performed with criminal intent, except for cases of recklessness or negligence

specifically established by statute. (Standard Penal C. for Latin America, sec. 24).

**Culpable.** Guilty, at fault, culpable, culprit, liable.

**Culpado.** Accused, charged.

**Culpar.** To accuse, blame, charge, fault, impute.

**Culposo.** Guilty, culpable.

**Cumplidor.** Trustworthy, dependable, reliable.

**Cumplimiento.** Fulfillment, accomplishment, completion, performance.

**Cumplimiento anticipado.** Earlier performance.

The obligee may reject an earlier performance unless it has no legitimate interest in so doing. Acceptance by a party of an earlier performance does not affect the time for the performance of its own obligations if that time has been fixed irrespective of the performance of the other party's obligations. (Unidroit, Prin., art. 6.1.5).

**Cumplimiento de obligación dineraria.** Performance of monetary obligation.

**Cumplimiento de obligaciones no-dinerarias.** Performance of non-monetary obligation. Where a party who owes an obligation other than one to pay money does not perform, the other party may require performance, unless (a) performance is impossible in law or in fact; (b) performance or, where relevant, enforcement is unreasonably burdensome or expensive; (c) the party entitled to performance may reasonably obtain performance from another source; (d) performance is of an exclusively personal character; or (e) the party entitled to performance does not require performance within a reasonable time after it has, or ought to have, become aware of the non-performance. (Unidroit, Prin., art. 7.2.2).

**Cumplimiento de sentencia.** Satisfaction of judgment.

**Cumplimiento específico.** Specific performance. Upon an obligor's failure to perform an obligation to deliver a thing, or not to do an act, or to execute an instrument, the court shall grant specific performance plus damages for delay if the obligee so demands. (Louisiana Civil Code art. 1986).

**Cumplimiento instantáneo o en etapas.** Performance at one time or in installments.

A party must perform its obligations at one time if that performance can be rendered at one time and the circumstances do not indicate otherwise. (Unidroit, Prin., art. 6.1.2).

**Cumplimiento parcial.** Partial performance. The obligee may reject an offer to perform in part at the time performance is due, whether or not such offer is coupled with an assurance as to the balance of the performance, unless the obligee has no legitimate interest in so doing. Additional expenses caused to the obligee by partial performance are to be borne by the obligor without prejudice to any other remedy. (Unidroit, Prin., art 6.1.3).

**Cumplimiento sustituto.** Substituted performance.

**Cumplimiento único.** Performance at one time.

**Cumplir.** To comply, heed, obey. To discharge, perform.

**Cumulativo, acumulativo.** Cumulative, aggregate, compounded.

**Cúmulo.** Accumulative, concurring, converging. Abundance, great number, plethora of circumstances.

**Cuota.** Quota, allotment, assignment, part, portion, share.

**Cupo.** Quota, ceiling, pre-determined amount.

**Cupón.** Coupon, stub. Stock certificate.

**Cura, curación.** Cure, recovery, rehabilitation, remedy. Antidote, panacea.

**Curado.** Cured, healed. Mended.

**Curador.** Curator, conservator, guardian, trustee. The person appointed to take care of the property and business of a person who, on account of his minority, insanity, imbecility, absence, interdiction, or declared prodigality, is not in a condition to personally administer or manage the same. (Escriche, Diccionario de Legislación y Jurisprudencia).

**Curador ejemplar.** Curator for incapacitated people.

**Curador para los bienes.** Curator *ad bona*.

**Curador para pleitos, *ad litem*.** Curator *ad litem*. Persons still under the parental authority, shall be represented in court by the persons having them under their authority. Persons not under parental authority, shall be so represented by their tutors and curators. (Sp. L. Civ. P., sec. 1851).

**Curaduría.** Curatorship, guardianship, tutelage, tutorship. Office of the public defender of insane people.

**Curandero.** Quack doctor, charlatan

**Curatela.** Curatorship.

**Curia.** Organized church. The Catholic Church.

**Curso.** Course. Development, progression. Path, track. Class, lecture, lesson. Flow, current. Circulation of money, rate of exchange.

**Curso forzoso.** Legal tender.

**Curso legal.** Legal tender, lawful currency.

**Curso ordinario de los negocios.** Ordinary course of business.

**Curva.** Curve, arch, curve, droop, bend, loop, turn.

**Custodia.** Custody. Escort, guard. Protection, care.

**Custodia de una cosa.** Custody of a thing. Who is the custodian of the thing? The presumption of liability bears on the person who has "actual control" over the thing. Generally it is the owner. However, the owner might keep legal control over the thing and convey, i.e., through a contract for the operation of a facility, its "actual control" to a particular contractor. Such conveyance is not required to be specified in the agreement since this matter of fact and not of law. (Barrios-Mannucci).

**Custodiar.** To guard, protect.

**Custodio.** Custodian, guard, protector.

# D

**Dación.** Delivery, tender. Offer of giving something.

**Dación en pago.** Giving in payment. The giving in payment is an act by which a debtor gives a thing to the creditor, who is willing to receive it, in payment of a sum which is due. That giving in payment differs from the ordinary contract of sale in this, that the latter is perfect by the mere consent of the parties, even before the delivery, while the giving in payment is made only by delivery. (Lou. Civ. C. art. 2655 and 2656).

**Dactilografía.** Typing.

**Dactilografiado.** Typed.

**Dactilógrafo.** Typist.

**Dactilograma.** Fingerprint sample.

**Dactiloscópico.** Relating to fingerprints.

**Dactiloscopista.** Person who studies fingerprints.

**Dactioloscopía.** Dactyloscopy, study of fingerprints.

**Dádiva.** Donation, endowment, gift, present.

**Dado bajo mi firma y sello oficial.** Given under my hand and seal of office.

**Dador.** Person who gives, donor. Issuer.

**DAF. Entregada En Frontera (...lugar convenido).** DAF. Delivered at Frontier (...named place). "Delivered at Frontier" means that the seller fulfills his obligation to deliver when the goods have been made available, cleared for export, at the named point and place at the frontier, but before the customs border of the adjoining country. (Incoterms).

**Damnificado.** Person who suffered damages. Victim.

**Damnificar.** To damage, harm, injure.

**Dañado.** Damaged, blemished, harmed.

***Damnum absque injuria* (L).** Loss or detriment to one party but without a correlative obligation to indemnify by the other party.

**Dañar.** To damage, harm, injure.

**Dañino.** Damaging. Malevolent, malignant.

**Daño.** Damage, injury, loss.

**Daño directo e indirecto.** Direct and indirect damages.

**Daño, dos sentidos.** Damages, two meanings. As in Common Law, the concept of damage (*daño*) has also two meanings. First, damage is the loss, injury or deterioration, caused by negligence or imprudence of one person to another, in respect of the latter's person or property. Second, it means compensation or indemnity recoverable in court by a person who has suffered loss, injury or deterioration. In Common Law, this distinction is generally denoted using the plural term for the latter and its singular for the former. Nevertheless, in Civil Law the distinction is made upon the context the world is found, regardless of whether plural or not. (Barrios-Mannucci).

**Daño emergente, *damnum emergens* (L).** It means the losses suffered by a creditor immediately after the culpable breach of debtor's obligations. It is the actual damage or loss contrasted with future loss or expectancy. In the terms of the owner of property, it is a diminution of owner's estate happening immediately after the occurrence of the default. For instance, an owner contracts with a contractor to repair certain buildings. The value of the building lost is the damnum emergens suffered by the owner. (Barrios-Mannucci). (See *lucro cesante*).

**Daño emocional.** Emotional distress.

**Daño imputable parcialmente a la parte agraviada.** Harm due in part to aggrieved party. Where the harm is due in part to an act or omission of the aggrieved party of to another event as to which that party bears the risk, the amount of damages shall be reduced to the extent that these factors have contributed to the harm, having regard to the conduct of each of the parties. (Unidroit, Prin., art. 7.4.7).

**Daño por cuasidelito causado al cónyuge.** Harm caused by tort against other spouse.

**Daño moral, contratos.** Moral damages, contracts. Latin American doctrine and jurisprudence adopts controversial positions as to whether or not moral damage arises as a consequence of breach of contracts, or if it shall only be recognized in torts. In Mexico and Argentina, by express disposition of their Civil Codes, moral damage is recoverable not only in torts, but also for breach of contract. The Peruvian Civil Code does not differentiate between moral damage in contracts and moral damage in torts, referring only to moral damage in general. In Colombia, the Supreme Court has recognized moral damages in torts, rejecting its application in contracts. The Venezuelan Civil Code only recognizes moral damages for torts. (Barrios-Mannucci).

**Daño moral, material y físico.** Moral, material and physical damages. In the Common Law, torts are divided into general classes, namely, property torts, which involve injury or damage to property, whether realty or personalty, and personal torts, which involve injuries to the person, whether to the body, reputation or feelings. In Civil Law, moral damage, as opposed to material damage, consists of personal injury, bodily harm or physical harm, and moral, physical, spiritual or emotional distress, pain and suffering that a person may experience as a consequence of the wrongful conduct of another. (Barrios-Mannucci).

**Daño terrestre producido desde aeronaves.** Ground damage from aircraft.

**Daños.** Damages, losses.

**Daños, clasificación.** Damages, classification. Within the concept of damage are two sub concepts: foreseeable damages (and unforeseeable damages), and direct damages (and indirect damages). Foreseeable damages are those objectively reasonable to expect, not merely what might conceivably occur, thus, unforeseeable damages are those resulting from *force majeure* or any other fortuitous event. Direct damages are those that flow immediately from the act done or not done. They arise naturally or ordinarily as a consequence of the act or omission that breaches the legal or contractual duty. Indirect damages and consequential damages refer to those damages that do not flow directly and immediately as a consequence of the act or omission that breaches the legal or contractual duty. With the exception of Argentina, indirect damages are recoverable when there is willful misconduct. (Barrios-Mannucci).

**Daños contractuales.** Contractual damages. Any nonperformance gives the aggrieved party a right to damages either exclusively or in conjunction with any other remedies except where the nonperformance is excused under these Principles. (Unidroit, Prin., art. 7.4.1).

**Daños previsibles.** Foreseeable damages.

**Daños y perjuicios.** Damages. Irrespective of whether or not the contract has been avoided, the party who knew or ought to have known of the ground for avoidance is liable for damages so as to put the other party in the same position in which it would have been if it had not concluded the contract. (Unidroit, Prin., art. 3.18).
Losses and damages, damages.

**Dañosos.** Damaging, detrimental, hurtful, injurious, prejudicial.

**Dar.** To give, award, assign, confer, deliver, donate.

**Dar aviso.** To give notice.

**Dar constancia.** Certify, authenticate, establish, demonstrate, prove.

**Dar copia.** To extend a copy, usually certified.

**Dar de baja.** To write off, to discharge, to cancel.

**Dar fe.** To certify, attest, verify.

**Dar poder.** To give power of attorney.

**Dar por recibido.** Acknowledge receipt.

**Dar por sentado.** Assume, believe, it goes without saying.

**Dar por válido.** Assume the validity or lawfulness of something.

**Darse cuenta.** To realize.

**Datar.** To date.

**Dativo.** Dative.

**Dato.** Datum, fact, information.

**Datos.** Elements, facts, data, information.

**DDP. Entregada Derechos Pagados (...lugar de destino convenido).** DDP. Delivered Duty Paid (...named place of destination). "Delivered duty paid" means that the seller fulfills his obligation to deliver when the goods have been made available at the named place in the country of importation. The seller has to bear the risks and costs, including duties, taxes and other charges of delivering the goods thereto, cleared for importation. Whilst the EXW term represents the minimum obligation for the seller, DDP represents the maximum obligation. (Incoterms).

**DDU. Entregada Derechos No Pagados (...lugar de destino convenido).** DDU. Delivered Duty Unpaid (...named place of destination). "Delivered duty unpaid" means that the seller fulfills his obligation to deliver when the goods have been made available at the named place in the country of importation. (Incoterms).

**De acuerdo con.** According to, following, in harmony with, pursuant to.

**De ahora en adelante.** Hereinafter.

**De derecho.** *De jure*, at law.

**De hecho.** *De facto*, in practice.

**De lege ferenda (L).** Law in a formal sense, statutory law.

**De lege lata (L).** Law in a broad sense, what is formally the law and, for instance, what should be enacted as law.

**De lo cual, de los cuales.** Whereof.

**De officio.** Sua sponte on the court's own motion, *ex officio*.

**De puro derecho.** No controverted facts, summary judgment.

**De uno y otro.** Of either, both.

**Dean.** Dean. Dignitary of the Catholic Church.

**Debate.** Debate, controversy, discussion, polemic.

**Debatir.** To debate, argue, contend.

**Debenture.** Debenture, bond.

**Deber.** Duty, liability, obligation, responsibility.

**Deber de alimentos.** Alimentary duty. Children are bound to maintain their father and mother and other ascendants, who are in need, and the relatives in the direct ascending line are likewise bound to maintain their needy descendants, this obligation being reciprocal. (Lou. Civ. C. art. 229).

**Deber de confidencialidad.** Duty of confidentiality.

Where information is given as confidential by one party in the course of negotiations, the other party is under a duty not to disclose that information or to use it improperly for its own purposes, whether or not a contract is subsequently concluded. (Unidroit, Prin., art. 2.16).

**Deber de controlar la conducta de terceros.** Duty to control conduct of third persons.

**Deber de no obstruir el cumplimiento de una sentencia.** Duty not to obstruct compliance with judgment.

**Deberá.** Should. In interpreting statutes the term should means may—thus making directive what is apparently mandatory—when it is necessary to conform the language of the statute to the legislative purpose. (Secretary of Justice v. Superior Court, 95 PRR 156 (1967)).

**Deberes.** Duties, chores, tasks.

**Deberes filiales.** Filial duties. A child, whatever be his age, owes honor and respect to his father and mother. As long as the child remains under the authority of his father and mother, he is bound to obey them in every thing which is not contrary to good morals and the laws. (Lou. Civ. C. art. 215 and art. 217).

**Deberes no delegables del empleador.** Non-delegable duties of master.

**Debidamente.** Duly.

**Debido a.** Due to, because.

**Debiente.** Owing.

**Debil.** Weak, feeble, frail.

**Debilidad.** Debility, impairment, weakness.

**Debilidad mental.** Mental deficiency; mental impairment.

**Debitar.** To debit.

**Débito.** Debit, debts.

**Débito conyugal.** Reciprocal obligation which spouses have of living together and of treating each other with love, care and respect.

**Década.** Decade.

**Decadencia.** Decadence, decline, deterioration, fall.

**Decaer.** To go down.

**Decano.** Dean, director, most senior member.

**Decapitación.** Execution by beheading.

**Decencia.** Decency, honesty.

**Deceso.** Death, decease, expiration. Demise, departure.

**Decidir.** To decide, conclude, determine, find, judge, order, rule.

**Decir.** To say, express, state.

**Decisión.** Decision, conclusion, determination, finding, judgment, ruling, order, verdict.

**Decisión judicial.** Court decision, judicial decision, judgment.

**Decisorio.** Decisive, conclusive, final.

**Declaración.** Declaration, announcement, deposition, report, statement, testimony.

**Declaración de derechos.** Bill of rights.

**Declaración de quiebra.** Adjudication in bankruptcy, declaration of bankruptcy.

**Declaración exculpatoria.** Exculpatory statement. Statement by a defendant through which he tries to protect himself by declaring that he had no participation in the criminal act under investigation. (Ppl. v. Andrades, 83 PRR 818 (1961)).

**Declaración judicial.** Judicial determination, adjudication, finding of fact or of law, judgment, sentence.

**Declaración jurada.** Affidavit, sworn statement.

**Declaración y pago de dividendos.** Declaration and payment of dividends.

**Declaraciones de testigos.** Testimony of witnesses.

**Declarado.** Declared, mentioned.

**Declarante.** Affiant, declarant, deponent, witness.

**Declarar.** To declare, affirm, depose, report, state.

**Declarar con lugar.** Sustain, rule in favor.

**Declarar sin lugar.** Overrule, rule against, throw out of court.

**Declarativo.** Declaratory. By way of example, not necessarily binding.

**Declaratoria.** Declaration, assertion, statement, testimony.

**Declaratoria de herederos.** Proceedings to declare heirship. Declaration of heirship.

**Declaratorio.** Declaratory. Not binding but by way of an example or as statement of intent.

**Declinar.** To decline, refuse. To step down, to turn down. To remove oneself. To deteriorate, regress, worsen. To lose strength.

**Declinatoria.** Declinature. The declinature shall be submitted to the judge or court considered incompetent, requesting that he or it cease to act in the matter and to transmit the record to the judge or court considered competent. (Sp. L. Civ. P., sec. 72).

Voluntary withdrawal by the judge from a case under his jurisdiction.

**Declinatorio.** Declinatory.

**Decomisable.** That can be confiscated or taken by the state.

**Decomisar.** To confiscate, appropriate, expropriate, impound, seize. To commandeer.

**Decomiso.** Confiscation, appropriation, expropriation, seizure.

**Decreciente.** Decreasing, diminishing, dwindling.

**Decretar.** To decree, announce, order, proclaim.

**Decrétase.** Let it be enacted.

**Decreto.** Decree, dictum, edict, order, command, proclamation.

**Decreto-ley.** Decree-law. A decree by the executive with force of a statute. Way in which *de facto* governments legislate.

**Dedicación.** Dedication. Commitment, consecration.

**Deducción.** Deduction, conclusion, implication, inference. Discount, rebate, reduction.

**Deducción hereditaria.** Hereditary deduction. By *deduction* is understood a portion or thing which an heir has a right to take from the mass of the succession before any partition takes places. (Lou. Civ. C. art. 1358 and art. 1359).

**Deducible.** Deductible.

**Deducir.** To infer, conclude. To deduct, subtract. To file, raise, present.

**Deductivo.** Deductive, analytical, inferential.

**Defecto.** Defect, deficiency, flaw, shortcoming, vice.

**Defecto o vicios ocultos, jurídicos y de hecho.** Juridical and factual hidden faults or defects. For the effect of the warranty obligation on the part of the vendor, limitations in the property right of the thing sold are designated as juridical hidden faults or defects, while inherent defects in the thing sold are known as hidden faults or defects of fact. (Ferrer v. General Motors Corp., 100 PRR 244 (1971)).

**Defectuoso.** Defective, blemished, faulty, deficient. Seconds.

**Defender.** To defend, guard, justify, protect, shield. To represent.

**Defendible.** Defendable, defensible, justifiable.

**Defensa.** Defense, excuse, justification. Attenuating or extenuating circumstances. Mitigating factors.

**Defensa de derecho o de hecho.** Defense in law or fact.

**Defensa de pobres.** *Pro bono* work. The attorneys whose duty it is to defend the poor can not excuse themselves therefrom, except for a personal and just cause, which shall be passed upon according to the prudent judgment by the deans of the college, where there is such, and in their absence by the judge or court before which the defense is to be made. (Sp. L. Crim. P., art. 120).

**Defensa propia, doctrina de.** Self-defense, doctrine of. A court may apply the doctrine of self-defense in a criminal or civil procedure only when it is established that the force or violence, exercised by whoever invokes said defense, was only that which is necessary to repel the attacks of which he was object, not having caused to the prejudiced party more injury than that necessary to attain that purpose. (In re De Castro, 100 PRR 182 (1971)).

**Defensas afirmativas.** Affirmative defenses.

**Defensas y negaciones.** Defenses and denials.

**Defenso.** Person being defended.

**Defensor.** Defendant's attorney.

**Deferir.** To delay, postpone. To relent, yield.

**Deficiencia.** Deficiency, insufficiency.

**Déficit.** Deficit, deficiency, imbalance, lack, need, scarcity, shortage.

**Deficitario.** Losing money. In the red.

**Definición.** Definition, description, explanation, meaning. Decision, final choice.

**Definimiento.** Definition, taking a clear and formal position.

**Definitivo.** Definitive, absolute, conclusive, final.

**Defraudación.** Fraud, deceit, hoax, swindle.

**Defraudador.** Fraud, charlatan, impostor, trickster.

**Defraudar.** To defraud, cheat, deceive, swindle.

**Defunción.** Death, decease, demise expiration.

**Degeneración.** Degeneration, decline, deterioration. Dissolution.

**Degenerado.** Degenerate, monster, pervert.

**Degenerar.** To degenerate.

**Degradación.** Degradation. Debasement, dishonor, disgrace. Loss of rank. Deterioration.

**Degradar.** To degrade. To debase, humiliate.

**Degüello.** Slitting of the throat, beheading.

**Dejación.** Abandonment, indifference, indolence.

**Dejadez.** Negligence, sloppiness.

**Dejar.** To abandon, leave. To depart, flee. To let, permit.

**Dejar cesante.** Discharge, dismiss, fire.

**Dejar sin efecto.** Annul, cancel, quash, rescind.

**Del país.** Inland, locally manufactured.

**Delación.** Information, denunciation, accusation, charge.

**Delatante, delator.** Informant, informer, snitch, squealer. Whistle blower.

**Delatar.** To denounce, accuse, snitch, squeal. To blow the whistle. To grass (G.B.).

**Delegable.** Delegable, assumable, transferable.

**Delegación.** Delegation, agency, commission, committee, council. Entourage. Assignment, appointment, commission.

**Delegación de cumplimiento.** Delegation of performance. A delegation of performance by an obligor to a third person is effective when that person binds himself to perform. A delegation effects a novation only when the obligee expressly discharges the original obligor. (Lou. Civ. C. art. 1886).

**Delegado.** Delegate, agent, deputy, envoy, representative, spokesman.

**Delegante.** Person who delegates. Elector, voter. Constituent. Principal.

**Delegar.** To delegate, assign, charge, entrust, impose.

**Delegatorio.** Delegatory.

**Deliberación.** Deliberation, conference, debate. Intent, intention, premeditation.

**Deliberadamente.** Deliberately, consciously, intentionally.

**Deliberado.** Deliberate, conscious, intentionally.

**Deliberar.** To deliberate, debate, discuss.

**Delictivo, delictuoso.** Criminal, illegal, illicit, unlawful.

**Delincuencia.** Crime, malfeasance, villainy.

**Delincuente.** Delinquent. Criminal, felon, offender

**Delincuente habitual o profesional.** Habitual or career criminal.

**Delincuente *in fraganti.*** Flagrant criminal. One who is surprised during, or immediately after the commission of a crime with effects or instruments in his possession which permit a strong presumption of his participation therein. (Sp. L. Crim. P., sec. 779, para 3).

**Delinquir.** To commit a crime, to break the law.

**Delito.** Crime, felony, misdemeanor, tort, transgression, wrong.

**Delito continuo, de ejecución continuada.** Continuing offense. A continuing offense means one enduring, not terminated by a single act or fact, that is subsisting for one definite period or intended to cover or apply to successive similar obligations or occurrences; there is a breach of the criminal law not terminated by a single act or fact, but which subsists for a definite period and is intended to cover or apply to successive similar obligations or occurrences. (Ppl. v. Serrano, 85 PRR 658 (1962)).

**Delito, estado extranjero.** Offense, foreign state. Those committing an offense against the internal or external security of a con-

tracting State or against its public credit, whatever the nationality or domicile of the delinquent person, are subject in a foreign country to the penal laws of each contracting State. (Bustamante C., arts. 305-307).

**Delito fragante.** Flagrant crime. A flagrant crime shall be considered such crime which is being committed or has been committed when the criminal or criminals are surprised. (Sp. L. Crim. P., sec. 779, para. 1 and 2).

**Delito, fuera de territorio nacional.** Offense, outside national territory. Piracy, trade in negroes and slave traffic, white slavery, the destruction or injury of submarine cables, and all other offenses of a similar nature against international law committed on the high seas, in the open air, and on territory not yet organized into a State, shall be punished by the captor in accordance with the penal laws of the latter. (Bustamante C., art. 308).

**Delito imposible.** Impossible crime. The punishment for attempt will not be applied when the consummation of the crime is an absolute impossibility. (Standard Penal C. for Latin America, sec. 41).

**Delito, lugar de comisión.** Crime, where accomplished. The offense is considered committed: 1) At the place where the criminal acts of authors and accomplices were carried out, totally or partially. 2) At the place where the result was caused or should have been caused. Omission offenses are considered committed at the place where the omitted act should have been performed. (Standard Penal C. for Latin America, sec. 14).

**Delito por comision y por omisión.** Crime through acts or omissions. Offenses may be committed through acts or omissions. When an act is punished in view of its results, responsibility will likewise attach to those who did not prevent said results, provided they were under a legal duty to prevent them and could have done so under the circumstances. (Standard Penal C. for Latin America, sec. 12).

**Delito, tiempo de comisión.** Crime, when accomplished. The act is considered accomplished at the time of the act or the omission, even if the result occurred at a different time. Omission offenses are considered committed at the time the omitted act should have been performed. (Standard Penal C. for Latin America, sec. 13).

**Delitos conexos.** Connected crimes. The following are considered connected crimes: 1) Those committed simultaneously by two or more persons together, provided that they are subject to the jurisdiction of different ordinary or special judges or courts, or who might be so on account of the nature of the crime. 2) Those committed by two or more persons at different places or times, if there shall have been a previous agreement between them. 3) Those committed as a means to perpetrate others or to facilitate their execution. 4) Those committed to secure immunity from others crimes. (Sp. L. Crim. P., art. 17).

**Delitos contra la honestidad.** Sex crimes.

**Demagogo.** Demagogue.

**Demanda, contenido.** Petition, content. The petition shall necessarily contain the following.

1) The names, surnames, particulars of the parties and their ID numbers.

2) The facts on which it is based, stated one by one and well specified.

3) The legal texts that support our thesis.

4) The specific request.

5) When damages are additionally requested, the reason that originates them must be specified, what they consist of and the specific assessment of each of them.

6) The offer of evidence, indicating, in its case, the name and other particulars of the witnesses.

7) Assessment of damages.

8) A procedural domicile to receive notifications. (C.R. C. of Civ. P., art. 290).

**Demanda contra coparte.** Cross-claim against co-party.

**Demanda obligada.** Forced petition. Except for an action of jaccitation (*acción de jactancia*), nobody can be forced to sue.

**Demanda y contestación, defectos.** Petition and answer, defects. If the petition, or its answer, had any defect, or if a legal requirement were missing, the judge may, at the time of filing, issue a verbal warning to the plaintiff or the defendant, indicating the defects in question, so that the pleading may be corrected or completed. The interested party may, if he so wishes, to insist that the pleading be filed. In such case the Judge shall order a correction ruling that in the term of five days the plaintiff or defendant remedy the defects, which the Judge will specify, indicating what requirements have not been met. (Panamanian Judicial Code, arts. 675, 676).

**Demandada, demandado.** Defendant.

**Demandante, demandador.** Plaintiff, claimant, complainant.

**Demandar.** To sue, to file a claim, to take to court. To request, demand, petition.

**Demasía.** Excess, doing much more than necessary.

**Demencia.** Insanity, dementia, derangement, madness. Absurdity, folly.

**Demente.** Insane, demented, deranged, mad.

**Democracia.** Democracy.

**Demora.** Delay, adjournment, deferral, postponement, recess, wait.

**Demora en el pago del precio.** Delay in paying the price. The delay in paying the price of the thing purchased in a commercial sale binds the purchaser to pay—in the absence of other legal interest agreed upon —the legal interest on the amount he owes the vendor. (Waterman Export Corp. v. Valdejully, 88 PRR 483 (1963)).

**Demostrable.** Demonstrable, explainable, provable.

**Demostración.** Demonstration, display, illustration, presentation. Evidence, proof.

**Demostrar.** To prove, convince, demonstrate, show.

**Demostrativo.** Demonstrative, affectionate, open.

**Denegación.** Denial, negation, rejection, refusal, veto.

**Denegación de informes.** Withholding information.

**Denegar.** To deny, negate, reject, refuse, veto.

**Denegatorio.** Denying, negating, refusing, rejecting.

**Denominación.** Denomination, commercial name, tradename. Appellation, designation.

**Denuncia.** Denunciation, accusation, arraignment, charges, complaint indictment, imputation.

**Denuncia de un delito.** Reporting a crime. He who shall be present at the commission of any public crime shall be obliged to inform immediately the nearest judge of examination, municipal judge, or official, under a penalty of paying a fine. (Sp. L. Crim. P., art. 259).

**Denuncia de un delito, deber profesional.** Reporting a crime, professional duty. Those who, by reason of their position, profession, or trade, should have information of some public crime, shall be obliged immediately to denounce the same to the public prosecutor, the court of competent jurisdiction, the judge of examination, and, in his absence, the municipal judge or the police officer nearest to the place, if a flagrant crime be involved. (Sp. L. Crim. P., art. 262).

**Denunciable.** That can be denounced or terminated.

**Denunciante.** Accuser, denouncer. Informant, informer. Claimant.

**Denunciar.** To denounce, accuse, arraign, bring charges, indict.

**Deontología jurídica.** Legal ethics.

**Dependencia.** Dependence, dependency. Reliance. Addiction.

**Dependendiente.** Dependent, helpless, reliant.

**Depender.** To depend.

**Dependiente de comercio.** Commercial employee.

**Deponente.** Affiant, attestant, declarant, deponent, witness.

**Deponer.** To depose, attest, testify, witness. To dethrone, remove, unseat. To cease. To disarm oneself.

**Deportación.** Deportation, banishment, exile, expulsion.

**Deportar.** To extradite, expel.

**Deportivo.** Sportive.

**Deposición.** Deposition, affidavit, attestation, declaration, statement, testimony.

**Depositante.** Depositor.

**Depositar.** To deposit. To accumulate, gather. To drop. To file. To save in a bank.

**Depositario.** Receiver. A receiver shall be:
I. The spouse of the absent person;
II. One of the children of legal age and resident in the same address as the absent person. If there is more than one child, the judge will select the most qualified one;
III. The closest relative to the absent person, in an ascending order;
IV. In the absence of the before mentioned, or when it were inconvenient, because of their notorious bad conduct, or due to their ineptitude, the judge will name the presumptive heir as the receiver. (Mex. Civ. C., art.653).

**Depósito.** Deposit. Down payment, earnest money. Sediment. Warehouse.

**Depósito, depositum, depósito voluntario.** Voluntary *depositum*. A *depositum* is constituted from the time a person receives a thing belonging to another with the obligation of keeping and returning it. An extrajudicial *depositum* is either necessary or voluntary. A voluntary *depositum* is that in which delivery is made by the will of the bailor. (Sp. Civ. C., sec. 1660, 1664, 1665).

**Depósito mercantil.** Commercial deposit. In order that a deposit may be considered commercial, it is necessary: 1) That the depositor, at least, be a merchant. 2) That the wares deposited be commercial objects. 3) That the deposit constitute in itself a commercial transaction, or be made by reason of commercial transactions. (Sp. Com. C., sec. 303/305).

**Depósito mercantil, obligaciones del depositario.** Commercial deposit, depositary's duties. The depositary is obliged to preserve the article deposited in the manner he receives it, and return it with its increase, should there be any, when the depositor request it of him. (Sp. Com. C., sec. 306).

**Depósito necesario.** Necessary *depositum*. A *depositum* is necessary. 1) When made in compliance with a legal obligation. 2) When it takes place on account of any calamity such as fire, ruin, pillage, shipwreck, or other similar cases. (Sp. Civ. C., sec. 1683).

**Depravación.** Depravity, evilness, perversity.

**Depravación moral.** Moral turpitude. Moral turpitude is a state or condition of the individual consisting in an inherent deficiency of his sense of morale and righteousness; of the person's disregard for the respect and security of the human life, and all his actions are essentially wrongful, deceitful, fraudulent, immoral, mean in nature, and consequently, harmful. (Morales Merced v. Superior Court, 93 PRR 411 (1966)).

**Depravado.** Depraved, evil, perverted, wicked.

**Depreciable.** Subject to loss of value.

**Depreciación.** Depreciation, devaluation, reduction in price.

**Depreciación monetaria.** Inflation.

**Depreciar.** To depreciate, deflate, devalue.

**Depredación.** Depredation. Abuse of the environment. Wastefulness.

**Depredador.** Predator. Pollutor. Wasteful person.

**Depresión.** Depression. Deflation, recession, economic slump. Dejection, melancholy.

**Depuración.** Purification, purge.

**Depuración de créditos.** Writing off bad debts and of assets of doubtful value.

**Depurar.** Purify, cleanse, purge.

**Deputación.** Office of a deputy. Agency, representation.

**DEQ. Entregada En Muelle (Derechos Pagados) (...puerto de destino convenido).** DEQ. Delivered *Ex Quay* (Duty Paid) (...named port of destination). "Delivered *Ex Quay* (duty paid)" means that the seller fulfills his obligation to deliver when he has made the goods available to the buyer on the quay (wharf) at the named port of destination, cleared for importation. (Incoterms).

**Derecho.** Law, legislation. Right. Regulation, rules. Legality, lawfulness, rule of law. Straight, upright.

**Derecho a asistencia de abogado.** Right to assistance of counsel. The right to assistance of counsel does not mean the right to assistance of a particular counsel, but of an attorney admitted to practice before the courts, of the free choice of other defendant when this is feasible, and in default thereof, of a public defenders or of one designated by the court and who in the particular case makes a *bona fide*—as in this case—rather than a merely *pro forma* defense. (Ppl. v. Pardo Toro, 90 PRR 618 (1964)).

**Derecho administrativo.** Administrative law. Latin American countries have built bodies of administrative law which, as in France, result from synthesis of doctrine. Many specialized administrative courts have also been set up. At the same time, however, almost all these countries have adopted the Anglo-Saxon system that empowers the judiciary to determine, at least on appeal, the legality of actions taken by public officiais. Almost everywhere administrative jurisprudence is the work of the supreme courts which in many cases also include a specialized division. These courts give very real protection to individuals through various procedures. The most widely used is the *habeas corpus*, imported from England and introduced into Latin American constitutions or practice. (W. Eur. & LA Leg. Sys.).

**Derecho a la cosa.** Right to enjoy the thing.

**Derecho al voto de los accionistas.** Voting rights of stockholders.

**Derecho aplicable.** Applicable law. The applicable law will be determined in accordance with the following rules:

I. The legal acts rightfully created in the entities of the Republic or in a foreign State in accordance to their law, must be recognized;

II. The status and legal capacity of physical persons is governed by their domiciliary law;

III. The creation, type of tenure and extinguishment of estates in realty, as well as leasing agreements and rental contracts of realty or personalty, will be governed by the laws of the place where the are found, regardless of the foreign nationality of their holders or owners;

IV. The formalities required of juridical acts are ruled by the laws of the place where they are performed. In the event such acts will impact within the Federal District, or the Republic and relate to Federal matters, they will also be valid if they comply with the requirements of this Code;

V. Except for the preceding paragraphs, the legal consequences of acts and contracts are subject to the laws of their place of performance, unless the parties have validly designated a different law. (Mex. Civ. C., art.13).

**Derecho aplicable en ausencia de una elección efectiva.** Applicable law in absence of an effective choice.

**Derecho civil, derecho romano.** Civil law, Roman legal system. The term civil law refers to the juridical principles of Roman, European, and South American origin, generally codified. (Morales v. Met. Pack. & Ware. C., 86 PRR 3 (1962)).

**Derecho colectivo del trabajo.** Collective labor law. Although strictly speaking not a legal term, the concept of collective Labor Law is firmly established in several countries. It expresses the notion that at least one of the interested parties, the workers, have the right to act collectively, independently of whether employers agree to do so collectively or individually. It also conveys the notion that the parties, by themselves, can act to create standards that regulate the work relationship. (Mex. Labor Law).

**Derecho colectivo de trabajo, contenido.** Collective labor law, content. The main elements of collective labor law are: right of association; collective bargaining agreements; work rules; modification, suspension and termination of collective agreements, including rules to deal with modernization; and right to strike. (Mex. Labor Law).

**Derecho colectivo de trabajo, objeto.** Collective labor law, purpose. As opposed to individual labor law, collective labor law does not seek to protect the worker in order to attain a balance in his relations with the employer. Its purpose is to permit the parties to attain such a balance for themselves, relying on fundamental institutions such as the right of association, collective bargaining, and strikes. (Mex. Labor Law).

**Derecho de defensa penal.** Right to criminal defense. The persons accused must be represented by a solicitor and defended by an attorney, whom they may appoint as soon as they are notified of the indictment. If they do not designate them themselves or should they not have the legal power to do so, they shall be appointed *ex officio,* upon their request. If the accused should not have designated a solicitor or attorney, he shall be

required to do so or they shall be appointed *ex officio,* if they should not have been appointed by him when the cause reaches a stage where he needs their counsel or some step should be taken wherein their intervention is necessary. (Sp. L. Crim. P., art. 118 and 119).

**Derecho de fondo y de forma.** Substantive and procedural law. The Judge, when issuing his rulings, must bear in mind that the object of the proceedings is the recognition of the rights created by substantive law and it is with such criterium that the norms of this Code must be construed. (Panamanian Judicial Code, art. 293).

**Derecho de los socios a examinar cuentas.** Right of stockholders to examine accounts. The managers or directors of commercial associations can not refuse to permit partners or stockholders to examine all the vouchers of the balances drawn up showing the condition of the management. (Sp. Com. C., sec. 173).

**Derecho de retracto.** Right of redemption. The right of redemption is an agreement or paction, by which the vendor reserves to himself the power of taking back the thing sold by returning the price paid for it. (Lou. Civ. C. art. 2567)

**Derecho de superficie.** Surface right. The surface right, according to the modern concept, is the real right to have or maintain, temporarily or indefinitely, on another person's land or real property, a building or erection as separate property, obtained by the exercise of the accessory right to build or erect or by means of an act of acquisition of the preexistent building or erection. (Lozada Ocasio v. Registrar, 99 PRR 423 (1970)).

**Derecho de tanteo.** Right of preemption.

**Derecho de uso.** Right of use. The personal servitude of right of use confers in favor of a person a specified use of an estate less than full enjoyment. (Lou. Civ. C. art. 639 and notes).

**Derecho español, orígenes.** Spanish law, origins. The roots of Spanish law can be traced back to the customs of two tribes of early inhabitants of the Peninsula—the Celts and the Iberians. Both tribal groups were intruders; the Iberians appear to have crossed over from North Africa sometime prior to the sixth century B.C., while the Celts moved southward across the Pyrenees in the seventh and sixth centuries B.C. These ancient peoples gradually mixed with each other, and with the late-coming invaders—the Carthaginians, Romans, Visigoths, and Moors—to form the ethnic amalgam from which the modern Spaniard and Portuguese have developed. Roman law first arrived about 250 B.C., when the Romans conquered the Peninsula. Though Roman law quickly dominated the area's public law, Celto-lberian customary law continued to play a role, albeit minor, in the area's private law. (L & D in LA).

**Derecho extranjero, Argentina.** Foreign law, Argentina. The application of foreign law is subject to certain limitations, some of which are contained in Article 14 of the Civil Code. Foreign law for example, may not be applied when to do so would be contrary to the public or criminal law of the republic, to the religion of the state, to freedom of worship, or to morality and good customs. It would also be inappropriate to apply foreign law that would be incompatible with the spirit of the code, or when application of the code would be more favorable to the validity of the acts in question. (LA Laws & Inst.).

**Derecho extranjero, México.** Foreign law, Mexico. In applying foreign law, the following shall be observed:

I. The law shall be applied as a judge would apply it in that foreign country, for which the judge shall obtain all necessary information regarding the text, applicability, reach, and meaning of such foreign law.

II. Foreign substantive law shall be applied, except when given the circumstances, it must be taken into account, with exceptional characteristics, the conflict rules of this foreign law, that make the applicable Mexican substantive norms or those of a third State.

III. It will not be an impediment for the application of foreign law, that Mexican law does not provide institutions or procedures essential for the applicable foreign institution, if analogous institutions or procedures exist.

IV. Preliminary or incidental issues that may arise with the main issue, need not necessarily be resolved necessarily in accordance with the law applicable to the latter.

V. When diverse aspects of the same case are regulated by different laws, they shall be applied harmoniously, trying to achieve the aims of each of the legal systems involved. The difficulties caused by the simultaneous application of those laws will be resolved taking into account the equitable requirements of the case.

The above rules will also be used if the law of a different Federal entity within the country becomes applicable. (Mex. Civ. C., art.14).

**Derecho hipotecario.** Mortgage law. The mortgage law is to a great extent a specialty of the civil law, which lacks self-substantiveness and is not interested in the structure and contents of property rights, but rather in the dynamics thereof, that is, their acquisition, conveyance, and loss. (Lozada Merced v. Registrar, 100 PRR 97 (1971)).

**Derecho internacional privado.** Private international law, conflict of laws. Latin America is comprised of civil law countries. Therefore, the primary source of every branch of law is found in codes and statutes as well as in executive decrees and rulings. No Latin American country has, as yet, enacted a comprehensive system of private international law as part of its domestic legislation. Those that have incorporated in their laws either the Montevideo Treaties or the Bustamante Code, have done so through international agreements and with specific reservations. A few countries have included these rules either in their civil codes or in special statutes (Argentina, Brazil, and Uruguay). Nevertheless, legal provisions in this field are few; they are usually scattered throughout different bodies of legislation, and are not collected in one organized system. In general, the Latin American countries have taken a conservative approach to private international law; in many cases, the rules have remained almost unaltered since their original enactment. (LA Laws & Inst.).

**Derecho internacional privado, Argentina.** Private international law, Argentina. Private international law in Argentine derives from several sources. It is embodied primarily in the national substantive codes and statutes (civil and commercial) and in some provincial procedural codes. The Argentine Civil Code was authored by Dalmacio Velez, based upon conflict of laws rules in Story's work, Commentaries on the Conflict of Laws. Articles 8-10, 159-63, and 1205-08 of the code are a translation of the principles contained in Chapter IV of the Commentaries. The articles deal with capacity, status, condition of persons, real property, validity of marriage, rights and duties arising therefrom, marriage contracts, matrimonial property regime, and validity of contracts in general. (LA Laws & Inst.).

**Derecho internacional privado, Brasil.** Private international law, Brazil. Brazil is a member of the Pan-American system of private inernational law through its adherence to the Bustamante Code. In 1916, a number of conflicts rules were adopted in the introduction to the Brazilian Civil Code. In 1942, this law was replaced by a new introduction, which today is the basic source of conflicts law. Nevertheless, only a minimal part of the conflicts law was incorporated in the legislation and enormous gaps still remain. Many Brazilian courts often do not refer to previous decisions, and, in many cases, neither the courts nor counsel are aware of their existence. In view of the incompleteness of the legislation and in the absence of easily accessible case law, there is a general reliance upon doctrine as a source second only to written law itself. This approach reflects a strong European theoretical influence, which many times proves unsuitable to specific Brazilian problems. Although the Bustamante Code as a whole has not been iacorporated into the Brazilian conflicts practice, it is used as a source of authority to be cited in briefs or opiaions. To some extent, it has influenced Brazilian jurisdictional concepts. For example, the code has been credited with either liberalizing or facilitating the recognition of voluntary election of foreign courts, investigation of paternity, succession upon death, foreign divorces and foreign marriages. (LA Laws & Inst.).

**Derecho internacional privado, Chile.** Private international law, Chile. The Chilean Civil Code established certain rules of private international law that have had a wide influence over the rest of Latin America. These rules first appeared in the civil code drafted by Andres Bello at the request of the Chilean government. His submission was enacted in 1855, and the code follows the basic principles and general arrangement of the French Civil Code (*Code Napoléon*). In many instances, however, it adopts solutions different from those in its model. The main sources used in the Chilean Civil Code were Roman law; Spanish laws, especially the Partidas; the *Nueva Recopilación* and the *Fuero Real*; the French Civil Code as commented upon by Rogron; the works of Pothier; the Civil Codes of Louisiana, Sardinia, Austria, Prussia, and the two Sicilies; and the works of Savigny, Delvincourt, Merlin, Escriche and Garcia Goyena. (LA Laws & Inst.).

**Derecho internacional privado, Colombia.** Private international law, Colombia. Colombia is governed by a constitution adopted in 1886. The basic code of the nation is the Civil Code, adopted as national law in 1886, and, substantially, a copy of the Chilean Civil Code of 1855. The provisions on private international law, contained in Articles 18-22 and in a few other scattered provisions, have not been amended. The fundamental principle is that of territoriality (Article 18). (LA Laws & Inst.).

**Derecho internacional privado, fuentes.** Private international law, sources. Latin America is comprised of civil law countries. Therefore, the primary source of every branch of law is found in codes and statutes as well as in executive decrees and rulings. Those that have incorporated in their laws either the Montevideo Treaties or the Bustamante Code, have done so through international agreements and with specific reservations. (LA Laws & Inst.).

**Derecho internacional privado, influencia de Chile.** Private international law, Chile's influence. The code was drafted with a sense of social adaptation to the New World that made it an excellent model for other nations of the continent. The entire Chilean Civil Code, including its private international law provisions, was adopted by Ecuador (1861) and Colombia (1886). Although the Uruguayan Code of 1868 followed the Chilean model very closely, the provisions relating to private international law were completely modified in 1941 to adjust to the system based upon domicile established by the Montevideo Treaties. The private international law schemes of Nicaragua and Honduras belong to the Chilean group, as they are based on Bello's system. (LA Laws & Inst.).

**Derecho Internacional Privado, desarrollo.** Private international law, development.

Private international law was transformed into a scientific, structured discipline under the influence of the German jurist Savigny. Savigny's premise was that the applicable law must be that which is most closely related to the action. His theory considers the law of the domicile as the personal law. It applies the territorial law to all real and Personal property. The law of the decedent's last domicile governs questions of succession. Autonomy of will may decide the law for contractual obligations, but if such a provision is absent, the law of the place of execution is applied. Savigny's theories were widely accepted in many Latin American nations. The Bustamante Code, drafted by the Cuban jurist Antonio Sanchez de Bustamante y Sirven, though based on the principle of nationality, also includes the principle of domicile in determining the applicable personal law. In this manner, Bustamante sought to devise a uniform code acceptable to Latin American nations adhering to either the nationality principle or the domicile principle. (LA Laws & Inst.).

**Derecho laboral, evolución.** Labor law, development. Labor-management relationships in civil law countries were originally a part of the law of contracts and were regulated by the hiring-of-services section of the civil codes and in some instances by the commercial code. The contractual origin of labor law proved to be unsatisfactory to the labor movement and, consequently, labor provisions became an independent body of

law. In some countries it was raised to the level of constitutional law. (LA Laws & Inst.).

**Derecho laboral, principios.** Labor law, principles. Every legal system is based on a series of principles that guide the development of standards. Listing these principles is risky since omissions may occur unless an exhaustive analysis of the entire body of legislation, its legal interpretation, and assessments in the legal literature is carried out. As an example, the most relevant principles of the Mexican labor system (excluding principles of procedural labor rights) are: a) Labor standards provide a balance and social justice in the relations between employees and employers. The basic concept is that the work relationship must be balanced and take into account both the economic condition of firms and the needs of workers. b) Work is a right and a social duty. The right to work appears in the Federal Labor Law fundamentally as a right to employment security, except in cases of illegal conduct, physical disability, or economic grounds. The obligation to work appears in several ways; the violation of the obligation is cause for dismissal. c) Work is not an article of commerce. The employee does not rent or sell himself, but rather transmits only his energy. The price of his effort (the salary) must take into account not only the value of the service performed, but also the personal and family needs of the employee. d) Work must be performed under a system of freedom and dignity for the persons providing it. This alludes to past Instances of exploitation, that led to the creation of a paternalistic system for the employees. e) Work must guarantee life, health, and a decent economic level of living for employees and their families. f) There may not be differences among employees on the basis of race, sex, age, religious or political beliefs, or social standing. However, Mexican nationality is grounds for preference in obtaining some forms of employment. g) There is the freedom to work in legal activities. h) Labor standards are mandatory in nature and workers' rights are Irrevocable. The former means that labor standaray not be superceded by agreement between management and labor. Any renunciation of workers' rights is void. i) The scope of a labor standard is construed In favor of the employee when there is doubt. j) It is presumed that a work relationship exists between the person providing a personal service and the person receiving it. k) There is no time limit on the length of the work relationship, unless It Is explicitly defined as being for a set time or for a specific job. (Mex. Labor Law).

**Derecho litigioso.** Litigious right. Litigious rights are those which can not be exercised without undergoing a lawsuit. (Lou. Civ. C. art. 3556).

**Derecho local, aplicabilidad.** Local law, applicability. The Mexican laws apply to all the persons located in the Republic [of Mexico], as well as to the acts and factual situations which have taken place within its territory or jurisdiction, and to those who have submitted to said laws, save when those laws provide for the application of a foreign law and save, also what is provided by the treaties and conventions to which Mexico has become a party. (Mex. Civ. C., art.12). (J. A. Vargas).

**Derecho minero, Argentina.** Mining law, Argentina. Mining activities in Argentina are regulated by the Mining code of Argentine Republic. This Code, which evolved into many separate laws, was amended and consolidated in 1977 and 1980. In 1995 it was again modified, primarily to address procedural matters and impose new limitations on the number of exploration permits to be held by each province.

Although the mineral rights belong to the state, a declaration of discovery can be made to allow the discoverer to be awarded the orebody or *mina*. The granting of a *mina* accords its holder the permanent, fully transferable right to extract designated minerals from a defined area. *Minas* are issued in units called *pertenencias*, each of which covers six hectares. The discoverer, if an individual, can hold up to thirty *pertenencias*; a corporation can hold up to seventy *pertenencias*. he owner of a *mina* must pay an annual fee or royalty in order to maintain its *mina* claim; otherwise the *mina* reverts to the state. (Orihuela).

**Derecho minero, Chile.** Mining law, Chile.

Mining concessions are granted in the form of court resolutions or "constitutional sentences" by means of a proceeding initiated before the judicial tribunals.

Once mining concession has been granted, the judge orders its registration in accordance with the Code, which also requires a form of public notice in the Official Mining Bulletin.

"All mining concessionaires have the exclusive right to extract samples and to excavate for mining purposes the lands under their dominion and within the boundaries of their concession" and to "undertake all acts that fulfill these objectives," including the establishment of necessary facility, the free use of water sources to open exploratory perforations, and other exploratory activities. In addition, mining concessionaires are allowed to take title to the minerals and substance for which concessions may be granted; to be indemnified, in the event of expropriation; and to defend the concession by all means under the law, both against the state and against private parties. (Orihuela ).

**Derecho minero, Perú.** Mining law, Peru. Mining activities in Peru are regulated by the General Mining Law. This law regulates the use of mineral substances from the soil or subsoil within the national maritime (200 miles) territory, but excludes oil, hydrocarbons, guano deposits, geothermal resources, and mineral-medical waters. Mining activities are defined as sampling, prospecting, exploration, exploitation, general labor, mining benefits, trading, and transportation. Mining activities can be executed by local or foreign individuals or corporations under the concession provisions of the General Mining Law.

The Peruvian General Mining Law, unlike the mining law in most Latin American countries, specifically covers opinion agreements. The law defines an option agreement as "an unconditional and irrevocable obligation for the optionor to enter into a final agreement, provided the optionee exercises the opinion within an agreed upon term," but provides that the term under the mining option agreement shall not exceed five years measured from the date of its execution.

Finally, foreign mining ventures must be duly incorporated under Peruvian law to due business in Peru and may choose any entity from covered General Corporations Law, such as the limited liability company, limited or general partnership, corporation (subsidiary), joint venture or branch. Although 100 percent foreign participation is allowed, the board of directors must be composed of Peruvian residents. (Orihuela).

**Derecho penal, aplicación a las personas.** Criminal law, personal scope. State law applies to every person, with the only following exceptions: 1) Foreign Heads of State within national territory, diplomatic agents of other States, and other persons similarly protected by principles of International Law. 2) Those who, according to the State's Constitution, enjoy privileges and immunities in certain areas. (St. P.C. for LA, sec. 11).

**Derecho penal, aplicación en el tiempo.** Criminal law, applicability time. Criminal acts will be tried according to the law in force at the time when they were committed.

If a new statute is enacted after the criminal act was committed, defendant will be prosecuted under the more benign law applicable to the specific case, but is forbidden to choose from laws during different periods in order to obtain a more favorable rule, through their joint consideration.

If a more benign statute is enacted while the convict is serving his sentence, the court with jurisdiction will modify said sentence accordingly. (St. P.C. for LA, sec. 7-10).

**Derecho penal, aplicación territorial.** Criminal Law, territorial scope. The penal laws of the State apply to criminal acts committed within its territory and in other places subject to its jurisdiction.

The criminal laws of the State likewise apply to criminal acts committed abroad that endanger the external security of the State, its economic welfare or its public health. It shall also apply to criminal acts committed abroad against the national administration, by State officials, regardless of their citizenship. (St. P.C. for LA, sec. 1, 2).

**Derecho penal, aplicación territorial. Aplicación residual de ley nacional.** Criminal law, territorial scope. Residual applicability of the national law. The national laws will further apply: 1) To criminal acts committed on board of national vessels and aircraft, commercial or private, located abroad and provided that said criminal acts are not prosecuted at the place of commission. 2) To criminal acts committed abroad by nationals when, due to their citizenship, the extradition requested by another State for their prosecution is refused. 3) The criminal acts committed abroad by State officials when, due to their diplomatic or functional immunity, they were not prosecuted at the place of commission. (St. P.C. for LA, sec. 3).

**Derecho penal, aplicación territorial. Cosa juzgada.** Criminal law, territorial scope. *Res judicata*. Foreign criminal judgments involving crimes against the local state do not constitute *res judicata* under State Law.

However, the sentence or part thereof served, under such judgments, will be subtracted from the sentence imposed by the national laws, provided both are of a similar nature. If the types were different, the penalty shall be equitably reduced. In any other case, a foreign judgment of acquittal will constitute *res judicata* for all legal purposes.

A judgment of conviction will constitute *res judicata* for purposes of determining the person's status as a repeat offender or habitual criminal, and for the civil consequences of said judgment, all of which shall be determined by State law. (St. P.C. for LA, sec. 5, 6).

**Derecho penal, aplicación territorial. Derecho internacional.** Criminal law, territorial scope. International law. The criminal laws of the State also apply to criminal acts that, according to international covenants or principles of international law, are subject to the State law for reasons other than those indicated above. Priority shall be given, however, to the foreign Nation in whose territory the criminal act was committed, provided that such Nation requests to try the case before proceedings start in the State. (St. P.C. for LA, sec. 4).

**Derecho procesal, orígenes.** Procedural law, origins. The procedural law which the New World colonies inherited from Spain and Portugal was at least as confused and chaotic as the substantive law. The *Fuero Juzgo*, the *Fuero Viejo*, the *Siete Partidas*, the *Ordenações* and the various recompilations all contained detailed procedural rules derived largely from Roman, Germanic and canon law. The French Code of Civil Procedure of 1807, like its civil and commercial code counterparts, was highly influential in Latin America. (L & D in LA).

**Derechos mineros.** Mining rights. The different approaches of the common and civil law traditions to structuring business relationships affect the nature of mining rights and property rights in general. While the common law focuses on the concepts of estates in land, the civil corpus juris is a law of ownership. Therefore, the legal structure law countries from the in the civil law countries of Latin America.

For example, in Latin America, ownership of all minerals in place is in the state, and miners obtain their right to work mineral deposits at the sufferance of the state, through concessions or other forms of permission. In contrasts, the US common law generally provides that the surface owner also owns the underlying minerals in fee simple. Under the civil law system, ownership of the subsoil minerals is always in the state, inalienable and imprescriptible.

Generally, all Latin American countries from Mexico to Argentina follow the principle of state ownership of all continental and maritime underground land within their territorial boundaries. Hence, in Latin America, mining rights granted to private interest are not a grant of an ownership interest in the mineral in place. Rather, the rights are concessions or licenses that merely provide a right to attach the minerals and reduce them to ownership upon separating them from the reserves. Moreover, the concessions or licenses are considered separate property from the real estate where they are located. "The state retains the right to control, in the public interest, any property rights it has not given away." (Orihuela).

**Derecho procesal internacional.** International procedural law. The law of each State determines the competence of courts, as well as their organization, the forms of procedure and of execution of judgments, and the appeals from their decisions. No State shall organize or maintain in its territory special tribunals for members of the other States. Competence *ratione loci* is subordinated, in the order of international relations, to the law of the State which establishes it. Competence *ratione materiae* and *ratione personae*, in the order of international relations should not be based by the States on the status as nationals or foreigners of the interested parties, to the prejudice of the latter. (Bustamante C., arts. 314-317).

**Derecho romano, influencia.** Roman law, influence. Iberian legal culture has been heavily influenced by Rome, which dominated the peninsula for more than six hundred years prior to the fifth century. Fundamental to the Roman concept of law was the effort to set out ethical standards of behavior to which society ought to aspire. Roman lawyers and jurists continually searched for universal, rational principles inherent in nature. By elevating moral principles determined from natural equity and universal reason over custom and tradition as a source of law, the Romans, particularly in the late Empire, produced an impressive body of abstract, idealized legal rules that were frequently honored in their breach. This legislative style was passed on virtually intact from Portugal and Spain to their colonies. (W. Eur. & LA Leg. Sys.).

**Derechohabiente.** Successor, assign, beneficiary, heir.

**Derechos.** Charges, duties, fee. Assessment, tariff.

**Derechos constitucionales.** Constitutional rights. In these matters Latin America is often misunderstood. Since political unrest impedes proper functioning of political institutions, all too frequently generalizations are based on countries where such unrest is most prevalent; the generalities in turn lead to statements that constitutional guarantees are deceiving and that the Latin Americans' love of freedom expresses itself in words instead of deeds. This is completely untrue: the limits set on arbitrary government by private law, penal procedure, administrative law, or social law are much more faithfully respected than any limits deriving from the balance of powers. On the whole, Latin America is a land of personal freedoms, and the exercise of those freedoms is more apt to be curtailed through the helplessness of governments than by their despotism. (W. Eur. & LA Leg. Sys.).

**Derechos laborales mínimos.** Minimum worker rights. The minimum worker rights guaranteed under the Mexican Constitution and the Federal Labor Law may be enhanced through a variety of mechanisms, such as individual labor contracts, collective bargaining agreements, or law-contracts. However, they can never be diminished. (Comparison of Labor Law).

**Derechos y acciones por incumplimiento.** Remedies for nonperformance.

A party is not entitled to avoid the contract on the ground of mistake if the circumstances on which that party relies afford, or could have afforded, a remedy for nonperformance. (Unidroit, Prin., art. 3.7).

**Derogable.** Voidable. Subject to invalidity or nullity.

**Derogación.** Abrogation, abolishment, abolition, annulment, derogation, repeal.

**Derogación de leyes.** Repeal of laws. Laws are repealed, either entirely or partially, by other laws. A repeal may be express or implied. It is express when it is literally declared by a subsequent law. It is implied when the new law contains provisions that are contrary to, or irreconcilable with, those of the former law. The repeal of a repealing law does not revive the first law. (Lou. Civ. C., art. 8).

**Derogación expresa.** Express repeal.

**Derogación por revisión.** Repeal by revision. The repeal by revision operates when the Legislature approves an act covering anew the entire subject matter of another former act, and the comparison of both acts indicates that the legislative intent was to substitute the new act for the old one. (Gonzalez Saldaña v. Industrial Commission, 89 PRR 262 (1963)).

**Derogación tácita.** Repeal by implication, implied repeal.

**Derogar.** To derogate, abrogate, repeal, quash.

**Derogatoria.** Derogation, repeal.

**Derramamiento.** Overfill, overflow. Spilling.

**Derramar.** To spill.

**Derrame.** Spill, spillage.

**Derrocamiento.** Deposal, ouster, overthrowing.

**Derrocar.** To depose, dethrone, oust, overthrow, unseat. To stage a successful coup or revolution.

**DES. Entregada Sobre Buque (...puerto de destino convenido).** DES. Delivered Ex Ship (...named port of destination). "Delivered Ex Ship" means that the seller fulfills his obligation to deliver when the goods have been made available to the buyer on board the ship uncleared for import at the named port of destination. The seller has to bear all the costs and risks involved in bringing the goods to the named port of destination.

This term can only be used for sea or inland waterway transport. (Incoterms).

**Desacatar.** Disobey, rebel, resist.

**Desacato.** Contempt, contempt to court, disrespect.

**Desaconsejar.** To discourage, to advice or counsel against.

**Desacuerdo.** Disagreement, discrepancy, dispute.

**Desafiante.** Challenging, confrontational.

**Desafiar.** To challenge, dare.

**Desafío.** Challenge, confrontation, dare.

**Desaforado.** Disbarred. Enraged, furious.

**Desaforar.** To disbar. To revoke a license to practice law.

**Desaforo, desafuero.** Disbarment. Loss of license to practice law.

**Desagravio.** Rectification of an unfair situation. The redress of a wrong.

**Desahogado.** In a comfortable economic position. Solvent.

**Desahogo.** Alienation, assuagement, relief.

**Desahuciador.** Party who evicts another.

**Desahuciar.** To evict, dislodge, dispossess, eject, expel. To throw out. To consider that someone has no chances of success.

**Desahucio.** Eviction, dislodgment, dispossession, ejection, expulsion. Eviction notice.

**Desairar.** Rebuff, ignore, reject, shun, snub.

**Desaire.** Rebuff, disregard, rejection, rebuke, snub.

**Desalojar.** To evict, dislodge, dispossess, eject, expel. To throw out. To empty, vacate.

**Desalojo, desalojamiento.** Eviction, dislodgment, dispossession ejection, expulsion, ouster.

**Desamparar.** To abandon, desert, forsake. To leave unprotected.

**Desamparar la apelación.** To overrule an appeal.

**Desamparo.** Abandonment, defection, desertion, forsaking.

**Desaparecido.** Person illegally abducted and killed by the armed forces and about whom no explanations are given (AR).

**Desaparición.** Disappearance, departure.

**Desapoderar.** To dispossess, to deprive from possession. To cancel a power of attorney.

**Desaprobar.** To disapprove, censure, criticize.

**Desapropiar.** To convey property away.

**Desasegurar.** To drop an insurance.

**Desatender.** To neglect, disregard, ignore.

**Desautorización.** Removal of permission. Withdrawal of authority.

**Desautorizado.** Unauthorized.

**Desautorizar.** To withdraw authority. To disavow, repudiate.

**Desavenencia.** Disagreement, conflict, discrepancy, friction.

**Desavenirse.** To disagree, differ, object.

**Descalificación.** Disqualification, elimination, ouster.

**Descalificar.** To disqualify, eliminate, oust.

**Descansar.** To annul or void a marriage.

**Descanso.** Rest. During the work shift, the worker shall te given a rest period of at least one-half hour (FLL, Article 63). There are some restrictions on the length of the work shift for children. (Mex. Labor Law).

**Descargar.** To discharge, unload. To release. To get rid of.

**Descargo.** Criminal defense. Discharge. Release.

**Descendencia.** Descent, ancestry, lineage, origin. Issue. Bloodline.

**Descendiente.** Descendant.

**Descifrar.** Decipher.

**Desconfiado.** Distrustful, doubtful.

**Desconfianza.** Distrust, doubt, mistrust, suspicion.

**Desconfiar.** To distrust, doubt.

**Desconocer.** Not to know. To ignore. To deny, reject.

**Descontar.** To discount, reduce. To allow for. To pay cash for a not or check.

**Descripción.** Description, depiction. Portrait. Narrative.

**Descripto.** Described, depicted.

**Descubierto.** Uncovered. Discovered. Lacking in funds.

**Descuidado.** Inattentive, careless, negligent, unmindful.

**Descuidar.** To neglect, disregard, overlook.

**Desechar.** To reject, decline, throw away. To dismiss.

**Desembargar.** To vacate an attachment order.

**Desembargo.** Cancellation of an attachment.

**Desembolsar.** To disburse, pay.

**Desembolso.** Disbursement, expenditure, expense, payment.

**Desempatar.** To decide a tie. To end a deadlock situation.

**Desempate.** Tie break. Casting vote.

**Desempeñar.** To cancel a pledge on a chattel.

**Desempeño.** Accomplishment. Performance. Redemption or discharge of a pledge.

**Deserción.** Desertion, abandonment, forsaking. Defection.

**Desertar.** To desert, abandon, forsake. To defect.

**Desertor.** Deserter, defector, dissident.

**Desequilibrio ecológico.** Ecological imbalance. Alteration of the interdependent relationships between natural elements which form the environment, that negatively affects the existence, transformation, and development of humans and other living beings.

**Desestimación involuntaria.** Involuntary dismissal.

**Desestimar.** To dismiss, deny, overrule, reject.

**Desestimatorio.** Dismissing, rejecting.

**Desfalcador.** Embezzler, cheat, crook, swindler.

**Desfalcar.** To embezzle, defraud, misappropriate, swindle.

**Desfalco.** Embezzlement, defalcation, misappropriation, swindle.

**Desfloración.** Defoliation.

**Desflorar.** To deflower, defile, rape, ravish.

**Desgaste.** Wear and tear.

**Desglosar.** To remove pages from a judicial record.

**Desglose.** Removal of a page or more from a dossier.

**Desgracia.** Calamity, misfortune, mishap.

**Desgravación.** Tax benefit.

**Desgravar.** To cancel or to remove an encumbrance. To remove a tax.

**Deshacer.** To undo, annul, rescind, void.

**Deshecho.** Undone, annulled, rescinded, void.

**Desheredación.** Disinherison.

Disinheritance. Disinheritance can only take place for one of the reasons expressly fixed by law. Disinheritance can only be made in a will mentioning therein the legal reason on which it is based. Sufficient causes for disinheritance are, in the respective cases, those of disqualification to succeed by reason of unworthiness.

A subsequent reconciliation of the offender with the offended deprives the latter of the right to disinherit and renders a disinheritance already made without effect. (Sp. Civ. C., sec. 825, 826, 829, 833).

**Desheredación de descendientes.** Disinherison of descendants. The ascendants may disinherit their descendants, coming to their succession, for the first nine and the eleventh and twelfth causes expressed in the preceding Article, when the acts there mentioned have been committed toward them or toward the parents, but they can not disinherit their descendants for the tenth cause. (Lou. Civ. C. art. 1622).

**Desheredación de hijos.** Disinherison of children. The just causes for which parents may disinherit their children are twelve in

number. There shall be a rebuttable presumption as to the facts set out in the act of disinherison to support these causes.

These causes are, to wit: 1) If the child has raised his or her hand to strike the parent, or if he or she has actually struck the parent; but a mere threat is not sufficient. 2) If the child has been guilty, towards a parent, of cruelty, of a crime or grievous injury. 3) If the child has attempted to take the life of either parent. 4) If the child has accused a parent of any capital crime, except, however, that of high treason. 5) If the child has refused sustenance to a parent, having means to afford it. 6) If the child has neglected to take care of a parent become insane. 7) If the child refused to ransom them, when detained in captivity. 8) If the child used any act of violence or coercion to hinder a parent from making a will. 9) If the child has refused to become security for a parent, having the means, in order to take him out of prison. 10) If the son or daughter, being a minor, marries without the consent of his or her parents. 11) If the child has been convicted of a felony for which the law provides that the punishment could be life imprisonment or death. 12) If the child has known how to contact the parent, but has failed without just cause to communicate with the parent for a period of two years after attaining the age of majority, except when the child is on active duty in any of the military forces of the United States. (Lou. Civ. C. art. 1621).

**Desheredación de padre y madre.** Disinherison of parents. Legitimate children, dying without issue, and leaving a parent, can not disinherit him or her, unless for the seven following causes, to wit: 1) If the parent has accused the child of a capital crime, except, however, the crime of high treason; 2) If the parent has attempted to take the child's life; 3) If the parent has, by any violence or force, hindered the child from making a will; 4) If the parent has refused sustenance to the child in necessity, having the means of affording it; 5) If the parent has neglected to take care of the child while in a state of insanity; 6) If the parent has neglected to ransom the child when in captivity; 7) If the father or mother have attempted the life, the one of the other, in which case the child or descendant making a will may disinherit the one who has attempted the life of the other. (Lou. Civ. C. art. 1623).

**Desheredar.** To disinherit, to repudiate an heir.

**Deshipotecar.** To cancel or to remove a mortgage.

**Deshonestidad.** Dishonesty, immorality, turpitude.

**Deshonesto.** Dishonest, dishonorable, immoral.

**Deshonor.** Dishonor, discredit, disgrace, humiliation, ignominy, shame. Lack of payment or performance.

**Deshonorar, deshonrar.** To dishonor, discredit, disgrace.

**Deshonra.** Dishonor, humiliation, ignomy, shame.

**Deshonroso.** Dishonorable, disgraceful, shameful.

**Desierto.** Desert, deserted.

**Designar.** Appoint, designate, name, nominate.

**Desintoxicación.** Disintoxication.

**Desistimiento.** Withdrawal. Whoever voluntarily withdraws from the commission of a criminal act prevents its results, will only be liable for the punishable acts performed prior to abandonment. (Standard Penal C. for Latin America, sec. 40).

Nonsuit, voluntary dismissal, dropping of charges. Relinquishment, abdication, surrender, waiver.

**Desistimiento de la construcción.** Discontinuance of work.

**Desistimiento será sin perjuicio.** Dismissal shall be without prejudice.

**Desistimiento voluntario.** Voluntary dismissal.

**Desistir.** To cease and desist. To move for voluntary dismissal. To relinquish, waive.

**Desleal.** Disloyal, deceitful, false, treacherous.

**Deslindar.** To set boundaries.

**Deslinde.** Land survey and marking of boundaries. Separation and distribution of rights and liabilities among several parties.

**Deslinde y amojonamiento.** Surveys and demarcation. The survey and demarcation of a piece of land may be requested not only by the owner thereof, but also by any person having a property right therein for its use or enjoyment.

The petition shall state whether the survey is to be made of the entire area within the perimeter of the land, or only in the part which borders upon some determined estate, and shall designate the names and residence of the persons to be cited to appear at the survey, or that such persons are unknown to the petitioner.

The judge shall set a day and hour upon which the survey is to begin, notice being given long enough in advance so that all persons interested may be present, who shall previously be legally cited to appear. (Sp. L. Civ. P. sec. 2060, 2061).

Fixing of boundaries and placing of landmarks. (Sp. Civ. C., sec. 392, 394).

**Desmedro.** Detriment, disadvantage, drawback. Unfavorable situation.

**Desmembar.** To dismember, separate.

**Desmembramiento.** Dismemberment, break, rupture, separation.

**Desmoronamiento.** Collapse, crumbling, falling.

**Desmoronar.** To collapse, crumble. To go down, fall.

**Desnaturalizado.** Unkind person, dehumanized, perverse.

**Desnaturalizar.** To denaturalize. To revoke citizenship. To abuse, debase, misuse.

**Desobediencia.** Disobedience.

**Desobligar.** To release from an obligation, to liberate from a duty.

**Desocupación.** Unemployment, lay off. Lack of occupancy.

**Desocupado.** Unemployed. Idle. Vacant.

**Desocupar.** To vacate, abandon, empty, evacuate.

**Desorden.** Disorder, anarchy, chaos, confusion.

**Despacho.** Dispatch. Message, report. Delivery, shipment. Judicial chambers. Office.

**Despedida.** Farewell.

**Despedir.** To fire, lay off. To bid farewell.

**Despido.** Firing from a job, discontinuance of services.

**Despido ilegal.** Unlawful discharge. The voluntary and arbitrary actions of an employer tending to compel an employee to abandon his position constitute a discharge, where the only reasonable alternative left to the employee is the abandonment of the position. (Velez Reilova v. Palmer Bros., Inc. 94 PRR 166 (1967)).

**Despido sin previo aviso.** Dismissal without notice.

**Despojante.** Depriver, dispossessor.

**Despojar.** To deprive, dispossess, divest. To take away.

**Despojo.** Deprivation, dispossession. Robbery.

**Desposeer.** To dispossess. To evict, eject.

**Desposeimiento.** Dispossession, eviction.

**Desposesión.** Dispossession.

**Déspota.** Despot, tyrant.

**Despotismo.** Despotism, autocracy.

**Desprender.** To unbutton. To follow as a logical consequence.

**Desproporción excesiva.** Gross disparity.

A party may avoid the contract or an individual term of it if, at the time of the conclusion of the contract, the contract or term unjustifiably gave the other party an excessive advantage. Regard is to be had, among other factors, to (a) the fact that the other party has taken unfair advantage of the first party's dependence, economic distress or urgent needs, or of its improvidence, ignorance, inexperience or lack of bargaining skill; and (b) the nature and purpose of the contract. (Unidroit, Prin., art. 3.10).

**Destajo, a.** Type of a work where payment is made by the number of pieces produced.

**Destierro.** Exile, banishment, deportation, ostracism.

**Destinación.** Destination, goal, objective.

**Destinar.** To destine. To have plans for something.

**Destinatario.** Recipient, receiver.

**Destino.** Destiny, fate, future, lot.

**Destitución.** Dismissal from a job or position, discharge, firing, ouster.

**Destituir.** To remove from office, to vote out, to vote down. To remove authorities by force.

**Destripador.** Ripper.

**Destripar.** To rip open.

**Destrucción.** Destruction, annihilation, devastation, ruin.

**Destructor.** Destructor, annihilator, destroyer.

**Desuso.** Non use, disuse, lack of use.

**Desvalijamiento.** Theft of valuables from a home.

**Desvalijar.** To burglarize, plunder, rob.

**Desvaloración monetaria.** Inflation.

**Desviación, desvío.** Deviation. Abnormality. Variation. Improper channelling or use of funds.

**Desvincular.** To sever all links.

**Detallar.** To detail, enumerate, itemize. To give a breakdown.

**Detalle.** Details, particulars, specifics. Minutia. De minimis.

**Detalle de las partidas de la cuenta.** Itemized statement of the account.

**Detective.** Detective, investigator, private agent, sleuth.

**Detector.** Detector, sensor.

**Detención.** Arrest. Any person may be placed under arrest: 1) He who shall attempt to commit a crime, at the moment he is about to commit it. 2) A delinquent captured *in fraganti*. 3) He who shall escape from a penal institution in which he may be serving a sentence. 4) He who shall escape from a prison in which he may be awaiting his transfer to a penal institution or place in which he is to serve the sentence which may have been imposed upon him by a final sentence. 5) He who shall escape while being conducted to the institution or place mentioned in the foregoing number. 6) He who shall escape while under arrest or detention awaiting trial. 7) A person accused or convicted who may be in default. (Sp. L. Crim. P., art. 489 and 490).

Detention, apprehension, capture. Confinement, imprisonment.

**Detener.** To arrest, detain. To apprehend, capture. To block, stop.

**Detenido.** Detained, arrested. Stopped, restrained.

**Detentación.** Tenancy, tenure. Possession. Use and enjoyment. Control, dominium. Ownership, proprietorship.

**Detentador.** Holder of a thing or a right.

**Detentar.** To hold. To have, possess.

**Deterioro.** Deterioration, degradation, impairment, waste, wear and tear.

**Deterioro ambiental.** Environmental degradation.

**Determinación.** Determination, clarification, finding. Firmness, tenacity. Conclusion, final decision.

**Determinación de causa probable.** Probable cause finding.

**Determinación de daños.** Measure of damages.

**Determinación de la calidad de la prestación.** Determination of quality of performance. Where the quality of performance is neither fixed by, nor determinable from, the contract a party is bound to render a performance of a quality that is reasonable and not less than average in the circumstances. (Unidroit, Prin., art. 5.6).

**Determinación del daño por referencia a precio corriente.** Proof of harm by current price. Where the aggrieved party has terminated the contract and has not made a replacement transaction but there is a current price for the performance contracted for, it may recover the difference between the contract price and the price current at the time the contract is terminated as well as damages for any further harm.

**Determinación del precio.** Price determination.

(1) Where a contract does not fix or make provision for determining the price, the parties are considered, in the absence of any indication to the contrary, to have made reference to the price generally charged at the time of the conclusion of the contract for such performance in comparable circumstances in the trade concerned, or if no such price is available, to a reasonable price. (2) Where the price is to be determined by one party and that determination is manifestly unreasonable price shall be substituted notwithstanding any contract term to the contrary. (3) Where the price is to be fixed by a third person, and that person cannot or will not do so, the price shall be a reasonable price. (4) Where the price is to be fixed by reference to factors which do not exist or have ceased to exist or to be accessible, the nearest equivalent factor shall be treated as a substitute. (Unidroit, Prin., art. 5.7).

**Determinaciones de hechos por la corte.** Findings by the court.

**Detrimento.** Detriment, damage, drawback, injury, loss.

**Deuda.** Debt, debit, deficit, liability, obligation.

**Deuda mancomunada.** Debt in severalty.

**Deuda revivida.** Revival of debt.

**Deuda total.** Aggregate indebtedness.

**Deudas de valor.** Debts expressed in a way different from a sum of money.

**Deudas dinerarias.** Debts expressed in an amount of money.

**Deudor.** Obligor, debtor. Obligor or debtor is the person who has engaged to perform some obligation. (Lou. Civ. C. art. 3556).

**Deudor de la cuenta.** Account debtor.

**Deudor de regreso.** Endorser of a negotiable instrument liable for payment.

**Deudor solidario.** Several debtor, joint debtor, joint and several debtor.

**Deudos.** Surviving family of a decedent.

**Devaluación.** Devaluation, inflation.

**Devaluar.** To devaluate.

**Devengado.** Accrued, earned, generated, produced yielded.

**Devengar.** To accrue, generate, produce, yield.

**Devolución.** Reimbursement, refund. Return.

**Devolutivo.** That is referred to another court for decision of a particular issue.

**Devolver.** To return, replace, restore. To reimburse, refund.

**Día.** Day.

**Día feriado.** Bank holiday, legal holiday.

**Diagnóstico.** Diagnose, assessment, prognosis.

**Diario.** Newspaper. Journal, diary. Chronicle. Bulletin, gazette. Daybook. Record, register.

**Diario de sesiones.** Congressional bulletin. Federal Register.

**Días feriados, de fiesta.** Public holidays, bank holidays.

**Días hábiles.** Legal working days. Legal working days are all days of the year excepting Sundays, full religious or civil holidays, and the days when courts are ordered closed. (Sp. L. Civ. P., sec. 257). Working days. Business days.

**Dicente.** Deponent, speaker, witness.

**Dicho.** Said, reported, stated. Adage, maxim, saying.

**Dictado.** Dictated. Ordered.

**Dictamen.** Legal opinion, assessment, appraisal, conclusion, decision, judgment, resolution.

**Dictamen de peritos.** Opinion of experts. Expert testimony may be used when, in order to determine or consider some fact of influence in the action, scientific, artistic, or practical knowledge becomes necessary. (Sp. L. Civ. P. sec. 609, 610).

**Dictaminado.** Assessed, decided, judged.

**Dictaminar.** To issue a legal opinion. To express a conclusion, a decision. To pass judgment.

**Dictar.** To dictate, decree, direct, order, ordain.

**Dictar sentencia.** To enter a judgment, to pass a judgment.

**Dictar un auto.** To issue a writ.

**Dieta.** Per diem, fee. Emolument.

**Difamación.** Defamation, libel, slander.

**Difamación de empresas.** Defamation of corporations.

**Difamación de personas fallecidas.** Defamation of deceased persons.

**Difamación de personas privadas.** Defamation of a private person.

**Difamación de un grupo o clase de personas.** Defamation of a group or class.

**Difamación que no requiere prueba de perjuicio.** Defamation actionable *per se*.

**Difamar.** To defame, libel, slander. To present in a false light.

**Difamatorio.** Defamatory, libelous, slanderous.

**Diferir.** To differ, disagree, clash. To adjourn, postpone, suspend.

**Difunto.** Deceased, decedent, dead.

**Digesto.** Digest, precis, summary. Compilation or collection of laws.

**Digital.** Digital.

**Dignatario.** Dignitary, emissary, envoy, representative.

**Dignidad.** Dignity.

**Digno.** Dignified, deserving. Meritorious, praiseworthy, worthy.

**Dilación.** Delay. Deferral, deferment, postponement, stay.

**Dilapidación.** Dilapidation, squandering. Extravagant spending, overspending. Waste.

**Dilapidado.** Dilapidated.

**Dilapidar.** To dilapidate, squander, overspend.

**Dilatar.** To delay, defer, postpone. To make larger.

**Dilatorio.** Dilatory. With the intent to gain time.

**Diligencia.** Diligence, expediency, industry. Errand, commission. Course of action.

**Diligencia de reconocimiento.** Lineup. The identification shall take place by placing before the person who is to make it the person to be identified, producing said person in union with other similar external circumstances. In the presence of all of them or from a point where he can not be seen, as the judge may consider more advisable, the person to make the identification shall state if the person to whom he may have referred in his declarations is in the group, and in an affirmative case he shall designate him in a clear and specific manner. (Sp. L. Crim. P., art. 369).

**Diligenciado.** Served, notified to the parties.

**Diligenciador.** Process server. Court officer in charge of notifications.

**Diligenciamiento de citaciones y emplazamientos.** Service of citations and summons. Service of citations and summons shall be made in the manner prescribed for notifications, with the following differences: The writ of citation shall contain: 1) The name of the judge or court issuing the order, the date of the latter, and the matter on which it is based. 2) The names and surnames of the parties to be cited, the address of their dwellings; and, should they be unknown, any other data by which their whereabouts may be ascertained. 3) The purpose of the citation. 4) The place where and the day and hour when the person cited is to appear. 5) The obligation, should there by any, of appearing upon the first call under a fine; or, if it be the second call, the obligation of attending with the admonition of being proceeded against as guilty of the crime of refusing aid, as provided for in the penal code with regard to jurors, experts, and witnesses. (Sp. L. Crim. P., art. 175).

**Diligenciamiento de notificaciones.** Service of notices. For the service of notices the secretary acting in the cause shall prepare a writ which shall contain: 1) A statement of the object of said cause and the names and surnames of the parties thereto. 2) A copy of the resolution which is to be served. 3) The name and surname of the person or persons upon whom notice is to be served. 4) The date on which the writ is issued. 5) The signature of the clerk. Service shall consist of the reading of the entire order to be served, delivering the copy of the writ to the person notified, and making a brief entry of service at the foot of the original writ. (Sp. L. Crim. P. art. 167 and 170).

**Diligencias preliminares.** Preparatory proceedings.

**Diligente.** Diligent, attentive, hard working, industrious.

**Dimisión.** Resignation, departure from a job or position.

**Dinero.** Money, cash, currency, legal tender.

**Diploma.** Diploma, certificate.

**Diplomado.** Certified, licensed, registered.

**Dipsomanía.** Dipsomania, alcoholism.

**Diputado.** Representative, congressman. Delegate, deputy.

**Diputar.** To commission, appoint, empower.

**Dique.** Dike, dam. Barrier, barricade, obstruction.

**Dirección.** Direction, course, path. Address, domicile. Government, supervision.

**Directiva.** Directive, decree, instruction.

**Directivo.** Executive, director. Belonging to the top management.

**Directo.** Direct, straight.

**Director.** Director, executive, manager.

**Directorio.** Board of directors.

**Dirigente.** Leader, ruler.

**Dirigir.** To direct, lead. To address. To aim at.

**Dirigismo.** State intervention in the economy.

**Dirimente.** Type of defect that cannot be remedied.

**Dirimir.** To arbitrate a dispute.

**Discernimiento.** Discernment, knowledge, understanding. Attribution of an honor, prize or reward.

**Discernir.** To understand. To award a prize.

**Disciplina.** Discipline, conduct, behavior. Method, order, regime.

**Disconforme.** In disagreement, dissenting.

**Disconformidad.** Dissension, dissent. Discord, objection.

**Discordancia.** Lack of harmony, dissent.

**Discordia.** Discord, conflict, strife.

**Discreción.** Discretion. Free will exercised reasonably.

**Discrecional.** Discretional, discretionary.

**Discrepancias idiomáticas.** Linguistic discrepancies.
     Where a contract is drawn up in two or more language versions which are equally authoritative there is, in case of discrepancy between the versions, a preference for the interpretation according to a version in which the contract was originally drawn up. (Unidroit, Prin., art. 4.7).

**Discreto.** Discreet, cautious, prudent.

**Discrimen (P.R.), discriminación.** Discrimination.

**Discriminación por organización obrera.** Discrimination by labor union.

**Disculpa** Apology, excuses, repentance. Excuse, justification. Defense.

**Disculpar.** To excuse, absolve, forgive.

**Discurso.** Speech, address, lecture, talk.

**Discusión.** Discussion, debate, deliberation. Confrontation.

**Discutible.** Arguable, debatable, questionable. Not certain.

**Discutir.** To discuss, debate, deliberate.

**Diseminar.** Disseminate, divulge, spread.

**Disenso.** Dissension, dissent.

**Disentir.** To dissent, differ, disagree.

**Disfraz.** Costume, disquise. Deception, front.

**Disfrazar.** To disguise. To conceal, screen, shroud.

**Disfrutar.** To enjoy, use.

**Disfrute.** Use and enjoyment.

**Disidencia.** Dissension, dissent.

**Disidente.** Dissident, dissenter, objector. Dissenting.

**Disimulo.** Concealment, pretense.

**Disminución.** Decrease, cutback, decline. Discount.

**Disminuido.** Disable, handicapped. Decreased, reduced.

**Disminuyente.** Diminishing, dwindling.

**Disolución.** Dissolution, liquidation, winding up.

**Disolución contractual.** Dissolution of contract. When the obligor fails to perform, the obligee has a right to the judicial dissolution of the contract or, according to the circumstances, to regard the contract as dissolved. In either case, the obligee may recover damages. In an action involving judicial dissolution, the obligor who failed to perform may be granted, according to the circumstances, an additional time to perform.

Upon dissolution of a contract, the parties shall be restored to the situation that existed before the contract was made. (Lou. Civ. C. art. 2013 and 2018).

**Disolver.** To dissolve.

**Disparar.** To shoot, fire. To launch. To dart, spurt.

**Disparate.** Absurdity, nonsense.

**Disparo.** Shot, discharge.

**Dispensa, dispensación.** Dispensation, exception, favor.

**Dispensa de ser testigo.** Privilege not to be a witness. The following are excused from the obligation of testifying: 1) The relatives of the accused in a direct ascending or descending line, his spouse, his uterine brothers or sisters, and his lateral blood relatives up to and including the second civil degree, as well as the natural parents. The examining judge shall inform the witness included in the foregoing paragraph that he is not obliged to testify against the accused, but that he may make the statements which he may deem proper, the answer which he may give to this notice being recorded. 2) The attorney of the accused, with regard to the facts which the latter may have confided to him as his counsel. (Sp. L. Crim. P., art. 416).

**Dispensable.** Excusable, justifiable.

**Dispensar.** To excuse, justify, pardon. To distribute, to give out.

**Disponente.** Conveyor, party who sells or who transfers.

**Disponer.** To alienate, convey, sell. To order, mandate.

**Disponibilidad.** Availability, existence. Cash.

**Disponible.** Available, free, present, ready.

**Disponiéndose.** Being ordered that.

**Disponiéndose (en una ley).** Provided clause (in a statute). Generally the mission of a provided clause is to establish an exception to the general provisions of a statute or to some of the, or to quality or modify them in some aspects. (Bull Insular Line v. Superior Court, 86 PRR 148 (1962)).

**Disponiéndose bajo la condición de.** Proviso, provided that.

**Disponiéndose que.** Proviso saying that.

**Disposición.** Disposition, clause, provision, proviso. Decree, order, ruling. State of mind, character.

**Disposición inoficiosa.** Inofficious clause. Those dispositions which fathers and mothers and other ascendants make of their property to the prejudice of their descendants, beyond the proportion reserved to them by law, are called inofficious. (Lou. Civ. C. art. 3556).

**Disposición testamentaria.** Testamentary disposition. Testamentary dispositions are either universal, under a universal title, or under a particular title. Each of these dispositions, whether it be made under the name of institution of heir, or under the name of legacy, shall have its effect, according to the rules hereafter established for universal legacies, for legacies under a universal title, and for particular legacies. (Lou. Civ. C. art. 1605).

**Dispositivo.** Dispositive, conclusive, decisive.

**Disputa.** Dispute, confrontation, controversy, disagreement.

**Disputa obrera, de trabajo.** Labor dispute.

**Disputabilidad.** Argumentability, contestability.

**Disputable.** Arguable, debatable, questionable.

**Disputar.** To argue, challenge, object, question.

**Disputas de trabajo.** Labor disputes. In principle, labor disputes can be resolved by any of the following mechanisms: a) direct settlement between the parties; b)conciliation; c) mediation; d) arbitration; and e) settlement by the courts. In Mexico, there is a preference for direct settlement of labor disputes between the parties, conciliation through the intervention of a specialized authority, and settlement by the Courts. Mediation and binding arbitration are less widely practiced. (Mex. Labor Law).

**Distancia.** Distance, gap, span. Aloofness, remoteness.

**Distinción.** Distinction, prominence. Difference, differentiation, discrimination.

**Distintivo.** Distinct, special, uncommon, unique.

**Distracción.** Distraction. Oversight, negligence. Lack of attention. Removal of a thing. Misappropriation. Conversion.

**Distracto.** Rescission, cancellation of a contract.

**Distraer.** To misappropriate, to take wrongfully. To remove, separate.

**Distribución.** Distribution. Circulation, dissemination. Dispatching, delivering, shipping. Arrangement.

**Distribuir.** To distribute. To circulate, disseminate. To deliver, send. To arrange.

**Distrito.** District, area, circuit, precinct.

**Disturbio.** Disturbance, disruption, interference, intrusion.

**Disturbio de la tranquilidad pública.** Breach of peace.

**Disyuntivo.** Disjunctive.

**Diversidad.** Diversity.

**Dividendo.** Dividend, bonus, premium, quota.

**Divisa.** Type of currency. Flag, emblem, symbol.

**Divisas.** Foreign convertible currency.

**Divisibilidad.** Divisibility.

**Divisible.** Divisible.

**División de bienes matrimoniales.** Division of matrimonial assets. Once the nullity of the marriage has been established, the division of assets will be commenced. The divisible assets, if the two spouses acted in good faith, will be divided between them in the fashion accorded in the pre-nuptial agreement. If only one party acted in good faith, this person will receive the assets. If there was bad faith by both parties, the assets will be given in favor of their children. (Mex. Civ. C., art.261).

**División de la cosa común.** Division of the thing held in common. Part-owners cannot compel a division of the thing held in common to be made, when by so doing they may render it unserviceable for the use for which it was intended. The rules relating to the division of inheritances shall apply to the division amongst part-owners. (Sp. Civ. C., art. 408, 413).

**Divorciar.** To grant a divorce. To separate.

**Divorcio.** Divorce, estrangement, separation. Breach, division.The causes for divorce are as follows: 1) Adultery on the part of either of the parties to the marriage. 2) Conviction of one of parties to the marriage of a felony, which may involve the loss of civil rights. 3) Habitual drunkenness or the continued and excessive use of opium, morphine, or any other narcotic. 4) Cruel treatment or grave injury. 5) The abandonment of the wife by the husband or of the husband by the wife for a longer period of time than one year. 6) The absolute, perpetual and incurable impotency occurred after marriage. 7) The attempt of the husband or wife to corrupt their sons or to prostitute their daughters, and connivance in their corruption or prostitution. 8) The proposal of the husband to prostitute the wife. A divorce carries with it a complete dissolution of all matrimonial ties, and the division of all property and effect between the parties to the marriage. (Sp. Civ. C., sec. 164, 173).

**Divorcio, causas.** Divorce, grounds. The causes of divorce and separation shall be subject to the law of the place in which they are sought, if the married couple is domiciled there. (Bustamante C., art. 54).

**Divorcio, consecuencias judiciales.** Divorce, judicial consequences. The law of the court before which the litigation is pending determines the judicial consequences of the action and terms of the judgment in respect to the spouses and the children. (Bustamante C., art. 55).

**Divorcio, derechos.** Divorce, rights. The right to separation and divorce is regulated by the law of the matrimonial domicile, but it cannot be founded on causes prior to the acquisition of said domicile, if they are not authorized with equal effect by the personal law of both spouses. (Bustamante C., art. 52).

**Divorcio, perdón.** Divorce, forgiveness. The innocent spouse may, at any time before the entry of a final judgment, grant forgive the other spouse. In that case, the innocent party may not ask for a divorce based on the same grounds the forgiveness was granted. A new divorce may be granted for new reasons, even if they are of the same nature, or for different facts that legally constitute a sufficient cause for divorce. (Mex. Civ. C., art.281).

**Divorcio, reconciliación.** Divorce, reconciliation. Reconciliation by the spouses terminates the divorce decree in whatever states the divorce was, if there still was not a final judgment. In that case, the parties must state their reconciliation to the judge, but failure to do so does not prevent the effects of a reconciliation. (Mex. Civ. C., art.280).

**Divorcio, reconocimiento.** Divorce, recognition. Each contracting State has the right to permit or recognize, or not, the divorce or new marriage of persons divorced abroad, in cases, with effects or for causes which are not admitted by their personal law. (Bustamante C., art. 53).

**Divulgación.** Dissemination, publication.

**Doble.** Double, duplicate, reproduction. Clone. Twice.

**Doble estiba.** Double stacking.

**Doble exposición por el mismo delito.** Double jeopardy.

**Doble inmatriculación.** Double registration. If a person who has a property recorded in his name believes that another property registration entered with a different number refers to the same real estate and to the same titleholder, he may request that the corresponding court summon all interested parties and, provided that the identity of both properties as a single piece of real estate can be proved, shall issue a ruling resolving which of the two entries shall subsist. (PR Mort. Law 1979, sec. 251).

**Doctor en leyes, doctor en derecho.** Doctor of laws, LL.D., J.D.

**Doctrina.** Doctrine. Legal writing.

**Doctrina de los contactos dominantes.** Doctrine of dominant contacts. The doctrine on the matter of conflict of laws on damages—to be applied when it must be determined which of the laws of two different states which are in conflict is to be applied by a court in a case for damages—known as the Doctrine of Dominant Contacts, requires that the rights and liabilities in tort be determined by the local law of that jurisdiction which has the most significant relationship with the occurrence and with the parties. (Widow of Fornaris v. Amer. Surety Co. of N.Y., 93 PRR 28 (1966)).

**Doctrina de los riesgos de la calle.** Street-risk doctrine.

**Doctrina de recibos implícitos.** Constructive receipts doctrine.

**Doctrina, México.** Legal writing, Mexico. If the publication of primary-source material in Mexico leaves something to be desired, the secondary literature, i.e., commentary on the law in books and journals, is of high quality. In Mexico, legal commentary, *la doctrine*, enjoys high prestige and authority. The leading treatise in a field of law has in effect the standing of a formal source of law. The main law schools in Mexico, including the LTNAM, the Escuela Libre de Derecho, the Universidad Iberoamericana, and the Universidad Panamericana, publish high-quality academic law journals. (Pratter).

**Doctrinal.** Doctrinal.

**Doctrinario.** Doctrinaire.

**Documentación.** Documentation, documents. Written evidence.

**Documental, documentario.** Documentary.

**Documentar.** To document, certify, demonstrate, prove.

**Documento.** Document, certificate, credential, instrument.

**Documento de la sucesión hereditaria, registro.** Hereditary succession document, registration. For Registry purposes, the hereditary succession document is the one that contains the will or the judicial declaration of abintestate heirs. (PR Mort. Law 1979 sec. 95).

**Documento auténtico.** Authentic document. An authentic document is not a mere private writing but a legalized document, which is publicly attested, that is, which is legally valid in itself. A document verified before a notary is an authentic document. (Ramos Mimoso v. Superior Court, 93 PRR 538 (1966)).

**Documento de resguardo.** Document of title.

**Documento negociable.** Negotiable instrument. An instrument—a check—is negotiable if it is payable to order or to bearer. (E.M.L. Insurance Company v. Banco Popular, 91 PRR 626 (1965)).

**Documento pagadero a la orden.** Instrument payable to order. An instrument is payable to order where it is drawn to the order of a particular person or of any person or his order. (E.M.L. Insurance Company v. Banco Popular, 91 PRR 626 (1965)).

**Documento pagadero al portador.** Instrument payable to bearer. An instrument is payable to bearer: a. when it is payable to the order of a fictitious or nonexisting person, and such fact is known by the persons making is so payable; or b. when the only or last endorsement is in blank. (E.M.L. Insurance Company v. Banco Popular, 91 PRR 626 (1965)).

**Documento privado, prueba.** Private instrument, proof. A private instrument legally acknowledged shall have, with regard to those who signed it and their legal representatives, the same force as a public instrument. (Sp. Civ. C., sec. 1193).

**Documento público, prueba.** Public instrument, proof. Public instruments are those authenticated by a notary or by a competent public official, with the formalities required by law. Public instruments are evidence, even against a third person, of the fact which gave rise to their execution and of the date of the latter. They shall also be evidence against the contracting parties and their legal representatives with regard to the declarations the former may have made therein. (Sp. Civ. C., sec. 1184, 1186).

**Documentos extranjeros.** Foreign documents.

Documents executed in other countries shall have the same validity in an action as those executed in Spain, providing they possess the following requisites: 1) That the subject matter of the act or contract be lawful and permitted under the laws of Spain. 2) That the contracting parties have legal power and capacity to contract according to the laws of their own country. 3) That in the execution thereof all formalities and requirements prescribed in the country wherein the acts or contracts were made have been observed. 4) That the document be legalized and possess the other requisites necessary to prove its authenticity in Spain.

To every document drafted in any language other than Spanish there shall be accompanied a translation thereof, and copies of both the original and translation. (Sp. L. Civ. P., sec. 599, 600).

**Dolo.** Fraud.

There is fraud when, with words or insidious machinations by one party, the other party is induced to enter into a contract when, without said words or machinations, he/she would not have entered into it. For the fraud to annul the contract, it must be serious and must not have been employed by both parties. Fraud that is not substantial only forces the party who used it to pay damages. (Sp. Civ. C., sec. 1269, 1270).

**Dolo (Crim.).** Criminal intent. A person acts with criminal intent when he wishes the occurrence of the act legally classified as a crime, or accepts it after having foreseen at least the possibility of its occurrence. (Standard Penal C. for Latin America, sec. 25).

Deceit. There is deceit when by words or insidious machinations on the part of one of the contracting parties the other is induced to execute a contract which without them he would not have made. Fraud, deception, misrepresentation, ruse, trickery, swindle.

**Doloso.** Fraudulent, deceitful, deceptive, dishonest.

**Doméstico.** Domestic. Internal, national. Relating to a home or to a family.

**Domiciliado.** Domiciled.

**Domiciliario.** Domiciliary, residential.

**Domiciliarse.** To be domiciled.

**Domicilio.** Domicil(e), habitual, residence, residence. Address, home, place of abode. Place of business. Headquarters.

**Domicilio conyugal.** Conjugal domicile. The conjugal domicile is the place where the spouses live together, without prejudice to the right of each spouse to have his or her domicile determined separately. (Inter-American Convention On Domicile of Natural Persons In Private International Law, art. 4).

**Domicilio de elección.** Domicil(e) of choice.

**Domicilio de origen.** Domicil(e) of origin.

**Domicilio, diplomáticos.** Domicile, diplomats. The domicile of diplomatic agents shall be their last domicile in the territory of the accrediting State. The domicile of natural persons temporarily residing abroad in the employment or commission of their Government shall be that of the State that appointed them. (Inter-American Convention On Domicile of Natural Persons In Private International Law, art. 5).

**Domicilio habitual.** Habitual residence. A person's domicile is the place where he resides habitually, and in lack thereof, the place of his business; in lack thereof, in the place where he actually lives, and if none, the place where he is found. It is presumed that a person habitually resides in the place he stays for more than six months. (Mex. Civ. C., art.29).

**Domicilio, jefe de familia.** Domicile, head of the family. The legal domicile of the head of the family extends to the wife and children, except children who have reached their majority or have been emancipated, and that of the tutor or guardian extends to the minors or incapables under his guardianship unless otherwise provided by the personal legislation of those to whom the domicile of another is ascribed. (Bustamante C., art. 24).

**Domicilio legal.** Legal domicile. The legal domicile of an individual is the place where the law determines his place of residency for the exercise of his rights and compliance of his obligations, even though he is not physically present there. (Mex. Civ. C., art.30).

**Domicilio, persona física**. Domicile, natural person. The domicile of a natural person shall be determined by the following circumstances in the order indicated: 1. The location of his habitual residence; 2. The location of his principal place of business; 3. In the absence of the foregoing, the place of mere residence; 4. In the absence of mere residence, the place where the person is located. When a person has his domicile in two States Parties, he shall be considered to be domiciled in the State Party where he resides and, if he resides in both, the place in which he is located shall be preferred. (Inter-American Convention On Domicile of Natural Persons In Private International Law, arts. 2 and 6).

**Domicilio, persona incompetente.** Domicile, incompetent person. The domicile of incompetent persons is that of their legal representatives, except when they are abandoned by those representatives, in which case their former domicile shall continue. (Inter-American Convention On Domicile of Natural Persons In Private International Law, art. 3).

**Dominante.** Dominant, commanding, controlling, ruling. Central, main, principal.

**Dominar.** To dominate, control, rule.

**Dominical.** Relating to Sunday.

**Dominio.** Ownership, fee simple, property. Domination, control.

**Dominio público de la nación y dominio particular del estado.** Public ownership of the nation and private ownership of the state. Public ownership of the nation relates to those things whose use is common because of their very nature or the purpose to which they are devoted—such as seashores, rivers, roads, public piers and ports—its principal characteristic being that it is not subject to conveyance or prescription.

Private ownership of the state relates to those things which are destined to its service, that is, to satisfy its collective necessities, and not for the common use, things of which it disposes as the individuals do with respect to those constituting their patrimony, among others, forests, mines, arsenals, fortresses, and military buildings. (Rubert Armstrong v. Commonwealth, 97 PRR 573 (1969)).

**Don.** Natural talent, gift of nature. Mister.

**Donación.** Donation, gift. A gift is an act of liberality by which a person disposes gratuitously of a thing in favor of another, who accepts it. (Sp. Civ. C., sec. 625).

**Donación antenupcial.** Gift in contemplation of marriage. Prenuptial gifts are those given from one spouse to another before marriage, regardless of what name practice has given it. (Mex. Civ. C., art.219).

**Donación entre vivos.** Donation *inter vivos*. Gifts *inter vivos* may be of three kinds: 1) A purely gratuitous gift, or one made without any condition attached and through mere liberality. 2) An onerous gift, or one in with the donee is burdened with a charge upon the value of the thing donated. 3) A remunerative gift or one made to a person by reason of his merits or for services rendered to the donor provided such services do not constitute recoverable debts.

**Donación gratuita.** Gratuitous donation. The donation purely gratuitous, or that which is made without condition and merely from liberality. (Lou. Civ. C. art. 1523 and notes).

**Donación inoficiosa.** Voidable donation. No person can give nor receive, by way of gift, more than what he can give or receive by will. A gift shall be considered void in all that exceeds said limits. (Sp. Civ. C., sec. 644).

**Donación manual.** Manual gift. The manual gift, that is, the giving of corporeal movable effects, accompanied by a real delivery, is not subject to any formality. (Lou. Civ. C. art. 1539).

**Donación matrimonial.** Gift by reason of marriage. Gifts by reason of marriage are those bestowed before its celebration, in consideration of the same, and in favor of one or of both spouses. (Sp. Civ. C., sec. 1294).

**Donación onerosa.** Onerous donation. The onerous donation, is that which is burdened with charges imposed on the donee.

The onerous donation is not a real donation, if the value of the object given does not manifestly exceed that of the charges imposed on the donee. (Lou. Civ. C. art. 1523 and art. 1524 and note).

**Donación por causa de muerte.** Donation *mortis causa*. A donation *mortis causa* (in prospect of death) is an act to take effect, when the donor shall no longer exist, by which he dispossess of the whole or a part of his property, and which is revocable. (Lou. Civ. C. art. 1469).

**Donación, reducción.** Donation, reduction. Gifts which, may be void after computing the net value of the property of the donor at the time of his death must be reduced with regard to the excess, but this reduction shall not prevent them from being valid during the life of the donor nor the donee from appropriating the fruits.

The reduction of gifts can be demanded only by the persons who have a right to a legal portion or to an aliquot part of the estate and their heirs or legal representatives. (Sp. Civ. C., sec. 662, 663).

**Donación remunerativa.** Remunerative donation. The remunerative donation, is that, the object of which, is to recompense for services rendered.

The remunerative donation is not a real donation, if the value of the services to be recompensed thereby being appreciated in money, should be little inferior to that of the gift. (Lou. Civ. C. art. 1523 and art. 1525 and note).

**Donación, reversión.** Donation, reversion. The reversion in favor of the donor only in any case and under any circumstances, may also be validly established, but not in favor of other persons, except in the same cases and under similar limitations, as prescribed for testamentary substitution.

The reversion stipulated by the donor in favor of a third person in contravention of the provisions of the foregoing paragraph, is void, but it shall not cause the annulment of the gift. (Sp. Civ. C., sec. 649).

**Donación, revocación.** Donation, revocation. Every gift *inter vivos* made by a person having no legitimate children nor descendants nor legitimized by a subsequent marriage is revoked by the mere fact of the occurrence of any of following cases: 1) When the donor, after the gift should have legitimate or legitimized or acknowledged illegitimate children, even should they be posthumous. 2) When the child of the donor, whom he supposed dead when he bestowed the gift, is found to be alive.

A gift may also be revoked at the instance of the donor, by reason of ingratitude, in the following cases: 1) When donee commits any crime against the person, the honor, or the property of the donor. 2) When the donee charges the donor with any of the crimes giving rise to official proceedings or public accusation, even though he proves it, unless the crime should have been committed against the donee himself, his wife, or the children under his authority. 3) When the latter improperly refuses him support. (Sp. Civ. C. sec. 652, 656).

**Donante.** Donor.

**Donar.** To donate, bequeath, devise, give.

**Donatario.** Donee

**Donativo.** Donation, gift.

**Dorso.** The back part of a page.

**Dotación.** Allowance, sum of money. Crew, team of workers. Grant.

**Dotal.** Related to dowry.

**Dotar.** To furnish, contribute, dispense, equip, supply. To endow. To pay a dowry.

**Dote.** Dowry. A dowry is composed of the property and rights brought as such by the wife to the marriage at the time of contracting it, and of those which she acquires during the same by gift, inheritance, or legacy, as dowry property.

**Doy fe.** "I so certify." Expression used by notary publics. It is associated to notaries to the point that the latter are also knows as *fedatarios* (dispensers of faith).

**Drenaje.** Drainage.

**Droga.** Drug. Medication, medicine. Drugs, hallucinogen, narcotic.

**Drogarse.** To take drugs. To commit substance abuse.

**Duda.** Doubt, qualms, query, question. Skepticism, uncertainty.

**Duda razonable.** Reasonable doubt. The doubt which justifies the acquittal of a defendant should not only be reasonable, but it should also arise from serene, fair, and impartial consideration of the evidence as a whole, or from the insufficiency of the evidence in support of the information. (Ppl. v. Malave Sanchez, 95 PRR 384 (1967)).

**Dudoso, dudable, dubitable.** Doubtful, dubious. Ambiguous, debatable, disputable. Unreliable.

**Duelista.** Duelist, one fighting a duel.

**Duelo.** Duel. Challenge to fight. Grief from a relative's death.

**Dueño.** Owner, master, proprietor.

**Dueño directo.** Legal owner.

**Dúplica.** Rejoinder.

**Duplicado.** Duplicate, copy, replica. Imitation, forgery.

**Duplicar.** To duplicate, copy. To forge, counterfeit.

**Duplicidad.** Duplicity, double dealing, double standards.

**Duración.** Duration, lapse, length of time.

**Durante.** During, while.

# E

**Ebriedad.** Drunkenness, alcoholism, inebriation, intoxication, dipsomania.

**Ebrio.** Drunk, drunkard, alcoholic, inebriated, intoxicated, dipsomaniac. Bombed, smashed.

**Ebrio habitual.** Habitual drunkard.

**Echar.** To throw away, to cast, chuck, toss. To fire, boot, discharge.

**Echazón (mar).** Jettison (mar). The captain shall supervise the jettison, and shall order the goods cast overboard in the following order: 1) Those which are on deck, beginning with those which embarrass the handling of the vessel or damage her, preferring, if possible, the heaviest ones and those of least utility and value. 2) Those in the hold, always beginning with those of the greatest weight and smallest value, to the amount and number and absolutely indispensable (Sp. Com. C., sec. 815).

**Eclecticismo.** Pragmatism. Forming a doctrine or a philosophy by borrowing from several other doctrines or philosophies.

**Eclesiástico.** Belonging to the church.

**Ecología.** Ecology.

**Economía.** Economy, finance. Austerity, frugality, saving.

**Economista.** Economist, financier.

**Ecosistema.** Ecosystem. The basic functional unit for interaction of living organisms among themselves and these with the environment, in a determined space and time.

**Ecuánime.** Steady, stable.

**Edad de consentimiento.** Legal age, when a person can obligate him or herself contractually.

**Edición.** Edition, issue, printing, publishing. Year when a book was printed.

**Edicto.** Edict, decree, order, ruling, proclamation.

**Edictos judiciales.** Service of process by publication.

**Edificio.** Building. A building is any structure made or devoted to shelter persons or animals, or to keep things. (Ppl. v. Cosme Vargas, 96 PRR 815 (1969)).

Construction, edifice. Block of flats (G.B.).

**Edificios ruinosos y árboles que amenazan caerse.** Unstable buildings and trees about to fall. When a building wall, column or any other construction is in danger of falling, the owner shall be obliged to demolish it, or to do whatever is necessary to prevent its falling.

Should the owner of the unstable thing fail to do so, it may be ordered demolished at his expense by the authorities. e.g. should a tree or building fall, the owner shall be liable for the damages caused, except in cases of vis major. (Sp. Civ. C., sec. 396, 398).

**Edil.** Prefect. alderman.

**Edilicio.** Urban. Relating to zoning laws or to the government of a city. Municipal.

**Editor.** Editor, publisher.

**Editorial.** Printing house. Main article in a newspaper.

**Efectivo.** Effective, effectual. Forceful, strong. Actual, real. Cash, currency, money.

**Efectivo en caja.** Cash, cash on hand.

**Efecto.** Effect consequence, result. Impression caused or received.

**Efecto retroactivo.** Retroactive effect.

**Efecto retroactivo de la anulación.** Retroactive effect of avoidance.

(1) Avoidance takes effect retroactively. (2) On avoidance either party may claim restitution of whatever it has supplied under the contract or the part of it avoided, provided that it concurrently makes restitution of whatever it has received under the contract or the part of it avoided or, if it cannot make restitution in kind, it makes an allowance for what it has received. (Unidroit, Prin., art. 3.17).

**Efecto vinculante del contrato.** Binding character of contract.

A contract validity entered into is binding upon parties. It can only be modified or terminated in accordance with its terms or by agreement or as otherwise provided in these principles. (Unidroit, Prin., art. 1.2).

**Efectos.** Effects, belongings, patrimony, property, possessions. Commercial paper.

**Efectuar.** To accomplish, achieve. To do, perform.

**Eficacia, efectividad.** Efficacy, efficiency. Mastery, power. Ability to cause change or to make an impact.

**Eficaz.** Efficient, effective. Capable, competent. Practical.

**Efracción.** Getting in or out of a building by breaking walls or windows.

**Efusión.** Gush, flood, flow, spill.

**Ejecución.** Execution, enforcement of a judgment. Death penalty. Performance, completion.

**Ejecución de sentencias, Código Bustamante.** Enforcement of judgments, Bustamante Code. Every civil or contentious administrative judgment rendered in one of the contracting States shall have force and may be enforced in the others if it combines the following conditions: (1) That the judge of the court which has rendered it have competence to take cognizance of the matter and to pass judgment upon it, in accordance with the rules of this Code. (2) That the parties have been summoned for the trial either personally or through their legal representative. (3) That the judgment does not conflict with the public policy or the public laws of the country in which its execution is sought. (4) That it is executory in the State in which it was rendered. (5) That it be authoritatively translated by an official functionary or interpreter of the State in which it is to be executed, if the language employed in the latter is different. (6) That the document in which it is contained fulfil the requirements necessary in order to be considered as authentic in the State from which it proceeds, and those which the legislation of the State in which the execution of the judgment is sought requires for authenticity.

The execution of the judgment should be requested from a competent judge or tribunal in order to carry it into effect, after complying with the formalities required by the internal legislation.

In the case reffered to in the preceding article, every recourse against the judicial resolution granted by the laws of that State in respect to final judgments rendered in a declarative action of greater import shall be granted. (Bustamante C., arts. 423-425).

**Ejecutable.** Executionable, enforceable, performable. Capable of being completed.

**Ejecutado.** Person against whom a judgment is enforced.

**Ejecutante.** Party who enforces a judgment or who sues. Performer.

**Ejecutar.** To perform, carry out, enforce.

**Ejecutividad.** Power or ability to be executed.

**Ejecutivo.** Executive. Executive power. Corporate officer. Entrepreneur. Manager.

**Ejecutor.** Executor. Judicial officer in charge of enforcement procedures.

**Ejecutoria.** Copy of a judgment. *Ejecutoria*, the public and formal instrument in which a final decision is entered for enforcement.

Enforceability. The Supreme Court of Justice shall declare the enforceability (*ejecutoria*) of decisions (*sentencias*) rendered by foreign authorities, without which declaration they shall have no effect as a means of proof, nor for the purpose of *res judicata* or enforcement.

**Ejecutoria, carta ejecutoria.** Writ of execution. In a strict sense *ejecutoria* or *carta ejecutoria* means—pursuant to law of civil procedure—the public instrument formally drafted by the competent judicial officer, in which a final judgment is literally inserted, transcribed or set forth. (Ramírez v. Registrar, 96 PRR 332 (1968)).

**Ejecutoria, sentencia ejecutoria.** Final judgment. The word *ejecutoria* and the phrase *sentencia ejecutoria* (final judgment) mean the same thing, that is, the judgment which, because of its having been consented in first instance or affirmed in last instance, has acquired the finality and authority of *res judicata*. (Ramírez v. Registrar, 96 PRR 332 (1968)).

**Ejecutoría.** Judgment that is enforceable.

**Ejecutoriar.** To obtain the enforcement of a judgment.

**Ejecutoriedad.** Binding power of a judgment.

**Ejecutorio.** Executory, enforceable.

**Ejemplar.** Copy, issue. Facsimile. Exemplary, commendable, worthy of admiration and following.

**Ejercer.** To practice a profession or trade.

**Ejercer como abogado.** To practice law, to practice.

**Ejercer un cargo.** Hold an office by appointment. To discharge a duty.

**Ejercer un oficio.** To engage in an occupation or trade.

**Ejercicio.** Exercise, activity, drill, workout.

**Ejercicio de acciones penales.** Exercise of prosecution functions. All penal actions must be prosecuted *ex officio,* excepting: 1) those which require the complaint of the victim; 2) those which are only prosecuted by private action. (Argentine Crim. C. art. 71).

**Ejercicio de la profesión.** Practice of law, lawyering.

**Ejercitable.** That can be put into practice or enforced.

**Ejercitar.** To perform, execute. To carry out.

**Ejército.** Army. Battalion, military, soldiers, troops.

**Ejidatario.** The term "ejidatario" refers to an individual who has participated as a beneficiary in a grant of land in accordance with the agrarian laws. The totality of *ejidatarios* participating in a given grant, together with their families and the lands which they received, constitute an *ejido.* Thus the term "ejido" refers to a community, while "ejidatario" refers to a specific individual. (W. Eur. & LA Leg. Sys.).

**Ejido.** The term "ejido," as now used in Mexico, refers to an agrarian community which has received and continues to hold land in accordance with the agrarian laws growing out of the Revolution of 1910. The lands may have been received as an outright grant from the government or as a restitution of lands that were previously possessed by the community and adjudged by the government to have been illegally appropriated by other individuals or groups; or the community may merely have received confirmation by the government of titles to land long in its possession. Ordinarily, the *ejido* consists of at least twenty individuals, usually heads of families (though not always), who were eligible to receive land in accordance with the rules of the Agrarian Code, together with the members of their immediate. (W. Eur. & LA Leg. Sys.).

**Elaboración.** Manufacture, construction, making.

**Elaborado.** Manufactured, made. Detailed, ornate, ostentation.

**Elección.** Election, choice, decision, selection.

**Elección del derecho aplicable.** Choice of applicable law.

**Electivo.** Elective, chosen by the people.

**Elector.** Elector, voter. Person who chooses or selects.

**Electrocución.** Electrocution.

**Electrocutar.** To electrocute.

**Elegir.** To elect, choose, decide, select.

**Elegir un jurado.** To impanel a juror.

**Elemento natural.** Natural element. Physical, chemical, and biological elements that present themselves in a determined time and space without the human influence.

**Elevar.** To elevate, hoist, lift. To anoint. To raise, boost, increase.

**Eliminación.** Elimination, annihilation, deletion, eradication, ouster.

**Eliminar.** To strike out, cancel, cross out, delete, erase.

**Eliminatorio.** Eliminatory.

**Eludido.** Eluded, avoided.

**Eludir.** To elude, avoid, bypass, dodge, evade, skint.

**Emancipación.** Emancipation. The minor who is emancipated has the full administration of his estate, and may pass all acts which are confined to such administration, grant leases, receive his revenues and moneys which may be due to him, and give receipts for the same. He can not bind himself legally by promise or obligation for any sum exceeding the amount of one year of his revenue. (Lou. Civ. C. art. 370 and art. 371).

**Emanicipación, acta.** Emancipation, record. Emancipation by marriage can be proven with the certificate of marriage, without the need of a separate certificate of emancipation. (Mex. Civ. C., art.93).

**Emancipación, clases.** Emancipation kinds. The law recognizes four kinds of emancipation: 1) Emancipation conferring the power to administer property. 2) Emancipation by marriage. 3) Judicial emancipation. 4) Emancipation by reason of having attained the age of majority. (Sp. Civ. C., sec. 302).

**Emancipación judicial.** Emancipation judicially granted. A minor sixteen years of age or older may be judicially emancipated and relieved of the disabilities which attach to minority. (Lou. Civ. C. art. 385).

A minor who has lost both parents may obtain the benefit of majority by concession of the Court of his domicile, after a hearing of the Public Attorney.

**Emancipación para administrar bienes.** Emancipation to administer property. A minor, although not married, may, for the sole purpose of administering his property, be emancipated by his father, or in default thereof, by his mother, when the said minor shall have completed the age of eighteen years.

This emancipation takes place by a declaration of the father or mother, before a notary public and in the presence of two witnesses, and with the consent of the minor. It shall be recorded in the civil registry and, until then, shall not produce any effect against third persons. (Sp. Civ. C., sec. 303).

**Emancipación por acto notarial.** Emancipation by notarial act. The minor, although not married, may be emancipated by his father, or if he has no father, by his mother, when he shall have arrived at the full age of fifteen years.

This emancipation takes place by the declaration to that effect of the father or mother, before a notary public in presence of two witnesses. (Lou. Civ. C. art. 366).

**Emancipación por mal trato.** Emancipation by reason of ill treatment. The minor may be emancipated against the will of his father and mother, when they ill treat him excessively, refuse him support, or give him corrupt examples. (Lou. Civ. C. art. 368).

**Emancipación por matrimonio.** Emancipation by marriage. A minor, whether male or female, becomes emancipated of right by marriage. This emancipation cannot be revoked. (Lou. Civ. C. art. 379 and art. 383).

**Emancipar.** To emancipate.

**Embajada.** Embassy, diplomatic, legation.

**Embajador.** Ambassador, diplomat, emissary, envoy.

**Embarazo.** Pregnancy.

**Embarazo, derechos laborales.** Pregnancy, labor rights. During pregnancy, female employees are entitled to six weeks' leave prior to giving birth, and six weeks' leave thereafter, with full salary. If they are unable to work because of pregnancy or childbirth, the maternity leave may be extended for as long as it is necessary, with the worker earning 50 percent of her salary during for up to 60 days. Maternity leaves do no affect seniority rights (FLL Article 170). (Mex. Labor Law).

**Embargable.** Attachable.

**Embargado.** Garnishee. Party whose property has been attached or garnished.

**Embargante.** Garnisher. Party who attaches or garnishes.

**Embargar.** To attach, arrest, garnish, seize.

**Embargo.** Attachment. Attachment is a juridical interdiction in the debtor's patrimony, decreed at ex parte request of the claimant creditor, one of the procedural effects of which is to subject or submit the attached goods to the performance of an obligation or claim in the main action; that is, to secure the effectiveness of the judgment rendered in the case if the action exercised should prosper. (Alum Torres v. Campos del Toro, 89 PRR 299 (1963)).

Arrest, garnishment, seizure. Embargo.

**Embargo, sin.** However, notwithstanding.

**Embarque por el vendedor.** Shipment by seller.

**Embaucador.** Con man, charlatan, cheat, fraud, swindler.

**Embaucar.** To con, cheat, swindle.

**Emborracharse.** To get drunk

**Emboscada.** Ambush, decoy, trap.

**Embriagado.** Drunk, inebriated, intoxicated.

**Embriaguez.** Drunkenness, alcoholism, inebriation, intoxication, dipsomania.

**Embrujamiento.** Bewitchment.

**Embrujar.** To bewitch, enchant, possess. To beguile, fascinate.

**Embuste.** Lie, falsehood, misrepresentation. Swindle.

**Embustero.** Liar, cheat, trickster.

**Emergencia ecológica.** Ecological emergency. A situation deriving from human activities or natural phenomena that upon severely affecting natural elements places one or several ecosystems in danger.

**Emisible.** Issuable.

**Emisión.** Issue. Copy, edition, printing. Emission. Utterance.

**Emisionismo.** Economic policy that relies heavily on the printing of money. One of the causes of inflation.

**Emisor, emitente.** Issuer. Drawer of a document. Party who signs a declaration.

**Emitir.** To issue, emit, proffer, utter.

**Emitir un cheque.** To draw a check.

**Emoción violenta.** Heat of passion, extreme anger. It is normally raised as an extenuating factor in criminal proceedings.

**Emolumento.** Emolument, fee, payment.

**Empadronamiento.** Registration for purposes of voting.

**Empadronar.** To register those who can vote.

**Empalme.** Junction, connection, link.

**Empatar.** To tie, draw.

**Empate.** Tie, deadlock, draw, stalemate.

**Empeñar.** To pledge, pawn.

**Empeño.** Act of pledging or pawning. Determination, firmness, steadfastness, tenacity.

**Empezar.** To begin, establish, generate, institute, originate.

**Empezar a regir.** Become effective, take effect.

**Emplazado.** Party that has been summoned.

**Emplazador, emplazante.** Party or person who summons.

**Emplazamiento.** Citation, summons. Site, situation.

Summons. Once the petition is legally filed, or its defects are corrected, the judge shall summon the defendant, granting the latter a term of thirty days to answer.

If the defendant is domiciled abroad, the term shall also determine, according to the case, that allowed to offer evidence. (C.R. C. of Civ. P., art. 295).

**Emplazamiento a los Estados Unidos.** Summons upon the United States.

**Emplazamiento a un funcionario o agencia.** Summons upon an officer or an agency.

**Emplazamiento a un individuo.** Summons upon an individual.

**Emplazamiento a un menor o a un incapaz.** Summons upon an infant or an incompetent person.

**Emplazamiento a una empresa.** Summons upon an enterprise.

**Emplazamiento en país extranjero.** Service in a foreign country.

**Emplazamiento por correo.** Summons through the mail.

**Emplazar.** To summon. To command appearance. To establish a non-extendable period of time for performance.

**Empleado.** Employee, laborer, worker.

**Empleado permanente.** Permanent employee. The term permanent employee means an employee who has passed the probationary period, who is entitled to all the benefits offered by the employer and who can not be discharged except on preferment and proof of charges or for economic reasons affecting the industry or establishment. (Cassasus v. Escambron Beach Hotel, 86 PRR 356 (1962)).

**Empleado probatorio, a prueba.** Probationary employee. The term probationary employee means generally the employee who according to the employment contract, is subject to a probationary period and is not entitled to the benefits offered by his employer to his permanent employees. (Cassasus v. Escambron Beach Hotel, 86 PRR 356 (1962)).

**Empleador.** Employer, boss, manager, principal.

**Empleo.** Employment, job, occupation, work. Position, post.

**Empresa.** Enterprise. For the purposes of labor rules, an enterprise is an economic unit for the production or distribution of goods or services, and an establishment is a technical unit which as a branch, agency, or other similar form, is an integral part and contributes to carrying out the purposes of the enterprise. Thus, the enterprise Is an economic reality that assumes legal responsibilities. Enterprises or corporations that come together for a common purpose are considered as one under labor law and as holding a trove of common responsibilities for working conditions and other obligations to workers. Employees of each enterprise or corporation also are entitled to equal working conditions for equal work performed. (Mex. Labor Law).

Enterprise, business, company, concern, establishment. Project, endeavor, task, venture.

**Empresa común.** Joint venture.

**Empresario.** Entrepreneur, businessman, executive.

**Empréstito.** Loan, public debt.

**En beneficio propio.** Self-serving.

**En blanco.** In blank.

**En curso del empleo.** In the course of employment. For the purposes of the Workmen's Accident Compensation Act, the phrase in the course of employment refers to factors of time and place, and means that an injury to be compensable must arise within the time and space boundaries of the employment. (Gallart, Manager v. Industrial Commission, 87 PRR 16 (1962)).

**En fe de lo cual.** In faith whereof.

**En ocasión del trabajo, como consecuencia del empleo.** Arising out of employment. For the purpose for the Workmen's Accident Compensation act, the phrase arising out of employment is expressive of the requirement that there must be a causal connection between the conditions which the employer puts about the employee and the employee's resulting injury. (Gallart, Manager v. Industrial Commission, 87 PRR 16 (1962)).

**En su nombre.** On his or her behalf.

**En testimonio de lo cual.** In witness whereof.

**En vigor.** In effect, in force, effective.

**Enajenable.** Alienable, marketable, saleable.

**Enajenación.** Conveying of property, sale.

**Enajenación de un inmueble.** Conveyance, sale. The term sale is comprised within the term conveyance currently used in the English language to denote the transfer of the title or any interest in real estate. (First Nat'l. City Bank v. Registrar, 89 PRR 749 (1964)).

**Enajenación mental**. Delusion, mental incapacity.

**Enajenante.** Seller, alienor.

**Enajenar.** To sell, alienate, convey, transfer.

**Enamorarse.** To fall in love. Lover

**Enbarque.** Shipment, cargo, freight, load.

**Encaje.** Relation between the money a bank holds and the amount it can loan.

**Encalladura.** Grounding, stranding.

**Encarcelación, encarcelamiento.** Imprisonment, incarceration, jailing. Confinement.

**Encarcelar.** To imprison, incarcerate, jail. To confine, lock up.

**Encarecer.** To endear. To set higher paces.

**Encargo.** Chore, task. Request. Assignment, charge.

**Encarpetar.** To file. To receive a request.

**Encartado.** Accused, defendant.

**Encartar.** To charge with the commission of a crime. To accuse.

**Encausable.** That can be charged with a crime.

**Encausado.** Accused, defendant.

**Encausar.** To prosecute.

**Enchalecar.** To place in a straitjacket, to restrict someone's movement or options.

**Encierro, encerramiento.** Imprisonment, confinement, incarceration, jailing.

**Enclave.** Colonial possession. Region accessible only by crossing a foreign country.

**Encomendar.** To appoint, name. To charge, empower. To entrust. To recommend. To commission.

**Encomienda.** Charge, duty. Parcel.

**Encubierto.** Concealed, camouflaged, hidden.

**Encubridor.** Person who harbors a criminal, accessory to a crime.

**Encubrimiento.** Harboring a crime, concealment.

**Encuesta.** Analysis, examination, investigation. Survey, poll.

**Endeudado.** Indebted, in the red, deficitary.

**Endeudarse.** To acquire debts, liabilities, obligations.

**Endosable.** Endorsable.

**Endosado.** Endorsed, endorsee.

**Endosante.** Endorser.

**Endosar.** To endorse.

**Endosatario.** Endorsee.

**Endoso.** Endorsement. Approval, authorization, support.

**Endoso en blanco.** Blank endorsement. An endorsement in blank: does not mention endorsee and is signed by the endorser. (E.M.L. Insurance Company v. Banco Popular, 91 PRR 626 (1965)).

**Enemistad.** Enmity, animosity, antagonism, hatred, malevolence.

**Enfermedad.** Illness, ailment, disease, infirmity, malaise, malady, sickness.

**Enfiteusis.** Emphyteusis.

**Enfitéutico.** Emphyteutic.

**Enganchado.** Person who joined the professional army after completion of the military service.

**Enganche.** Clasp, crook, hook. Joining the professional army after the military service. Recruitment of soldiers.

**Engañar.** To deceive, betray, cheat, dupe, fool. To defraud, swindle.

**Engaño.** Deceit, deception, chicanery, fabrication, fraud, trickery.

**Engañoso.** Misleading, deceptive, deluding, false, fraudulent, illusive, illusory.

**Enjuiciable.** Actionable, amenable to litigation.

**Enjuiciado.** Accused, defendant.

**Enjuiciamiento.** Suit, judicial proceedings, litigation.

**Enjuiciar.** To sue, to bring to trial, to prosecute.

**Enlace.** Matrimony, nuptials, wedding, wedlock. Alliance, union. Link.

**Enmascarado.** Masked, veiled.

**Enmendadura.** Crossing out, altering a writing. Mending.

**Enmendar.** To amend, alter, change, modify. To improve, connect.

**Enmienda.** Amendment, alteration, change, modification. Legal reform. Rider. Improvement.

**Enriquecimiento.** Enrichment, financial improvement.

**Enriquecimiento ilegítimo.** Unjust enrichment. He who without cause enriches himself at the expense of another, will be obligated to indemnify the latter in the proportion that the former was enriched. (Mex. Civ. C., art. 1882).

**Enriquecimiento indebido, sin causa.** Unjust enrichment. The general principle of law based on equity called the doctrine of unjust enrichment—which, if not applied to a specific situation gives rise to the inequity that someone may unjustly enrich himself at the expense of another—operates in the entire ambit of the law—including labor law—its application not being limited to a case in which a contract or quasi-contract exists. (Silva v. Industrial Commission, 91 PRR 865 (1965)).

**Enrolamiento.** Enrollment, draft, enlistment, recruitment.

**Ensayar.** To attempt, endeavor, try.

**Ensayo.** Essay, article, thesis. Test, trial.

**Ensenada.** Roadstead.

**Enseña.** Ensign, emblem, flag.

**Enseñanza.** Teaching, education, instruction, schooling.

**Enseres.** Chattels, fixtures, furniture.

**Entablar.** To present, to file. To bring to the authority's attention. To start (legal) proceedings.

**Entablar demanda.** To file a lawsuit, sue, take to court.

**Ente, entidad.** Entity, establish-ment, institution.

**Entender.** To understand, comprehend, discern. To exercise jurisdiction in a specific case.

**Enterarse.** To realize, to get to know.

**Entero.** Whole, complete, entire, total, unbroken.

**Enterramiento, entierro.** Burial, interment, funeral.

**Entidad.** Entity. Used many times as a synonym of corporation or organization.

**Entorpecer.** To disturb, interfere, perturb, trouble, upset.

**Entrada.** Entry, admission, entrance. Booking at a police station.

**Entrada en vigor.** Effective date of a statute.

**Entrada y registro.** Entry and search. No one can enter the domicile of a Spaniard or foreigner residing in Spain without his consent, excepting in the cases and in the manner expressly provided by law.

Useless inspections shall be avoided in making the searches, it being sought not to prejudice nor importune the person interested more than necessary, and all precautions possible shall be taken not to compromise his reputation, his secrets being respected, should they not interest the investigation. (Sp. L. Crim. P., sec. 545, 552).

**Entradas.** Revenue, gains, income, profits. Entries.

**Entrampamiento.** Entrapment. For a peace officer to procure a person to commit a crime, which he otherwise would not have committed, for the purpose of apprehending and prosecuting him, is entrapment. (Ppl. v. Verdejo Meléndez, 88 PRR 202 (1963)).

**Entre.** Between.

**Entredicho.** Brawl, tussle.

**Entrega.** Delivery, consignment, dispatch, shipment. Surrender, capitulation.

**Entrega "ex-barco."** Delivery "ex-ship."

**Entrega manual.** Manual delivery.

**Entregado.** Delivered, shipped. Defeated.

**Entregador.** Person who delivers. One who betrays the confidence of a criminal and furnishes information for his arrest.

**Entregar.** To deliver, consign, dispatch, ship.

**Entregarse.** To surrender, capitulate. To abandon a fight or a struggle.

**Entrelineado, entre líneas.** Between the lines.

**Entrelinear.** To write between the lines.

**Entrevista.** Conference, meeting.

**Entuerto.** Inequitable or unjust situation.

**Enumeración.** Enumeration, list.

**Enunciado.** Said, stated.

**Enunciar.** To enunciate, announce, declare, state.

**Enunciativo.** Not strictly binding. By way of introduction or example.

**Envenenamiento.** Poisoning, contamination, infection.

**Envenenar.** To poison, contaminate, infect.

**Enviar.** To send, dispatch, direct, mail, route, ship, transmit.

**Envío.** Sending, dispatch, mailing, shipment, transmission.

**Epidemia.** Epidemic.

**Epígrafe, epígrafo.** Title, subtitle.

**Epistolar.** Related to letters, mail or missives.

**Época.** Epoch, age, period, time.

**Equidad.** Equity, fairness, justice.

**Equilibrio ecológico.** Ecological equilibrium. The interdependent relationship between elements forming the environment that make possible the existence, transformation, and development of man and other living beings.

**Equipo.** Equipment, kit, tools. Gear, outfit. Team, crew, squad.

**Equitativo.** Equitable.

**Equivalencia.** Equivalence, of similar value or strength.

**Equivocación.** Error, fault, flaw, mistake.

**Equívoco.** Equivocal, cryptic, uncertain, unclear.

**Era.** Era. The term era in Law CIII of Title XVIII of the Third Partida of the laws of the Seven Partidas means "year." (Heirs of Carrasquillo v. Registrar, 95 PRR 900 (1968)).

**Erario.** Public funds.

**Erótico.** Erotic, sexually passionate.

**Erotismo.** Eroticism.

**Erotomanía.** Erotomania.

**Error.** Mistake. Mistake is an erroneous assumption relating to facts or to law existing when the contract was concluded. (Unidroit, Prin., art. 3.4).

**Error de concepto.** Error of construction. In the mortgage law an error of construction is understood to be the one committed by a registrar when, in setting forth in the record some of the terms in the deed, their meaning is altered or changed without such fault necessarily producing the nullity thereof in accordance with the provisions of Art. 30 of the Mortgage Law. (Guibas v. Registrar, 98 PRR 563 (1970)).

**Error en la expresión o en la transmisión.** Error in expression or transmission.

An error occurring in the expression or transmission of a declaration is considered to be a mistake of the person from whom the declaration emanated. (Unidroit, Prin., art. 3.6).

**Error evidente.** Plain error.

**Error invencible (Crim.).** Invincible error. No criminal liability attaches to whoever, due to an invincible error, is convinced that the act committed is not punishable.

If the error is not invincible, the act will be punishable with a sentence not less than half the minimum, nor more than half the maximum legally prescribed for the corresponding crime. (Standard Penal C. for Latin America, sec. 28).

**Error no perjudicial.** Harmless error.

**Error no punible (Crim.).** Non-punishable error. No punishment applies to whoever performs a criminal act convinced that it lacks some element required under the corresponding statutory definition. However, if the person is recklessly or negligently mistaken, the act will be punishable only when the law contemplates the reckless or negligent commission of the criminal act.

The same rules apply to those who wrongfully assume the existence of justifying circumstances. (Standard Penal C. for Latin America, sec. 27).

**Error punible (Crim.).** Punishable error. If by a mistake the act committed was different from the one the person had in mind, the punishment corresponding to the less serious act will apply. (Standard Penal C. for Latin America, sec. 29).

**Error relevante.** Relevant mistake.

A party may only avoid the contract for mistake if, when the contract was concluded, the mistake was of such importance that a reasonable person in the same situation as the party in error would only have concluded the contract on materially different terms or would not have concluded it at all if the true state of affairs had been known, and (a) the other party made the same mistake, or caused the mistake, or knew or ought to have known of the mistake and it was contrary to reasonable commercial standards of fair dealing to leave the mistaken party in error; or (b) the other party had not at the time of avoidance acted in reliance on the contract. (Unidroit, Prin., art. 3.5).

**Error sobre la causa.** Error that concerns cause. Error may concern a cause when it bears on the nature of the contract, or the thing that is the contractual object or a substantial quality of that thing, or the person or the qualities of the other party, or the law, or any other circumstance that the parties regarded, or should in good faith have regarded, as a cause of the obligation. (Lou. Civ. C. art. 1950).

**Error sobre la persona.** Mistake, as to the person.

**Es decir.** That is, namely.

**Escala.** Scale, proportion. Stop, stopover, leg.

**Escalador.** One who climbs a wall or fence to commit a crime.

**Escalamiento.** Climbing, aggravating circumstance of a crime.

**Escalar.** To climb, ascend, escalate, mount.

**Escalo.** Aggravated type of housebreaking.

**Escamoteador.** Charlatan, cheat, con man, fraud, swindler, trickster.

**Escamotear.** To cheat, con, defraud, swindle, trick. To steal something with a sudden movement. (Slang).

**Escamoteo.** Fraud, petty theft. (Slang).

**Escándalo.** Scandal, sensation, uproar. Disgrace, embarrassment, ignominy.

**Escaño.** Bar, forum, platform, podium.

**Escapar.** To escape, break away, flee, run away.

**Escapatoria.** Outlet, only possibility left.

**Escape.** Escape, breakout, flight.

**Escapismo.** Escapism.

**Escaramuza.** Scuffle, brawl, melee, rumpus, struggle.

**Escarmiento.** Punishment or penalty aimed at preventing the party receiving it to commit the same mistake again.

**Escisión.** Surgical cut, separation, split.

**Esclavitud.** Slavery.

**Esclusa.** Water lock, sluice.

**Escondrijo.** Cache, refuge, hideout.

**Escopeta.** Rifle, firearm.

**Escribanía.** Notarial office.

**Escribano.** Notary public, notary. In Spain and in Latin America notaries are highly paid and highly respected professionals. In many cases their rank is higher than that of attorneys.

**Escribano de actuaciones.** Recording clerk.

**Escribano de cámara.** Clerk of chamber.

**Escribiente.** Court employee of low rank. Amanuensis.

**Escrito.** Written motion, brief.

**Escritorio.** Lawyer's office. Desk.

**Escritos de conclusión.** Final pleadings. The final pleadings shall be limited to the following: 1) In numbered paragraphs there shall be stated, with clearness and with the greatest possible conciseness, each one of the facts which have been the object of the contention, making a short and methodic brief of the evidence which, in the judgment each party, sustains or disproves them. 2) In paragraphs, also brief and numbered, and following the same order as that of the facts, the evidence of the opposite party shall be discussed. 3) The principles of law respectively alleged in the complaint and answer, and, in a proper case, in the replication and rejoinder, shall be fully and concisely stated, if contended or in whole or in part. (Sp. L. Civ. P. sec. 669).

**Escritura.** Deed. Certificate, document. Something in writing.

**Escritura de traspaso.** Deed of conveyance.

**Escritura de venta.** Deed, bill of sale.

**Escritura sobre un derecho inmobiliario.** Indenture.

**Escriturar.** To sign a deed. To convey real estate. To file a document with a notary public.

**Escrúpulo.** Scruples, morals, mores. Ethical standards.

**Escrutinio.** Counting of votes.

**Escudo de armas.** Coat of arms.

**Escuela.** School, trend of thought.

**Esencial.** Essential, basic, main, most important. Indispensable.

**Espacio.** Space, cosmos, galaxy, universe. Expanse, distance. Gap. Locale, place.

**Espalda.** Back. Reverse. End, rear.

**Espaldas, a.** Surreptitiously, covertly, secretly.

**Especialidad.** Specialty, speciality. Professional interest or activity.

**Especie.** Specie, category, class, kind, type, variety. Currency, legal tender.

**Especies.** Goods, commodities, merchandise, wares.

**Especificaciones.** Specification, classification, designation.

**Especificar.** To specify, classify.

**Especioso.** Deceptive, false, misleading.

**Especulativo.** Speculative, uncertain. With the intention of making a profit.

**Espera.** Waiting, deferment, delay, postponement, reprieve, respite, stay, time extension.

**Esperma.** Sperm.

**Espía.** Spy, secret agent, double agent. Undercover detective.

**Espionage.** Espionage, spying, surveillance.

**Espíritu.** Spirit, goal, objective of a law.

**Esponsales.** Betrothal, engagement, espousal.

**Esposa.** Wife, consort, spouse.

**Esposas.** Manacles, handcuffs.

**Esposo.** Husband, consort, spouse.

**Espureo, espurio.** Spurious, bogus, fake, false, fraudulent, treacherous.

**Esquela.** Short letter, note.

**Esqueleto.** Skeleton.

**Esquilmar.** To wipe out, to swindle.

**Esquizofrenia.** Schizophrenia.

**Estabilidad.** Stability, aplomb, balance, calm, equilibrium, poise, steadiness.

**Establecer.** To establish, found, install, settle. To prove, to obtain a finding.

**Establecido.** Established. Provided, agreed, settled.

**Establecimiento.** Establishment, concern, business. Settlement, colony.

**Estación.** Station, base, camp, position, post. Season, term, time.

**Estadía.** Stay, sojourn, stopover, visit.

**Estadista.** Statesman.

**Estadística.** Statistics.

**Estado.** State. Country, kingdom, land, nation, republic. Condition, circumstances, situation. Status. Civil status.

**Estado civil, modificación.** Civil status, modification. The judicial authorities that declare a person's absence, guardianship, presumption of death, divorce, or loss or limitations in the competency to administer assets, will transmit to the corresponding judge of the Civil Registry, within eight days, a certified copy of the respective decree. (Mex. Civ. C., art.131).

**Estado de buena fe civil.** Status of civil good faith. This name designates that requisite demanded from a person who alleges being a third-party mortgagee, consisting in that status which shows that the subsequent acquirer of a real property or of a promissory note guaranteed by mortgage did not have knowledge outside of the registry of property about the "disagreement" of the facts between what appeared in the registry at the time of the acquisition and what the reality could be. (Sánchez v. Colón, 97 PRR 481 (1969)).

**Estado de cuenta.** Bank statement, statement of account.

**Estados Unidos (de América).** United States of America, U.S.A., U.S., America.

**Estafa.** Fraud, hoax, swindle.

**Estafador.** Swindler, charlatan, cheat, con man, crook, fraud.

**Estafar.** To cheat, con, defraud, swindle. To dupe, fool. To misrepresent, mislead.

**Estampar.** Affix, place, stamp.

**Estampilla.** Stamp, mark, seal.

**Estancia.** Stay, sojourn, stopover, visit. Ranch.

**Estanco.** Small retail business where goods monopolized by the state—such as tobacco and lottery tickets—are sold. (SP).

**Estatal.** Related to the state or government.

**Estatismo.** Statism, publicism.

**Estatuir.** To establish, command, decree, enact, legislate, order, pass.

**Estatutario.** Statutory.

**Estatuto.** Statute, edict, mandate, regulation. Articles of incorporation, bylaws.

**Estelionato.** Stellionate.

**Esterilidad.** Sterility, impotency, infertility.

**Estiba.** Stowage.

**Estibador.** Longshoreman, stevedore.

**Estilo.** Style, method, technique. Elegance.

**Estimación.** Estimation, estimate, appraisal, calculation, evaluation. Fondness, estime.

**Estimar.** To estimate, appraise, assess, evaluate. Guess, reckon. To be fond of.

**Estimativo.** Estimated, appraised, assessed.

**Estipendio.** Stipend, allowance, grant, subsidy.

**Estipulación.** Stipulation, clause, condition, proviso, term.

**Estipulación de hechos.** Agreed statement of facts.

**Estipulaciones sorpresivas.** Surprising terms. No term contained in standard terms which is of such a character that the other party could not reasonably have expected it, is effective unless it has been expressly accepted by the party. (Unidroit, Prin., art. 2.20).

**Estipulante.** Stipulator, party to a contract, offeror or offeree.

**Estipular.** To stipulate, provide, specify.

**Estirpe.** Stirpes. Descendance, family origin, lineage.

**Estorbar.** To annoy, bother, vex. To disturb, interfere, molest.

**Estorbo.** Nuisance, annoyance, hindrance, obstacle.

**Estrado.** Platform, podium, pulpit, stage.

**Estrangulación.** Strangulation, strangling, asphyxiation, choking, smothering, suffocation.

**Estrangulador.** Strangler.

**Estrangular.** To strangle, asphyxiate, choke, smother, suffocate.

**Estraperlo.** Profiteering, black market, opportunism.

**Estropear.** To spoil, decay, decompose, go off, rot.

**Estructura.** Structure, building, edifice. Formation, organization, pattern. Composition.

**Estructura legal, México.** Legal structure, Mexico. Mexico's 1917 Constitution contains a broad grant of powers to the federal government, including the power to legislate with respect to hydrocarbons, mining, commerce, money, banking and credit, communications, nuclear and electrical energy, foreign investment, technology, and labor.' Powers not expressly granted to the federal government are reserved to the states.' Unlike the other Latin American countries, Mexico permits the states to enact their own basic codes, with the exception of commercial and labor codes. Nonetheless, the states' civil, criminal, criminal procedure, and civil procedure codes are virtually carbon copies of the codes for the federal district. (Rosenn).

**Estudiantes de derecho.** Law students. Latin American law students typically enter law school immediately after secondary school, or after a brief cram course to enable them to pass university entrance examinations. The only general liberal arts training they receive at the university comes during the first two years of law school, when political science, economics, history, and sociology courses are mixed with some perspective courses like Introduction to the Science of Law. The remaining three years are devoted almost exclusively to required legal subjects. (L & D in LA).

**Estudiar.** To study, analyze, examine, investigate, research, scrutinize.

**Estudio.** Study, education, learning. Analysis, investigation. Law firm.

**Estupefaciente.** Narcotic, barbiturate, drugs, hallucinogen.

**Estúpido.** Stupid, dimwit, moronic, obtuse.

**Estupro.** Sexual intercourse with someone below the legal age for informed consent. Rape.

**Ética.** Ethics, morals, professional standards.

**Ético.** Ethical.

**Eufiteuta.** Emphyteuticary.

**Eutanasia.** Euthanasia.

**Evacuación.** Evacuation, depletion. Abandonment, removal.

**Evacuar.** To evacuate, deplete, empty. To abandon, leave, vacate.

**Evadido.** Escaped prisoner.

**Evadir.** To evade, avoid, dodge, escape.

**Evaluación.** Evaluation, appraisal, estimation, estimate, calculation.

**Evaluar.** To evaluate, appraise, assess estimate.

**Evasión.** Escape, breakout, flight. Tax fraud, underreporting, nonreporting.

**Evasiva.** Ambiguous and evasive conduct.

**Evasivo.** Evasive, ambiguous, elusive, slippery.

**Evasor.** Tax evader.

**Evento.** Event, circumstance, happening, incident, occurrence.

**Eventual.** Eventual, conceivable, contingent, feasible, possible, potential.

**Eventualidad.** Eventuality, chance, likehood, possibility, probability, prospect.

**Evicción.** Eviction. Eviction is the loss suffered by the buyer of the totality of the thing sold, or of a part thereof, occasioned by the right or claims of a third person. (Lou. Civ. C. art. 2500).

Ejection, expulsion, ouster, removal, throwing out.

**Evicción en saneamiento.** Eviction, warranty. For the effects of the obligation of a vendor to give a warranty, eviction means to defeat at a trial and it means the loss of a right as a consequence of a judicial judgment. (Ferrer v. General Motors Corp., 100 PRR 244 (1971)).

**Evidencia.** Evidence, proof, showing. Corroboration, indication.

**Evidencia circunstancial.** Circumstantial evidence. Circumstantial evidence is nothing more than the inferences—deductions which the reason of the judge or jury make —said to arise from a series of proven facts. (Ppl. v. Cortes, 86 PRR 208 (1962)).

**Evidenciar.** To evidence, prove, show.

**Evidente.** Evident, conspicuous, obvious.

**Evitable.** Avoidable, escapable, preventable.

**Evitar el abuso de derecho.** Avoid abuse of right. The principle of avoiding the "abuse of right" means avoiding that juridical situation which, though legal in the ordinary course of the contract, results in evident inequality between the obligations. (Rodríquez v. Lema, 87 PRR 587 (1963)).

**Evocación.** Evocation, commemoration, memorial, remembrance.

**Exacción.** Exaction, forced contribution.

**Exactor.** One who obtains an exaction.

**Exageración.** Exaggeration, overstatement, stretching of the truth.

**Examen.** Exam, examination, test. Analysis, inspection, research, scruting.

**Examinador.** Examiner, professor, teacher. Tribunal, jury.

**Examinar.** To examine, review, test. To analyze, inspect, research, scrutinize.

**Excarcelación.** Release from jail on parole or because the arrest warrant is quashed.

**Excarcelar.** To excarcelate. To release from jail.

**Excedente.** Excess, balance, surplus.

**Excepción.** Exception. Appeal, objection, procedural recourse. Anomaly, irregularity. Exclusion, exemption.

**Excepción previa.** Demurrer.

**Excepcionable.** That admits an appeal, objection or procedural recourse.

**Excepcionar.** To appeal or object.

**Excepciones de previo pronunciamiento.** Preliminary exceptions. The following questions or pleas shall be the subject of preliminary exceptions: 1) a declinatory plea; 2) a plea of *res judicata*; 3) the prescription (statute of limitations) of a crime; 4) the plea of amnesty or pardon; 5) the lack of administrative authority to conduct proceedings in cases in which it is necessary in accordance with the constitution and special laws. (Sp. L. Crim. P., sec. 666).

**Excepciones dilatorias.** Dilatory exceptions. If the defendant should plead any dilatory exception, he shall not be obliged to answer the complaint until the same has been disposed of, which must always be done before any further proceeding in the action. The following only shall be admissible as dilatory exceptions: 1) Lack of jurisdiction. 2) Want of personality on the part of the plaintiff on account of the lack of some qualification necessary to appear in an action, or because he does not prove the character or representative capacity under which he sues. 3) The want of personality in the solicitor of the plaintiff, on account of the insuffi-

ciency or illegality of the power to attorney. 4) Want of personality on the part of the defendant, because he does not have the character or representative capacity under which he is sued. 5) The pendency of another action in another competent superior or inferior court. 6) A legal defect in the manner in which the complaint is made. It shall be understood that this defect exists when the general requisites are not complied with in the complaint. 7) The absence of a prior demand made administratively, when the complaint is directed against the public treasury. (Sp. L. Civ. P. sec. 531-533).

*Exceptio non adimpleti contractus* **(L).** Literally it means "exception of non-fulfilled contract". It is raised by the defendant when plaintiff himself has not performed his side of the contract.

*Exceptio veritatis* **(L).** Raising truth as a defense, for instance in an action for slander.

**Exceptuar.** To except, exempt. To exclude, reject.

**Excesiva onerosidad.** Hardship. There is hardship where the occurrence of events fundamentally alters the equilibrium of the contract either because the cost of a party's performance has increased of because the value of the performance a party receives has diminished, and (a) the events occur or become known to the disadvantaged party after the conclusion of the contract; (b) the events could not reasonably have been taken into account by the disadvantaged party at the time of the conclusion of the contract; (c) the events are beyond the control of the disadvantaged party; and (d) the risk of the events was not assumed by the disadvantaged party. (Unidroit, Prin., art. 6.2.2).

**Excesiva onerosidad, efectos.** Hardship, effects.

(1) In case of hardship the disadvantaged party is entitled to request renegotiations. The request shall be made without undue delay and shall indicate the grounds on which it is based. (2) The request for renegotiation does not in itself entitle the disadvantaged party to withhold performance. (3) Upon failure to reach agreement within a reasonable time either party may resort to the court. (4) If the court finds hardship it

may, if reasonable, (a) terminate the contract at a date and on terms to be fixed; or (b) adapt the contract with a view to restoring its equilibrium. (Unidroit, Prin., art. 6.2.3).

**Exceso.** Excess, balance, surplus.

**Excitación.** Excitement, exhilaration, thrill. Instigation, encouragement, incitement.

**Exclusión.** Exclusion, exception, barring, expulsion, prohibition, removal.

**Exclusivista.** Exclusivist, elitist.

**Exclusivo.** Exclusive.

**Excluyente.** Excluding factor.

**Exculpación.** Exculpation, absolution, acquittal, exoneration.

**Excursión.** Excursion, expedition, voyage.

**Excusa.** Excuse, apology, justification, extenuating circumstance.

**Excusar.** To excuse, forgive.

**Excusarse.** To apologize. To withdraw.

**Exención.** Exemption, exclusion, pardon, reprieve.

**Exención contributiva.** Tax exemption.

**Exento.** Exempt, exonerated, liberated.

**Exequatur.** Procedure or order to enforce a foreign judgment. Let it be enforced (lit.).

**Exequatur, Chile.** Exequatur, Chile. The Chilean Supreme Court has exclusive jurisdiction to review the enforcement application and to decide on whether to grant the *exequatur*. A legalized and translated transcript of the judgment must be filed with the applications. The enforcement application will be transmitted to the party against whom enforcement is sought and to the Office of the Attorney General. If the Supreme Court grants the *exequatur*, the matter is referred to the lower court which would have had jurisdiction had the original lawsuit been brought in Chile. (Amado).

**Exhibición.** Exhibition, display, showing. Presentation in court.

**Exhibicionismo.** Exhibitionism.

**Exhibir.** To exhibit, display, show.

**Exhibitorio.** Exhibitory.

**Exhortante.** Judge who issues a letter requisitorial.

**Exhortar.** Sending of a letter requisitorial by one court to another. To exhort, implore, pray, request.

**Exhorto.** Letter requisitorial, letter rogatory.

**Exhorto, Convención Interamericana.** Letter Rogatory, Inter-American Convention On Letters Rogatory. This Convention shall apply to letter rogatory, issued in conjunction with proceedings in civil and commercial matters held before the appropriate authority of one of the States Parties to this Convention, that have as their purpose: a. The performance of procedural acts of a merely formal nature, such as service of process, summonses or subpoenas abroad; b. The taking of evidence and the obtaining of information abroad, unless a reservation is made in this respect. (Inter-American Convention On Letters Rogatory, arts. 2, 13, and 16).

**Exhorto, ejecución.** Letters rogatory, execution.
Letter rogatory shall be executed in accordance with the laws and procedural rules of the State of destination. (Inter-American Convention On Letters Rogatory, art. 10).

**Exhorto, formalidades.** Letter rogatory, formalities. The formalities of execution of letters rogatory are subject to the laws of the country where the witnesses are to be examined. Nevertheless, the examination and the weight of the evidence obtained are governed by the *lex fori* and *lex rei sitate*. (LA Laws & Inst.).

**Exhorto, gastos.** Letter rogatory, expenses. The costs and other expenses involved in the processing and execution of letters rogatory shall be borne by the interested parties. The effects of a declaration *in forma pauperis* shall be regulated by the law of the State of destination. (Inter-American Convention On Letters Rogatory, art. 12).

**Exhorto, interés estatal.** Letters Rogatory, public policy. The State of destination may refuse to execute a letter rogatory that is manifestly contrary to its public policy ("ordre public"). (Inter-American Convention On Letters Rogatory, art. 17).

**Exhorto internacional.** International letter rogatory. Letters rogatory directed to foreign courts shall be sent through diplomatic channels in the manner prescribed by treaty, and in the absence thereof, as prescribed by the general regulations of the government. In all other cases principles of reciprocity shall govern. (Sp. L. Crim. P., art. 193).

**Exhorto, jurisdicción.** Letter rogatory, jurisdiction. The authority of the State of destination shall have the jurisdiction to determine any issue arising as a result of the execution of the measure requested in the letter rogatory. Should such authority find that it lacks jurisdiction to execute the letter rogatory, it shall *ex officio* forward the documents and antecedents of the case to the authority of the State which has jurisdiction. (Inter-American Convention On Letters Rogatory, art. 11).

**Exhorto, reconocimiento.** Letter Rogatory, recognition. Execution of letters rogatory shall not imply ultimate recognition of the jurisdiction of the authority issuing the letter rogatory or a commitment to recognize the validity of the judgment it may render or to execute it. (Inter-American Convention On Letters Rogatory, art. 9).

**Exhumación.** Exhumation, disinterment.

**Exigencia.** Demand, command, order, requirement.

**Exigibilidad.** Demandability, with binding force.

**Exigible.** Demandable, past and clue, matured.

**Exigir.** To demand, command, order, require.

**Exilio.** Exile, banishment, expulsion. Ostracism.

**Eximente.** Exempting, exculpatory, exonerating.

**Eximir.** To exempt, excuse, exculpate, exonerate, pardon.

**Existencia.** Existence. Permanence. Merchandise in stock.

**Exoneración.** Exoneration, exemption, pardon, release.

**Exoneración en quiebra.** Discharge in bankruptcy.

**Exonerar.** To exonerate, exempt, pardon.

**Exorbitante.** Exorbitant. Too big, costly or powerful. Outrageous.

**Exordio.** Presentation of a brief or motion where the petitioner states introductory matters.

**Expectante.** Expectant, hopeful, waiting.

**Expectativa.** Expectation, anticipation, foreseeability.

**Expedición.** Expedition, excursion. Consignment, dispatch, shipment. Sending, mailing.

**Expedidor.** Shipper, dispatcher, sender.

**Expediente.** File, dossier, record. Practical maneuver to achieve a result.

**Expediente de apelación.** Record of appeal.

**Expedir.** To ship, dispatch, mail, send.

**Expeler.** To expel, discharge, dismiss, eliminate, evacuate.

**Expendedor.** Dealer, dispenser, distributor, merchant, middleman, retailer.

**Expender.** To deal, dispense, market. To consume, disburse, spend.

**Expensas.** Legal costs. Charges, expenditure, expense.

**Experto.** Expert, authority, professional, specialist.

**Expiación.** Expiation, atonement, penance.

**Expiar.** To expiate, to undergo punishment, to serve a sentence.

**Expiración.** Expiration, end of a term or period. Cessation, finish, termination. Death.

**Expirar.** To expire, conclude, lapse, terminate. To die, perish.

**Explicable.** Explicable, discernable, understandable. Logical.

**Explicativo.** Explanatory. Precatory, not binding.

**Explícito.** Explicit, clear, precise, specific.

**Exploración.** Exploration. Works carried out on the ground with the purpose of identifying mineral deposits, as well as quantifying and evaluating the economically usable reserves contained therein.

**Explosión.** Explosion, blast, outburst.

**Explotación.** Exploitation. Marketing, commercial use.

**Explotador.** Person who develops a commercial opportunity. Pimp.

**Expoliación.** Spoliation. Abuse, misuse.

**Expoliar.** To abuse, misuse, mishandle, mistreat.

**Exponente.** Exponent. Person who testifies or deposes. Model or standard.

**Exponer.** To declare, demonstrate, explain, show, state.

**Exportación.** Export, exportation, international sales.

**Exportar.** To export, to sell or market abroad.

**Exposición.** Statement, account, assertion, declaration, report, statement.

**Exposición de motivos.** Statement of motives, of legislative intent.

**Expósito.** Foundling, abandoned child.

**Expositor.** Person who declares or states.

**Expresar.** To express, communicate, convey, declare, state, say, verbalize.

**Expreso.** Express. Intentional, deliberate, premeditated. With full knowledge.

***Expressio unius est exclusio alterius* (L).** Literally it means that what is specifically included excludes what is not. A technique of legislative interpretation assuming that, when a statute mentions something specifically—e.g. list of reasons for which a will may be challenged—it is implicitly banning any other grounds.

**Expropiable.** Condemnable, expropriable.

**Expropiación inversa.** Inverse condemnation.

**Expropiación.** Expropriation, condemnation. The first law of society being that the general interest shall be preferred to that of individuals, every individual who possesses under the protection of the laws, any particular property, is tacitly subjected to the obligation of yielding it to the community, wherever it becomes necessary for the general use.

If the owner of a thing necessary for the general use, refuses to yield it, or demands an exorbitant price, he may be divested of the property by the authority of law.

In all cases, a fair price should be given to the owner for the thing of which he is dispossessed. (Lou. Civ. C. art. 2626, 2627, and 2628).

**Expropiado.** Person whose property is condemned.

**Expropiador.** Party who expropriates, the state.

**Expropiar.** To condemn, expropriate.

**Expulsar.** To expel, discharge, dismiss, fire, eliminate, evacuate.

**Expulsión.** Expulsion, discharge, dismissal. Ejection, eviction.

**Extender.** To extend, enlarge, lengthen. To present to another party.

**Extensible.** Extendible, prolongable.

**Extensión.** Extension. Continuation, postponement. Length.

**Extinción.** Extinction, cessation, conclusion, ending.

**Extinguir.** To extinguish, end, terminate. To put out, to smother.

**Extinguirse.** To cease, expire, lapse, terminate.

**Extintivo.** Extinctive.

**Extorsión.** Extortion, blackmail, bribery, duress, intimidation.

**Extorsionador, extorsionista.** Extortioner.

**Extorsionar.** To blackmail. To exact a sum of money. To coerce payment.

**Extorsivo.** Extortionate, exorbitant, outrageous.

***Extra petitum* (L).** Part of the judgment that awards a relief not requested.

**Extracción.** Extraction, pulling, removal.

**Extracontractual.** Derived from a source other than a contract.

**Extraconyugal.** Extraconjugal.

**Extracto.** Abstract, excerpt, summary, synopsis. Extract.

**Extradición, Código Bustamante.** Extradition, Bustamante Code. In order to render effective the international judicial competence in penal matters, each of the States shall accede to the request of any of the others for the delivery of persons convicted or accused of crime, if in conformity with the provisions of this title, subject to the dispositions of the international treaties and conventions containing a list of penal infractions which authorize the extradition. (Bustamante C. art. 344).

**Extraditable.** Extraditable. Subject to extradition.

**Extrajudicial.** Extrajudicial, without the court's intervention, privately.

**Extralimitación.** Trespass, breach, infringement, violation.

**Extranjería.** Alienage.

**Extranjero.** Alien, foreigner, immigrant, stranger.

**Extraoficial.** Not public yet, confidential.

**Extraterritorial.** Extraterritorial, international.

**Extraviado.** Lost.

**Extravío.** Loss of a thing, of sense of direction or of sanity.

**Extremo.** Extreme, excessive, exorbitant, unreasonable. Farthest, most removed.

**Extrínsico.** Extrinsic, external, on the surface.

**EXW. En Fábrica (...lugar convenido).** EXW. Ex Works (...named place). "Ex works" means that the seller fulfills his obligation to deliver when he has made the goods available at his premises (i.e. works, factory, warehouse, etc.) to the buyer. In particular, he is not responsible for loading the goods on the vehicle provided by the buyer or for clearing the goods for export, unless otherwise agreed. (Incoterms).

# F

**Fábrica.** Factory, mill, plant, workshop, works.

**Fabricación.** Manufacture, manufacturing, building, construction, production.

**Fabricado.** Fabricated, trumped. Manufactured.

**Facción.** Faction, divergence, split. On duty, watchman.

**Fachada.** Facade, front.

**Facilidades de pago.** Extension of credit, payment by installments.

**Facilitar.** To facilitate, assist, ease. To furnish, loan, provide.

**Facsimil.** Facsimile. Exact copy, duplicate or reproduction from the original. Fax.

**Factor.** Factor, component, element. Clerk, commercial agent, store keeper.

**Factoring.** Factoring.

**Factura.** Invoice, bill, charges. Manufacture.

**Facturar.** To bill, charge, invoice.

**Facultad.** Faculty, ability, capability. Authority, authorization, right. Body of professors, college.

**Facultades y deberes del tribunal.** Powers and duties of the court. The court must treat the petition, requests, recourse and motions in the way the law indicates, even if the way suggested by the parties is erroneous.

Magistrates and Judges have the general duties: [...]

To indicate what is wrong with pleadings (*funciones de saneamiento*) *sua sponte*;

To rule *sua sponte (de oficio)* on the procedural steps conducive to avoid procedural nullities [...] (Panamanian Judicial Code, arts. 471 and 199).

**Facultar.** To authorize, empower, license, permit.

**Facultativo.** Optional, discretional, elective, permissive, voluntary.

**Faena.** Labor, chore, job, task, work.

**Fajo.** Bundle, neat packet or parcel.

**Falacia.** Fallacy, falsehood, fiction. Deceit clothed as truth.

**Falaz.** Fallacious.

**Falencia.** Bankruptcy, insolvency. Defect, deficiency, flaw.

**Falla.** Failure, breakdown, deficiency, insufficiency. Error, fault, mistake. Defect, flaw.

**Fallar.** To fail, breakdown, to make a mistake. To enter a judgment or a ruling.

**Fallecimiento.** Death. Bankruptcy.

**Fallecimiento, notificación.** Death, notice. All persons who reside at the house where the death occurred; the directors or administrators of the detention centers, hospitals, colleges or any other community housing, the guests of the hotels, inns or neighborhoods, have the obligation to notify the Civil Registry judge. (Mex. Civ. C., art. 120).

**Fallido.** Bankrupt, insolvent, broke, ruined.

**Fallir.** To go bankrupt.

**Fallo.** Judgment, decision, order, ruling, veredict. Conclusion, opinion.

**Falsa representación.** Misrepresentation.

**Falsario.** Forger, falsifier.

**Falseado.** Forged, counterfeit, insincere, untrue.

**Falsear.** To falsify, counterfeit, doctor, forge. To lie, misrepresent.

**Falsedad.** Falsehood, fabrication, fib, invention, lie.

**Falsía.** Deceit, backstabbing, deception, duplicity.

**Falsificación.** Falsification, forgery, fabrication, fake, imitation, reproduction.

**Falsificador.** Forger, falsifier.

**Falsificar.** To falsify, counterfeit, fake, forge, reproduce.

**Falso.** False, bogus, counterfeit, fraudulent, sham, spurious. Disloyal, treacherous, unfaithful, untrue.

**Falso testimonio.** Perjury, lying under oath.

**Falta.** Fault, defect, deficiency. Blame, culpability, liability. Error, mistake. Shortage, lack of, scarcity. Misdemeanor, offense, tort, traffic violation, violation, wrong.

**Falta de competencia.** Want of competence, lack of jurisdiction.

**Falta de pago.** Nonpayment, default, dishonor.

**Falta grave.** Gross negligence.

**Faltante de caja.** Missing cash.

**Faltar.** To commit a fault, a wrong. To be absent. To be lacking in something.

**Fama.** Fame, notoriety, prominence, renown, reputation, repute.

**Familla.** Family. Family in a limited sense, signifies father, mother, and children. In a more extensive sense, it comprehends all the individuals who live under the authority of another, and includes the servants of the family. It is also employed to signify all the relations who descend from a common root. (Lou. Civ. C. art. 3556). Common ancestry, offspring, progeny, relatives. Category, class.

**Fardo.** Bale.

**Faro.** Lighthouse, strong light, beacon.

**FAS. Franco Al Costado Del Buque (...puerto de carga convenido).** FAS. Free Alongside Ship (...named port of shipment). "Free Alongside Ship" means that the seller fulfills his obligation to deliver when the goods have been placed alongside the vessel on the quay or in lighters at the named port of shipment. This means that the buyer has to bear all costs and risks of loss of or damage to the goods from that moment. (Incoterms).

**Fatal.** Fatal, deadly, lethal. Fateful, inevitale, unavoidable. Destructive, disastrous. Final, not extendable.

**Fauna silvestre.** Wild fauna. All terrestrial animal species who exist subject to natural selection processes that inhabit either temporarily or permanently live on national territories, including once domesticated animals that have been abandoned or returned to their natural habitat. Any development of fauna natural resources, areas or habitats, especially when endangered species are involved, must occur in a manner that does not alter the necessary conditions for the subsistence, development and evolution of such species.

**Fautor.** Abettor, accessory, promoter, supporter.

**Favor.** Favor, accommodation, courtesy, gesture, service.

**Favorecedor.** One who favors or supports something.

**Favorecido.** Person who receives a favor or any kind of advantage. Winner.

**FCA. Franco Transportista (...lugar cnvenido).** FCA. Free Carrier (... named place). "Free Carrier" means that the seller fulfills his obligation to deliver when he has handed over the goods, cleared for export, into the charge of the carrier named by the buyer at the named place or point. If no precise point is indicated by the buyer, the seller may choose within the place or range stipulated, where the carrier shall take the goods into his charge. When, according to commercial practice, the seller's assistance is required in making the contract with the carrier (such as in rail or air transport) the seller may act at the buyer's risk and expense. (Incoterms).

**Fe.** Faith, conviction. Belief, credence, confidence. Evidence, persuasion, proof.

**Fe de bautizmo.** Proof of baptism, birth certificate.

**Fe de erratas.** Erratum.

**Fe notarial.** Notarial certification.

**Fecha.** Date, day, time. Done, made (old Spanish).

**Fecha cierta.** Day certain.

**Fecha de vigencia.** Effective date.

**Fechar.** To date.

**Fecho.** Done, made, accomplished, achieved, executed, performed (old Spanish but still used as a term of art).

**Fechoría.** Illegal behavior. Highly offensive conduct. Wrong doing.

**Fedatario.** Notary public. Professional who certifies as to the truth or authencity of acts performed before him.

**Federación.** Federation, alliance, association, coalition, compact, confederation, league.

**Federal.** Federal, nation wide.

**Federalismo.** Federalism. The federalist traditions of Canada and the U.S., although they differ in various important respects, are quite distinct from those of Latin America. Canada and the U.S. were colonized by Great Britain, which allowed its colonies substantial freedom in governing themselves. In both countries, federalism was perceived as a useful technique for integrating substantially autonomous colonies into a single nation. Latin America, on the other hand, was colonized by Spain and Portugal, whose heavily centralized regimes permitted their colonies little freedom to govern their own affairs. In Latin America, federalism was perceived as a means to decentralize governments that had been heavily concentrated. Both the U.S. and Canada, with the exception of Quebec, were products of colonizations that synthesized Protestantism. Locke's social compact theory, and the natural rights of Englishmen. This North American inheritance of theology and political theory was far more conducive to the structured dispersal of power among many regional centers than Latin America's inheritance of the centralized, hierarchical organization of Roman Catholicism and Bourbon absolutism. It should not be surprising, therefore, that power in all the Latin American federal nations is far more centralized than in Canada or the U.S. (Rosenn).

**Federalismo, comparación.** Federalism, comparison. The text of the constitutions of Argentina, Brazil, Mexico, and Venezuela sugests that these countries have federal systems that resemble the U.S. and Canada. But the reality is quite different. Political power has been so heavily centralized in the national governments, particularly in the executive, that, with the exception of Brazil, the states or provinces have minimal autonomy. On the other hand, the power of the central governments has not always penetrated into the interior of these countries, which traditionally have been ruled by local large landholders or *caudillos*. A strong *de facto* system of local rule emerged in Latin America, despite what the laws or constitutions proclaimed. (Rosenn).

**Federalismo, economía.** Federalism, economy. Argentina, Brazil, Mexico, and Venezuela have not had similar court battles about federalist constraints upon the powers of the federal government to regulate the economy. This is partly because they are civil law countries whose legal systems are

predicated upon basic codes, and the constitutions of all these countries have conferred the power to enact the commercial codes upon the federal government. It is also partly because frequent periods of political instability have led to domination of the states and provinces by the central government through military intervention and frequent changes in constitutional texts. (Rosenn).

**Federalismo, México.** Federalism, Mexico. In theory, federalism has been the Mexican form of political organization since its first constitution in 1822, when there were twenty-two states. Article 40 of the Mexican Constitution characterizes the country as a `representative, democratic, and federal republic formed by free and sovereign states in all manners concerning their internal governments, but united in a stabilized federation—Article 124, modeled after the 10th Amendment to the U.S. Constitution, provides that the powers of the federal government are limited to those specifically delineated, the remainder being reserved for the states. But Mexico, like Argentina, suffers from what the late Carlos Nino called "hyperpresidentialism." Virtually all real political power is concentrated in the federal government, and more precisely in the hands of the president and the PRI. Decentralization did increase somewhat in the six years under President Salinas, but what Jorge Carpizo wrote in 1973 is essentially true today: A good part of the federated states' autonomy is under central will. In this fashion, what really exists in Mexico is a centralized government with some decentralized aspects. (Rosenn).

**Federalismo, Venezuela.** Federalism, Venezuela. Venezuela's 1961 Constitution grants to the national government a broad array of powers covering virtually all aspects of a modern state, such as foreign affairs, defense, naturalization, currency, taxation, armed forces, mineral resources, expropriation, navigation, transportation, communications, banking, and agrarian reform. Like Brazil's, Venezuela's Constitution also grants the national government the power to enact civil, commercial, criminal, and procedural codes, in addition to a broad specific grant of powers to the federal government, the Venezuelan Constitution also gives the federal government power over all other matters that this Constitution attributes to the National Power or which corresponds to it by its type or nature. The counties (municipios) are granted the power to regulate local concerens, such as urban growth, traffic, culture, health, social assistance, and popular credit institutions. On the other hand, the states are granted virtually no significant powers other than organizing their own governments. Although the states have the residual powers, the powers granted to the federal government are so broad that little is left to the various states. To counterbalance this centralist tilt, the federal legislature, by two-thirds vote, may grant powers to the states in the intrest of decentralization. (Rosenn).

**Federalizar.** To federalize.

**Federarse.** To become a member of a federation, association or a similar collective body.

**Fehaciente.** That carries probative value as to its authenticity. Authentic, credible, dependable, reliable, truthful.

**Felón.** Felon, criminal, convict, law-breaker, malefactor, offender, outlaw.

**Felonía.** Felonious conduct, criminal act, crime. Betrayal, perfidy.

**Feria.** Market, fair. Legal holiday when courts are closed.

**Feriado.** Holiday, leave, vacation.

**Ferrocarril.** Railroad, railway (G.B.).

**Feticida.** Person who commits a feticide.

**Feticidio.** Feticide, abortion.

**Feudo.** Feud.

**Fiable.** Dependable, reliable, trustworthy.

**Fiado.** Sale of goods on credit.

**Fiador.** Person who extends credit. Bailor, guarantor, surety.

**Fiador-solidario.** Joint-surety. In the relations between a creditor, a joint debtor and a mere surety there exists another eclectic figure, which as a matter of fact and law participates simultaneously of the nature of the figure of the joint debtor and the surety, called the joint-surety, who is the person who signs an obligation as joint debtor for the only purpose of allowing that a loan be granted to the principal debtor, and who has no personal or monetary interest in obtaining same and does not benefit himself from the transaction. (Carr v. Nones, 98 PRR 230 (1970)).

**Fianza.** Security. By security a person binds himself to pay or perform for a third person in case the latter should fail to do so.

The security may be conventional, legal, or judicial, gratuitous, or for a valuable consideration. It may also be constituted, not only in favor of the principal debtor, but in favor of the other surety, either with the consent, ignorance, and even against the opposition of the latter. A surety may bind himself to less but not to more than the principal debtor as in quantity as well as to the burden of the conditions. Should he have bound himself for more, his obligation shall be reduced to the limits of that of the debtor.

Security is not presumed; it must be express and can not be extended further than that specified therein.

Bond, collateral, guarantee.

**Fianza (Crim.).** Bail (Crim.). In order to determine the amount and character of the bail, the naure of the crime, the social status and the antecedents of the accused shall be taken into consideration, as well as all other circumstances which may bear upon the greatr or lesser interest of the latter to place himself beyond the jurisdiction of the judicial authority.

The purpose of the bail shall be to answer for the appearance of the accused when called by the judge or court taking cognizance of the cause. (Sp. L. Crim. P., art. 531 and 532).

**Fianza comercial.** Commercial surety—ship. A commercial suretyship is one in which: 1) The surety is engaged in a surety business; 2) The principal obligor or the surety is a business corporation, partnership, or other business entity; 3) The principal obligation arises out of a commercial transaction of the principal obligor; or 4) The suretyship arises out of a commercial transaction of the surety. (Lou. Civ. C. art. 3042).

**Fianza legal.** Legal suretyship. A legal suretyship is one given pursuant to legislation, administrative act or regulation, or court order. (Lou. Civ. C. art. 3043).

**Fianza ordinaria.** Ordinary suretyship. An ordinary suretyship is one that is neither a commercial suretyship nor a legal suretyship. An ordinary suretyship must be strictly construed in favor of the surety. (Lou. Civ. C. art. 3044).

**Fianza para auto de suspensión.** Supersedeas bond.

**Fiar.** To extend credit. To accept collateral or a guarantee.

**Fiat.** Decree or ruling of a court.

**Ficción.** Fiction, fantasy, myth. Not real.

**Ficción jurídica.** Legal fiction.

**Ficha.** File. Account. Data card.

**Fichero.** File cabinet, archive.

**Ficto.** Constructive, implied, fictional. Imaginary, invented. Illusory.

**Fidedigno.** Credible, believable, dependable, reliable, trustworthy, veracious.

**Fideicomisario.** Trustee, administrator, agent, delegate, guardian, representative.

**Fideicomiso.** Trust.

**Fideicomitente.** Settlor of a trust, trustor.

**Fidelidad.** Fidelity, faithfulness. Devotion, loyalty.

**Fiducia.** Trust, confidence, reliance.

**Fiduciario.** Fiduciary.

**Fiel.** Faithful, loyal, true. The needle of a scale.

**Fijación.** Determination or establishment of something. Joinder of the issue. Fixation. Fixing.

**Fijación de precios.** Official prices set by the government, usually in the form of a ceiling.

**Fijar.** To affix, fix. To ascertain. To conclude, settle.

**Fila.** Line, queue, sequence.

**Filiación.** Filiation, derivation, origin.

**Filibustero.** Buccaneer, corsair, pirate, privateer.

**Filigrama.** Watermark.

**Filosofía del derecho.** Jurisprudence.

**Fin.** End, finish, termination. Aim, goal, intention.

**Finado.** Deceased, decedent.

**Financiar.** To finance, endow, fund, underwrite.

**Financiero.** Financial, monetary. Related to money.

**Finca.** Farm, plantation, ranch. House.

**Finca asensuada.** Estate subject to an annuity.

**Fincas rústicas y urbanas.** Rural and town property.

**Fingimiento.** Lie, pretense, simulation.

**Finiquitar.** To conclude, end, settle, terminate.

**Finiquito.** Discharge, release of an obligation or debt.

**Firma.** Signature, autograph. Enterprise, trade name.

**Firma por poder.** Signature by procuration.

**Firmado.** Signed.

**Firmante.** Signer, subscriber. Person who issues a document.

**Firmar.** To sign, autograph, execute, initial.

**Firme.** Firm. Final, conclusive, irrevocable. Unappealable. Uncompromising.

**Firmo la presente.** I have hereunto set my hand.

**Fiscal.** District Attorney, D.A., prosecutor, prosecution. A belonging to the state or government. Financial. Related to taxes.

**Fiscalía.** District attorney's office. The prosecution.

**Fiscalización.** Supervision, administration, control.

**Fiscalizador.** Person or body with control or supervision.

**Fisco.** The state or government. Financial branches of government.

**Físico.** Bodily, carnal, corporeal, physical. Material, concrete. Physicist.

**Flagrante.** Flagrant, clearly seen, evident, exposed, obvious, patent.

**Fletador.** Shipper, charterer, freighter, sender.

**Fletamento.** Affreightment, charter, freightment. Consignment, dispatch.

**Fletante.** Affreighter, charterer.

**Fletar.** To charter. To send, consign, dispatch.

**Flete.** Freight. Cost of transportation.

**Fletero.** Carrier of goods.

**Flojedad.** Debility, feebleness, fragility, weakness.

**Flora silvestre.** Wild flora. The land vegetable species, as well as mushrooms, that exist subject to natural selection processes and develop freely, including populations or specimens of these species found under human control. Any development of flora natural resources, areas or habitats, especially when endangered species are involved, must occur in a manner that does not alter the necessary conditions for the subsistence, development and evolution of such species.

**Flota.** Fleet, flotilla, navy.

**Flotar.** To float.

**Flote.** Float, buoy.

**Fluctuación.** Fluctuation, oscillation, shift. Repeated changes.

**Fluctuante.** Changing between two extremes, relatively unstable.

**Flujo y reflujo.** Movement of the tide between its upper and lower ebb.

**FOB. Franco A Bordo (...puerto de embarque convenido).** FOB. Free on Board (...named port of shipment). "Free on Board" means that the seller fulfills his obligation to deliver when the goods have passed over the ship's rail at the named port of shipment. This means that the buyer has to bear all costs and risks of loss of or damage to the goods from that point. (Incoterms).

**Foja.** Folio, page, sheet (old Spanish, but still used as a forensic term).

**Foliar.** To number and or initial pages.

**Folio.** Page or group of pages.

**Fomentador.** Developer, promoter. Person who moves other people into action.

**Fomentar.** To promote, awaken people's interest.

**Fomento.** Aid, encouragement, promotion.

**Fondisia.** Innkeeper.

**Fondo.** Fund. Stock, supply. Bottom.

**Fondo de comercio.** Physical and intangible assets of a corporation. The whole corporation.

**Fondo de reserva.** Reserve fund.

**Fondo Monetario Internacional.** International Monetary Fund. IMF.

**Fondos.** Funds, endowment, grant, money.

**Fondos suficientes.** Sufficient funds. In those agencies which require the existence of funds the agent will not be obligated to perform any transactions while the principal does not provide the sufficient funds, the agent having the right to suspend his performance when the necessary funds have been exhausted. (Mex. Com. C., art. 281).

**Forajido.** Dangerous criminal, fugitive, outlaw.

**Foral.** Related to one particular jurisdiction or forum.

**Foraneo.** Foreign, alien, imported (often used despectively).

**Forastero.** Foreigner, alien, stranger.

**Forense.** Forensic. Legal, legalistic.

**Forma.** Form. Configuration, shape. Style.

**Forma fehaciente.** Authentic manner.

**Formación.** Formation.

**Formal.** Formal. Proper, dependable. Customary, standard.

**Formalidad.** Formality, ceremony, rite.

**Formalidades.** Formalities. Bureaucratic or legal procedures.

**Formalismo.** Formalism. There is an amazing proliferation of requirements for legal permissions and official documents in all sorts of legal relationships. The mere cashing of a traveler's check can become a complicated, time-consuming operation, and dealing with customs agents is likely to be a Kafkaesque experience. There is a marked tendency to presume that every citizen is lying unless one produces written, documentary proof that one is telling the truth. The formal legal systems of Latin American countries, whether ascertaining criminal guilt or issuing employment benefits, display a decided tendency to believe only documents and not people. (L & D in LA). (See *Legalismo.*)

**Formalizar.** To formalize, to render final and enforceable. To sign, execute.

**Formar.** To form. To create, set up. To organize.

**Fórmula.** Formula, equation.

**Formular.** To formulate. To express, state.

**Formulario.** Form, application.

**Formulismo.** Empty formality.

**Fornicación.** Fornication. Sexual intercourse out of wedlock.

**Fornicar.** To fornicate.

**Foro.** Forum, jurisdiction, court.

**Fortaleza.** Fortress, fort, bastion, stronghold.

**Fortuito.** Fortuitous, accidental, casual, unplanned. Depending on chance or fate.

**Forzoso.** Compulsory, binding, mandatory.

***Forum non conveniens*, Costa Rica.** *Forum non conveniens*, Costa Rica. This country rejects cases filed in it under the mentioned theory, due to lack of jurisdiction. The excerpts that follow are citations from their complete text, filed in Delgado v. Shell Co., 890 F. Supp. (S.D. Tex. 1995). The judicial decisions partially transcribed below, all the way to the Supreme Court, derive from the same case. It should be added that in Latin America, the decision of a foreign judge, with jurisdiction over the case, ordering the plaintiffs to file such case in another country, is seen as politically offensive.

**Decision of the Fourth Civil Court of San José**, by the Honorable Ricardo González Mora, of 9/5/95:

[In reference to *forum non conveniens*] This institution is unknown and therefore cannot be applied in the Costa Rican legal system, nor can it be the legal ground for determining the competence of this Court. (Page 6).

In fact, article 323 of the Bustamante Code provides that in personal suits the competent judge shall be a judge of the place where the obligation is to be performed or the place of the defendant's domicile and secondarily, the place of the latter's residence. (Page 8).

[...] the issue is directed, instead, at finding liability on the part of the manufacturers and distributors of an allegedly defective product. Therefore, the causal event of the claim lies outside Costa Rican territory, and does not meet the linkage requirements set forth in Costa Rican law. Consequently, it may be clearly concluded that the law applicable to this case is Article 323 of the Bustamante Code and that the plaintiffs were proceeding in accordance with the law when they filed their suits in the courts of the State of Texas, which is the domicile or place of residence of the defendant companies. (Page 9).

By virtue of the Private International Law Code (Bustamante Code), the competent court is that of the defendants' domicile or place of residence, which is not Costa Rica. (Page 10).

The fact that judge Lake deems it more convenient for the plaintiffs to have the case heard in another jurisdiction, even against their express will, is not relevant to the issue immediately at hand before this Court, since, as Dr. Arguedas Salazar writes, "Jurisdiction is one of the fruits of sovereignty, and it should therefore not be exported or sacrificed." (Page 10).

This being the case, the proper course of action is to expressly decline to hear or try this case on the grounds that it is not a matter for Costa Rican judges, since it does not meet the linkage requirements set forth in national or international rules of competence applicable to the Costa Rican legal system. (Page 10).

**Decision of the Superior Tribunal de Apelaciones de San José**, overruled an appeal of the above decision, on 9/25/95.

**Decision of the Supreme Court of Costa Rica**, affirmed the District Court's judgment, on 2/21/96:

III. [...] the decision [of the District Court] establishing that adjudication of the present case does not correspond to a Costa Rican judge, is affirmed.

**Decision of the Juzgado Civil y de Trabajo de Limón**, signed by the Honorable Javier Víquez Herrera, on 5/20/96:

[Referring to *forum non conveniens*] A procedural decision, issued by a Court of the United States of America, cannot determine the territorial jurisdiction within this country, to adjudicate the present case, since that would violate National Sovereignty. (Part II).

[S]uch decisions [pesticed manufacturing and distribution] were taken in said country [USA], which is where the defendants are domiciled and where their assets are located; and it is not the case of a lawsuit against the branches that the defendants have in our country. (Part IV).

[The Bustamante Code, article 323] establishes that concerning personal actions, the judge with jurisdiction is the one where the obligation must be performed or the one of the defendant's domicile, and subsidiarily the defendant's residence. Accordingly [...] there is no doubt that [...] filing the claim in that country of the North [USA] was the correct thing to do [...] (Part V).

Therefore. This lawsuit should not be heard by this Court, due to which jurisdiction is declined, according to the rules of national and international jurisdiction. (Final paragraph).

**Forum non conveniens, Dominica.** *Forum non conveniens*, Dominica. The Commonwealth of Dominica is a jurisdiction based on the English Common Law. At the same time, due to its Caribbean location, it also receives some influences of Latin American law, for instance, through CARICOM. Dominica protects its nationals from the effects of *forum non conveniens* with its Act No. 16 of 1997, which can be officially cited as **Transnational Causes of Action (Product Liability) Act 1997**. In its introductory statement, it mentions it is "An Act to make provision for the expeditious and just trial in the Commonwealth of Dominica of transnational product liability actions where any such action was dismissed in a foreign forum on the basis of *forum non conveniens*, comity or on a similar basis."

The most relevant sections of the present law follow:

Sec. 3. Application. This Act shall apply to all transnational causes of action brought against a foreign defendant where:

(a) any such action was dismissed in a foreign forum on the basis of *forum non conveniens*; or

(b) on the basis of comity or other similar basis the Courts in Dominica provide a more convenient forum for trial of the action.

Sec. 5. Posting of bond. (1) Subject to section 4 [that the Dominican Courts have jurisdiction and that proceedings are not stayed] the Court shall order that any defendant who enters an appearance makes a deposit in the form of a bond int he amount of one hundred and forty percent per claimant of the amount proved by plaintiff to have been awarded in similar foreign proceedings.

(2) The terms and conditions for the posting and disposal of a bond under subsection (1) shall be determined by the Court.

Sec. 8. Strict liability. (2) Any person, whether a national of or domiciled, resident or incorporated in a foreign country, or otherwise carrying on business abroad, who manufactures, produces, distributes or otherwise puts any product or substance into the stream of commerce shall be strictly liable for any and all injury, damage or loss, caused as a result of the use or consumption of that product or substance.

Sec. 10. Orders of the Court. (1) Where a transnational cause of action is established under this Act to the satisfaction of the Court, the Court shall make an award of exemplary or punitive damages, in addition to any general or special damages which it awards, in the circumstances specified in section 11.

(2) Without prejudice to the generality of subsection (1), the Court is hereby empowered to make any order it considers appropriate in the circumstances, including:

that an apology be made by the defendant to the plaintiff;

publication of the facts about the defendant's products in the newspapers, health magazines and journals in Dominica and abroad;

the placing of advertisements and warnings about the defendant's products; and

the publication of the health, environmental, and economic consequences of the wrongful act of the defendant.

Sec. 11. Exemplary and punitive damages. (1) The Court shall make an award of exemplary or punitive damages in the following circumstances, where the Court is satisfied that:

(a) the defendant acted in bad faith or in reckless disregard for the welfare of others; or

(b) having knowledge of the harm which his wrongful act was likely to cause, nevertheless persisted in the relevant action with a view to making a profit.

(2) In awarding exemplary or punitive damages, the Court shall take account of all the circumstances of the case and in particular the following factors:

that the defendant continued to produce or sell any products or substances after the product or substance was banned or its use restricted in the country of manufature or in any other country in which it was used or consumed;

that the defendant failed to issue a warning to the Government of Dominica or to any other relevant person of the harmful effects of the product or substance;

that where a warning was issued under subparagraph (b) the nature of the warning and any inherent inadequacies in that warning; and

the past conduct and culpability of the defendant.

Sec. 12. Levels of damages. (1) In awarding damages, whether exemplary of punitive, the Court shall consider and be guided by awards made in similar proceedings or for similar injuries in other jurisdictions, in particular damages awarded in the Courts of the country with which the defendant has a strong connection whether through residence, domicile, the transaction of business or the like.

(2) For the purposes of this section, the Court shall take judicial notice of awards made in relevant foreign courts.

Sec. 14. Limitation period. (1) The limitation period for bringing a transnational cause of action under this Act shall be six years.

(2) For the purposes of this Act the period of limitation under subsection (1) shall begin to run from the date on which the cause of action arose; plaintiff knew or ought to have known that he had a cause of action and the person or persons against whom he could proceed; or action was stayed or finally dismissed in a foreign forum whichever of the above was latest.

Sec. 15. Retro-activity. This Act shall have retroactive effect on all actions which are pending at the date of its enactment.

### *Forum non conveniens*, **Ecuador.** *Forum non conveniens*, Ecuador. This country rejects cases filed in it under the mentioned theory, due to lack of jurisdiction. The excerpts that follow are citations from their complete text, filed in Delgado v. Shell Co.,

890 F. Supp. (S.D. Tex. 1995). The declaration of Congress, as well as the opinion of the Attorney General's Office, partially transcribed below, derive from the same case. A complete version of the opinion from the Attorney General's Office can fe found in Maria Aguinda et al. v. Texaco, Inc., USDC, S.D., NY. It should be added that in Latin America, the decision of a foreign judge, with jurisdiction over the case, ordering the plaintiffs to file such case in another country is seen as politically offensive.

**Public Declaration of the President of the International Affairs Commission of the Honorable National Congress of Ecuador**, Don Gustavo Larrea, signed on 1/25/95:

Companies of highly industrialized countries import technical procedures and goods capable of causing accidents of catastrophic proportions, with hundreds or thousands of victims, or causing severe damage to the environment. Our judicial system, in responding to a socioeconomic reality that is different from that of highly industrialized countries, is not designed to resolve massive accidents of catastrophic proportions as a result of the application of dangerous industrial techniques or the use of a highly noxious substance. It is not just, or proper, that the harm caused by products or highly noxious techniques from societies of great industrial development be redressed only by our Judiciary Power, which, logically, is not adequately equipped with the infrastructure or mechanisms necessary for these cases. (Page 2).

Our legal system accords the plaintiff in a personal action the right to choose the defendant's domiciliary courts as the forum. When there is concurrent jurisdiction between our courts and a foreign court—and when the foreign country concerned also considers that there is concurrent jurisdiction—the choice of the foreign court by a national plaintiff is completely valid according to both legal systems in question. In that case, if the foreign court imposes on the national plaintiff the obligation to return to his country and to refile the petition here, it is also imposing upon our Judiciary Power to adjudicate the case and to completely disregard the mentioned legal principle that accords the plaintiff the choice of forum. (Page 2).

The application of the theory of *forum non conveniens* violates various multilateral international treaties, among which: the Convention to Determine the Condition of Foreigners in the Territory of the Contracting Parties, article 5, the American Declaration of the Rights and Liberties of Man, arts. II, XVII and XVIII and the Universal Declaration of the Rights of Man, arts. VII and VIII. Ecuador has also signed bilateral treaties with the United States of America that give access to citizens of another country to their courts, such as the Treaty of Peace, Friendship and Commerce signed by both countries on June 13, 1839. (Page 3).

**Official Opinion of the Attorney General's Office**, signed by Don Leonidas Plaza Verduga, on 15/1/97, in a letter addressed to the US Attorney General, Ms. Janet Reno:

If according to this Treaty [bilateral treaty of Peace, Friendship, commerce and navigation] the access to the courts is open and free, it is not clear how the application of a judicial theory ("*forum non conveniens*"), inferior in ranking to international treaties, can close the doors of American courts to citizens of my country. (Page 2).

The bilateral treaty makes certain that the doors of our courts are not closed on American plaintiffs because of their condition as foreigners. It is because of that, among other reasons, that the Ecuadorian plaintiffs in the two cases, to which this letter obeys, expected reciprocity from American judges. (Page 2).

Such reciprocity is not only a basic element of international comity, but it facilitates juridical cooperation between our two countries, which Ecuador has a genuine desire to increase, to help fighting common problems, such as the illicit traffic of drugs and others that, unfortunately, has received a strong blow with the behavior of American courts concerning cases where Ecuadorian citizens have an interest. (Page 2).

My country considers that our citizens are treated in a discriminatory way due to the application of the "*forum non conveniens*" theory. An example of such discrimination is reflected in the order handed down by the

Honorable Judge Sim Lake, the pertinent part of which says, in Spanish, as follows:

"While the district courts must respect the choice of forum made by an American plaintiff, the choice of an American forum made by a foreign plaintiff *deserves less deference.*" (Lineas Maritimas Argentinas v. Schichau-Unter Wesser) (Emphasis added) (Case cited by Judge Sim Lake in his decision of Jully 11, 1995, pages 1365 and 1366). (Page 3).

It would then seem that citizens of my country, just for being foreign, are considered as second class citizens and receive a less favorable treatment than that afforded to American nationals. This does not happen in my country, since Ecuadorian courts treat American citizens in the same way as Ecuadorian citizens, without any kind of discrimination. (Page 3).

What does behoove us is to state our deep regret when seeing that Ecuadorian citizens are given, in the United States of America, a discriminatory treatment in court, notwithstanding that the bilateral treaties in force between both nations preclude such situation. (Page 3).

**Interpretative Law of Articles 27, 28, 29 and 30 of the Code of Civil Procedure for Cases of International Concurrent Jurisdiction**, published in the Registro Oficial, 1/30/98, pp. 1 and 2:

Art. 1 Without prejudice to their literal meaning, articles 27, 28, 29 and 30 of the Code of Civil Procedure shall be interpreted in the sense that in case of concurrent international jurisdiction, the plaintiff may freely choose between bringing suit in Ecuador or in a foreign country, except when an explicit statute provides that the matter shall be exclusively settled by Ecuadorian courts, such as in the case of a divorce action of an Ecuadorian national who contracted marriage in Ecuador. If a suit were to be filed outside Ecuador, the national competence and jurisdiction of Ecuadorian courts shall be definitely extinguished.

Art. 2 This law shall become effective after its publication in the Registro Oficial, it is a special law and, as such, it shall prevail over any opposing law, whether general or special.

**Forum non conveniens, Guatemala.** This country rejects cases filed in it under the mentioned theory, due to lack of jurisdiction. The excerpts that follow are citations from their complete text, filed in Delgado v. Shell Co., 890 F. Supp. (S.D. Tex. 1995). The opinion of the Attorney General's Office, as well as the decisions, partially transcribed below, derive from the same case. At the end a statute that completely clarifies the issue, is transcribed. It should be added that in Latin America, the decision of a foreign judge, with jurisdiction over the case, ordering the plaintiffs to file such case in another country is seen as politically offensive.

**Official Opinion of the Attorney General's Office**, signed by Don Acisclo Valladares Molina, Attorney General for Guatemala, dated 5/3/95:

According to the provisions of Article 17 of Decree 107 contained in the Code of Civil and Commercial Procedures of the Republic of Guatemala, "The plaintiff in all personal actions, will have the right to exercise his/her action before the judge of the defendant's domicile, notwithstanding any waiver or submission of the latter." (Page 1).

The Code of International Private Law (an instrument not ratified by the United States of America, but internal law for Guatemala), says in Article 323: "Outside of cases of express or tacit submission, and except for local law to the contrary, the judge having jurisdiction over the bringing of personal actions will be the judge of the place of compliance with the obligation or of the domicile of the defendants and subsidiarily that of their residence." (Page 1).

Guatemala does not recognize the *Forum non conveniens* theory. According to our legal system, affected workers have the protected right to bring suit in the domicile of the defendants. Once this right is exercised it is invested with the quality of an acquired right and seeking to subvert it would be illegal. The jurisdictional standards in our system are mandatory and do not lend themselves to being manipulated by any tribunal whether domestic or foreign. Once the plaintiffs have exercised the right to bring suit in the domicile of the defendants, whether in this country or abroad, it is illegal for a Guatemalan judge to disturb this choice of tribunal. (Page 2).

We trust that, in the same way that a Guatemalan court would not dare to require an American judge to violate American law, the American Judiciary Power would also abstain from requesting that the Guatemalan Judiciary Power violate Guatemalan law. (Page 2).

As expressed above, Guatemala does not accept nor does it recognize the Doctrine of *Forum non conveniens*. But, even in the hypothetical case that this Doctrine were to exist in Guatemala, it would not apply to the case in question; since Guatemalan legislation itself through Article 17 of Decree Law 107 establishes the right of the presumed affected person to bring suit in the domicile of the defendant. (Page 2).

It was not our citizens but rather American firms, American marketing and American technology that caused the facts on which the suit is sustained. Therefore, although we are sensitive to the small inconveniences which prosecution of the trial in the United States may cause American citizens individually, we understand that the reason for going to and staying in American courts are amply justified. (Page 3).

We understand that the acts are based on American civil liability [...] surely it is there [the USA] where you have the most advanced and sophisticated resources to allow the Judge greater clarity in the matter. Since it involves American civil liability, we do not see why American courts would not be able to try it. As far as we are concerned it is clear that it is a matter of company civil responsibility, conceived and directed from the Unites States. (Page 3)

Since Guatemala does not recognize the theory of Forum Non Conveniens, such theory in not applicable in Guatemala. (Page 4).

**Decision of the Seventh Civil District Court**, signed by the Honorable Elsa Noemí Falla de Galdamez, dated 8/17/95:

According to the Code of Civil and Commercial Procedures, the plaintiff in all personal actions has the right to file the action before the defendant's domiciliary court, notwithstanding any waiver or submission of the latter. (Page 1).

From a study of the documents included and the statement of facts in the claim, this judge establishes her lack of jurisdiction in the case at bar, since it also appears in the enclosed documents that the plaintiffs renounced to their domiciliary courts. (Page 2).

Holding: The court abstains from hearing this present case since, from the statements made and the documents enclosed, it emerges that this court lacks territorial jurisdiction to adjudicate and orders the interested party to apply to the corresponding [judge], in which case, at plaintiff's request, the file shall be transmitted to the court or agency with jurisdiction in the case. (Page 2).

**Decision by the Court of Appeals**: Appeal was denied as being improper.

**Law for the Defense of Procedural Rights of Nationals and Residents**, unanimously enacted by Congress on May 14, 1997:

CONSIDERING

That up to date two cases have already occurred where the application of the "Theory of *Forum non conveniens*" by foreign judges has negated the right of Guatemalan citizens to file and to prosecute to an end petitions before foreign courts against enterprises that manufacture and market products that are harmful to human beings, although the plaintiffs in these actions had voluntarily chosen the foreign court. This makes it necessary to enact a law that controls the applicability of legal theories unknown in our system and to guarantee the right to justice as a basic human right.

THEREFORE

In exercise of the faculties conferred in article 171 (a) of Guatemala's Political Constitution,

The following LAW FOR THE DEFENSE OF PROCEDURAL RIGHTS OF NATIONALS AND RESIDENTES

IS DECREED

Article 1. Because it is in violation of the rights that the Political Constitution of the Republic and the judicial order of Guatemala guaranteed to its nationals and residents, the theory called "*Forum non conveniens*" is declared unacceptable and invalid, when it intervenes to prevent the continuation of a lawsuit in the domiciliary courts of the defgendants.

Article 2. The personal action that a plaintiff validly establishes abroad before a judge having jurisdiction, forecloses national jurisdiction, which is not revived unless a new lawsuit is filed in the country, brought spontaneously and freely by the plaintiff.

Article 3. If having informed the foreign judge about the reach of this law and the same refuses to hear the case submitted to his jurisdiction, as an exceptional measure and to avoid procedural abandonment of the Guatemalan nationals and residents, the national judges can reassume jurisdiction. But in specific cases they will have to observe the following methods:

a) The defendants that do not have their principal property in the Republic of Guatemala, shall deposit in the treasury of the Judicial Organization as bond, the entire amount in damages they are sued for and the fees and expenses that are evidenced by agreements signed with national or foreign attorneys who were involved in the original proceeding.

b) In case the plaintiffs win, the presiding Guatemalan court will take as a minimum guide the concepts and levels of indemnification in substantially similar cases in the country where the lawsuit was originally established, consistent with the legal documents that prove the levels of indemnification.

c) The State of Guatemala will benefit from this law when it is a plaintiff in a lawsuit.

Article 4. Enforcement: this decree will enter into force the day after it is published in the official gazette.

***Forum non conveniens*, Honduras.** This country rejects cases filed in it under the mentioned theory, due to lack of jurisdiction. The excerpts that follow are citations from their complete text, filed in Delgado v. Shell Co., 890 F. Supp. (S.D. Tex. 1995). The opinion of the Attorney General's Office, as well as the Resolution of the Honduran Congress, partially transcribed below, derive from the same case. It should be added that in Latin America, the decision of a foreign judge, with jurisdiction over the case, ordering the plaintiffs to file such case in another country is seen as politically offensive.

Official Opinion of the Attorney General's Office, signed by the Honorable Jorge Reyes Días, Attorney General of Honduras, on June 2, 1995.

In personal actions, Honduran law protects the plaintiff's right to bring suit in the defendant's domicile. Honduras honors this principle in national law as well as in international agreements that Honduras has signed. (Page 1).

[...] the first rule of Article 146 of the Law on the Organization and Attributes of the Courts, which has been in force since 1906, provides that in personal actions, the court of the place where an obligation is to be honored shall be competent, otherwise, at the election of the plaintiff, a judge of the defendant's domicile or a judge of the place of the contract shall be competent. Further developing the same principle, the second paragraph of the same article provides that if a suit is filed simultaneously against several defendants residing in different locations, when said defendants may be jointly or severally liable, a judge of the domicile of any of said defendants shall be competent, at the plaintiff's election. (Page 2).

Further, the Bustamante Code, the Code of International Private Law, an international agreement signed by Honduras, which has had the force of national law since 1930, provides under Article 323 for the right to file personal suits in the courts of the defendant's domicile. (Page 3).

Honduran jurisdictional rules are mandatory. A Honduran judge has no power to modify, overrule or ignore these rules. This is true even in the event of a foreign decision. (Page 2).

Honduran procedural law does not recognize the "depositions" or "discovery" of American law. (Page 2).

All testimonial evidence must be produced in court. Attorneys cannot question the witnesses privately as a means of gathering evidence. Witnesses may only answer questions in court. The parties to a suit, their spouses and close relatives are expressly prohibited by Honduran law from being witnesses in Honduran proceedings. (Page 3).

Honduran industry is that of a developing country, and the Honduran legal system and legislation have therefore not evolved substantive rules of specific procedures for trying cases involving the massive contamination or collective sterilization of workers, genetic mutations, or cancer caused by chemical agents. (Page 3).

In contrast, it would seem that the United States does have far-reaching procedural legislation expressly tailored to industrial disasters; therefore, it is to be presumed that a [U.S.] judge has the elements of law and advanced material resources and techniques providing greater guidance in deciding such cases. (Page 3).

## Resolution in the Defense of Legislative Sovereignty, Judicial Independence and Procedural Rights, Honduran Congress, March 1996:

### I. Introduction

It is noticeable with increasing frequency that, while international contacts continue to grow, some enterprises of highly developed countries import goods and techniques capable of massive destruction and generalized harm. These goods or techniques are able to maim or kill thousands of people and can also destroy our environment in just one event. Our legal system obeys to a socioeconomic reality different from that of highly industrialized countries and, logically, it has not been designed to cope with accidents of massive and catastrophic proportions.

On the other hand, it is also noticeable that when our nationals are the victims of such accidents and they choose to file a lawsuit in the country where the responsible enterprise is domiciled, such enterprise sometimes resorts to the theory of *forum non conveniens* to convince the foreign judge to decline adjudication of the case ordering our nationals to refile the lawsuit in our courts. The reason alleged by these enterprises is that most of the evidence is in our country and that, to defend itself adequately, it is just, practical and convenient that the case be prosecuted in our country and not abroad, where it was originally filed. The foreign judge who accepts this theory closes the doors of his court on our nationals and orders them to refile the case in our courts.

The present Resolution pursues three ends: a) fillling a legislative gap produced when the theory of *forum non conveniens* prevents our citizens or residents from continuing prosecuting a case abroad; b) dissuading foreign enterprises from violating our environment; and c) protecting our workers and consumers who suffer the effects of industrial products or procedures causing them massive injuries.

It is a fact that certain enterprises of highly industrialized countries eventually market or use products and/or technical procedures that constitute an enormous source of danger. There even are some enterprises capable of marketing or using products in our nation after they have been banned in their country of origin once their unreasonably dangerous nature has been scientifically proven.

A specific situation that this law tries to remedy is the one created when high technology harms the environment or a great number of citizens. It sometimes happens that when our people file a lawsuit abroad, in the domicile of the responsible enterprises, the latter seek refuge in the theory of *forum non conveniens* to dodge facing liability in their own country. The problem that this causes is that when the case is refiled in our courts, they lack an adequate system to solve these massive torts. It is not that our legal system is inefficient but, naturally, it reflects the situation of our country. Since our nation, fortunately, does not produce goods capable of causing massive harm and its industry does not threaten the life and health of entire cities, our legal system is not ideally equipped to deal with such evens.

It is not just, nor proper, that the harm and conflict caused by catastrophic products, manufactured by highly industrialized countries, be only redressed by our Judiciary Power which, logically, was not equipped to deal with cases of catastrophic destruction and of massive harm. It is with pride that we notice that our nation does not have an adequate legal infrastructure to deal with these

catastrophes, not because of lack of preparation but because our country is a peace-loving one, that does not manufacture and does not produce catastrophic goods able to impair the life and physical integrity of workers and consumers in a massive scale.

It seems adequate to us that the Judiciary Power of the country that produces such lethal goods also share in the work of solving the problems caused by such products. Because it is precisely these highly industrialized countries, where these goods originated, that have the most suitable laws to deal with the realities that they create.

After all, if foreign judges persist in closing the doors of their courts on our citizens and residents, and continue to refuse hearing cases legally brought before them, the application of the present Resolution, made to defend our people from catastrophes, could not be criticized.

## II. Drawbacks of the *Forum non conveniens* Theory

Some of the serious obstacles for the results that the *forum non conveniens* theory triggers in our country are as follows:

1. **Illegality.** Our legal system accords to the plaintiff in a personal action the right to choose the defendant's domiciliary courts. When there is concurrent jurisdiction between our courts and a foreign court—and when the foreign country concerned also considers that there is concurrent jurisdiction—the choice of the foreign court by a national plaintiff is completely valid according to both legal systems in question. In that case, if the foreign court imposes on the national plaintiff the obligation to return to his country and to refile the petition here, it is also imposing on our Judiciary Power to adjudicate the case and to disregard completely the mentioned legal principle that accords to plaintiff the choice of the forum. Our judges cannot lend themselves to such moves because their principal constitutional duty is to uphold our legal system, not a foreign one.

2. **Impracticability.** Our legal system is not made to solve massive torts of catastrophic proportions. A foreign system that counts with procedural techniques for col-

lective or global methods to process cases with a high number of parties, as the class action, bifurcation, or powerful devices to produce evidence, such as discovery, is much better equipped than our own to solve industrial disasters, massive torts and catastrophic events.

3. **Opportunism.** It is observed in practice that the great majority of defendants resort to *forum non conveniens* for reasons different than the ones alleged to the foreign judge. Experience shows that whe they are really looking for is for a lengthier case in our country and far more reduced damages that they would be exposed to if the case remained before the original court. Defendants also speculate with the possibility that the second lawsuit will never be refiled in our country, or that if refiled, it will be eventually abandoned by plaintiffs.

4. **Difficulty.** Experience also shows that when the foreign court closes its doors through a *forum non conveniens* ruling, the dificulty in refiling in our courts is so great that only very exceptionally is the case prosecuted up to its final disposition on the merits.

5. **Discrimination.** The effects of the mentioned theory cause a procedural discrimination against our citizens abroad because, in practice, it is against the latter that forein courts close their doors and not against the nationals of the foreign judge. Accordingly, the *forum non conveniens* theory leads to xenophobic results.

6. **Inequality.** Our system does not discriminate procedurally against foreigners. As long as our courts have jurisdiction, they have to continue adjudicating the case. Our courts cannot close their doors just because some facts—domicile of witnesses, parties' nationality, their residence, their language, etc.—are predominantly foreign.

7. **No jurisdiction.** As stated above, our system grants to plaintiff the right to choose the defendant's domiciliary courts. When the plaintiff effects such a choice legally for our system and for the foreign one, our courts lose their jurisdiction. Said jurisdiction can only be activated again for reasons recognized by our law, for instance, the nonsuit of the foreign action and the filing of a second lawsuit, independent from the first one, before our courts. Because *forum non conveniens* is an unknown institution to our system, it cannot reactivate our jurisdiction. The plaintiff that resorts to our courts, not of his own free will but compelled to do so by a foreign judge, does not reactivate our jurisdiction with his petition—even if it is formally valid—because a spontaneous and authentic will is lacking.

8. **International treaties.** The theory of *forum non conveniens* breaches several multilateral international treaties, among which: the **Convention Regarding the Status of Aliens in the Respective Territories of the Contracting Parties, article 5; the American Declaration of Rights and Duties of Man**, articles II, XVII and XVIII; and the **Universal Declaration of Rights of Man**, approved and proclaimed by the United Nations General Assembly, in Paris, on December 10, 1948, articles 7 and 8. All these treaties, among others, guarantee access to the courts of law in order to uphold rights and obligations. The theory of *forum non conveniens* consists on exactly the opposite, that is, on closing the doors of the court to litigants. This doctrine then contradicts both the letter and the spirit of these international treaties. To the extent that it bars foreign plaintiffs from access to courts with jurisdiction, the theory of *forum non conveniens* constitutes a violation of international law. The Nation has also signed bilateral treaties that guarantee open access to courts by the nationals of the other country. For instance, the **Treaty of Friendship, Commerce and Consular Rights**, signed with the United States of America in the city of Tegucigalpa, on December 7, 1927, and that became effective on July 19, 1928. Article I, paragraph 3 of this bilateral treaty warrants to the citizens of one country "free access to the courts" of the other country, as well as "the prosecution of their rights, at all court levels established by law." Article II of said bilateral treaty grants national treatment in cases of civil liability for physical harm or death. The theory of *forum non conveniens* breaches international law since it closes the doors of a court with jurisdiction, against a foreign litigant.

9. **Justice.** It seems unfair that highly industrialized countries, from where massive torts are caused and directed, would distance themselves from the lawsuits triggered by such massive torts. It also seems unfair that the enterprises causing such catastrophes could refuse to defend a lawsuit in their own territory.

10. **Atomization.** It is not unusual for massive torts to be so huge that their effects go beyond the borders of a single country. In fact, they can produce victims spread over many countries and over several continents. Against this background, a basic sense of judicial economy dictates that the lawsuit should be tried in a single country. In these cases the most reasonable and practical solution is to choose a country with a common link to all the others, and this would normally be the country where all defendants are domiciled.

11. **Imperialism.** What is normal, and what is normally expected is that a court with jurisdiction would adjudicate cases before it. It is surprising that a court with jurisdiction would decide to stop the case and unilaterally order that proceedings should continue in another country. This is an imperialistic attitude since the original court behaves as a superior court deciding that the case shall continue in this or that subordinated district. Such unilateral decision is summarized in the expression "I abandon this because I want to, you take charge of it now," and it violates international law and international comity.

12. **Comparative law.** The international application of the *forum non conveniens* theory constitutes a procedural aberration which is practiced only by a very reduced number of countries. For the great majority of nations this theory is unknown. It is telling that nations with a legal culture that goes back for thousands of years, such as several systems of continental Europe, do not apply *forum non conveniens*. Despite its misleading Latin name, this theory is not Roman but a relatively recent Scottish invention.

13. **Gap.** Our procedural rules do not expressly contemplate the situation of a national plaintiff on whom the doors of the foreign court have been closed due to the theory of *forum non conveniens*.

### III. Text of the Resolution

For the above reasons, the following Resolution is issued:

### Resolution On defense Of Legislative Sovereignty, Judicial Independence and Procedural Rights

Our procedural law grants to citizens and residents the right to file personal lawsuits in the defendant's domiciliary courts. This is a right of constitutional import, based on principles of due process.

Elemental reasons of national sovereignty and of judicial independence prevent our Judiciary Power to implement a foreign court's order imposing the theory of *forum non conveniens*. This would violate our jurisdictional norms and would disregard the valid choice of forum effected by our citizens or residents.

When a personal action is validly filed in the domiciliary courts of a foreign defendant, national jurisdiction for that particular case becomes extinguised. Thereafter, such jurisdiction can only be activated when plaintiffs nonsuit the first case and file the case in our courts, on their own absolutely free and spontaneous will.

The filing of a petition in our courts following an order of a foreign judge and/or which has been dictated by such judge based on the theory of *forum non conveniens*, does not generate national jurisdiction, even if said petition has no vice as to its form.

The procedural rights of our citizens and residents cannot be manipulated or diminished by any foreign judge. And with greater reason, no national judge can lend himself to continue, at a domestic level, such diminishment of rights.

### Documentary Supplement

The following documents substantiate the reasons and the juridical arguments used to propose the enactment of this bill.

A) The Legal Opinions of the Attorney Generals of: 1) Guatemala, 2) Honduras and 3) Nicaragua supporting the reasons explained in numered paragraphs 1, 2, 7, 8 and 11.

B) An English translation of the judgments rendered by the trial courts of 1) Costa Rica, 2) Guatemala, 3) Nicaragua and 4) Panama, and of 5) the Constitutional Court of Panama, supporting the reasons explained in numbered paragraphs 1, 2, 4, 7 and 8.

C) Article in English language, *Forum non conveniens in American and England*: "A Rather Fantastic Fiction," by Professor David W. Robertson, published in The Law Quarterly Review, July 1987, pp. 398-432, supporting the reasons explained in numbered paragraph 3 and 4. A Spanish summary of this article is enclosed.

D) A complete copy, in Spanish, of the treaties mentioned in numbered paragraph 8. A full copy, in English of the Treaty of Friendship, Commerce and Consular Rights, signed with the United States of America. A transcription of the articles specifically cited is added, including a Spanish unofficial translation of articles I and II of the mentioned bilateral treaty.

E) Definition in Spanish of the expression *forum non conveniens*, taken from *Diccionario Jurídico Dahl* (*Dahl's Law Dictionary*), New York, 1993, pp. 115, 116.

## Forum non conveniens, Islas Filipinas.

*Forum non conveniens*, Philippine Islands. Other jurisdictions, outside Latin America, also reject the consequences of *forum non conveniens*. Such is the case of The Philippines, all the more interesting since this country does use, internally, *forum non conveniens*. Such position is illustrated in the case of Bernabé L. Nacida et al. v. Shell Oil et al., civil case Nr. 5617, decided in 1996 by the Regional Court, Judicial District 11, Section 37, General Santos City. Bernabé derives from the American case Delgado v. Shell Co., 890 F. Supp. (S.D. Tex. 1995). The complete text of Bernabé, of another similar decision, as well as of an opinion by the Department of Justice of The Philippines, all of them rejecting the international use of *forum non conveniens*, can be found in Delgado.

## Forum non conveniens, Nicaragua. This

country rejects cases filed in it under the mentioned theory, due to lack of jurisdiction. The excerpts that follow are citations from their complete text, filed in Delgado v. Shell Co., 890 F. Supp. (S.D. Tex. 1995). The opinion of the Attorney General's Office, as well as the decision from the District Court and from the Court of Appeals, partially transcribed below, derive from the same case. A bill, clarifying the situation is transcribed at the end. It should be added that in Latin America, the decision of a foreign judge, with jurisdiction over the case, ordering the plaintiffs to file such case in another country is seen as politically offensive.

**Official Opinion of the Attorney General's Office**, signed by Don Carlos José Hernández López, Attorney General for Nicaragua, dated 5/24/95.

The procedural rules of our country do not grant jurisdiction to Nicaraguan courts against pesticide manufacturers who have only manufactured and sold their product abroad, without having performed any acts in Nicaraguan territory. Code of Civil Procedure, article 265, paragraph 1. (Page 1).

The Nicaraguan judge is forced to respect the jurisdictional rules established in our Code of Civil Procedure, including the one that guarantees, in personal actions, the choice of the defendant's court, duly exercised by plaintiff. Code of Civil Procedure, article 298. (Page 1).

Our procedural rules do not know, nor do they accept the "depositions" or the "discovery," recognized in American law. (Page 2).

In Nicaragua a person cannot be a witness and a party in the same case. Spouses of the parties are also precluded from being witnesses. Code of Civil procedure, article 1317, paragraphs 2 and 10). (Page 2).

Nicaraguan law does not allow the request of documents in an undetermined way. It is necessary to identify the document that a party wants to introduce into the case as evidence. [...] (Page 2).

**Decision of the Second District Civil Court of León,** signed by the Honorable Teresa de Jesús Bustamante, dated 8/21/95.

To such effect [to determine jurisdiction], one must only take into consideration the personal circumstances of the defendant, those of plaintiffs is irrelevant. (Page 3).

[...] the defendant corporations have their domicile in the State of Texas, not in Nicaragua; the defendant corporations have their assets in the United States of America, not in Nicaragua. (Page 3).

[Referring to article 150 of the National Constitution]. The administration of justice guarantees the Principle of Legality; it protects and harbors human rights through the enforcement of the law in matters submitted to it. (Page 4).

Art. 265, paragraph 1 of the Code of Civil Procedure establishes that in cases concerning personal actions, the defendant's domiciliary court shall have jurisdiction. (Page 4).

Art. 298 of the Code of Civil Procedure prescribes that when the defendant is a juridical person, as in the case at bar, for purposes of determining the court with jurisdiction, the place where such corporation or foundation has its seat shall be reputed as its domicile. (Page 4).

The fact that the Nicaraguan plaintiffs in this case have filed the same lawsuit, requesting the same damages, before the Honorable Federal Court in Texas, amounts to a jurisdictional submission. (Page 4).

According to Art. 255 of the Code of Civil Procedure, once jurisdiction attaches it cannot be modified. (Page 4).

Finally, [...] our procedural system does not recognize, and therefore it does not accept nor does it admit, the imposition of the *Forum non conveniens* Theory by foreign courts. (Page 4).

The undersigned declares herself with lack of jurisdiction to adjudicate the present lawsuit. Plaintiffs shall continue with their case before the Honorable Federal Court of the State of Texas, where the petition was filed. (Page 4).

**Decision of the Court of Appeals of the Occidente, Civil and Labor Division**, dated 12/11/97, excerpts from pages 102, reverse up to 105:

**II)** [...] Considering the second ground of appeal, Nicaraguan law accepts both the tacit and the express submission. These two mean, paraphrasing Carnelutti, the subordination of one's will to that of another. Consequently, submission is the act or omission, through which one party acknowledges, expressly or tacitly, the court's

jurisdiction concerning a specific case. In the case at bar we have a tacit submission, due to which a group of Nicaraguans sued a group of foreign corporations or enterprises that are domiciled in the State of Texas, USA. First they filed their action before the Honorable Federal Judge Sim Lake, of the Southern District, Houston Division. This is in agreement with article 262 (1) of the procedural code, which states as follows:

A tacit submission takes place: 1st. By the plaintiff, for the mere fact of filing the petition before the court." A tacit submission emerges from acts committed by the parties or third parties with a legitimate interest when such acts are explicit and unequivocal. That is why the law establishes that, for the plaintiff, a clear and direct fact as evidence of tacit submission to a specific court: filing the petition there. Nicaraguan law is strict about such issue: the mere fact of filing a petition with a specific judge is sufficient to subject the plaintiff or plaintiffs to such judge's jurisdiction (in the present case to that of the Southern District, Houston Division, State of Texas, already mentioned); issuance of summons on the other party or any other act or procedural step leading to a more complete result are not required. The filing of a petition is enough. The fact that plaintiff has chosen the domicile of the corporations or enterprises (the State of Texas) to file the petition is in accord with the general rule established in article 290 of the procedural code stating that the defendant's domiciliary court has jurisdiction to decide a civil case, which agrees with the principle:

"Actor sequitur forum rei". Plaintiffs also have acted in harmony with article 265, para. 1 of the procedural code, which establishes (apart from cases of express or tacit submission) that in personal actions the court with jurisdiction can also be, according to plaintiff's choice, the one of defendant's domicile. As it can be seen, the legal texts leave the choice to the plaintiff. And, since the defendant is a juridical person, its domicile is reputed to be the place where the respective corporation or foundation has its seat (art. 298, para. one, procedural code.) In conclusion, this Court finds that since plaintiff has filed its petition before a Federal Judge with jurisdiction in the State of Texas, USA, such filing having been realized in a legal way, the court below had no other alternative but to declare its lack of jurisdiction, as ruled by art. 255 of the procedural code, as was done in the decision of 8:15 A.M. on August 22, 1995, issued by the Second Distriót court , for Civil Matters of Leon, due to which this appeal must be dismissed.

**III)** Additionally, it must be pointed out that the filing of the petition before the Nicaraguan court, at 12:35 P.M., on August 8, 1995, was caused by the fact that the defendant corporations or enterprises raised the defense of FORUM NON CONVENIENS before the Federal Judge of the State of Texas and the Federal Judge SIM LAKE ordered plaintiffs to file the petition in another country, theory which is unknown in Nicaragua's procedural system and cannot be admitted because it would be accepting the imposition of foreign courts, at the same time that it causes violence to the plaintiff's will, who has the freedom to choose or to select the defendant's domicile to file the a petition and, in the case at bar, to file the action before a court of the United States of America.

The opposite would mean to close the doors of the court to the plaintiff or plaintiffs who have chosen a foreign court with jurisdiction while such court has jurisdiction according to both legal systems involved. It would also mean contradicting those international law principles establishing that all Nations are equal, that no discrimination must be made among people and that every Nation must guarantee access to justice for all. However, "it may be that a foreign court legitimately declares itself without jurisdiction to adjudicate a claim, but that said declaration results in a denial of justice or in an avoidance of the law to the detriment of one of the parties" (Unanimous Affirmative Opinion, Permanent Juridical Committee, on the "Law for the Defense of Procedural Rights of Citizens and Residents," Dossier Nr. 12-655, Legislative Assembly, San Jose, Costa Rica, June 10, 1997). Such possibility, when the world undertakes procedures for the globalization of the economy, a greater internationalization of the law and a closer interrelation between Justice and Development, in their turn also internationalized (See Justicia y Desarrollo en América Latina y el Caribe, Interamerican Development Bank, Washington, D.C., 1993), has triggered a legislative movement for the defense of fellow citizens, as the case of Decree Nr. 34-97, of the Guatemalan Congress, which promulgated the "Law in Defense of the Procedural Rights of Citizens and Residentes," enacted and published in the "Diario de Centroamérica," an official publication of the Guatemalan Republic, volume CCLVI, Nr. 69, of June 12, 1997, pages 2033 and 2034, which in its article 1 "declares unacceptable, inapplicable and invalid, the theory called "*Forum non conveniens*," lack of jurisdiction due to inconvenient forum, when it is raised to avoid continuing with the case in the defendant's domiciliary courts." (Page 2034).

This Court holds that it is essential to law and justice to protect the plaintiff's will and freedom to select the judge who would have ordinary jurisdiction, being able to choose the court with jurisdiction of the defendant's domicile, which is in harmony with Nicaraguan procedural law, art, 1, 318, 319, 321, 322 and 323 of the Bustamante Code.

**IV)** In an analogous case the Civil Court Nr. 4 of San Jose, Costa Rica, issued its decision Nr. 353-95, of 5 P.M., September 1, 1995. In its Section III, while analyzing the federal theory called "FORUM NON CONVENIENS," it determined that "such theory is foreign to our legal system and to international jurisdictional rules subscribed by Costa Rica."; in section IV, discussing the jurisdictional rules applicable to the case, the judgment says that: "the liability claimed runs against the enterprises that manufactured and distributed the pesticides FUMAZONE and NEMAGON, so it is those facts or acts which shall determine what court has jurisdiction. If the said enterprises did not commit acts in Costa Rica, if they did not manufacture here the goods in question, then the claim to obtain damages from such enterprises does not satisfy the requirement of connection established in Art. 46, para 3 of the procedural code. As indicated in Section II, the action is not directed against the employers, nor is it based on a labor relationship of plaintiffs. Rather, it is about determining the eventual liability of manufaturers and distributors of a supposedly defective product. From this point of view, the cause of action is rooted outside our territory and does not satisfy the requirements of connection established by national law.

And so, the said Costa Rican judgment, cited in applying art. 443 of the procedural code, concludes with the following result:

"Consequently, it can be clearly concluded that the applicable rule to this case is Article 323 of the Bustamante Code and that plaintiffs acted legally when they filed their claims in the State of Texas, domicile or residence of the defendant enterprises" (Sec. IV).

And then, said judgment concluded that "it is fitting to expressly decline adjudication of this case since it is not of the kind that corrresponds to a Costa Rican Judge, according to national and international criteria of jurisdictional connection, operative in our system" (Sec. V).

Further, this Court also finds that, beyond what has been debated and expressed in sections II and III of this judgment, and supported by the Code of Private International Law (Bustamante Code, art. 323), signed and ratified by Nicaragua, the Court with jurisdiction is that of the defendants' domicile: the Southern District of the State of Texas, Houston Division, USA, where the case was started and, due to the Federal theory of that nation, plaintiffs were sent to the Nicaraguan courts, without such event necessarily meaning the lack of jurisdiction of the American judge, since Judge SIM LAKE may reassume the case through "RETURN," as he himself has stated in his decision of July 11, 1995, which says:

"Notwithstanding the dismissals that may result from this Memorandum and Order, in the event that the highest court of any country finally affirms the dismissal for lack of jurisdiction of any action commenced by plaintiffs in this action in his home country or the country in which he was injured, that plaintiff may return to this court and, upon proper motion, the court will resume jurisdiction over the action as if the case had never been dismissed for f.n.c." (See page 81 of the appellate record.)

**V)** [...] consequently, nothing more remains for this Court than to affirm the appealed judgments. The parties must now go before the Federal Judge of the District Court for the Southern District of Texas, Houston Division, USA. It must be mentioned that it has not been easy for this Court to obtain information about "FORUM NON CONVENIENS" since it is a theory foreign, not only to Nicaraguan law, but in general to Central American, to Latin American law, and to the rules of international jurisdiction suscribed and ratified by Nicaragua and in general also by Central American countries.

THEREFORE

Due to the considerations raised, the rules cited and arts. 413, 414 and 424 of the procedural code and art. 90, para. 1. L.O.T.T., the Undersigned Judges of the Civil and Labor Section of the Court of Appeals of Occidente, Republic of Nicaragua, DECIDE:

The judgments of 3:24 P.M. of August 21, and of 8:15 A.M., of August 22, 1995, issued by the Second Civil Court of the León District, Nicaragua, are affirmed. Consequently, the parties shall apply to the District Federal Court for the Southern District of the State of Texas, Houston Division, USA. [...]

**Draft Law for the Defense of Procedural Rights of Nationals and Residents in Nicaragua; filed on May 12, 1997:**

[...] This bill aspires to protect the environment and the health of the Nicaraguan people, it is convenient to clarify certain rules on international jurisdiction and on the applicable law to damages.

Concerning the former, the choice of forum made by the plaintiff must be strengthened, when such forum has jurisdiction according to both legal systems. Concerning the applicable law to damages and pecuniary sanctions, it must also be clarified that the plaintiff may require the applicability of the foreign legal system connected to the case.

These two norms are already incorporated in our legal system, but in a disperse way and not so expressly stated. Because of that it is necessary to clarify and to systematize them.

The rules about jurisdiction, for instance, we have inherited from classic Roman law, which established that in personal actions it was the defendant's domiciliary court that had jurisdiction. As an example of the validity of this rule, article 323 of the Bustamante Code can be cited, establishing the same principle.

This law would benefit the victims of ecological wrongs and, in general, those who have suffered damages caused in or from another country.

Article 1 makes sure that if the plaintiff chooses a foreign court with jurisdiction, such judge will not be able to close the doors of the court on him as, for instance, has been happening with the theory of *forum non conveniens*.

Article 2 also favors the victims of ecological wrongs since it strengthens the possibility that the indemnity and pecuniary sanctions be in accordance with foreign law.

In summary, what the law clarifies is that those who incur in international tort liability, will not be able to escape their domiciliary courts and, additionally, that they will be sanctioned, at the victim's option, whether by the law of the place where the wrong is suffered, or by the law of the place where damages are generated. [...]

### Draft Law for the Defense of Procedural Rights of Nationals and Residents of Nicaragua

Art. 1 The petition that is validly filed, according to both legal systems, in the defendant's domiciliary court, extinguishes national jurisdiction. The latter is only reborn if the plaintiff nonsuits of his foreign petition and files a new petition in the country, in a completely free and spontaneous way.

Art. 2 In cases of international tort liability, the national court may, at the plaintiff's request, apply to damages and to the pecuniary sanctions related to such damages, the relevant standards and amounts of the pertinent foreign law, duly proven according to Nicaraguan law.

Art. 3 When the national judge cannot apply what is established in article 2 of this law to the case at bar, he will determine, in a discretionary way, the amount or amounts to which the plaintiff is entitled.

Art. 4 The present Law is a matter of Public Order.

### *Forum non conveniens*, **Panamá.** *Forum non conveniens*, Panama. This country rejects cases filed in it under the mentioned theory, due to lack of jurisdiction. The excerpts that follow are citations from their complete text, filed in Delgado v. Shell Co., 890 F. Supp. (S.D. Tex. 1995). The decisions, partially transcribed below, including two from the Supreme court, derive from the same case. At the end a statute that completely clarifies the issue, is transcribed. It should be added that in Latin America, the decision of a foreign judge, with jurisdiction over the case, ordering the plaintiffs to file such case in another country is seen as politically offensive.

### Decision of the Second Civil Circuit Court of the First Judicial Circuit of Panama, signed by the Honorable Carlos Strah Castrellón, on 9/20/95:

> The Court notes that each and every one of the defendant companies is foreign, with head offices in various states in the United States of America and some were incorporated under the law of the State of Israel and have offices in Israel and legal domiciles in Houston, Texas, United States of America.

With respect to competence to hear causes to which legal persons are a party, Article 254 of the Judicial Code states as follows:

> "254. Unless the law provides otherwise, in actions brought against a legal person, a judge with jurisdiction over said legal person's domicile shall be the competent judge."

This case corresponds to the situation described in the law cited above, since each and every defendant companies has its head offices or domicile, as has already been noted, in various states in the United States of America, and the Court therefore believes that it is not competent to hear the suit. (Page 2).

In a similar case, the First Superior Court of Justice, in a decision handed down on April 18, 1995, pointed out that:

> "Since this cause involves three companies as defendants, the judge who is com-

petent to hear suits brought against said defendants is a judge with jurisdiction over the place where said companies have head offices." (Page 2).

It is therefore prudent in this cause, which clearly falls under this category and the law cited in the above Superior court ruling, to decline to hear this cause on the grounds of lack of competence. (Page 2).

Therefore, in the cause referenced hereinabove, the Second Civil Circuit Judge of the First Judicial Circuit of Panama hereby DECIDES

To decline to hear this cause on the grounds of lack of competence to do so.

**Decision of the First Superior Court of Justice**, signed by the Honorable Nelson H. Ruiz C., Eva Cal and Elitza A. Cedeño, on 10/6/95:

Attorney [for defendant] filed with this Court a motion for protection, for breach of constitutional guarantees, against resolution number 2276 of September 20, 1995, signed by Mr. Carlos Strah [...] in which the latter ordered to abstain from hearing the case against [...] due to lack of jurisdiction. (Page 1).

Because of the considerations expressed by the First Superior Court of Justice, administering justice in the name of the Republic and under the authority given by the law, the motion for protection from breach of constitutional guarantees is OVERRULED [...] (Page 5).

**Supreme Court of Justice.** Judgment of March 28, 1996, signed by the Honorable Rafael González, Arturo Hoyos and José Manuel Faundes:

[...] the Chamber of General Affairs of the Supreme Court, administering justice on behalf of the Republic and by the authority invested in me by the law, hereby rules that the foreign legal order of November 17, 1995, handed down by the District Court for the Southern District of the State of Texas, Houston Division, which conditionally declines competence in favor of the jurisdiction of each of the countries of origin of the plaintiffs in the suit brought by SANTOS ABREGO MORALES ET AL., against SHELL OIL COMPANY, [Et Al.], is not enforceable IN THE Republic of Panama.

Supreme Court of Justice. Certification issued on December 10, 1996, considering the decision by the Second Civil District Court as *res judicata*:

Whereas the decision No. 2276 of September 20, 1995, handed down in the case of SANTOS ABREGO ET AL. v. SHELL OIL [ET AL.] is duly completed and the respective file has been sent to the archive.

Whereas such decision was not subject to attack, due to Article 702 of the Judicial Code, according to which such decision cannot be challenged and is invested with the authority of *res judicata*.

**Forum non conveniens, PARLATINO.**
*Forum non conveniens,* PARLATINO. As its name indicates, PARLATINO, also known as Latin American Parliament, is an institution that groups representatives of all legislative congresses of Latin America. Although its decisions are not mandatory, they still have a high persuasive value. PARLATINO's official position towards *forum non conveniens* is representative of that of all its member-countries.

**Model Law**, approved by the Permanent Forum of Regional Parliaments for the Environment and for a Sustainable Development, on January 27, 1998.

### Model Law on International Jurisdiction and Applicable Law to Tort Liability

To protect the environment and the health of the Peoples of Latin America, it is convenient to clarify certain rules on international jurisdiction and on the applicable law to damages. Concerning the former, the choice of forum made by the plaintiff must be strengthened, when such forum has jurisdiction according to both legal systems. Concerning the applicable law to damages and pecuniary sanctions, it must also be clarified that the plaintiff may require the applicability of the foreign legal system connected to the case.

These two norms are already incorporated in the majority of our legal systems, but in a disperse way. Because of that it is necessary to clarify and to systematize them. The rules about jurisdiction, for instance, we have inherited from classic Roman law, which established that in personal actions it was the defendant's domiciliary court that had jurisdiction. As an example of the validity of this rule, article 323 of the Bustamante Code can be cited, establishing the same principle.

Concerning pecuniary liability, it is also known that the national court may apply foreign law. However, in several countries this notion is not clearly articulated. Because of that, it is convenient to enact a law as the one proposed.

This law would benefit the victims of ecological wrongs and, in general, those who have suffered damages caused in or from another country. Article 1 makes sure that if the plaintiff chooses a foreign court with jurisdiction, such judge will not be able to close the doors of the court on him as, for instance, has been happening with the theory of *forum non conveniens*. Article 2 also favors the victims of ecological wrongs since it strengthens the possibility that the indemnity and pecuniary sanctions be in accordance with foreign law.

In summary, what the law clarifies is that those who incur in international tort liability, will not be able to escape their domiciliary courts and, additionally, that they will be sanctioned, at the victim's option, whether by the law of the place where the wrong is suffered, or by the law of the place where damages are generated.

One hopes that the enactment of the bill will help towards the respect of the environment and the health of our Peoples.

### Text of the Model Law

Art. 1 National and international jurisdiction. The petition that is validly filed, according to both legal systems, in the defendant's domiciliary court, extinguishes national jurisdiction. The latter is only reborn if the plaintiff nonsuits of his foreign petition and files a new petition in the country, in a completely free and spontaneous way.

Art. 2 International tort liability. Damages. In cases of international tort liability, the national court may, at the plaintiff's request, apply to damages and to the pecuniary sanctions related to such damages, the

relevant standards and amounts of the pertinent foreign law.

***Forum non conveniens*, posición latino-americana.** Forum non convens, Latin American view. *Forum non conveniens* (FNC) is an unknown institution in Latin America, where the effects it causes are illegal. Accordingly Latin America does not offer an alternative jurisdiction in a FNC situation. Among the illegalities that FNC causes in Latin America, the following can be mentioned: *1. Plaintiff forced to file a claim.* The plaintiff who refiles in Latin America does not do it of his own free and spontaneous will but constrained by the FNC order. This is deeply offensive to the procedural freedom that people enjoy in Latin America, where nobody can force a person to file a claim, much less a foreign court. Admittedly, plaintiff may opt for not filing the second claim. However that would be tantamount to abandoning the claim and losing the case. The choice to lose is not really a choice. *2. Plaintiff deprived from right to sue in defendant's court.* In Latin America the plaintiff in a personal action has the unfettered right to choose the defendant's court. This is a very old principle, which existed already in Roman law under the name of *"actio sequitur forum rei"* and adopted by the Bustamante Code. Such rule is a standard feature in the regional codes of civil procedure. FNC effectively deprives plaintiff from the right to sue in defendant's domicile, which of course contravenes Latin American law. A Latin American court cannot be expected to disregard its own law and become complicit in a system that denies plaintiff's right to choose defendant's court. *3. Procedural equality.* A basic Latin American rule is that every individual is equal before the law. According "less deference" to the plaintiff's choice of forum, as *Piper Aircraft Co. v. Reyno* indicates, triggers unconstitutional consequences in all Latin American jurisdictions. Foreign governments have complained about such discrimination. *4. Pre-emptive jurisdiction.* The Spanish term of art is *"competencia preventiva"*. It is a concept that comes from Roman law where it was known as *"forum praeventionis"* and it applies to instances of concurrent jurisdiction. Once a court starts hearing a case, the other court that had concurrent jurisdiction loses such jurisdiction. The US court that hears the case first cannot dismiss it on FNC grounds because the Latin American court has lost the jurisdiction that it might have had initially. *5. Indelibility of jurisdiction.* This is a principle that comes from Roman law, where it was known as "*perpetuatio jurisdictionis.*" It means that once a court with jurisdiction starts hearing a case, that court cannot be changed for another. *6. Lis pendens.* In Latin America this institution is known as "*litispendencia.*" In some instances lis pendens even has constitutional rank. FNC normally grants the US judge continuing jurisdiction and, as such, it triggers lis pendens in Latin America. Pre-emptive jurisdiction, lis pendens and indelibility of jurisdiction are manifestations of the same basic premise: once a court with jurisdiction hears a case all other courts lose jurisdiction. *7. Sovereignty.* In a FNC situation, the US Court predetermines several important issues on how the case will be litigated in the foreign country. The US Court orders plaintiff to refile the lawsuit abroad, normally within a certain period. Usually the US Court also includes in the order some language as to how the statute of limitations can be raised as well as certain conditions as to what evidence can be presented. All this is extremely illegal in Latin America. FNC is perceived as a vehicle through which a US judge issues direct orders intended to be executed in the respective Latin American country. For elementary reasons of sovereignty a foreign court cannot tell a party what to do or what not to do in a Latin American lawsuit. *8. Treaty supremacy.* Art. 27 of the Vienna Convention on the Law of Treaties determines that domestic law cannot prevent the exercise of a treaty right. FNC violates a series of bilateral conventions that specifically establish equal treatment and open courts. FNC also violates some multilateral treaties that provide for equal treatment, such as the International Covenant of Civil and Political Rights, which has been signed by the US and by most Latin American nations. *9. Jurisdictional waivers, submissions and stipulations are void.* It is sometimes said that any

illegality that FNC may cause abroad is purged by the jurisdictional waivers that the parties make: plaintiff by filing the claim abroad and defendant by making a general appearance. This is a flawed argument. Plaintiff's "waiver" is not such. To trigger effects, a waiver must satisfy the same basic requirements as the filing of a claim, i.e. it must be the product of the party's free and spontaneous will. The submission that defendant may make, before the US court or directly to the Latin American one does no cure the FNC illegalities and, consequently, does not generate jurisdiction. Similarly, stipulations made to the US court that contravene Latin American law are illegal in the respective countries. Defendant's stipulations before the US judge are meaningless in Latin America. *10. Honesty towards the foreign court.* Latin American litigants must be loyal and truthful to their respective courts. This means that the plaintiff who has been dismissed by the US court on FNC grounds should disclose to his or her court the full procedural history of the case. Further, the plaintiff that honestly believes that the foreign court lacks jurisdiction should be free—even duty bound—to state so. Honesty towards the foreign court, however, could be fatal for the chances of having the case re-instated in the US. Defendant could challenge the reinstatement of the claim accusing plaintiff of having sabotaged the foreign lawsuit. It is difficult to see how US law could punish plaintiff for being honest to the foreign court. *11. Appeals in the US.* The case could be refiled abroad while a US appeal is pending. Assume, for instance, that two years after filing abroad the corresponding US Appellate Court overrules the FNC decision. The case is then pulled away from the foreign judge, without any consultation whatsoever. A Latin American court cannot be expected to assume "jurisdiction" over a case where a US appellate court has the power to pull the case away. *12. Appeals in Latin America.* In some cases the FNC order requires that "the highest court" of the foreign country rule for lack of jurisdiction before the case can be reinstated in the US. Such modality forces the plaintiff to appeal an intermediate foreign decision for lack of jurisdiction, even if plaintiff believes the decision to be correct. The US judgment is in fact forcing an appeal in bad faith. *13. Latin American court lacks power to constrain defendants that lack assets in Latin America.* A US defendant in a lawsuit filed in Latin America pursuant to a FNC decision can disregard an condemnatory judgment and challenge the enforcement of the Latin American decision before a US court, where the assets are. This is strange considering that the case was transferred to Latin America at defendant's request. It is also very disadvantageous for plaintiff who after having won the case now has to battle to enforce the decision. It would seem that it is inconvenient for the case to litigate it in a forum where the defendant cannot be compelled to comply with an adverse decision. Without the power to constrain there is no jurisdiction. *14. Effect of the illegality.* It is clear that a situation of illegality cannot be allowed to create its intended illegal effect. In this case, a claim filed in Latin America pursuant to a FNC order cannot be allowed to generate jurisdiction. The effects of FNC violate the principle of legality present in every system and also specifically upheld in some constitutions. The illegalities created by FNC in Latin America prevent Latin American courts from assuming jurisdiction. *15. Instance where FNC would not be illegal.* There is a type of case where the effects of FNC would probably not violate the law of the Latin American country concerned. Such is the instance when the defendant is Latin American. This party could effectively raise FNC when sued in the US because it would be in conformity with the principle of *actio sequitur forum rei.* In other words, FNC would transfer the case to defendant's domiciliary courts, which is what Latin American systems dictate anyway.

**Fosa.** Tomb, crypt, grave. Depression, hole, pit.

**Fotocopia.** Photocopy, copy.

**Fotografía.** Photo, photograph, picture, print.

**Fotostático.** Photostatic.

**Fracasar.** To fail, falter. To be unsuccessful.

**Fracaso.** Failure.

**Fraguar.** To forge. To make, manufacture. To counterfeit, falsify. To plan, scheme.

**Franco.** Frank. Honest. Non working day. Exempt, clear.

**Franco a bordo.** See *FOB.*

**Franco al costado.** See *FAS.*

**Francotirador.** Sniper, guerrilla.

**Franquear.** To pay, prepay. To get through customs. To stamp an envelope for mailing. To dispatch.

**Franqueo.** Postage, stamps. Administrative clearance.

**Franquicia.** Franchise, license, privilege. Tax exemption.

**Fratricida.** Fratricide, murderer of a sibling.

**Fratricidio.** Fratricide, the murder of a sibling.

**Fraude.** Fraud. Fraud is misrepresentation or a suppression of the truth made with the intention either to obtain an unjust advantage for one party or to cause a loss or inconvenience to the other.

Fraud may also result from silence or inaction. Fraud does not vitiate consent when the party against whom the fraud was directed could have ascertained the truth without difficulty, inconvenience, or special skill. This exception does not apply when a relation of confidence has reasonably induced a party to rely on the other's assertions or representations. (Lou. Civ. C. art. 1953 and 1954).

Deceit, deception, misrepresentation, swindle.

**Fraude al tribunal.** Fraud upon the court.

**Fraudulento.** Fraudulent.

**Freno.** Brake. Constraint, deterrence.

**Frente.** Front, Forepart. Exterior. Sham exterior.

**Frívolo.** Frivolous, superficial, trivial.

**Frontera.** Frontier, border, boundary, limit.

**Fronterizo.** Belonging to the frontier. Extreme. Insane.

**Fructuoso.** Lucrative, fruitful, gainful, profitable. Productive.

**Frustración.** Frustration, disappointment, dissatisfaction. Failure, nonachievement.

**Frustración sobreviniente.** Supervening frustration.

**Frustrado.** Frustrated, disappointed.

**Frutos.** Fruits, crop, harvest, produce. Earnings, yield.

**Frutos civiles.** Civil fruits, rent. Civil fruits are the rents of buildings, the price paid for the lease of lands, and the amount of perpetual, life or other similar incomes. (Sp. Civ. C., sec. 362, par. 3).

**Frutos industriales.** Cultivated fruits. Cultivated fruits are those produced by lands of any kind, through cultivation or labor. (Sp. Civ. C., sec. 362, par. 2).

**Frutos naturales.** Natural fruits. Natural fruits are the spontaneous productions of the soil, and the broods and other products of animals. (Sp. Civ. C., sec. 362, par. 1).

**Fuego.** Fire.

**Fuente.** Source, derivation, origin. Basis, reason.

**Fuentes de derecho.** Sources of law. The sources of law are legislation and custom.

According to civilian doctrine, legislation and custom are authoritative or primary sources of law. They are contrasted with persuasive or secondary sources of law, such as jurisprudence, doctrine, conventional usages, and equity, that may guide the court in reaching a decision in the absence of legislation and custom. (Lou. Civ. C., art. 1 and note).

**Fuera.** Out, outside. Excluded.

**Fuera de matrimonio.** Out of wedlock.

**Fuero.** Forum, court. Privilege, exceptional right or power, license. Collection of laws.

**Fuero de atracción.** Unitary action.

**Fuerza.** Power, strength. Effectiveness. Force. Force means the effect of power which cannot be resisted. *Superior force.* Those accidents are said to be caused by superior force, which human prudence can neither foresee nor prevent. (Lou. Civ. C. art. 3556).

**Fuerza mayor.** *Force Majeure.* Nonperformance by a party is excused if that party proves that the nonperformance was due to an impediment beyond its control and that it could not reasonably be expected to have taken the impediment into account at the time of the conclusion of the contract or to have avoided or overcome it or its consequences. When the impediment is only temporary, the excuse shall have effect for such period as is reasonable having regard to the effect of the impediment on the performance of the contract. The pary who fails to perform must give notice to the other party of the impediment and its effect in its ability to perform. If the notice is not received by the other party within a reasonable time after the party who fails to perform knew or ought to have known of the impediment, it is liable for damages resulting from such non-receipt. Nothing in this article prevents a party from exercising a right to terminate the contract or to withhold performance or request interest on money due. (Unidroit, Prin., art. 7.1.7).

Act of God, irresistible force.

**Fuerzas armadas.** Armed forces.

**Fuga.** Escape, breakout, desertion, disappearance, flight.

**Fuga de cerebros.** Brain drain.

**Fugitivo.** Fugitive. Outlaw, renegade. Exile, refugee.

**Fullería.** Illicit gambling. Fraud, swindle.

**Fullero.** Professional gambler, card player. Cheat, crook.

**Fulminar.** To destroy, obliterate.

**Función.** Function. Purpose, role. Performance, show.

**Funcionario.** Officer, official, administrator, director, executive.

**Funcionarios que no pueden ejercer el comercio.** Officials forbidden to engage in commerce.

**Fundación.** Foundation. Organization not for profit. Corporation. Founding, settlement. Basis, justification.

**Fundado.** Founded, well supported.

**Fundador.** Founder, organizer, promoter.

**Fundándose en los auto y legajos.** Upon the record and files.

**Fundar.** To found, establish, settle.

**Fundir.** To consolidate, merge.

**Fundirse.** To go bankrupt.

**Fundo** Land, estate, property, tenement. Acreage, farm, plot.

**Funerales.** Funeral, burial, interment, last rites, requiem.

**Funerario.** Relating to funerals.

**Fungibilidad.** Fungibility, interchangeability.

**Fungible.** Fungible, interchangeable.

**Fungir.** To commingle, to mix.

**Fusil.** Rifle, firearm.

**Fusiliamiento.** Military execution, shooting by a firing squad.

**Fusilar.** To execute.

**Fusión.** Merging, amalgamation, consolidation.

**Fusionar.** To merge, amalgamate, consolidate.

**Futuro.** Future, hereafter.

# G

**Gabela.** Gabel tax, duty, burden, excise.

**Gabinete.** Office, law firm. Barrister's chambers (G.B.). Government ministers.

**Gaceta.** Gazette.

**Gaje del oficio.** Discomforts and setbacks inherent to a particular job or occupation.

**Galaxia.** Galaxy.

**Galera.** Galley. Printing draft.

**Galería.** Gallery.

**Ganado.** Cattle.

**Ganador.** Winner, winning party.

**Ganancia.** Earnings, benefit, gains, income, pay, proceeds, revenue, salary.

**Ganancia bruta.** Gross profit.

**Ganancia dejada de percibir.** Gain prevented, lost earning.

**Ganancia líquida o neta.** Net profit.

**Gananciales.** Property acquired during marriage that belongs to both spouses in equal shares. All that is acquired or increased during marriage, except by gift or inheritance.

**Ganancias de capital.** Capital gains.

**Ganancias y pérdidas.** Profit and loss.

**Ganancioso.** Profitable, advantageous, lucrative.

**Ganar.** To win, beat, prevail. To accomplish, to obtain. To gain, to earn.

**Ganar dinero.** To make money.

**Ganar interés.** To draw interest.

**Ganga.** Bargain.

**Gángster.** Gangster.

**Gangsterismo.** Gangsterism.

**Ganzúa.** Picklock, passkey.

**Garante.** Surety, bondsman, collateral, guarantor.

**Garantía.** Security, bond, collateral, guaranty, warranty.

**Garantía adecuada de mantenimiento.** Adequate assurance of due performance.

A party who reasonably believes that there will be a fundamental nonperformance by the other party may demand adequate assurance of due performance and may meanwhile withhold its own performance. Where this assurance is not provided within a reasonable time the party demanding it may terminate the contract. (Unidroit, Prin., art. 7.3.4).

**Garantías individuales.** Individual guarantees. Foreigners belonging to any of the contracting States shall also enjoy in the territory of the others identical individual guarantees with those of nationals, except as limited in each of them by the Constitution and the laws. Identical individual guarantees do not include, unless especially provided in the domestic legislation, the exercise of public functions, the right of suffrage, and other political rights. (Bustamante C. art. 2).

**Garantir, garantizar.** To secure, back, guarantee, warrant.

**Garantizado.** Secured, guaranteed.

**Garito.** Place where illegal gambling is conducted.

**Gas.** Gas, fume, vapor.

**Gastos.** Costs, bills, charges, disbursement, expenditure, expenses.

**Gastos bancarios.** Bank charges.

**Gastos causídicos.** Court costs and attorneys' fees.

**Gastos de cobranza.** Cost of collection.

**Gastos de conservación.** Preservation expenses, upkeep.

**Gastos de lujo y recreo.** Expenses for luxury or pleasure.

**Gastos particulares.** Personal expenses.

**Gatillo.** Trigger.

**General.** General.

**Generales de la ley.** Preliminary interrogation of witnesses on personal data, e.g. name, address, etc. Especially as to whether they have an interest in the outcome of the case.

**Generoso.** Generous, kind, unselfish.

**Genocidio.** Genocide.

**Gente.** People.

**Genuino.** Genuine, authentic, real, legitimate.

**Gerencia.** Management, board of directors, executives.

**Gerente.** Manager, director, executive.

**Gestión.** Agency. Measures, steps taken. Management.

**Gestión de negocios ajenos.** Management of another's business, *negotiorum gestio*. An officious manager must fulfill his charge with all the diligence of a good father of a family and indemnify for injuries which, through his fault or negligence, may be caused to the owner of the property or business he may be managing. Nevertheless, the courts may reduce the amount of the indemnity, according to the circumstances of the case. The ratification of the management by the owner of the business produces the effects of an express authorization.

**Gestionar.** To pursue, to handle.

**Gestor.** Agent, representative. Clerk. Promoter, managing partner.

**Gestor oficioso.** Officious manager.

**Girado.** Drawee.

**Girador, girante.** Drawer, maker.

**Girar.** To draw a commercial paper, to sign a check. To conduct business with a certain capital.

**Giro.** Draft, note. Money order through the mail. Turnover.

**Glosa.** Gloss, comment to a text.

**Glosador.** Glossator, commentator.

**Glosar.** To gloss, to write a comment.

**Gobernación.** Government, administration, executive.

**Gobernador.** Governor.

**Gobernante.** Ruler.

**Gobernar.** To govern, rule. To command, dominate.

**Gobierno.** Government, administration, executive. The ruling party.

**Goce.** Enjoyment, use of something. Ownership, possession.

**Golfo.** Gulf. Hooligan.

**Golpe.** Knock, blow. Revolution, coup, military uprising.

**Golpiza.** Beating.

**Gozar.** To enjoy, own, possess, use.

**Gozar de plena capacidad civil.** Enjoy full legal capacity.

**Gracia.** Forgiveness, mercy, pardon. Extension of time, prolongation. Graciousness.

**Graciable.** Gracious, as a favor, beyond what is strictly binding.

**Gracioso.** Gracious, free, gratis, gratuitous.

**Grado.** Degree, level.

**Grado levítico.** Degree of relationship distant enough to allow marriage.

**Graduación.** Graduation, grading. Classification, scaling. Assessment.

**Gran jurado.** Grand jury.

**Granizo.** Hailstorm.

**Gratificación.** Bonus, tip, gratuity, reward.

**Gratis.** Free, complimentary, gratuitous.

**Gratuidad.** Gratuity.

**Gratuito.** Gratuitous, complimentary, free.

**Gravable.** Assessable, taxable. Subject to encumbrances.

**Gravado.** Encumbered, taxed.

**Gravamen.** Tax, encumbrance.

**Gravamen por labor de operarios.** Mechanic's lien.

**Gravar.** To encumber, tax. To mortgage.

**Gravoso.** Expensive, onerous. Time consuming.

**Gremio.** Trade union.

**Grupo.** Group, association, organization.

**Grupos empresarios.** Groups of Enterprises. Such a concept arises when an enterprise which is the beneficiary of a service has entered into a binding arrangement with the enterprise that provides the service. Thus, for example, if an enterprise which performs work or services exclusively or mainly for another does not have sufficient means of its own to cover its obligations to the employees, the enterprise that receives the services is held responsible. Likewise, employees of the supplying enterprise have the right to working conditions equal to those of the employees of the first enterprise (FLL, Articles 13, 14, and 15). This reduces the possibility of evading obligations to workers through the creation of different legal entities. (Mex. Labor Law).

**Guarda.** Guard.

**Guardabosques.** Forest keeper.

**Guardacostas.** Coast guard.

**Guardaespaldas.** Body guard.

**Guardar secreto.** To preserve secrecy.

**Guardia.** Guard. Sentinel, sentry. Escort, custody.

**Guardia civil.** Police (SP).

**Guardián.** Guardian. Caretaker, custodian. Warden.

**Guardián *ad litem* (L).** Defensor judicial. Guardian ad litem. A guardian ad litem is a special tutor, designated by a court to represent an incompetent person or a minor in a particular suit. (Fernandez Martinez v. Superior Court, 89 PRR 737 (1964)).

**Guarismo.** Cipher, figure, number.

**Guarismos y por extenso.** In figures and letters.

**Gubernamental.** Governmental, official.

**Guerra.** War, battle, combat, warfare.

**Guerra civil.** Civil war, guerrilla, rebellion.

**Guerra fría.** Cold war.

**Guerrilla.** Guerrilla.

**Guerrillero.** Guerrilla, freedom fighter, mercenary, irregular.

**Guía.** Guide. Counselor. Customs receipt. Phone book.

**Guiar.** To guide. To drive, lead.

**Guiar sin licencia.** To drive a vehicle without a license.

**Guillotina.** Guillotine.

# H

**Ha lugar.** Sustained, favorable ruling.

**Habeas corpus (L).** Habeas corpus. In many countries the *habeas corpus* procedure has been broadened to provide protection not only against bodily restraint and arbitrary imprisonment, but also against violation of the various individual freedoms, such as worship, occupation, inviolability of the home, and so on. It has also been used to offer possessory protection against government agencies. Brazil is one of the countries where the *habeas corpus* is the broadest.

There are also more original and remarkably effective legal resorts. One of them, of Mexican origin, is the amparo, of which Mexican jurists are justly proud; the other is the Brazilian procedure *mandato de segurança*. (W. Eur. & LA Leg. Sys.).

**Haber.** Assets, belongings, possessions.

**Haber jubilatorio.** Pension, retirement pay.

**Haber social.** Capital, common capital.

**Haberes.** Salary, wages.

**Habiendo prestado debido juramento.** Being duly sworn.

**Hábil.** Of age and sound of mind. Capable, skilled.

**Habilidad.** Ability, competence, dexterity.

**Habilitación.** License, authorization, permit, qualification.

**Habilitación para comparecer en juicio.** Investiture of power to appear in court. Legitimate children not emancipated when not authorized to appear in court by law, must be vested with power therefor by the father or by the mother, if under parental control.

Investiture can only be granted when the person requesting it is included in one of the following cases: 1) When the parents are absent and their whereabouts is unknown, there being no good reason to believe that they will soon return. 2) When the father or the mother refuses to appear in court on behalf of the son or daughter. 3) When an action has been instituted against the petitioner. 4) When the petitioner would be greatly prejudiced if he did not institute the action for which he requests investiture. (Sp. L. Civ. P. sec. 1993, 1994).

**Habilitado.** Licensed, authorized.

**Habilitar.** To license, authorize, open.

**Habitación.** Habitation. Usual place where someone lives. Habitation is the nontransferable real right of a natural person to dwell in the house of another.

A person having the right of habitation may reside in the house with his family, although not married at the time the right was granted.

The right of habitation terminates at the death of the person having it unless a shorter period is stipulated. (Lou. Civ. C. art. 630 and art. 633 and art. 638).

**Habitante.** Inhabitant, citizen, resident.

**Hábito.** Habit. For the purpose of evidence in civil and criminal actions, habit means a course of behavior of a person regularly repeated in like circumstances. (Ppl. v. Martínez Lucena, 92 PRR 859 (1965)).

Custom, repeated practice.

**Habla.** Language, tongue. Speech.

**Hablar.** To speak, say, talk.

**Hacendado.** Person who exploits a ranch.

**Hacer.** To make, build, create, do.

**Hacer caso omiso.** Disregard, ignore, pay no notice.

**Hacer constar.** To certify. To enter in the record.

**Hacer efectivo.** Pay.

**Hacer estampar el sello.** Cause the seal affixed.

**Hacer fe.** Prove, demonstrate evidence. To authenticate, certify. Self authenticating.

**Hacer fe contra.** Evidence against.

**Hacer funcionar un vehículo.** Operate a vehicle. For the purposes of the statues under which it is prohibited to operate a motor vehicle by a person under the influence of intoxicating liquor, it is not necessary to prove that the automobile in which the person is found was in motion but is sufficient—as in the present case—to show that the person was inside the automobile, with the motor running and under his immediate control. (Ppl. v. Ramos García, 92 PRR 859 (1965)).

**Hacer suyo.** Appropriate, take for oneself.

**Hacer valer sus derechos.** To enforce his rights.

**Hacerse cargo.** Take over, take charge.

**Hacienda.** Ranch. The *hacienda* carries various names in Latin America *estancia* (Argentina, Uruguay, southern Brazil), *fundo* (Chile), *fazenda* (most of Brazil), *latifundia*, and so on. Whatever the name, the *hacienda* provides the nominal umbrella for the same unique cultural phenomenon. It dominates the landholding patterns of Latin America. (W. Eur. & LA Leg. Sys.).

**Hacienda pública.** Ministry of economy.

**Hágase saber.** Let it be known. Phrase usually used to end bills and judgments.

**Hallazgo.** Discovery, invention. Innovation. Breakthrough. Treasure.

**Hampa.** Crime, low life.

**Hampón.** Person belonging to the underworld. Crook, rogue.

**Hazaña.** Feat, great achievement, deed.

**Hechizo.** Bewitchment, curse, spell.

**Hecho.** Fact.

**Hecho falso.** False fact. A false fact is an uncertain act, feigned, simulated or fabricated. It is the deceitful semblance of a fact. (Ppl. v. Olivencia Román, 98 PRR 1 (1969)).

**Hecho jurídico.** Juridical act.

**Hecho por duplicado.** Done in duplicate.

**Hecho sobreviniente.** Supervening or intervening cause.

**Hechos controvertidos.** Facts in dispute.

**Hechos probados.** Proven facts.

**Hegemonía.** Hegemony, domination, predominance.

**Herbolar.** Lace with poison.

**Heredable, hereditable.** Heritable, inheritable.

**Heredad confinante.** Adjacent tenement.

**Heredad de caza.** Game preserve.

**Heredad, heredamiento.** Acreage, estate, farm, land, manor, plantation, property, tenement, ranch.

**Heredado.** Inherited, received mortis causa.

**Heredar.** To inherit.

**Heredera.** Heiress.

**Heredero.** Heir, inheritor, successor.

**Heredero presunto.** Presumptive heir.

**Heredero y legatario.** Heir and legatee. An heir is a person succeeding under an universal title; and a legatee, one succeeding under a special title.

A person who has no heirs by force of law may dispose by will of all his property or part of it in favor of any person qualified to acquire it. (Sp. Civ. C., sec. 668, 751).

**Hereditario.** Hereditary, transmissible.

**Herencia.** Inheritance, succession. The inheritance includes all the property, rights, and obligations of a person, which are not extinguished by his death. (Sp. Civ. C., sec. 667).

**Herencia, aceptación y repudio.** Inheritance, acceptance and repudiation. Acceptance or repudiation of the inheritance can not take place, either partially, for a certain period, nor conditionally. (Sp. Civ. C., sec. 957, 966).

**Herencia legítima.** Intestate succession. Intestate succession occurs:

I. When there is no will, or the will is null or invalid;

II. When the testator did not dispose of all his assets;

III. When the conditions imposed on the beneficiary are not complied;

IV. When the beneficiary dies before the testator, repudiates the will or is incapable of inheriting, if he has not named a substitute. (Mex. Civ. C., art.1599).

**Herencia vacante.** *Bona Vacantia.* The succession of persons dying ab intestato without heirs, and that of those who, leaving such heirs without their presenting themselves to claim the property of the inheritance in accordance with law, belongs to the State Treasury. (Sp. Civ. C., sec. 352).

**Herida.** Wound, injury, laceration.

**Herido.** Wounded, injured.

**Herir.** To wound, injure.

**Hermana.** Sister, sibling.

**Hermanastra.** Half-sister, step sister.

**Hermanastro.** Half-brother, step brother.

**Hermano.** Brother, sibling.

**Hermano de crianza.** Foster brother.

**Hermanos de doble vínculo.** Siblings of full blood.

**Hermanos uterinos.** Siblings on the maternal side.

**Hermenéutica.** Hermeneutics, construction, interpretation.

**Heroína.** Heroin.

**Herramienta.** Tools. Means.

**Hielo.** Ice.

**Hielo libre.** Floating ice not belonging to anyone in particular.

**Higiene.** Sanitation, health.

**Hija.** Daughter.

**Hijastra.** Step daughter.

**Hijastro.** Step son.

**Hijo.** Son, child, descendant.

**Hijo de crianza.** Foster child.

**Hijo incestuoso.** Incestuous child. An incestuous child may be acknowledged. The parents that acknowledge the child will have the right that their names appear in the birth certificate; but in it will not be stated that the child is of an incestuous nature. (Mex. Civ. C., art.64).

**Hijos, clasificación.** Children, kinds. Children are legitimate, illegitimate, or legitimatized.

Legitimate children are those born in wedlock. Illegitimate children are those born out of wedlock.

Illegitimate children may be legitimatized either by the marriage of their parents, or in accordance with the provisions of the Civil Code. (Sp. Civ. C., sec. 180).

**Hijos, ilegítimos.** Illegitimate children. Illegitimate children are those who are conceived and born out of marriage. (Lou. Civ. C. art. 180).

**Hijos ilegítimos, derechos sucesorios**. Illegitimate children, inheritance rights. The inheritance rights of illegitimate children are subject to the personal law of the father and those of illegitimate parents are subject to the personal law of the child. (Bustamante C. art. 65).

**Hijos, legítimos.** Legitimate children. Legitimate children are those born 180 days after the marriage has been celebrated and before 300 days have passed after the marriage has been dissolved. Against legitimacy no other proof shall be admitted than the physical impossibility of the husband to use his wife within the first one hundred and twenty days of the three hundred days that have preceded the birth of the child. (Sp. Civ. C., sec. 181).

**Hijuela.** Parts in which an inheritance can be divided.

**Hipnotismo.** Hypnotism.

**Hipoteca.** Mortgage. A real right that directly and immediately binds an estate and the rights on which it is imposed, whoever its owner or titleholder may be, to the fulfillment of the obligation for the security of which it was constituted. Recorded mortgages shall be strictly real encumbrances, permitting mortgage loans to be made regardless of any subsequent right that is acquired on the same property or mortgage rights. Mortgages are voluntary or statutory.

A mortgage covers natural accessions, improvements and the proceeds from an indemnity granted or owed to the owner by the insurers of the mortgaged property or by virtue of government eminent domain, and the surplus area of a mortgaged property, even though this eventuality was entered in the Registry after the registration of the mortgage. (PR Mort. Law 1979, sec. 155, 156, 160).

**Hipoteca convencional.** Conventional mortgage. *Conventional* mortgage is that which depends on covenants. (Lou. Civ. C. art. 3287 and 3290).

**Hipoteca, ejecución de.** Mortgage, foreclosure. Once a mortgage loan or its interest has wholly or partially become due, the procedure for its foreclosure and collection, when levied solely against the property encumbered with the mortgage, shall conform to summary proceedings. At his option, a mortgage creditor may also resort to ordinary judicial procedures to collect his loan. (PR Mort. Law 1979, sec. 210).

**Hipoteca especial.** Special mortgage. *Special* mortgage is that which binds only certain specified property. (Lou. Civ. C. art. 3288).

**Hipoteca, extensión.** Mortgage, coverage. The following shall be considered mortgaged along with the property, even if not mentioned in the contract, provided they belong to the owner: 1) Improvements consisting of new plantings, irrigation or drainage projects, repairs, safety measures, alterations, conveniences, decoration or additions of stories to buildings, or any other similar improvements, and the annexation of land by natural accession. 2) Indemnity granted or owed to the owner of the mortgaged property either from insurance, provided the damage took place after the mortgage was constituted, or by eminent domain. If any of these indemnities should be paid before the expiration of the obligation insured, and the one who is to pay it has been previously notified of the existence of the mortgage, the proceeds shall be deposited according to the wishes of the interested parties, or, if there is no such agreement, as provided by the court. (PR Mort. Law 1979, sec. 161, 162).

**Hipoteca general.** General mortgage. General mortgage is that which binds all the property, present and future, of the debtor. (Lou. Civ. C. art. 3288).

**Hipoteca judicial.** Judicial mortgage. Judicial mortgage is that which results from judgments. (Lou. Civ. C. art. 3287 and 3321).

**Hipoteca legal.** Legal mortgage. Legal mortgage is that which is created by operation of law. (Lou. Civ. C. art. 3287 and 3311).

Statutory mortgage. A statutory mortgage is constituted in favor of the state and its corresponding municipalities on the taxpayer's property for land taxes pertaining to the las five annual assessments and for current unpaid taxes encumbering it. This statutory mortgage is implicit and specifies a preference in favor of its titleholders above all other creditors and over the third acquirer, even though he may have recorded his rights. (PR Mort. Law 1979, sec. 200).

**Hipoteca, permuta o posposición.** Exchange or postponement of mortgage. A recorded mortgage may be exchanged for another of lower rank or postponed for another to be constituted in the future. (PR Mort. Law 1979, sec. 189).

**Hipoteca, postores.** Mortgage, bidders. The foreclosing creditor may bid in all the auctions. Should he turn out to be the highest bidder, the amount of his loan shall be totally or partially credited to the price offered by him. The holders of current mortgage loans and those made after the mortgage, which is being collected and foreclosed, who appear as such in the Registry certification, may also bid in all the auctions. In such a case, they may use the amount owed to them or any part thereof in their bids. (PR Mort. Law 1979, sec. 222).

**Hipoteca, subasta.** Mortgage, auction. When the time allotted for the judicial demand for payment has expired without the debtor or third owner's having made the payments for which he was summoned, and with the objections he made having been finally resolved against him, the Court, at the request of the foreclaser, the debtor or the third owner, shall order that, prior to the Clerk's issuance of the corresponding order, the marshal shall proceed to auction the mortgaged properties, advertising the auction. (PR Mort. Law 1979, sec. 219, 220).

**Hipoteca voluntaria.** Voluntary mortgage. Voluntary mortgages are those agreed to between parties, or imposed by order of the owner of the properties or rights on which they are constituted, and may only be established by those having free disposal of these properties or rights, or, if they do not have it, they do have the legal authority to do so. (PR Mort. Law 1979, sec. 182, 188).

**Hipoteca y prenda.** Mortgage and pledge. Mortgage differs from pledge in this: 1) That mortgage exists only on immovables, ships, steamboats and other vessels, or such other rights as shall be hereafter described, and that the pledge has for its object only movables, corporeal or incorporeal. 2) That, in pledge, the movables and effects subjected to it, are put into the possession of the creditor, or of a third person agreed upon by the parties, while the mortgage only subjects to the rights of the creditor the property on which it is imposed, without it being necessary that he should have actual possession. (Lou. Civ. C. art. 3281).

**Hipotecable.** Mortgageable.

**Hipotecador, hipotecante.** Mortgagor.

**Hipotecar.** To mortgage.

**Hipotecario.** Mortgage.

**Hipótesis.** Hypothesis, alternative, example, postulate, premise, supposition, theory.

**Hipotético.** Hypothetical.

**Hispanoamericano.** Hispanic, Spanish-American.

**Historial.** Background, history, record.

**Hito.** Boundary. Milestone.

**Hogar.** Home, dwelling house, family residence, homestead.

**Hogar seguro (P.R.).** Homestead.

**Hoja.** Page, folio, sheet.

**Hoja de servicios.** Work history.

**Hológrafo.** Holographic, hand written.

**Hombre.** Man, human, humanity

**Hombre de paja.** Middleman.

**Hombre prudente.** Average prudent person.

**Homicida.** Murderer, killer. Homicidal.

**Homicidio.** Murder, homicide.

**Homicidio culposo.** Manslaughter

**Homicidio intencional.** Murder.

**Homicidio involuntario.** Involuntary manslaughter.

**Homologación.** Homologation. Court approval.

**Homologar.** To homologate, approve.

**Honestidad.** Honesty, integrity, veracity.

**Honesto.** Honest, truthful.

**Honorabilidad.** Honorability, honor.

**Honorable.** Honorable.

**Honorario.** Honorary. Honorarium, fee.

**Honorarios.** Legal fees. Fees.

**Honradez.** Honesty, integrity, probity, veracity.

**Honrado.** Honest, honored. Sincere, upright.

**Honrar.** To honor, to perform on time.

**Hora.** Hour.

**Hora pico o punta.** Rush hour.

**Horario.** Schedule, timetable. Agenda.

**Horas extra.** Overtime.

**Horas hábiles.** Legal working days. Legal working hours are those between sunrise and sunset. (Sp. L. Civ. P., sec. 258).

**Horca.** Gallows.

**Hormigón.** Cement for construction of high buildings.

**Horrible.** Horrible, dreadful.

**Hospedar.** To lodge, accommodate, receive.

**Hospicio.** Hospital, asylum, sanitarium.

**Hospitalización.** Hospitalization.

**Hostigamiento.** Constant attack, offensive.

**Hostil.** Hostile, antagonistic, belligerent, quarrelsome, unfriendly.

**Hostilidades.** Hostilities, belligerence.

**Hotelero.** Innkeeper, hotel manager.

**Hoy.** Today.

**Huelga.** Strike. Industrial action (G.B.). A temporary suspension of work by a coalition of workers. The strike may cover an enterprise or one or more of its establishments.

**Huelga de brazos caídos.** Industrial action by which employees attend the place of work but do not labor.

**Huelga de servicios comunitarios esenciales.** Strikes in essential community services.

**Huelga ilegal.** Illegal strike. The Conciliation and Arbitration Board may rule that a strike is illegal. When a strike is declared to be illegal the workers who continue to strike may be fired (FLL, Article 934). (Mex. Labor Law).

**Huelga patronal.** Lockout.

**Huelguista.** Person who strikes.

**Huellas.** Tracks, fingerprints, imprints, prints, tracks.

**Huérfano, huérfana.** Orphan, foundling.

**Huída.** Escape, breakout, flight.

**Humo.** Smoke. Solid particles of extremely small dimensions, generally less than one micrometer, produced by condensation or incomplete combustion.

**Hurtar.** To burglarize, rob, steal, thieve.

**Hurto.** Larceny, petty larceny. Robbery, stealing. Burglary, theft.

**Hurto de uso.** Conversion.

# I

**Idealismo y religión.** Idealism and religion. The idealism and unreality of Iberian law were accentuated by the manner in which law and religion were fused in the Peninsula. The Spanish and Portuguese monarchs were the beneficiaries of the "divine right of kings" theory of sovereignty, which had developed during the Middle Ages. In the Peninsula, as in the rest of Europe, the theory operated to strengthen royal power. Since the king was God's representative on earth, disobedience to royal command became sinful as well as unlawful. (L & D in LA).

**Identidad.** Identity. Name. Individuality.

**Identificación.** Identification, papers.

**Identificación del cuerpo.** Identification of the body. In the case of flood, shipwreck, fire, or any other disaster where it is not easy to identify the body, the record shall state the information provided by the individuals who found the body. They will state as much as possible the particular signs of the body and the clothing or objects which it was found with. (Mex. Civ. C., art.123).

**Identificar.** To identify, name, point out. To associate with, to relate to. To sympathize with.

**Idioma.** Language, tongue.

**Idiosincracia.** Idiosyncrasy, general trait, peculiarity.

**Idiota.** Idiot, fool, simpleton.

**Idiotez.** Idiocy, madness, stupidity.

**Idoneidad.** Competence, capability, proficiency, skill.

**Idóneo.** Competent, capable, proficient, skilled. Credible, believable.

**Ignorancia.** Ignorance, lack of knowledge. Inexperience. Unawareness.

**Iguala.** Type of payment in a contract for services.

**Igualar.** To balance equal, level.

**Igualdad.** Equality. The constitutions of Latin American countries have affirmed in one form or another that men are born free and equal and, as the Uruguayan constitution puts it, differ only in talent and virtue. In all these countries where slavery prevailed during the colonial period and sometimes long afterward, it was thought advisable to stress that any involuntary servitude was forbidden. Since most Latin American nations are multiracial and legal discrimination prevailed in colonial times against Amerindians, Africans, mestizos, and mulattoes, racial equality is often emphasized as well. (Western European and Latin American Systems).

Equivalence. Fairness, neutrality, impartiality, justice.

**Igualdad ante la ley.** Equality before the law.

**Igualitario.** Equalizing.

**Ilegal.** Illegal, illicit, unlawful. Banned, prohibited. Criminal, felonious. Tortious.

**Ilegalidad.** Illegality, lawlessness, unlawfulness. Crime.

**Ilegitimidad.** Illegitimacy.

**Ilegítimo.** Illegitimate.

**Ilicitud.** Illegality.

**Ilíquido.** Unliquidated.

**Imbécil.** Imbecile, cretin, fool.

**Imbecilidad.** Imbecility, foolishness, idiocy.

**Imitación.** Imitation, copy, emulation, reproduction, simulation.

**Imitado.** Counterfeit, false, fraudulent, spurious.

**Impagable.** Unpayable, exorbitant.

**Impago.** Unpaid, liability.

**Imparcial.** Impartial, neutral, unbiased. Fair, just.

**Impedido.** Precluded. The term precluded as used in the Code of Commerce includes not only the estoppel but also the ratification in cases of acts in excess of, or without authority. (The Bank of Nova Scotia v. Velez Rullan, 91 PRR 347 (1964)).

Crippled, disabled, handicapped, impaired, incapacitated, estopped, stopped.

**Impedido de negar.** Estopped to deny.

**Impedimento dirimente.** Marriage impediment that does not annul the marriage in question.

**Impedimento impediente.** Marriage impediment that results in the annulment of such marriage.

**Impedimento, impeditivo.** Impediment. Disability, handicap, hindrance, impairment. Estoppel.

**Impedimento legal.** Legal bar or obstacle.

**Impedimentos matrimoniales, extranjeros.** Marriage impediments, foreigners. Local legislation is applicable to foreigners in respect to the impediments which it establishes as indispensable, to the form of consent, to the binding or non binding force of the betrothal, to the opposition to the marriage, the obligation of notifying impediments and the civil consequences of a false notice, to the form of preliminary procedure, and to the authority who may be competent to perform the ceremony. (Bustamante C. art. 38).

**Impedir.** To prevent, avert, avoid, deflect, deter, estop, frustrate, hinder, obstruct, preclude, thwart.

**Imperativo.** Imperative, necessity, requirement, requisite.

**Imperativo legal.** Commanded by the law.

**Imperdonable.** Unforgivable, indefensible, inexcusable, irretrievable, unjustifiable, unpardonable. Dishonorable, shameful.

**Imperfecto.** Imperfect, inferior. Defective, deficient, faulty, flawed. Substandard.

**Imperio.** Binding power of the courts. Jurisdiction. Empire, kingdom. Sovereignty.

**Impersonal.** Impersonal, cold, detached, distant.

**Impertinencia.** Impertinence, effrontery, impudence, insolence. Irrelevance, immateriality, incongruity, inconsistency. Redundancy.

**Impertinente.** Impertinent, impudent, insolent. Irrelevant, immaterial, incongruous, inconsistent. Redundant.

**Impetración.** Commission of a crime.

**Implantar.** To establish, install, introduce, settle, set up.

**Implicar.** To implicate, embroil, ensnare, entangle, involve. To accuse, charge, inculpate. To imply, hint, insinuate, suggest.

**Implícito.** Implicit, implied, constructive, tacit, suggested, understood, unexpressed, unspoken.

**Imponente.** Party, usually the state, that imposes something. Imposing, stately, towering.

**Imponer.** To impose, assess charge, exact, levy, tax.

**Imponibilidad.** Taxation, taxability.

**Imponible.** Taxable, assessable, excisable.

**Importación.** Importation, import.

**Importante.** Important, meaningful, momentous, significant.

**Importe.** Amount, price, value.

**Importe razonable.** Reazonable value.

**Importunar.** To disturb, intrude, perturb, trouble.

**Imposibilidad.** Impossibility, infeasibility. Disability.

**Imposibilidad de cumplimiento.** Impossibility of performance. An obligor is not liable for his failure to perform when it is caused by a fortuitous event that makes performance impossible.

An obligor is, however, liable for his failure to perform when he has assumed the risk of such a fortuitous event. An obligor is liable also when the fortuitous event occurred after he has been put in default. (Lou. Civ. C. art. 1873).

**Imposibilidad legal.** Legal impossibility.

**Imposibilidad sobreviniente.** Supervening impracticability.

**Imposibilitar.** To disable. To make impossible.

**Imposible.** Impossible, infeasible, preposterous.

**Imposición.** Imposition. Tax.

**Impositivo.** Related to taxes.

**Impostergable.** Most urgent, that cannot be relegated.

**Impostura.** Imposture, deception, fraud, lie, misrepresentation.

**Impotencia.** Impotency, helplessness, weakness.

**Imprenta.** Press, printing press.

**Imprescindible.** Indispensable, essential, necessary, vital.

**Imprescriptible.** Not subject to the statute of limitations.

**Impresión.** Impression. Effect, impact. Imprint, mark.

**Impresión digital.** Fingerprint.

**Imprevisible.** Unforeseeable, unpredictable.

**Imprevisión.** Unforeseeability, unpredicibility.

**Imprevisto.** Unexpected.

**Imprevistos.** Contingency, eventuality, incident.

**Ímprobo.** Dishonest, mendacious.

**Improcedencia.** Irrelevancy, immateriality. Rejection of a motion.

**Improcedente.** Irrelevant, immaterial.

**Impronta.** Impression, mark, seal. Track, imprint.

**Impropio.** Improper, dishonest, incorrect, wrong.

**Imprudencia.** Imprudence, recklessness, temerity. Indiscretion. Audacity, gall, nerve.

**Imprudente.** Imprudent. An imprudent person is a negligent person, wanting in foresight, who creates a serious risk for himself or for another, without obligation, necessity, or benefit.
Reckless. Indiscrete. Audacious.

**Impúber.** Minor, under age. Adolescent, teenager, youth.

**Impúdico.** Shameless, immoral, indecent, lewd.

**Impuesto.** Tax, assessment, contribution, duty, excise, tariff.

**Impuesto a las ganancias eventuales.** Capital gains tax.

**Impuesto al valor agregado.** Value added tax, V.A.T.

**Impuesto de justicia.** Stamp tax.

**Impuesto inmobiliario.** Real estate tax.

**Impuesto sobre la renta.** Income tax.

**Impugnabilidad.** Possibility or availability of a legal challenge.

**Impugnable.** Challengeable.

**Impugnación.** Challenge, attack, objection. Action for annulment, invalidity or voidness.

**Impugnador, impugnable.** Challenger, objector.

**Impugnar.** To challenge, attack, object. To move for annulment, invalidity or voidness.

**Impulso.** Prosecution of a case. Procedural diligence. Impulse, impetus.

**Impulso procesal.** Motions that move the lawsuit forward.

**Impune.** Without punishment or sanction.

**Impunidad.** Impunity, nonaccountability. Immunity.

**Imputabilidad.** Criminal responsibility. No responsibility attaches to whoever, at the time of the act or omission, and due to mental illness, incomplete mental development or retardation, to a severe disturbance of conscience, lacked the capacity to understand criminality of his act or to conduct himself in accordance with said understanding. (Standard Penal C. for Latin America, sec. 19).

**Imputabilidad, alcohol o drogas.** Criminal responsibility, alcohol or drugs. Punishment will not be attenuated simply because the person in question was only partially able, at the time of the act or omission, to understand the criminality of the act or to conduct himself in accordance with said understanding, if the disturbance of conscience was caused by consuming alcoholic beverages intentionally or carelessly, or to facilitate the commission of the act or to create an excuse. (St. P.C. for LA, sec. 22).

**Imputabilidad, falta de capacidad plena.** Criminal responsibility, lack of full understanding. Whoever, at the time of the act or the omission, lacked full capacity to understand the criminality of his act or to conduct himself with said understanding, will be sentenced to not less than one third of the minimum, nor longer than one third of the maximum legally prescribed for the corresponding crime.

If punishment is deemed inimical to proper treatment due to pathological reasons, only medical measures will be taken. (St. P.C. for LA, sec. 20).

**Imputabilidad, minoridad.** Criminal responsibility, minority. A person who at the time of the act has not reached the age indicated by the corresponding statute, cannot be punished. (St. P.C. for LA, sec.23).

**Imputabilidad, perturbación mental autoprovocada.** Criminal responsibility, self induced mental disturbance. When the severe disturbance of conscience was self-induced by the person in question, responsibility will attach for the criminal intent, recklessness or negligence in relation to the criminal act, present at the time when the severe disturbance of conscience was induced. (Standard Penal C. for Latin America, sec. 21).

**Imputable.** Imputable, attributable, chargeable.

**Imputación.** Imputation. Assignation of fault or liability. Accusation, charge.

**Imputación de pago.** Application of payment. A person having several debts of the same kind in favor of a single creditor may declare, at the time of making a payment, to which of them it is to be applied. If the debtor should accept a receipt from the creditor, setting forth the application of the payment, he can not make a claim against it, unless there should be some cause which may invalidate the contract. (Sp. Civ. C., sec. 1140).

**Imputar.** To impute. To accuse, blame, charge.

**In dubio pro operario (L).** In case of doubt the issue is resolved in favor of the worker. A principle particular to labor law that works as an interpretation technique. Of course, if the issue is clear, this phrase is not applicable.

**In dubio pro reo (L).** Applicable only in criminal cases this principle of interpretation states that doubts are resolved in favor of the accused.

**In fraudem legis (L).** In a fraudulent way. Strictly speaking the expression means "defrauding the law". It is used mainly to highlight that the law has been breached although no person has yet been individualized yet as a victim.

**In rem verso (L).** Sometimes this expression is preceded by the Latin word *actio*, for action. It was indeed an old Roman action to obtain that a thing be returned to its lawful possessor. In American law one could find an equivalent in restitution or replevin.

**Inabrogable.** That cannot be annulled or voided.

**Inacción.** Inaction, lack of taking proper steps.

**Inaceptable.** Unacceptable, inadequate, inadmissible, inappropriate, improper.

**Inacumulable.** Noncumulative.

**Inadmisible.** Inadmissible, inadequate, inappropriate, improper, unacceptable.

**Inadvertencia.** Inadvertence, oversight.

**Inafectable.** Out of commerce. That cannot be alienated or encumbered.

**Inajenable, inalienable.** Inalienable. Out of commerce.

**Inalienabilidad.** That cannot be sold or transferred.

**Inamistoso.** Unfriendly, bellicose, hostile. Cold, distant.

**Inamovible.** That cannot be removed or replaced.

**Inamovilidad.** Tenure. Job security.

**Inapelable.** Unappealable, final, firm.

**Inaplicable.** Inapplicable, immaterial, irrelevant.

**Inatacable.** Unimpeachable, unchallengeable. Incontestable.

**Incapacidad.** Incapacity, disability. Impossibility.

**Incapacidad total.** Total disability. Such injuries as result in the total and permanent disability of the workman or employee to engage in any kind of remunerative work or occupations shall be considered total disability. (Arzola Maldonado v. Industrial Commission, 92 PRR 534 (1965)).

**Incapacitado, discapacitado.** Disabled, incompetent. Disqualified.

**Incapacitarse.** To become disabled, incompetent or disqualified.

**Incapaz.** Incapable, unable.

**Incautación.** Attachment, capture, confiscation, expropriation, forfeiture, impoundment, seizure.

**Incautar.** To attach, capture, confiscate, seize.

**Incautarse.** To confiscate, commandeer, impound, seize. To appropriate for oneself. To steal.

**Incendiar.** To set on fire, to burn down.

**Incendio.** Fire, hostile fire.

**Incesibilidad.** Intransferability, legal impossibility to convey.

**Incesto.** Incest.

**Incestuoso.** Incestuous.

**Incidencia.** Incidence. Effect, consequence. Frequency, occurrence.

**Incidental.** Incidental. Accidental, indirect. Insignificant, negligible.

**Incidente.** Incidental issue. Incidental issues which must be decided before the main issue can be proceeded with, which may be raised in any kind of an action, except oral actions, and for which no special procedure is prescribed in this law, shall be heard and determined according to the procedure prescribed in this title. Such questions, in order to be classified as incidental issues, must be immediately related to the main question which is the object of the action in which they are raised, or with the validity of the procedure.

The incidental issues which, requiring a previous decision, are an obstacle to the continuation of an action, shall be heard and determined in the same proceedings, the course of the principal action being meanwhile suspended. (Sp. L. Civ. P. sec. 740-744).

Incident. Derivation from a main judicial case. Episode, event.

**Incipiente.** Incipient, beginning, nascent.

**Inciso.** Subsection, subparagraph, subclause.

**Incitación a la separación de un matrimonio.** Alienation of spouse's affection.

**Incitador.** Instigator, abettor. Provocation.

**Incitar.** To incite, arouse, goad, induce, provoke, stimulate.

**Incluir.** To include, embrace, encompass, involve. To consist of.

**Inclusión.** Inclusion, encompassing, involvement.

**Incoación.** Inception. Commencement.

**Incoado.** Inchoate, formally filed.

**Incoar.** To file charges.

**Incoar pleito.** To file a lawsuit.

**Incobrable.** Uncollectible, bad debt.

**Incógnito.** Incognito, secret, undercover.

**Incómodo.** Annoying, inconvenient, bothersome.

**Incomparecencia.** Nonappearance, failure to make a judicial appearance.

**Incompatibilidad.** Incompatibility, incongruity, mismatch.

**Incompatible.** Incompatible. Antagonistic, hostile. Contradictory, irreconcilable.

**Incompetencia.** Incompetence. Lack of jurisdiction, improper venue. Inexperience, lack of skill or knowledge.

**Incompetencia dictada de oficio.** *Sua sponte* ruling on lack of jurisdiction. Except in cases of submission, if the judge believes he lacks jurisdiction, he shall so declare *sua sponte*, and shall order the case to be sent to the judge that he believes should take cognizance of the matter. (C.R. C. of Civ. P., art. 43).

**Incompetencia por foro inconveniente.** See *Forum non conveniens*. It is not an instance of lack of jurisdiction. For such reason, the term incompetencia is not proper.

**Incompetente.** Incompetent. Without jurisdiction. Inexperienced, unskilled.

**Incomunicación.** Incommunication, isolation. Solitary confinement.

**Incomunicado.** Incommunicado, isolated.

**Inconciliable.** Irreconcilable, discordant, incompatible.

**Inconcluso, inconcluyente.** Inconclusive, unachieved, unfinished.

**Inconcuso.** Unaffected, untouched. Without having suffered the least damage.

**Incondicionado, incondicional.** Unconditional, absolute, complete.

**Inconexo.** Disconnected, unconnected. Irrelevant, immaterial.

**Inconfirmado.** Unconfirmed, unofficial.

**Inconforme, disconforme.** Dissenting, objecting. Unaccepting.

**Inconformidad, disconformidad.** Disapproval, dissent, nonconformity.

**Incongruencia.** Variance, contradiction, disagreement, divergence, inconsistency, incompatibility.

**Inconmutable.** Unpardonable, unforgivable. Irretrievable.

**Inconsecuente.** Inconsequential, irrelevant. Negligible, *de minimis*.

**Inconstitucional.** Unconstitutional.

**Inconstitucionalidad.** Unconstitutionality.

**Inconsumible.** Durable, that can be used many times without loss or destruction.

**Incontestabilidad.** Incontestability, indisputability, unchallengeable, unimpeachable.

**Incontestable.** Incontestable, indisputable, incontrovertible.

**Incontrovertible.** Incontrovertible.

**Incorporación.** Incorporation. Assimilation. Acceptance, reacceptance.

**Incorporador.** Incorporator, promotor.

**Incorporal, incorporeo.** Incorporal, intangible.

**Incorporar.** To incorporate. To set up a corporation. To assimilate, accept. To absorb, swallow. To merge. To consolidate.

**Incorporar en autos.** To file, to read into the record.

**Incorruptible.** Incorruptible. Of great integrity.

**Incremento.** Increase, expansion, growth, raise.

**Incriminar.** To incriminate. To accuse, arraign, charge, indict. To implicate, impute, involve. To inculpate.

**Incruento.** With little physical damage.

**Inculpabilidad.** Lack of culpability, fault or liability.

**Inculpable.** Innocent, without guilt or fault.

**Inculpado.** Accused, charged, defendant.

**Inculpar.** To accuse, arraign, blame, charge, indict. To report, to inform on someone. To blow the whistle.

**Inculpatorio.** Inculpatory, incriminating, implicating. Compromising.

**Incumbencia.** Pertinence, relevance. Tenure. Administration.

**Incumbir.** To incumb, to be pertinent, to be of concern.

**Incumplido.** Unperformed, unachieved. Incomplete.

**Incumplimiento.** Nonperformance.

Nonperformance is failure by a party to perform any of its obligations under the contract, including defective performance or late performance. (Unidroit, Prin., art. 7.1.1).

Breach, default, noncompliance.

**Incumplimiento anticipado.** Anticipatory nonperformance. Where prior to the date for performance by one of the parties it is clear that there will be a fundamental nonperformance by the party, the other party may terminate the contract. (Unidroit, Prin., art. 7.3.3).

**Incumplimiento substancial.** Material breach.

**Incuria.** Laches.

**Incurrir.** To incur, to become subject to.

**Incurrir en error.** Make a mistake, be in error.

**Incurrir en mora.** Fall in default, default.

**Incurso.** Having committed a certain crime or act.

**Indagación.** Investigation, enquiry.

**Indagador.** Enquirer, examiner, investigator.

**Indagar.** To investigate, to ask.

**Indagatoria.** Formal interrogation of the accused in a criminal proceeding.

**Indebido.** Undue, illegal, illicit, unlawful. Tortious, wrongful.

**Indecencia.** Indecency, immorality.

**Indecente.** Indecent, dissolute, immoral, obscene, pornographic.

**Indeciso.** Undecided, not final.

**Indeclinable.** Unwaivable, unrefutable.

**Indefendible.** Indefensible, untenable. Preposterous.

**Indefensión.** Defenselessness.

**Indefenso.** Undefended.

**Indelegable.** What cannot be delegated; undelegable.

**Indelicado.** Rash, coarse, imprudent.

**Indemnidad.** Indemnity, compensation, damages, recompense, reimbursement, reparation, restitution. Redress, settlement.

**Indemnizable.** Subject to an indemnity or damages.

**Indemnización.** Indemnification, compensation, compensation, damages, indemnity, recompense, reimbursement, reparation, restitution. Redress, settlement.

**Indemnización, alcances.** Damages scope.

Damages shall include, not only the value of what has been lost, but also of profits prevented, except for what is mentioned in the following articles. (Sp. Civ. C., sec. 1106).

**Indemnización basada en justas expectativas.** Damages based on reliance.

**Indemnización, cuantía.** Damages, measure. Damages are measured by the loss sustained by the obligee and the profit of which he has been deprived. (Lou. Civ. C. art. 1995).

**Indemnización en daños y perjuicios.** Damages. Indemnity for losses and damages includes not only the amount of the loss which may have been suffered, but also that of the profit which the creditor may have failed to realize, reserving the provisions contained in the following sections. (Sp. Civ. C., sec. 1073, 1074).

**Indemnización especulativa.** Uncertain damages.

**Indemnización genérica.** General damages.

**Indemnización nominal.** Nominal damages.

**Indemnización por dolo.** Damages for fraud.

Damages for fraud shall be actionable in all obligations. An action for fraud cannot be validly waived. (Sp. Civ. C., sec. 1102).

**Indemnización por incumplimiento estipulada en el contrato.** Agreed payment for nonperformance. Where the contract provides that a party who does not perform is to pay a specified sum to the aggrieved party for such nonperformance, the aggrieved party i entitled to that sum irrespective of its actual harm. (Unidroit, Prin., art, 7.4.13).

**Indemnización por incumplimiento parcial.** Damages for partial breach.

**Indemnización por mora.** Damages for delay. Performance of an obligation is owed from the time the obligor is put in default. Other damages are owed from the time the obligor has failed to perform.

Moratory damages presuppose a performance actually rendered, although delayed.

In such a case, the object of the obligee's recovery is compensation for the injury his interest has sustained because of the obligor's untimeliness in performing.

Compensatory damages presuppose, instead, total or partial nonperformance, or defective performance by the obligor. (Lou. Civ. C. art. 1989 and notes).

**Indemnización por pérdida no pecuniaria.** Damages for nonpecuniary loss. Damages for nonpecuniary loss may be recovered when the contract, because of its nature, is intended to gratify a nonpecuniary interest and, because of the circumstances surrounding the formation or the nonperformance of the contract, the obligor knew, or should have known, that his failure to perform would cause that kind of loss. (Lou. Civ. C. art. 1998).

**Indemnización punitiva.** Punitive damages.

**Indemnización punitoria.** Punitive damages. *Damnum emergens, lucrum cessans* and moral damages constitute the only types of damages recognized by the Latin American legislation. Punitive or exemplary damage is a concept rejected by Civil law Tradition, and hence, it neither exists in contracts nor in torts. Except for Argentina, these three damages may be indirect damages. On the other hand, they may be either foreseeable or unforeseeable damages depending upon the circumstances of the case. (Barrios-Mannucci).

**Indemnizado.** Party who receives an indemnity.

**Indemnizador.** Party who pays an indemnity.

**Indemnizar.** To indemnify, compensate. To pay damages.

**Indemnizatorio.** Compensatory.

**Independiente.** Independent, autonomous, free.

**Inderogable.** That cannot be derogated or annulled.

**Indeterminado.** Indeterminate, indefinite, undetermined.

**Indexación.** Linkage of debts to inflation.

**Indicador.** Indicator, sign, signal. Indication, symptom.

**Indicatorio.** Indicatory, indicative. Denotative, representation, telling, symptomatic.

**Índice.** Index list, table.

**Indiciamiento.** Indictment.

**Indicio.** Indication, indicia. Clue, demonstration, manifestation, sign.

**Indiferente.** Indifferent. Without a formed opinion. Unbiased. Careless, imperious, unconcerned.

**Indignidad.** Unworthiness. They are called unworthy, in matters of succession, those who, by the failure in some duty towards a person, have not deserved to inherit from him, and are in consequence deprived of his succession.

Indignity. Humiliation, shame.

**Indignidad e incapacidad.** Unworthiness and incapacity. There is this difference between being unworthy and incapable of inheriting, that he who is declared incapable of inheriting, has never been heir, whilst he who is declared unworthy, is not the less heir on that account, if he has the other qualities required by law to inherit. Thus a person unworthy of inheriting remains seized of the succession, until he is deprived of it by a judgment, which declares him divested of it for cause of unworthiness. (Lou. Civ. C. art. 965).

**Indigno.** Unworthy.

**Indiligencia.** Negligence, carelessness.

**Indirecto.** Indirect, oblique, vague. Secondary, derived, incidental.

**Indisciplina.** Undiscipline.

**Indisolubilidad.** Indissolubility, that cannot be broken or separated.

**Indispensable.** Indispensable, essential, fundamental, imperative, necessary, needed, vital.

**Indisponibilidad.** Lack of, shortage. unavailability. Intransferability, inalienability.

**Indisponible.** Intransferable, inalienable.

**Indisputable.** Indisputable, incontestable, unchallengeable, unimpeachable.

**Individual.** Individual, personal, private, single.

**Individuo.** Individual, person.

**Indivisible.** Whole.

**Indivisión.** Indivision, whole.

**Indiviso.** Undivided, whole.

**Indocumentado.** Illegal alien. Immigrant lacking a visa and a work permit. Without documents.

**Indubitable.** Unquestionable, certain, undoubted.

**Inducción.** Induction, initiation. Recruitment.

**Inducir a error.** To lead to error.

**Indulgencia.** Indulgence. Forgiveness, clemency, leniency, mercy, pardon. Gratification.

**Indultar.** To pardon, to decree an amnesty.

**Indulto.** Pardon. A pardon extinguishes all or part of the punishment imposed, or converts it into a more benign punishment. Other consequences, ancillary to the punishment, are not affected by a pardon. Ancillary penalties are removed by a pardon only when specifically included.

A pardon is an act of executive clemency which does not form pat in itself of the criminal process which culminates in the accused's conviction. (Ppl. v. Albizu, 77:843, followed) (Reynolds v. Delgado, Warden, 91 PRR 294 (1964)). Amnesty.

**Industria.** Industry. Manufacture. Business, trade. Diligence, hard work.

**Industrial.** Industrial.

**Ineficacia.** Inefficiency, inoperativeness, uselessness.

**Ineficaz, ineficiente.** Ineffective, ineffectual.

**Inejecución.** Failure to execute or to enforce.

**Inembargable.** That cannot be attached or seized. Exempted property.

**Inenajenable.** That cannot be sold.

**Ineptitud.** Inability, incompetence, ineffectiveness.

**Inepto.** Inept, awkward, clumsy, incapable, unable.

**Inequitativo.** Inequitable, unfair, unjust.

**Inequívoco.** Unequivocal, clear.

**Inescrupuloso.** Unscrupulous, corrupt, dishonest, unprincipled.

**Inestimado.** Unassessed, unappraised.

**Inevitable.** Inevitable, unavoidable.

**Inexcusable.** Inexcusable. Unforgivable, unpardonable. Forceful, mandatory, necessary.

**Inexistencia.** Inexistence. Nullity.

**Inexistente.** Inexistent. Null and void.

**Inexpugnable.** Invulnerable. Indefeasible, incontestable, unchallengeable.

**Infamante.** Calumnious, libelous, slanderous. Type of felony.

**Infamatorio.** Defamatory.

**Infame.** Infamous, disgraceful, nefarious.

**Infamia.** Infamy, ignominy, shame.

**Infancia.** Infancy, childhood. Beginning.

**Infante.** Infant, child. Soldier.

**Infanticida.** Person who murders a child.

**Infanticidio.** Infanticide, murder of a child.

**Inferencia.** Inference is the deduction from the fact proved or fully established made by the trier in his discernment. (Murcelo v. H.I. Hettinger & Co., PRR 398 (1965)).

Sometimes characterized as *"hominis"* presumption—is the deduction from the facts proved or fully established made by the trier in his discernment. (Widow of Delgado v. Boston Ins. Co., 99 PRR 693 (1970)).

Deduction, implication.

**Inferior.** Inferior, lesser, lower. Subordinate. Substandard.

**Inferir.** To infer, deduct, imply. To assume, gather, presume, suppose.

**Infidelidad.** Infidelity, unfaithfulness. Disloyalty, treachery.

**Infidencia.** Indiscretion, breach of confidence.

**Infidente.** Disloyal, indiscrete, double crosser.

**Infiel.** Unfaithful.

**Infiltración.** Infiltration, filtering through. Going in undetected.

**Infligir.** To inflict, administer, create, impose.

**Influencia.** Influence, control, power.

**Influenciar.** To influence, persuade, sway.

**Influyente.** Influential.

**Información.** Information, data, knowledge, news.

**Información sumaria.** Judicial proceeding to establish the truth of a certain fact that is not contested but cannot be ascertained otherwise for reasons such as lack of recordation, loss of pertinent documents, etc.

**Informaciones para perpetuar memoria.** Proceedings to perpetuate testimony. Judges shall admit and order that all proceedings to perpetuate testimony instituted before them be taken, provided they do not relate to facts which may prejudice some determinate and certain person. (Sp. L. Civ. P. sec. 2001).

**Informador, informante.** Informer. Announcer, reporter, speaker.

**Informal.** Informal. Direct. Unreliable.

**Informar.** To inform, notify, tell.

**Informativo.** Informative, newsworthy, revealing.

**Informe.** Report, account, paper.

**Informe final.** Closing argument.

**Informe pericial.** Expert report.

Expert evidence. The judge shall call for an expert opinion if, to ascertain or weigh some important fact or circumstances in the case, scientific or artistic knowledge should be necessary or advisable.

**Infortunio.** Calamity, misadventure, misfortune.

**Infracción.** Infraction, breach, infringement, nonperformance, trespass, violation.

**Infractor.** Transgressor, trespasser, violator.

**Infrascripto.** Undersigned.

**Infringir.** To infringe, breach, nonperform, trespass, violate.

**Infundado.** Unfounded. With no basis or reason.

**Infungible.** Non fungible, not interchangeable.

**Ingerencia.** Interference, encroachment, impingement, invasion.

**Ingerencismo.** State intervention, statism.

**Ingratitud.** Ingratitude, ungratefulness, unappreciative.

**Ingreso.** Income, revenue. Access, admission.

**Ingresos.** Income, earnings, salary, wages.

**Inhabil.** Incompetent, unfit, unsuited, unqualified.

**Inhabilidad.** Disability, incompetence, unsuitability.

**Inhabilitación.** Disqualification, disbarment.

**Inhabilitación absoluta.** Absolute disqualification. Absolute disqualification includes: 1) Loss of any State employment or position held by the convict, even if he was elected by the people. 2) Disqualification to obtain any State employment. 3) Inability to vote and be elected and to join any political association. 4) Inability to exercise parental rights or to be appointed tutor or guardian. (Standard Penal C. for Latin America, sec. 49).

**Inhabilitación accesoria**. Attendant disqualification. Disqualification, as an attendant penalty to imprisonment, is subject to the following rules: a.) If imprisonment was for ten years or more, the court may also impose an attendant disqualification for 5 to 15 years. b.) If imprisonment was less than 10 years but more than 2, the court may also impose an attendant disqualification from 2 to 10 years. (Standard Penal C. for Latin America, sec. 51).

**Inhabilitación especial.** Specific disqualification. Specific disqualification consists in the deprivation, restriction, loss, or suspension of the right to practice a profession or trade, be it regulated or not. (Standard Penal C. for Latin America, sec. 50).

**Inhabilitado.** Disqualified, disbarred.

**Inherente.** Inherent, innate, intrinsic.

**Inhibición.** Inhibition. The justices and judges included in any of the cases mentioned as grounds for a challenge shall abstain from taking cognizance of the cause without waiting to be challenged. (Sp. L. Crim. P., art. 55).

Constraint, impediment.

**Inhibición ante un tribunal penal.** Inhibitory plea before a criminal court.

**Inhibirse.** To withdraw, to decline, step down.

**Inhibitoria.** Declinature. The inhibition shall be presented to the judge or court considered competent, requesting that a writ be issued forbidding the court not considered as having jurisdiction to proceed in the cause and ordering it to transmit the record. (Sp. L. Civ. P., sec. 72).

**Inhibitorio.** Inhibitory.

**Inhumar.** To bury, entomb, inter.

**Iniciar.** To begin, commence, start.

**Iniciativa.** Initiative. Drive.

**Inicuo.** Evil.

**Inimpugable.** Unimpeachable, unchallengeable, uncontestable.

**Ininteligible.** Unintelligible, incomprehensible, confusing.

**Injuria.** Injury, damage, grievance.

**Injuriador.** Offender, wrongdoer.

**Injuriar.** To slander, libel. To insult.

**Injurioso.** Slanderous, libelous. Offensive. Insulting.

**Injusticia.** Injustice, inequity, unfairness.

**Injustificable.** Unjustifiable, indefensible, inexcusable.

**Injustificado.** Unjustified.

**Injusto.** Unjust, unfair.

**Inmaterial.** Immaterial, irrelevant.

**Inmatriculación por el estado.** Registration by state. The State, its agencies, instrumentalities or municipalities may register properties belonging to them, provided they have possessed by property, as shown in their records, for more than thirty years as owners, quietly, continuously, publicly and peacefully. (PR Mort. Law 1979, sec. 249).

**Inmemorial.** Immemorial.

**Inmobiliario.** Related to land and buildings.

**Inmoderado.** Exorbitant, extravagant, unreasonable.

**Inmoral.** Immoral, dissolute, unethical.

**Inmoralidad.** Immorality. By immorality is meant all those acts or practices which are in contravention of mutually established standards in order to attain decency, good order, and correct personal conduct; hence, everything that is hostile to the welfare of the general public and contrary to good morals is immoral; it is not confined to sexual matters, but includes conduct inconsistent with rectitude or indicative of corruption, indecency, depravity, dissoluteness, or as willful, flagrant, or shameless conduct showing moral indifference to the opinion of respectable members of a community, and as an inconsiderate attitude toward good order and the public welfare. (Velez v. Secretary of Education, 86 PRR 717 (1962)).

**Inmotivado.** Without a motive or reason. Baseless.

**Inmueble.** Immovable, real estate.

**Inmuebles incorporales.** Incorporeal immovables. Rights and actions that apply to immovable things are incorporeal immovables. Immovables of this kind are such as personal servitudes established on immovables, predial servitudes, mineral rights, and real or possessory actions. (Lou. Civ. C. art. 470).

**Inmuebles no inscriptos.** Real property not recorded.

**Inmuebles por accesión.** Component parts of tracts of land, fixtures doctrine. Buildings, other constructions permanently attached to the ground, standing timber, and unharvested crops or ungathered fruits of trees, are component parts of a tract of land when they belong to the owner of the ground.

**Inmune.** Immune, exempt, invulnerable, privileged.

**Inmunidad.** Immunity, exemption, privilege.

**Inmunidad soberana.** Sovereign immunity.

**Innavegable.** Impossible to navigate.

**Innominado.** Innominate.

**Innovación.** Innovation, breakthrough, invention.

**Inobservancia.** Nonobservance, breach, disregard, noncompliance.

**Inocencia.** Innocence, candor, guiltlessness, lack of liability.

**Inocente.** Innocent, non liable, not guilty.

**Inoficioso.** Ineffective, inoperative.

**Inoperante.** Inoperative, ineffectual, theoretical.

**Inoponible.** That cannot be raised.

**Inquilinato.** Cheap rental, asylum.

**Inquilino.** Tenant, lessee.

**Inquirir.** To inquire, enquire. To ask, query. To request information.

**Inquisición.** Inquisition. Examination, probe.

**Insacular.** Inclusion of names that later will be drawn out by chance.

**Insanable.** Irretrievably damaged or void.

**Insania.** Insanity, dementia, derangement, lunacy, madness.

**Insano.** Insane, lunatic, mad man.

**Insasicular un jurado.** To draw a juror.

**Insatisfecho.** Unsatisfied, unpaid, unperformed.

**Inscribible.** Recordable.

**Inscribir.** To record, list, register.

**Inscribirse.** To enlist, enroll, sign up.

**Inscripción.** Inscription, enlistment, enrollment, recordation, registration.

**Inscripción de títulos, actas y contratos.** Registration of titles, transactions and contracts. In order to be recordable, titles must appear in deeds, judgments or official documents issued by judicial authority or a competent official, in the manner prescribed by law and regulations, except in cases where the law establishes a different procedure. (PR Mort. Law 1979, sec. 38, sec. 42).

**Inscripción o anotación preventiva.** Preventive recording or entry. When any document recorded or entered preventively in the Registry constitutes, conveys, modifies or extinguishes real property rights, no other document may be recorded with the same or an earlier date which may be contrary to or incompatible with it which conveys or encumbers said property. (PR Mort. Law 1979, sec. 56).

**Inscripciones registrales.** Entries in the property registry. Entries made of any property in the Registry shall include the following data in the most concise form possible: 1) The nature, location and boundaries of real properties subject to registration or affected by the right that must be recorded and their surface area measurements in the metric decimal system, as well as the name and number if they appear in the title and conforming to their description and official nomenclature when there is one, also consigning all those specifications leading to the complete individualization of the real property. 2) The nature, extension, suspensive or resolutory conditions and encumbrances on the right which is being recorded, and their value. (PR Mort. Law 1979, sec. 87).

**Inscripto, inscrito.** Recorded.

**Insecuestrable.** Exempt from seizure or attachment.

**Inseparable.** Inseparable.

**Inserción.** Insertion, addition, rider.

**Insertar.** To insert, add, inject.

**Insinuación.** Insinuation, hint, implication, inference, suggestion.

**Ínsito.** Intrinsic, inborn, inherent, natural.

**Insobornable.** Impossible to bribe.

**Insolvencia.** Insolvency, bankruptcy, indigence, paucity, poverty.

**Insolvente.** Insolvent, bankrupt, destitute, indigent, pauper, poor.

**Insostenible.** Untenable, indefensible, unconceivable.

**Inspección.** Inspection, audit, examination, scrutiny.

**Inspección ocular.** Inspection on sight. If the crime prosecuted shall have left traces or material evidence of its commission, the examining judge or person acting in his stead shall collect and keep them for the oral trial, if possible, proceeding for this purpose to make an ocular inspection and a description of all that which might have any connection with the existence and nature of the act. For this purpose he shall include in the record of the proceeding a description of the place of the commission of the crime, the location and condition of the objects found there, the topography or location of the dwellings, and any other details which might be utilized for the accusation or for the defence. (Sp. L. Crim. P., art. 326).

**Inspección personal del juez.** Personal inspection by the judge. Evidence by personal inspection by the court or judge shall only be effective in so far as it clearly permits the court to judge, by the external appearance of the thing inspected, of the fact which he desires to ascertain. (Sp. Civ. C., sec. 1208).

**Inspector.** Inspector, auditor, detective, examiner, investigator.

**Inspectoría.** Control board or department.

**Instancia.** Instance. Case. Example, illustration.

**Instar.** Incite, encourage, provoke.

**Instigación.** Instigation. Whoever has caused another to commit a criminal act will be sentenced to the penalty provided for the principal. (Standard Penal C. for Latin America, sec. 34).
Encouragement, provocation.

**Instigador.** Instigator.

**Instigar.** To instigate, encourage, provoke.

**Institución.** Institution. Establishment. Generally accepted habit or conduct.

**Institucional.** Institutional. Corporate, collective.

**Instituir.** To institute. To enact, legislate. To create, found. To establish.

**Instituto.** Institute, institution. Organization. School.

**Instituyente.** Founder, creator.

**Instrucción.** Instruction. Investigation of facts during criminal proceedings.

**Instructivo.** Instructive, educational.

**Instructor.** Instructor. First instance criminal judge in charge of investigating the facts.

**Instrumental.** Instrumental. Equipment, instruments, tools. Related to documentary evidence.

**Instrumentar.** To execute, to document in writing.

**Instrumento.** Instrument. Written document.

**Instrumento de venta.** Bill of sale.

**Instrumento negociable.** Commercial paper.

**Instrumento privado.** Private document.

**Instrumento público.** Public document.

**Insubordinación.** Insubordination disobedience, rebellion.

**Insubsanable.** Irretrievably damaged or void.

**Insubsistente.** No longer present or in existence.

**Insuficiencia.** Insufficiency, inadequacy.

**Insuficiente.** Insufficient, inadequate.

**Insultar.** To insult, offend, ridicule.

**Insurrección.** Insurrection, disobedience, rebellion.

**Intachable.** Unimpeachable, beyond reproach or suspicion.

**Intangible.** Intangible. Exempt from attachment or seizure. Beyond people's reach.

**Integración.** Integration, amalgamation, consolidation, synthesis.

**Integración del contrato.** Supplying an omitted term.
(1) Where the parties to a contract have not agreed with respect to a term which is important for a determination of their rights and duties, a term which is appropriate in the circumstances shall be supplied. (2) In determining what is an appropriate term regard shall be had, among other factors, to

(a) the intention of the parties; (b) the nature and purpose of the contract; (c) good faith and fair dealing; (d) reasonableness. (Unidroit, Prin., art. 4.8).

**Integral.** Integral, complete, through.

**Integrante.** Member, partner, part of, party. Component, constituent. Associate, fellow.

**Integrar.** To integrate, desegregate, blend, unite.

**Íntegro.** Entire, complete, whole. Intact, undamaged. Honest, trustworthy.

**Inteligencia.** Intelligence, intellect. Point of agreement. Sense. Secret information.

**Inteligencia errónea.** Wrong assumption, mistaken belief.

**Inteligible.** Intelligible.

**Intempestivo.** Abruptly, precipitous, without notice. Suddenly and untimely.

**Intención.** Intention, intent, object, purpose.

**Intención de las partes.** Intention of the parties.

(1) A contract shall be interpreted according to the common intention of the parties. (2) If such an intention cannot be established, the contract shall be interpreted according to the meaning that reasonable persons of the same kind as the parties would give to it in the same circumstances. (Unidroit, Prin., art. 4.1).

**Intencional.** Intentional, conscious.

**Intencionalidad.** Intent, premeditation.

**Intencionalmente.** Intentionally, advisedly, consciously, purposefully.

**Intendencia.** Mayor's office. Body of janitors.

**Intendente.** Mayor. President of a club.

**Intentar.** To attempt, endeavor, try, undertake.

**Intento.** Attempt, endeavor, try out, undertaking.

**Intercambio.** Interchange, exchange, swap, switch.

**Interdicción, interdicto.** Interdiction, injunction, prohibition, restraining order.

**Interdicción por incapacidad física.** Interdiction for physical incapacity. Not only lunatics and idiots are liable to be interdicted, but likewise all persons who, owing to any infirmity, are incapable of taking care of their persons and administering their estates. Such persons shall be placed under the care of a curator, who shall be appointed and shall administer in conformity with the rules contained in the present chapter. (Lou. Civ. C. art. 422).

**Interdicción por incapacidad mental.** Interdiction for mental incapacity. No person above the age of majority, who is subject to an habitual state of imbecility, insanity or madness, shall be allowed to take care of his own persona and administer his estate, although such person shall, at times, appear to have the possession of his reason. (Lou. Civ. C. art. 389).

**Interdictal.** Related to an interdiction or injunction.

**Interdicto.** Summary proceedings related to property. Summary proceedings relating to property can only be instituted: 1) To acquire possession. 2) To retain or recover possession. 3) To prevent a new construction. 4) To prevent that damage be caused by a ruinous construction.

**Interdicto de adquirir, posesorio.** Summary proceedings to acquire property. In order that summary proceedings to acquire possession may be instituted, it shall be an indispensable requisite that no person be in the possession as owner or usufructuary of the property whose possession is requested.

**Interdicto de obra nueva.** Summary proceedings based upon a new construction. After the complaint in summary proceedings based upon a new construction has been filed, the judge shall issue any order restraining the owner of the construction from continuing the same, under an admonition to destroy what is being built, and citing the parties interested to appear at an oral hearing upon the nearest day possible after the three days following the notification of said injunction, and to present thereat the documents upon which they base their contentions. A copy of the complaint must be attached to the same, drafted on ordinary paper, which shall be delivered to the defendant when the citation is served upon him. The judgment rendered in summary proceedings based upon a new construction does not decide the question, which can be subsequently discussed in an ordinary action, relating to the right to continue the erection of the construction involved. (Decision of November 26, 1864).

**Interdicto de obra ruinosa.** Summary proceedings against ruinous construction. Summary proceedings against ruinous constructions may have two objects: 1) The adoption of urgent measures of precaution for the purpose of avoiding the dangers which may arise from the bad condition of some building, tree, column, or any another similar object, the fall of which may cause injury to persons or property. 2) The total or partial demolition of a ruinous construction. (Sp. L. Civ. P. sec. 1674-1677).

**Interdicto de retener o de recobrar.** Summary proceedings to retain or recover possession. Summary proceedings to retain or recover possession shall lie with the person who is in possession or in the tenancy of a thing which has been disturbed therein by acts that show the intention of molesting dispossessing said party, or when said party has already been disseized of his possession or tenancy. (Sp. L. Civ. P. sec. 1649, 1650).

**Interdicto prohibitorio.** Injunction.

**Interés.** Interest. Attention, curiosity, desire to know. Dividend, profit, revenue.

**Interés asegurable.** Insurable interest.

**Interés garantizado.** Security interest.

**Interesado.** Interested party. Interested.

**Interesarse.** To acquire an interest. To request about.

**Intereses compuestos.** Interest on interest, compound interest.

**Intereses moratorios.** Interest on delay.

**Interestatal.** Interstate. International.

**Intereses por incumplimiento de obligaciones dinerarias.** Interest for failure to pay money. If a party does not pay a sum of money when it falls due the aggrieved party is entitled to interest upon that sum from the time when payment is due to the time of payment whether or not the non-payment is excused. (Unidroit, Prin., art. 7.4.9).

**Intereses sobre el monto de la indemnización.** Interest on damages. Unless otherwise agreed, interest on damages for nonperformance of non-monetary obligations accrues as from the time of nonperformance. (Unidroit, Prin., art. 7.4.10).

**Interferencia de la otra parte.** Interference by the other party. A party may not relay on the nonperformance of the other party to the extent that such nonperformance was caused by the first party's act or omission or by another event as to which the first party bears the risk. (Unidroit, Prin., art. 7.1.2).

**Interino.** Temporary, acting, interim, provisional.

**Interior.** The provinces. Internal, domestic, indigenous, national. Interior, inside.

**Interlinear.** To interline. To write between the lines.

**Interlocutorio.** Interlocutory. Court rulings on routine procedural matters.

**Intermediario.** Intermediary, broker, middleman. Agent, representative. Mediator. Amicable compounder.

**Intermedio.** Intermediate. Conduit. By means of.

**Internación.** Commitment. Commitment measures will last for a maximum of 15 years. Measures of surveillance will last for a maximum of 10 years. (Standard Penal C. for Latin America, sec. 59).

**Internacional.** International, transnational. Universal, worldwide.

**Internamiento.** Internment, confinement, reclusion, seclusion.

**Interpelación.** Interpellaltion. Questioning. Challenge. Examination, cross examination.

**Interpelar.** To examine, cross examine. To question. To challenge.

**Interpol.** Interpol.

**Interpolación.** Interlineations, between the lines, interpolation.

**Interponer.** To interpose. To mediate, arbitrate. To intervene, step in. To file a motion. To move. To raise a defense.

**Interponer apelación.** To file an appeal.

**Interposición.** The filing of a motion or of an appeal. Brokerage, mediation. Intervention.

**Interpósito.** Placed in between.

**Interpretación.** Interpretation, construction. Clarification, explanation, elucidation. Translation.

**Interpretación auténtica.** Legislative construction of a statute.

**Interpretación *contra proferentem*.** *Contra proferentem* rule.

If contract terms supplied by one party are unclear, an interpretation against that party is preferred. (Unidroit, Prin., art. 4.6).

**Interpretación de contratos.** Contractual interpretation. If the terms of a contract are clear and leave no doubt as to the intentions of the contracting parties, the literal sense of its stipulations shall be observed.

**Interpretación de declaraciones y otras conductas.** Interpretation of statements and other conduct. (1) The statements and other conduct of a party shall be interpreted according to that party's intention of what the other party knew or could not have been unaware of. (2) If the preceding paragraph is not applicable, such statements and other conduct shall be interpreted according to the meaning that a reasonable person of the same kind as the other party would give to it in the same circumstances. (Unidroit, Prin., art. 4.2).

**Interpretación de normas procesales.** Interpretation of procedural rules. When interpreting a procedural rule, the judge shall take into account that the object of a procedural rule is to implement substantive law. In cases of doubt the judge can resort to the general principles of Procedural Law. (C.R. C. of Civ. P., art. 3).

**Interpretación de testamentos.** Construction of wills. The construction of wills consists in an intellectual operation the finality of which is to inquire into the testator's will, clarifying and ascertaining the actual meaning of its expression and, if necessary, filling the gaps of its declarations. (Rivera Padró v. Rivera Correa, 98 PRR 195 (1966)).

**Interpretación judicial.** Judicial construction of a statute.

**Interpretativo.** Interpretative.

**Intérprete.** Interpreter, translator, court translator. Commentator. Communication.

**Interpuesto.** Interposed, in the middle.

**Interrogador.** Interrogator, examiner, questioner.

**Interrogante.** Question, doubt, enquiry, query.

**Interrogar.** To interrogate, ask, enquire, examine, quiz.

**Interrogativo, interrogatorio.** Interrogatory. List of questions. Examination. Test.

**Interrogatorio bajo custodia.** Custodial interrogation. Questioning initiated by law enforcement officers after a person has been taken into custody or otherwise deprived of his freedom of action. (Ppl. v. Beltrán Santiago, 97 PRR 89 (1969)).

**Interrupción.** Interruption, interference. Discontinuance. Adjournment, deferment. Stay, suspension. Intermission, recess.

**Interrupción de la prescripción.** Interruption of the statute of limitations or of adverse possession.

**Interrupción del proceso.** Stay of proceedings.

**Interruptivo.** Interruptive, disruptive. Discontinuing.

**Intervención.** Intervention.

**Intervención adhesiva.** Intervention in support. A third party may intervene in a lawsuit without alleging a right for himself, but only with the purpose of helping a party win the case, the intervenor having a interest in the outcome of the case. The intervenor will continue in the case in the state the case happens to be at the time of the intervention. (C.R. C. of Civ. P., art. 112).

**Intervención en el pago.** Payment for honor.

**Intervenir.** To intervene, to take action. To participate. To be or to become a party to proceedings.

**Interventor.** Interventor. Auditor, inspector, observer. Officer sent by central authorities to take control of and to supervise a local emergency.

**Interventor en el pago.** Payor for honor.

**Interventoría.** Interventor's mandate, office or work.

**Interviniente.** Intervener, intervening party. Person involved or who has acted.

**Intestado.** Intestate, without a valid will.

**Intimación.** Order. Summons. Intimation, inference, suggestion.

**Intimación, quebrantamiento.** Commitment, infringement. If a commitment measure is infringed the court may extend such measure for a period reasonable necessary to achieve its purpose. (Standard Penal C. for Latin America, sec. 60).

**Intimado.** Party served with the summons. Party ordered to pay or to defend herself.

**Intimar.** To order. To summon. To intimate, imply, suggest.

**Intimatorio.** With due judicial notice. Under penalties of law.

**Intimidación.** Intimidation, fear, terror. Coercion, threats.

**Intimidar.** To intimidate, frighten, scare. To coerce, threaten.

**Intoxicado.** Intoxicated, inebriated.

**Intraestatal.** Intrastate. Domestic, local, internal, purely national.

**Intransferible.** Untransferable, unconveyable. Out of commerce. Inalienable.

**Intransmisible, intraspasable.** Intransmissible.

**Intromisión.** Interference, intrusion, intromission, meddling.

**Intrusión.** Intrusion, encroachment, imposition, impingement. Interruption. Invasion.

**Intruso.** Intruder, invader, trespasser.

**Inutilidad.** Futility, ineffectiveness, uselessness.

**Invalidar.** To invalidate, annul, cancel, nullify. Repeal, reverse, revoke, quash. To disable, damage, impair.

**Invalidarse.** To become disabled or impaired.

**Invalidez.** Invalidity, voidness, cancellation, nullity. Disability.

**Inválido.** Invalid, annulled, null, void. Disabled.

**Invasión.** Invasion, military aggression, raid.

**Invención, invento.** Invention, breakthrough, discovery, innovation. Fabrication, fantasy, lie, mendacity.

**Invenciones de los trabajadores.** Inventions by employees. In instances in which an employee develops an invention in the course of his work, he is entitled to have his name appear as the inventor. However, if his job is research-related, ownership of the invention, and the right to patent its use, will belong to the employer. In the latter case, the inventor will be entitled to compensation by mutual agreement or, in its absence, as decided by the Conciliation and Arbitration Board. If the employee does not work in research activities, the ownership of the invention will be his. (Mex. Labor Law).

**Inventariar.** To inventory, appraise, assess, catalog, list.

**Inventario.** Inventory, catalog, appraisal, list of assets.

**Inventor.** Inventor, creator, discoverer.

**Inversión.** Investment, placement of money.

**Inversión extranjera, Argentina.** Foreign investment, Argentina.

Foreign investors are entitled to utilize any of the corporate structures recognized by Argentine law, and are therefore free to enter the market via the most convenient vehicle available, whether through a merger, acquisition, joint venture, etc. As a result of the no-discrimination principle, foreign and domestic companies are treated equally under the law, including access to short, medium or long-term domestic or foreign currency financing in the local market, as well as full eligibility for economic development incentive programs. Competitive equality is applied to markets and credit. Additionally, foreign firms may also participate in publicly financed research or subsidized research and development programs on a national treatment basis.

The new Constitution, enacted in 1994, declares the citizens' right to enjoy a healthy and balanced environment, suitable for human development and for productive activities, without compromising the rights of future generations. It also states that ecological damage must be repaired. (Alonso Peña).

**Inversionista, inversor.** Investor.

**Inversiones extranjeras, Chile.** Foreign investments, Chile. Chile's Constitution establishes some basic principles on which foreign investors may rely.

First, article 19 of the Constitution guarantees uniformity in the application of the law, both to Chileans and foreigners. Second, articles 19, 22, and 98 prohibit arbitrary differences or discrimination. Third, article 19 further guarantees the right to develop any economic activity not contrary to the morals, nation security, or public order of the country. Fourth, article 19 also guarantees the right to ownership of both physical goods and incorporeal assets. In addition, expropriation is allowed only when a law passed by the Chilean Congress authorizes expropriation based on public interest. (Orihuela).

**Invertir.** To invest.

**Investidura de título.** Vesting of title.

**Investigación.** Investigation, search. Research, analysis.

**Investir.** To award, accord, confer, bestow, grant, invest, vest.

**Inviolable.** Inviolable, intangible, unbreachable.

**Invitado.** Invitee.

**Invocar.** To invoke, conjure, evoke, summon. To implore, petition, pray, supplicate.

**Involuntario.** Involuntary, unconscious.

**Inyectar.** To inject, insert, introduce. To shoot up.

**Irrazonable.** Irrational, unreasonable, exorbitant, inconceivable, untenable.

**Irrebatible.** Irrebuttable, indisputable, unchallengeable.

**Irrecuperable.** Irrecoverable, irretrievable. Bad debt.

**Irrecurrible.** Final, *res judicata*, unappealable.

**Irrecusable.** Unchallengeable, unimpeachable.

**Irredimible.** Irredeemable, irretrievable.

**Irrefutable.** Irrefutable, unrebuttable.

**Irregular.** Irregular. Illegal, wrong.

**Irregularidad.** Irregularity. Departure from established norms.

**Irreivindicable.** That cannot be claimed back. Beyond the plaintiff's power of replevin.

**Irrelevante.** Irrelevant, immaterial, inconsequential, unconnected.

**Irremediable.** Unavoidable, inescapable, inevitable.

**Irremisible.** Irremissible, unforgivable.

**Irrenovable.** Not renewable, final, non extendable.

**Irrenunciable.** Unwaivable.

**Irreparable.** Irreparable, hopeless, irreversible.

**Irresponsabilidad.** Irresponsibility.

**Irresponsable.** Irresponsible, unaccountable.

**Irretroactividad.** Irretroactivity.

**Irretroactivo.** Irrectroactive, non retroactive.

**Irreversible.** Irreversible, final, irretrievable.

**Irrevisable.** Non revisable.

**Irrevocabilidad.** Irrevocability, finality.

**Irrevocable.** Irrevocable, final, unappealable.

**Islote.** Small island.

***Iura novit curia* (L).** Old Roman adage meaning that the court knows the law. The practical consequence is that if the law is not plead, or even the wrong statute is cited, the court may still apply the proper legal principle.

***Iure gestionis* (L).** An act performed by the State but not in a strict governmental capacity. The practical test usually is to consider if a private entity could perform, or usually performs the same type of act. For instance, if the State owns and exploits and opera theater or a railway company. The importance of this classification usually arises in the context of a defense based on sovereign immunity. The most common position is that acts performed by the State and which are iure gestionis, are not covered by sovereign immunity.

***Iure imperii* (L).** It applies to acts of authority performed by the State in its governmental capacity. For instance, arresting an individual, declaring war on another nation or enacting legislation. These acts are usually considered immune from prosecution under the theory of sovereign immunity. Although it is not strictly necessary both expressions, iure gestionis and iure imperii are preceded by the preposition "de" (of) when used in a Spanish phrase.

***Iuris et de iure* (L).** Phrase applied to a legal presumption that is irrebuttable.

**Iuris tantum (L).** Phrase applied to a legal presumption that is rebuttable.

**Ius cogens (L).** Part of the law that is absolutely mandatory and cannot be waived or contracted away.

**Ius dispositivum (L).** Part of the law that can be contractually altered by the parties concerned.

**Ius posterius derogat priori (L).** Principle of interpretation stating that the law enacted later in time prevails over the more ancient one.

**Ius preferendi (L).** Preference right.

**Ius utendi (L).** Right to use something.

**IVA.** Value added tax, V.A.T.

# J

**Jactancia.** Claiming rights one is not entitled to, especially inheritance rights. Boasting.

**Jefatura.** Headquarters, head office.

**Jefe.** Leader, boss, chief, director, ruler.

**Jefe de familia.** Family head, bread winner.

**Jerarquía.** Hierarchy, rank, category.

**Jerga.** Jargon. Legalese. Gibberish.

**Jornada.** Day, 24 hours, work period in a day.

**Jornada de trabajo.** Full working day

**Jornada de trabajo, menores.** Work shift, minors. The work shift of minors may not exceed six hours, divided into two periods of a maximum of three hours by a rest period of at least one hour. Minors may not work overtime, on holidays, or on mandatory rest days. (Mex. Labor Law).

**Jornada de Trabajo.** Work Shift. The work shift is the time in which the worker is at the disposal of the employer in order to perform work. (Mex. Labor Law).

**Jornal.** Salary paid to workers by the day.

**Jornalero.** Jobber, manual worker hired by the day.

**Jubilación.** Pension, retirement.

**Jubilado.** Pensioner, retired worker.

**Jubilar.** To pension, retire.

**Judicatura.** Judicature, bench, judiciary power, judgeship.

**Judicial.** Judicial, judiciary.

**Juego.** Game. Gambling.

**Juego y apuesta.** Gambling and betting. The law does not permit any action to claim what is won in a game of chance, luck, or hazard; but the person who loses can not recover what he may have voluntarily paid, unless there should have been fraud, or should he be a minor or incapacitated to administer his property.

**Juez.** Judge, magistrate, justice.

**Juez *a quo*.** Trial judge.

**Juez *ad quem*.** Judge who decides on appeal.

**Juez arbitral.** Arbitrator.

**Juez de paz.** Justice of the peace. Although the names are quite similar, the Latin American version could be hard to distinguish from the district judge.

**Juez de Registro Civil.** Civil Registry Judge. In the Federal District, the judges of the Civil registry will be in charge of the legalization of matters related to the civil status of individuals, the issuance of birth certificates, the acknowledgment of paternity, adoptions, marriages, administrative divorces and the death of Mexicans and foreigners residing within their districts, as well as the recording of final judgments declaring absence, presumption of death, judicial dissolution of marriage, custody or its loss and limitations on the legal capacity to administer one's own assets. (Mex. Civ. C., art.35).

**Juez instructor.** Criminal judge who intervenes in the evidentiary part of the case.

**Juez lego.** Lay judge.

**Juez ponente.** Judge who expresses the view of the majority in one tribunal.

**Juicio.** Suit, lawsuit, litigation. Legal action. Wisdom, prudence. Opinion, belief.

**Juicio cabal.** Sound mind.

**Juicio de apeo.** Proceeding to fix limits and boundaries.

**Juicio de consignación.** Lawsuit depositing with the court a payment that the defendant refuses to accept.

**Juicio de desahucio.** Action for unlawful detainer. All persons legally entitled to the possession of the estate either as owners, beneficiaries, or by virtue of another title which gives them the right to enjoy the estate, and their representatives, shall be considered legal parties to institute an action of unlawful detainer.

**Juicio ejecutivo.** Executory action. *Juicio ejecutivo*: An action the purpose of which is to enforce what is already determined or which appears from a title which has the same force of law as a judicial decision. (Escriche,

Diccionario de Legislación y Jurisprudencia).

An executory action must be based upon a document importing a confession of judgment. Such documents are: public instruments, bills of exchange, commercial papers payable to order, etc. (Spanish L. Civ. P., sec. 1427, 1462-1465).

**Juicio en rebeldía.** Proceeding in default. From the time when the defendant has been declared in default, there shall be ordered, if the opposite party so requests it, the seizure of all kinds of personal property and an attachment of the real property to the amount considered necessary to insure that which is the object of the action. (Sp. L. Civ. P. sec. 761).

**Juicio ordinario posterior.** Ordinary action after executory proceedings. Judgments rendered in executory actions shall not give rise to the exception of *res judicata*, the parties reserving their rights to institute an ordinary action upon the same question. (Sp. L. Civ. P. sec. 1477).

**Juicio pericial.** Lawsuit that depends on the outcome of an expertise.

**Juicio político.** Impeachment. Proceeding whereby Congress convenes as a court to judge the acts of one of its members.

**Juicio por jurado.** Jury trial.

**Juicio por la corte.** Trial by the court.

**Juicio rápido y público.** Speedy and public trial.

**Juicio sumario.** An expedited type of proceedings characterized by allowing shorter periods for the different procedural steps.

**Juicio sumarísimo.** The quickest type of proceedings, allowing the shortest delays for the different procedural steps.

**Juicio universal o general.** Bankruptcy and testamentar proceedings. The proceeding in which all the actions and rights which all creditors have against the property of another are heard and determined, such as bankruptcy, testamentary, and intestate proceedings. (Escriche, Diccionario de Legislación y Jurisprudencia).

**Juicios civiles (derecho laboral).** Civil trials (labor law). They are used to deal with disputes (individual or collective) regarding the interpretation and compliance with labor standards. The process has several stages: a) a conciliation hearing, involving presentation of complaints and admission of evidence; b) as many hearings as are needed to gather all relevant evidence; c) procedures outside of the Board's offices, or in their own offices, by officials or law clerks, or with the aid of other officials, to provide evidence. (Mex. Labor Law).

**Junta.** Board, commission, committee, council. Military government.

**Junta consultiva.** Advisory board.

**Junta de acreedores.** Creditors' meetings.

**Junta directiva.** Board of directors.

**Jura.** Taking of an oath.

**Jura de la bandera.** Swearing allegiance to the flag.

**Jurado.** Jury, jurors, panel.

**Jurados suplentes.** Alternate jurors.

**Juramentar, jurar.** To take an oath.

**Juramento.** Oath, solemn promise, vow.

**Juramento de cargo.** Oath taken by an appointee to a specific public office.

**Juramento decisorio o indecisorio.** Decisory or indecisive oath. Every litigant is obligated to make his statement under oath when the opposite party requires it. A decisory oath shall be considered full proof even though there be additional evidence. An indecisive oath shall prejudice only the person who testifies. (Sp. L. Civ. P. sec. 578).

**Juramento indecisorio.** Answer to request for admissions that is only considered if it is detrimental to the person who answers.

**Jurídicamente.** Juridically, legally.

**Juridicidad.** Legality.

**Jurídico.** Juridical, legal.

**Jurisconsulto.** Attorney-at-law, lawyer, jurist.

**Jurisdicción.** Jurisdiction. The term jurisdiction means the power or authority of a court to hear and determine the causes or controversies. (Gearheat v. Hashell, 87 PRR 53 (1963)).

Venue.

**Jurisdicción contenciosa.** Contentious jurisdiction. That jurisdiction exercised when one invokes the aid of the law against one that disputes his demands, as distinguished from voluntary jurisdiction, when the person having the right to resist the demand appears as a consenting applicant. (Century Dictionary).

**Jurisdicción extranjera.** Foreign jurisdiction. For the purposes of private international law, those jurisdictions having their own laws on certain matters, who laws may be in conflict with each other, are considered foreign among themselves even though those jurisdiction are not necessarily foreign for the purposes of public international law. (Armstrong v. Armstrong, 86 PRR 387 (1962)).

**Jurisdicción penal ordinaria.** Ordinary criminal jurisdiction. The ordinary jurisdiction shall take cognizance of criminal causes in which persons subject to the ordinary as well as to other special jurisdictions appear guilty, with the exceptions expressly mentioned in the laws with regard to the competency of another jurisdiction.

**Jurisdicción voluntaria.** Voluntary jurisdiction. All proceedings in which the intervention of the judge is requested or is necessary, without there being actual litigation, or in which no question is raised between known and determined parties, shall be considered an act of voluntary jurisdiction. (Sp. L. Civ. P., sec. 1810).

**Jurisdiccional.** Jurisdictional.

**Jurisprudencia.** Case law, legal decisions.

**Jurisprudencial.** Related to case law.

**Jurista.** Jurist.

**Justa causa.** Just cause.

**Justicia.** Justice, equity, fairness.

**Justicia gratuita.** Legal aid to the poor.

Persons declared poor shall enjoy the following privileges: 1) The right to use in their defense stamped paper of their class. 2) The right to have an attorney and a solicitor appointed, without being obliged to pay them any fees or charges. 3) Exemption from the payment of all kinds of charges to the assistants and subaltern officials of the superior and inferior courts. 4) To give promise under oath to pay if their fortune should improve, instead of making the deposits necessary in order to request and obtain relief. 5) The right to have all letters rogatory and other communications re-

quested by them acted upon, and complied with *de oficio* , should they demand it. (Sp. L. Civ. P., sec. 13, 14).

**Justiciable.** Amenable to court, defendant.

**Justiciar.** To sue, prosecute. To execute.

**Justiciero.** That imposes justice and redresses wrongs.

**Justificable.** Justifiable, excusable, explainable.

**Justificación.** Justification. No crime is committed by those who act in the performance of a legal duty or in the lawful exercise of a right. (Standard Penal C. for Latin America, sec. 15). Excuse, explanation. Attenuating reason, extenuating circumstance, mitigating factor.

**Justificación de la rebeldía.** Excuse from default.

**Justificación, defensa propia o ajena.** Justification, defense of self or others. No crime is committed by those who act in defense of persons or rights—their own or someone else's—provided all the following circumstances concur: 1) Unlawful attack. 2) The means employed to prevent or repel the attack were reasonable. (St. P.C. for LA, sec. 16).

**Justificación, exceso.** Justification excess. Whoever causes excessive harm, will not be justified. However, the court may reduce the sentence, which shall be not less than one third of the minimum nor greater than one third of the maximum legally established for the crime in question.

Excessive conduct resulting from the excitement or a disturbance justified under the circumstances, is not punishable. (St. P.C. for LA, sec. 18).

**Justificación, prevención de un mal mayor.** Justificación, prevention of a greater harm. Whenever one's own lawful rights, or those of another, are endangered, no crime is committed by whoever injures another legal right in order to avoid a greater harm, provided all the following circumstances concur: concurrently: 1) That the danger is clear and present or imminent. 2) That the danger has not been intentionally provoked by the person in question. 3) That the danger cannot be prevented otherwise. If the person whose lawful rights are endangered is duty bound to assume the risk involved, this article will not apply. (St. P.C. for LA, sec. 17).

**Justificador.** Justifier, diminisher of liability.

**Justificante, justificativo.** Certificate, evidence, proof. Corroborating document.

**Justipreciador.** Appraiser, assessor.

**Justipreciar.** To appraise. To assess, estimate the value.

**Justiprecio.** Appraisal, estimate, valuation.

**Justo.** Just, equitable, fair.

**Juvenil.** Juvenile, youthful.

**Juventud.** Youth, adolescence, puberty.

**Juzgado.** Court, tribunal. Courthouse.

**Juzgado correccional.** Criminal court for lesser offenses.

**Juzgado de primera instancia.** District court.

**Juzgado promiscuo.** Court that hears civil and criminal cases.

**Juzgador.** Judge, court, tribunal. Judiciary.

**Juzgamiento.** Trial, legal proceeding, legal process. Judgment, ruling, verdict.

**Juzgar.** To judge. To pass or render judgment. To decide a case. To adjudicate.

# K

**K.** The twelfth letter of the Spanish alphabet. Only words of foreign origin begin with this letter.

**Kártell.** Cartel (Sp).

**Kilo.** Prefix, means thousand.

**Kilómetro.** Kilometer.

**Kilovatio.** Kilowatt.

**Kopek.** Kopeck. A Russian coin equal to $\frac{1}{100}$ of the rouble.

# L

**La cosa habla por sí sola.** *Res ipsa loquitur* (L).

**Labor.** Labor. The work or labor of an employee is not limited exclusively to the exertion of physical or mental effort, but, under particular circumstance, that an employee may engage an employee to do nothing but simply to wait some occurrence which may call for his activity, either of his own initiative or at the employe's request. (Heirs of Meledez v. Central San Vicente, 86 PRR 377 (1962)).

Job, work. Strain, toil. Chore, task. Period before birth or child delivery.

**Laboral.** Related to work.

**Laboratorio.** Lab, laboratory.

**Labradío.** Fertile land that can be cultivated.

**Labranza.** Husbandry.

**Labrar.** To draft a legal document. To cultivate the land.

**Labriego.** Farmhand.

**Lacerar.** To cause physical injury with a cutting instrument.

**Lacrar.** To seal a document with wax. To seal a door, box or envelope as a precaution.

**Lacre.** Wax used for sealing.

**Ladrón.** Thief, burglar, crook, robber.

**Laguna.** Lagoon, small lake.

**Laguna del derecho.** Areas where the law remains silent. Legal gap, situation that has not been foreseen by the law.

**Laguna jurídica.** Legal gap. Legal gaps found in this Book shall be filled with rules applicable to analogous cases and, if the latter are missing, with constitutional principles and general principles of procedural law. (Panamanian Judicial Code, art. 465.)

**Lagunas procesales.** Procedural gaps. Cases not foreseen by this Code shall be ruled by established norms, be they by analogy or by constructions *a contrario sensu*. If these means are not possible, the gaps shall be filled with constitutional principles and with the general principles of Procedural Law. (C.R. C. of Civ. P., art. 4).

**Lanzamiento.** Eviction, dislodgement, dispossession, ejection, expulsion, ouster.

**Lanzar.** To evict, dislodge, eject, oust. To throw, hurl, pitch.

**Lapidación.** Causing death by stoning.

**Lapso.** Lapse, time running between two given points.

**Lascivia.** Lasciviousness, lewdness.

**Lastimado.** Injured, damaged, hurt, wounded.

**Lastimadura.** Injury, laceration, lesion.

**Lastre.** Weight, counterweight.

**Lateral.** Lateral, collateral.

**Latifundio.** Large expanse of land, usually unproductive, in the hands of a single family.

**Latifundismo.** System that favors ownership of enormous areas of land.

**Lato.** Ample, broad, irrestricted.

*Lato sensu* **(L).** In a broad sense, generally speaking.

**Latronicio.** The killing of a thief when caught in the act of stealing.

**Laudar.** To award an arbitral decision, to render a judgment.

**Laudemio.** Laudemio, laudemium.

**Laudo.** Award, judgment.

**Laudo no ejecutable.** Non-enforceable award.

1. The recognition and execution of the decision may be refused, at the request of the party against which it is made, only if such party is able to prove to the competent authority of the State in which recognition and execution are requested:

a. The parties to the agreement were subject to some incapacity; or

b. That the party against which the arbitral decision has been made was not duly notified; or

c. That the decision concerns a dispute not envisaged in the agreement; or

d. That the constitution of the arbitral tribunal or the arbitration procedure has not been carried out in accordance with the terms of the agreement; or

e. That the decision is not yet binding on the parties or has been annulled or suspended. (Conv. on Intl. Comm. Arb., art. 5).

**Leal.** Loyal, devoted, faithful.

**Leal saber y entender.** To the best of one's knowledge.

**Lealtad.** Loyalty, allegiance, faithfulness, fidelity.

**Lealtad contractual.** Good faith and fair dealing.

**Lealtad y probidad.** Loyalty and honesty. The parties and their attorneys are under the duty:

1. To behave with loyalty and honesty in all their acts;

2. To behave reasonably in their requests or exceptions and in the exercise of their procedural rights.

The parties must behave with loyalty and honesty during the proceedings. (Panamanian Judicial Code, arts. 215, 462).

**Lecho.** Bed.

**Lecho conyugal.** Marital bed.

**Lectura.** Reading.

**Lectura de la acusación.** Arraignment

**Legación.** Legation, mission, representation, ambassadorship.

**Legado.** Legacy, bequest, device. Testamentary gift. Gift *mortis causa.*

**Legado bajo título universal.** Legacy under universal title. The legacy, under a universal title, is that by which a testator bequeaths a certain proportion of the effects of which the law permits him to dispose, as a half, a third, or all his immovables, or all his movables, or a fixed proportion of all his immovables or of all his movables. (Lou. Civ. C. art. 1612).

**Legado de parte alícuota.** Legacy of aliquot. The figure of legacy of an aliquot share or legacy of aliquot part in a will—also called partial legacy or hereditary legacy—is a legacy the contents of which are determined by the testator as an arithmetical fraction of his total patrimony, as an abstract and ideal part or share thereof, or, a legacy by virtue of which the testator disposes under specific title of a proportional part of his inheritance. (Vivaldi v. Registrar, 86 PRR 596 (1962)).

**Legado particular.** Particular legacy. Every legacy, not included in the definition before given of universal legacies and legacies under a universal title, is a legacy under a particular title. (Lou. Civ. C. art. 1625).

**Legado universal.** Universal legacy. A universal legacy is a testamentary disposition, by which the testator gives to one or several persons the whole of the property which he leaves at his decease. (Lou. Civ. C. art. 1606).

**Legajo.** File, dossier.

**Legajo de la sentencia.** Judgment roll.

**Legal.** Legal, lawful, legitimate, licit. Forensic. Juridical. Judicial.

**Legalidad.** Legality, lawfulness, legitimacy.

**Legalismo.** Legalism. Latin American legal culture is highly legalistic; that is, society places great emphasis upon seeing that all social relations are regulated by comprehensive legislation. There is a strong feeling that new institutions or practices ought not be adopted without a prior law authorizing them. Laws, regulations, and decrees regulate with great specificity seemingly every aspect of Latin American life, as well as some aspects of life not found in Latin America. It often appears that if something is not prohibited by law, it must be obligatory. (L & D in LA). (See Formalismo.)

**Legalista.** Legalistic. Formalistic.

**Legalización.** Authentication, legalization, certification.

**Legalizar.** To legalize. To certify authenticity. To authenticate. To comply with required formalities.

**Legalmente.** Legally, lawfully.

**Legar.** To bequeath, devise. To pass over. To leave behind.

**Legatario.** Legatee, beneficiary, donee, devisee.

**Legión.** Legion, army, company, squadron.

**Legislación.** Legislation. Legislation is a solemn expression of legislative will. (Lou. Civ. C., art. 2).

Statutory law. Law. Legal System.

**Legislación ambiental.** Environmental law. Any statute or regulation, or provision thereof, the primary purpose of which is the protection of the environment, or the prevention of a danger to human life or health, through (i) the prevention, abatement or control of the release, discharge, or emission of pollutants or environmental contaminants, (ii) the control of environmentally hazardous or toxic chemicals, substances, materials and wastes, and the dissemination of information related thereto, or (iii) the protection of wild flora or fauna, including endangered species, their habitat, and specially protected natural areas in the Party's territory, but does not include any statute or regulation, or provision thereof, directly related to worker safety or health.

**Legislador.** Legislator, law maker, law giver. Senator, representative.

**Legislar.** To legislate, enact, pass laws, to promulgate.

**Legislativo.** Legislative, congressional, parliamentary.

**Legislatura.** Legislature, congress, parliament.

**Legista.** Forensic, pertaining to the law or the legal system.

**Legítima defensa.** Self-defense, legitimate defense.

**Legítima, porción legítima.** Legal portion. The legal portion is that part of the property which the testator cannot dispose of because the law has reserved it for specified heirs, called on that account forced heirs. (Widow of Sambolin v. Registrar, 94 PRR 303 (1967)).

**Legitimación.** Legitimation.

**Legitimación, capacidad.** Legitimation, capacity. The capacity to legitimate is governed by the personal law of the father, and the capacity to be legitimated by the personal law of the child, legitimation requiring the concurrence of the conditions prescribed by both. (Bustamante C. art. 60).

**Legitimación por acto notarial.** Legitimation by notarial act. A father or mother shall have the power to legitimate his or her illegitimate children by an act passed before a notary and two witnesses, declaring that it is the intention of the parent making the declaration to legitimate such child or children. (Lou. Civ. C. art. 200).

**Legitimación por matrimonio.** Legitimation by marriage. Illegitimate children are legitimated by the subsequent marriage of their father and mother, whenever the latter have formally or informally acknowledged them as their children, either before or after the marriage. (Lou. Civ. C. art. 198).

**Legitimar.** To legitimize. To give credence or respectability.

**Legitimario.** Forced heir.

**Legitimidad.** Legitimacy, lawfulness, legality. Genuiness. Rightfulness.

**Legitimidad, presunción.** Legitimacy, presumption. Rules concerning the presumption of legitimacy and its conditions, those conferring the right to the name, and those which determine the evidence of filiation and regulate the inheritance of the child are rules of an internal public order, the personal law of the child if different from that of the father being applied. (Bustamante C. art. 57).

**Legítimo.** Legitimate, lawful, legal. Genuine. Rightful.

**Lego.** Layman, nonprofessional. Amateur, dilettante.

**Leguleyo.** Lawyer proven to play tricks and given to chicanery.

**Lengua.** Language, speech, tongue.

**Lenocinio.** Brothel, bordello, whorehouse.

**Leña.** Wood, lumber, timber.

**Leonino.** Abusive, one sided, overreaching, unfair.

**Lesbiana.** Lesbian.

**Lesión.** Damage. Injury, laceration, lesion, wound. Economic damage.

**Lesión enorme.** A ground for rescinding a transaction when one of the parties was injured in half or more of the market value. Transaction that is grossly unfair to one of the parties.

**Lesión subjetiva.** Lesion. Lesion can be alleged only by the vendor in no other sale than one of corporeal immovable.

If the vendor has been aggrieved for more than half the value of an immovable estate by him sold, he has the right to demand the rescission of the sale, even in case he had expressly abandoned the right of claiming such rescission, and declared that he gave to the purchaser the surplus of the thing's value. (Lou. Civ. C. art. 2593 and 2589).

**Lesionado.** Injured, damaged, wounded.

**Lesionar.** To damage, injure, wound.

**Lesivo.** Damaging, injurious, noxious, prejudicial.

**Letal.** Lethal, deadly, fatal, mortal.

**Letra.** Letter. Handwriting. Bill of exchange, draft.

**Letra de cambio.** Bill of exchange. The drawer may draw the bill of exchange: 1) To his own order, stating that he reserves the value thereof. 2) On a person, in order that he may make the payment at the domicile of a third person. (Sp. Com. C., sec. 446).

**Letra de cambio, capacidad.** Bills of exchange, capacity. Capacity to enter into an obligation by means of a bill of exchange shall be governed by the law of the place where the obligation is contracted. (Inter-American Convention on Conflicts of Laws Concerning Bills of Exchange, Promissory Notes, and Invoices, art. 1).

**Letra de cambio, endoso.** Bill of exchange, endorsement. The endorsement shall render each and every endorser liable as security for the amount of the bill, if it is not accepted, and for its repayment, with the costs of the protest and reexchange, if not paid when due, provided the proceeding of presentation and protest took place at the time and in the manner prescribed by law. (Sp. Com. C., sec. 467).

**Letra de cambio, forma**. Bills of exchange, form. The form of the drawing, endorsement, guaranty, intervention, acceptance or protest of a bill of exchange shall be governed by the law of the place in which each one of those acts is performed. (Inter-American Convention on Conflicts of Laws Concerning Bills of Exchange, Promissory Notes, and Invoices, art. 2).

**Letra de cambio, intervención en la aceptación y el pago.** Bill of exchange, intervention in acceptance and payment. If after a bill of exchange should be protested for nonacceptance or nonpayment a third person should appear offering to accept or pay the same for the account of the drawer or for the account of any of the endorsers, even though there is no prior mandate to do so, the intervention for the acceptance or payment shall be admitted, one or the other being entered immediately after the protest, under the signature of the person who intervened and that of the notary, the name of the person for whose account the intervention took place being stated in the instrument. (Sp. Com. C., sec. 511).

**Letra de cambio, protesto.** Bill of exchange, protest. The nonacceptance or nonpayment of bills of exchange must be proven by means of a protest, without the first protest having been made exempting the holder from making the second, and without the death of the person on whom it is drawn nor his condition of bankruptcy permitting the holder to not make the protest. (Sp. Com. C., sec. 502).

**Letra de cambio, provisión de fondos.** Bill of exchange, supply of funds. The supply of funds shall be considered made, when the bill being due, the person on whom it was drawn is the debtor of an equal or greater sum than the bill of exchange to the drawer or to the third person for whose account the bill was drawn. (Sp. Com. C., sec. 457).

**Letra de cambio, recambio y resaca.** Bill of exchange, rechange and redraft. The holder of a protested bill of exchange may recover the amount thereof and the costs of protest and reexchange by drawing a new bill against the drawer or one of its endorsers and attaching thereto the original bill of exchange as well as the certified copy of the protest and the account of the redraft. (Sp. Com. C., sec. 527).

**Letra de cambio, término.** Bill of exchange, term. Bills of exchange may be drawn for cash or on time for one of the following periods: 1) At sight. 2) At one or more days, and at one or more months after sight. 3) At one or more days or at one or more months from date. 4) At one or more usances. 5) At a fixed or determined day. 6) At fairs. (Sp. Com. C., sec. 460).

**Letra de cambio, valor en cuenta y valor entendido.** Bill of exchange, "value on account" and "value understood." The phrases "value on account" and "value understood" shall render the person accepting the bill responsible for the amount of the same in favor of the drawer, in order to demand it or compensate him in the manner and at the time which both may have agreed upon in making the exchange contract. (Sp. Com. C., sec. 445).

**Letra en diversos ejemplares.** Bills in a set.

**Letra y firma.** Handwriting and signature.

**Letrado.** Attorney, counselor.

**Letrado patrocinante.** Attorney of record.

**Leva.** Recruitment of soldiers for the army. Military service.

**Levantamiento.** Uprising, coup, rebellion. Cancellation, removal.

**Levantar.** To raise.

**Levantar la sesión.** To adjourn.

**Levantar un acta.** To draft and sign a document, usually through a notary, describing a given situation; e.g. nonpayment.

**Levantar un cargo.** Bring charges, accuse, report a crime.

**Levantar un embargo.** To vacate an attachment order.

**Levantar un pagaré.** To pay a note.

**Ley, aplicación.** Application of the law. Mexican law shall apply to all persons that are in the Republic, as well as to the acts and events that occur in this territory or jurisdiction and to those that submit themselves to these laws, except when these provide the application of foreign law, and except when, also, as stated in the applicable treaties and conventions signed by Mexico. (Mex. Civ. C., art.12).

**Ley, silencio, laguna.** Law, silence, gap. Any court which shall refuse to render a decision on the pretext of silence, obscurity or unintelligibility of the laws, or for any other reason, shall be held liable therefor.

When there is no statute applicable to the case at issue, the court shall decide in accordance with equity, which means that natural justice, as embodied in the general principles of jurisprudence and in accepted and established usages and customs, shall be taken into consideration. (Sp. Civ. C., sec. 7).

**Ley.** Law, act, legislation, statute.

**Ley agraria.** Agrarian Law.

**Ley contra monopolios.** Antitrust act.

**Ley de compensaciones a obreros por accidentes de trabajo.** Workmen's accident compensation act.

**Ley de proscripción.** Bill of attainder.

**Ley del caso.** Law of the case.

**Ley, derogación.** Law, repeal. Laws shall only be repealed by means of subsequent laws; and disuse, custom or practice to the contrary shall not impede their enforcement. Laws may be repealed either entirely or in part by other laws.

The repeal is either express or implied. It is express, when it is literally declared by a subsequent law; it is implied, when the new law contains provisions either contrary to or irreconcilable with those of the former law.

**Ley, ignorancia.** Law, ignorance. Ignorance of the law does not excuse from compliance therewith. (Sp. Civ. C., sec. 2).

**Ley, interpretación.** Law, interpretation. When a law is clear and free from all ambiguity, the letter of the same shall not be disregarded, under the pretext of fulfilling the spirit thereof.

The words of a law shall generally be understood in their most usual signification, taking into consideration, not so much the exact grammatical rules governing the same, as their general and popular use.

Technical terms and phrases used in the arts and sciences shall be interpreted according to their perceived meaning and acceptation with the experts and authorities in the science, art of profession to which they refer. (Sp. Civ. C., sec. 13-20).

**Ley minera.** Mining Law.

**Ley, retroactividad.** Law, retroactivity. Laws shall not have a retroactive effect unless they expressly so decree. In no case shall the retroactive effect of a law operate to the prejudice of rights acquired under previous legislative action. (Sp. Civ. C. sec. 3).

**Leyes de Toro.** The Laws of Toro consisted of 83 laws promulgated in 1505. The first of these laws reproduced the *Ordenamiento de Alcalá* in modified form, filling certain lacunae. The remainder of the provisions dealt with succession, marriage, prescription, contracts, and criminal law. (L & D in LA).

**Libelista.** Person who commits libel.

**Libelo.** Libel. Complaint, original petition.

**Liberación.** Liberation, discharge, emancipation, freedom, release.

**Liberar, libertar.** To free, deliver, liberate, release.

**Liberatorio.** Liberating, discharging, releasing.

**Libertad.** Liberty, autonomy, independence, freedom.

**Libertad condicional.** Parole. The court may grant parole to a convict sentenced to prison for over two years, provided that the following circumstances are met: a). The convict has served half the sentence if he is a first offender, and two thirds if he is a repeat offender. b). The convict has displayed good conduct, evidenced by affirmative acts while serving his sentence and is capable of engaging in a lawful occupation or trade. c). The convict has redressed the damage caused by his crime, or seriously promises to do so, according to his means, and d). Studies of the convict's personality and other data warrant the conclusion that he will not commit further crimes. (Standard Penal C. for Latin American, sec. 82).

**Libertad condicional, revocación.** Parole, revocation. Parole will be automatically revoked if the parolee commits a new intentional crime.

When parole is revoked, the remainder of the sentence must be served. The court may further order that the convict serve all or part of the term he spent on parole. (Standard Penal C. for Latin America, sec. 84 and 85).

**Libertad de contratación.** Freedom of contract. The parties are free to enter into a contract and to determine its content. (Unidroit, Prin., art. 1.1).

**Libertad de culto.** Freedom of worship and of religion. After independence, there was general agreement to proclaim freedom of conscience and worship. Separation of Church and state was proclaimed in many countries.

The fact that Church and state are separate in so many countries does not imply any disagreement between them. Whether separated or not, Latin America as a whole remains Catholic. In almost all the countries the Church is still a strong political force, and the clergy is consulted by the governments. Since the clergy has been a conservative force, a segment of public opinion is complaining about lingering clericalism. (Western European and Latin American Legal Systems).

**Libertad de opinión y de palabra.** Freedom of speech and of the press. Latin American constitutions guarantee freedom of speech, and most of them frown upon press censorship. The effectiveness of these provisions is what foreign observers, North Americans especially, are most skeptical about, not only because the constitutional guarantees are suspended all too often, but also because they think the government has too much control over the press even under normal circumstances. (W. Eur. & LA Leg. Sys.).

**Libertad vigilada.** Freedom under surveillance. Measures of surveillance consist of: 1) establishment of a fixed domicile; 2) prohibition to visit certain places; 3) duty of reporting to the police and other special surveillance authorities; 4) duty to abstain from drinking alcohol, and 5) duty to abstain from using narcotic, hallucinatory or other addictive substances. (Standard Penal C. for Latin America, sec. 57).

**Libra.** Pound (weight), pound sterling.

**Librado.** Drawee, person in whose name a commercial paper is drawn.

**Librador, librante.** Drawer, person who issues a commercial paper.

**Libramiento.** Issuance of a commercial paper.

**Libranza.** Commercial paper.

**Libranzas vales y pagarés a la orden.** Drafts, bill or promissory notes payable to order. Draft payable to order between merchants and the bills or promissory notes likewise payable to order, which arise from commercial transactions, shall produce the same obligations and effects as bills of exchange, except with regard to acceptance, which is a quality pertaining to latter only. (Sp. Com. C., sec. 532).

**Librar.** To issue. To emit. To free, discharge, release.

**Libre.** Free. Autonomous, independent. Complimentary.

**Libre a bordo.** See *FOB*.

**Libre al lado.** See *FAS*.

**Libre de gravamen.** Unencumbered, free, clear.

**Libreta.** Notebook. Certificate. Report.

**Libro.** Book, tome, volume. Publication. Text.

**Libro de registro de accionistas.** Stock ledger.

**Libro diario de navegación.** Log book.

**Libro mayor.** Ledger. The accounts referring to each object or person in particular shall, moreover, be opened with a credit and debit in the ledger, and the entries referring to these accounts in the daybook shall be transferred to the former in strict order of dates. (P.R. Com. C. sec. 32, 10 LPRA sec. 1077).

**Libros comerciales, copiador.** Commercial books, copying book. All letters which a merchant may write regarding his business and the telegrams he may send shall be transferred to the copying book, either by hand or through any mechanical means, completely and consecutively, by order of dates, including the subscribing clause and signature. (Sp. Com. C., sec. 41).

**Libros comerciales, diario.** Commercial books, daybook. The first entry in the daybook shall consist of the result of the inventory mentioned in the foregoing article, divided into one or several consecutive accounts, according to the system of bookkeeping adopted. There shall thereafter follow, day by day, all their transactions, each entry stating the credit and debit of the respective accounts. (Sp. Com. C., sec. 38).

**Libros comerciales, exhibición.** Commercial books, exhibition. The inspection shall be made in the office of the merchant, in his presence, or in that of the person he may delegate, and shall be limited exclusively to the points which relate to the matter in question, said points being the only ones which may be verified. (Sp. Com. C., sec. 47).

**Libros comerciales, fuerza probatoria.** Commercial books, evidence value. Books of merchants shall be evidence against themselves, no proof to the contrary being admitted, but the opponent can not accept the entries which are favorable to him and reject those which prejudice him; but, having admitted this means of evidence, he shall abide by the result which they may show in their entirety, taking into equal consideration all the entries relating to the matter in litigation. (Sp. Com. C., sec. 48).

**Libros comerciales, inventarios y balances.** Commercial books, inventory and statements. The book of inventories and balances shall begin with the inventory which must be made by the merchant at the time of commencing business, and shall contain an exact statement of assets and debts. (Sp. Com. C., sec. 37).

**Libros comerciales, libro de actas.** Commercial books, book of minutes. In the book of minutes which shall be kept by each association there shall be entered verbatim all resolutions adopted at their meetings or at those of their managers, stating the date of each one, the persons who were present at the same, the votes cast, and anything else which will aid in arriving at an exact knowledge of what was decided. (Sp. Com. C., sec. 40).

**Libros comerciales, mayor.** Commercial books, ledger. The accounts referring to each object or person in particular shall, moreover, be opened with a credit and debit in the ledger, and the entries referring to these accounts in the daybook shall be transferred to the former in strict order of dates. (Sp. Com. C., sec. 39).

**Libros commerciales, autenticación.** Commercial books, authentication. Merchants shall present their books bound, ruled, and foiled, to the municipal judge of the district where they have their commercial establishment, in order that he may make on the first folio of each one a signed memorandum of the number contained in the book. The seal of the municipal court which authenticates them shall, moreover, be stamped on all the sheets of each book. (Sp. Com. C., sec. 36).

**Libros y contabilidad del comerciante.** Commercial books and bookkeeping. Merchants shall be required to keep: 1) A book of inventories and balances. 2) A daybook. 3) A ledger. 4) A copying book for letters and telegrams. 5) The other books required by special laws.

**Licencia.** License, certificate, credential, permit. Authorization, permission.

**Licencia de enfermedad.** Sick leave.

**Licenciado, lcdo.** Attorney, advocate, lawyer.

**Licenciar.** To license. To lay off, to fire from work.

**Licenciarse.** To graduate. To become licensed.

**Licenciatario.** Licensee

**Licenciatura.** License.

**Licitación.** Tender. Call for bids.

**Licitador.** Bidder, offeror.

**Licitar.** To sell through a bid. To bid at auction or on public works.

**Lícito.** Licit, lawful, legal, legitimate, permissible.

**Licitud.** Legality, lawfulness, legitimacy.

**Líder.** Leader, chief, commander, ruler.

**Liderazgo.** Leadership.

**Lidia.** Fighting, contest, match.

**Ligazón.** Link, bond, connection.

**Limitado.** Limited, confined, narrow, restricted.

**Limitar.** To limit, confine, restrict.

**Límite.** Limit, border, frontier. Extreme.

**Limítrofe.** Bordering.

**Linaje.** Lineage, ancestry, bloodline, genealogy. Family, kin, progeny.

**Linchar.** To lynch, execute, hang.

**Lindante.** Neighboring, adjacent, adjoining, next.

**Lindero.** Neighboring, adjacent, adjoining, next.

**Línea.** Line. Column, file, string. Lineage, descent.

**Línea ascendente.** Ascending line. Line of ancestors.

**Línea colateral.** Collateral line, formed by family members who are not in a direct line as, for instance, siblings, cousins, etc.

**Líneas generales.** General lines.

**Liquidación.** Liquidation. Final bill. Payment of a debt or ending a right.

**Liquidador.** Liquidator, adjuster, treasurer, trustee.

**Liquidar.** To liquidate. To turn into cash. To pay a debt or to end a right.

**Liquidez.** Liquidity, cash availability.

**Líquido.** Liquid. Expressed in money. Net and final.

**Líquido y exigible.** Determined and demandable, matured, past due and owing.

**Lista.** List, register, roll, roster, schedule.

**Lista negra.** Black list.

**Lite.** Lawsuit, court proceedings, litigation.

**Literal.** Literal. Precise, verbation. Related to writings and documents.

**Literalidad.** Literality.

**Literatura jurídica.** Legal writing.

**Litigación.** Litigation, court proceedings.

**Litigador, litigante.** Litigant, litigator, party.

**Litigante victorioso.** Prevailing party.

**Litigar.** To litigate.

**Litigio.** Lawsuit, court proceedings, suit.

**Litigioso.** Litigious, contested, challenged, unclear.

***Litis* (L).** Lawsuit, court proceedings, litigation.

**Litisconsorcio.** Joinder.

**Litisconsorcio necesario.** Necessary party. When according to law, or due to the nature of the case, the decision must be made considering several persons, these must sue or be sued in the same lawsuit. If the claim, or the counterclaim does not include all the necessary parties, the judge shall order to the party that, within the term of eight days, the claim or the counterclaim be enlarged by adding those who are missing. In Costa Rica a defendant does not have the right to name a third party defendant. The same is true in other systems, like Ecuador. See also *Intervención adhesiva.*

**Litisconsorte.** Co-party in a lawsuit.

**Litiscontestación.** Filing of the answer in a lawsuit. Answer.

**Litisexpensas.** Litigation expenses.

**Litispendencia.** *Lis pendens.* Local jurisdiction is not excluded by the pendency of the same case or a connected one before a foreign judge.

Once a lawsuit has been filed, a new lawsuit cannot be had between the same parties, for the same purpose and based on the same facts, regardless of the type of procedure chosen, as long as the first case is still pending. (Panamanian Judicial Code, arts. 231, 663).

**Litoral.** Littoral, land contiguous to a river, coast, shore.

**Llamada a licitación.** Call for bids.

**Llamamiento.** Summons, calling.

**Llamar a concurso.** Call for bids. Opening a position.

**Llamar a juicio.** To sue, to implead.

**Llamar al orden.** Call to order.

**Llegar a un acuerdo.** To reach an agreement.

**Llevar a término.** To achieve something, to realize.

**Llevar a pleito.** To sue.

**Llevar registro.** To keep a record.

**Locación.** Lease, employment, rent. Precise place in a geographic area.

**Locación de servicios.** Letting out of labor or industry. Labor may be let out in three ways: 1) Laborers may hire their services to another person. 2) Carriers and watermen hire out their services for the conveyance either of persons or of goods and merchandise. 3) Workmen hire out their labor or industry to make buildings or other works. (Lou. Civ. C. art. 2745).

**Locador.** Lessor, employer.

**Local.** Local, domestic, national.

**Locatario.** Lessee, worker.

**Locativo.** Relating to a lease.

**Lock-out.** Lock-out.

**Loco.** Crazy, insane, lunatic, madman.

**Locura.** Madness, derangement, lunacy, madness.

**Locus regit actum (L).** *Locus regit actum.* The formalties of foreign documents are governed by the principle *locus regit actum.* This Latin expression means that formalities are subject to the law of the place where the act

in question was performed. To prove that a document executed abroad has complied with the laws of the place where it was executed, a consular or diplomatic statement duly supported by a citation of law is normally sufficient. If the document is not in Spanish, a translation must be provided. The document must be legalized and executed in accordance with the formalities prescribed at the place of execution. (LA Laws & Inst.).

**Logro.** Achievement, accomplishment, success.

**Longitud.** Longitude. Length.

**Lonja.** Market, market place, produce exchange, rural market.

**Lote.** Lot, parcel, tract.

**Lotería.** Lottery, sweepstakes.

**Luces.** Lights, luminosity.

**Lucha.** Fight, strife, struggle.

**Lucidez.** Lucidity, intelligence, wit.

**Lucrativo.** Lucrative, advantageous, beneficial, gainful, remunerative.

**Lucro.** Gains, earnings, proceeds, profit.

**Lucro cesante.** Lost profit, *lucrum cessans* (L). Lost profit—recognized as an element of damages which must be considered when a court fixes the corresponding compensation in an action for damages—consists properly of loss of earnings caused to the person injured and the decrease of his earning capacity. (Rodríguez v. Ponce Cement Corp., 98 P.R.R 196 (1969)).

Gains prevented.

**Lugar.** Place, site, space.

**Lugar de cumplimiento.** Place of performance. Performance shall be rendered in the place either stipulated in the agreement or intended by the parties according to usage, the nature of the performance, or other circumstances. In the absence of agreement or other indication of the parties' intent, performance of an obligation to give an individually determined thing shall be rendered at the place the thing was when the obligation arose.

**Lugarteniente.** Lieutenant, acting, deputy.

**Lujo.** Luxury, lavishness. Extravagance, wastefulness.

**Lunar.** Relating to the moon.

**Lunático.** Lunatic.

**Lunfardo.** Slang (AR).

**Lupanar.** Brothel.

**Lustro.** Term of five years.

**Luto.** Mourning.

**Luxación.** Sprain of a muscle, dislocation of a bone.

**Luz.** Light. Clarity, luminosity.

# M

**Macabro.** Macabre, gory, morbid.

**Macero.** Sergeant at arms.

**Machismo.** Male chauvinism.

**Macho.** Male. It is normally used to denote the sex of animals rather than of humans.

**Mácula.** Blemish.

**Madrastra.** Stepmother.

**Madre.** Mother, parent.

**Madre política.** Mother-in-law.

**Madrina.** God mother. Woman who protects or who sponsors a cause.

**Maestranza.** Janitorial staff.

**Maestro.** Master, educator, teacher, professor.

**Magistrado.** Magistrate, judge, justice.

**Magistrado ponente.** Justice "*ponente*." A justice "ponente" shall be selected for each cause. It shall be the duty of the ponente to draft the rulings and judgments agreed upon by the chambers, even though his vote has not been in accordance with that of the majority. In such case, the presiding judge of the chamber may intrust the drafting of the judgment to another justice, if he considers it advisable by reason of special circumstances. (Sp. L. Civ. P. sec. 335, 336).

**Magistral.** Magisterial.

**Magistratura.** Magistracy, judicature, judiciary, the bench.

**Magnicidio.** Killing of a head of state or of someone who is otherwise very famous.

**Mal.** Wrong, fault. The opposite of good.

**Mala fe, dolo.** Bad faith, fraud.

The issue of bad faith has strong authority in Roman law, where it was known as mala fides. By contrast, good faith was known as bona fides, or simply fides. In the same way that the party in bad faith loses access to substantive or procedural rights otherwise available, the party in good faith to the same transaction is protected. In Roman law this was expressed as *mala fides superveniens non nocet* (the bad faith of one party does not taint the party who acts in good faith) (conf. Dig. 41, 1, 48, 1; Dig. 41, 10, 4). This notion has been fully received by Spanish and Latin American law. That is the reason why in all these jurisdictions the purchase in good faith and for value (*de buena fe y a título oneroso*) of a chattel (*bien mueble*) conveys ownership to the buyer, even if the seller is in bad faith. In some countries this is also known as the theory of the invincible *error (teoría del error invencible).*

**Mala conducta.** Misconduct, bad acts.

**Mala fe.** Bad faith, malice.

**Maleante.** Thief.

**Malecón.** Dike, jetty. Levee, mole.

**Maleficio.** Malediction, curse. Bewitchment, spell.

**Maléfico.** Malignant, evil, sinister.

**Malentendido.** Misunderstanding, misconception. Mutual error.

**Malevo.** Ruffian, hooligan.

**Malevolente.** Malevolent, malignant, spiteful, venomous.

**Malhechor.** Malefactor, criminal, offender.

**Malicia.** Malice. Bad faith, malevolence. The term malice denotes a wrongful and intentional act without a just cause or excuse—a conscious violation of the law to the prejudice of another. (Ppl. v. Reyes Lara, 100 PRR 676 (1971)).

**Malicia premeditada.** Malice aforethought. The concept of malice aforethought implies the absence of just cause or excuse in causing the death and the existence of the intent to kill a fellow creature. (Ppl. v. Rosario Centeno, 90 PRR 851 (1964)).

**Malicioso.** Malicious, malevolent.

**Maligno.** Malignant, malevolent, mean venomous.

**Malintencionado.** Ill-intended.

**Malo.** Bad, faulty, unsatisfactory. Harmful. Evil. Naughty. Adverse.

**Malos antecedentes.** Bad reputation, criminal record.

**Malos tratos.** Abusive behavior including physical injury.

**Maltratar.** To abuse, maltreat. To use roughly. To spoil, destroy.

**Maltrato.** Abuse, mistreatment.

**Malversación.** Embezzlement, misappropriation, swindle.

**Malversador.** Embezzler, crook, swindler.

**Malversar.** To embezzle, misappropriate, swindle.

**Manantiales.** Springs.

**Manceba.** Concubine, lover.

**Mancomún.** Debt with co-debtors or co-creditors.

**Mancomunada y solidariamente.** Jointly and severally.

**Mancomunadamente.** Jointly.

**Mancomunar.** To sign or to assume a debt jointly.

**Manda.** Bequest, donation, gift, legacy.

**Mandamiento.** Mandate. A mandate shall be employed for the purpose of ordering the issue of certificates, or transcripts, or the fulfillment of any judicial order, the execution of which is imposed upon registrars of property, notaries, assistants, or subordinate officials of inferior or superior courts. (Sp. L. Civ. P. sec. 288).

Mandamus. Court order, ruling. Writ.

**Mandamiento de arresto.** Arrest warrant.

**Mandamiento de concurso.** Writ of assistance.

**Mandamiento de desalojo.** Eviction order.

**Mandamiento de ejecución.** Writ of execution.

**Mandamiento embargo.** Attachment order.

**Mandamientos de posesión.** Writ of possession.

**Mandante.** Principal, mandator.

**Mandante manifiesto.** Disclosed principal.

**Mandante oculto.** Undisclosed principal.

**Mandante parcialmente manifiesto.** Partially disclosed principal.

**Mandar.** To command, direct, dictate, order. To convey, sled, deliver, dispatch, mail, ship.

**Mandas y legados.** Legacies and bequests. A testator may charge with legacies and bequests, not only his heir, but also the lega-tees. The latter shall not be liable for the charge only to the extent of the value of the legacy. (Sp. Civ. C., sec. 834).

**Mandatario.** Agent, representative. Attorney, attorney-in-fact. Proxy. Delegate, deputy.

**Mandatario especial.** Special agent.

**Mandatario general.** General agent.

**Mandato.** Mandate, agency. By the contract of agency, a person binds himself to render some service, or to do something for the account or at the request of another.

A mandate, *procuration* or *letter of attorney* is an act by which one person gives power to another to transact for him and in his name, one or several affairs. (Lou. Civ. C. art. 2985).

Command, order. Ruling, writ.

**Mandato en blanco.** Mandate in blank. A blank may be left for the name of the attorney in fact in the letter of attorney. In that case, the bearer of it is deemed the person empowered. (Lou. Civ. C. art. 2993).

**Mandato general o especial.** General or special agency. Agency is general or special. The former includes all the business of the principal. The latter, one or more specific transactions.

An agency stated in general terms only includes acts of administration. In order to compromise, alienate, mortgage, or to execute any other act of strict ownership an express commission is required. (Sp. Civ. C., sec. 1614, 1615).

**Mandato, renuncia.** Agency, withdrawal. An agent may withdraw from the agency by giving notice to the principal. Should the latter suffer any losses through the withdrawal, the agent must indemnify him therefor, unless said agent bases his withdrawal upon the impossibility of continuing to act as such without serious detriment to himself. (Sp. Civ. C., sec. 1638).

*Mandatum solvitur morte* **(L).** Death revokes a power of attorney.

**Mando.** Command, order, control.

**Manera de vivir.** Livelihood, means of living.

**Manera de vivir conocida.** Visible means of support.

**Manglar.** Mangrove.

**Manía.** Mania, fixation, obsession.

**Maniatar.** To chain, manacle.

**Manicomio.** Mental asylum, hospital.

**Manifestación.** Manifestation, declaration, statement. Demonstration, march, parade.

**Manifestante.** Declarant, deponent, witness. Demonstration.

**Manifestar.** To declare, depose, express, say, state. To demonstrate.

**Manifiesto.** Manifest. Patent, obvious.

**Maniobra.** Maneuver, strategy.

**Mano de obra.** Manufacture, cost of manufacturing. Labor.

**Mano dura.** Harsh, severe, without pity.

**Mano muerta.** Mortmain.

**Mantener y asegurar.** Preserve and enforce.

**Mantenido.** Dependent. Sustained. Pimp.

**Mantenimiento, manutención.** Maintenance, conservation, upkeep. support, living expenses, subsistence.

**Manufactura.** Manufacture.

**Manumisión.** In roman law, the act of granting freedom to a slave.

**Manumitir.** To liberate, emancipate, set free.

**Manuscribir.** To write by hand.

**Manuscrito.** Manuscript, draft.

**Mañoso.** Unduly, quirky.

**Mapa.** Map, chart, diagram.

**Maquiladora.** In-bond company. A Mexican Corporation, usually set up as a sociedad anónima, that can import industrial machinery without paying customs duties. As part of the preferential treatment received, such company must export at least 80% of its production. A minimum of five shareholders are needed. As an exception to Mexico's general laws, all shareholders of in-bond companies can be foreign.

This type of industries are usually found in the North of Mexico, near the U.S. border. The basic legislation is in the presidential decree of 8/15/83.

**Máquina.** Machine, apparatus, engine, mechanism.

**Maquinación.** Machination, conspiracy, plot, scheme.

**Máquinas vendedoras de seguros.** Insurance vending machine.

**Mar.** Sea, ocean.

**Marca.** Frame. Mark. Background. Trademark, brand, trade name, mark, sign.

**Marca de fábrica.** Trademark, industrial name.

**Marca registrada.** Registered trademark. Trade name.

**Marcario.** Related to trademarks, patent rights and intellectual property.

**Marchar.** To walk, trek. To march, parade. To demonstrate.

**Maremoto.** Seaquake.

**Margen.** Margin, edge, rim. Protection, insurance, reserve, surplus.

**Marginal.** Marginal. Quasicriminal, belonging to the underworld.

**Marido.** Husband, consort, spouse.

**Mariguana, marihuana, marijuana.** Marihuana.

**Marina.** Navy.

**Marino.** Sailor, mariner, navigator, seamen, seawolf. Naval officer. Related to the sea.

**Marisma.** Marshes. Marshes—which are considered as "forests"—have been defined as low lands contiguous to the seashores or riverbanks which are flooded by the overflowing waters of the seas and rivers. (Rubert Armstrong v. Commonwealth, 97 PRR 573 (1969)).

**Marital.** Marital, matrimonial, spousal.

**Marítimo.** Maritime.

**Martillar.** To sell in an auction.

**Martillero.** Auctioneer, realtor.

**Martillo.** Hammer, gavel. Auction room.

**Más.** More, beyond, further.

**Más adelante.** Further, hereinafter.

**Masa.** Mass. Estate, patrimony. Collection of assets, and liabilities.

**Masa común.** Common funds.

**Masa de la quiebra.** Bankruptcy assets.

**Matadero.** Slaughter house.

**Matador.** Assassin, killer, murderer. Executioner.

**Matar.** To kill, assassinate, murder, slain.

**Materia.** Matter, element, substance, subject.

**Materia no privilegiada.** Non-privileged matter.

**Material.** Material. Important, relevant. Physical, solid, tangible. Cloth, fabric.

**Material peligroso.** Hazardous material. Dangerous substances, remnants, their containers, packaging, or other components which comprise all or part of a cargo to be transported.

**Maternidad.** Maternity, motherhood, pregnancy.

**Matorral.** Bush.

**Matrero.** Outlaw who inhabits rural areas (AR).

**Matricida.** Matricide, murderer of one's mother.

**Matricidio.** Matricide, murder of one's mother.

**Matrícula.** License, registration number. List or roster of those who are registered.

**Matriculación.** Enrollment, enlistment, registration. Signing up.

**Matricular.** To matriculate, enroll, list, recruit. To license.

**Matrimonial.** Matrimonial, marital, spousal.

**Matrimonio.** Marriage. Marriage is a legal relationship between a man and a woman that is created by civil contract. The relationship and the contract are subject to special rules prescribed by law. The marriage contract differs from other contracts in that it creates a social status that affects not only the contracting parties, but also their posterity and the good order of society. It is thus subject to legislative control, independent of the will of the parties. (Lou. Civ. C. art. 86 and note).

Alliance, matrimony, nupcials, wedlock.

**Matrimonio absolutamente nulo.** Absolutely null marriage. A marriage is absolutely null when contracted without a marriage ceremony, by procuration, or in violation of an impediment. A judicial declaration of nullity is not required, but an action to recognize the nullity may be brought by any interested person. (Lou. Civ. C. art. 94).

**Matrimonio, acta.** Marriage record. Persons who intend to get married must submit their petition to the Civil Registry judge of their domicile, setting forth:

I. The names, last names, age, occupation, and address, of the bride and groom, as well as the parents, if they are known. If either the bride or groom have been previously married, it will be stated the name of the previous spouse, the reason for dissolution, and that date it became effective;

II. That they do not have a legal impediment to marry;

III. That it is their will to marry.

**Matrimonio, acto voluntario.** Marriage, voluntary act. A betrothal agreement does not obligate to marry, nor can the agreement stipulate any penalty for non-compliance. (Mex. Civ. C., art.142).

**Matrimonio, bienes propios.** Marriage, property belonging to each of the spouses. The following is the separate property of each of the spouses: 1) That brought to the marriage as his or her own. 2) That acquired for a good consideration by either of them during the marriage. 3) That acquired by right of redemption or by exchange for other property belonging to one of the spouses only (Sp. Civ. C., sec. 1335).

**Matrimonio, Argentina.** Marriage, Argentina. Under the Argentine Law of Civil Marriage, all marriages must be performed before an officer of the Civil Registry at the domicile of one of the parties. Registration of a foreign marriage requires evidence that same was performed in compliance with foreign law, approval of the general director of the Registry, and an order signed by a competent judge. (LA Laws & Inst.).

**Matrimonio, disolución.** Marriage, dissolution. The bond of matrimony is dissolved, 1) By the death of the husband or wife; 2) By a divorce legally obtained; 3) Whenever the marriage is declared null and void. Separation from bed and board does not dissolve the bond of matrimony, since the separated husband and wife are not at liberty to marry again; but it puts an end to their conjugal cohabitation, and to the common concerns, which existed between them. (Lou. Civ. C. art. 101).

**Matrimonio, nulidad.** Marriage, nullity. When a marriage has not been contracted according to the requirements of the law, the same is null and void. The right to an action for a declaration of nullity of a marriage, belongs to the parties to the marriage, to the public attorney, and to such other persons as may have an interest in the annulment of the same. In case of violence or intimidation, the action of nullity can only be exercised by the innocent party. (Sp. Civ. C., sec. 178, 179).

**Matrimonio, obligaciones.** Marriage, obligations. The spouses are obligated to contribute each one with their part to all the ends of matrimony and to help each other. All persons have a right to decide freely, responsibly and knowingly the number of and at what intervals to have children. In regards to marriage, this right will be exercised in common accordance between the husband and the wife. (Mex. Civ. C., art.163).

**Matrimonio putativo.** Putative marriage. An absolutely null marriage nevertheless produces civil effects in favor of a party who contracted it in good faith for as long as that party remains in good faith. (Lou. Civ. C. art. 96)

**Matrinonio relativamente nulo.** Relatively null marriage. A marriage is relatively null when the consent of one of the parties to marry is not freely given. Such a marriage may be declared null upon application of the party whose consent was not free. The marriage may not be declared null if that party confirmed the marriage after recovering his liberty or regaining his discernment. (Lou. Civ. C. art. 95)

**Matrimonio, separación de bienes.** Marriage, separation of property. In the absence of a specific declaration of the marriage contract, the separation of the property of the spouses during the marriage, shall not take place except by virtue of a judicial decree. (Sp. Civ. C., sec. 1342).

**Matrimonio, sociedad de gananciales.** Marriage conjugal partnership. By virtue of the conjugal partnership the earning of profits indiscriminately obtained by either of the spouses during the marriage shall belong to the husband and the wife, share and share alike, upon the dissolution of the marriage. The conjugal partnership shall always begin on the same day that the marriage is celebrated. The community of goods terminated when the marriage is dissolved

or is declared null. (Sp. Civ. C., sec. 1310, 1311, 1330).

**Matrimonio, validez.** Marriage, validity. A marriage shall be held valid everywhere in respect to its form if it has been celebrated in the manner prescribed as valid by the laws of the country where it has taken place. (Bustamante C. art. 41-42).

**Matriz.** Matrix, cast, mold. Original.

**Matute.** Smuggling, bootlegging. Chaos, strife.

**Matutear.** To smuggle.

**Matutero.** Smuggler, crook. Person who causes trouble.

**Máxima.** Maxim, aphorism, proverb, saying.

**Mayor.** Major. Bigger, larger. Old, older. Ledger.

**Mayor cuantía.** Greater import. These actions are such as involve interest valued at more than a minimum amount, questions relating to political or honorary rights, those in which the interest involved can not be appraised or determined, personal exemptions and privileges, filiations, paternity, and other questions involving the civil status and conditions of persons. (Alcubilla, Diccionario de la Administración española).

**Mayor de edad.** Of legal age.

**Mayorazgo.** Primogeniture.

**Mayordomo.** Butler. Head employee in a ranch (AR).

**Mayoría.** Majority, plurality. Legal age, full age, of age.

**Mayoría, mayor edad.** Majority. Majority begins at the age of twenty-one years. A person having attained the age of majority is capable of executing all the acts of civil life with the exceptions established in special cases by the Civil Code. (Sp. Civ. C., sec. 317).

**Mayoridad.** Legal age, full age, of age.

**Mayoritario.** Concerning a majority.

**Mecanografiar.** To type.

**Media firma.** Signing with initials only.

**Media prueba.** Testimony of only one witness.

**Mediación.** Mediation, brokerage. Arbitration. Good offices.

**Mediador.** Broker, intermediary. The broker or intermediary is he who is employed to negotiate a matter between two parties, and who, for that reason, is considered as the mandatary of both. (Lou. Civ. C. art. 3016).
Mediator, middleman. Arbitrator, amicable compounder.

**Medianería.** Party walls and fences, part ownership. Rural partnership.

**Mediante.** Through, by means of.

**Mediar.** To mediate, intervene.

**Medible.** Measurable.

**Medicina forense.** Forensic medicine.

**Medicine.** Medicine, drug, medication.

**Medición antropométrica.** Anthropometrical data.

**Médico.** Doctor, practitioner, physician, surgeon.

**Médico forense.** Coroner.

**Medida.** Measure, measurement. Portion, ration. Step, action.

**Medidas de seguridad.** Security measures. Security measures will be imposed by the court in those cases specifically established by law. Security measures are applied according to the law in force at the time when they are to be carried out. Security measures can be: therapeutic, commitment to an institution and surveillance. (Standard Penal C. for Latin America, sec. 55, 56, 57).

**Medidas de seguridad curativas.** Therapeutic security measures. Therapeutic measures will be indeterminate. They will cease by court order, once experts establish that the person in question no longer poses a threat to himself or to others. Therapeutic measures consist in following an adequate treatment, to be administered in specialized centers or in dependencies thereof. Measures of commitment consist in the imposition of a program of work and education (Standard Penal C. for Latin America, sec. 57 and 58).

**Medidas de seguridad, substitución.** Safety measures, substitution. The court may substitute a security measure, being carried out, for another one deemed more appropriate in view of the subject's personality and the effectiveness of the measure. (Standard Penal C. for Latin America, sec. 61).

**Medidas laborales disciplinarias.** Disciplinary labor measures. The following forms of disciplinary measures are permissible: a) oral or written reprimands; b) suspension of up to eight days without wages; c) termination. Before a reprimand or suspension may be issued, the worker must have an opportunity to have his case heard through a grievance procedure. (Mex. Labor Law).

**Medidas preventivas.** Preventive measures. The terms "preventive measures" or "guarantee measures" are deemed to be equivalent when they are used to mean procedures or measures whose propose is to guarantee the findings or effects of a pending or future proceeding concerning the security of persons, property, or of obligations to give, to do or not do a specific thing in civil, commercial or labor matters, or in criminal trials in which civil damages are sought. (Conv. on Prev. Meas., art. 1).

**Medidas preventivas, causas.** Preventive measures, grounds. The grounds for a preventive measure shall be decided in accordance with the laws and by the judges of the place of the proceedings. However, its execution and the counterproductive measure or guaranty shall be determined by the judges of the place where execution is sought, in accordance with its law. (Conv. on Prev. Meas., art. 3).

**Medidas preventivas, consulados.** Preventive measures, consulates. Without prejudice to the rights of third parties, the consular authorities of a State may receive the personal effects of a national of that State when, because of death, they are placed at the disposal of the relatives or heirs presumptive of the national and there are no such relatives or heirs. (Conv. on Prev. Meas., art. 8).

**Medidas preventivas, custodia de menores.** Preventive measures, custody of minors. When the preventive measure relates to the custody of minors, the judge or court of the State of destination may limit, in his territory, the scope of the effects of the measure pending the final judgment of the judge of the principal proceedings. (Conv. on Prev. Meas., art. 9).

**Medidas preventivas, ejecución.** Preventive measures, enforcement. Preventive measures abroad shall be enforced by means of letter rogatory, which may be transmitted to the judge or court addressed by the interested parties themselves, through judicial channels, through consular or diplomatic agents, or through the Central Authority of the State of origin or of the State of destination, as the case may be. (Conv. on Prev. Meas., art. 13).

**Medidas preventivas, exhortos.** Preventive measures, letters rogatory. Letters rogatory shall be executed provided that they meet the following requirements: a. The letter rogatory is legalized. The letter rogatory shall be presumed to be duly legalized in the State of origin when legalized by competent consular or diplomatic agent. b. The letter rogatory and the accompanying documentation are duly translated into the official language of the State of destination. (Conv. on Prev. Meas., art. 14-15).

**Medidas preventivas, orden público.** Preventive measures, public policy. The State of destination may decline to execute a letter rogatory concerning preventive measures that are manifestly contrary to its public policy (ordre public). (Conv. on Prev. Meas., art. 12).

**Medidas preventivas, propiedad.** Preventive measures, property. When an attachment or any other preventive measure involving property has been executed, the person affected by this measure may plead his third-party claim or pertinent objections before the judge to whom the letter rogatory was addressed, for the sole purpose of having that claim communicated to the judge of origin when the letter rogatory is returned to him. If the third-party claim excludes ownership or rights *in rem* over the property attached, or the objection is based on possession or ownership of the property attached, it shall be decided by the judges in accordance with the law of the place where the property is located. (Conv. on Prev. Meas., art. 5).

**Medio.** Middle, center, median, medium.

**Medio ambiente.** Environment. Nature, climate. Ambiance, atmosphere.

**Medio social.** Social circle.

**Medios.** Means, method, way. Resources. Money.

**Medios de prueba.** Means of proof. The means of proof which may be employed in an action are the following: 1) Confession in court. 2) Formal public documents. 3) Private documents and correspondence. 4) Commercial books kept as prescribed by the Code of Commerce. 5) Opinions of experts. 6) Judicial examination. 7) Witnesses. (Sp. L. Civ. P. sec. 577).

**Megalomanía.** Megalomania.

**Mejor.** Better, best. Finer, superior. More advantageous or convenient.

**Mejora.** Improvement, amelioration, betterment. Restoration, repairs. Progress.

**Mejorador.** Person who makes improvements.

**Mejorar.** To improve, ameliorate, better. To make progress.

**Mejoras por el poseedor de buena fe.** Improvements by possessor in good faith. When constructions, plantings, or works are made by a possessor in good faith, the owner of the immovable may not demand their demolition and removal. He is bound to keep them and at his option to pay to the possessor either the cost of the materials and of the workmanship, or their current value, or the enhanced value of the immovable. (Lou. Civ. C. art. 496).

**Mejoras por el poseedor de mala fe.** Improvements by possessor in bad faith. When constructions, plantings, or works are made by a bad faith possessor, the owner of the immovable may keep them or he may demand their demolition and removal at the expense of the possessor, and, in addition, damages for the injury that he may have sustained. If he does not demand demolition and removal, he is bound to pay at his option either the current value of the materials and of the workmanship of the separable improvements that he has kept or the enhanced value of the immovable. (Lou. Civ. C. art. 497).

**Mejoría.** Improvement, particularly concerning health.

**Melancolía.** Melancholy, depression, gloom.

**Memorandum.** Memo, memorandum.

**Memoria.** Memory. Report, account, statement. Appellate brief.

**Memorial.** Appellate brief, petition, record.

**Menaje.** Furniture.

**Mención.** Mention. A mention is a mere notice entered by a registrar of the existence of an unrecorded interest. A mention is also defined, as concerns registration, as the mere indication of the existence of a lien or encumbrance on a property, made in an entry concerning the same. In addition, it is defined as the allusion made in an entry, of a personal or property right different from that giving rise thereto. (Postigo v. Registrar, 96 PRR 536 (1968)).

Allusion, reference.

**Mencionado.** Aforesaid.

**Mendicidad.** Mendacity, begging, panhandling.

**Mendigar.** To beg, implore, panhandle.

**Mendigo.** Beggar, medicant, panhandler, pauper.

**Menester.** Need. Task, chore, occupation.

**Menor.** Minor. Child, infant, underage. Less, smaller. Least, smallest.

**Menor cuantía.** Actions involving interests of over a certain minimum and not exceeding a certain maximum. (Alcubilla, Dicionario de la Administración española).

**Menoría.** Age minority.

**Menoscabar.** To block, impair, obstruct.

**Menoscabo.** Damage, detriment, impairment, prejudice.

**Menospreciar.** To snub, rebuff. To undervalue, underestimate.

**Menosprecio.** Disdain, scorn. Undervaluation.

**Mensaje.** Message, communication, missive.

**Mensajería.** Messenger service, courier.

**Mental.** Mental, cerebral, intellectual, rational.

**Mente sana.** Sound mind, sane.

**Mentir.** To lie, deceive, misrepresent.

**Mentira.** Lie, falsehood, fabrication.

**Mercader.** Merchant, businessman, dealer, salesman, wholesaler.

**Mercadería.** Merchandise, commodities, goods, wares.

**Mercado.** Market.

**Mercado de valores.** Stock exchange.

**Mercancía.** Goods, merchandise.

**Mercanchifle.** Retailer of cheap and insignificant goods.

**Mercante, mercantil.** Mercantile, commercial, related to trade.

**Merced.** Privilege, concession. Mercy.

**Mercenario.** Mercenary, hireling, soldier of fortune.

**Merecer.** Meritorious, deserving, worthy.

**Mérito.** Merit, worth, worthiness.

**Meritorio.** Meritorious. Law student who works for free at court.

**Mero.** Mere, sheer, just.

**Merodeador.** Marauder, looter, raider.

**Mesa.** Table, board.

**Mesa de entrada.** Reception.

**Mesa directiva.** Board of directors.

**Mesonero.** Hostel keeper.

**Meta.** Goal, object, objective, purpose.

**Metales preciosos, amonedados o en pasta.** Precious metals, either coined or in bullion.

**Metálico.** Made of metal. Cash.

**Metralleta.** Sub-machinegun.

**Metrópoli.** Mother country, metropolis.

**México, investigación jurídica.** Mexico, legal research. The best way to begin researching Mexican law is to know something about Mexico in general—its history, its culture(s), its political and social traditions. Of course, that approach implies learning about Mexico and its law before a specific question arises in the course of legal practice. There really is no other way of putting the question into the proper context. (Pratter).

**México, Lexis.** Lexis now has a library of Mexican law (in Spanish). This at least makes it possible to get current texts of the Mexican Constitution and laws. The Lexis library is called MEXICO. It is divided into files such as the Constitution (MXCNST), Federal Laws (MXFED), Environmental Law (MXAMB), and so on. For those who read Spanish, the Lexis MEXICO library is a true advance in researching Mexican law. (Pratter).

**México, sistema legal.** Mexico, legal system. Mexico is a federal republic with a centralizing tradition. It has a heterogeneous legal system, which, like those of other Latin American countries, bears the influence of what is often called the "civil law tradition." (Pratter).

**Miedo.** Fear, apprehension. Anxiety, worry.

**Miembro.** Member. Component, participant. Associate. Fellow.

**Milicia.** Militia.

**Militante.** Militant, activist.

**Militar.** Miliary.

**Millonario.** Millionaire, highroller, tycoon.

**Mina.** Mine.

**Minería, Argentina.** Mining, Argentina. In 1991 Argentina created the Secretariat of Natural Resources and Human Environment to oversee the coordination of environmental regulations in this federated country. However, Argentina has been labeled as the latecomer in Latin America environmental legislation, since many of its laws fail to appreciate the need to incorporate environmental concerns into policies affecting economic activities. Currently, Argentina has no comprehensive set of environmental regulations for the mining industry, and coordination of the country's provincial mining regulations is still a pending development. (Orihuela).

**Minería, Chile.** Mining, Chile. Chile's exceptional economic growth over the past several years has increased air, soil, and water pollution. Similarly, industrial, urban, and technological developments have placed an excessive strain on the ability of government agencies to engage in monitoring and enforcement activities. Environmental safeguards are based largely on US Environmental Protection Agency standards, as is most of Chile's environmental legislation. Other bodies administering environment regulations in Chile are the Chilean Copper Commission and the National Geology and Mining Service Institute. (Orihuela).

**Minería, registro.** Mining, registry. Registry which records all official mining documents, including; concession certificates for exploration and exploitation; mining assignment certificates; declarations of nullity or cancellations; notarized notices of mining related contracts; and judicial notices of denials, verifications, modifications, nullifications, cancellations, etc. of inscriptions.

**Minería y medio ambiente.** Mining and the environment.

In most of the developing countries of Latin America, mining has higher landuse priority while environmental policies for mining are limited to mining codes, subsidiary regulations, and mineral investment agreements. Most current mining codes and most mineral investment agreements contain very generally formulated provisions that usually include an obligation, formulated as a general principle, to minimize environmental degradation and to adhere to good environmental practices (usually not specified); an obligation to submit an environmental impact assessment as part of the feasibility study, which is usually the basis for the mining right authorizing construction and operation of the mine; and sometimes, a general formation on reclamation. While these open-ended provisions do not impose any specific obligation, they could become a vehicle for an energetic environmental policy specifying, by watt of regulations, agreements, and periodic or continuous government/operator consultations, the definitive content and scope of environmental obligations as environmental problems are identified and mitigation techniques involve. (Orihuela).

**Minero.** Miner (n). Mining (a).

**Miniaturización.** Miniaturization, reduction, shrinking.

**Mínimo.** Minimum, *de minimis*, minimal.

**Ministerial.** Ministerial.

**Ministerio.** Ministry. Conduct, means.

**Ministerio de Comercio.** Commerce Department.

**Ministerio de Economía de Hacienda.** Treasury Department.

**Ministerio de Estado.** State Department.

**Ministerio de Relaciones Exteriores, del Exterior.** State Department. Foreign office. (G.B.)

**Ministerio de Salud.** Health Department.

**Ministerio del Interior.** Ministry of the Interior. French influence is felt in the widespread institution of a Ministry of the Interior which does not exist under that name in the United States. The existence of such a ministry is easy to justify, since many Latin American countries are unitary states and local administration is controlled by the central government. Such a ministry even in the federal countries is construed as evidence of a trend toward centralization more marked than in the United States. (W. Eur. & LA Leg. Sys.).

**Ministerio Fiscal, Público.** Justice Department.

**Ministerior de Trabajo.** Labor Department.

**Ministro.** Minister, supreme court judge, justice.

**Minoría, minoridad.** Minority. Non-age, infancy, underage.

**Minoritario.** Related to a minority.

**Minuta.** Minutes, proceeds of a meeting, note.

**Minuta del convenio.** Memorandum of agreement.

**Místico.** Mystic, mystical, mysterious. Ghostly, occult.

**Mistización.** Miscegenation.

**Mita.** Tax levied by viceroys in Latin America.

**Mitad hereditaria.** Moiety.

**Mitigación.** Mitigation, attenuation, moderation, reduction.

**Mitigador.** Mitigator, moderator.

**Mitigar.** To mitigate, attenuate, moderate, reduce.

**Mitin.** Meeting.

**Mitómano.** Mythomaniac, liar.

**Mixto.** Mixed, combined.

**Mobiliario.** Movables, chattels, personal property.

**Moblaje.** Furniture.

**Moción.** Motion, proposal, suggestion.

**Mocionante.** Movant, petitioner.

**Mocionar.** To move, petition.

**Modalidad.** Modality. Formalities.

**Modelo.** Model, archetype, replica, standard. Prototype.

**Modificable.** Modifiable, not final.

**Modificación.** Modification, amendment, alteration, change, reform.

**Modificar.** To modify, amend, alter, change, reform.

**Modo de aceptación.** Mode of acceptance.
A statement made by or other conduct of the offeree indicating assent to an offer is an acceptance. Silence or inactivity does not in itself amount to acceptance. An acceptance of an offer becomes effective when the indication of assent reaches the offeror. (Unidroit, Prin., art. 2.6).

**Mojón.** Boundary mark, landmark, milestone. Turning point.

**Molestia.** Disturbance, nuisance.

**Molestia privada.** Private nuisance.

**Molestia pública.** Common nuisance.

**Moneda.** Coin, cash, currency, legal tender, money.

**Moneda, La (CH).** Government house.

**Moneda de pago.** Currency of payment.
If a monetary obligation is expressed in a currency other than of the place for payment, it may be paid by the obligor in the currency of the place for payment unless (a) that currency is not freely convertible; or (b) the parties have agreed that payment should be made only in the currency in which the monetary obligation is expressed. (Unidroit, Prin., art. 6.1.9).

**Moneda que no ha sido especificada.** Currency not expressed. Where a monetary obligation is not expressed in a particular currency, payment must be made in the currency of the place where payment is to be made. (Unidroit, Prin., art. 6.1.10).

**Monedaje.** Monetary, monetage.

**Monismo.** Monism. Theory that supports the same origin for national as for international law.

**Monopólico.** Monopolistic.

**Monopolio.** Monopoly, cartel, control, trust.

**Monopolista, monopolístico.** Monopolist, monopolistic.

**Montante, monto.** Amount, aggregate, sum, total, quantity.

**Monte.** Hill, mound.

**Montepío.** Pension fund, gratuity fund for widows and orphans. Pawnshop operated by the state.

**Mora.** Default, delay. Persons obliged to deliver or to do something are in default from the moment when the creditor demands the fulfillment of their obligation, judicially or extrajudicially. However, the demand of the creditor, in order that default may exist, shall not be necessary: 1) If the obligation or law declares it expressly. 2) If by reason of its nature and circumstances it may appear that the fixing of the period within which the thing was to be delivered or the service rendered was a determinate cause to constitute the obligation. (Sp. Civ. C., sec. 1067).

**Morada.** Abode, domicile, house, residence.

**Moratoria.** Moratorium.

**Moratorio.** Moratory.

**Mordida (ME).** Bribe, graft, payoff.

**Morfinomanía.** Morphinomania.

**Morfinómano.** Morphinomaniac.

**Morganático.** Morganatic, a type of marriage where spouses acquire restricted rights.

**Moribundo.** About to die.

**Morir.** To die, expire, perish. To pass away.

**Morosidad.** Nonpayment or delay in paying a debt.

**Moroso.** In default, delinquent.

**Mortalidad.** Mortality, death rate, death.

**Mostrenco.** Chattel with no owner.

**Mote.** Alias, nickname. Pseudonym.

**Motín.** Mutiny, insurrection, riot, uprising.

**Motivar.** To motivate, incentivate, stimulate. To lay grounds or reasons. To justify.

**Motivo.** Cause, consideration. Motive, objective, reason.

**Motivo fundado.** Probable cause.

**Movil.** Motive, incentive, reason.

**Movilización.** Civil commotion, mobilization.

**Movilizar.** To set into action, trigger. To cause an official response. To stir the people.

**Movimiento.** Movement, activity, motion. Broad political group or coalition.

**Muchacha.** Girl, lass, young lady.

**Muchacho.** Boy, lad, youth, young man.

**Mudo.** Dumb.

**Muebles.** Movables. All things, corporeal or incorporeal, that the law does not consider as immovables, are movables. (Lou. Civ. C. art. 475).

Furniture. Whenever the word "furniture" (*muebles*) alone is used, the following objects shall not be considered as comprised therein: Money, credits, commercial effects, stocks, jewels, scientific or artistic collections, books, medals, arms, clothing, riding beasts or carriages and their harnesses, breadstuffs, liquids and merchandise, nor other things which have not for principal object the furnishing or ornamenting of living rooms, except where, by the context of the law or of the individual declaration, the contrary clearly appears. (Sp. Civ. C., sec. 346).

**Muebles corporales.** Corporeal movables. Corporeal movables are things, whether animate or inanimate, that normally move or can be moved from one place to another. (Lou. Civ. C. art. 471).

**Muebles incorporales.** Incorporeal movables. Rights, obligations, and actions that apply to a movable thing are incorporeal movables. Movables of this kind are such as bonds, annuities, and interests or shares in entities possessing juridical personality. (Lou. Civ. C. art. 473).

**Muebles por anticipación.** Movables by anticipation. Unharvested crops and ungathered fruits of trees are movables by anticipation when they belong to a person other than the landowner. (Lou. Civ. C. art. 474).

**Muelle.** Dock, pier, quay, wharf.

**Muerte.** Death, decease, demise.

**Muerte civil.** Civil death.

**Muerte del procesado.** Death of the accused. The death of the accused extinguishes the penal action. The death of the convict extinguishes any remaining punishment. (Standard Penal C. for Latin America, sec. 98).

**Muerte natural.** Natural death.

**Muerte violenta.** Violent death. When the Civil Registry judge suspects that the death of a person was due to violent means, he will notify the attorney general's office, communicating all the information that he possess, so that the investigation may proceed in accordance to with the law. (Mex. Civ. C., art.122).

**Muerto.** Dead, deceased.

**Muestra.** Sample, example, specimen.

**Muestrario.** Set of samples.

**Mujer.** Woman, female. Wife, spouse.

**Multa.** Fine, assessment, penalty.

**Multa penal.** Fines in criminal proceedings. Fines will be paid to the State in quotas, and satisfied in legal tender. A quota is equivalent to the daily income of the convict and will be determined in accordance with his financial situation, considering especially his net worth, revenues, means of subsistence, levels of expenditure and other factors that the sentencing judge consider appropriate. (Standard Penal C. for Latin America, sec. 45).

**Multa penal, pago.** Fines in criminal proceedings, payment. At the time of imposing a fine, or by subsequent judicial order and in view of the financial situation of the convict, the court may grant an extension or authorize payment in installments, with a personal surety or with collateral. At the court's discretion, the surety or collateral requirements can be waived. (Standard Penal C. for Latin America, sec. 46).

**Multable.** Finable, subject to a penalty.

**Multar.** To fine, penalize, tax.

**Multiplicidad.** Multiplicity, diversity, profession. Abundance, variety.

**Municiones de boca y guerra.** Provisions and munitions of war.

**Municipal.** Municipal, domestic, local.

**Municipalidad.** Municipality, town, city hall.

**Municipalizar.** To municipalize, to incorporate a town.

**Municipio.** Municipality, township.

**Muro.** Wall.

**Mutilación.** Mutilation, mayhem. Disfigurement, dismemberment, laceration. Defacement.

**Mutilar.** To mutilate, disfigure, lacerate. To deface.

**Mutismo.** Absence of communication. Silence.

**Mutual.** Association that loans money to its members.

**Mutualidad.** Mutuality, reciprocity.

**Mutuante.** Lender.

**Mutuario.** Borrower.

**Mutuo.** Mutual, bilateral, common, reciprocal, loan, mutuum.

# N

**Nacido.** Born.

**Nacimiento.** Birth, delivery. Beginning, creation.

**Nacimiento, declaración.** Birth declaration. The declarations of birth will be made presenting the child before the Civil Registry judge in his office or in the place where the birth occurred. (Mex. Civ. C., art. 54).

**Nacimientos múltiples.** Multiple births. When there are multiple births, there will be a birth certificate for each new born, noting the particularities that distinguish the newborn and the order of their birth, with accordance to the information that the doctors provide, the surgeon, the midwife, or the persons who helped in the birth. (Mex. Civ. C., art. 76).

**Nación.** Nation, country, state.

**Nacional.** National. Citizen, inhabitant, subject. Domestic, local.

**Nacionalidad.** Nationality, citizenship.

**Nacionalidad, asociaciones**. Nationality, associations. The nationality of origin of associations shall be the nationality of the country in which they are constituted. (Bustamante C. art. 17).

**Nacionalidad, atribución.** Nationality, attribution. Each state shall apply its own law for the determination of the nationality of origin of any individual or juristic person and of its acquisition, loss and recuperation thereafter. (Bustamante C., art. 9).

**Nacionalidad de corporaciones y fundaciones.** Nationality of Corporations and Foundations. The nationality of origin of corporations and foundations shall be determined by the law of the State which authorizes or approves them. (Bustamante C. art. 16).

**Nacionalidad de origen.** Nationality of origin. In questions relating to nationality of origin in which the State in which they are raised is not interested, the law of that one of the nationalities in issue in which the person concerned has his domicile shall be applied. (Bustamante C. art. 10).

**Nacionalidad, pérdida.** Loss of Nationality. In the case of loss of nationality, the law of the lost nationality should be applied. Resumption of nationality is controlled by the law of the nationality which is resumed. (Bustamante C. arts. 14-15).

**Nacionalidad, sociedades anónimas.** Nationality, stock corporations. With respect to stock corporations, nationality shall be determined by the articles of incorporation or, in an applicable case, by the law of the place where the general meeting of shareholders is normally held, and in the absence thereof, by the law of the place where its principal governing or administrative board or council is located. (Bustamante C. art. 19).

**Nacionalismo.** Nationalism.

**Nacionalista.** Nationalistic. Patriotic.

**Nacionalización.** Nationalization.

**Nacionalizar.** To nationalize, confiscate, expropriate.

**Naciones riparias.** Riparian nations, countries that share a river as a border.

**Naciones Unidas.** United Nations, U.N., O.N.U.

**Nada.** Nothing.

**Narcótico.** Narcotic, drugs.

**Narcotraficante.** Drug dealer, drug pusher.

**Narcotráfico.** Drug-trafficking.

**Natal.** Related to one's birth.

**Natalicio.** Birthday.

**Natalidad.** Birth rate, population growth, demographic expansion.

**Nativo.** Native, domestic, local, natural.

**Nato.** Born. Spontaneous. Naturally talented.

**Natural.** Natural, organic, wild. Spontaneous.

**Naturaleza.** Nature. Wilderness. Character, temper.

**Naturalización.** Naturalization, citizenship.

**Naufragar.** To shipwreck, sink.

**Naufragio.** Shipwreck. The losses and damages suffered by a vessel and her cargo by reason of shipwreck or stranding shall be individually suffered for the account of the owners, the part of the wreck which may be saved belonging to them in the same proportion. (Sp. Com. C., sec. 840).

**Náufrago.** Survivor of a shipwreck, sinking.

**Náutico.** Nautical, naval.

**Naval.** Naval, marine.

**Nave.** Vessel, ship, aircraft.

**Navegación.** Navigation, cruising, sailing.

**Navegación a flote común o a tercio.** Navigation for freight in common or in shares. If a captain navigates for freight in common or on shares he can not make any transaction for his exclusive account, and should he do so the profit shall belong to the other persons in interest, and the losses shall be his. (Sp. Com. C., sec. 613).

**Navegabilidad.** Seaworthiness, airworthiness. Fitness to navigate.

**Navegante.** Navigator, sailor.

**Navegar.** To navigate, cruise, sail.

**Naves, nacionalidad.** Ships, nationality. The nationality of ships is proved by the navigation license and the certificate of registration and has the flag as an apparent distinctive symbol. (Bustamante C. art. 274).

**Naviero.** Ship agent.

**Navío.** Vessel, boat, craft, sip.

**Necesidad.** Necessity, need. Poverty, want.

**Necesidad del original.** Best evidence rule.

**Necrología.** Obituary.

**Necropsia.** Autopsy.

**Negable.** Deniable, dismissable, rejectable.

**Negación.** Denial, refusal, rejection. Rebuttal, refutation.

**Negador.** Denier.

**Negante.** Party who denies.

**Negar.** To deny, refuse, reject.

**Negarse.** To refuse.

**Negativa.** Refusal, denial, rejection.

**Negatorio.** Negatory.

**Negligencia.** Negligence, carelessness, oversight, slip.

**Negligencia concurrente.** Concurrent negligence.

**Negligencia contribuyente.** Contributory negligence.

**Negligencia contribuyente como obstáculo.** Contributory negligence as bar to action.

**Negligencia criminal.** Criminal negligence. The term negligence for the purpose of the Penal Code, imports a want of such attention to the nature or probable consequences of the act or omission, as a prudent man ordinarily bestows in acting in his own concern. (Ppl. v. Ortiz, 86 PRR 431 (1962)).

**Negligencia grave.** Gross negligence.

**Negligencia sobreviniente.** Supervening negligence.

**Negligente.** Negligent, careless. Inattentive, distracted.

**Negociabilidad.** Negotiability, marketability.

**Negociable.** Negotiable, marketable.

**Negociación.** Negotiation, bargain, deal. Settlement.

**Negociaciones con mala fe.** Negotiations in bad faith.
It is bad faith for a party to enter into or continue negotiations when intending not to reach an agreement with the other party. (Unidroit, Prin., art. 2.15).

**Negociado.** Illegal deal. Embezzlement. Oficina (PR).

**Negociador.** Negotiator, agent, dealer.

**Negociante en bienes raíces, operador inmobiliario.** Real estate dealer, realtor. In general terms, it may be said that a real estate dealer is a person who is engaged in certain activities which constitute the ordinary operation of a business for which he acquires property for the purpose of selling it later at a profit, while an investor is one who acquires property by reason of the income which it will yield rather than for the profit which may be obtained in the resale. (Valldejuli Rodríquez v. Sec. of Treas., 89 PRR 17 (1963)).

**Negociar.** To negotiate, bargain, deal, trade. To market, retail, wholesale.

**Negocio.** Business, occupation. Shop, store.

**Negocio en marcha.** Going concern.

**Negocio jurídico disimulado.** Concealed juridical business. The valid and tacit acts concealed by apparent contracts but which have no specific consideration necessary for their existence, constitute concealed juridical business. (Hernández v. Sec. of the Treas., 86 PRR 12 (1962)).

**Negotiorum gestio (L).** Implied agency based on a factual situation. For instance, my neighbor is out on a vacation and his roof collapses. To avoid damage from an approaching storm I have his roof repaired and I pay for it. The result is that my neighbor has now an enforceable debt towards me for the amount of the repairs. Before an emergency situation the law implies reasonable consent on the party that is absent or incapacitated.

**Negro.** Black. Illegal, forbidden. Evil, nefarious. Threatening. Somber.

**Neonatal.** Neonatal, concerning a new-born.

**Nepotismo.** Nepotism, cronysm.

**Neurastenia.** Neurasthenia.

**Neurópata.** Neuropath.

**Neurosis.** Neurosis.

**Neutral, neutro.** Neutral, impartial, unbiased.

**Neutralidad.** Neutrality, objectivity. Fairness.

**Neutralismo.** Neutrality.

**Neutralización.** Neutralization. Annulment.

**Nexo.** Link, bond, connection, Tie.

**Ni afirmo ni niego.** I neither confirm nor deny. No contest.

**Niebla.** Fog, mist.

**Nieta.** Granddaughter.

**Nieto.** Grandson.

**Niña.** Girl, child.

**Ninfómana.** Nymphomaniac.

**Ninfomanía.** Nymphomania.

**Ningún.** None.

**Niñez.** Childhood, infancy.

**Niño.** Child, boy, infant.

**Niño adoptivo.** Adopted child. An adopted child is considered a legitimate child of the adopter, and that is the family status recognized for all legal purposes. (Valladars de Sabater v. Rivera Lazu, 89 PRR 249 (1963)).

**Niño expósito.** Foundling.

**Niño incorregible.** Incorrigible child. For the purpose of the Minors Act, an incorrigible child is one whose conduct jeopardizes his own or the community's welfare. (People ex rel. M.G.G., 99 PRR 898 (1970)).

**Nivel.** Level, degree, layer.

**Nivel de vida.** Standard of living.

**No.** No, not.

**No aplicabilidad del derecho extranjero.** Non applicability of foreign law. Foreign law shall not be applied:

When fundamental principles of national law have been evaded artificially, having the judge to determine the fraudulent intention of such evasion; and

When the provisions of foreign law or the result of its application is contrary to the fundamental principles or institutions of the national public order. (Mexican Civ. Code, art. 15). (J. A. Vargas).

**No apto.** Not fit, inappropriate.

**No comparecencia.** Nonappearence.

**No culpable.** Not guilty. Innocent.

**No devengado.** Unearned.

**No ha lugar.** Overruled, denied.

**No navegable.** Nonnavigable.

**No negociable.** Nonnegotiable.

**No obstante.** However, notwithstanding, nonetheless, still.

**Nobleza.** Nobility. Integrity, virtue. Aristocracy, royalty.

**Nocturnidad.** Aggravating factor of a crime committed by night.

**Nómade.** Nomad.

**Nombramiento.** Appointment, designation, nomination.

**Nombrar.** To appoint, elect, select. To name.

**Nombre.** Name, appellation. Reputation.

**Nombre comercial.** Trade name. Firm name.

**Nombre social.** Firm name.

**Nómina de pago.** Payroll.

**Nominación.** Nomination, appointment, selection.

**Nominador.** Person who appoints. Designator.

**Nominal.** Nominal, academic, theoretic.

**Nominalidad.** Nominality.

**Nominar.** To appoint, elect, select. To name.

**Nominativo.** Nominative.

**Nominatorio.** Nominee.

***Non bis in idem* (L).** Used in criminal law this phrase means that no one can be punished twice by the same act.

***Non compos mentis* (L).** Insane.

**Norma.** Norm, rule, standard. Average. Legal principle. Law.

**Norma de seguridad y salud ocupacional.** Occupational safety and health standard.

**Norma jurídica.** Juridical norm or rule.

**Normal.** Normal, ordinary, regular, usual.

**Normalización.** Normalization.

**Normas imperativas.** Mandatory rules.

**Normativo.** Normative, statutory.

**Nota.** Memorandum, memo, note, notice.

**Nota marginal.** Marginal note. A marginal note is an entry which complies with any of the following purposes: (a) to facilitate the mechanism of the registry office; (b) to state circumstances which modify recorded rights; or (c) to replace other entries. (Colon & Cia, Inc. v. Registrar, 88 PRR 77 (1963)).

**Notable.** Notorious. Famous.

**Notaría.** Notary's office.

**Notariado.** Professional organization of notaries. College of notaries.

**Notarial.** Notarial.

**Notario público.** Notary, official notary. Notary public (G.B.). In Spain and in Latin America notaries are highly trained professionals. In many instances notaries rank higher than attorneys.

**Noticia.** News, information.

**Noticiar.** To inform, report.

**Notificación.** Notice. Notice of all orders, rulings, and judgments shall be given to the parties to the action on the day of their rendition, and should this not be possible, on the day following. Notices shall be served by the clerk, secretary, or official of the chamber authorized thereof, who shall read in full the order to the person upon whom service is made, and shall at the same time deliver to him a true copy thereof, signed by the recording clerk. (Sp. L. Civ. P., sec. 260-262). Notification. Summons. Service of process.

**Notificación de demanda.** Service of process. In every suit the original service of summons must be made upon the defendant in person. If the party summoned cannot be located by the bailiff, the opposing party may produce evidence showing that the party to be served has a residence within the territory of the forum and is, therefore, within the court's jurisdiction. If the court is satisfied with this proof, it may order that the summons be served by schedule. (LA Laws & Inst.).

**Notificación defectuosa.** Irregular notice.

**Notificación en los estrados.** Service of notifications in the court room. In all actions and proceedings in which a litigant shall place himself or be declared in default for not appearing in the action after he has been formally cited, no further effort shall be made to secure his appearance. (Sp. L. Civ. P. sec. 281).

**Notificación y emplazamiento.** Service of process. Service of citations and summonses upon those who are or who should be parties to the action, shall be made by writ delivered to the person to be cited instead of the copy of the order, a statement of said service being made in the proceedings. (Sp. L. Civ. P., sec. 271, 272).

**Notificaciones, citaciones y emplazamientos.** Notifications, citations and summonses. Notifications, citations, and summonses which are served beyond the limits of the court room or chamber, shall be respectively served by a bailiff or an officer of the chamber. Those within the court room shall be served by reading the entire order to the person in interest, giving him at the same time a copy thereof. (Sp. L. Crim. P., art. 166).

**Notificador.** Process server.

**Notificar.** To notify. To serve.

**Notoriedad.** Notoriety, fame, publicity.

**Notorio.** Notorious, evident, obvious. Patent.

**Novación.** Novation. Obligations may be modified: 1) By the change of their object or principal conditions. 2) By substituting the person of the debtor. 3) By subrogating a third person in the rights of the creditor. (Sp. Civ. C., sec. 1171, 1172).

**Novación objetiva.** Objective novation. Novation takes place when, by agreement of the parties, a new performance is substituted for that previously owed, or a new cause is substituted for that of the original obligation. If any substantial part of the original performance is still owed, there is no novation. Novation take place also when the parties expressly declare their intention to novate an obligation. Mere modification of an obligation, made without intention to extinguish it, does not effect a novation. The execution of a new writing, the issuance or renewal of a negotiable instrument, or the giving of new securities for the performance of an existing obligation are examples of such a modification. (Lou. Civ. C. art. 1881).

**Novación subjetiva.** Subjective novation. Novation takes place when a new obligor is substituted for a prior obligor who is discharged by the obligee. In that case, the novation is accomplished even without the consent of the prior obligor, unless he had an interest in performing the obligation himself. (Lou. Civ. C. art. 1882).

**Novar.** To make a novation, to substitute.

**Novatorio.** Novatory, pertaining to a novation.

**Novia.** Bride, fiancee.

**Noviazgo.** Betrothal, courtship, engagement.

**Novio.** Bridegroom, fiance.

**Núbil.** Nubile, celibate. Of proper age for marriage.

**Nuca.** Nape.

**Nuda propiedad.** Legal title without the right of use and enjoyment.

**Nudo.** Knot. Nude.

***Nudum pactum* (L).** A mere agreement where performance has not yet started. The phrase is used primarily in property law to distinguish situations where possession has been granted from others where only the consent of both parties has been exchanged. A *nudum pactum* could be just as binding as one where possession has already changed heads. The importance of this classification can be appreciated when the rights of third parties come into play. For instance, a *nudum pactum* does not usually put third parties on notice while a transfer of possession usually does.

**Nuera.** Daughter-in-law.

**Nuevo.** New, fresh, moved.

**Nuevo juicio.** New trial.

**Nuevo matrimonio.** Remarriage. Divorce returns to the parties their capacity to remarry. (Mex. Civ. C., art.289).

**Nugatorio.** Nugatory. Ineffective.

**Nulidad.** Nullity, invalidity, voidness.

**Nulidad absoluta contractual.** Absolute nullity of contracts. A contract is absolutely null when it violates a rule of public order, as when the object of a contract is illicit or immoral. A contract that is absolutely null may not be confirmed. (Lou. Civ. C. art. 2030).

**Nulidad contractual.** Nullity of contracts. A contract is null when the requirements for its formation have not been met. (Lou. Civ. C. art. 2029).

**Nulidad contractual, efectos.** Nullity of contracts, consequences. An absolutely null contract, or a relatively null contract that has been declared null by the court, is deemed never to have existed. The parties must be restored to the situation that existed before the contract was made. If it is impossible or impracticable to make restoration in kind, it may be made through an award of damages. (Lou. Civ. C. art. 2033).

**Nulidad relativa contractual.** Relative nullity of contracts. A contract is relatively null when it violates a rule intended for the protection of private parties, as when a party lacked capacity or did not give free consent at the time the contract was made. A contract that is only relatively null may be confirmed. (Lou. Civ. C. art. 2031).

**Nulificar.** To annul, nullify, rule out. To veto, void.

**Nulla poena sine lege (L).** This is the short version of the phrase *nullum crimen, nulla poena sine lege penale.* It means that for a crime to be committed there must exist a violation of a specific criminal law.

**Nullum crimen sine lege (L).** See *nulla poena.*

**Nulo.** Null, invalid, null and void. Ineffectual, inoperative.

**Numerario.** Money, cash, currency.

**Número.** Number, cipher, digit, figure, numeral.

**Numeroso.** Numerous, abundant, many.

**Nuncupativo.** Nuncupative.

**Nupcialidad.** Marriage, wedding.

**Nupcias.** Marriage, wedding.

# O

**O.N.U.** Organization of the United Nations, U.N.O, U.N.

**O.N.G.** NGO, non-governmental organization.

**Obedecer.** To obey, comply with.

**Obediencia.** Obedience, compliance, submission.

**Obediencia a órdenes militares.** Obedience to military orders.

**Obediencia debida.** Due obedience. No liability attaches to whoever acts under superior orders, provided all the following circumstances concur: 1) That the order originates from the proper authority and fulfills all legal formalities. 2) That the person in question is duty bound to follow such order. 3) That the order is not manifestly a criminal act. (St. P.C. for LA, sec. 32).

**Óbito.** Death.

**Objeción.** Objection, challenge, exception, demurrer. Opposition. Complaint, protest.

**Objetable.** Objectionable. Controversial, questionable. Offensive.

**Objetante.** Objector, challenger, demurrant.

**Objetar.** To object, challenge. To take exception. To oppose. To protest.

**Objetivo.** Objective. Goal, purpose. Neutral, unbiased.

**Objeto.** Object, article, thing. Objective.

**Oblación.** Payment, disbursement.

**Oblar.** To pay, disburse.

**Obligación.** Obligation. Every obligation consists in giving, doing, or not doing something. Those arising from acts or omissions, in which faults or negligence, not punished by law, occur, shall be subject to the law of torts. (Sp. Civ. C., sec. 1055, 1060).

Duty, liability. Bond, commitment. Burden.

**Obligación a plazo.** Obligation subject to a time period. Obligations, the fulfillment of which has been fixed for a day certain, shall only be demandable when the proper day arrives. A day certain is understood to be one which must necessarily arrive, even though its date be unknown. (Sp. Civ. C., sec. 1092).

**Obligación alimentaria.** Child support, spouse support.

**Obligación alternativa.** Alternative obligation. An obligation is alternative when an obligor is bound to render only one of two or more items of performance. When an obligation is alternative, the choice of the item of performance belongs to the obligor unless it has been expressly or impliedly granted to the obligee. (Lou. Civ. C. art. 1808 and 1809).

**Obligación bajo condición resolutoria.** Obligation subject to a resolutory condition. If the obligation may be immediately enforced but will come to an end when the uncertain event occurs, the condition is resolutory. (Lou. Civ. C. art. 1767).

**Obligación bajo condición suspensiva.** Obligation subject to a suspensive condition. If the obligation may not be enforced until the uncertain event occurs, the condition is suspensive.

A suspensive condition that depends solely on the whim of the obligor makes the obligation null.

**Obligación condicional.** Conditional obligation. A conditional obligation is one dependent on an uncertain event.

Conditions may be either expressed in a stipulation or implied by the law, the nature of the contract, or the intent of the parties. (Lou. Civ. C. art. 1767 and 1768).

**Obligación conjunta.** Joint obligation. When different obligors owe together just one performance to one obligee, but neither is bound for the whole, the obligation is joint for the obligors.

When one obligor owes just one performance intended for the common benefit of different obligees, neither of whom is entitled to the whole performance, the obligation is joint for the obligees. (Lou. Civ. C. art. 1788).

**Obligación conjuntiva.** Conjunctive obligation. An obligation is conjunctive when it binds the obligor to multiple items of performance that may be separately rendered or enforced. In that case, each item is regarded as the object of a separate obligation.

The parties may provide that the failure of the obligor to perform one or more items shall allow the obligee to demand the immediate performance of all the remaining items. (Lou. Civ. C. art. 1807).

**Obligación de pagar el precio.** Obligation to pay the price. The obligation to pay the price of a commercial purchase, unless otherwise agreed upon, begins after the merchandise is placed at the disposal of the purchaser and after the latter has stated his satisfaction. (Waterman Export Corp. v. Valdejulli, 88 PRR 483 (1963)).

**Obligación de resultado y obligación de medios.** Duty to achieve a specific result. Duty of best efforts. (1) To the extent that an obligation of a party involves a duty to achieve a specific result, that party is bound to achieve that result. (2) To the extent that an obligation of a party involves a duty of best efforts in the performance of an activity, that party is bound to make such efforts as would be made by a reasonable person of the same kind in the same circumstances. (Unidroit, Prin., art. 5.4).

**Obligación, definición.** Obligation, definition. An obligation is a legal relationship whereby a person, called the obligor, is bound to render a performance in favor of another, called the obligee. Performance may consist of giving, doing, or not doing something. (Lou. Civ. C. art. 1756).

**Obligación divisible.** Divisible obligation. An obligation is divisible when the object of the performance is susceptible of division. (Lou. Civ. C. art. 1815).

**Obligación divisible e indivisible.** Divisible and indivisible obligation. The obligations to give specified things and all those which are not capable of partial fulfillments shall be considered as indivisible. The obligations of doing shall be divisible when their purpose is the prestation of a number of days of work, the execution of works by units of measurement, or other similar things which by reason of their nature are capable of partial fulfillment. In obligations of not doing the divisibility or indivisibility shall be decided by the character of the prestation in each particular case. (Sp. Civ. C., sec. 1118, 1119).

**Obligación, efectos.** Obligation, effects. An obligation may give the obligee the right to: 1) Enforce the performance that the obligor is bound to render; 2) Enforce performance by causing it to be rendered by another at the obligor's expense; 3) Recover damages for the obligor's failure to perform, or his defective or delayed performance. (Lou. Civ. C. art. 1758).

**Obligación estrictamente personal.** Strictly personal obligation. An obligation is strictly personal when its performance can be enforced only by the obligee, or only against the obligor. When the performance requires the special skill or qualification of the obligor, the obligation is presumed to be strictly personal on the part of the obligor. All obligations to perform personal services are presumed to be strictly personal on the part of the obligor. (Lou. Civ. C. art. 1766).

**Obligación, extinción.** Obligation, extinction. Obligations are extinguished: By their payment or fulfillment. By the loss of the thing due. By the remission of the debt. By the merging of the rights of the creditors and debtor. By compensation. By novation. (Sp. Civ. C., sec. 1124).

**Obligación, fuentes.** Obligation, sources. Obligations arise from contracts and other declarations of will. They also arise directly from the law, regardless of a declaration of will, in instances such as wrongful acts, the management of the affairs of another, unjust enrichment and other acts or facts. (Lou. Civ. C. art. 1757).

**Obligación hereditable.** Heritable obligation. An obligation is heritable when its performance may be enforced by a successor of the obligee or against a successor of the obligor. Every obligation is deemed heritable as to all parties, except when the contrary results from the terms or from the nature of the contract. A heritable obligation is also transferable between living persons. (Lou. Civ. C. art. 1765).

**Obligación indivisible.** Indivisible obligation. An obligation is indivisible when the object of the performance, because of its nature or because of the intent of the parties, is not susceptible of division. (Lou. Civ. C. art. 1815).

**Obligación mancomunada.** Several obligation. When each of different obligors owes a separate performance to one obligee, the obligation is several for the obligors. When one obligor owes a separate performance to each of different obligees, the obligation is several for the obligees. A several obligation produces the same effects as a separate obligation owed to each obligee by an obligor or by each obligor to an obligee. (Lou. Civ. C. art. 1787).

**Obligación mancomunada, conjunta y solidaria.** Several joint and solidary obligation. When an obligation binds more than one obligor to one obligee, or binds one obligor to more than one obligee, or binds more than one obligor to more than one obligee, the obligation may be several, joint, or solidary. Lou. Civ. C. art. 1786).

**Obligación, modificación.** Obligation, modification. Obligations may be modified: 1) By the change of their object or principal conditions. 2) By substituting the person of the debtor. 3) By subrogating a third person in the rights of the creditor. (Sp. Civ. C., sec. 1171, 1172).

**Obligación natural.** Natural obligation. A natural obligation arises from circumstances in which the law implies a particular moral duty to render a performance.

Examples of circumstances giving rise to a natural obligation are: 1) When a civil obligation has been extinguished by prescription or discharged in bankruptcy. 2) When an obligation has been incurred by a person who, although endowed with discernment, lacks legal capacity. 3) When the universal successors are not bound by a civil obligation to execute the donations and other dispositions made by a deceased person that are null for want of form. (Lou. Civ. C. art. 1760 and 1762).

**Obligación natural, efectos.** Natural obligation, effects. A natural obligation is not enforceable by judicial action. Nevertheless, whatever has been freely performed in compliance with a natural obligation may not be reclaimed. (Lou. Civ. C. art. 1761).

**Obligación o derechos no inscrible.** Obligation or rights nor recordable.

**Obligación ofrecimiento de pago y consignación.** Obligation, tender of payment and consignation. If the creditor to whom the tender of payment has been made should refuse to accept it, without reason, the debtor shall remain released from all liability by the consignation of the thing due. (Sp. Civ. C., sec. 1144).

**Obligación pagadera a la vista.** Demand liability.

**Obligación real.** Real obligation. A real obligation is a duty correlative and incidental to a real right. A real obligation attaches to a thing.

Because a real obligation is a duty incidental and correlative to a real right, and because such a right may apply to both movables and immovables, a real obligation may attach either to a movable or an immovable. For example, when a movable is subject to a usufruct, the real obligation attaches to the movable; when an immovable is burdened with a predial servitude, the real obligation attaches to the immovable. (Lou. Civ. C. art. 1763 and note).

**Obligación real, efectos.** Real obligation, effects. A real obligation is transferred to the universal or particular successor who acquires the movable or immovable thing to which the obligation is attached, without a special provision to that effect. But a particular successor is not personally bound, unless he assumes the personal obligations of his transferor with respect to the thing, and he may liberate himself of the real obligation by abandoning the thing. (Louisiana, Civ. C. art. 1764).

**Obligación simple y condicional.** Obligation not subject and subject to a condition. Every obligation, the fulfillment of which should not depend upon a future or uncertain event or upon a past event, unknown to the parties in interest, shall be immediately demandable. (Sp. Civ. C., sec. 1080, 1081).

**Obligación solidaria.** Solidary obligation. An obligation is solidary for the obligees when it gives each obligee the right to demand the whole performance from the common obligor. An obligation is solidary for the obligors when each obligor is liable for the whole performance. A performance rendered by one of the solidary obligors relieves the others of liability toward the obligee. (Lou. Civ. C. art. 1790 and 1794).

**Obligación, término para el cumplimiento.** Obligation, term for performance. A term for the performance of an obligation is a period of time either certain or uncertain. It is certain when it is fixed. It is uncertain when it is not fixed but is determinable either by the intent of the parties or by the occurrence of a future and certain event. It is also uncertain when it is not determinable, in which case the obligation must be performed within a reasonable time. (Lou. Civ. C. art. 1778 and 1777).

**Obligaciones alternativas.** Alternative obligations. A person who is alternatively obliged to make different prestations must fully comply with one of them. A creditor can not be compelled to receive a part of one and a part of another. The option pertains to the debtor unless it has been expressly granted the creditor. (Sp. Civ. C., sec. 1098, 1099).

**Obligaciones de dar.** Obligations to give a certain thing, including money.

**Obligaciones de hacer.** Obligations to perform a certain act, for instance, to build a wall, to paint a picture, etc.

**Obligaciones de no hacer.** Obligations to refrain from doing something.

**Obligaciones implícitas.** Implied obligations. Implied obligations stem from (a) the nature and purpose of the contract; (b) practices established between the parties and usages; (c) good faith and fair dealing; (d) reasonableness. (Unidroit, Prin., art. 5.2).

**Obligado.** Obligor, debtor, liable party.

**Obligado de regreso.** Endorser of a commercial paper liable for payment.

**Obligante.** Obligee, creditor.

**Obligar.** To coerce, constrain, compel, force, require.

**Obligatoriedad.** Condition of being mandatory. One of the attributes of the law.

**Obligatorio.** Obligatory, binding, compulsory, mandatory.

**Obra.** Work, work product.

**Obra en juicio.** Is included in the records.

**Obra por pieza.** Work by piece.

**Obrar.** To act, behave, operate.

**Obrar en juicio.** To be in the record. To be a party to a lawsuit.

**Obras Públicas.** Public works, such as roads, bridges and highways.

**Obrero.** Worker, employer, jobber, workman.

**Obscenidad.** Obscenity, indecency, pornography.

**Obsceno.** Obscene, indecent. Lascivious, lecherous, lustful. Erotic, libidinous.

**Obsequio.** Gift, present, donation.

**Observancia de normas procesales.** Observance of procedural ruels. Procedural rules are a matter of strong public policy and, consequently, completely mandatory, for the judge as much as for the parties, as well as for third parties. The exception to these principles are those rules that, although procedural, are of an optional nature, because they refer to private interests of the parties. (C.R. C. of Civ. P., art. 5.)

**Observar.** To comply. To notice.

**Obsesión.** Obsession, fixation, mania.

**Obtemperar.** To comply.

**Obstrucción.** Obstruction.

**Obtención.** Attainment.

**Obviar.** To render unnecessary.

**Ocasional.** Occasional. From time to time.

**Occiso.** Murdered, corpse.

**Ociosidad.** Idleness.

**Ocultación.** Concealment, hiding, removal.

**Ocultamiento.** Concealment.

**Ocultamiento doloso.** Fraudulent concealment.

**Ocupación.** Retention. Things are acquired by retention which can be appropriated by reason of their nature, which have no owners, such as animals which are the object of hunting and fishing, hidden treasure, and abandoned property. (Sp. Civ. C., sec. 617).

Occupation. Business, career, job. Invasion. Occupancy, residence, tenancy. Possession. Control.

**Ocupación, apropiación.** Occupancy, appropriation. Occupancy is the taking of possession of a corporeal movable that does not belong to anyone. The occupant acquires ownership the moment he takes possession. (Lou. Civ. C. art. 3412 and notes).

**Ocupante.** Occupier, tenant, inhabitant, squatter.

**Ocupar.** To occupy, inhabit, reside. To possess, squat. To employ.

**Ocurrencia.** Occurrence, event, happening, incident.

**Ocurrir.** To occur, happen. To pursue a way of appeal.

**Ofendedor, ofensor.** Offender, trespasser, wrongdoer.

**Ofender.** To offend, affront, aggravate. Insult. To infringe, trespass, violate.

**Ofendido.** Victim. Offended.

**Ofensa.** Offense, Crime, infraction, tort, transgression. Abuse, affront, insult.

**Oferente, ofertante.** Offeror, bidder.

**Oferta.** Offer. A proposal for concluding a contract constitutes an offer if it is sufficiently definite and indicates the intention of the offeror to be bound in case of acceptance. (Unidroit, Prin., art. 2.2).

Offer, bid, proposal, submission, tender.

**Oferta de prueba.** Offer of proof.

**Oferta irrevocable.** Irrevocable offer. An offer that specifies a period of time for acceptance is irrevocable during that time. An irrevocable offer expires if not accepted within the time prescribed in the preceding Article. (Lou. Civ. C. art. 1928 and 1929).

**Oferta revocable.** Revocable offer. An offer not irrevocable may be revoked before it is accepted. A revocable offer expires if not accepted within a reasonable time. (Lou. Civ. C. art. 1930 and 1931).

**Ofertar.** To offer, bid, propose, quote, submit, tender.

**Oficial.** Official, clerk, officer. Official, formal, governmental.

**Oficial de sala.** Official of the chamber.

**Oficial jurídico.** Law clerk.

**Oficialismo.** Officialism.

**Oficialista.** Follower of the party presently in power.

**Oficializar.** To accept publicly. To legalize.

**Oficialmente.** Officially.

**Oficiar.** To officiate. To perform a certain roll. To act in a certain capacity.

**Oficina.** Office, bureau. Law firm.

**Oficio.** Judicial request. When judges or courts are obliged to direct requests to authorities or officials of another department, they shall do so by official communications or statements, as the case may require. (Sp. L. Crim. P., art. 187).

Occupation, trade.

**Oficioso.** Officious, official. Assiduous, diligent.

**Ofrecedor.** Offeror.

**Ofrecer.** To offer, bid, propose, quote, submit, tender.

**Ofrecido.** Offered.

**Ofrecimiento de pago.** Tender of payment.

**Oído el fiscal.** Upon the recommendation of the district attorney.

**Oidor.** Auditor, judge.

**Oír.** To hear, listen. To heed.

**Ojear.** To examine casually. To peruse.

**Ojos.** Eyes.

**Ola.** Wave, surge.

**Oligofrenia.** Oligophrenia.

**Ológrafo.** Holograph, hand written.

**Olor.** Odor, smell. Aroma, perfume, scent.

**Omisión.** Omission. Exception, exclusion, oversight. Disregard, negligence.

**Omitir.** To omit. To forget, neglect, overlook. To exclude, reject.

**Onerosidad.** For value, that requires payment.

**Oneroso.** Onerous.

**Onirismo.** Lyricism.

**Onomástico.** Nameday, saint's day.

**Opción.** Option, alternative, choice.

**Opción de compra.** Option of purchase. Option of purchase is a contract sui generis having its own substantivity and defined contours, very similar to the contract of unilateral promise of accepted sale which is distinguished only by the requirement of the premium or price which may be stipulated in the latter by the acquisition of the right to choose within a certain period between the execution or withdrawal of the proposed sale. (Pérez v. Sanpedro, 86 PRR 498 (162)).

**Opción para anticipar a discreción.** Option to accelerate at will.

**Opcional.** Optional.

**Operación.** Transaction. Operation. Surgery.

**Operación al contado.** Cash transaction.

**Operación de bolsa.** Exchange transaction.

**Operar.** To operate. To act, behave, perform. To handle, manage, use. To do business. To work.

**Operario.** Worker who performs routines.

**Opinión.** Opinion. Memorandum. Belief, idea, view.

**Oponente.** Opponent, adversary, enemy.

**Oponer, oponerse.** To raise, object, challenge. To take exception. To oppose. To protest.

**Oponible.** That can be raised, objected or opposed.

**Oportunidad.** Opportunity, chance, occasion.

**Oportunidad de cumplimiento.** Time of performance. A party must perform its obligations: (a) if a time is fixed by or determinable from the contract, at that time; (b) if a period of time is fixed by or determinable from the contract, at any time within that period unless circumstances indicate that the other party is to choose a time; (c) in any other case, within a reasonable time after the conclusion of the contract. (Unidroit, Prin., art. 6.1.1).

**Oposición.** Opposition. Antagonism, resistance. Enemy, opponent. Counterpart.

**Opositor.** Opponent, adversary, competitor, enemy.

**Oprobio.** Opprobrium, censure.

**Optativo.** Optional, elective, voluntary.

**Orador.** Orator, speaker, talker. Rhetorician. Lecturer. Person who prays.

**Oral.** Oral, spoken, verbal, vocal. Parol.

**Oralidad.** Orality. Verbosity.

**Ordalía.** Ordeal, trial by combat.

**Orden.** Order. System, sequence, command, directive, mandate, ruling, writ.

**Orden de allanamiento o registro.** Search warrant.

**Orden de arresto.** Arrest warrant.

**Orden de entredicho.** *Ex parte* temporary restraining order.

**Orden del día.** Order of the day.

**Orden público.** Public policy. In Spanish the term is much stronger than its English version. Public policy is usually used to denote a sense of urgency that allows for actions that ordinarily would not be permissible. Public policy, for instance, justifies retroactivity of the law.

Latin American Civil Codes do not define the concept of public order apart from making clear the private agreement cannot derogate from laws which are a matter of public order. The approach in determining public order issues has been *a posteriori* rather than *a priori*. As a consequence courts have wide discretion to determine whether or not an agreement is unenforceable for violation of public order. This discretion is even broader if we note the precedents have no binding value for Civil Law. (Barrios-Mannucci).

**Ordenación.** Entrance into priesthood.

**Ordenador de datos.** Computer.

**Ordenamiento.** Legal system, law legislation. Decree, edict, ruling. Placing in a proper order.

**Ordenanza.** Ordinance, decree, regulation.

**Ordenar.** To order. To command, rule.

**Ordenar se abstenga.** To enjoin.

**Ordinario.** Ordinary, common, routine, standard.

**Organismo.** Organism, association, body, group.

**Organización.** Organization.

**Organización de Estados Americanos, OEA.** Organization of American States, OAS. The functions of the OAS, as defined in Article 2 of the Revised Charter, are: (a) To strengthen the peace and security of the continent; (b) To prevent possible causes of difficulties and to ensure the pacific settlement of disputes that may arise among the Member States; (c) To provide for common action on the part of those States in the event of aggression; (d) To seek the solution of political, juridical and economic problems that may arise among them; and (e) To promote, by cooperative action, their economic, social and cultural development. (L & D in LA).

**Organización de las Naciones Unidas.** United Nations Organization, U.N.O., U.N.

**Organizador.** Organizer, incorporator, promotor.

**Organizar.** To organize, create, settle, set up.

**Órgano.** Organ, organism. Dependency, instrumentality.

**Orientación.** Orientation, direction, sense, trend. Briefing. Explanation.

**Origen.** Origin, genesis, root, source.

**Original.** Original. Ingenious, inventive. Authentic, genuine. First, forerunner, precursor.

**Originario.** From a certain origin. Natural or native of.

**Orina.** Urine.

**Oro.** Gold.

**Ortografía.** Spelling.

**Ortográfico.** Orthographic, related to spelling, in writing.

**Ostensible.** Ostensible, apparent, seeming.

**Otorgador, otorgante.** Obligor, conveyor, grantor, maker.

**Otorgamiento.** Grant, authorization.

**Otorgar.** To concede, convey, grant. To sign, execute.

**Otrosí, otrosí digo.** Furthermore. Added paragraph(s) at the end of a motion.

**Oyente.** Auditing student, one who does not take credit.

# P

**P.p.** In representation of.

**Pabellón.** Top part of a ship. Flag, banner, ensign.

**Pacotilla.** Bauble, bric-a-brac, junk, trinket.

**Pactado.** Agreed, accorded, concurred.

**Pactante.** Party who agrees or contracts.

**Pactar.** To contract, agree, bind oneself.

**Pacto.** Pact, compact, accord, agreement, arrangement, bargain, compromise, contract, convention, covenant, deal, treaty, settlement, understanding.

**Pacto de cuota litis.** Contingency fee.

**Pacto de no agresión.** Non-aggression treaty.

**Pacto de recompra.** Repurchase agreement.

**Padrastro.** Stepfather.

**Padre.** Father, ancestor, forefather, progenitor. Author, inventor.

**Padre político.** Father-in-law.

**Padrino.** Godfather.

**Padrón.** Voting list.

**Paga.** Pay, payment, compensation, earning, salary, wages. Profit, return, revenue.

**Paga doble.** Double wages.

**Pagable.** Payable.

**Pagadero.** Payable on such a time, at such a place.

**Pagadero a la orden.** Payable to order.

**Pagadero a la vista.** Payable on demand.

**Pagadero al portador.** Payable to bearer.

**Pagado.** Paid, compensated, defrayed, disbursed, expended.

**Pagador.** Party who pays.

**Pagar.** To pay, clear, compensate, defray, disburse, honor, settle.

**Pagaré.** Note, promissory note.

**Pagaré a la orden.** Note made to order.

**Pagaré hipotecario.** Mortgage note.

**Pago.** Payment, compensation, remuneration, reward. Revenge, vengeance.

**Pago a su debido tiempo.** Payment in due course.

**Pago con cheque u otro instrumento.** Payment by cheque or other instrument.

**Pago de obligaciones.** Payment of obligations. A debt shall not be considered as paid until the full amount of the thing has been delivered, or the prestation of which the obligation consisted has been made. (Sp. Civ. C., sec. 1125, 1126, 1139).

**Pago en cesión de bienes.** Payment by assignment of property. The debtor may assign his property to creditors in payment of his debts. This assignment releases the former from liability only to the net amount of the property assigned, unless there is an agreement to the contrary. (Sp. Civ. C., sec. 1143).

**Pago global.** Lump sum.

**Pago mediante transferencia de fondos.** Payment by funds transfer.
Unless the obligee has indicated a particular account, payment may be made by a transfer to any of the financial institutions in which the obligee has made it known that it has an account. (Unidroit, Prin., art. 6.1.8).

**País.** Country, kingdom, nation, republic, state.

**Palabra.** Word, utterance. Assurance, promise.

**Palabras y frases técnicas.** Technical terms and phrases, terms of art.

**Palaciego.** Pertaining to a palace or government house. It is used, despectively, about measures political taken by the authorities without consulting with the people.

**Palacio.** Palace, castle. Mansion.

**Palacio de justicia.** Law courts.

**Paliar.** To alleviate or to palliate.

**Paliativo.** Palliative.

**Paliza.** Beating. Knocking, striking. Defeat, setback.

**Palmario.** Obvious, easy to prove.

**Palo.** Stick, pole, rod.

**Palo, garrote.** Club. A club is not a deadly weapon *per se* when it is used within the common and ordinary use of wood; however, when it is used as an assault instrument capable of producing great bodily injury, it may become a deadly weapon. (Ppl. v. Rodríquez Ocana, 88 PRR 325 (1963)).

**Pan y agua.** Bread and water.

**Pandilla.** Gang, band, group, pack of criminals or hooligans.

**Pandillero.** Member of a gang.

**Panel.** Panel, board, committee, jury.

**Panfleto.** Pamphlet. Flier, handbill, handout. Booklet, brochure.

**Papel.** Paper, document.

**Papel moneda.** Money, bills, legal tender.

**Papel sellado.** Stamped paper.

**Papeleo.** Bureaucracy, red tape.

**Papeles.** Personal identification. Documents.

**Papeleta.** Ballot.

**Par.** Pair, couple, twosome.

**Para mejor proveer.** Order from the court requesting additional evidence. Literally it means "to render a better decision."

**Parada.** Stop, stoppage. Parade, march, procession.

**Parada o partidor.** Stop lock or sluice gate.

**Paradero.** Whereabouts, destination.

**Paraestatal.** Semi-official, semi-private.

**Paraje.** Area, landscape. Panorama, view. Rural countryside.

**Paralegal.** Paralegal. Not illegal but in a gray area.

**Paralización del proceso.** Stay of proceedings for an indefinite time.

**Paranoia.** Paranoia.

**Parapolicial.** Done unofficially by the police or other groups.

**Parar.** To stop, prevent. To place upright.

**Parcela.** Tract of land, lot.

**Parcelación.** Division of land into regular plots.

**Parcelar.** To divide the land into regular plots following administrative guidelines.

**Parcial.** Partial. In part only, incomplete. Biased, prejudiced.

**Parcialidad.** Partiality. Incompleteness. Bias.

**Parecer.** Opinion, belief, supposition, view.

**Pared.** Wall, obstacle.

**Pared divisoria.** Dividing wall, party wall.

**Pareja.** Couple, pair. Partner in a marriage or common-law marriage.

**Parentesco.** Relationship, kinship. The nearness of relationship is determined by the number of generations. Each generation forms one degree. A series of degrees forms the line, which may be direct or collateral. (Sp. Civ. C., sec. 889, 890).
　Affinity, ancestry, lineage, relationship.

**Parentesco civil.** Legal kinship. Legal kinship results from adoption and only exists between adapting parent and adopted child. (Mex. Civ. C., art.295).

**Parentesco por afinidad.** Kinship by affinity. Kinship by affinity is the one that exists by marriage, between the husband's and the wife's relatives, and the wife's and the husband's relatives. (Mex. Civ. C., art.294).

**Parentesco por consanguinidad.** Kinship by consanguinity. Kinship by consanguinity is the one that exists between persons that descend from the same ancestor. (Mex. Civ. C., art.293).

**Paridad.** Parity, correspondence, equivalence, symmetry.

**Pariente.** Relation, relative, family, kin.

**Paritario.** Related to agreements between employers and unions, entered on a basis of equality.

**Parlamentario.** Parliamentary, congressional.

**Parlamento.** Parliament, legislative power.

**Paro.** Strike, industrial action (G.B.). Unemployment, underemployment.

**Párrafo.** Paragraph.

**Parricida.** Parricide, person who murders his father.

**Parricidio.** Parricide, murder of one's father.

**Parroquia.** Small church.

**Parroquiano.** Patron, client, customer, regular.

**Parte.** Party, litigant. Part, portion.

**Parte acomodante.** Accommodation party.

**Parte agraviada.** Aggrieved party.

**Parte contraria.** Adverse party.

**Parte interesada propiamente dicha.** Real party in interest.

**Parte solicitante.** Moving party, movant.

**Parte vencida.** Losing party, defeated party.

**Partes con un interés similar.** Parties aligned on the same side.

**Partes en un pleito.** Parties to an action.

**Partible.** That can be divided, divisible, separable.

**Partición.** Partition, distribution, grouping.

**Partición hereditaria.** Hereditary partition. Fathers and mothers and other ascendant may make a distribution and partition of their property among their children and legitimate descendants, either by designation the *quantum* of the parts and partitions (portion) which they assign to each of them, or in designating the property that shall compose their respective lots. These partitions may be made by act *inter vivos* or by testament. (Lou. Civ. C. art. 1724 and 1725).

**Participación.** Participation. Interest. Co-authorship. Commission, share of profits.

**Participación en las ganancias.** Share of profits.

**Participante, partícipe.** Participant. Co-author.

**Participar.** To participate. To enter, take part. To notify.

**Particular.** Particular. Special. Private.

**Particular querellante.** Private complainant. The private complainant, whatever jurisdiction he be subject to, shall be subject for all purposes of the action instituted by him to the judge of examination or court having jurisdiction of the crime which is the subject matter of the complaint. (Sp. L. Crim. P., sec. 274).

**Particularizar.** To go into detail. To explain completely.

**Partida.** Departure, exodus, exit. Assortment, batch, lot.

**Partida de nacimiento.** Birth certificate.

**Partidario.** Partisan, adherent, follower, supporter, sympathizer.

**Partido.** Political party. Parted.

**Partidor.** Person who apportions or divides.

**Partija.** Division, separation.

**Partir.** To partition, divide, split. To apportion, distribute. To share. To depart, exit, leave.

**Parto.** Birth, delivery.

**Pasador.** Person who transports others or things between two points.

**Pasajero.** Passenger, traveler, voyager, wanderer.

**Pasante.** Law clerk, articled clerk (G.B.).

**Pasantía.** Clerkship in a law firm.

**Pasaporte.** Passport.

**Pasar.** To pass. To convey, sell.

**Pasar lista.** To call the roll.

**Pasavante.** Permit used in customs.

**Pase.** Pass, authorization, license, permission.

**Pasividad.** Passivity, inactiveness.

**Pasivo.** Passive. Debt, liability, obligation. Inactive, placid.

**Paso.** Passage, path, way. Speed.

**Pastura.** Pasture, forage, grass. Meadow.

**Patentable.** Patentable.

**Patentado.** Patented.

**Patentar.** To patent.

**Patentatario.** Related to patents and inventions.

**Patente.** Patent. Charter, concession, copyright, franchise, license, permit, trademark. License plate. A patent, in general terms, is an exclusive right or privilege-monopoly—created under the protection of the law and it has the attributes of personal property. (Gonzalez Chemical v. Sec. of the Treas., 86 PRR 67 (1962)).

**Patente de corso.** Letter of marque.

**Patente de navegación.** Navigation certificate.

**Patentizar.** To prove beyond any doubt, to render obvious.

**Paternalismo.** Paternalism. The paternalism which stemmed from the Iberian monarchies and the extended patriarchal family still permeates Latin American society. (L & D in LA).

**Paternidad.** Paternity, fatherhood.

**Paterno.** Paternal, fatherly.

**Patíbulo.** Scaffold, stockade.

**Patria potestad.** Parental authority. The *patria potestas* over the legitimate children not emancipated belongs to the father and the mother jointly. If there should be any disagreement between the husband and the wife, the issue will be decided by the court. (Sp. Civ. C., sec. 22).

Custody, managing conservatorship, patria potestas.

**Patrimonial.** Patrimonial, economic, related to money.

**Patrimonio.** Patrimony, assets and liabilities net worth.

**Patrimonio familiar.** Family patrimony is:
I. The family residence;
II. In some cases a parcel of agricultural land. (Mex. Civ. C., art.723).

**Patrón, patrono.** Employer, manager, supervisor.

**Patrón de buque.** Master of vessel.

**Patrón, empleador.** Employer, boss. The employer is the individual or legal entity which employs the services of one or more employees. (Mex. Labor Law).

**Patrón, representante.** Employer, representative. This refers to the directors, administrators, managers, and other individuals who perform functions of direction or administration in the enterprise or establishment. (FLL, Article 11).

**Patronato.** Association, usually for charity. Board of trustees, administration.

**Patrulla.** Patrol, guard, sentry, watch.

**Pauta.** Important factor or element to be considered.

**Pavimento.** Road, street.

**Paz.** Peace, armistice, truce. Calm, tranquility, cease fire, harmony.

**Peaje.** Toll.

**Peatón.** Pedestrian, walker.

**Pecado.** Sin, offense. Immorality, vice.

**Pecuario.** Related to cattle.

**Peculado.** Embezzlement, misappropriation of funds.

**Peculio.** Capital, net worth.

**Pecuniario.** Pecuniary, patrimonial, related to money.

**Pederasta.** Pederast, pervert.

**Pederastía.** Pederasty.

**Pedido.** Request, application, behest, petition, plea, requirement, solicitation. Favor.

**Pedir.** To request, ask, require, seek, pray, supplicate.

**Pelea.** Fight, strife, struggle.

**Peligro.** Danger, hazard, jeopardy, risk, threat.

**Peligroso.** Dangerous, perilous. Threatening, risky, unsafe.

**Pelotera.** Fight, tumult, quarrel.

**Pena aflictiva.** Corporal punishment. Jail term over a certain minimum time.

**Pena atenuada.** Attenuated sentence.

**Pena capital.** Death penalty.

**Pena, criterios de regulación.** Penalty, criteria to fix it. The court will fix the sentence within the limits provided for each crime, taking into account the extent of the harm of danger caused. (Standard Penal C. for Latin America, sec. 73).

**Pena de cadena perpetua.** Life sentence.

**Pena judicial.** Judicial penalty. Where the court orders a party to perform, it may also direct that this party pay a penalty if it does not comply with the order. (Unidroit, Prin., art. 7.2.4).

**Pena pecuniaria.** Fine. Sentence ordering the payment of a sum of money.

**Pena, penalidad.** Penalty, castigation, correction, disciplinary action, penance, punishment, retribution.

**Pena privativa de la libertad.** Jail term.

**Pena suspendida.** Suspended sentence.

**Penado.** Prisoner, captive, convict, criminal.

**Penal.** Prison, jail, penal colony, penitentiary. Penal, punitive.

**Penalista.** Penalist, specialist in criminal law.

**Penalizador.** Penalizing, enforcer of discipline.

**Penalizar, penar.** To condemn, sentence. To castigate, to discipline, penalize.

**Penas, clasificación.** Penalties, classification. The only punishments that can be imposed for a crime are the following: *Principal punishments*: Imprisonment and fine. *Supplementary punishments*: Total or partial disqualification. (Standard Penal C. for Latin America, sec. 42).

**Pendencia.** Pendency.

**Pendiente.** Pending, due and owning, outstanding, unpaid, unsettled.

**Peninsular.** Peninsular.

**Penintenciaría.** Penitentiary, prison, jail, penal colony.

**Penititenciario.** Related to administrative aspects of prisons.

**Penología.** Penology, criminology.

**Pensado.** Conscious, aforethought, premeditated.

**Pensión.** Pension, annuity, retirement, subsidy, support. Alimony.

**Pensión alimenticia.** Alimony.

**Pensionado.** Pensioner. Pensioned.

**Pensionar.** To pension, retire.

**Pensionista.** Person who receives an annuity or other regular income. Lodger.

**Penuria.** Pain, distress, suffering.

**Peón.** Rural, manual or unskilled worker.

**Pequeño.** Small, minute, reduced.

**Percepción.** Perception. Knowledge, understanding. Perceiving, charging, pocketing.

**Perceptible a los sentidos.** Cognizable, perceptible, by the senses.

**Perdedor.** Loser, defeated party.

**Perder.** To lose, be defeated. To fall. To mislay.

**Pérdida.** Loss. Damages, destruction, harm, injury. Beating, defeat. Forfeiture, penalty.

**Pérdida de competencia.** Loss of jurisdiction. Jurisdiction is lost in a specific case:
   a. When it is decided that the case belongs to another court; and
   b. When the case, procedural step, recourse or commission reaches an end. (Panamanian Judicial Code, art. 238.)

**Pérdida de la cosa debida.** Loss of the thing due. An obligation, consisting in the delivery of a specified thing, shall be extinguished when said thing should be lost or destroyed without fault of the debtor and before he should be in default. (Sp. Civ. C., sec. 1150).

**Pérdida de la patria potestad.** Termination of the parent-child relationship, removal of parental rights and duties.

**Pérdida total de un vehículo.** Total loss of a vehicle.

**Perdón.** Pardon, absolution, amnesty, clemency, forgiveness, grace, mercy, leniency, remission.

**Perdón del ofendido.** Condonation by the victim. The condonation of the victim—or, in case of incapacity of his/her legal representative—extinguishes the penal action in crimes prosecuted by private action. (Standard Penal C. for Latin America, sec. 101).

**Perdonar.** To pardon, absolve, forgive, remit.

**Perecer.** To perish, die, succumb.

**Perención.** Peremption. Peremption is a period of time fixed by law for the existence of a right. Unless timely exercised, the right is extinguished upon the expiration of the preemptive period. (Lou. Civ. C. art. 3458). Lapsing, expiration, laches, prescription, statute of limitations. Dismissal for lack of prosecution.

**Perentorio.** Peremptory, conclusive, final.

**Perfección.** Perfection. Formal establishment of a right.

**Perfeccionamiento.** Formalization.

**Perfeccionar.** To perfect. To improve. To comply with all formalities.

**Perfecto.** Perfect. Completely binding.

**Perfidia.** Perfidy.

**Pergamino.** Old document, parchment. Diploma. Papyrus, scroll.

**Pericia.** Expertise. Ability, skill.

**Pericial.** Relating to an expertise.

**Perimir.** To lapse, to become time barred, to expire.

**Periodicidad.** Periodicity.

**Período.** Period, duration, interval, lapse, term. Era, epoch, time. Phase, stage.

**Período de enfriamiento.** Cooling period.

**Período de veda.** Closed season.

**Peritaje.** Expert testimony, expertise.

**Perito.** Expert, expert witness. Person with a specialized area of knowledge.

**Perjudicado.** Injured. Aggrieved, offended, party. Party who suffers damages. Plaintiff. Victim.

**Perjudicar.** To prejudice. To damage, hurt, injure.

**Perjuicio.** Prejudice. Damages, impairment, loss. Profits lost, gains prevented.

**Perjuicioso.** Damaging, injurious, wasteful.

**Perjurar.** To perjure. To lie under oath.

**Perjurio.** Perjury. A conscious lie under oath. Falsehood, prevarication.

**Permanencia.** Occupancy, occupation, possession, tenancy. Fact of remaining somewhere.

**Permisible.** Permissible, allowable, lawful.

**Permisión, permiso.** Permission, permit, authorization.

**Permisivo.** Permissive, lenient, liberal tolerant. Assenting, consenting.

**Permitir.** To permit, allow, authorize, tolerate. To turn a blind eye.

**Permuta.** Exchange, barter. Exchange is a contract by which each of the contracting parties binds himself to give a thing in order to receive another. (Sp. Civ. C., sec. 1441).

**Permuta mercantil.** Commercial exchange, barter.

**Pernoctar.** To spend the night.

**Perpetrador.** Perpetrator.

**Perpetrar.** To perpetrate, to commit an act.

**Perpetuación.** Perpetuation.

**Perpetuidad.** Perpetuity.

**Perpetuo.** Perpetual.

**Persecución.** Persecution. Harassment, oppression, tyranny.

**Perseguir.** To persecute. To follow. To claim a right.

**Persistir.** To persist, persevere. To continue, carry on, insist.

**Persona.** Person, citizen, individual, man, woman. Juridical person.

**Persona en libertad condicional.** Parolee.

**Persona incierta.** Unknown person.

**Persona interpuesta real.** Real person interposed. In the field of contracts a contractual intermediary is designated as real person interposed, went the latter intervenes in the contract as actual contracting party, establishing the juridical relationship in his own name. (Hernandez v. Sec. of the Treasury, 86 PRR 12 (1962)).

**Persona interpuesta simulada, testaferro.** Simulated person interposed, name lender.

**Personal.** Personal, individual, private. Particular, special.

**Personalidad.** Rights and liabilities of natural and juridical persons. Personalty. Famous person.

**Personalidad civil.** Civil personality. The capacity of individual persons is governed by the personal law. (Bustamante C. arts. 27-28).

**Personalidad civil, extinción.** Civil personality, extinction.

**Personalidad jurídica.** Civil personality and capacity. Birth determines civil personality and capacity. A child shall be considered as born when completely separated from his mother's womb. (Sp. Civ. C., sec. 24, 25).

**Personas.** Persons.

According to the Romanist tradition, persons are divided into natural persons and juridical persons. A natural person is a human being. Only human beings may be natural persons. A juridical person is an entity to which the law attributes personality, such as a corporation or a partnership. (Lou. Civ. C., art. 24 and note).

**Personas jurídicas.** Juridical person. Artificial persons may acquire and possess property of all kinds and also contract obligations and institute civil and criminal actions, in accordance with the law and regulation of their establishment. (Sp. Civ. C., sec. 30).

**Personas jurídicas públicas y privadas.** Public and private juridical persons. According to civilian doctrine, juridical persons are classified either as private persons or public persons. A public person is governed by rules of public law; a private person is governed by rules of private law. (Lou. Civ. C. art. 24 and note).

**Personas jurídicas, reconocimiento.** Juristic persons, recognition. The concept and recognition of juristic persons shall be governed by the territorial law. (Bustamante C., art. 32).

**Personas morales.** Legal entities. Legal entities are:

The Nation, the states, and the municipalities;

The remaining public corporations recognized by law;

Civil associations or mercantile companies;

The unions, professional associations; Cooperative and mutual associations;

Other associations not mentioned above that have political, scientific, artistic, recreation, or any other legal end, as long as they are allowed by law;

Foreign private entities. (Mex. Civ. C., art.25).

**Personería.** Standing. Right to participate in a legal case. Capacity to exercise a right.

**Personero.** Agent, representative.

**Pertenecer.** To appertain, concern.

**Pertenencia.** Belonging, ownership, proprietorship.

**Pertenencias.** Belongings, assets, holdings, possessions. Accessories, adornments, appurtenances.

**Pertinencia.** Relevance, relevancy, materiality, pertinence.

**Pertinente.** Pertinent, relevant, material.

**Pertrecho.** Stores.

**Perturbación.** Disturbance, disruption, distraction, interference, intrusion. Nuisance, infringement, perturbation, trespass.

**Perturbador.** Nuisance. Wrongdoer.

**Perversidad, perversión.** Perversity, depravation.

**Pesar.** To weigh. To assess. To calculate.

**Pesca.** Fishing.

**Peso.** Weight, burden, onus.

**Pesquisa.** Criminal investigation.

**Pesquisante.** Criminal investigator, detective, sleuth.

**Petición.** Claim, petition, motion. Application.

**Petición peticionario.** Petitioner, applicant, movant, plaintiff, relator.

**Peticionar.** To petition, apply, claim, move, request. To demand.

**Petitorio.** Prayer for relief.

**Picapleitos.** Ambulance chaser, shyster.

**Picardía.** Chicanery, deception, duplicity, trickery.

**Picota.** Pillory, stockade.

**Pieza.** Piece. Certain number of pages in the record. Evidence offered. Room.

**Pignorable.** Subject to being pledged.

**Pignoración.** Pledge, chattels given as security of a debt.

**Pignorar.** To pledge, pawn.

**Pignoraticio.** Related to a pledge.

**Pilotaje.** Pilotage. Control of an aircraft or vessel.

**Pillaje.** Pillage, loot, plunder, raid, sacking.

**Pillar.** To pillage, loot, plunder, raid, sack.

**Pilluelo.** Hooligan, petty thief.

**Piquete.** Picket, formation of demonstrators.

**Piquete de huelga.** Strike picket.

**Pirámide.** Pyramid.

**Pirata.** Pirate, buccaneer, corsair, privateer. Bootlegger, counterfeiter.

**Piratear.** To breach copyright laws. To bootleg.

**Piratería.** Piracy, pirating. Copyright violation.

**Piromanía. Piromancia.** Pyromania.

**Pirómano.** Pyromaniac.

**Pisada.** Footprint, track. Imprint, trail.

**Pista.** Clue, lead, tracks.

**Pistola.** Pistol, gun.

**Pistolero.** Gangster, robber.

**Pito.** Whistle, siren. Signal.

**Placa.** Plate. License plate. X-ray.

**Plagiar.** To plagiarize, lift, steal an intellectual product. To pirate.

**Plagiario.** Plagiarist.

**Plagio.** Plagiarism.

**Planificación.** Planning, plannification. Order, system.

**Planilla.** Return, chart, form, model.

**Plantear.** To raise and issue or objection. To throw an idea.

**Plata.** Silver. Cash, money.

**Plausible.** Plausible, believable, credible, possible.

**Playa.** Seashore. Seashore is the space of land over which the waters of the sea spread in the highest tide during the winter season. (Lou. Civ. C. art. 451).

**Plaza.** Market. Area. Park.

**Plazo.** Term, period. Duration. Time or date when an obligation becomes due.

**Plazo adicional para el cumplimiento.** Additional period for performance.

(1) In case of nonperformance the aggrieved party may by notice to the other party allow an additional period of time for performance. (2) During the additional period the aggrieved party may withhold performance of its own reciprocal obligations and may claim damages but may not resort to any other remedy. (Unidroit, Prin., art. 7.1.5).

**Plazos procesales.** Procedural terms. The terms indicated for the completion of procedural acts are strict and not subject to be extended, except when the contrary is expressly stated. (Panamanian Judicial Code, arts. 497, 499.)

**Plebiscito.** Plebiscite, referendum.

**Pleiteador.** Litigious person.

**Pleiteante.** Litigant, party to a case.

**Pleitear.** To litigate, sue. To file an action. To take to court.

**Pleito.** Lawsuit. Dispute, disagreement.

**Plenario.** Plenary.

**Plenipotenciario.** Plenipotentiary.

**Pleno.** *En banc*, complete, full.

**Plica.** Escrow.

**Pliego.** Questions in writing submitted to the counterparty for an answer.

**Pliego de posiciones.** Written interrogatory.

**Plural.** Plural.

**Pluralidad.** Plurality, variety. Majority.

**Pluriempleo.** Holding more than one job per person.

**Plus.** Advantage, bonus, plus.

**Plus petitio** (L). Action claiming more than what is reasonable.

**Plusvalía.** Goodwill.

**Plusvalor.** Additional value, unearned value.

**Plutocracia.** Plutocracy. Government of the rich.

**Pluvioso.** Rainy.

**Pobre.** Poor, indigent, pauper.

**Pobreza.** Poverty, paucity.

**Poder.** Power, authority, energy, force, strength, vigor. Power of attorney, proxy, mandate, representation. Agency.

**Poder de mandato inherente.** Inherent agency power.

**Poder de representación, aceptación.** Power of attorney, acceptance. The agent need not state his acceptance in the instrument itself for the power of attorney to be valid. This acceptance shall result from the use of the power of attorney. (Conv. on Power of Att., art. 11).

**Poder de representación, atestación.** Power of attorney, attestation.

**Poder de representación, en el extranjero.** Power of attorney, abroad. The formalities and solemnities to be observed in giving a power of attorney to be used abroad shall be governed by the law of the place in which it was given unless the principal chooses to submit to the law of the State in which the power of attorney is to be used. (Conv. on Power of Att., art. 2).

**Poder de representación, orden público.** Power of attorney, public policy. The State of destination may refuse to execute a power of attorney if it is manifestly contrary to its public policy ("ordre public"). (Conv. on Power of Att., art. 12).

**Poder de representación, publicidad.** Power of attorney, publicity. The requirements with respect to publicity pertaining to a power of attorney shall be governed by the law of the State in which it is to be used. (Conv. on Power of Att., art. 4).

**Poder de representación, traducción.** Power of attorney, translation. Powers of attorney granted in a language different from the official language of the State in which they are to be used shall be translated into that official language. (Conv. on Power of Att., art. 9).

**Poderdante.** Principal.

**Poderhabiente.** Attorney-in-fact, agent.

**Poderío.** Power, control, omnipotence, potential. Great wealth.

**Podrá.** May. The term may in a statute means shall, when the principal aim or purpose of the statute is that the thing permitted be done. (Espasas Dairy, Inc. v. M.W.B., 94 PRR 781 (1967)).

**Poliandra.** Polyandrous.

**Policía.** Police, police force. Constabulary.

**Policía judicial.** Judicial police. The object of the judicial police, as well as the obligation of all individuals composing the same, is to ascertain the public crimes committed within its territory or district; to take, according to their powers, the steps necessary to verify said crimes and discover the delinquents and collect all the effects, instruments, or proof of the crime which may be in danger of disappearing, and to place the same at the disposal of the judicial authority. (Sp. L. Crim. P., art. 282).

**Policíaco, policial.** Police related.

**Policitación.** Pollicitation, offer made to the general public.

**Poligamia.** Polygamy.

**Polígamo.** Polygamist.

**Política.** Politics, state affairs, public matters. Policy, goal, strategy. Public order.

**Politicastro, politiquero.** Minor political figure.

**Político.** Politician. Political.

**Politiqueo.** Political maneuvering.

**Politiquería.** Low politics.

**Póliza.** Insurance policy.

**Polizonte.** Policeman.

**Ponencia.** Thesis, argument, assertion, proposition, statement. Article, desertion, essay. Opinion, judgment.

**Ponente.** Speaker. Movant. Opining judge.

**Poner.** To place, keep, put.

**Poner a cubierto.** Except. Harbor, protect. Hold harmless.

**Poner a prueba.** Demand strict proof. Test.

**Poner por escrito.** Reduce to writing.

**Pontazgo.** Bridge toll.

**Por.** Through, by, for.

**Por cabeza.** Per head, per person, individually.

**Por cuanto.** Whereas.

**Por día.** Per day, daily.

**Por escrito.** In writing.

**Por lo tanto, resuélvese.** Now, therefore, be it resolved.

**Por ministerio de la ley.** By operation of law.

**Por oficio de piedad.** By way of charity.

**Por orden de la corte.** By order of the court.

**Por propia iniciativa.** Of its own motion.

**Por razón de oficio.** On business.

**Por semana.** Per week, weekly.

**Porcentaje.** Percentage, proportion, rate. Interest, bonus.

**Porción.** Portion, allotment, part, share.

**Porción marital.** Marital portion. The marital portion is an incident of any matrimonial regime and a charge on the succession of the deceased spouse. It may be claimed by the surviving spouse, even if separated from the deceased, on proof that the separation occurred without his fault. (Lou. Civ. C. art. 2432 and 2433).

**Porción por estirpe.** Stirpital share.

**Pormenorizar.** To explain in detail.

**Pornografía.** Pornography, obscenity.

**Portable.** Portable, movable, transportable.

**Portadocumentos.** Briefcase, folder.

**Portador.** Bearer, carrier, holder.

**Portafolios.** Briefcase.

**Portar armas.** To bear arms, to be armed.

**Portavoz.** Spokesman, representative. Megaphone, mighty voice.

**Porte.** Frame, body. Physical appearance. Transportation.

**Porteador.** Carrier.

**Portero.** Porter. Bailiff. Janitor.

**Pórtico.** Entrance to a building.

**Porvenir.** Future, outlook, prospect.

**Posdatar.** To postdate.

**Poseedor.** Possessor, holder, tenant, occupant.

**Poseedor de buena fe.** Good faith possessor. He is bona fide possessor who possesses as owner by virtue of a title sufficient in its terms and conditions to transfer the ownership, and the defects of which he is ignorant of. (Sp. Civ. C., sec. 366).

**Poseer.** To posses, control, enjoy, have hold, use.

**Posesión.** Possession. Natural possession is the holding of a thing or the enjoyment of a right by any person. Civil possession is the same holding or enjoyment joined to the intent of holding the thing or right as one's own.

Control, enjoyment, tenure, use.

**Posesión, adquisición.** Possession, acquisition. Only things and rights susceptible of being appropriated can be the objects of possession. Acts merely tolerated and those clandestinely executed, without the knowledge of the possessor of a thing, or with violence, do not affect possession. (Sp. Civ. C., sec. 439, 441, 443, 445, 446).

**Posesión autorizada de un vehículo.** Authorized possession of a vehicle. The operation of a vehicle by a third person authorized by the person to whom the owner entrusted it is equivalent to the authorized possession of the vehicle by that third person. (McGee Quiñones v. Palmer, 91 PRR 450 (1964)).

**Posesión civil.** Civil possession. Once acquired, possession is retained by the intent to possess as owner even if the possessor ceases to possess corporeally. (Lou. Civ. C. art. 3431).

**Posesión clandestina.** Clandestine possession. Possession in clandestine when it is not open or public, discontinuous when it is not exercised at regular intervals, and equivocal when there is ambiguity as to the intent of the possessor to own the thing. (Lou. Civ. C. art. 3436).

**Posesión corporal.** Corporeal possession. Corporeal possession is the exercise of physical acts of use, detention, or enjoyment over a thing. (Lou. Civ. C. art. 3425).

**Posesión de animales fieros.** Possession of wild animals. Wild animals are only possessed so long as they are under control. (Sp. Civ. C., sec. 467).

**Posesión de bienes hereditarios.** Possession of hereditary property. The possession of hereditary property is understood as transferred to the heir without interruption and from the moment of the death of the testator, in case the inheritance be accepted. Any person who rejects an inheritance in a valid manner is considered as never to have possessed the same. (Sp. Civ. C., sec. 442, 444).

**Posesión de buena y de mala fe.** Possession in good and bad faith. A bona fide possessor is deemed to be person who is not aware that there exists in his title or the manner of acquiring it, any flaw invalidating the same. It is presumed that possession, is continued under the same understanding by which it was acquired, until the contrary be proven.

**Posesión de cosa raíz.** Possession of a tenement. The possession of any tenement presumes the possession of the furniture and objects therein, so long as it be not shown or proven that they should be excluded. (Sp. Civ. C., sec. 451).

**Posesión en común.** Possession in common. Each one of the participants of a thing possessed in common, is deemed to have possessed the part allotted to him upon the division thereof during the whole time that the property remained intact. (Sp. Civ. C., sec. 452).

**Posesión ficta.** Constructive possession. One who possesses a part of an immovable by virtue of a title is deemed to have constructive possession within the limits of his title. (Lou. Civ. C. art. 3426).

**Posesión indivisible.** Indivisible possession. Possession, as a fact, cannot be recognized in two different personalities, unless in cases of indivisibility. (Sp. Civ. C., sec. 447).

**Posesión, pérdida.** Possession, loss. A possessor may lose possession: 1) By abandonment of the thing. 2) By an assignment made to another person, either for a valuable consideration or by a deed of gift. 3) By the destruction or total loss of the thing, or because the same becomes unmarketable. 4) By the possession of another person, even against the will of the former possessor, if the new possession has lasted longer than a year. (Sp. Civ. C., sec. 462, 464, 466, 468).

**Posesión precaria.** Precarious possession. The exercise of possession over a thing with the permission of or on behalf of the owner or possessor is precarious possession. (Lou. Civ. C. art. 3437 and 3438).

**Posesión, protección.** Possession, protection. Every possessor has a right to be respected in his possession; and if he be disturbed therein, he shall be protected or reinstated in such possession by the means established in the laws of procedure. (Sp. Civ. C., sec. 448).

**Posesión sobre muebles por la fuerza.** Forcible taking of chattels.

**Posesión viciosa.** Faulty possession.

**Posesión violenta.** Violent possession. Possession is violent when it is acquired or maintained by violent acts. (Lou. Civ. C. art. 3436).

**Posesión y propiedad.** Possession and ownership. The possession of property and rights may be considered in one of two different aspects: either in that of the owner, or in that of the holder of the thing or right to keep and enjoy them, the ownership belonging to another person. Only the possession acquired and enjoyed by a person in the belief that he is the owner can serve as a title to acquire ownership. (Sp. Civ. C., sec. 435, 449, 450, 466).

**Posesionarse.** To appropriate for oneself. To take, to take possession. To break in. To occupy.

**Posesiones.** Possessions, colonies, domains. Assets, belongings, property.

**Posesor.** Possessor, holder, tenant.

**Posesorio.** Possessory.

**Posibilidad.** Possibility, probability.

**Posición.** Position, location, place site. Posture, Opinion. Circumstance.

**Posiciones.** Written questions for the counterparty to answer. Interrogatories.

**Positivo.** Positive. Affirmative. Certain.

**Post data.** P.S., post scriptum.

**Posta.** Post, post office.

**Postal.** Postal, related to the mail.

**Poste.** Pole, post.

**Posteridad.** Posterity, descent. Future.

**Posterioridad.** After, afterwards, later.

**Postor.** Bidder, offeror.

**Postulación.** Candidacy, nomination.

**Postular.** To petition, propose, submit, subject.

**Póstumo.** Posthumous.

**Postura.** Bid. Opinion, belief. Position.

**Potencia.** Potency, strength. Sovereign power, foreign country.

**Potestad.** Authority, capability, faculty, power.

**Potestativo.** Facultative, elective, optional, voluntary.

**Potro de tormento.** Medieval torture machine designed to dislocate joints through increasing tension.

**Pozo.** Well, pit.

**Práctica.** Practice, experience. Custom, habit, procedure.

**Práctica ilícita de trabajo.** Unfair labor practice.

**Práctica profesional prevaleciente en la comunidad.** Professional practice prevailing in the community. For the purposes of measuring the care exercised and the treatment administered by a physician to his patient in a specific case, the phrase professional practice prevailing in the community means that practice which complies with the acknowledged professional requirements, that is, the acceptable practice, professionally speaking, in a specific place and time. (Pérez v. E.L.A., 95 PRR 745 (1968)).

**Practicable.** Practical, feasible, possible, viable.

**Practicar.** To practice, perform. To prepare, rehearse.

**Prácticar la religión.** To worship.

**Prácticas desleales.** Unfair tactics.

**Prácticas engañosas.** Deceptive practices.

**Práctico.** Pilot of a ship.

**Preámbulo.** Preamble, foreword, introduction, prologue.

**Preaviso.** Notice. Notice previous to terminating employment.

**Prebenda.** Bribe.

**Preboste.** Provost.

**Precario.** Precarious, provisional, temporary. At will at sufferance. Revocable. Dangerous, hazardous, risky.

**Precarista.** Possessor subject to eviction.

**Precaucional, precautorio.** Precautionary, as a matter of protection or safeguard, preventive.

**Precedencia.** Precedence, greater urgency, preeminence, priority, superiority.

**Precedente.** Precedent. Case law, legal authority, source. Antecedent, foregoing, preceding, previous.

**Preceptivo.** Binding, mandatory, obligatory.

**Precepto.** Precept, dictate, principle, order, regulation, rule.

**Preceptuar.** To rule, dictate, establish, order.

**Preciador.** Assessor, appraiser.

**Preciar.** To appraise, assess, estimate, evaluate. To appreciate, treasure.

**Precintar.** To seal, to secure against unauthorized opening, to tie with bale wire.

**Precinto.** Security seal to detect an unauthorized opening.

**Precio.** Price, charge, bill, cost, expense. Consequence, result.

**Precio corriente.** Current price.
Current price is the price generally charged for goods delivered or services rendered in comparable circumstances at the place where the contract should have been performed or, if there is no current price at that place, the current price at such other place that appears reasonable to take as a reference. (Unidroit, Prin., art. 7.4.6).

**Preclusión.** Preclusion, estoppel.

**Preclusión de una cuestión.** Issue preclusion.

**Precontractual.** Precontractual.

**Predecesor.** Predecessor, originator.

**Predial.** Predial.

**Predio.** Tenement, estate, land, lot, patch, tract.

**Predio dominante y sirviente.** Dominant and servient tenements.

**Predio inferior.** Lower tenement.

**Predisponer.** To predispose, influence, prejudice.

**Predisposición.** Bias, prejudice.

**Prefacio.** Preface, foreword, introduction, prologue.

**Prefecto.** Prefect, person in charge of an organization.

**Prefectura.** Prefecture, central office.

**Preferencia.** Choice, option, predilection, selection.

**Preferente.** Preferential, chosen, preferred, selected. Previous, stronger, superior.

**Pregón.** Announcement by shouting, herald, proclamation.

**Pregonero.** Announcer, crier, herald.

**Pregunta.** Question, doubt, enquiry, interrogation, query, quiz.

**Preguntar.** To ask, demand, examine, enquire.

**Preguntas al jurado.** Poll of jury.

**Preguntas capciosas.** Leading questions. Trick questions. No captious or suggestive questions shall be put to the witness, nor shall coercion, deceit, promises, or artifices of any kind be employed to force or induce him to testify in a specific sense. (Sp. L. Crim. P. sec. 439).

**Preguntas sugestivas.** Leading questions.

**Preindicado.** Above said, prementioned.

**Prejudicial.** Prejudicial, pretrial.

**Prejuicio.** Prejudice, bias, bent, leaning, preconception, prejudgment.

**Prejuzgar.** To prejudge.

**Prelación.** Preeminence, precedence, preference, rank.

**Prelación de créditos.** Preference of credits.

**Prelativo.** Of a higher rank.

**Preliminar.** Preliminary, introductory, preparatory.

**Premeditación.** Premeditation, deliberation, malice aforethought, predetermination.

**Premeditado.** Premeditated, calculated, deliberate, express, planned.

**Premiado.** Prize winner.

**Premio.** Prize, premium. Bonus, gift, tip. Reward.

**Premisa.** Premise, assumption, postulate, proposition, supposition.

**Premoriente.** Predeceased person.

**Premuerto.** Predeceased.

**Premura.** Urgency, gravity, seriousness.

**Prenda.** Pledge. Collateral, security. The following are essential requisites of the contracts of pledge and of mortgage: 1) That they be constituted to secure the fulfillment of a principal obligation. 2) That the thing pledged or mortgaged is owned by the person who pledges or mortgages it. 3) That the persons who constitute the pledge or mortgage have the free disposition of their property, and, should they not have it, that they are legally authorized for the purpose. (Sp. Civ. C., sec. 1758, 1759, 1764).

**Prendador.** Pledge.

**Prendar.** To pledge, guarantee, pawn.

**Prendario.** Relating to a pledge.

**Preparado.** Prepared, alert, fit, ready, set.

**Preparar.** To prepare, to get read.

**Prerrogativa.** Prerogative, alternative, decision, pick, preference, privilege.

**Presbiofrenia.** Presbyophrenia.

**Prescribir.** To prescribe, announce, decree, dictate, command, ordain, order, rule.

**Prescripción.** Statute of limitations. Ownership and other property rights are acquired by prescription in the manner and under the conditions specified by law. Rights and actions, of any kind whatsoever, also are extinguished by prescription in the same manner. (Sp. Civ. C., sec. 1831).

Adverse possession, prescription. Time bar. Legal mandate or rule.

**Prescripción adquisitiva.** Adverse possession.

Acquisitive prescription. Acquisitive prescription is a mode of acquiring ownership or other real rights by possession for a period of time. (Lou. Civ. C. art. 3446).

**Prescripción adquisitiva, buena fe del poseedor.** Adverse possession, possessor's good faith. Good faith of the possessor consists in his belief that the person from whom he received the thing was the owner of the same, and could convey his title. (Sp. Civ. C. sec. 1851).

**Prescripción adquisitiva, inmuebles.** Adverse possession, real property. Ownership and other property rights in real property shall prescribe by possession for ten years as to persons present, and for twenty years with regard to those absent, with good faith and with a proper title. (Sp. Civ. C., sec. 1858, 1861).

**Prescripción adquisitiva, justo título.** Adverse possession, proper title. By a proper title is understood that which legally suffices to transfer the ownership or property right, the prescription of which is in question. (Sp. Civ. C., sec. 1853, 1855).

**Prescripción adquisitiva, muebles.** Adverse possession, personal property. The ownership of personal property prescribes by uninterrupted possession in good faith for a period of three years. The ownership of personal property also prescribes by uninterrupted possession for six years, without the necessity of any other condition. (Sp. Civ. C. sec. 1856).

**Prescripción adquisitiva, muebles robados.** Adverse possession, stolen movables. Personal property stolen or robbed can not prescribe to the persons who stole or robbed the same, nor to their accomplices, or harborers. (Sp. Civ. C. sec. 1857).

**Prescripción de delitos múltiples.** Time barring for multiple crimes. When several criminal acts are being tried, the corresponding statutes of limitations, with their respective terms, will apply separately to each. (Standard Penal C. for Latin America, sec. 107).

**Prescripción de diez años.** Prescription of ten years. The requisites for the acquisitive prescription of ten years are: possession of ten years, good faith, just title, and a thing susceptible of acquisition by prescription. (Lou. Civ. C. art. 3473 and 3475).

**Prescripción de la acción.** Statute of limitations, time bar. Prescription of actions is interrupted by their institution before the courts, by extrajudicial claim of the creditor, and by any act of acknowledgment of the debt by the debtor. (Sp. Civ. C., sec. 1862, 1874).

**Prescripción de la acción penal.** Time barring for prosecutions. Prosecutions are time barred: 1) After twenty years, for crimes punishable by imprisonment not exceeding fifteen years. 2) After lapse of a term equal to the maximum established for the corresponding crime, when such crime is punishable by imprisonment of not less than one year nor more than fifteen. 3) After three years, in crimes punished with fines or disqualification. (Standard Penal C. for Latin America, sec. 102).

**Prescripción de la acción penal, comienzo.** The statute of limitations will start running the day the crime was committed; or—for a continuing crime—when its commission ceased. (Standard Penal C. for Latin America, sec. 103 and 106).

**Prescripción de la acción penal, interrupción.** Time barring for prosecutions, interruption. The statute of limitations ceases running when a subsequent criminal act is committed. (Standard Penal C. for Latin America, sec. 105).

**Prescripción de la acción penal, suspensión.** Time barring for prosecutions, tolling. The statute of limitations is tolled in the following cases: 1) When prosecution cannot be initiated nor the process continued pending a special authorization, or when other prior or prejudicial issues must be adjudicated in a separate trial. 2) By any court decision against a specific person procedurally involved in the case, provided that there is a minimum of evidence against such person. (Standard Penal C. for Latin America, sec. 104).

**Prescripción de la pena, cómputo.** Time barring for penalties, computation. The statute of limitations applicable to the punishments will start running when the sentence becomes final, or when the punishment was evaded, if service had begun. (Standard Penal C. for Latin America, sec. 109).

**Prescripción de la pena de inhabilitación.** Time barring for the penalty of disqualification. The punishment consisting of disqualification cannot be enforced after 5 years. (Standard Penal C. for Latin America, sec. 108).

**Prescripción de la pena de multa.** Time barring for the penalty of fines. The punishment consisting of fines cannot be enforced after 5 years. (Standard Penal C. for Latin America, sec. 8).

**Prescripción de la pena de prisión.** Time barring for the penalty of imprisonment. A punishment of imprisonment cannot be enforced after a period equal to the time imposed in the sentence, increased by one third, has lapsed. (Standard Penal C. for Latin America, sec. 108).

**Prescripción de la pena, interrupción.** Time barring for penalties, interruption. The statute of limitations applicable to punishments will cease running, canceling the effects of any period already passed, when the convict commits a new criminal act before the limitation period runs, or when he voluntarily surrenders, or when he is captured. (Standard Penal C. for Latin America, sec. 110).

**Prescripción de treinta años.** Prescription of thirty years. Ownership and other real rights in immovables may be acquired by the prescription of thirty years without the need of just title or possession in good faith. (Lou. Civ. C. art. 3486).

**Prescripción, interrupción.** Prescription interruption. If prescription is interrupted, the time that has run is not counted. Prescription commences to run anew from the last day of interruption. (Lou. Civ. C. art. 3466).

**Prescripción liberatoria.** Liberative prescription. Liberative prescription is a mode of barring of actions as a result of inaction for a period of time. (Lou. Civ. C. art. 3447).

**Prescripción por no uso.** Prescription of nonuse. Prescription of nonuse is a mode of extinction of a real right other than ownership as a result of failure to exercise the right for a period of time. (Lou. Civ. C. art. 3448).

**Prescripción positiva.** Adverse possession. Adverse possession necessary for prescription must be:
As an owner;
Peaceful;
Continuous;
Open and notorious. (Mex. Civ. C., art.1151).

**Prescripción sobre muebles.** Prescription over movables. One who has possessed a movable as owner, in good faith, under an act sufficient to transfer ownership, and without interruption for three years, acquires ownership by prescription. (Lou. Civ. C. art. 3490 and 3491).

**Prescripción, suspensión.** Prescription, suspension. The period of suspension is not counted toward accrual of prescription. (Lou. Civ. C. art. 3472).

**Prescriptible.** Subject to the statute of limitations.

**Prescriptivo.** Prescriptive.

**Prescrito.** Time barred, no longer actionable, lapsed.

**Presencia.** Presence, attendance, appearance, company. Deportment.

215

**Presenciar.** To attend, appear, participate. To witness.

**Presentación.** Presentation, demonstration, display. Introduction.

**Presentación al pago.** Presentment for payment.

**Presentante.** Person who presents.

**Presentar.** To present, demonstrate, display. To introduce. To file.

**Presentarse en concurso.** File for bankruptcy.

**Presente.** Present, now, current. Gift, donation.

**Preservativo.** Preventive, protective. Condom.

**Presidencia.** Presidency, control, chair.

**Presidente.** President, chairman, executive, ruler.

**Presidente de la Corte Suprema.** Chief justice.

**Presidente del jurado.** Foreman.

**Presidiario.** Prisoner, captive, convict, detainee, inmate.

**Presidio.** Prison, jail, penitentiary. Penal colony. Reformatory.

**Presidir.** To preside, chair, control, rule.

**Presión.** Pressure. Stress, tension. Coercion, constraint. Influence.

**Preso.** Prisoner, captive, convict, detainee, inmate.

**Presupuesto.** Budget, allowance, financial plan. Logical basis, premise, supposition.

**Prestación.** Performance, compliance, payment of an obligation. Prestation. Delivery of an object.

**Prestador.** Supplier of goods or services. Lender.

**Prestador a la gruesa.** Lender on bottomry.

**Prestamista.** Lender, especially of money.

**Préstamo.** Loan. There are two kinds of loans: a) The loan of things, which may be used without being destroyed; b) the loan of things, which are destroyed by being used. (Lou. Civ. C. art. 2891).

**Préstamo a la gruesa o préstamo a riesgo marítimo.** Loans on bottomry or *respondentia*. A loan on bottomry or *respondentia* shall be considered that of which the repayment of the sum loaned and the premium stipulated, under any condition whatsoever, depends on the safe arrival in port of the goods on which it is made, or of their value in case of accident. (Sp. Com. C., sec. 719).

**Préstamo con garantía.** Loan secured by collateral.

**Préstamo con vencimiento fijo.** Loan for fixed time.

**Préstamo mercantil.** Commercial loan. A loan shall be considered commercial when the following conditions are present: 1) That one of the contracting parties is a merchant. 2) When the articles loaned are destined to commercial transactions. 3) Loans shall not draw any interest unless there is an agreement in writing to that effect. (Sp. Com. C., sec. 311, 314).

**Préstamo mercantil con garantía de efectos o valores públicos.** Commercial loan guaranteed by public bonds or securities. A loan with a guaranty of securities quoted on exchange, contained in an instrument with the intermediation of licensed agents, shall always be considered commercial. (Sp. Com. C., sec. 320).

**Préstamo mercantil, dinero, valores, mercadería.** Commercial loan, money, bonds, goods. If the loan consists of money, the debtor shall pay it by returning an amount equal to that received, in accordance with the legal value the money may have at the time of the return, unless there was an agreement with regard to the kind of money in which the payment was to be made, in which case the fluctuations in value shall be lost or taken advantage of by the lender. (Sp. Com. C., sec. 312).

**Préstamo simple.** Simple loan. A person receiving money or any other perishable thing on loan acquires its ownership, and is bound to return to the creditor an equal amount of the same kind and quality. (Sp. Civ. C., sec. 1655).

**Prestar.** To lend, loan. To provide services.

**Prestar buena y suficiente fianza.** To give good and sufficient security.

**Prestar fianza.** To give bail, furnish bail.

**Prestar juramento.** Take an oath.

**Prestatario.** Borrower, debtor.

**Presumir.** To presume, assume, infer, gather, suppose, surmise. To boast, brag, flaunt.

**Presunción.** Presumption. A presumption is a consequence that the law or the court attaches to a known fact for the purpose of establishing the existence of another and unknown fact. (Lou. Civ. C. art. 1849).

Assumption, supposition. Gall, impudence.

**Presunción controvertible.** Rebuttable, disputable presumption.

**Presunción de paternidad.** Presumption of paternity. The husband of the mother is presumed to be the father of all children born or conceived during the marriage. (Lou. Civ. C. art. 184 and art. 185).

**Presunción de propiedad sobre muebles.** Presumption of ownership of movables. The possessor of a corporeal movable is presumed to be its owner. (Lou. Civ. C. art. 530).

**Presunción del ejercicio habitual del comercio.** Presumption of regular engagement in commerce. The legal presumption of a regular engagement in commerce exists from the time the person who desires to trade gives notice through circulars, newspapers, handbills, posters exhibited to the public, or in any other manner whatsoever, of an establishment, the purpose of which is to conduct any commercial transaction. (Sp. Com. C., sec. 3).

**Presunción legal.** Presumption established by law. Legal presumptions are rebuttable or conclusive. A rebuttable legal presumption is established in the interest of private parties and may be controverted. A conclusive legal presumption is established for reasons of public policy and may not be controverted. (Lou. Civ. C. art. 1850 and 1851).

**Presunción no establecida por ley.** Presumption not established by law. A presumption not established by law is left to the discretion of the court. (Lou. Civ. C. art. 1852).

**Presuntivo, presunto.** Presumptive, assumed, presumed.

**Presupuestario.** Budgetary.

**Pretender.** To attempt, aim, endeavor, strive, try. To claim, petition, request.

**Pretendiente.** Applicant, claimant, petitioner, relator.

**Pretensión.** Cause of action, claim, prayer for relief, relief.

**Preterición.** Pretermition. Heir born after will was made.

**Preterintencional.** Beyond the person's intention.

**Preterir.** To leave out, disregard, omit.

**Pretexto.** Pretext, excuse, pretense. Attenuating factor, extenuating circumstance, justification.

**Prevalecer.** To prevail, dominate, predominate, win.

**Prevaricación, prevaricato.** Representation by an attorney of two clients with opposing interest. Prevarication.

**Prevaricar.** To prevaricate.

**Preveer.** Foresee. In its usual and common meaning, to foresee is to see with anticipation, to guess what is going to happen; to provided against, to anticipate or to avoid an injury or danger. (Salva Matos v. Díaz Const. Corp., 95 PRR 880 (1968)).

**Prevención.** Prevention, avoidance, deterrence, discouragement, ending, evading, stopping. Admonition, warning.

**Prevención de un mal mayor.** Prevention of a greater harm. No criminal liability attaches to whoever commits an unjustifiable act to prevent a clear and present, or imminent, harm that cannot be prevented otherwise. (St. P.C. for LA, sec. 30).

**Prevenir.** To avoid, block, deter, discourage, end, evade, neutralize, warn, admonish, advise.

**Preventivo.** Preventive, guarding, protective.

**Previa notificación.** Upon notice.

**Previo.** Previous, anticipated, before, earlier. Prior, above, foregoing, former.

**Previsibilidad.** Foreseeability. Foreseeability—element characteristic of fault—consists of the possibility of foreseeing the damaging result of an action not effectively foreseen in the case involved. (Salva Matos v. Díaz Const. Corp., 95 PRR 880 (1968)).

**Previsibilidad del daño.** Foreseeability of harm. The nonperforming party is liable only for harm which it foresaw or could reasonably have foreseen at the time of the conclusion of the contract as being likely to result from its nonperformance. (Unidroit, Prin., art. 7.4.4).

**Previsión.** Foresight. In its usual and common meaning foresight—the act of foreseeing—is the act of providing what is necessary to attend to foreseeable risks or necessities, that is, attend to that which is susceptible of being foreseen. (Salva Matos v. Díaz Const. Corp. 95 PRR 880 (1968)).

**Prima.** Premium, award, bonus, reward.

**Primar.** To prevail upon, predominate, sway.

**Primer.** Number one, first, earliest. Most important.

**Primera y segunda leva.** First and second lift.

**Primeras diligencias.** First steps. The following are considered first steps: Those taken to protect the injured parties, record the evidence of the crime which may disappear, collect and place under custody all that may conduce to the proof thereof and to the identification of the delinquent, and, in a proper case, arrest the presumed criminals. (Sp. L. Crim. P., art. 13).

**Primogénito.** First-born son.

**Primogenitura.** Primogeniture. System awarding exclusive inheritance rights to the first-born child.

**Primordial.** Basic, first, fundamental, overriding.

**Principal.** Principal, basic, most important.

**Príncipe.** Prince, heir, noble.

**Principio.** Beginning. Norm, rule.

**Principio de derecho.** Legal norm or rule.

**Principio de legalidad.** Principle of legality. Illegal pacts do not trigger any obligation or action, even if they refer to business transactions. (Sp. Com. C., sec. 53).

**Prioridad.** Priority, preeminence, preference, stronger, right.

**Prisión.** Imprisonment. The penalty of imprisonment consists in the temporary deprivation of freedom. Imprisonment will be served wherever the law establishes and will try to bring about the prisoner's rehabilitation. (Standard Penal C. for Latin America, sec. 43, 44).

Prison, jail, penal colony, penitentiary, reformatory.

**Prisión provisional.** Provisional imprisonment. In order to decree the provisional imprisonment, the following circumstances shall be necessary: 1) That the existence of an act presenting the characteristics of a crime is established in the cause. 2) That a penalty higher than prisión correccional be affixed thereto according to the general scale embraced in the penal code, or that even though a lower penalty be affixed thereto the judge shall consider provisional imprisonment necessary, in view of the circumstances of the act and the antecedents of the accused, until he shall give the bond which he may require. 3) That there shall appear in the case motives sufficient to believe that the person against whom the writ of imprisonment is to issue is criminally liable for the crime. (Sp. L. Crim. P., art. 503 and 528).

**Prisionero.** Prisoner, captive, convict, detainer, inmate.

**Privación.** Deprivation. Hardship, suffering. Denial, withholding.

**Privar.** To deprive, deny, refuse, restrict, withhold.

**Privatista.** Specialist in private law.

**Privativo.** Exclusive.

**Privilegiado.** Privilege, preferred.

**Privilegiar.** To accord special treatment.

**Privilegio.** Privilege. Privilege is a right, which the nature of a debt gives to a creditor, and which entitles him to be preferred before other creditors, even those who have mortgages. (Lou. Civ. C. art. 3186).

Exclusive right, superior right.

**Privilegio de no denunciar un delito.** Privilege not to report a crime. Nor shall the following be obliged to report a crime: 1) The spouse of the delinquent. 2) The ascendant and descendants by consanguinity or affinity of the delinquent and his collateral relatives by consanguinity or uterine, and by affinity up to and including the second degree. (Sp. L. Crim. P., art. 261).

**Privilegio del confidente.** Informer's privilege. What is known as informer's privilege is the Government's privilege to withhold from disclosure the identity of persons who furnished information of violations of law to the authorities. (Ppl. v. Lopez Rivera, 91 PRR 672 (1965)).

**Privilegio del vendedor de un inmueble.** Vendor's privilege on immovables. The vendor of an immovable only preserves his privilege on the object, when he has caused to be duly recorded at the office for recording mortgages, his act of sale. (Lou. Civ. C. art. 3271).

**Privilegio, extinción.** Privilege, extinction. Privileges become extinct: 1) By the extinction of the thing subject to the privilege. 2) By the creditor acquiring the thing subject to it. 3) By the extinction of debt which gave birth to it. 4) By prescription. (Lou. Civ. C. art. 3277).

**Privilegio general sobre bienes muebles.** General privilege on all movables. The debts which are privileged on all the movables in general, are those hereafter enumerated, and are paid in the following order: 1) Funeral charges. 2) Law charges. 3) Charges, of whatever nature, occasioned by the last sickness, concurrently among those to whom they are due. 4) The wages of servants for the year past, and so much as is due for the current year. 5) Supplies of provisions made to the debtor or his family, during the last six months, by retail dealers, such as bakers, butchers, grocers; and, during the last year, by keepers of boarding houses and taverns. 6) The salaries of clerks, secretaries, and other persons of that kind. (Lou. Civ. C. art. 3191).

**Privilegio sobre bienes muebles particulares.** Privilege on particular movables. The debts which are privileged on certain movables, are the following: 1) The appointments or salaries of the overseer for the current year, on the crops of the year and the proceeds thereof. 2) The debt of a workman or artisan for the price of his labor, on the movable which he has repaired or made, if the thing continues still in his possession. 3) The rents of immovable and the wages of laborers employed in working the same, on the crops of the year, and on the furniture, which is found in the house let, or on the farm, and on every thing which serves to take working of the farm. 4) The debt, on the pledge which is in the creditor's posses-

sion. 5) That of a depositor, on the price of the sale of the thing by him deposited. 6) The debt due for money laid out in preserving the thing. 7) The price due on movable effects if they are yet in the possession of the purchaser. 8) The things which have been furnished by an innkeeper, on the property of the traveler which has been carried to his inn. (Lou. Civ. C. art. 3217).

**Privilegio sobre embarcaciones.** Privilege on ships and vessels. The following debts are privileged on the price of ships and other vessels, in the order in which they are placed: 1) Legal and other charges incurred to obtain the sale of a ship or other vessel, and the distribution of the price. 2) Debts for pilotage, towage, wharfage and anchorage. 3) The expenses of keeping the vessel from the time of her entrance into port until sale, including the wages of persons employed to watch her. 4) The rent of stores, in which the rigging and apparel are deposited. 5) The maintenance of the ship and her tackle and apparatus, since her return into port from her last voyage. 6) The wages of the captain and crew employed on the last voyage. 7) Sums lent to the captain for the necessities of the ship during the last voyage, and reimbursement of the price of merchandise sold by him for the same purpose. (Lou. Civ. C. art. 3237).

**Privilegio sobre inmuebles.** Privilege on immovables. Creditors who have a privilege on immovables, are: 1) The vendor on the estate by him sold, for the payment of the price or so much of it as is unpaid, whether it was sold on or without a credit. 2) Architects, undertakers, bricklayers, painters, masters builders, contractors, subcontractors, journeymen, laborers, cartmen and other workmen employed in constructing, rebuilding or repairing houses, buildings, or making other works. 3) Those who have supplied the owner or other person employed by the owner, his agent or subcontractor, with materials of any kind for the construction or repair of an edifice or other work, when such materials have been used in the erection or repair of such houses or other works. The above named parties shall have a lien and privilege upon the building, improvement or other work erected. (Lou. Civ. C. art. 3249).

**Privilegio sobre muebles e inmuebles.** Privilege on movables and immovables. The privileges which extend alike to movables and immovables are the following: 1) Funeral charges. 2) Judicial charges. 3) Expenses of last illness. 4) The wages of servants. 5) The salaries of secretaries, clerks and other agents of that kind. (Lou. Civ. C. art. 3252).

**Privilegios concurrentes.** Concurrent privileges. The creditors who are in the same rank of privileges, are paid in concurrence, that is on an equal footing. (Lou. Civ. C. art. 3181).

**Probabilidad.** Probability, likelihood, possibility, prospect, viability.

**Probable.** Probable, feasible, possible.

**Probanza.** Evidence, proof. Confirmation, data, demonstration, discovery, documentation, exhibit, indication, indicia, sign, testimony, validation, verification.

**Probar.** To prove, ascertain, certify, confirm, demonstrate, determine, discover, document, establish, evidence, validate, verify. To test, try.

**Probatorio.** Probatory, evidential, evidentiary.

**Probidad.** Probity, character, decency, fidelity, honesty, honor, integrity.

**Problema.** Problem, dilemma, quandary.

**Probo.** Honorable, honest, reliable, upright.

**Procedencia.** Origin, point of departure, point of origin, source. Nationality.

**Procedente.** Viable according to procedural and substantive law. Originating from.

**Proceder.** Act, behavior, conduct. To proceed, to carry on.

**Procedimiento.** Proceeding, case, lawsuit, litigation. Procedure, process. Method, routine, system, technique.

**Procedimiento criminal.** Criminal procedure. Latin America adheres to the continental model frequently denominated as "inquisitorial." As applied to modern codes of criminal procedure, the term "inquisitorial" is likely to mislead; present-day continental criminal procedure is more accurately described as a mixed system, blending elements of the "accusatorial" and "inquisitorial" systems. (L & D in LA).

**Procedimiento criminal, etapas.** Criminal procedure, stages. The typical Latin American criminal proceeding is divided into two stages: the investigative (*sumario* or *instrucción*) and the trial (*plenario* or *juicio oral*). The investigative stage is orchestrated by an examining magistrate, who conducts a complete, secret investigation into the facts surrounding the crime. The police, at least in theory, work under the direction of the examining magistrate. The examining magistrate does not sit passively in a courtroom waiting for counsel to present evidence. One might say the magistrate makes house calls: interviewing witnesses, inspecting the scene of the crime, and interrogating the accused. (L & D in LA).

**Procedimiento de apremio.** Compulsory process to enforce the judgment. After the order for the judicial sale has been made and affirmed by the audience, or after the security has been given in case the fulfillment thereof is requested when an appeal has been taken, payment of principal and costs shall be made at once, after a taxation of the latter, if the property attached be money, salaries, pensions, or credits which may immediately be realized upon. (Sp. L. Civ. P. sec. 1447).

**Procesable.** Actionable, triable. That which can be taken to court and litigated.

**Procesado.** Defendant in a criminal action. Accused, arraigned, indicted.

**Procesal.** Procedural, adjective, formal.

**Procesalista.** Specialist in procedural law.

**Procesamiento.** Prosecution, accusation, arraignment, indictment. Trial of a criminal case.

**Procesar.** To start a criminal action, to file criminal charges. To prosecute, arraign, indicted.

**Proceso.** Action, case, lawsuit, litigation, proceedings, trial. Process, procedure, method, routine, system, technique.

**Proclamación, proclama.** Proclamation, official announcement, declaration, pronouncement.

**Proclamar.** To proclaim, announce, declare, pronounce.

**Proclividad.** Proclivity, inclination, predilection, propensity, tendency.

**Procreación.** Procreation, fathering, siring. Creation, genesis.

**Procuración.** Practice of law supervised by an attorney. Legal representation. Power of attorney.

**Procurador.** Solicitor. The distinction between *procurador* and *abogado* is not in every particular that between solicitor and attorney, but the translation conveys the idea. (Sp. L. Civ. P., sec. 3).

Attorney's aid, person who without being a fully fledged attorney is allowed a limited intervention in litigation. District attorney. Person who buys, obtains or secures something.

**Procurador, fiscal general.** Attorney general.

**Procuraduría.** Office of the attorney general.

**Procurar.** To buy, obtain, secure.

**Procurarse.** To obtain or purchase for oneself.

**Pródigo.** Prodigal, spendthrift, squanderer.

**Producir.** To produce, exhibit, present, show. To bear fruit, to yield.

**Productivo.** Productive, fruitful, gainful, profitable, remunerative.

**Producto.** Product, earnings, gains, proceeds, reward, yield.

**Profanación.** Profanation, debasement, desecration, violation.

**Profano.** Heretic, nonbeliever. Layman, person without the necessary skill.

**Proferir.** To proffer, announce, declare, say, state.

**Profesar.** To profess, affirm, support. To practice.

**Profesión.** Profession, career, calling, occupation, work. Affirmation, statement.

**Profesional, profesionista.** Professional person, expert, specialist.

**Profesor.** Professor, scholar, teacher.

**Profesores de derecho.** Law professors. The full-time law professor is still a rarity in Latin America. Most law professors are busy practitioners, who dash into the law school to give a lecture and disappear immediately thereafter. Absenteeism, both by professors and students, tends to be rather high. (L & D in LA).

**Prófugo.** Fugitive, deserter, exile, runaway.

**Progenie.** Progeny, descent, issue, offspring.

**Progenitura.** Progeny, children, descent, offspring, successors.

**Programa de estudios.** Curriculum. The curriculum of the National University's Faculty of Law is typical of leading Mexican and other Latin American law schools. Its standard law course lasts five years, and includes annual subjects offered two or three hours per week. All subjects are required, with the exception of two elective courses, which must be opted from a list. (W. Eur. & LA Leg. Sys.).

**Progreso.** Progress. Headway, advancement, breakthrough, development, improvement. Modernization, industrialization. Civilization.

**Prohibición.** Prohibition, ban, injunction, prevention.

**Prohibir.** To prohibit, ban, enjoin, prevent, restrain.

**Prohibitivo, prohibitorio.** Prohibitive. Too expensive.

**Prójimo.** Other people, others. The rest of the community.

**Prole.** Progeny, descent, family, issue.

**Prólogo.** Prologue, foreword, introduction. Prelude.

**Promesa.** Promise, assurance, commitment, oath, pledge. Good prospect, potential.

**Promesa contra la libertad de matrimonio.** Promise in restraint of marriage.

**Promesa de matrimonio incumplida.** Breach of promise of marriage. The liability or non liability for breach of promise of marriage or for the publication of bans in such case is governed by the common personal law of the parties and in the absence thereof by the local law. (Bustamante C., art. 39).

**Prometedor.** Promisor, promising party, obligor. Promising, showing good signs or symptoms.

**Promisorio.** Promissory.

**Promitente.** Promisor, promising party. Obligor.

**Promoción.** Class or year. Advancement, raise. Publicity. Encouragement, support.

**Promotor, promovedor.** Promoter, incorporator.

**Promover.** To promote, further, upgrade.

**Promoviente.** Petitioner, plaintiff, relator, promoter.

**Promulgar.** To promulgate, enact, pass, legislate.

**Pronunciamiento.** Pronouncement, announcement, declaration, proclamation.

**Pronunciar.** To pronounce. To render a judgment. To enunciate.

**Propiedad.** Ownership. Ownership is the right that confers on a person direct, immediate, and exclusive authority over a thing. (Lou. Civ. C. art. 477). Property, proprietorship. Land, farm, house.

**Propiedad, accesión.** Ownership, accession. The ownership of property, whether movable or immovable, carries with it the right, by accession, to everything which is produced thereby, or which is united thereto or incorporated therewith, either naturally or artificially. (Sp. Civ. C., sec. 360-361).

**Propiedad, accesión respecto de inmuebles.** Ownership, accession with respect to immovables. Whatever is built, planted or sown on another's land, and the improvements or repairs made thereon, belong to the owner thereof. (Sp. Civ. C., sec. 367, 369).

**Propiedad, accesión respecto de muebles.** Ownership, accession with respect to movables. When two movable things, belonging to different owners, are united in such a way that they come to form a unit, without bad faith on the part of either owner, the owner of the principal thing acquires the accessory thing by indemnifying the former owner thereof for its value. (Sp. Civ. C., sec. 383, 386).

**Propiedad de inmuebles, prueba.** Ownership of immovables, proof. One who claims the ownership of an immovable against another in possession must prove that he has acquired ownership from a previous owner or by acquisitive prescription. (Lou. Civ. C. art. 531).

**Propiedad de los frutos por accesión.** Ownership of fruits by accession. In the absence of rights of other persons, the owner of a thing acquires the ownership of its natural and civil fruits. (Lou. Civ. C. art. 483 and art. 484).

**Propiedad, derecho de superficie.** Owner surface right. The owner of a parcel of ground is the owner of its surface and of everything under it, and he can construct thereon any works or make any plantations and excavations which he may deem proper, without detriment to the usufructs legally established thereon. (Sp. Civ. C., sec. 357).

**Propiedad, dominio, señorío.** Ownership. Ownership is the right by which a thing belongs to some one in particular, to the exclusion of all other persons. Ownership confers the right to enjoy and dispose of things without further limitations than those established by law. The owner holds a right of action against the holder and the possessor of the thing in order to recover it. (Sp. Civ. C., sec. 353, 354).

**Propiedad ejecutada.** Foreclosed property.

**Propiedad, formas de adquisición.** Ownership, ways of acquiring it. Ownership and other property rights are acquired and transmitted by law, by gift, by testate or intestate succession, and in consequence of certain contracts, by tradition. A gift is consummated upon the donor having knowledge of its acceptance by the donee. All persons who are not especially disqualified by law therefore may accept gifts. (Sp. Civ. C., sec. 616, 631, 633, 643).

**Propiedad intelectual e industrial.** Copyrights and industrial property. Copyrights and industrial property shall be governed by the provisions of the special international conventions at present in force or concluded in the future. (Bustamante C. art. 115).

**Propiedad, tesoro.** Ownership, treasure. Hidden treasures belong to the owner of the land on which they are found. By treasure is understood, for legal effects, any hidden or unknown deposit of money, jewelry, or other precious objects, the lawful ownership of which is not proven. (Sp. Civ. C., sec. 358, 359).

**Propiedad y posesión.** Ownership and possession. The ownership and the possession of a thing are distinct. Ownership exists independently of any exercise of it and may not be lost by nonuse. Ownership is lost when acquisitive prescription accrues in favor of an adverse possessor. (Lou. Civ. C. art. 481).

**Propietario.** Owner, proprietor.

**Propina.** Tip, gratuity, small gift or reward.

**Proponente.** Proponent. Person who suggests or requests. Applicant, petitioner, supplicant. Sidder, offeror.

**Proponer.** To propose. Request, suggest. To bid, offer.

**Proponerse.** To intend, try.

**Proposición, propuesta.** Proposition, proposal. Requirement, suggestion. Bid, offer.

**Propósito.** Purpose, aim, design, goal, intention, plan, object, objective.

***Propter rem* (L).** Literally "that follows the thing." Used in property law, this phrase attaches to the obligations that remain unchanged even if the debtor disappears from the scene.

**Prorrata.** Pro rata, percentage, proportional.

**Prorratear.** To prorate, to distribute proportionally.

**Prorrateo.** Prorating, proportional distribution.

**Prórroga.** Time extension, delay, postponement. Deferral, suspension.

**Prórroga de competencia.** Waiver of jurisdiction. Jurisdiction that accrues by reason of the place where the case must be tried, may be waived.

**Prórroga de competencia expresa o tácita.** Waiver of jurisdiction, express or tacit. Submission to jurisdiction may be express or tacit.

Submission is express when in the contract itself, or in a later document, the parties designate clearly the court they submit themselves to.

There is tacit submission on the plaintiff's part when he files a petition in a specific Court, and on the defendant's part by taking, after filing the answer, any step that does not raise a nullity based on lack of jurisdiction. (Panamanian Judicial Code, arts. 246, 247, and 248.)

**Prórroga de competencia, formas.** Jurisdictional submission, forms. Submission to jurisdiction can be reached in an express or in a tacit way.

A tacit submission occurs:

1) Concerning the plaintiff, by the mere fact of filing a lawsuit, not only as to such petition but also as to any counterclaim.

2) Concerning the defendant in regular or summary proceedings, by making any appearance or filing any request, before opposing an exception of lack of jurisdiction, except any appearance leading to prepare or substantiate such an exception. (C.R. C. of Civ. P., art. 34.)

**Prórroga de jurisdicción penal.** Prorogation of criminal jurisdiction. Prorogation of jurisdiction is prohibited in criminal matters, so that only the judge competent in accordance with the provisions of this law may take cognizance of crimes and misdemeanors which may be committed. (Sp. L. Crim. P., art. 8 and note).

**Prorrogable.** Subject to a time extension or postponement.

**Prorrogar.** To extend, delay, postpone. To defer, suspend.

**Prosapia.** Ancestry, bloodline, family, lineage.

**Proscribir.** To proscribe, ban, outlaw.

**Proscripción.** Proscription, banning, prohibition, restriction.

**Proscriptor.** Proscriptive, banning.

**Prosecretario.** Under secretary.

**Prosecución.** Prosecution. Carrying a case forward.

**Proseguir.** To proceed, to carry on, to continue.

**Prospecto.** Prospect. Brochure, prospectus.

**Prosperidad.** Prosperity, affluence, financial success, wealth.

**Prostíbulo.** Brothel, cathouse, whorehouse.

**Prostitución.** Prostitution, streetwalking. Degradation, commercialization.

**Prostituta.** Prostitute, hooker, streetwalker, whore.

**Protección.** Protection, care, custody, guard, preservation, safety.

**Proteccionista.** Protectionist.

**Protesorero.** Deputy treasurer.

**Protesta.** Protest, complaint, criticism, objection. Demonstration, rally. Assert, declare.

**Protestable.** Protestable, objectionable.

**Protestar.** To protest, challenge, complain, dissent, object.

**Protesto.** Protest.

**Protesto por falta de pago.** Protest for non-payment.

**Protocolar.** According to protocol, ceremonious, formal, stately. Relating to a notary's recordations.

**Protocolización.** Protocolization, notarial registration. Recording of a document in an official register. Typically it is what a notary public does with documents submitted or issued by him.

**Protocolizar.** To record in a notarial register.

**Protocolo.** Protocol. Diplomatic formalities. Record kept by notaries following strict procedures.

**Protutor.** Protutor.

**Provecho.** Advantage, benefit, earnings, gains, profit.

**Provechoso.** Advantageous, beneficial, gainful, profitable.

**Proveer.** To decide by a court. To supply, equip, furnish, provide.

**Proveído.** Court decision or order.

**Provenir.** To originate from.

**Proveyendo.** Provided.

**Providencia.** Order. Used to decide a matter of mere practice. (Sp. L. Crim. P., art. 141). Interlocutory order.

**Providencia judicial.** Judicial ruling.

**Provincial.** Provincial.

**Provisión.** Provision, supply. Existence of funds.

**Provisional, provisorio.** Provisional, conditional, contingent, interim, temporary.

**Provocación.** Provocation, incitement, instigation.

**Provocador.** Instigator, initiator. Provocateur.

**Proxenitismo.** Prostitute trafficking.

**Próximo.** Proximate, alongside, by, close, near, neighboring, next.

**Proyecto.** Draft. Project, plan, scheme.

**Proyecto, borrador.** Draft.

**Proyecto de ley.** Bill, draft law.

**Prudencia.** Prudence, care, caution, poise, reasonableness, steadiness, wisdom.

**Prudencial.** Prudent, circumspect, discreet.

**Prudente arbitrio.** Sound discretion.

**Prueba.** Proof, evidence. Confirmation, data, demonstration, discovery, documentation, exhibit, indication, indicia, sign, testimony, validation, verification. Test, trial.

**Prueba, conflicto de leyes.** Evidence, conflict of laws. The form of the evidence is regulated by the law in force in the place where it is taken. The weight of the evidence depends on the law of the judge. (Bustamante C. arts. 398-401).

**Prueba de obligaciones.** Proof of obligations. Proof may be given by instruments, by confession, by the personal inspection of the court or judge, by experts, by witnesses, and by presumptions. (Sp. Civ. C., sec. 1182, 1183).

**Prueba de peritos.** Proof of expert evidence. This kind of evidence may only be made use of when, in order to weigh the facts, scientific, artistic, or practical knowledge is necessary or advisable. (Sp. Civ. C., sec. 1210).

**Prueba de referencia.** Hearsay.

**Prueba de testigos.** Evidence of witnesses, testimony. Evidence of witnesses shall be admissible in all cases in which it should not have been expressly forbidden. (Sp. Civ. C., sec. 1212, 1216).

**Prueba del daño en caso de una operación sucedánea.** Proof of harm in case of replacement transaction. Where the aggrieved party has terminated the contract and has made a replacement transaction within a reasonable time and in a reasonable manner it may recover the difference between the contract price and the price of the replacement transaction as well as damages for any further harm. (Unidroit, Prin., art. 7.4.5).

**Prueba del derecho extranjero.** Proof of foreign law. Foreign law can be proven by a duly authenticated copy of the pertinent part of the statute, or by the testimony of two or more lawyers who are in practice in the country whose law must be proven. (LA Laws & Inst.).

**Prueba del diligenciamiento.** Return.

**Prueba documental.** Documentary evidence. The court shall examine in person the books, documents, papers and other exhibits which may contribute to an elucidation of the facts or to a more certain investigation of the truth. (Sp. L. Crim. P., sec. 726).

**Prueba en Latinoamérica.** Evidence in Latin America. Latin American evidentiary systems know of testimonial proof, public and private documents, confession, opinions by experts, judicial inspections and presumptions. At first blush the system is not so different from its US counterpart. However, a closer inspection reveals that Latin American rules are structurally weak and very restrictive. It would not be an exaggeration to estimate that if transferred to a Latin American jurisdiction the evidence obtainable there would be at least 80% weaker than if the case remained in the US. That is so for the following reasons. In Latin American systems there are no depositions and no discovery, witnesses are very restricted and the court has very little power to compel document production.

**Prueba, evaluación.** Evaluation of evidence. The judge's power to evaluate evidence is much more circumscribed than that of the common law judge. The codes of civil procedure commonly set out detailed rules as to how the judge should weigh testimony, specifying considerations about motivation, precision, clarity, the witness' capacity to perceive, and his interest in the case. Latin American courts display a decided tendency to believe documents and to disbelieve people. The innate distrust of oral testimony is reflected in broad disqualifications of witnesses related to any of the parties. (L & D in LA).

**Prueba, presunciones.** Proof, presumptions. Presumptions are not admissible, except when the fact from which they are to be deduced is fully proven. Presumptions established by law exempt those favored thereby from producing any further proof. (Sp. Civ. C., sec. 1217, 1218, 1220).

**Psicosis.** Psychosis.

**Psiquiatra.** Psychiatrist.

**Pubertad.** Puberty, pubescence, adolescence, youth.

**Publicación.** Publication, announcement, printing, proclamation.

**Publicación de casos, México.** Case reporting, Mexico. Case reporting in Mexico is nothing like in the U.S. There is one famous series of law reports, the *Semanario Judicial de la Federación*, now in its eighth "epoch." The *Semanario* is devoted exclusively to the decisions of the Supreme Court and the federal appellate courts. Only a devoted student of Mexican law will be prepared to expend the effort required to learn how to use the *Semanario*. (Pratter).

**Publicación de leyes, México.** Publication of statutes, Mexico. The official source of legislative enactments in the civil-law countries is the *official gazette*. The U.S. has no equivalent, although the Federal Register and the state registers have that form. At the national level it is called the *Diario Oficial de la Federación*. It is published every business day. It contains all federal legislative and administrative acts of any significance. (Pratter).

**Publicidad.** Publicity, advertisement.

**Publicidad de los debates.** Publicity of oral arguments. The arguments at the oral trial shall be public, under pain of nullity. Nevertheless, the presiding judge may order that the proceedings be held behind closed doors when necessary for reasons of morality or public order, or the respect due to the person offended by the crime or to his family. (Sp. L. Crim. P., sec. 680, 682).

**Publicista.** Publicist, specialist in public law.

**Público.** Public, audience, community, people, population.

**Publíquese y hágase saber.** Let it be known.

**Pudor.** Sexual decency, decorum or modesty. Delicate sense of shame or constraint.

**Puerto.** Port, harbor. Sanctuary, shelter.

**Pugna.** Argument, conflict, contest, disagreement, dispute.

**Puja.** Competition, conflict, contest, match, rivalry.

**Pujar.** To struggle in competition. Move to outbid a rival.

**Punible.** Punishable, subject to a fine or penalty.

**Punición.** Punishment, castigation, correction, discipline, penalty.

**Punitivo.** Punitive, correctional, disciplinary.

**Puntapié.** Kick.

**Punto.** Point. Detail, particular. Issue, item.

**Puntualizar.** To explain in detail.

**Puñal.** Dagger, small knife or blade.

**Puñalada.** Stabbing, wound inflicted with a dagger or a knife.

**Puñetazo.** Punch, blow, jab. Knock with a clenched fist.

**Pupilaje.** Pupilage, guardianship. Care of minors.

**Pupilar.** Relating to minors under guardianship.

**Pupilo.** Ward, minor under guardianship.

**Purga del incumplimiento.** Cure by nonperforming party. The nonperforming party may, at its own expense, cure any nonperformance, provided that (a) the nonperforming party without undue delay gives notice of cure indicating the proposed manner and timing of the cure; (b) cure is appropriate to the circumstances; (c) the aggrieved party has no legitimate interest in refusing cure; and (d) cure is effected promptly. (Unidroit, Prin., art. 7.1.4).

**Purgación.** Purge.

**Purgar.** To purge, to remove selectively.

**Puro y claro.** Unclouded, free of any lien or restraint.

**Puta.** Hooker, prostitute, whore.

**Putativo.** Putative, assumed, reputed, supposed, commonly esteemed.

# Q

**Quasi posesión.** Quasi possession. The exercise of a real right, such as a servitude, with the intent to have it as one's own is quasi-possession. The rules governing possession apply by analogy to the quasi-possession of incorporeals. (Lou. Civ. C. art. 3421 and note).

**Que se declare de puro derecho.** Motion for summary judgment.

**Quebrado.** Broken. Bankrupt, insolvent.

**Quebrantador.** Person who breaks the law.

**Quebrantamiento.** Breach, infringement, violation.

**Quebrantar.** To breach, infringe, violate.

**Quebranto.** Economic loss or damage.

**Quebrar.** To break, breach. To go bankrupt.

**Queja.** Complaint, grievance, protest.

**Quejarse.** To complain, protest.

**Quejoso.** Complainant, aggrieved party.

**Quemarropa.** At point-blank range.

**Querella.** Complaint. The complaint shall always be submitted through a solicitor having a sufficient power subscribed by an attorney. It shall be drafted on official paper, and shall state: 1) The judge or court before whom it is made. 2) The name, surname, and residence of the complainant. 3) The name, surname, and residence of the person charged. If these details be unknown, the description of the person charged must state such distinctive marks as may best tend to his identification. 4) A detailed statement of the act, with a statement of the place, year, month, day, and hour it was committed, if known. (Sp. L. Crim. P., art. 277).

Criminal prosecution. Criminal accusation.

**Querellado.** Accused in criminal proceedings.

**Querellante.** Plaintiff in criminal proceedings.

**Querellar.** To file criminal charges.

**Quid.** Essence, heart of the matter, main issue.

**Quid pro quo (L).** One thing for another.

**Quiebra.** Bankruptcy. The declaration of bankruptcy shall be proper: 1) When the bankrupt itself requests it. 2) On a well-founded request of a legitimate creditor. (Sp. Com. C., sec. 874/75). Insolvency.

**Quiebra accidental.** Accidental bankruptcy. An accidental bankruptcy shall be considered that of a merchant who is the victim of misfortunes. (Sp. Com. C., sec. 887).

**Quiebra, acreedores prendarios.** Bankruptcy, creditors secured by pledge. Creditors who are secured by a pledge established in a public instrument or in a certificate in which an agent or broker has taken part, shall not be obliged to turn in the assets the securities or objects they may have received as security, unless the receivers in bankruptcy should desire to recover the same by paying the credit in question in full. (Sp. Com. C., sec. 918).

**Quiebra, clases.** Bankruptcy, kinds. For legal purposes three different kinds of bankruptcy shall be distinguished, viz: 1) Accidental insolvency. 2) Culpable insolvency. 3) Fraudulent insolvency. (Sp. Com. C., sec. 886).

**Quiebra culpable.** Culpable bankruptcy. A culpable bankruptcy shall be considered that of merchants who are embraced in any of the following cases: 1) If the household and personal expenses of the bankrupt should have been excessive and not in proportion with his net profits, taking into consideration the circumstances of his standing and family. 2) If he should have suffered losses at any kind of play which exceed that which a careful father of a family should risk in this kind of entertainment. (Sp. Com. C., sec. 888).

**Quiebra fraudulenta.** Fraudulent bankruptcy. A merchant shall be considered a fraudulent bankrupt when his acts bring him within any of the following conditions: 1) Flight with all or a part of his property. 2) The inclusion in the balance, memoranda, books or other documents relating to his business or transactions, of fictitious property, credits, debts, losses, or expenses. 3) If they have not kept books, or, if they have done so, they include therein, to the prejudice of a third person, entries not made in the proper place and at the proper time. (Sp. Com. C., sec. 890/91).

**Quiebra, graduación de crédito.** Bankruptcy, graduation of credits. The graduation of the credits shall be made by dividing them into two sections. The first one shall include the credits which are to be paid from the proceeds of the personal property of the bankruptcy, and the second those which are to be paid from the proceeds of the real estate. (Sp. Com. C., sec. 912).

**Quiebra, rehabilitación del quebrado.** Bankruptcy, discharge of bankrupts. Fraudulent bankrupts can not be discharged. With the discharge of the bankrupt all the legal interdictions which a declaration of bankruptcy gives rise to shall cease. (Sp. Com. C., sec. 920/11).

**Quien calla otorga.** He who remains silent, consents.

**Quieta y pacífica posesión.** Enjoyment of a property without being disturbed.

**Quincena.** Fortnight.

**Quincenal.** Fortnightly, bimonthly.

**Quinquenio.** Five years.

**Quirografario.** Unsecured creditor.

**Quirografía.** Documentary, handwriting.

**Quiropráctica.** Chiropractice. The science of the treatment of the human body by means of adjustments and manipulations for the purpose of correcting partial misalignment and subluxation of the spinal column, causing compression on the nerves, thus hindering the transmission of vital energy from the brains to the organs, tissues, and cells of the human body. (Ppl. v. Rodriquez, 91 PRR 699 (1965)).

**Quita.** Allowance, rebate.

**Quita, espera.** Respite. A respite is an act by which a debtor, who is unable to satisfy his debts at the moment, transacts with his creditors and obtains from them time or delay for the payment of the sums which he owes to them. (Lou. Civ. C. art. 3084).

**Quitación, quitamiento.** Release, quitclaim, waiver.

**Quitanza.** Accord and satisfaction, complete release, discharge of an obligation.

**Quórum.** Quorum, necessary number of votes to proceed with a meeting.

# R

**Rábula.** Shyster.

**Rabulería.** Chicanery.

**Racionalización.** Rationalization, explanation. Act of making a government body more cost effective.

**Racismo.** Racism.

**Racista.** Racist.

**Rada.** Roadstead.

**Radicación.** Filing.

**Radicar.** To file. To apply for.

**Radicarse.** To settle in.

**Radio.** Radio. Radius. A circular geographic area.

**Rama.** Branch, division. Area of law.

**Ramera.** Prostitute, hooker, streetwalker, whore.

**Ramo.** Line of business. Category, class.

**Rango.** Rank, degree, level, status. Order of importance.

**Rapiña.** Robbery, burglary, larceny, theft.

**Rapiñar.** To steal, lift, pilfer, snatch.

**Raptar.** To kidnap, abduct, steal.

**Rapto.** Kidnapping, abduction.

**Raptor.** Kidnapper, abductor.

**Raspadura.** Erasure, cancellation, crossing, out, deletion.

**Rastro.** Track, footprints, imprint, steps, trail.

**Ratería, raterismo.** Small thefts, pilfering.

**Ratero.** Petty thief.

**Ratificación.** Ratification. Ratification is a declaration whereby a person gives his consent to an obligation incurred on his behalf by another without authority. An express act of ratification must evidence the intention to be bound by the ratified obligation. Tacit ratification results when a person, with knowledge of an obligation incurred on his behalf by another, accepts the benefit of that obligation. (Lou. Civ. C. art. 1843).

Approval, confirmation, corroboration, verification.

**Ratificar.** To ratify, approve, confirm, corroborate, verify.

**Rayadura.** Crossing out, cancellation, deletion, erasure.

**Rayar.** To cross out, to cancel. To border or something, to be close.

**Raza.** Race. Breed.

**Razón.** Reason. Argument, cause, explanation. Sanity, mental health.

**Razón de dicho.** Grounds for one's statements.

**Razón social.** Corporate name, trade name.

**Razonable.** Reasonable, rational, sensible. Conceivable, logical, moderate. Fair, just.

**Razonamiento.** Reasoning.

**Reabrir.** To reopen. To undo or unlock once more.

**Reaceptación.** Reacceptance, to consent or approve once more.

**Readaptación.** Readaptation, rehabilitation.

**Readquirir.** To acquire once more, to purchase again.

**Reafirmar.** To reaffirm. To maintain or profess once more.

**Reagrupación.** Regrouping.

**Reajustar.** To readjust, reaccommodate, readapt.

**Reajuste.** Readjustment. Alteration in price. Change, correction.

**Real.** Royal. Actual, certain, proven. Relating to real estate.

**Real Decreto.** Royal Decree.

**Realizable.** That can be turned into cash.

**Realizar.** To realize. To turn into cash. To comprehend, perceive, understand. To fulfill, perform.

**Reanimación.** Reanimation, resuscitation.

**Reanudar.** To continue, proceed, resume.

**Reapertura de la causa.** Reopening of proceedings.

**Reargüir.** To reargue, relitigate.

**Reaseguro.** Reinsurance.

**Reaseguro en masa.** Bulk reinsurance.

**Reavaluar, revaluar.** To reappraise, reassess.

**Reavalúo, revalúo.** Reappraisal, reassessment.

**Rebaja.** Rebate, cutback, discount, reduction. Abatement, remission.

**Rebajar.** To rebate, discount. To abate, remit. To debase, degrade, lower.

**Rebaje.** Discount. Remission.

**Rebatir.** To rebut, counter, object, refute.

**Rebelde.** In default. A person accused who shall not appear within the period fixed in the requisitions or who can not be found and brought before the judge or court taking cognizance of the cause shall be declared in default. (Sp. L. Crim. P., art. 834).

Contemnor. Rebel, dissenter, revolutionary.

**Rebeldía.** Default, contempt to court, nonappearance.

**Rebelión.** Rebellion, coup, insubordination, insurgence, insurrection, revolt, revolution.

**Rebote.** Bounce.

**Rebus sic stantibus (L).** This phrase is mostly used in the context of contract law. It is the equivalent of the theory of changed circumstances, hardship or of frustration of contract. Literally it means a substantial change of circumstances or events.

**Recabar.** To obtain, e.g. information.

**Recalada.** Sighting land.

**Recalar.** Stand in shore. The convenience or the interests of the passengers shall not obligate nor empower the captain to stand in shore or enter places which may take the vessel out of her course, nor to remain in the ports he must or is under the necessity of touching for a period longer than that required for the business of the service. (Sp. Com. C., sec. 701).

**Recámara.** Place where bullet is lodged before firing.

**Recambio.** A new bill of exchange to replace an old one.

**Recapacitar.** To stop to think, meditate. To rehabilitate, reeducate.

**Recapitalización.** Recapitalization.

**Recapitulación.** Summary, abridgement, condensation, outline.

**Recapturar.** To recapture. To seize once more.

**Recargo.** Surcharge, additional cost. Markup in price.

**Recaudable.** Collectible. Viable claim.

**Recaudación.** Collection, contributions, funds, income, revenue.

**Recaudador.** Collector, receiver.

**Recaudar.** To collect, cash in, obtain, perceive, receive.

**Recaudatorio.** Relating to collection purposes.

**Recaudo.** Precaution, protection, safety, shelter. Requirement, requisite.

**Recepción.** Reception. Acceptance. Incorporation. Welcome.

**Recepción de la revocación, rechazo o aceptación.** Reception of revocation, rejection or acceptance. A written revocation, rejection, or acceptance is received when it comes into the possession of the addressee or of a person authorized by him to receive it. (Lou. Civ. C. art. 1938).

**Recepcionista.** Receptionist. Person who receives or accepts.

**Receptador.** Party who receives.

**Receptar.** To receive, accept, adopt, acquire, establish.

**Receptor.** Receiver, acceptor, adopter.

**Receptoría.** Tax office, tax collection bureau.

**Recesar.** To recess, adjourn, break, pause, stay.

**Receso.** Recess, break, intermission, pause.

**Recetar.** To prescribe. To suggest as a solution.

**Rechazable.** Declinable, discardable, refusable, rejectable.

**Rechazamiento.** Denial, refusal, rejection, veto. Dismissal.

**Rechazar.** To decline, disavow, discard, disown, refuse, reject, repudiate. To dismiss, to throw out of court. To recant, retract, rescind. To deny, refuse, reject, veto.

**Rechazo.** Refusal, rejection, repudiation. Disavowal. Dismissal of an action. Rescission.

**Rechazo de la oferta.** Rejection of offer. An offer is terminated when a rejection reaches the offeror. (Unidroit, Prin., art. 2.5).

**Recibí.** Paid, payment received.

**Recibido.** Received. Graduated from high school or college.

**Recibimiento a prueba.** Period for producing evidence. The ordinary period for the taking of evidence shall be divided into two parts common to all parties. The first period of twenty days, which can not be extended, shall be for the purpose of stating in one or more written instruments all the matters upon which they desire evidence to be taken. The second period of thirty days, which can not be extended either, shall be for the purpose of taking all the evidence proposed by the parties. (Sp. L. Civ. P. sec. 552).

**Recibir.** To receive, accept, collect, gather, take.

**Recibir juramento.** Administer oaths.

**Recibirse.** To obtain a high school or a college degree. To become admitted to practice.

**Recibo.** Receipt, stub.

**Recidivismo.** Duplication, recurrence, reiteration of a criminal act.

**Recidivista.** Recidivist, repeat offender, professional criminal.

**Recién nacido abandonado.** Abandoned newborn child. Any person who finds a newborn child or finds him in his house or property, must bring him before the Civil Registry judge. (Mex. Civ. C., art.65).

**Recinto.** Closed area.

**Reciprocidad.** Reciprocity, mutuality.

**Recíproco.** Reciprocal, joint, common, complemental, mutual, shared.

**Reclamable.** Claimable, demandable.

**Reclamación.** Claim, demand, litigation, suit.

**Reclamaciones opuestas.** Adverse, conflicting claims.

**Reclamante.** Plaintiff, claimant.

**Reclamar.** To claim, demand, insist, request, require.

**Reclamo.** Demand, urgent request. Advertisement, commercial.

**Recluir.** To seclude, imprison, isolate. To insulate.

**Reclusión.** Seclusion, imprisonment, isolation.

**Recluso.** Prisoner, convict, inmate. Hermit, loner.

**Reclutamiento.** Recruiting, chafing, enlistment, enrolling. Signing up.

**Recobrable.** Recoverable, collectible. Retrievable, redeemable.

**Recobrar.** To recover, recapture, recoup, regain, repossess, rescue, retrieve.

**Recobro.** Recovery, repossession, rescue, retrieval. Health improvement.

**Recogedor.** Person who picks up or receives.

**Recoger.** To receive, pick up.

**Recomendado.** Recommended, approved, endorsed, praised.

**Recomendar.** To recommend, approve, endorse, praise.

**Recomendatorio.** Person who is recommended.

**Recompensa.** Reward, award, bonus, compensation, payment, prize, remuneration.

**Recompensable.** Compensable, payable.

**Recompensar.** To reward, award, compensate, pay, remunerate.

**Recomprar.** To repurchase. Buying the same thing for a second time.

**Reconciliación.** Reconciliation.

**Reconducción.** Extension of a contract for another term.

**Reconducir.** To extend the duration of a contract for one more term.

**Reconocer.** To admit, acknowledge, concede, confess, grant, recognize. To inspect, examine, investigate, probe, study.

**Reconocimiento.** Admission, acknowledgment, concession, confession, recognition. Inspection, exam, examination, investigation, probe, study.

**Reconocimiento de progenitura.** Parenthood acknowledgment. In the event the father or the mother or both of a child born out of wedlock produce the child for the recording of its birth, the proceeding have the effect of a legal acknowledgment of the parenthood for the person who appears. (Mex. Civ. C., art.77).

**Reconocimiento en rueda de presos.** Lineup, identification. The identification shall take place by placing before the person who is to make it the person to be identified, producing said person in union with others of similar external appearance. In the presence of all of them or from a point where he cannot be seen, as the judge may consider more advisable, the person to make the identification shall state if the person to whom he may have referred in his declarations is in the group. (Sp. L. Crim. P., sec. 369).

**Reconocimiento judicial.** Judicial inspection. If for the purpose of elucidating and weighing the facts, it should be necessary for the judge to personally examine some place or the thing which is the object of the litigation, a judicial inspection shall be made at the instance of any of the parties. (Sp. L. Civ. P. sec. 632, 633).

**Reconsiderar.** To reconsider.

**Reconstitución.** Reenactment, reconstitution.

**Reconstituir.** To restructure, reset.

**Reconvención.** Counterclaim.

**Reconvención en exceso de la demanda.** Counterclaim exceeding opposing claim.

**Reconvencional.** Relating to a counterclaim.

**Reconvenir.** To counterclaim.

**Reconversión.** Change to the original state.

**Recopilación.** Compilation.

**Recopilador.** Compiler, chronicler, historian, narrator, recorder.

**Recopilar.** To compile, accumulate, amass, assemble, collect, gather, stack.

**Recordatorio.** Reminder.

**Recorrido.** Itinerary, circuit, course, route.

**Recorte.** Cutting.

**Recriminación.** Recrimination, countercharge. Accusation, complain.

**Recriminador.** Recriminator. Accuser.

**Recriminar.** To recriminate, countercharge. To accuse.

**Rectificación.** Rectification, amendment, correction, improvement.

**Rectificación de cabida.** Rectification of size of properties. Rectification of the size of all properties already recorded may be entered in the Registry by any of the following means: 1) By an unappealable verdict handed down in a regular procedure of judicial survey or to establish the dimensions. 2) By public document when it is a question of reduction of the area or an excess of no more than twenty percent of the recorded area, and it is done by proven technical sur-

veying methods. (PR Mort. Law 1979, sec. 247).

**Rectificar.** To rectify, amend, change, correct, improve.

**Rectificativo.** Rectifying.

**Recuento.** Recount.

**Recuerdo.** Recollection, remembrance, memory. Fame, impression.

**Recuperable.** Recoverable, collectible. Retrievable, redeemable.

**Recuperación, recupero.** Recovery, repossession, rescue, retrieval. Health improvement.

**Recuperar.** To recover, recapture, recoup, regain, repossess, rescue, retrieve.

**Recurrencia.** Recurrence.

**Recurrente.** Complainant, petitioner, plaintiff, relator, appellant, applicant.

**Recurrible.** Not firm or final. Appealable.

**Recurrido.** Subject to an appeal or a revision.

**Recurrir.** To sue, appeal, apply, petition, request.

**Recurso.** Appeal, motion for a revision.

**Recurso aclaratorio de sentencia.** Motion to clarify a decision. Courts can not amend their decisions after the same have been signed, but on the first legal day after the notice is served they may elucidate some obscure point, supply any omission, or correct any important mistake therein. (Sp. L. Crim. P., art. 161).

**Recurso de apelación.** Appeal. An appeal can not be interposed until a petition for amendment has been filed; but both may be interposed in the same instrument. (Sp. L. Crim. P., art. 222).

**Recurso de casación.** Appeal for annulment of judgment. An appeal for annulment of judgment for violation of law lies from all sentences rendered in first and last instance. (Sp. L. Crim. P., art. 847).

**Recurso de casación por nulidad de sentencia, casos.** Appeal for annulment of judgment, cases. An appeal for annulment of judgment shall lie in the cases established in this law: 1) From final judgments rendered by audiences. 2) From final judgments rendered by judges of the first instance in actions of unlawful detainer of which they take cognizance on appeal. 3) From judgments of amicable compounders. (Sp. L. Civ. P. sec. 1684-1690).

**Recurso de casación por quebrantamiento de forma.** Appeal for annulment of judgment for breach of form. An appeal for annulment of judgment for a breach of form may be interposed: 1) When the taking of some evidence considered pertinent proposed in due time and form by the parties shall have been denied. 2) When the citation of the accused shall have been omitted, whether he be imprisoned or at liberty, and of the accusing party and civil plaintiff for appearance at the oral and public trial, unless said parties should have appeared in due time considering themselves cited. (Sp. L. Crim. P., art. 911).

**Recurso de fuerza en conocer.** Complaint against ecclesiastical decision. The complaint made by a person who considers himself unjustly treated by an ecclesiastical judge to a secular judge, imploring his protection, and requesting that the former be ordered to repair the injustice done the appellant. (Novísima Recopilación, book 2, title 2, law 1).

**Recurso de queja.** Complaint. A complaint lies from all rulings of a judge which can not be appealed from and from decisions disallowing an appeal. (Sp. L. Crim. P., art. 218).

**Recurso de reforma.** Petition for amendment. Petitions for amendment lie from all rulings of a judge of examination. (Sp. L. Crim. P., art. 217).

**Recurso de revisión.** Appeal for review. The review of a final judgment shall be proper: 1) If, after judgment has been rendered, decisive documents should be recovered which were detained by *force majeure* or by an act of the party in whose favor judgment was rendered. 2) When the judgment was rendered by virtue of documents which at the time said judgment was rendered, were acknowledged and declared false without the knowledge of one of the parties. (Sp. L. Civ. P. sec. 1794, 1795).

**Recurso de revisión (Crim.).** Appeal for review (crim.). An appeal for review shall lie from final sentences in the following cases: 1) When two or more persons are serving a sentence by virtue of contradictory sentences for the same crime which could not have been committed by more than one person. 2) When a person is serving a sentence as the principal, accomplice, or accessory to the homicide of a person whose existence is established after the sentences. (Sp. L. Crim. P., art. 954).

**Recursos naturales.** Natural resources.

**Recusable.** Impeachable, recusable.

**Recusación.** Challenge to the judge. Justices and judges, whatever their rank or hierarchy, and assessors to municipal judges who substitute those of first instance and subordinate officials of superior and inferior courts, may be challenged only for a legitimate cause. The following are legitimate cause of challenge: 1) Relationship by affinity or consanguinity within the fourth civil degree with any of the litigants. 2) The same relationship within the second degree with the attorney of any of the parties to the action. This should be understood without prejudice to the prohibition which is imposed upon attorneys to act as such in actions in which any of their relatives within the same degrees are to act as judges. (Sp. L. Civ. P., sec. 188).

**Recusación (Crim.).** Challenge to the judge (crim.). In criminal matters only the following persons are permitted to challenge: The prosecuting officials. The private accuser or his legal representatives. The accused. Those civilly liable for a crime or misdemeanor. Legitimate causes of challenge are: 1) Relationship by consanguinity or affinity within the fourth civil degree to any of the persons mentioned in the foregoing article. 2) The same relationship within the second degree to the attorney of any of the parties to the cause. 3) To be or have been denounced or accused by any of said parties as the principal, accomplice, or accessory to a crime or as a principal in a misdemeanor. (Sp. L. Crim. P., art. 53 and 54).

Recusal, challenge, impeachment.

**Recusación de peritos.** Challenge of experts. The following are causes for challenge of experts: 1) relationship by consanguinity or affinity within the fourth degree with the complainant or the accused; 2) a direct or indirect interest in the cause or in another similar one; 3) intimate friendship or manifest enmity. (Sp. L. Crim. P., sec. 468).

**Recusante.** Party who challenges.

**Recusar.** To recuse, challenge, impeach.

**Red.** Net, system.

**Redacción.** Drafting, writing.

**Redactar.** To draft, author, pen, scrawl.

**Redada.** Raid, storming.

**Redención.** Absolution, acquittal, clearance, exculpation, exoneration, forgiveness, pardon, redemption, remission.

**Redescuento.** Rediscounting.

**Redhibición.** Redhibitory action. Redhibition is the avoidance of a sale on account of some vice or defect in the thing sold, which renders it either absolutely useless, or its use so inconvenient and imperfect, that it must be supposed that the buyer would not have purchased it, had he known of the vice. (Lou. Civ. C. art. 2420).

Redhibition, action for hidden vices for the thing purchased.

**Redhibitorio.** Redhibitory.

**Redimible.** Redeemable.

**Redimir.** To redeem. For a corporation, to reacquire its own shares previously sold. To reclaim, recover, regain. To free, release, save.

**Rédito.** Revenue, benefits, earnings, gains, income, lucre, proceeds, return, wages.

**Reducción.** Reduction. Cutback, decrease, discount. Abatement, attenuation, remission. Compression, shortening.

**Reeducación.** Reeducation, readaptation, rehabilitation.

**Reembargo.** Reattachment.

**Reembolso de gastos médicos.** Reimbursement of medical expenses. This concept is included in the rule that repartion must be complete. Historically, the obligation to reimburse medical expenses can be traced back to Roman law, in the Lex Aquilia, of about 287 BC.

**Reembolsable.** Reimbursable, returnable. Claimable, deductible.

**Reembolsar.** To reimburse, compensate, indemnify, recompense, refund, remunerate, return.

**Reembolso.** Reimbursement, compensation, indemnification, recompense, refund, remuneration, return, reward.

**Reemplazante.** Replacement, agent, deputy, proxy, representative, substitute, surrogate.

**Reencarcelar.** To send back to prison.

**Reenvío.** Remand. Renvoi.

**Reexaminación.** Re-examination, reappraisal, restudy.

**Reexportación.** Reexportation.

**Refacción.** Type of rural loan, agricultural loan.

**Refaccionar.** To recondition, reconstruct, renew, repair, restore.

**Referendum.** Referendum.

**Referente.** In reference to, concerning.

**Refletar.** To recharter.

**Reflujo.** Receding tide. Backlash action.

**Reforma.** Reform. Amendment. Alteration, change, correction, improvement, modification, transformation, revision, variation.

**Reformatorio.** Reformatory.

**Refrenda.** Authentication, confirmation, corroboration, ratification, validation, verification.

**Refrendar.** To authenticate, confirm, corroborate, ratify, validate, verify.

**Refrendata.** Countersignature.

**Refriega.** Fight, riot, skirmish.

**Refugiado.** Refugee, desperado, expatriate, escapee, exiled, fugitive, runaway.

**Refugio.** Shelter. Haven, protection, shield. Asylum, refuge, sanctuary.

**Refutable.** Refutable, arguable, rebuttable, questionable.

**Refutación.** Refutation, argument, contradiction, objection, rebuttal.

**Refutar.** To refute, argue, contradict, object, rebut.

**Regalía.** Royalty.

**Regatear.** To bargain, dicker, haggle.

**Regateo.** Bargaining, dickering, haggling.

**Regente.** Regent. Person ruling in the king's name.

**Regicida.** Murderer of a king.

**Regicidio.** Murder of a king.

**Regidor.** Governor, ruler, Spanish colonial official, city councilman.

**Régimen.** Regime, method, order, routine, strategy, system.

**Régimen de separación de bienes.** Separation of property regime. A regime of separation of property is established by a matrimonial agreement that excludes the legal regime of community of acquest and gains or by a judgment decreeing separation of property. (Lou. Civ. C. art. 2370).

**Régimen matrimonial.** Matrimonial regime. A matrimonial regime is a system of principles and rules governing the ownership and management of the property of married persons as between themselves and toward third persons. (Lou. Civ. C. art. 2325).

**Régimen presidencial.** Presidential regime. The characteristic feature of the presidential regime in Latin America is that, although the institutions resemble those of the United States, the president usually succeeds in gaining control. Even if we disregard the frequent periods when legality is suspended, his power may be said to verge on hegemony. (W. Eur. & LA Leg. Sys.).

**Región.** Area, region, zone.

**Regir.** To rule, command, govern. To be in force, applicable, binding, mandatory, obligatory. To control.

**Registrable.** Recordable.

**Registración, registro.** Examination, inspection, pat down, probe, search. Registry, register. Entry, annotation, record.

**Registrado.** Recorded, filed, registered.

**Registrador.** Registrar, recorder.

**Registral.** Concerning recordation of titles and encumbrances to real estate.

**Registrante.** Party who records or registers.

**Registrar.** To examine, inspect, pat down, probe, search. To record, register. To make an entry. To annotate, record.

**Registro.** Roster, list, register.

**Registro, anotación preventiva.** Registration, cautionary notice. The following may request that cautionary notices on their respective rights be entered in the Registry: 1) A person who, in a lawsuit, claims ownership to real property or the constitution, declaration, modification or extinction of any recordable right or one who files his claim in an action that affects a title to real property, or on the validity and force, or the lack of validity or force. of the title or titles involved in the acquisition, constitution, declaration, modification or extinction of the above-cited recordable rights. 2) A person who lawfully obtains an attachment order in his favor on real property belonging to the debtor. (PR Mort. Law 1979, sec. 112).

**Registro, anotación preventiva de crédito refaccionario.** Registration, attachment by administrative collection proceedings. Attachment ordered by administrative collection proceedings shall be governed by the provisions applicable to them, and to this effect the authorities who decree them on real property may present a certification containing the attachment order and the data needed to record it in the corresponding section. (PR Mort. Law 1979, sec. 118).

**Registro, cancelación de asientos.** Registration, cancellation of entries. Cancellation of Registry entries may be total or partial. Cancellation of an entry made without any external curable defect shall become totally effective with regard to the third party who, because of it, has acquired and recorded a right, even though said cancellation is later annulled for some reason that does not clearly originate from that entry or the Registry. (PR Mort. Law 1979, sec. 129, 131, 143).

**Registro civil.** Civil registry. Acts relating to the civil status of persons shall be recorded in the registry devoted to that purpose. The records in the registry shall be evidence of the civil status. (Sp. Civ. C., sec. 318, 320).

**Registro de inmuebles.** Search of premises. Useless inspections shall be avoided in making the searches, that being sought not to prejudice nor importune the person interested more than necessary. (Sp. L. Crim. P., art. 552).

**Registro de la propiedad.** Property registry. The purpose of the Property Registry is the registration of transactions and contracts relating to real property through a public record system of titles containing the acquisitions, modifications and extinctions of domain and other real rights on said property, and the recordable rights on same, and those judicial opinions which may affect the legal capacity of the owners of record. (PR Mort. Law 1979, sec. 7).

**Registro de penados.** Register of convictions. Every judge of examination shall keep a book which shall be called "Register of Convictions." The leaves of this book shall be numbered, sealed, and rubricated by the judge of examination and his secretary of administration. (Sp. L. Crim. P., art. 254).

**Registro de procesados en rebeldía.** Register or persons accused in default. In the latter book shall be entered all causes in which the persons accused have been declared in default, and the proper entry shall be made upon the record of each cause when the person in default is found. (Sp. L. Crim. P., art. 255).

**Registro, derechos de un tercero.** Registration, third person's rights. Despite the fact that registration does not validate transactions or contracts that are null according to the law, nor does it alter the legal relationship of those intervening as parties in said transactions or contracts, a third person who, in good faith and by paying a price, validly acquires a right from a person who according to the Registry, appears with the power to convey it, shall be sustained in his acquisition after he has recorded his right. (PR Mort. Law 1979, sec. 105).

**Registro e incautación.** Search and seizure.

**Registro fiel y exacto.** True and faithful record.

**Registro, inexactitud.** Registration, inaccuracies. Inaccuracy of the Record is understood to mean any disagreement on recordable rights which may exist between the Record and the legal reality outside the Registry. Rectification of the Registry may be requested by the titleholder of dominion or real right which is not recorded, which is recorded erroneously, or which is impaired by the inaccurate entry. (PR Mort. Law 1979, sec. 110).

**Registro mercantil, inscripciones.** Commercial registry, records. A commercial registry shall be opened in all the capitals of provinces, composed of two independent books, in which there shall be recorded: 1)

Private merchants. 2) Associations. The registrar shall enter in chronological order in the registry and general index all the merchants and associations which have their names registered, giving each sheet the proper correlative number. The commercial registry shall be public. (Sp. Com. C., sec. 16, 17, 19, 20, 30).

**Regla.** Rule, canon, dictate, law, norm, precept, principle, standard.

**Reglamentación, reglamento.** Regulation, command, decree, dictate, direction, order, standing order. Bylaws.

**Reglamentar.** To regulate, control, handle, manage, monitor, supervise, oversee.

**Reglamentario.** Regulatory, administrative.

**Reglamento interior de trabajo.** Work rules. Those provisions which bind workers in carrying out the work in an enterprise or establishment.

**Reglar.** To settle, agree, establish, fix. To pay, acquit oneself, clear discharge.

**Regreso.** Return, reappearance. Reinstatement, recovery, replacement, restoration.

**Regularización.** Regularization, normalization.

**Regularizar.** To bring back to normal conditions.

**Rehabilitación.** Rehabilitation, re-adaptation. Reestablishment, reinstallation, reinstatement, restoration.

**Rehabilitación, causales.** Reinstatement of rights, grounds. Rehabilitation will be granted if all the following requisites are met: a) After six years of extinguishment of the principal penalty; or twelve years for a professional of repeat offender. If the convict received a security measure of commitment following the penalty, the time will start counting at the end of such security measure; b) Satisfactory conduct of the convict during the time expressed above. (Standard Penal C. for Latin America, sec. 89).

**Rehabilitación, naturaleza.** Reinstatement of rights, scope. Reinstatement will restore the convict to the full enjoyment of the rights that were withdrawn or restricted from him by the judgment of conviction. (Standard Penal C. for Latin America, sec. 87, 88).

**Rehabilitación, revocación.** Reinstatement of rights, revocation. Reinstatement will be revoked *ipso jure* if the person in question commits a new intentional crime. (Standard Penal C. for Latin America, sec. 91).

**Rehabilitar.** To rehabilitate, readapt. To reestablish, reinstall, reinstate, restore.

**Rehabilitarse.** To rehabilitate oneself.

**Rehén.** Hostage, captive, prisoner.

**Rehipotecar.** To remortgage.

**Rehuir.** To avert, avoid, dodge, elude, evade.

**Rehusar.** To decline, refuse, step down.

**Reimpresión.** Reprint. Offprint (GB).

**Reincidencia.** Recidivism, repeat offender. Whoever commits a crime, after a prior final judgment of conviction, can have his sentence increased by up to one half of the maximum established for the crime in question. (St. P.C. for LA, sec. 69, 70, and 71).
Recidivism. Duplication, recurrence, reiteration of a criminal act.

**Reincidente.** Repeat offender, recidivist.

**Reincidir.** To commit a second crime.

**Reincorporar.** To reincorporate, reinstate, restore. To condone, forgive.

**Reiniciar.** To start again.

**Reinstalación.** Reinstatement, rehabilitation, restoration.

**Reinstalar.** To reinstall.

**Reintegrable.** Refundable, actionable, collectible, reimbursable, returnable.

**Reintegración, reintegro.** Refunding, compensation, reimbursement, remuneration, repayment. Reestablishment, reinstallation, reinstatement, restoration.

**Reintegrar.** To refund, compensate, reimburse, remunerate, repay. To reestablish, reinstall, reinstate, restore.

**Reiteradamente.** Repeatedly, several times.

**Reiteración.** Reiteration, recidivism. Duplication, recurrence.

**Reiterado.** Reiterated, repeated.

**Reiterante.** Intermittent, periodic, reappearing, recurrent, redundant, repeated, repetitious.

**Reiteratorio.** For a second time, repeated, repetitious.

**Reivindicable.** Claimable, reclaimable, recoverable, retrievable. Subject to replevin.

**Reivindicación.** Reivindication. Suit to recover, repossess or retrieve a thing. Replevin.

**Reivindicador.** Plaintiff in an action to recover or replevin.

**Reivindicar.** To reivindicate, recover, replevin, repossess, retrieve.

**Reivindicatoria.** Replevin.

**Reivindicatorio.** Relating to a replevin action.

**Relación.** Description of facts in a judgment. Narration, report. Statement of facts. Relation. Description of previous owners in a deed. Account, declaration, recital.

**Relación de acreedores.** Creditor's schedule.

**Relación de trabajo, relación laboral.** Work Relationship. The rendering of a personal service by one person to another, under the latter's direction and control, in consideration for the payment of a salary. Once there is such a work relationship, regardless of what may be the origin of the relationship, statutes that establish and protect the rights of workers automatically apply. (Mex. Labor Law).

**Relacionar.** To relate. To recount, report, state. To compare, correlate.

**Relativo.** Relative. Depending on various external factors. Uncertain.

**Relato.** Description of facts in a judgment. Narration, report, statement of facts.

**Relator.** Clerk who drafts the statement of facts for the judge. Narrator. Relator, reporter, draftsman. The person appointed in each superior court to make the briefs of the causes.

**Relegación.** Loss of rank, demotion, set back.

**Relevación, relevo.** Exemption from a particular task or duty.

**Relevamiento.** Finding or research of facts. Exemption from a particular task or duty.

**Relevancia.** Relevance, bearing, connection, materiality, significance.

**Relevante.** Relevant, connected, consequential, material, significant.

**Relevar.** To clear, acquit. To take someone's task or job, to exchange, fill in, relieve, substitute, supplant, switch.

**Relicto.** Quality of an estate whose owner has died and is subject to probate proceedings.

**Remanente.** Remnant, balance, excess, remainder, remains, residue, surplus.

**Rematador.** Auctioneer, person conducting a public sale.

**Rematar.** To auction, to perform a judicial sale.

**Remate.** Auction, judicial sale.

**Remediable.** Remediable, actionable. That can be settled through litigation.

**Remediar.** To remedy, alleviate, ameliorate, assuage, palliate. To mitigate, redress, restore.

**Remedio.** Remedy, action, appeal, hope, recourse, resort.

**Remesa.** Shipment, dispatch, lot, remittance.

**Remesar.** To ship, dispatch, remit, send.

**Remisión de deuda.** Remission of debt. A remission of debt by an obligee extinguishes the obligation. That remission may be express or tacit. (Lou. Civ. C. art. 1888 and 1889).

**Remisor.** Shipper, dispatcher, sender.

**Remisoria.** Sending back a case to the original court, remand.

**Remisorio.** Related to a remittance or dispatch.

**Remitente.** Shipper, dispatcher, sender.

**Remitir.** To remit. To forgive, pardon. To ship, dispatch, send.

**Remoción.** Removal, dislodgement, taking. Discharger, dismissal. Elimination.

**Remolque.** Towing, dragging.

**Rémora.** Handicap, hindrance, impediment, load, restriction.

**Remordimiento.** Remorse, repentance, sorrow.

**Remover.** To stir, mix. To remove, take away.

**Remunerable.** Remunerable, compensable, payable.

**Remuneración.** Remuneration, compensation, recompense, retribution, payment.

**Remunerar.** To remunerate.

**Remuneratorio.** Remunerative, advantageous, beneficial, fruitful, gainful, lucrative.

**Rendición.** Account stated, breakdown, itemized bill. Capitulation, relinquishment, surrender. Margin of gain or profit, yield.

**Rendición de cuentas.** Accounting, state of account.

**Rendimiento.** Productivity, product, production, turnout, yield. Profits, gain, revenue. Capitulation, surrender.

**Rendir.** To produce, give, make, turn out, yield. To take an exam. To render, present, offer, submit, supply.

**Renegociable.** Renegotiable.

**Renegociar.** To renegotiate.

**Renglón.** Line, item, subject.

**Reniego.** Denial, defection, disaffirmance, rejection, renunciation, retraction. Breach.

**Renombre.** Renown, fame, reputation, repute.

**Renovación.** Renovation, recondition, renewal, restoration. Extension of time.

**Renovar.** To renew, renovate.

**Renta.** Rent, annuity, dividends, earnings, income, payment, salary, remuneration.

**Renta vitalicia.** Life annuity. An aleatory contract of annuity binds the debtor to pay a pension or annual income to one or more specified persons for life, for a principal in personal or real property the ownership of which is at once transferred to said debtor charged with the income. (Sp. Civ. C., sec. 1704, 1705).

**Rentable.** Profitable, advantageous, beneficial, money making.

**Rentado.** Rental.

**Rentar.** To rent.

**Rentista.** Investor, annuitant, person who lives on income from investments and from dividends.

**Renuncia.** Waiver. The term waiver is defined as the resignation or voluntary relinquishment of a thing possessed, or of the right thereto. (Fenning v. Superior Court, 96 PRR 602 (1968)).

Resignation, departure, quitting. Disclaimer, release, relinquishment, renunciation, waiver. Abdication, concession.

**Renuncia al puesto sin responsabilidad para el trabajador.** Abandonment of the job without resposibility for the worker. An employer may refrain from dismissing a worker because of the belief that sufficient grounds or effective evidence to do so may be lacking. In these instances, employers often resort to noncompliance with some of their obligations: abstaining from paying the salary; unilateral change in some working condition (such as the schedule); bad treatment of the worker; etc. Should this be the case, the law may permit the employee to take the initiative and remove himself from the enterprise, terminating the work relationship. (Mex. Labor Law).

**Renuncia de un derecho.** Waiver of a right. The constituent elements of the waiver of a right are: a) an existing right; b) knowledge of such right; and c) the intention to relinquish it. (Fenning v. Superior Court, 96 PRR 602 (1968)).

**Renuncia justificada, indemnización.** Resignation for cause, compensation. When the worker resigns from employment with just cause, the compensation is three months' salary, plus twenty days of salary payments for every complete year of seniority, and the accrued salaries and bonuses. (Mex. Labor Law).

**Renunciable.** Renounceable, waivable.

**Renunciar.** To resign, depart, leave, quit. To disclaim, release, relinquish, renounce, waive. To abdicate, cede.

**Reo.** Captive, convict, criminal, felon, prisoner.

**Reo con antecedentes penales.** Repeat offender, recidivist.

**Reo sin antecedentes penales.** First offender.

**Reorganización.** Reorganization, rearrangement, reconstruction.

**Reorganizar.** To reorganize.

**Repagable.** Repayable, reimbursable, refundable.

**Repagar.** To repay.

**Reparación integral.** Full compensation. The aggrieved party is entitled to full compensation for harm sustained as a result of the nonperformance. Such harm includes both any loss which it suffered and any gain of which it was deprived. (Unidroit, Prin., art. 7.4.2).

**Reparación por delitos.** Compensation for crimes. The commission of a crime generates an obligation to compensate for all damages derived therefrom. Whoever has suffered damages derived from a crime, has a right to be compensated for such damages. (Standard Penal C. for Latin America, sec. 93-95).

**Reparación por delitos, extinción.** Compensation for crimes, lapsing. Civil liability derived from crime expires in accordance with time limitations prescribed by civil statutes commencement of criminal proceedings toll the action for a civil suit. (Standard Penal C. for Latin America, sec. 96).

**Reparación y reemplazo de cumplimiento defectuoso.** Repair and replacement of defective performance. The right to performance includes in appropriate cases the right to require repair, replacement, or other cure of defective performance. (Unidroit, Prin., art. 7.2.3).

**Reparaciones.** Repairs.

**Reparar.** To repair, reestablish, reinstall, reinstate, restore. To pay, compensate, recompense, redress, reimburse, remunerate. To counterbalance, offset.

**Reparo.** Objection, protest, opposition. Safety, shelter, shield, protection. Adjustment, repair, restoration.

**Repartidor.** Distributor, arbitrator.

**Repartimiento de negocios.** Distribution of business, of cases. All civil matters,whether of contentious or voluntary jurisdiction, shall be distributed among the courts of first instance when there is more than one in the town, and in all cases among the different clerks offices of each court. (Sp. L. Civ. P. sec. 429, 430).

**Repartimiento, reparto.** Allocation, allotment, apportionment, distribution, grouping.

**Repartir.** To distribute, allocate, allot, apportion, divide, group, partition, separate, share.

**Reparto.** Apportionment.

**Repatriación.** Repatriation. Sending back. Allowing to be sent back. Deportation, expulsion from a country.

**Repentino.** Sudden, unanticipated, unexpected, unforeseen. Impulsive, rash.

**Repertorio.** Compilation, collection, digest. Repertoire, accumulation, assortment, series, variety.

**Repetición.** Right to obtain reimbursement from a third party. Indemnity, recovery, refund. Repetition.

**Repetir.** To claim reimbursement from a third party. To indemnify, recover, refund. To repeat.

**Repetitivo.** Repetitive, redundant, repetitious. Cyclical, constant. Recurrent.

**Réplica.** Answer, rebuttal, reply, response, retort.

**Replicante.** Respondent, appellee, defendant.

**Replicar.** To answer, rebut, reply, respond, retort.

**Reponer.** To reestablish, reinstall, reinstate, restore. To refund, repay, replenish.

**Reposesión.** Repossession, recapture. Ejection of an intruder.

**Reposición.** Replacement, return.

**Repositario.** Depositary, recipient.

**Repregunta.** Cross examination.

**Repreguntar.** To cross examine.

**Reprender.** To chide, reprimand, reproach, scold.

**Represalia.** Reprisal, counterattack, counterstroke, punishment, retaliation, retribution, revenge, vengeance, vindication.

**Representación.** Representation, description, presentation. Agency.

**Representación de indigentes.** Legal aid. Although the administration of justice in Latin American countries long ago accepted the legal-philosophical precepts of legal aid, with few exceptions Latin American legal systems have moved very slowly toward developing adequate mechanisms for giving the poor effective participation in the legal process. (W. Eur. & LA Leg. Sys.).

**Representación hereditaria.** Representation of heirs. Representation is a fiction of the law, the effect of which is to put the representative in the place, degree, and rights of the person represented. Representation takes place ad infinitum in the direct line of descendants. (Lou. Civ. C. art. 881, 882).

**Representado.** Principal, owner.

**Representante.** Agent, representative.

**Representar.** To represent, introduce, present.

**Representativo.** Representative, ordinary, standard, usual.

**Represión.** Repression, dictatorship, tyranny. Oppression. Control, domination, restraint, subjugation. Avoidance, deterrence, forestallment, prevention.

**Represivo.** Repressive, oppressive, suppressive.

**Reprimenda.** Reprimand, admonishment, censure, reproach, scolding.

**Reprobación.** Disapproval, condemnation, objection, rejection, repudiation.

**Reprobar.** To fail an exam. To censure, criticize. To oppose, protest. To disapprove, refuse, reject.

**Reproducción.** Reproduction. Breeding, procreation. Copy, fake, imitation, reprint.

**Repudiar.** To repudiate, disavow, disclaim, recant, retract. To annul, ignore, rescind.

**Repudio.** Repudiation, disaffirmance, disavowal, retraction.

**Repuesto.** Spare part. Placed back in its previous position. Restore.

**Repugnancia.** Repugnance, abhorrence, aversion, revulsion.

**Repugnante.** Repugnant, disgusting, revolting.

**Repulsa.** Rejection, refusal, resistance.

**Repulsar.** To repulse, avert, deflect, divert, repel. To refuse, reject, repudiate, spurn.

**Reputación.** Reputation, fame, renown, repute.

**Requerido.** Defendant, appellee, respondent. Required.

**Requerimiento.** Requirement, condition, essential, must, necessity, prerequisite, requisite. Requisition, demand, injunction, summons. Command, order.

**Requerir.** To require. Command, enjoin, order.

**Requiriente, requirente.** Judge who issues an order.

**Requisa.** Search and seizure. Appropriation, confiscation, expropriation, forfeiture.

**Requisar.** To search and seize. To appropriate, commandeer, expropriate, impound.

**Requisición.** Search and seizure.

**Requisito.** Requisite, condition, essential, must, necessity, prerequisite, requirement.

**Requisitorio.** Requisitional.

**Res nullius (L).** A thing that does not belong to anyone and that can be acquired by simple appropriation. For instance, a fish in high sea would be a *res nullius*.

**Resaca.** New bill of exchange issued to cover another one, or part thereof, that remained unpaid.

**Resacar.** To issue a new bill of exchange.

**Resarcimiento.** Damages, compensation, indemnity, redress, reparation, restitution, settlement. Earnings, income, payment, recompense, reward.

**Resarcir.** To pay damages, to compensate, indemnify, redress, settle. To pay, recompense, reward.

**Rescatable.** Redeemable, claimable.

**Rescatar.** To redeem. To deliver, free, recapture, recover, recuperate, regain, release, repossess, rescue, retrieve, salvage, save.

**Rescate.** Redemption. Ransom. Rescue.

**Rescindible.** Rescindable, annullable, revocable, voidable.

**Rescindir.** To rescind, annul, cancel, invalidate, nullify, repudiate, revoke, void.

**Rescisión.** Rescission. The following may be rescinded: 1) The contracts which may be executed by guardians without the authorization of the competent District Court provided the persons they represent have suffered lesion of more than one-fourth part of the value of the things which may have been the object thereof. 2) Those executed in representation of absentees, provided the latter have suffered the lesion referred to in the preceding number. (Sp. Civ. C. sec. 1258, 1261).

Annulment, cancellation, nullity, repudiation, revocation.

**Rescisión de la relación de trabajo, despido.** Dismissal. Dismissal must be for cause. It cannot take place except for the specific causes contemplated by the law. A labor contract or collective bargaining agreement may not create additional causes for dismissal. (Mex. Labor Law).

**Rescisorio.** Rescinding.

**Reseña.** Review. Abstract, outline, summary, synopsis.

**Reserva.** Reserve, reservation. Caveat. Disposable funds. Discretion, restraint.

**Reserva, de prioridad.** Reservation of priority. Priority may be reserved for a contract being negotiated, which may affect a recorded right, at the request by a notary public to the Registrar, provided there is notarized proof of the consent of the owners of the registered right. (PR Mort. Law 1979 sec. 54).

**Reservar.** To reserve. To book. To keep, to preserve for the future, to maintain in abeyance.

**Resguardar.** To secure, to insure, to protect.

**Resguardo.** Protection. Security, guarantee. Shelter.

**Residencia.** Residence, abode, domicile, dwelling, home, house, residency, quarters. Environment.

**Residente.** Resident, citizen, denizen, dweller, inhabitant, occupant. Neighbor.

**Residir.** To reside, to be domiciled.

**Residual.** Residual, excessive.

**Residuo.** Residue, balance, left over, remainder, remnant.

**Residuo agrícola.** Agricultural waste.

**Residuos peligrosos.** Hazardous Residues. All residues, in any physical state, that due to corrosive, toxic, poisonous, reactionary, explosive, flammable, infectious or irritating biological properties, represent a danger to ecological equilibrium or to the environment.

**Resistencia.** Resistance, opposition, struggle.

**Resistente.** Resistant, firm, unyielding.

**Resolución.** Resolution. Decision declaration, order, judgment. Conclusion, settlement, solution. Determination, tenacity.

**Resolución conjunta.** Joint resolution.

**Resoluciones judiciales.** Rulings. The resolutions of superior and inferior courts in matters of a judicial character shall be called:

*Providencias*, when they are of mere practice.

*Autos* (rulings), when deciding incidental issues or points.

*Sentencias* (judgments), when finally deciding the questions at issue in an action in one instance, or in an extraordinary remedy.

Final judgments, when, by their nature or by agreement of the parties, there should be no ordinary or extraordinary remedy against them.

*Ejecutoria*, the public and formal instrument in which a final judgment is entered for enforcement. (Sp. L. Crim. P. sec. 368-370).

**Resolutivo, resolutorio.** Resolutory.

**Resolver.** To resolve, solve, conclude, decide. To cancel, rescind.

**Respaldo.** Support, backing, certification, endorsement. Cover, collateral, guarantee, security.

**Respiración.** Breath. Respiration.

**Responder.** To answer, react, rebut, rejoin, respond, reply, reply.

**Responsabilidad.** Responsibility, accountability, blame, burden, culpability, fault, guilt, liability.

**Responsabilidad civil de jueces y magistrados.** Civil liability for judges and associate justices. The civil liability which may be incurred by judges and associate justices, when, in the discharge of their duties, they violate the law through inexcusable negligence or ignorance, can be enforced only at the instance of the party prejudiced or of his legal representatives in a declaratory action and before the court immediately superior to the one in which the liability may have been incurred. (Sp. L. Civ. P. sec. 902-904, 916).

**Responsabilidad contractual.** Contractual liability. Generally, liability in contracts arises when the obligated person defaults (totally or partially) in the performance of his contractual obligations, or delay in such performance, and thus the damages due are only those directly related to the scope and object of the contract. (Barrios-Mannucci).

**Responsabilidad de terceros.** Third-party liability.

**Responsabilidad del agente.** Liability of agent. When the agent contracts under his own name, he will have a direct right and obligation with the parties he contracts with, without having to declare who is the principal, except in insurance cases. (Mex. Com. C., art.284).

**Responsabilidad del constructor.** Builder's liability. The liability attributed to the constructor of a "building" or a "work of certain magnitude" when its collapse is due to a defect in its original construction deserves particular analysis. This is what is called in many countries "Decennial Liability" since it generally stands for a period of ten years (five years in Brazil, Costa Rica, Chile, and Peru). This liability is contractual in nature, and may be considered as a warranty implied in law. (Barrios-Mannucci).

**Responsabilidad del constructor, terceros.** Builder's liability, third parties. As far as damages to third parties is concerned, the owner and constructor are considered joint and severally liable in torts. (Barrios-Mannucci).

**Responsabilidad del empleador.** Master's liability.

The basis of this liability is that its presumption, established in most of Latin American Civil Codes against the person in custody of an inanimate object that has caused harm to another person, can only be rebutted by proving *force majeure* or an act of God, or an external factor that cannot be imputed to him; it does not suffice to prove that he was not an fault, or that he cause of the harmful act has been ascertained. (Barrios-Mannucci).

**Reponsabilidad del empleador, defensas.** Master's liability, defenses. Three factors only may discharge the custodian of the thing: the fault of the victim, the act of a third party, or the occurrence of a fortuitous event. (Barrios-Mannucci).

**Responsabilidad del mandante.** Principal's liability. When the agent expressly contracts under the principal's name, the agent will not be liable, his actions being treated as those of a common mercantile agent, under the dispositions of the civil code. (Mex. Com. C., art.285).

**Responsabilidad extracontractual.** Tort liability. Most civil codes contain an article with a provision similar to the following language: "he who by his act, or by his negligence or imprudence causes damage to another, obliges himself to repair the damages caused." This provision constitutes the basis for the Civil Law of Torts. This liability applies to all relations between individuals who are not bound by contract. (Barrios-Mannucci).

**Responsabilidad objetiva, sin culpa.** Strict liability, no-fault liability.

**Responsabilidad por artículos y bienes.** Liability for articles and goods. The agent shall be liable for the articles and goods that he receives, under the terms and conditions, as stated in the delivery invoice, unless he certifies under two brokers, or two merchants in the absence of the former, that the products were defective or damaged. (Mex. Com. C., art.294).

**Responsabilizarse.** To take responsibility.

**Responsable.** Responsible, accountable, culpable, at fault, guilty, liable. Answerable.

**Resposabilidad patronal por accidentes.** Employer's liability for accidents. Employers are not absolved of responsibility even if: a) workers explicitly or implicitly assumed the occupational risks; b) an accident occurs due to the employee's own clumsiness or negligence; c) or an accident results from the carelessness or negligence of a fellow worker (Article FLL, 489). (Mex. Labor Law).

**Respuesta.** Answer, reaction, rebuttal, rejoinder, reply.

**Restablecer.** Reestablish, reinstall, reinstate, restore, replace.

**Restante, resto.** Remainder, balance, excess, remnant, residue, surplus.

**Restitución.** Restitution, compensation, refund, recovery, reimbursement, repair, repayment. Return, replacement.

**Restituciones.** Restitution. On termination of the contract either party may claim restitution of whatever it has supplied, provided that such party concurrently makes restitution of whatever it has received. If restitution in kind is not possible or appropriate allowance should be made in money whenever reasonable. (Unidroit, Prin., art. 7.3.6).

**Restituir.** To compensate, refund, recover, reimburse, repair, repay. To return, replace. To reinstate, restore.

**Restitutorio.** Restitutory.

**Restricción.** Restriction, caveat, condition, constraint, limitation, proviso, qualification.

**Restrictivo.** Restrictive, constraining, limiting.

**Restringir.** Restrain, ban, contain, prohibit, repress.

**Resuélvase.** Where it is ordered.

**Resultantes.** Whereas.

**Resumen.** Summary abridgement, abstract, delineation, digest, outline, synopsis.

**Resumiendo.** In summary.

**Resumir.** To summarize.

**Retasa.** New appraisal.

**Retención.** Withholding, holding, keeping. Retainer. Suppression. Conversion.

**Retener.** To withhold, hold, keep, retain. To suppress. To convert.

**Retentor.** Party who withholds, retains or suppresses. Converter.

**Retirar.** To withdraw. remove, take away. To recant, retract, revoke.

**Retirarse.** To retreat, recoil.

**Retiro.** Withdrawal, removal. Recantation, retraction. Retirement, pension.

**Retiro de la aceptación.** Withdrawal of acceptance. An acceptance may be withdrawn if the withdrawal reaches the offeror before of at the same time as the acceptance would have become effective. (Unidroit, Prin., art. 2.10).

**Retiro de la oferta.** Withdrawal of offer. (1) An offer becomes effective when it reaches the offeree. (2) An offer, even if it is irrevocable, may be withdrawn if the withdrawal reaches the offeree before or at the same time as the offer. (Unidroit, Prin., art. 2.3).

**Retorsión.** Counterstroke, reprisal, retaliation, retribution, vengeance.

**Retractación.** Retraction, rescission.

**Retractar.** To retract, rescind.

**Retracto.** Redemption. The right which by law, custom, or agreement a person has to annul a sale and himself take the thing sold to another for the same price. (Escriche, Diccionario de Legislación y Jurisprudencia). In order that an action for redemption may be allowed is necessary: 1) That it be instituted within nine days, counted from the date of the execution of the deed of sale. 2) That the price, if known, be deposited, and otherwise that security be furnished to do so as soon as the price becomes known. 3) That some evidence of the title upon which the redemption is based be attached to the complaint, even if not conclusive. (Sp. L. Civ. P. sec. 1616).

**Retracto convencional.** Redemption by agreement. Conventional redemption shall take place when the vendor reserves to himself the right to recover the thing sold. (Sp. Civ. C. sec. 1410, 1421).

**Retracto legal.** Redemption by operation of law. Legal redemption is the right to be subrogated, with the same conditions stipulated in the contract, in the place of the person who acquires a thing by purchase or in payment of a debt. (Sp. Civ. C., sec. 1424).

**Retraer.** To hold close.

**Retransferir.** To retransfer, to convey again.

**Retransmisión.** Retransmission.

**Retrasado.** Delayed, late, in arrears.

**Retraso.** Delay, arrearage.

**Retrato.** Mere agreement. Picture, description.

**Retribución.** Compensation, payment, recompense, remuneration, reward, salary, wages. Retribution. Punishment, vengeance.

**Retributivo.** Reciprocating. Advantageous, lucrative, profitable.

**Retribuyente.** Reciprocating.

**Retroactividad.** Retroactivity.

**Retroactividad de la leyes.** Retroactivity of laws. In the absence of contrary legislative expression, substantive laws apply prospectively only. Procedural and interpretative laws apply both prospectively and retroactively, unless there is a legislative expression to the contrary. (Lou. Civ. C., art. 6 and note).

**Retroactivo.** Retroactive.

**Retrocesión.** Retrocession. Buy back.

**Retrotraer.** To backdate.

**Retrovender.** To sell back.

**Retroventa.** Repurchase. Sell back to previous owner.

**Reunión.** Meeting, appointment, assembly, gathering.

**Reunión pacífica.** Peaceable assembly.

**Reunirse.** To meet, convene, converge, gather.

**Reválida.** Exam for a professional license in another country. Bar exam.

**Revalidación.** Authentication, corroboration, verification.

**Revalorizar, revaluar.** To reassess, reappraise. To correct prices, to mark up.

**Revalúo.** Revaluation.

**Revelar.** To reveal, disclose, discover, evince, expose.

**Reventa.** Resale, repurchase.

**Rever.** To reconsider, reexamine, retry, review. To countermand, quash, revoke.

**Reversión.** Reversión. Regression. Reversal. Return.

**Reversión al Estado.** Escheat.

**Reverso.** Back of a page.

**Revertir.** To revert, regress, return.

**Reversible.** Invertible, transposable. Revertible.

**Revisable.** Reviewable. Subject to appeal.

**Revisador.** Inspector, controller.

**Revisar.** To examine, check, inspect, probe, scrutinize. To review on appeal. To retry.

**Revisión.** Remittance, remission, remittal. Forgiveness, pardon. Shipment, dispatch, lot. Review, exam, examination. Retrial.

**Revisión judicial.** Judicial review. Argentina and Mexico have constitutional provisions directly modeled on the U.S. Supremacy Clause. Brazil has a similar provision. Venezuela achieves the same result by denying to the states the power to do anything that does not conform to the Constitution and requiring that all exercise of public power conform to the Constitution. (Rosenn).

Judicial review. Latin American codes abound with procedural devices for securing review of judicial decisions, a legacy from a colonial past which demonstrated a distrust of inferior courts by permitting multiple appeals, with a final appeal to the king. Interlocutory appeals are frequently permitted. (L & D in LA).

**Revisión judicial federal, Argentina.** Federal judicial review, Argentina. In Argentina, the procedure for federal review of provincial court decisions resembles that of the U.S. In 1863, Argentina enacted a procedural law adopting the writ of error from the U.S. Judiciary Act of 1789. Decisions of provincial courts involving issues of federal or provincial law normally terminate in the provincial courts. (Rosenn).

**Revisión judicial federal, México.** Federal judicial review, Mexico. In Mexico, federal judicial control over state court decisions and state law is even more centralized. A clause in Article 14 of the Mexican Constitution provides: "In civil cases the final judgment shall be according to the letter of the law or the juridical interpretation of the law; in the absence of the latter, it shall be based upon general principles of law." Read literally, this clause would appear to establish a constitutional right to have all decisions made correctly, and that is precisely the interpretation that the Mexican Supreme Court has given to it. Consequently, the Mexican federal courts routinely review state court decisions in which the only federal question is whether the state court correctly interpreted or applied state law. (Rosenn).

**Revisor.** Inspector, controller. Accountant, auditor.

**Revista.** Magazine, bulletin.

**Revista jurídica.** Law journal, law review.

**Revocabilidad.** Revocability.

**Revocable.** Revocable, reviewable, subject to appeal.

**Revocación.** Revocation, annulment, cancellation, rescission, repeal.

**Revocación de donación.** Revocation of donation. Donations *inter vivos* are liable to be revoked or dissolved on account of the following causes: 1) The ingratitude of the donee; 2) The nonfulfillment of the eventual conditions, which suspend their consummation; 3) The nonperformance of the conditions imposed on the donee; 4) The legal or conventional return of the thing donated. (Lou. Civ. C. art. 1559).

**Revocación de la oferta.** Revocation of offer. Until a contract is concluded an offer may be revoked if the revocation reaches the offeree before it has dispatched an acceptance. (Unidroit, Prin., art. 2.4).

**Revocación por ingratitud.** Revocation for ingratitude. Revocation on account of ingratitude can take place only in the three following cases: 1) If the donee has attempted to take the life of the donor; 2) If he has been guilty towards him of cruel treatment, crimes or grievous injuries; 3) If he has refused him food when in distress. (Lou. Civ. C. art. 1560).

**Revocación por testamento posterior.** Revocation by a later will. A revocation made in a posterior testament has its entire effect, even though this new act remains without execution, either through the incapacity of the person instituted, or of the legatee, or through his refusal to accept it, provided it is regular as to its form. (Lou. Civ. C. art. 1694).

**Revocar.** To revoke, abrogate, annul, rescind, repeal, quash, vacate.

**Revocatoria.** Revocation, annulment, rescission.

**Revocatorio.** Revocatory, canceling.

**Revolución.** Revolution, coup, insurgence, insurrection, rebellion, revolt, riot, subversion, uprising.

**Revolucionario.** Revolutionary, insurgent, subversive.

**Revuelta.** Coup, riot.

**Rey.** King, majesty, monarch, sovereign.

**Rezago.** Waste, refuse, salvage.

**Ribazos.** Moats, sloping banks.

**Ribereño.** Riperian owner, tenant or settle.

**Riesgo.** Uncertainty, danger, hazard, jeopardy, menace, risk, threat.

**Riesgo de la calle, doctrina de.** Street risks doctrine. In order to determine the compensability of an accident under the provisions of the Workermen's Accident

Compensation Act, the doctrine of street risks establishes that, when the nature of the work demands the worker's constant presence on the public thoroughfare thereby exposing him to the ordinary street risks with greater frequency, an accident sustained by such person on the public thoroughfare is compensable if his presence thereat is due to his employment, provided there is causal nexus between the work and the accident. (Gallart, Manager v. Industrial Commission, 87 PRR 16 (1962)).

**Riesgo profesional.** Professional liability. Owners of the businesses are responsible for accidents in the workplace and ailments by the workers suffered because or under the exercise of the work or profession that they perform; likewise, the business owners must pay indemnification correspondingly, according to what has happened, such as death, temporary or permanent incapacity to work. This liability shall exist even if the business owners obtains contract labor. (Mex. Civ. C., art.1935).

**Riesgos de trabajo.** Occupational safety. Title IX of the FLL (Articles 472 to 515) deals with occupational safety and health. It creates a system that places the entire responsibility on the employer for compensating workers affected by occupational hazards, both in terms of in-kind benefits that must be provided to workers as well as monetary compensation in the event that a hazard results in incapacitation or death of the worker. (Mex. Labor Law).

**Riguroso.** Stern, demanding, firm, harsh, rigorous, strict, severe, tough.

**Rito.** Rite, formality, procedure.

**Robar.** To rob, burglarize, snatch, steal, take.

**Robo.** Burglary, larceny, robbery, stealing, theft, thievery.

**Robo a mano armada.** Armed robbery.

**Robo con escalo.** Burglary with breaking an entry.

**Robo de cantidades menores.** Petty larceny.

**Robo de cantidades mayores.** Grand larceny.

**Rogatorio.** Rogatory.

**Rollo.** Roll. List, roster. Dossier, file, record.

**Romanista.** Romanist, civilian, continental.

**Romper.** To break. To breach, infringe, violate. To divide, separate.

**Rompimiento.** Break, breach, trespass, violation.

**Rotura.** Breaking, hole.

**Rúbrica.** Line drawn under a signature as part thereof.

**Rubricado.** Book that has been officially stamped and signed.

**Rubricar.** To give official value to commercial books by signing and stamping them.

**Rubro.** Line of business. Items, title.

**Rueda.** Session, turn. Wheel.

**Ruego.** Prayer, petition, request.

**Rumor.** Rumor, gossip, hearsay.

**Ruptura.** Breaking, e.g. of a contract.

**Rural.** Rural.

**Rutina.** Routine.

# S

**S.A.** Corporation.

**S.A. de C.V.** Corporation of variable capital (*de capital variable*).

**S.C.** Limited partnership.

**S.R.L.** Limited-liability company.

**Saber y entender.** Knowledge and information.

**Sabotaje.** Sabotage, damage caused by insiders.

**Saboteador.** Saboteur.

**Sabotear.** To sabotage, undermine.

**Sacar.** To take, make, receive.

**Sacerdote.** Priest, cleric, clergyman, pastor, preacher, reverend.

**Sacerdotes y otros ministros del evangelio.** Ordained priests and other ministers of the gospel.

**Sádico.** Sadist.

**Sadismo.** Sadism.

**Sala.** Court's main room. Division of the Appeal's court.

**Salariado.** Worker, employee, jobber. Person receiving a salary.

**Salario.** Salary, compensation, earnings, pay, wages.

**Salario mínimo.** Minimum salary. The minimum salary is the lowest minimum cash payment that a worker may receive for services rendered in a given work period (FLL, Article 90).

**Salario, sueldo.** Salary. Salaries may be established (FLL, Article 83) on the basis of a unit of time (day, week, biweekly, or month); a unit of work (piece-rate); a lump sum; in the form of commissions; or any other manner. Salaries must be adequate and never be below the minimum established by law (FLL, Article 85).

**Saldar.** To pay completely.

**Saldar una deuda.** Pay a debt.

**Saldo.** Balance. Remainder of a debt.

**Saldo vencido.** Balance due.

**Saldos.** Seconds, leftovers going on sale.

**Salir.** To go, exit, leave.

**Saliva.** Saliva, spit, spittle.

**Salteador.** Bandit, thief, robber.

**Saltear.** To rob. To disregard, omit, pass over.

**Salteo.** Robbery in a public place.

**Salvaguarda, salvaguardia.** Safeguard, precaution, protection.

**Salvamento.** Rescue operation, salvage.

**Salvar.** To save, salvage. To amend, correct, rectify. To overcome.

**Salvedad.** Exclusion, exception, particularity, reservation.

**Salvo.** Safe. Except for.

**Salvoconducto.** Safe conduct, pass.

**Sana crítica.** One of the methods for issuing judgment, based on a reasonable appreciation of all the facts and evidence presented.

**Sanar, sanear.** To remove encumberments or charges. To cure. To become healthy.

**Sanción.** Approval, authorization, endorsement, praise. Penalty, punishment, reproval.

**Sancionable.** Sanctionable.

**Sancionar.** To approve, authorize, endorse, praise. To penalize, punish, reprove.

**Sancionatorio.** Sanctioning.

**Saneado.** Cleared, improved.

**Saneamiento.** Warranty. By virtue of an implied warranty the vendor shall warrant to the vendee: 1) The legal and peaceful possession of the thing sold. 2) That there are no hidden faults or defects therein. (Sp. Civ. C., sec. 1377).

Improvement by removing vices, defects or encumbrances.

**Saneamiento en caso de evicción.** Eviction. Eviction shall take place when by a final judgment, and by virtue of a right prior to the sale, the vendee is deprived of the whole or of a part of the thing purchased. The vendor shall be liable for the eviction even though no stipulation has been included in the contract on the subject. (Sp. Civ. C., sec. 1378).

**Saneamiento o garantía.** Warranty or surety. For the purposes of the Civil Code the two traditional forms of the obligation of warranty—designated as surety in foreign law and in the doctrine—consist: 1) in the obligation of the vendor to warrant the peaceful possession of the thing sold; and 2) in the obligation to give a warranty against the hidden faults or defects it may have. (Ferrer v. General Motors Corp., 100 PRR 244 (1971)).

**Saneamiento por los defectos o gravámenes ocultos de la cosa vendida.** Warranty for hidden defects or burden of the thing sold. The vendor is bound to give a warranty against hidden defects which the thing sold may have should they render it unfit for the use to which it was destined. (Sp. Civ. C., sec. 1387).

**Sanear.** To remove encumbrances. To rectify error or mistakes. To render back to the original state.

**Sangre.** Blood.

**Sangre fría.** Balance, calmness, poise.

**Sanidad.** Health, hygiene, sanitation.

**Sano juicio.** Sound of mind, sane.

**Sano y salvo.** Safe and sound.

**Santa Sede.** Holy See.

**Santo y seña.** Password.

**Saqueo.** Pillage, theft, storming and looting.

**Sargento.** Sergeant.

**Satisfacción.** Satisfaction, accord and satisfaction.

**Satisfacer.** To satisfy, to cancel an obligation, to pay a debt.

**Satisfecho.** Satisfied, canceled, paid.

**Se resuelve.** Be it resolved.

**Sección.** Section, article, paragraph. Department, division. Part, sector, segment.

**Secretaría.** Secretariat.

**Secretariado.** Secretariat, career as a secretary.

**Secretarial.** Secretarial.

**Secretario.** Secretary, court clerk.

**Secretario de despacho.** Member of the cabinet.

**Secretario de hacienda.** Secretary of the treasury.

**Secreto.** Secret, concealed, undisclosed.

**Secreto de estado.** State secret.

**Secreto profesional.** Professional secret.

**Sector.** Sector, area, district, region, zone. Part, segment, section.

**Secuela.** Remains, vestige. Remaining consequences of a trial.

**Secuencia en el cumplimiento.** Order of performance. To the extent that the performance of the parties can be rendered simultaneously, the parties are bound to render them simultaneously unless the circumstances indicate otherwise. (Unidroit, Prin., art. 6.1.4).

**Secuestrable.** Attachable. Non exempt property.

**Secuestrador.** Abductor, kidnapper. Receiver.

**Secuestrar.** To abduct, kidnap. To attach, seize.

**Secuestro.** Sequestration. A judicial deposit or sequestration takes place when an attachment or placing in security of property in litigation is ordered. (Sp. Civ. C., sec. 1687, 1688).
Abduction, kidnapping. Seizure, attachment.

**Secuestro convencional.** Conventional sequestration. Sequestration is a kind of deposit, which two or more persons, engaged in litigation about anything, make of the thing in contest to an indifferent person, who binds himself to restore it, when the issue is decided, to the party to whom it is adjudged to belong. (Lou. Civ. C. art. 2973).

**Secularización.** Passage from the church to the state.

**Secundario.** Secondary, inferior, subordinate. Ancillary, lateral.

**Sede.** Seat, central administration, headquarters, place of business.

**Sedición.** Sedition, coup, insurgency, insurrection, palace coup, rebellion, revolution, subversion, treason.

**Sedicioso.** Seditious, insurgent, subversive.

**Sediente.** Located, with headquarters in.

**Seducción.** Seduction, attraction, charm, lure, temptation.

**Seducir.** To seduce, attract, charm, tempt.

**Seductor.** Seducer.

**Seglar.** Layman.

**Segregación.** Segregation. Segregation is the act within the discretion and option of the owner of a property by which a parcel is separated from the main property to constitute a different property. (Mattei v. Registrar, 94 PRR 444 (1967)).

**Seguidores.** Followers.

**Seguir.** To follow, ensue. To succeed, supplant.

**Según.** Depending on. According to.

**Segunda instancia.** Procedure before the court of appeals.

**Segundas nupcias.** Second marriage.

**Segundo.** Second.

**Seguridad.** Safety, protection, security. Certainty, certitude. Confidence, assurance, conviction.

**Seguridad e higiene, obligación patronal.** Safety and health, employers' duty. Employers have the obligation to set up enterprises in accordance with the principles of worker safety and health, and to take necessary actions to ensure that contaminants do not exceed the maximum levels allowable under the regulations and instructions issued by competent authorities. (FLL, Article 132 XVI). (Mex. Labor Law).

**Seguridad social, beneficios.** Social security, benefits. Social security benefits may be in cash or in kind. Cash benefits take the form of transfer payments In the early stages of illness or incapacitation, depending on the medical condition and effects on work and pensions. (Mex. Labor Law).

**Seguridad social de los trabajadores.** Workers' social security. The social security system protects employees in matters of: a) occupational illness; b) maternity; c) old age; d) retirement, and survivor pensions for retired workers; and e) day care for insured employees. (Mex. Labor Law).

**Seguridad social, financiamiento.** Social security, financing. The social security system is financed from contributions by workers, employers, and the government. The contributions are based on salary levels. Workers earning the minimum salary do not make contributions, however. (Mex. Labor Law).

**Seguridad social, servicios generales.** Social security, general services. The social security system also provides services to non-workers. Examples include public information campaigns to promote health and hygiene, improve nutrition, encourage housing improvement, etc. (Mex. Labor Law).

**Seguro.** Insurance. Certain, confident, poised.

**Seguro contra accidentes.** Casualty insurance.

**Seguro de incapacidad física.** Disability insurance.

**Seguro de vida.** Life insurance.

**Seguro industrial.** Industrial insurance. Industrial insurance is a life insurance sold to workers, issued in small amounts, with premiums collected at frequent intervals— semi monthly or weekly—by an agent of the insurance company who calls at the door. (Rosario v. Atl. Southern Ins. Co. of P.R., 95 PRR 742 (1968)).

**Selección de jurados.** *Voir dire*, examination of jurors.

**Sellado.** Stamps, seals.

**Sellar.** To seal. To stamp.

**Sello.** Seal. Stamp.

**Sello de correos.** Postal stamp.

**Sello del juzgado.** Seal of the court.

**Semáforo.** Traffic light.

**Semanario.** Weekly publication.

**Semestral.** Publication appearing every six months.

**Seminario.** Seminar. Conference, meeting.

**Semovientes.** Livestock.

**Senado.** Senate.

**Senador.** Senator.

**Senda, sendero.** Path, course, way.

**Sentado.** Seated, filed, presented.

**Sentencia.** Decision. *Sentencias* (decisions), when they definitely decide the criminal question. Decisions shall be prepared subject to the following rules: They shall begin by stating the place at and date on which rendered; the facts which gave rise to the formation of the cause; the names and surnames of the private complainants, should there be any, and of the accused; the titles and nicknames by which they are known; their age, conjugal condition, nativity, domicile, trade or profession, and, in the absence thereof, all the other matters by which they may have figured in the cause, and also the name and surname of the justice *ponente*. (Sp. L. Crim. P., art. 141 and 142).

Judgments must be clear, precise, and congruent to the pleadings and other allegations duly advanced in the action, and shall contain the declarations required by the latter, deciding for or against the defendant all questions which have been the object of the arguments. If there should be several issues, the decisions pertaining to each shall be separately rendered. (Sp. L. Civ. P. sec. 358). Award, decision, ruling, sentence, verdict.

**Sentencia en rebeldía.** Judgment by default.

**Sentencia firme.** Final decision. Final judgment. A judgment becomes final when there is no ordinary or extraordinary remedy against the same, except review and discharge. (Sp. L. Crim. P., art. 141).

**Sentencia meramente declarativa.** Declaratory judgment.

**Sentencia sumaria.** Summary judgment.

**Sentenciador.** Judge, court.

**Sentenciar.** To issue a judgment.

**Sentencias extranjeras, Argentina.** Foreign judgments, Argentina. The Argentine Republic has a federal organization in which power is distributed between the federal government and twenty-two provinces. The recognition and enforcement procedures are governed by the law of the province where the judgment is sought to be enforced. Since the judgment enforcement rules of the various provinces are significantly similar, an analysis of the relevant provisions of the Code of Civil and Commercial Procedure for the Federal Capital is sufficiently representative. Argentine courts will grant recognition upon the mere verification that the judgment fulfills the requirements of article 517 of the Procedural Code. Enforcement, in contrast, requires an *exequatur* or confirmation procedure. (LA Laws & Inst.).

**Sentencias extranjeras, Chile.** Foreign judgments, Chile. The Chilean Code of Civil

Procedure requires an *exequatur* for both the recognition and the enforcement of foreign adjudications. Pursuant to the general rule of reciprocity set forth in Article 243 of the Code, foreign judgments must be accorded the same force in Chile that Chilean judgments are given in the State of origin. Therefore, Chilean courts will not enforce a foreign judgment when the courts in the State of origin do not enforce Chilean judgments. (Amado).

**Sentencias extranjeras, Chile, requisitos.** Foreign judgments, Chile, requirements. When reciprocity cannot be established, Chilean courts will still enforce the judgment if the following general requirements are met: (1) The judgment must be final according to the laws of the State of origin; (2) The judgment must not be adverse to the exclusive jurisdiction of Chilean courts; (3) The judgment must contain nothing contrary to substantive Chilean law; and (4) The defendant must have been personally notified of the complaint in the original action and given a fair opportunity to defend. (Amado).

**Sentencias extranjeras, Código Bustamante.** Foreign judgments, Bustamante Code. According to Article 423, a judgment rendered in one contracting state would have force in another if: (1) The court in the State of origin was competent to take cognizance of the matter and to pass judgment upon it, in accordance with the rules of this Code; (2) The parties have been summoned for the bW either personally or through their legal representatives; (3) The judgment does not conflict with the public policy of the country in which execution is sought; (4) The judgment is executory in the state in which it was rendered; (5) The judgment is oinciauy translated if the official language is different in the State addressed; (6) If the document in which the judgment is contained is authentic in the state from which it proceeds, and in the State addressed. (Amado).

**Sentencias extranjeras, México.** Foreign judgments, Mexico.

In addition to the reciprocity requirement, the federal rules require that the foreign adjudication meet the following conditions: (1) That the judgment is *res judicata* in the State of origin or no ordinary appeal or recourse be available to the defendant; (2) That the court in the State of origin had jurisdiction according to the rules of jurisdiction recognized in the international sphere which are compatible with Mexican Law; (3) That the defendant was personally served in order to guarantee the availability of a hearing and an opportunity to defend; (4) That the obligation being enforced is not contrary to Mexican public policy; (5) That the judgment does not result from an *in rem* action; (6) That the judgment does not result from an action which is subject to pending litigation between the same parties before a Mexican court; and (7) That the judgment fulfills all formal requisites to be regarded as authentic. (Mexican Federal Code of Civil Procedure, art. 571). (Amado).

**Sentencias extranjeras, Perú.** Foreign judgments, Peru. Peruvian law strictly adheres to the requirement of reciprocity, which is applied to deny enforcement of foreign adjudications both when the State of origin does not enforce Peruvian judgments—and when the courts of the State of origin engage in a revision au fond of Peruvian judgments. (Amado).

**Sentencias extranjeras, Venezuela.** Foreign judgments, Venezuela. Foreign judgments cannot be enforced in Venezuela or be given effect as *res judicata* unless granted *exequatur* by the Supreme Court. Occasionally, judgments rendered in matters of adoption, emancipation, and other cases may be granted *exequatur* by the lower courts. The state in which the judgment was rendered must be shown to grant execution to Venezuelan judgments without prior substantive review (reciprocity). (Venzuela, Código Procesal Civil, art. 851). (Amado).

**Sentido.** Sense, feeling, perception. Meaning, connotation, significance. Direction, guidance, orientation.

**Seña, anticipo.** Earnest money, down payment. But if the promise to sell has been made with the giving of earnest, each of the contracting parties is at liberty to recede from the promise; to wit: he who has given the earnest, by forfeiting it; and he who has

received it, by returning the double. (Lou. Civ. C. art. 2463).

**Señal.** Signal, gesture, warning. Sign, mark. Particular feature.

**Señalamiento de casos.** Assignment of cases.

**Señalar.** To indicate, to point out. To name, identify.

**Señalización.** Signalization.

**Señorío.** Ownership, property. Control, domain.

**Separable.** Separable, divisible.

**Separación.** Separation, divorce, estrangement.

**Separación de bienes.** Separation of property. In the absence of a specific declaration of the marriage contract, the separation of the property of the spouses during the marriage, shall not take place except by virtue of a judicial decree. (Sp. Civ. C., sec. 1342).

**Separación de cargos o de procesados.** Severance of charges or defendants.

**Separar.** To separate, detach, divide, segregate.

**Sépase.** Let it be known.

**Sepultura.** Sepulcher, crypt, grave, tomb.

**Sereno.** Watchman.

**Serio.** Serious, pensive, reflective. Believable, credible. Important, grave.

**Servicio.** Service. Assistance, help. Governmental department. Domestic servants.

**Servicio doméstico.** Domestic service. The contract to render domestic service is characterized by the personal and familiar nature of the services which are its object and by the ordinary living together which is presumed between its two members, called master and servant. (López Figueroa v. Valdes, 94 PRR 227 (1967)).

**Servicio secreto.** Secret service, state intelligence.

**Servidor.** Servant.

**Servidumbre.** Servitude. A servitude is a charge imposed upon an immovable for the benefit of another tenement belonging to a different owner. (Sp. Civ. C., sec. 536, 543). Easement. Domestic servants.

**Servidumbre afirmativa y negativa.** Affirmative and negative servitude. Predial servitudes are either affirmative or negative. Affirmative servitudes are those that give the right to the owner of the dominant estate to do a certain thing on the servient estate. Such are the servitudes of right of way, drain and support. Negative servitudes are those that impose on the owner of the servient estate the duty to abstain from doing something on his estate. Such are the servitudes of prohibition of building and of the use of an estate as a commercial or industrial establishment. (Lou. Civ. C. art. 706).

**Servidumbre aparente y no aparente.** Apparent and nonapparent servitude. Predial servitudes are either apparent or nonapparent. Apparent servitudes are those that are perceivable by exterior signs, works, or constructions; such as a roadway, a window in a common wall, or an aqueduct. Nonapparent servitudes are those that have no exterior sign of their existence; such as the prohibition of building on an estate or of building above a particular height. (Lou. Civ. C. art. 707).

**Servidumbre de abrevadero y de sacar agua.** Servitude for watering animals or drawing water. Compulsory servitudes for watering animals or drawing water may be imposed only for causes of public utility in favor of a town or hamlet (*caserío*), after payment of the proper indemnity. (12 LPRA sec. 761).

**Servidumbre de amarre de barcos de paso, embarcaciones.** Servitude for mooring or ferryboats, passing vessels and floating objects. Riparian estates are subject to a servitude for fastening or security the warps or cables necessary for the establishment of a ferryboat service, after indemnity for loss and damage, and also to permit temporary mooring, in extreme cases, of passing vessels or floating objects; also upon payment of indemnity. (12 LPRA sec. 779).

**Servidumbre de apoyo.** Servitude of support. The servitude of support is the right by which buildings or other constructions of the dominant estate are permitted to rest on a wall of the servient estate. (Lou. Civ. C. art. 700).

**Servidumbre de caminos de sirga.** Servitude for towpaths. Estates adjoining the banks of rivers which are navigable or down which logs or rafts may be floated are subject to a servitude for towpaths. The width thereof shall be one meter if a foot towpath, and two meters if a horse towpath. (12 LPRA sec. 771).

**Servidumbre de depósito de mercancías.** Servitude for deposit of merchandise. The riparian estates are also obliged to permit the deposit thereon of merchandise jettisoned and saved in case of accidents, shipwreck, or any other urgent necessity. (12 LPRA sec. 781).

**Servidumbre de depósito de objetos flotantes.** Servitude for deposit of floating objects for safety. If, in order to prevent floods from carrying away timber or objects floated down the river, it shall become necessary to remove and deposit them on the riparian estates, the owners of the latter shall not have the right to prevent it, and shall be entitled only to payment for loss and damage. (12 LPRA sec. 780).

**Servidumbre de desague de edificios.** Servitude of drainage of buildings. The owner of a building is obliged to construct his roofs or coverings in such manner that rainwater may fall on his own land or on the street or any public place, and not on the land of his neighbor. (Sp. Civ. C., sec. 593).

**Servidumbre de estribo de presa.** Servitude for dam abutments. A compulsory servitude for dam abutments may be imposed when the person who intends to build the dam is not the owner of the banks or ground upon which they are to be placed, and when the water to be taken thereby is destined to a public service or to one of the services of private interest. (12 LPRA sec. 751).

**Servidumbre de luces y vistas.** Servitude of light and views. No part-owner may, without the consent of the other, make in the party wall any window or opening whatever. The owner of a wall which is not a party wall, adjoining another's tenement, may make in it windows or openings to admit light, at the height of the ceiling joists or immediately under the ceiling, of the dimensions of thirty centimeters square, and, in any case, with an iron grate embedded in the wall and a wire screen. (Sp. Civ. C., sec. 587, 588).

**Servidumbre de luz.** Servitude of light. The servitude of light is the right by which the owner of the dominant estate is entitled to make openings in a common wall for the admission of light; this includes the right to prevent the neighbor from making an obstruction. (Lou. Civ. C. art. 703).

**Servidumbre de medianera.** Servitude of party walls and fences. The servitude of party walls and fences is presumed, unless there is a little or exterior sign or proof to the contrary: 1) In dividing walls of adjoining buildings, up to the point of common elevation. 2) In dividing walls of gardens or yards, situated in a town or in rural districts. 3) In fences, enclosures, and live hedges dividing rural tenements. (Sp. Civ. C., sec. 578, 579).

**Servidumbre de muro común.** Common wall servitude. A landowner who builds first may rest one-half of a partition wall on the land of his neighbor, provided that he uses solid masonry at least as high as the first story and that the width of the wall does not exceed eighteen inches, not including the plastering which may not be more that three inches in thickness. (Lou. Civ. C. art. 673).

**Servidumbre de parada o partidor.** Servitude for stop lock or sluice gates. Any person who, in order to irrigate or improve his estate shall find it necessary to construct stop locks or sluice gates in the irrigating ditch or canal through which he is to receive the water without annoyance to or diminishing the supply of other irrigators, may demand that the owners of the margins permit their construction, after paying for any loss or damage, including that caused by the new servitude. (12 LPRA sec. 754).

**Servidumbre de paso.** Servitude of passage. The servitude of passage is the right for the benefit of the dominant estate whereby persons, animals, or vehicles are permitted to pass through the servient estate. Unless the title provides otherwise, the extent of the right and the mode of its exercise shall be suitable for the kind of traffic necessary for the reasonable use of the dominant estate. (Lou. Civ. C. art. 705).

**Servidumbre de prohibición de luz.** Servitude of prohibition of light. The servitude of prohibition of light is the right of the owner of the dominant estate to prevent his neighbor from making an opening in his own wall for the admission of light or that limits him to certain lights only. (Lou. Civ. C. art. 704).

**Servidumbre de prohibición de vista.** Servitude of prohibition of view. The servitude of prohibition of view is the right of the owner of the dominant estate to prevent or limit openings of view on the servient estate. (Lou. Civ. C. art. 702).

**Servidumbre de tendido de redes y depósito de la pesca.** Servitude for spreading of nets and deposit of fish. The owners of the margins of rivers are obliged to permit fishermen to take out and spread their nets thereon, and to deposit temporarily the product of the catch, without trespassing upon the estate nor going beyond three meters from the edge of the river, unless the topography of the ground should require a greater width to be fixed in any case. (12 LPRA sec. 782).

**Servidumbre de vista.** Servitude of view. The servitude of view is the right by which the owner of the dominant estate enjoys a view; this includes the right to prevent the raising of constructions on the servient estate that would obstruct the view. (Lou. Civ. C. art. 701).

**Servidumbre en materia de aguas.** Servitude relating to water. Lower tenements are obliged to receive the waters which naturally and without the intervention of man descend from higher tenements, as well as the stone or earth which they carry with them. Neither may the owner of the lower tenement construct works preventing the servitudes nor the owner of the higher tenement works aggravating the same. (Sp. Civ. C., sec. 559, 560).

**Servidumbre forzosa de acueducto.** Compulsory aqueduct servitude. A compulsory aqueduct servitude may be imposed for the conveyance of waters intended for public service not requiring the condemnation of lands. (12 LPRA sec. 721).

**Servidumbre legal.** Legal servitude. A legal servitude is but a limitation of the property right imposed by the State for the public interest, which is governed by the provisions of the public or administrative law. (Borges v. Registrar, 91 PRR 106 (1964)).

**Servidumbre legal, objeto.** Legal servitude, object. The object of servitudes imposed by law is either public utility, or private interest. (Sp. Civ. C., sec. 556).

**Servidumbre natural de aguas.** Natural servitude for water. Lower tenements are obliged to receive the waters flowing thereon from higher tenements naturally and without the work of man, as well as the stones or earth which such waters carry with them in their course. (12 LPRA, sec. 701).

**Servidumbre personal.** Personal servitude. A personal servitude is a charge on a thing for the benefit of a person. There are three sorts of personal servitudes: usufruct, habitation, and rights of use. (Lou. Civ. C. art. 534).

**Servidumbre predial.** Predial servitude. A predial servitude is a charge on a servient estate for the benefit of a dominant estate. The two estates must belong to different owners. The definition indicates that predial servitudes are real rights burdening immovables that the creation of these rights requires the existence of two distinct immovables belonging to different owners and that these rights are for the benefit of an immovable rather than a person. (Lou. Civ. C. art. 646 and notes).

**Servidumbre predial, clases.** Predial servitude, kinds. Predial servitudes may be natural, legal, and voluntary or conventional. Natural servitudes arise from the natural situation of estates; legal servitudes are imposed by law; and voluntary or conventional servitudes are established by juridical act, prescription, or destination of the owner. (Lou. Civ. C. art. 654 and art. 699).

**Servidumbre predial, derecho de paso.** Predial servitude, right of passage. The owner of an estate that has no access to a public road may claim a right of passage over neighboring property to the nearest public road. He is bound to indemnify his neighbor for the damage he may occasion. (Lou. Civ. C. art. 690).

**Servidumbre predial legal.** Legal predial servitude. Legal servitudes are limitations on ownership established by law for the benefit of the general public or for the benefit of particular persons. The owner is bound to keep his buildings in repair so that neither their fall nor that of any part of their materials may cause damage to a neighbor or to a passer-by. He is answerable for damages caused by his neglect to do so.

**Servidumbre predial natural.** Natural predial servitude. An estate situated below is bound to receive the surface waters that flow naturally from an estate situated above unless an act of man has created the flow. (Lou. Civ. C. art. 655).

**Servidumbre voluntaria.** Voluntary servitude. Every owner of an estate has a right to charge it with all the servitudes he may deem fit, and in the manner and form he may consider as best, provided he does not violate the laws or public order. (Sp. Civ. C., sec. 601).

**Servir.** To serve. To be useful or helpful.

**Sesión.** Session, meeting, round, sitting, term.

**Sesionar.** To deliberate, to hold a session.

**Sesos.** Brains, brain, intellect, mind.

**Seudónimo, pseudónimo.** Pseudonym, alias, nickname, penname.

**Sevicia.** Unnecessary and excessive cruelty.

**Sexual.** Sexual.

**Sicario.** Professional murderer.

**Sicopatía, psicopatía.** Psychopathy.

**Sicosis, psicosis.** Psychosis.

**Siempre.** Always, forever, perpetually. Consistently, invariably. Routinely.

**Siglas.** Abbreviation, initials.

**Signatario.** Signer, signatory. Maker.

**Signo.** Sign, brand, mark.

**Signo aparente.** Apparent sign. The apparent sign mentioned in the Civil Code for the establishment of a servitude should be established by the property owner and should be permanent, not variable, nor accidental. (Goenaga v. O'Neill, 85 PRR 162 (1962)).

**Signo notarial.** Notarial mark or signature.

**Siguiente.** Next, ensuing, following, successive. Contiguous, neighboring.

**Silencio.** Silence, calm, peace, tranquility.

**Silla.** Chair, bench, stand.

**Simbólico.** Symbolic, representative.

**Simple.** Simple, plain, single.

**Simulación.** Simulation, fabrication, sham. A contract is a simulation when, by mutual agreement, it does not express the true intent of the parties. If the true intent of the parties is expressed in a separate writing, that writing is a counterletter. (Lou. Civ. C. art. 2025).

**Simulación absoluta.** Total simulation. A simulation is absolute when the parties intend that their contract shall produce no effects between them. That simulation, therefore, can have no effects between the parties. (Lou. Civ. C. art. 2026).

**Simulación absoluta contractual.** Contractual absolute simulation. In the field of contracts the assumption of absolute contractual simulation occurs when the contraction parties seek the apparent configuration of a feigned or nonexistent act. (Hérnandez v. Sec. of the Treas., 86 PRR, 12 (1962)).

**Simulación relativa.** Relative simulation. A simulation is relative when the parties intend that their contract shall produce effects between them though different from those recited in their contract. (Lou. Civ. C. art. 2027).

**Simulación relativa contractual.** Contractual relative simulation. In the field of contracts, the concept contractual relative simulation occurs when the contracting parties execute an apparent juridical business which concealed a real transaction and which the contracting parties wish to withdraw from the curiosity or indiscretion of third parties, which feigned or simulated transaction requires the existence of a licit consideration. (Hernandez v. Sec. of the Treasury, 86 PRR 12 (1962)).

**Simuladamente.** Surreptitiously.

**Simulado.** Simulated, fabricated, sham.

**Simular.** To simulate, fabricate, fake. To copy, imitate.

**Sin.** Without.

**Sin blancos.** Leaving no blank spaces.

**Sin cumplimentar.** Unexecuted, breached, unfulfilled.

**Sin efecto.** Inoperative, ineffective.

**Sin efecto ni valor.** Null and void.

**Sin gastos.** Without cost.

**Sin lugar.** Overruled, denied.

**Sin lugar a dudas.** Beyond reasonable doubt.

**Sin menoscabo.** Without affecting.

**Sin responsabilidad.** Without recourse.

**Sin ulterior recurso.** Without further remedy.

**Sinalagmático.** Synallagmatic, mutual, reciprocal.

**Sinarquismo.** Right-wing extremism.

**Sinarquista.** Fascist.

**Sindicado.** Accused, charged.

**Sindicalismo.** Syndicalism.

**Sindicalizar.** To join the unions, to unionize.

**Sindicar.** To accuse, charge. To consolidate, merge. To organize.

**Sindicato.** Trade union. In Mexico, article 356 of the Federal Labor Law defines a union as "the association of workers or employers for the study, advancement, and defense of their respective interests." (Comparison of Labor law).

**Sindicato, disolución.** Union, dissolution. A union cannot be dissolved or suspended nor its registration canceled by administrative decision (FLL, Article 370).

**Sindicatos, clasificación.** Unions, classification. Some unions, especially the larger ones, are divided into sections representing specific groups of workers, work areas, specialties, etc. These sections do not have, as a general rule, their own legal standing and in collective matters must act through the board of directors of the principal union. (Comparison of Labor Law).

**Sindicatos, estatutos.** Unions, by-laws. In Mexico, union by-laws must address a series of requirements (FLL, Article 371), including the name of the union, its address, its objectives, the time period for which it is established, conditions for membership, obligations and rights of the members, causes and procedures for expulsion, disciplinary measures, procedures for holding meetings, procedures for the election of a board of directors, regulations regarding the management of the assets of the union, form of payment and amount of union fees, dates for presentation of financial statements, rules for liquidating union assets, other regulations approved by the membership. (Comparison of Labor Law).

**Sindicatos, registro.** Unions, registration. In Mexico, to gain official recognition, unions must register with the Secretariat of Labor and Social Welfare in cases where the Federal Government has jurisdiction, and with the local Conciliation and Arbitration Board in cases of local jurisdiction. (Comparison of Labor Law).

**Sindicatura.** Receivership, trusteeship.

**Síndico.** Receiver, trustee. Representative of shareholders in a corporation.

**Sinecura.** Sinecure.

**Singular.** Singular. Unique.

**Siniestro.** Fire, accident, disaster.

**Sinopsis.** Synopsis, outline.

**Sinrazón.** Injustice, abuse, baseless act, unfairness.

**Siquiatra, psiquiatra.** Psychiatrist.

**Sirga.** Towing of barges.

**Sirviente.** Servant.

**Sirvientes, domésticos.** Domestic servants. Servants or domestics are those who receive wages, and stay in the house of the person paying and employing them for his service or that of his family; such are valets, footmen, cooks, butlers, and others who reside in the house. (Lou. Civ. C. art. 3205).

**Sismoterapia.** Seismotherapy.

**Sistema.** System, organization, structure.

**Sistema de acumulación.** Accrual method of accounting. In the accrual method system all income and expenses are reported when incurred, regardless of the date they are received or paid. (Ramos Hermanos v. Secretary of the Treasury, 89 PRR 541 (1963)).

**Sistema federal, México.** Federal system, Mexico. Each state of Mexico has a complete legislative, administrative and judicial system. However, it has to be conceded that legal research at the state level is difficult, especially from a distance. (Pratter).

**Sitial.** Place of honor and respect. Podium.

**Sitiar.** To siege, storm. To blockade. To surround.

**Situación.** Situation. Event, incident, occurrence. Circumstance, predicament, state. Place, position.

**Situar.** To situate. To discover, find, place, spot.

**So pena.** Subpoena, under penalty of.

**Soberanía.** Sovereignty, autonomy, independence, self determination, self rule.

**Soberano.** Sovereign, king, monarch, ruler.

**Sobornador.** Briber, suborner.

**Sobornar.** To bribe, buy off, corrupt, suborn.

**Soborno.** Bribe, graft, payoff, payola.

**Sobre.** Envelope.

**Sobreasegurado.** Overinsured.

**Sobrecapitalizar.** To overcapitalize, to build excessive reserves.

**Sobrecarga.** Overload. Additional tax or charge.

**Sobrecargos.** Supercargoes. Supercargoes shall discharge on board the vessel the administrative duties which the agent or shippers may have assigned them; they shall keep an account and registry of their transactions in a book which shall have the same conditions and requisites as required for the accounting book of the captain, and shall respect the latter in his duties as chief of the vessel.

**Sobregirar.** To overdraw, to be in the red, to bounce a check, to run out of funds.

**Sobregiro.** Overdraft.

**Sobreimposición.** Surtax, double taxing, multiple taxing.

**Sobreimpuesto.** Surtax, added tax.

**Sobreinterés.** Bonus interest points.

**Sobrelínea.** Interlineation.

**Sobrenombre.** Nickname, alias, also known as, a.k.a.

**Sobrentendido.** Implicit, implied, inferred, tacit, understood, unexpressed, unspoken.

**Sobrepasar.** To surpass, exceed, outdo, overtake, outstrip.

**Sobrepopulación.** Overpopulation.

**Sobresaliente.** Outstanding, excellent.

**Sobreseer.** To absolve, acquit, clear exonerate.

**Sobreseimiento.** Dismissal of proceedings. The dismissal of proceedings may be absolute or provisional, total or partial. If the dismissal of proceedings be partial, the institution of the oral trial with regard to the accused whom it may not favor shall be ordered. If it be total, the cause and exhibits whose owner is unknown shall be ordered filed after the taking of the steps necessary for the execution of what may have been ordered. (Sp. L. Crim. P., art. 634).

Absolution, acquittal, exoneration.

**Sobreseimiento libre.** Absolute dismissal. An absolute dismissal of proceedings shall lie: 1) Where there are no reasonable indications of the perpetration of the act which may have given rise to the institution of the cause. 2) When the act does not constitute a crime. 3) When the persons accused appear to be exempt from criminal liability as principals, accessories, or accomplices. (Sp. L. Crim. P., art. 637).

**Sobreseimiento provisional.** Provisional dismissal. A provisional dismissal of proceedings shall lie: 1) When the commission of the crime which may have given rise to the institution of the cause is not duly established. 2) If it shall appear from the sumario that a crime has been committed, and there are not sufficient grounds to accuse one or more specific persons as principals, accomplices, or accessories. (Sp. L. Crim. P., art. 641).

**Sobresello.** Raised seal, second seal.

**Sobresueldo.** Bonus, in addition to the normal salary.

**Sobretasa.** Surtax, surcharge.

**Sobreutilidad.** Earnings or profits beyond a certain mark.

**Sobreviniente.** Supervening, development or event that takes place at a later time.

**Sobreviviente.** Survivor, person who outlasts an accident or a group of people.

**Sobrevivir.** To survive, endure, outlast.

**Sobrina.** Niece.

**Sobrino.** Nephew.

**Social.** Social. Corporate.

**Sociedad.** Society. Community, people, population. Association, business entity, corporation, enterprise. Circle, club, group of people with a common aim.

**Sociedad accidental.** Joint venture.

**Sociedad anónima.** Corporation, stock company.

**Sociedad anónima, carácter mercantil.** Corporation, commercial character. The commercial character of a corporation depends upon the law provided in the articles of association; in the absence of such provision, upon the law of the place where the general meetings of shareholders are held, and in the absence thereof, the law of the place where the board of directors is normally located. (Bustamante C. art. 248).

**Sociedad cerrada.** Close corporation.

**Sociedad civil.** Association for a non business activity. Not-for-profit corporation. Civil partnership.

**Sociedad colectiva, en nombre colectivo.** General partnership.

**Sociedad colectiva o comanditaria, carácter mercantil.** Collective or silent partnership, commercial character. The commercial character of a collective or silent partnership is determined by the law to which the articles of partnership are subject, and in the absence thereof, by the law of the place where it has its commercial domicile. (Bustamante C. art. 247).

**Sociedad conjugal.** Community property.

**Sociedad de ahorro y préstamo.** Savings and loans association, S and L association.

**Sociedad de control.** Holding company.

**Sociedad de crédito.** Credit union.

**Sociedad de crédito inmobiliario.** Building and loan association, savings and loans association.

**Sociedad de economía mixta.** Enterprise where the state and private individuals hold an interest.

**Sociedad de familia.** Family corporation.

**Sociedad de gananciales.** Conjugal partnership. By virtue of the conjugal partnership the earning of profits indiscriminately obtained by either of the spouses during the marriage shall belong to the husband and the wife, share and share alike, upon the dissolution of the marriage. (Sp. Civ. C., sec. 1310, 1311, 1330). Community property.

**Sociedad de hecho.** Partnership in fact.

**Sociedad de responsabilidad limitada.** Limited partnership.

**Sociedad en comandita.** Limited partnership.

**Sociedad en comandita por acciones.** Joint-stock company.

**Sociedad en comandita simple.** Enterprise that combines general and limited partners.

**Sociedades mercantiles, personalidad jurídica.** Commercial partnership, juristic personality. Commercial partnerships duly constituted in a contracting State will enjoy the same juristic personality in the other contracting States except for the limitations of territorial law. (Bustamante C. art. 252).

**Sociedad minera.** Mining Company. A company legally capable, in accordance to the Law to hold mining concessions and survey activities.

**Sociedad por acciones.** Corporation.

**Sociedad vinculada.** Related enterprise.

**Societario.** Belonging to an enterprise.

**Socio.** Member, partner, share holder, associate.

**Socio accionista.** Partner who is a shareholder.

**Socio aparente.** Ostensible partner.

**Socio capitalista.** Limited partner.

**Socio colectivo.** General partner, managing partner.

**Socio comanditado.** General partner.

**Socio comanditario.** Silent partner, special partner.

**Socio general.** Member without any special attributes.

**Socio gerente, gestor, administrador.** Managing partner, manager.

**Socio solidario.** General partner.

**Socio vitalicio.** Member for life.

**Socorro.** Help, assistance, aid, cooperation.

**Sodomía.** Sodomy.

**Sofocación, sofocamiento.** Suffocation, asphyxiation, choking, smothering.

**Solar.** Tenement, acreage, land, lot, parcel, tract.

**Soldado.** Soldier, warrior.

**Solemne.** Solemn, ceremonious, formal.

**Solemnidad.** Solemnity, formality expressly required by law.

**Solemnizar.** To comply with all formalities required by law.

**Solicitante.** Movant, petitioner, applicant. Party who requests.

**Solicitud.** Petition, application, demand, request, prayer for relief, sulpplication. Form, blank. Solicitude, concern.

**Solicitud de autorización pública.** Application for public permission. Where the law of a State requires a public permission affecting the validity of the contract or its performance and neither that law nor the circumstances indicate otherwise (a) if only one party has its place of business in that State, that party shall take the measures necessary to obtain the permission; (b) in any other case the party whose performance requires permission shall take the necessary measures. (Unidroit, Prin., art. 6.1.14).

**Solidaria y mancomunadamente.** Joint and severally.

**Solidariamente.** Joint and severally.

**Solidaridad.** Solidarity, joint and several liability.

**Solidario.** Solidary, joint and several.

**Soltero.** Celibate, bachelor, unmarried. Spinster.

**Soltura.** Detachment, ease, facility, fluency.

**Solución de disputas.** Dispute resolution. The formal legal systems of Latin American countries are modern, developed institutional structures. Disputes are resolved by a hierarchical arrangement of courts on the basis of the wording and legislative history of legal norms, scholarly doctrine, opinions of distinguished jurists, and prior court decisions. (L & D in LA).

**Solutio indebiti (L).** Payment of what is not due.

**Solvencia.** Solvency. Affordability, having the means, wealth. Being up to the task.

**Solventar.** To pay, honor, settle.

**Solvente.** Solvent, able to pay. Dependable, reliable.

**Someter.** To submit, introduce, present.

**Someterse.** To submit oneself, to acquiesce, abide, comply, heed, observe.

**Sondeo.** Opinion poll, survey.

**Soñar.** To dream.

**Soplón.** Informant.

**Sordo.** Deaf.

**Sordomudo.** Deaf and dumb.

**Sorprender.** To surprise, amaze, astonish, astound, shock. To catch, capture, find.

**Sorpresa.** Surprise.

**Sorteo.** Lottery, drawing.

**Sosía.** Look alike.

**Sospecha.** Suspicion, distrust, doubt, reservation. Hunch, hypothesis, theory, idea, supposition.

**Sospechar.** To suspect, doubt, mistrust. To conjecture, speculate, surmise.

**Sospechoso.** Suspect (n), suspicious (adj).

**Sostén.** Support, livelihood, maintenance, sustenance.

**Sostén de familia.** Bread winner, person who supports a family.

**Sostener.** To sustain. To advocate, encourage, endorse, maintain, uphold. To support, assist, provide for a living, subsidize.

**Sostenible.** Sustainable, admissible, defensible, excusable, tenable, viable.

**Sostenimiento.** Support, backing. Adhering to an idea, policy or theory.

**SS.** The letters SS in a judicial document merely mean *scilicet*, that is, "to wit." (Ppl. v. Velez, 83 PR.R.R., 467 (1961).

**Status.** Status, level, social, position.

*Strictu sensu* **(L).** In a strict sense. This phrase is more general than legal since it does not have a specifically legal connotation.

**Subagente.** Sub-agent.

**Subalquilar.** To sublet, sublease.

**Subalquiler.** Sublet, sublease.

**Subalterno.** Assistant, employee. Person of lower rank, especially among the military. Ancillary, inferior, minor, subaltern, subordinate, subservient.

**Subarrendador.** Sublessor.

**Subarrendar.** To sublet, sublease.

**Subarrendatario.** Subtenant, sublessee.

**Subarriendo.** Sublet, sublease.

**Subasta.** Auction, judicial sale, public sale.

**Subasta pública.** Sale by auction. The sale by auction is that which takes place when the thing is offered publicly to be sold to whoever will give the highest price. (Lou. Civ. C. art. 2601).

**Subasta voluntaria judicial.** Voluntary judicial sale. Any person requesting that a judicial public sale be made shall, by presenting the proper documents therefor, prove the following: 1) That he has the legal capacity to make the proposed contract. 2) That he can dispose of the thing or object at public sale as proposed. (Sp. L. Civ. P. sec. 2047-2049).

**Subastador.** Auctioneer.

**Subastar.** To auction.

**Subcontratar.** To subcontract.

**Subcontratista.** Subcontractor.

**Subcontrato.** Subcontract.

**Subdirector.** Assistant director, deputy director, vice rector.

**Súbdito.** Subject, citizen, national. Serf, vassal.

**Subempleado.** Subservient.

**Subempleo.** Underemployment.

**Subida.** Augmentation, elevation, enlargement, raise, rise, upward trend.

**Subinquilino.** Subtenant, sublessee.

**Subjefe.** Assistant chief, deputy, vice director, vice president.

**Sublocación.** Sublease.

**Sublocador.** Sublessor.

**Sublocatorio.** Sublessee, subtenant.

**Submandatario.** Sub-agent.

**Suboficial.** Non-commissioned officer, petty officer.

**Subordinación.** Subordination, dependence, dependency, submission. Position of inferior rank that requires taking orders.

**Subordinado.** Subordinate, employee, person of lesser rank, person under order. Ancillary, residual, secondary, subservient, tangential.

**Subprefecto.** Subprefect, assistant prefect.

**Subprefectura.** Subprefecture.

**Subprocurador General.** Assistant attorney general.

**Subregistrador.** Assistant registrar.

**Subrepción.** Disloyal way of acting without other people's knowledge. Concealment, misrepresentation. Underhanded act.

**Subrepticio.** Subreptitious, concealed, in hiding, unnoticed.

**Subrogación.** Subrogation, transfer of rights. Subrogation is the substitution of one person to the rights of another. It may be conventional or legal. (Lou. Civ. C. art. 1825 and 1826).

**Subrogación convencional por el acreedor.** Conventional subrogation by the obligee. An obligee who receives performance from a third person may subrogate that person to the rights of the obligee, even without the obligor's consent. (Lou. Civ. C. art. 1827).

**Subrogación convencional por el deudor.** Conventional subrogation by the obligor. An obligor who pays a debt with money or other fungible things borrowed for that purpose may subrogate the lender to the rights of the obligee, even without the obligee's consent. (Lou. Civ. C. art. 1828).

**Subrogación por imperio de la ley.** Subrogation by operation of law. Subrogation takes place by operation of law: 1) In favor of an obligee who pays another obligee whose right is preferred to his because of a privilege, pledge, or mortgage; 2) In favor of a purchaser of movable or immovable property who uses the purchase money to pay creditors holding any privilege, pledge, or mortgage on the property. (Lou. Civ. C. art. 1829).

**Subrogante.** Person who transfers her rights.

**Subrogar.** To subrogate, to transfer one's rights.

**Subrogatorio.** Subrogating, passing from one head to another.

**Subrubro.** Subparagraph, subtitle. Detailed description of a particular aspect of a broader category.

**Subsanable.** Retrievable. Subject to improvement or rectification.

**Subsanar.** To amend, ameliorate, better, fix, improve, rectify, remedy, repair.

**Subscribir.** To subscribe. To sign, autograph, initial. To approve, endorse, support.

**Subsecretario.** Assistant secretary.

**Subsidiario.** Subsidiary, accessory, ancillary, residual, secondary, subordinate, supplementary, tangential.

**Subsidio.** Subsidy, allowance, annuity, financial aid, grant, *per diem*, scholarship, stipend.

**Substancial.** Substantial. Material, physical. Considerable, important, plentiful, substantive.

**Substanciar.** To substantiate, prove, show cause. To raise legal arguments or to offer evidence.

**Substantivo.** Substantive. Material, important, relevant.

**Substitución.** Substitution, change, replacement, subrogation, swap, switch. In lieu of.

**Substituido, substituto.** Substitute, agent, proxy, replacement, surrogate. Understudy.

**Substracción.** Subtraction. Unauthorized, taking, taking away, conversion, larceny, removal, theft, withdrawal.

**Substraer.** To subtract. To take illegally or without authorization. To remove unlawfully. To rob, steal.

**Subsuelo.** Subsoil, underground. Basement, cellar.

**Subteniente.** Second lieutenant.

**Subterfugio.** Subterfuge, artifice, chicanery, machination, maneuver, stratum, trick.

**Subtesorero.** Assistant treasurer.

**Subvención.** Subvention, allowance, annuity, financial aid, grant, pension, *per diem*, scholarship, stipend.

**Subvencionar.** To subsidize.

**Subversivo.** Subversive, dissident, guerrilla, revolutionary. Insurgent, seditious.

**Sucesión.** Succession, inheritance. Succession is the transmission of the rights and obligations of a deceased person to his heirs. Succession is granted either by the will of the man as expressed in a will or, in its absence by provision of law. (Sp. Civ. C., sec. 664a, 666).

Testamentary or probate proceedings. Estate, inheritance rights. Descendants, heirs. Chain of events, sequence.

**Sucesión bajo condición.** Succession subject to a condition. The conditions imposed upon heirs and legatees shall be governed by the rules established for conditional obligations in all that is not prescribed in this Article. (Sp. Civ. C., sec. 779, 780).

**Sucesión, Código Bustamante.** Succession, Bustamante Code. Successions, both intestate and testamentary, including the order of descent, the quantum of the rights of descent and the intrinsic validity of the provisions, shall be governed, except as hereinafter provided, by the personal law of the person from whom the rights are derived, whatever may be the nature of the estate and the place where it is found. (Bustamante C. arts. 144-145).

**Sucesión forzosa** Forced heirship. System where certain close relatives cannot be disinherited if not by a cause contemplated by the law.

**Sucesión, indignidad.** Succession, unworthiness. The following are disqualified to succeed by reason of unworthiness: 1) Parents who have abandoned their children or prostituted their daughters or made attempts against their chastity. 2) He who has been sentenced in a trial for having made attempts against the life of the testator, his spouse, descendants, or ascendants. (Sp. Civ. C., sec. 744, 745).

**Sucesión intestada, abintestato.** Intestate or legitimate succession. Legitimate succession takes place: 1) If a person dies without a will, or with a void will, or which may have lost its validity subsequently. 2) When the will does not contain the designation of heirship to all or part of the property, or does not dispose of all that belongs to the testator. In such case legitimate succession shall take place only with regard to the property of which the testator has not disposed. (Sp. Civ. C., sec. 886).

**Sucesión, la legítima.** Succession, legal portion. A legal portion is that part of the property which the testator cannot dispose of because the law has reserved it for specified heirs, called, on that account, heirs by force of law. (Sp. Civ. C., sec. 794, 795, 804, 805).

**Sucesión legítima.** Legitimate succession. Legitimate or lawful succession is that which the law has established in favor of the nearest relatives of the deceased. (Sp. Civ. C., sec. 666b).

**Sucesión, partición.** Succession, division. No heir shall be compelled to remain in possession of the inheritance without partition unless the testator expressly prohibits partition. (Sp. Civ. C., sec. 1018, 1035).

**Sucesión por causa de muerte.** Succession *mortis causa*. Succession is the transmission of the estate of the deceased to his successors. The successors thus have the right to take possession of the estate of the deceased after complying with applicable provisions of law.

There are two kinds of succession: testate and intestate. (Lou. Civ. C. art. 871 and art. 873).

**Sucesión, sustitución.** Succession, substitution. The testator may substitute one or more persons in the place of the heir or heirs designated in case they die before him or do not wish or can not accept the inheritance. (Sp. Civ. C., sec. 762).

**Sucesión testamentaria.** Testamentary succession. Testamentary succession is that which results from the institution of any heir or heirs contained in a will executed in accordance with law. (Sp. Civ. C., sec. 666(a)).

**Sucesión vacante.** Vacant succession. A succession is called vacant when no one claims it, or when all the heirs are unknown, or when all the known heirs to it have renounced it. (Lou. Civ. C. art. 1095).

**Sucesiones, Argentina.** Probate, Argentina. The right to succeed under Argentine law originates (in both testamentary [*testamantaria*] and intestate [*legítima*] successions) at the time of the decedent's death and at the place of his domicile. The right to succeed is governed by the law of this domicile whether the decedents are Argentine nationals or aliens, and jurisdiction over the estate belongs to the courts of this location. (LA Laws & Inst.).

**Sucesiones, Chile.** Probate, Chile. Chilean law follows the Roman principle of unity of succession. This means that, as a general rule, all questions concerning the estate are subject to a single law. This rule is strictly observed in Chile. For example, the courts have held succession subject to Chilean law (Article 71) if a married woman dies abroad while her husband is domiciled in Chile. (LA Laws & Inst.).

**Sucesiones, Venezuela.** Probate, Venezuela. The order of intestate succession to real and personal property located in Venezuela is determined by internal law, regardless of the nationality or domicile of the decedent. (LA Laws & Inst.).

**Sucesivo.** Successive, consecutive, continuous, ensuing, following, next, progressive, serial, succeeding.

**Suceso.** Circumstance, event, happening, incident, occurrence.

**Sucesor.** Successor. Successor is, generally speaking, the person who takes the place of another. (Lou. Civ. C. art. 3556).

Appointee, assignee, beneficiary, devisee, heir.

**Sucesor en derechos.** Successor in interest.

**Sucesor particular.** Particular successor. The particular successor succeeds only to the rights appertaining to the thing which is sold, ceded or bequeathed to him. (Lou. Civ. C. art. 3556).

**Sucesor universal.** Universal successor. The *universal* successor represents the person of the deceased, and succeeds to all his rights and charges. (Lou. Civ. C. art. 3556).

**Sucesores hereditarios.** Hereditary successors. There are two kinds of successors corresponding to the two kinds of succession described in the preceding articles: Testate successors, also called legatees. Intestate successors, also called legatees. Intestate successors, also called heirs. (Lou. Civ. C. art. 876, 877, 878, and 879).

**Sucesorio.** Related to inheritance or probate proceedings.

**Sucumbir.** To succumb. To capitulate, give in, surrender. To fall prey of something. To die, perish.

**Sucursal.** Agency, branch, division, office.

**Sudor.** Perspiration, sweat.

**Suegra.** Mother-in-law.

**Suegro.** Father-in-law.

**Sueldo.** Salary, compensation, earnings, income, pay, revenue, stipend, wages, remuneration.

**Suelo.** Ground, area, earth, land, soil, terrain, territory.

**Suero.** Serum.

**Suerte.** Chance, destiny, fate, fortune, luck.

**Suficiente.** Sufficient, adequate, enough.

**Sufragio.** Suffrage. Ballot, ticket, vote. Election, poll.

**Sufragista.** Vote, elector.

**Sufrimiento.** Suffering, ache, anguish, grief, pain, sorrow, woe.

**Suicida.** Person who attempts or commits suicide.

**Suicidarse.** To commit suicide.

**Suicidio.** Suicide, self-destruction.

**Sujetarse.** To abide by, comply with, follow.

**Sujeto.** A person, individual, man, subject, bound to, liable.

**Suma cierta.** Sum certain.

**Sumariamente.** Summarily, expeditely, immediately, without delay.

**Sumariante.** Judge in charge of clarifying the facts in a criminal case. Official who investigates charges brought in administrative proceedings.

**Sumariar.** To start administrative proceedings aginst someone. To accuse. To press criminal charges.

**Sumario.** Criminal dossier. The criminal dossier (*sumario*) consists of the proceedings had to prepare the trial and for the purpose of verifying and evidencing the commission of crimes with all the circumstances which may have a bearing upon their classification and the guilty of the delinquents, securing their persons and the pecuniary liabilities of the same. (Sp. L. Crim. P., art. 299). Record in an administrative or criminal proceedings. Summary outline, synopsis, summary.

**Suministrar.** To administer, allot, dispense, distribute, furnish, give, supply. Inflict.

**Suministro.** Allotment, cargo, consignment, dispatch, distribution, shipment, supply.

**Sumisión.** Submission, acceptance, acquiescence, compliance, conformity, deference, obedience, subjection.

**Sumisión arbitral.** Submission to arbitrate. A submission is a covenant by which persons who have a lawsuit or difference with one another, name arbitrators to decide the matter and bind themselves reciprocally to perform what shall be arbitrated. (Lou. Civ. C. art. 3099).

**Sumisión, Código Bustamante**. Submission, Bustamante Code. The submission can be made only to a judge having ordinary jurisdiction to take cognizance of a similar class of cases in the same degree. (Bustamante C. art. 319).

**Sumisión expresa o tácita**. Express or implied submission. By express submission shall be understood the submission made by the interested parties in clearly and conclusively renouncing their own court and unmistakably designating the judge to whom they submit themselves. Implied submission shall be understood to have been made by the plaintiff from the fact of applying to the judge in filing the complaint, and by the defendant from the fact of his having, after entering his appearance in the suit, filed any plea unless it is for the purpose of denying jurisdiction. (Bustamante Code, Articles 321-323).

**Suntuario.** Sumptuary, expensive, extravagant.

**Superavit.** Excess, surplus, glut, overabundance, over production, oversupply.

**Superchería.** Ignorant belief, old wives' tale, superstition.

**Superioridad.** Superiority, ascendancy, dominance, preeminence, primacy, supremacy. Person or body of a higher rank.

**Supernumerario.** Employee appointed exceeding the budget.

**Superpotencia.** Superpower.

**Supérstite.** Surviving.

**Superutilidad.** Gains or profits exceeding a certain mark.

**Superviniente, sobreviniente.** Supervening, development or event that takes place at a later time.

**Supervisación laboral.** Labor supervision. The term "supervision" must be understood as referring to the employee having to submit to the instructions given by his employer and having to fulfill them. (Mex. Labor Law).

**Supervisión.** Supervision, administration, care, control, direction, management, surveillance.

**Supervivencia.** Survival, remaining alive.

**Superviviente.** Survivor, person who outlasts an accident or a group of other people.

**Suplemental, suplementario, supletorio.** Supplementary, accessory, additional, ancillary, auxiliary, complementary, extra, spare, supplemental.

**Suplemento.** Supplement, additional, extra.

**Suplente.** Deputy, substitute. Acting, interim, provisional, temporary.

**Súplica, suplicación.** Prayer for relief, supplication. Petition, plea, prayer, request.

**Suplicante.** Supplicant, petitioner.

**Suplicar.** To ask, beg, entreat, petition, plead, pray, request, supplication.

**Suplicatoria, suplicatorio.** Letter rogatory.

**Suplicatorio, exhorto, carta-orden.** Letter requisitorial, letter rogatory. Judges and courts shall aid each other in the execution of all proceedings necessary and ordered in civil actions. (Sp. L. Civ. P. sec. 284, 285).

**Suposición.** Supposition, assumption, belief, conjecture, guess, hypothesis, hunch, inference, postulate, speculation, suspicion, surmise, theory.

**Supradicho.** Above, above mentioned, referred.

**Suprema Corte de Justicia.** Supreme Court.

**Suprema instancia.** Highest authority, Supreme Court, last instance.

**Suprimible.** Suppressible, dispensable, expendable, needless, nonessential, redundant, secondary, superfluous, unnecessary.

**Suprimir.** To suppress, abate, annul, cancel, nullify, repeal, rescind, reverse, revoke, void. To contain, quell, repress, restrain, subdue. To cross out, delete, erase.

**Supuesto.** Assumption, conjecture, hypothesis, supposition, postulate, theory.

**Surtir.** To supply, dispense, equip, give, furnish, outfit, provide.

**Surtir efecto.** Cause a consequence, trigger a result, be effective, binding.

**Suscribiente.** Undersigned. Adherent, follower, supporter.

**Suscripción.** Subscription, adherence, membership.

**Suscripto.** Undersigned. Member, listed.

**Suscriptor.** Subscriber.

**Susodicho.** Aforesaid, referred.

**Suspender.** To suspend. Defer, delay, discontinue, interrupt, postpone, put of, shelve, stay, table. To adjourn, suspend.

**Suspensión.** Suspension, adjournment, cessation, continual, deferment, interruption, stay.

**Suspensión colectiva de la relación de trabajo.** Collective suspension of the work relationship. Collective suspensions of a collective barganing agreement contrato colectivo de trabajo or a law-contract contrato-ley, may come about because of certain problems affecting the employer which reflect on the workers. These are matters which temporarily make it Impossible, or difficult, to continue to operate an enterprise or establishment. (Mex. Labor Law).

**Suspensión de ejecución.** Stay of execution.

**Suspensión de pagos.** Suspension of payments. A merchant who, possessing sufficient property to cover all his debts, foresees the impossibility of meeting them when they fall due, may suspend payments, which shall be declared by the judge of first instance of his domicile in view of his declaration. (Sp. Com. C., sec. 870).

**Suspensión de procedimientos.** Stay of proceedings.

**Suspensión temporal colectiva.** Collective temporary suspension. In addition to individual causes for suspension of a work relationship between an employer and an individual, there may also be "collective" causes for suspension of a work relationship between an employer and a group of employees. (Mex. Labor Law).

**Suspensión temporal individual.** Individual temporary suspension. The FLL does permit a temporary suspension of the work relationship. In the case of a suspension, the obligation to work and to pay salary may temporarily cease without a permanent termination of the work relationship under certain circumstances. (Mex. Labor Law).

**Suspensivo.** Suspensive. Producing effects at a later date.

**Suspenso.** Suspense, expectation, uncertainty.

**Sustancia corrosiva.** Corrosive substance. A substance that causes visible destruction of, or irreversible alterations in living tissue by chemical action at the site of contact.

**Sustancia irritante.** Irritant substance. A substance which is not corrosive, but which causes a reversible inflammatory effect on living tissue by chemical action at the site of contact.

**Sustanciación de una causa.** Having a hearing and rendering a decision.

**Sustancial.** Substantial, important, material, tangible, significant.

**Sustanciar.** To substantiate. To offer evidence. To decide on the merits.

**Sustantivo.** Substantive, material.

**Sustentable.** Sustainable, defensible, tenable, viable. Admissible, excusable, justifiable.

**Sustento.** Support, livelihood, living, maintenance, necessaries, subsistence.

**Sustitución.** Substitution, replacement, representation, subrogation.

**Sustituto.** Substitute, proxy, surrogate.

**Sustracción.** Subtraction. Removal, withdrawal. Conversion, larceny, robbery, theft.

# T

**Taberna.** Tavern, inn.

**Tabla.** Chart, blueprint, diagram, graph, index, list, schedule, table.

**Tabla de concordancia.** Table showing the correspondence.

**Tablero.** Board, panel, switchboard.

**Tacha.** Impeachment. Challenge, confrontation. Elimination, removal. Deletion.

**Tachable.** Impeachable.

**Tachadura.** Blot, cancellation, crossing out, challenge, deletion.

**Tachar.** To impeach. To challenge, confront. To eliminate, remove. To delete, cross out.

**Tachas de los testigos.** Challenge of witnesses. Each party may challenge the witnesses of the opposite party for any of the following reasons: 1) Relationship of the witness to the party for whom he appears by consanguinity or affinity within the fourth civil degree. 2) That the witness at the time of giving his testimony is a partner, employee, or servant of the party for whom he appears. (Sp. L. Civ. P. sec. 659).

**Tachón.** Crossing out, deletion, erasure.

**Tácita reconducción.** Implied renewal. Automatic extension of a contract.

**Tácito.** Tacit. Tacit is said of that which, although not expressed, is understood from the nature of the thing, or from the provision of the law. (Louisiana Civ. Code, art. 3556).

Assumed, constructive, implicit, implied, understood.

**Talión.** Talion, private justice, retaliation, revenge, vengeance.

**Talla.** Size, content, magnitude.

**Talón.** Stub, receipt.

**Talonario.** Stub book.

**También conocido como.** Also known as, aka. Alias.

**Tanteo.** Analysis, audit, examination, inspection, investigation, scrutiny.

**Tanteo y retracto.** Redemption. The right which certain persons have to acquire for themselves a thing purchased by another, rescinding the sale already made.

**Taquígrafo.** Stenographer, court reporter.

**Tarde.** Behind, belated, deferred, late, postponed.

**Tarifa.** Tariff, charge, duty, levy, tax, toll. Price, price list, schedule of payment.

**Tarificación.** Systematization of payments according to a schedule.

**Tarjeta.** Card, visit card, index card.

**Tasa.** Tax charged by the state in reference to precise services actually provided to each contributor.

**Tasable.** Taxable. Appraisable.

**Tasación.** Appraisal, appraisement, assessment, estimate, valuation, price.

**Tasación de costas.** Taxation of costs. When there is an adjudication of costs, as soon as it becomes final, payment shall be enforced by compulsory process, after their taxation, if the party adjudged to pay the same should not have done so before the opposite party requests said taxation. (Sp. L. Crim. P. sec. 420).

**Tasador.** Appraiser, assessor. Land surveyor.

**Tasar.** To appraise, assess, estimate, evaluate, value.

**Tatuaje.** Tattoo.

**Tatuar.** To tattoo.

**Taxativo.** Taxative. Limited to the examples or cases specifically stated.

**Técnico.** Technician, authority, expert, master, professional, specialist. A technical.

**Tela de juicio, en.** Argued about, challenged, questioned.

**Temario.** Agenda, calendar, docket. Program, schedule. List of topics to be considered.

**Temerario.** Reckless, careless, thoughtless. Exorbitant, groundless, wild.

**Temeridad.** Recklessness, audacity, gall, temerity.

**Temeridad y malicia.** Abuse of process, malicious prosecution, wrongful proceedings. Frivolous litigation.

**Temperamento.** Intention, objective, state of mind, spirit. Character.

**Tendencia.** Tendency, bent, bias, drift, inclination, leaning, penchant, preference, proclivity, propensity, trend. Particular school of thought within a political party or group.

**Tenedor.** Holder. Occupant.

**Tenedor de buena fe.** Holder in due course.

**Tenedor legítimo.** Holder in due course.

**Tenencia.** Tenancy, holding, tenure. Immediate control over a thing, holding, occupancy.

**Tener.** To control, have, hold, own, possess, retain.

**Tenida.** Conference, debate.

**Teniente.** Lieutenant. Second lowest rank as an army officer.

**Teniente coronel.** Lieutenant colonel.

**Tentativa.** Attempt. Whoever starts to execute a criminal act through conduct aimed directly at consummation, but fails to achieve it for reasons beyond his control, will be sentenced to not less than two-thirds of the minimum nor more than two-thirds of the maximum provided for the corresponding crime. (Standard Penal C. for Latine America, sec. 39).
Effort, endeavor, try.

**Teoría de la imprevisión.** Theory that allows rescission of a contract due to changed circumstances that turn it into excessively burdensome for one of the parties.

**Terapia.** Therapy, medication, medicine, prescription, treatment.

**Tercer hipotecario.** Third-party mortgagee. Assuming that the cause of nullity of the summary foreclosure proceeding of a property is not clearly recorded in the Registry of Property, the condition of third-party mortgagee of the vendee of said property should be judged considering the true date of the acquisitive title—which is the one which can oppose claims of other persons who did not take part in the contract—and the right should always be grounded on a recorded title, it being improper to consider for such purpose the previous date on which a meeting of minds on the object and consideration between the vendee and the vendor of the property took place. (Fuentes v. Heirs of Fuentes, 94 PRR 561 (1967)).

**Tercer poseedor.** Third party possessor.

**Tercería.** Intervention. Interventions must be based either upon the ownership of the property attached as belonging to the attachment debtor, or upon the right of the third person to recover his credit before the execution creditors is reimbursed. (Sp. L. Civ. P. sec. 1530).
Third party practice. Impleader, interpleader.

**Tercerista.** Impleaded or interpleaded party. Third party defendant.

**Tercero.** Third party. One who has no interest in the case at bar. Party not connected with a previous transaction.

**Tercero beneficiado.** Third party beneficiary. A contracting party may stipulate a benefit for a third person called a third party beneficiary. (Lousiana Civ. Code, art. 1979).

**Terceros.** Third persons. With respect to a contract or judgment, third persons are all who are not parties to it. In case of failure, third persons are, particularly, those creditors of the debtor who contracted with him without knowledge of the rights which he had transferred to another. (Louisiana Civ. Code, art. 3556).

**Terceros procesales.** Third-party practice.

**Terciar.** To mediate. To try to.

**Terminable.** Finite, limited, temporary.

**Terminación.** Termination.

**Terminación de contrato.** Termination of contrat. A party may terminate the contract where the failure of the other party to perform an obligation under the contract amounts to a fundamental nonperformance. (Unidroit, Prin., art. 7.3.1).

**Terminación de contrato, efectos.** Termination of contract, effects. Termination of the contract releases both parties from their obligation to effect and to receive future performance. (Unidroit, Prin., art. 7.3.5).

**Terminación de la relación de trabajo.** Termination of work relationship. An employer who wishes to terminate a work relationship without just cause may not do so without incurring a liability. If the employee enjoys job permanence, there is no legal way for the employer to dismiss the employee, since the Constitution (Article 123-A, Section XXII) and the FLL establish the right to mandatory reinstatement. (Mex. Labor Law).

**Término.** Term, date, deadline, duration, extent of time, period, span, time.

**Término de deliberación.** Term for deliberating. By term for deliberating is understood the time given to the beneficiary heir, to examine if it be for his interest to accept or reject the succession which has fallen to him.

**Terrateniente.** Land owner, farmer.

**Terremoto.** Earthquake, quake.

**Terreno.** Terrain, area, earth, land, plot, soil, territory, tract.

**Terreno baldío.** An empty plot of land.

**Terreno edificado.** Plot of land with a building or buildings.

**Terreno saneado.** Reclaimed land.

**Territorial.** Territorial, domestic, internal, local, national.

**Territorio.** Territory, area, belt, district, expanse, precinct, region, tract, sector, zone.

**Terror.** Terror, apprehension, dread, fear, fright, horror, panic.

**Terrorismo.** Terrorism.

**Tesorería.** Treasury.

**Tesorero.** Treasurer.

**Tesoro.** Treasure, riches, wealth. Public treasury.

**Testado.** Testate, with a valid will, included in a will.

**Testador.** Testator, deceased, decedent.

**Testadora.** Testatrix.

**Testadura.** Crossing out, blotch, cancellation, erasure.

**Testaferro.** Concealed agent, man of straw, middle man, name giver. Proxy, substitute. Dummy, feigned intermediary, name lender.

**Testamentaría.** Testamentary or probate proceedings. Testamentary proceedings may be voluntary or necessary. They are voluntary when instituted by a legitimate party. Testamentary proceedings shall be called necessary in the cases wherein the judge must institute them *ex officio*. (Sp. L. Civ. P., sec.

1035, 1036, 1040). See *Sucesión testamentaria.*

**Testamentario.** Related to a will.

**Testamento abierto.** Open will. A will is open whenever the testator expresses his last will in the presence of the persons who must authenticate the act, they being informed of its provisions. An open will must be executed before a notary. (Sp. Civ. C., sec. 687, 703).

Nuncupative will.

**Testamento cerrado.** Closed will. A will is closed when the testator, without revealing his last will, declares that it is contained in the instrument which he presents to the persons who are to authenticate the act. (Sp. Civ. C., sec. 688).

**Testamento, clases.** Will, kinds. Wills may be ordinary or special. Ordinary wills may be holographic, open, or closed. (Sp. Civ. C., sec. 684).

**Testamento conjunto o mancomunado.** Joint or reciprocal will.

**Testamento, disposición de última voluntad.** Will, testament. The act by which a person disposes of all his property or of a part of it, to take effect after his death, is called a will. A will is absolutely a personal act. The making of it, either wholly or partially, can not be left to the discretion of a third person, nor can it be made through a trustee or agent. (Sp. Civ. C., sec. 675, 678).

**Testamento, disposiciones contradictorias.** Will, contradictory dispositions. When a person had ordered two things, which are contradictory, that which is last written is presumed to be the will of the testator, in which he has persevered, and a derogation to what has before been written to the contrary. (Louisiana Civ. Code, art. 1723).

**Testamento especial.** Special will. Military and maritime wills and those executed in foreign countries are considered special. (Sp. Civ. C., sec. 685).

**Testamento hológrafo.** Holographic will.
Holographic wills may be executed only by persons of full age. In order that such will be valid, it shall be written in its entirety and signed by the testator, who shall state the year, month and day in which it is executed. If it contains words erased, corrected or

interlined, the testator shall make a note thereof under his signature. (Sp. Civ. C., sec. 696).

**Testamento marítimo.** Will made at sea. Testament, made during a voyage at sea may be received by the captain or master, in presence of three witnesses taken by preference from among the passengers; in default of passengers from among the crew. This testament, is subject to no other formality than that of being reduced to writing, and being signed by the testator, if he can write, by him who receives it, and by those in whose presence it is received. (Louisiana Civ. Code, art. 1601, 1603, and 1604).

**Testamento militar.** Military will. The wills of persons employed in armies in the field, or in a military expedition, may be received by a commissioned officer, in presence of two witnesses. (Louisiana Civ. Code, art. 1597, 1598, 1599, 1560).

**Testamento místico o cerrado.** Mystic or closed will. The mystic or secret testament, otherwise called the closed testament, is made in the following manner: The testator must sign his dispositions, whether he has written them himself or has caused them to be written by another person. The paper serving as their envelope must be closed and sealed. The testator shall present it thus closed and sealed. (Louisiana Civ. Code, art. 1584).

**Testamento nuncupativo por acto privado.** Nuncupative will by private act. A nuncupative testament, under private signature, must be written by the testator himself, or by any other person from his dictation, or even by one of the witnesses, in presence of five witnesses residing in the place where the will is received, or of seven witnesses residing out of that place. (Lousiana Civ. Code. art. 1581).

**Testamento nuncupativo por acto público.** Nuncupative will by public act. The nuncupative testaments by public act must be received by a notary public, in presence of three witnesses residing in the place where the will is executed, or of five witnesses not residing in the place. (Louisiana Civ. Code. art. 1578).

**Testamento, revocación.** Will, revocation. All testamentary provisions are essentially revocable, even though the testator should state in the will his wish or resolution not to revoke them. All clauses annulling future provisions shall be considered as not existing, as well as those in which the testator may order that the revocation of the will should not be valid unless made with certain words or marks. (Sp. Civ. C., sec. 727, 729).

**Testar.** To will, to make a will. To cross out, cancel.

**Testificador.** Witness, person who testifies.

**Testificante.** Attesting, certifying.

**Testificar.** To witness, attest, aver, certify, corroborate, demonstrate, determine, prove, show, testify.

**Testigo.** Witness, attestant, bystander.

**Testigo de cargo.** Prosecutor witness.

**Testigo idóneo.** Credible believable, unimpeachable witness.

**Testigos, comparecencia.** Witnesses, appearance. All persons residing within Spanish territory, whether natives or foreigners, who are not prevented therefrom, shall be obligated to appear upon a judicial citation to declare all they may know in the matter upon which they may be questioned, provided they be cited with the formalities prescribed by law. (Sp. L. Crim. P., sec. 410).

**Testigos, interrogatorio.** Witnesses, interrogation. The judge shall permit the witness to narrate without interruption the facts upon which he testifies, and shall only require of him such supplementary explanations as may tend to dissipate obscure or contradictory statements. Therupon he shall put such questions to him as he may deem proper to elucidate the facts. (Sp. L. Crim. P. sec. 436, 437).

**Testimonial.** Testimonial, related to witnesses.

**Testimoniar.** To witness, attest, aver, certify, corroborate, demonstrate, determine, prove, show, testify.

**Testimonio.** Mandate. A mandate shall be employed for the purpose of ordering the issue of certificates or transcripts or the fulfillment of any judicial proceeding, the execution of which is imposed upon registrars of property, notaries, assistants, or subordinate officials of inferior or superior courts, and member of the judicial police who are under the orders of the same. (Sp. L. Crim. P., art. 186).

Testimony, attestation, certification, corroboration, deposition. Certified transcript.

**Testimonio.** Testimony. Even if the judge is present at a hearing in which a witness is testifying, which is not always the case, he or she may pay little attention to the testimony until the written version is studied. Transcription of oral testimony often takes place simultaneously with its delivery; the clerk types while the witness talks. The parties submit their requests for examination of witnesses, along with the questions to be asked on direct or "cross examination," to the judge and opposing counsel prior to the hearing. (L & D in LA).

Conformed copy.

**Testimonio pericial.** Expert testimony.

**Texto.** Text, body, content, reading. Manual, primer.

**Tía.** Aunt.

**Tiempo.** Time, duration, moment, period, term. Weather.

**Tiempo de espera.** Waiting period.

**Tiempo hábil.** Timely, in good time.

**Tiempo inmemorial.** Time immemorial.

**Tiempo indeterminado.** Indefinite Duration. The duration of a work relationship is presumed to be indefinite. Only by exception are labor corttracts entered irtto by job or for a finite period of time (FLL, Article 35). (Mex. Labor Law).

**Tienda.** Store, business, market, mart, outlet, shop.

**Tierra.** Land, acreage, ground, plot, property, real estate, tract. Earth, soil.

**Tierra ribereña.** Riparian land.

**Tierras baldías.** Wasteland.

**Tierras labrantías.** Arable lands.

**Tierras mojadas.** Wetlands. The area of transition between terrestrial and aquatic systems which constitute areas of temporary or permanent inundation, whether or not subject to tidal influence, such as swamps, marshes, and bogs, whose limits are indicated by the type of hydrophilic vegetation present on a seasonal or permanent basis; areas of predominantly hydric soils; and lacustric areas or those where soils are constantly wet due to the natural discharge of aquifers.

**Timador.** Cheat, con man, swindler, trickster.

**Timar.** To cheat, con, swindle, trick.

**Timba.** Place where illegal gambling is held.

**Timbrar.** To stamp.

**Timbre.** Stamp.

**Timo.** Cheating, conning, fraud, misrepresentation, swindle, trick.

**Timonel.** First mate.

**Tinterillo.** Shyster, bureaucrat, paper pusher.

**Tío.** Uncle.

**Tipo.** Type, category, class, kind. Rate of exchange. Normal, ordinary, routine, standard.

**Tipo de descuento.** Rate of discount.

**Tirada.** Number of copies printed, circulation of a newspaper.

**Tirador.** Maker of a bill of exchange. Shooter.

**Tiro.** Shot, blast, blaze, discharge, fire.

**Titulación.** Vestment of title. Obtaining a university degree.

**Titulado.** University graduate, licensed, admitted to practice.

**Titular.** Owner, proprietor. Holder of a job.

**Titularidad.** Ownership, right, title.

**Título.** Title. For registration purposes, according to the preceding section, the word title is defined as the contents of the public document or documents on which the person in whose name registration is made bases his right, and which serve as evidence, by themselves or with other complementary documents, or by proven compliance with the rules. (PR Mort. Law 1979 sec. 43).

Cause, ground, interest, right. Certificate, deed. Degree, diploma. Name, caption, heading.

**Título de crédito.** Commercial paper.

**Título de la deuda pública.** Government bond.

**Título de nobleza.** Title of nobility.

**Título ejecutivo.** Lawsuit on a commercial paper. It is characterizes by the fact that only a few exceptions and defenses are allowed, for instance, forgery of signature.

**Título gratuito.** Without consideration. Gratuitously, gratis.

**Título oneroso.** Valuable consideration. The title is said to be onerous when it is acquired for a certain price, or under certain charges. It is the contrary of the lucrative title. (Louisiana Civ. Code art. 3556).

**Título traslativo de dominio.** Conveyance of ownership.

**Títulos.** Certificates, deeds, documents, securities.

**Títulos de acciones.** Certificates of shares. In all certificates of shares, either payable to order or to bearer, there shall always be entered the sum which has been paid on account of its par value or that they are fully paid. (Sp. Com. C., sec. 164).

**Títulos inscritos, efecto en cuanto a terceros.** Registered titles, effectiveness for third parties. Registered titles shall become effective for third parties from the date of their registration. (PR Mort. Law 1979 sec. 53).

**Tocante.** Concerning, pertaining.

**Tocar.** To touch. To concern. To reach.

**Todo daño debe indemnizarse.** All injury must be compensated. This is the rule for compensation in torts. It is also the title preceding article 1645 of the Guatemalan Civil Code, which states: "Every person who causes injury or detriment to another, whether intentionally, by negligently or imprudently, is obligated to redress such wrong, except if able to prove that the damage or injury was caused by the victim's fault or inexcusable negligence."

**Toga.** Gown, cloak, toga.

**Togado.** Attorney, barrister, judge.

**Tolerancia.** Tolerance, acceptance, endurance, equanimity, forbearance, resignation, patience, stamina.

**Toma.** Appropriation, capture, taking, seizure.

**Toma de posesión.** Entering in possession.

**Toma de razón.** Recordation, registration.

**Tomador.** Person who receives a commercial paper, payee.

**Tomar juramento.** Taking of an oath.

**Tomar en estudio.** To take under advisement.

**Tonelaje.** Tonnage, capacity, cargo, room, space, volume, weight.

**Tonto.** Fool, dimwit, dunce, idiot, imbecile, simpleton.

**Torcer.** To twist, bend, curve, turn. To distort, falsify, misrepresent.

**Tormento.** Torment, torture. Agony, suffering.

**Torpeza.** Turpitude. Unskilled or awkward action. Clumsiness.

**Torticero.** Tortious, wrongful. Unfair, unlawful.

**Total.** Total, grand total. Absolute, unrestricted, whole.

**Totalmente.** Totally, completely, fully.

**Toxicomanía.** Toxicomania, alcoholism, drug addiction.

**Toxicómano.** Drug addict, drug dependent, junky.

**Traba.** Moment when summons are received or when an attachment order is recorded. Point in time when a suit or an order therefrom becomes operational.

**Trabajador.** Worker, agent, assistant, employee, laborer, representative, servant, workman.

**Trabajador a domicilio.** Homeworker.

**Trabajador de confianza.** Employees in positions of Trust. These are individuals who carry out management, monitoring, oversight, and auditing functions in a business or enterprise, whenever these functions are of a general nature. (Mex. Labor Law).

**Trabajador, empleado.** Worker, employee. This is the individual who provides personal supervised labor to another person or legal entity. (Mex. Labor Law).

**Trabajadores, atención médica.** Workers, medical treatment. Article 487 of the FLL provides that workers who suffer from occupational hazards are entitled to medical and surgical attention, including: physical rehabilitation, hospftalization should the case so require, medications and medical supplies, prosthetic and orthopedic devices as needed, and monetary compensation as established by law. (Mex. Labor Law).

**Trabajar.** To work, labor, toil.

**Trabajo.** Work, labor, job, occupation, toil. Livelihood, trade or art. Chore, task.

**Trabajo de las mujeres.** Work by women. Currently, the regulation of women's work exclusively relates to the protection of the woman during the periods of pregnancy and nursing of children. During pregnancy and nursing, women may not engage in (FLL, Article 166) unhealthy or dangerous jobs. (Mex. Labor Law).

**Trabajo de los menores.** Work of minors. Workers between the ages of fourteen and sixteen are considered to be minors. The work of minors is subject to the strict oversight of the Labor Inspection Office (*Oficina de Inspeción del Trabajo*), an entity within the Secretariat of Labor and Social Welfare (FLL, Article 173). (Mex. Labor Law).

**Trabajo forzado.** Hard labor, forced labor.

**Trabajo por pieza.** Piecework.

**Trabajo prohibido a menores.** Work illegal for minors. Workers under 16 years of age are prohibited from engaging in the following types of work (FLL, Article 175): a) work in places where alcoholic beverages are sold for immediate consumption; b) work that may affect their morals or good habits, c) itinerant work. (Mex. Labor Law).

**Tracalería.** Swindle, deceit, deception, hoax, fraud, misrepresentation.

**Tracalero.** Swindler, crook, cheat.

**Tradición.** Delivery. The tradition or delivery in the transferring of the thing sold into the power and possession of the buyer. (Louisiana Civ. Code, art. 2477).

Transfer of possession. Cultural background, historical legacy, custom.

**Tradición de bienes muebles.** Delivery of movables. The tradition or delivery of movable effects takes place either by their real tradition, or by the delivery of the keys of the buildings in which they are kept; or even by the bare consent of the parties; if the things can not be transported at the time of sale, or if the purchaser had them already in his possession under another title. (Louisiana Civ. Code, art. 2478).

**Tradición de inmuebles.** Delivery of immovables. The law considers the tradition or delivery of immovables, as always accompanying the public, act, which transfers the property. (Louisiana Civ. Code, art. 2479).

**Tradicional.** Traditional.

**Traducción.** Translation, interpretation.

**Traducir.** To translate, interpret. To explain, decipher, decode.

**Traductor público.** Sworn translator, court interpreter.

**Traficante.** Dealer, drug peddler or pusher.

**Tráfico.** Traffic. Trade, illicit trade. Commute, transport.

**Traición.** Treason, betrayal, disloyalty, infidelity, sedition, treachery.

**Traicionar.** To betray, beguile, deceive, doublecross, mislead, trick.

**Traidor.** Traitor, betrayer, fifth column.

**Tramitación.** Red tape, bureaucratic requirements, paper pushing. General dealings with the public administration, such as filing documents, obtaining signatures and processing documents in general.

**Tramitar.** To do the paper work.

**Tramite judicial.** Procedural step, court proceeding.

**Trámite.** Red tape, paper work.

**Trampa, trampería.** Trap, ambush, scheme, ruse, trick.

**Trampeador, tramposo.** Cheat, crook, trickster.

**Trampear.** To cheat, trick. To incur in disloyal behavior.

**Transacción.** Settlement, compromise. A compromise is a contract by which each of the parties in interest, by giving, promising, or retaining something, avoids the filing of a suit or terminates one that has already been instituted. (Sp. Civ. C., sec. 1711).

Transaction, accord and satisfaction, bargain business. Contract, deal. Out-of-court settlement, private arrangement.

**Transacción, compromiso.** Transaction, compromise. A transaction or compromise is an agreement between two or more persons, who, for preventing or putting an end to a lawsuit, adjust their differences by mutual consent, in the manner which they agree on, and which every one of them prefers to the hope of gaining, balanced by the danger of losing. (Louisiana Civ. Code, art. 3071).

**Transaccional.** Transactional, consensual, contractual.

**Transacciones fraudulentas.** Fraudulent transactions.

Transactions made in accordance with the law but that seek a result prohibited by the law, or contrary to the legal system, shall be considered of a fraudulent nature and shall not escape the applicability of the prohibition they tried to avoid. (Sp. Civ. C., sec. 6 (4)).

**Transar.** To settle. To meet midway.

**Transcribir.** To transcribe, copy, transliterate. To plaigarize.

**Transcripción.** Transcription, copy transliteration, transcript.

**Transcurso.** Affluxion of time, unfolding of an event. Period.

**Transeunte.** Commuter, passenger, pedestrian, traveller, walker.

**Transferencia.** Transference, conveyance, bequest, reassignment, relocation, removal.

**Transferencia de créditos no endosables.** Transfer of nonnegotiable credits. Commercial credits, which are not negotiable nor payable to the bearer, may be transferred by the creditor without requiring the consent of the debtor, it being sufficient that the transfer be communicated to him. (Sp. Com. C., sec. 347).

**Transferencia de obligaciones.** Delegation of duties.

**Transferente.** Transferor, assignor, conveyor.

**Transferibilidad.** Transferability, assignability, conveyability, heritability.

**Transferible.** Transferable, assignable, conveyable, heritable.

**Transferir.** To transfer, assign, bequeath, devise, convey.

**Transgredir.** To transgress, breach, trespass, violate.

**Transgresión.** Transgression, breach, tort, trespass, violation.

**Transgresor.** Transgressor, infringer, tortfeasor, trespasser, wrongdoer.

**Transigible.** That can be settled out of court.

**Transigir.** To compromise, settle. To meet midway. To yield partially.

**Transitivo.** Transitive.

**Tránsito.** Transit, movement of goods and people, traffic. Transportation between two points.

**Transitorio.** Transitory, temporary. Impermanent, momentary. Transient, passing.

**Translación.** Transfer, passage of title.

**Translimitación.** Trespass. Excessive behavior.

**Transmisibilidad.** Transmissibility, contagiousness. Transferability, assignability.

**Transmisible.** Transmissible, contagious. Transferable, conveyable, sellable.

**Transmisión de créditos y demás derechos incorporales.** Assignment of credits and other incorporeal rights. The assignment of a credit, right, or action shall produce no effect against a third person but from the time the date is considered fixed. (Sp. Civ. C., sec. 1429).

**Transmitente.** Transferor, conveyor, grantor. Person who transfers.

**Transmitir.** To transmit. Communicate, inform, notify, tell. Convey, deliver, transport.

**Transporte.** Transport, transportation. Movement of goods or people.

**Transporte fluvial.** Transportation by river.

**Traslado.** Notification of a judicial order or of a certain development in a case.

**Traslativo.** Related to a transfer of title.

**Traspapelado.** Lost among many other papers.

**Traspasar.** To cross a particular limit, to exceed a certain point of reference. To transfer ownership or other rights.

**Traspaso.** Transfer of title or of other rights. Delivery, placing in possession.

**Traspaso de título.** Passing of title.

**Trastorno.** Setback, disadvantage, mishap, worry.

**Trasvestismo.** Transvestism.

**Trata.** Illicit trade, traffic.

**Tratadista.** Scholar who writes treatises. Authority, expert.

**Tratado.** Treaty. International agreement, compact, pact or settlement.

**Tratados de Montevideo.** Montevideo treaties. These treaties, together with the Bustamante Code, constitute the other main body of private international law in Latin America. (LA Laws & Inst.).

**Tratos.** Dealings, practical arrangements, previous contacts.

**Trauma.** Trauma, shock, strong disturbance.

**Traumatismo.** Traumatism, serious injury.

**Tregua.** Truce, ceasefire.

**Treintañal.** Thirty year limitation period.

**Tren.** Train, engine, locomotive. Caravan.

**Triángulo.** Triangle. Relationship among three people.

**Tribuna.** Platform, dais, podium, rostrum, stage.

**Tribunal.** Tribunal, court, judge. Board, committee, panel.

**Tribunal *a quo*.** Lower court, from the point of view of the court of appeals.

**Tribunal *ad quem*.** Court of appeals.

**Tribunal colegiado.** Collegiate court.

**Tribunal de almirantazgo.** Admiralty court.

**Tribunal de alzada.** Court of higher rank, sitting on appeal.

**Tribunal inferior.** Court below.

**Tribunalicio.** Forensic, procedural, relating to courts.

**Tributable.** Assessable, taxable. Non exempt.

**Tributación.** Taxation.

**Tributante.** Tax payer.

**Tributar.** To pay taxes. To pay tribute or homage.

**Tributario.** Related to the state's tax power.

**Tributo.** Tribute. Tax, assessment, contribution.

**Trifulca.** Disorderly fight, brawl, melee.

**Trimestre natural.** Calendar quarter.

**Trimestre.** Quarter.

**Tríplica.** Plaintiff's answer to defendant's rejoinder.

**Triplicado.** Triplicate, in three copies.

**Triplicar.** To answer defendant's rejoinder.

**Tripulación.** Crew. Personal or staff on board a plane or ship.

**Tripulante.** Staff of a ship or plane.

**Tronar.** To cause a commotion or great impact.

**Tronco.** Family line traced to a common ancestor.

**Trueque.** Barter, countertrade, exchange, swap, switch.

**Tumulto.** Mob, crowd, multitude. Riot, public disturbance.

**Tunda.** Beating.

**Tupamaro.** Urban guerrilla, from Tupac Amaruc, Indian chief who resisted the Spanish conquest of Latin America. (UR).

**Turbar.** To disturb, disrupt, upset.

**Turismo.** Tourism, travel.

**Turno.** Turn, shift. Judicial term. Time during holidays when certain courts remain open.

**Tutela.** Tutorship. The object of tutorship is the custody of the person and property, or of only the property, of such persons who, not subject to *patria potestas,* are incapable of governing themselves. (Sp. Civ. C., sec. 237, 238).

**Tutela, acta.** Guardianship, record. The guardianship record shall contain:
I. The name, last name, and age of the ward;
II. The type of disability for which the guardianship is created;
III. The name and other information about the persons who have had custody of the ward prior to the appointment of a guardian. (Mex. Civ. C., art.91).

**Tutela dativa.** Dative tutorship. When a minor is an orphan, and has no tutor appointed by his father or mother, nor any relations who may claim the tutorship by effect of law, or when the tutor appointed in some of the modes above expressed is liable to be excluded or disqualified, or is excused legally, the judge shall appoint a tutor to the minor. (Louisiana Civ. Code, art. 270).

**Tutela de pródigos y ebrios habituales.** Tutorship of prodigals and habitual drunkards. A decree of prodigality or habitual drunkenness shall be made by means of an ordinary suit prosecuted in an oral and public trial. The judgment shall prescribe the acts which shall be prohibited to the incapacitated person and the powers which the tutor shall exercise in his name. (Sp. Civ. C., sec. 257, 259).

**Tutela legal.** Tutorship by effect of law. When a tutor has not been appointed to the minor by father or mother dying last, or if the tutor thus appointed has not been confirmed or has been excused, then the judge shall appoint to the tutorship, from among the qualified ascendants in the direct line, collaterals by blood within the third degree and the surviving. (Louisiana Civ. Code, art. 263).

**Tutela legítima.** Tutorship by effect of law. In default of a testamentary tutor appointed by the father or mother, only the following persons shall exercise tutorship by effect of the law over unemancipated minors: 1) The paternal grandfather. 2) The maternal grandfather. 3) The paternal and maternal grandmothers. (Sp. Civ. C. sec. 248).

**Tutela natural.** Tutorship by nature. Upon the death of either parent, the tutorship of minor children belongs of right to the other. (Louisiana Civ. Code, art. 250).

**Tutela testamentaria.** Tutorship by will. The right of appointing a tutor, whether a relation or a stranger, belongs exclusively to the father or mother dying last. (Louisiana Civ. Code, art. 257).

**Tutor.** Tutor. The person in charge, primarily, of the education, rearing, and defense, and, secondarily, of the administration and government of the property of a person whose father died before the former had attained the age of majority.

**Tutoría.** Tutorship, guardianship.

# U

**Ubicación.** Placement.

**Ubicar.** To place.

**Ujier.** Bailiff, court clerk.

**Ulterior.** Ulterior, beyond, hidden, further, secret, undisclosed.

**Última oportunidad efectiva.** Last clear chance, helpless plaintiff.

**Ultimar.** To assassinate, massacre, murder, kill, slay.

**Ultimo domicilio.** Last known address.

**Ultimo testamento.** Last will.

***Ultra petita* (L).** This is said of a judgment that awards more than was requested in the petition. Literally it means "beyond what has been requested."

***Ultra vires* (L).** Beyond the power that the law grants.

**Ultrajador.** Rapist, criminal, felon.

**Ultrajar.** To affront, humiliate, offend. To rape.

**Ultraje.** Affront, atrocity, outrage. Rape.

**Unánime.** Unanimous, accordant, unified.

**Unanimidad.** Unanimity, accord, homogeneity, unity.

**Única instancia.** Proceeding that admits no appeal.

**Unicameral.** Only one chamber.

**Único.** Unique, only, rare, single, singular.

**Unidad.** Unit, block, component, division, part. Unity, oneness, wholeness. Accord, harmony.

**Unidad minera.** Mining unit. The mining claim, or aggregate adjoining or nearby claims granted to a single concessionaire, or to several concessionaires who exploit them under one management.

**Unilateral.** Unilateral.

**Unión.** Union. Consolidation, fusion, merger. Marriage.

**Uniones.** Labor unions.

**Unir.** To unite. Amalgamate, combine, consolidate, merge.

**Universalidad.** University, academy, college.

**Uno y otro.** One and another, both.

**Urbanismo.** Urbanism, city management or planning.

**Urbanización.** Urbanization, land development.

**Urbano.** Urban, belonging to a city or town. Urbane, polite, refined.

**Urbe.** City.

**Urgencia.** Urgency, crisis, emergency, importance, seriousness.

**Urna.** Urn.

**Usanza.** Usage.

**Usía.** Written or oral way of addressing a judge, abbreviation of *"vuestra señoría"* (Your Honor).

**Uso.** Use, custom, habit, practice, tradition. Usage.

**Uso de ganado.** Use of cattle. The person having the use of cattle may make use of the young, milk and wool thereof, insofar as may be sufficient for the consumption of himself and his family, as well as of the dung required for manuring the land he may cultivate. (Sp. Civ. C., sec. 528).

**Uso diferenciado del usufructo.** Use distinguished from usufruct. The usufruct of any property is distinguished from the use of the same in that the enjoyment of the thing by the usufructuary is not confined to what is necessary for the maintenance of himself and his family, but he may receive all the fruits and dispose of them as he pleases. (Sp. Civ. C., sec. 525).

**Uso impropio.** Improper use.

**Uso indebido.** Improper use, without authorization.

**Uso y habitación.** Use and occupancy. Use is the right granted to a person to make gratuitous use of a thing belonging to another or to receive a part of the fruits of the same, in so far as they be sufficient for the wants of the said person and his family. The rights of use and occupancy are established and extinguished in the same manner as usufruct. (Sp. Civ. C., sec. 522, 524, 533, 535).

**Uso y habitación, derechos y obligaciones.** Use and occupancy, rights and duties. The rights and obligations of a person having the use of a thing and of the one who has the right of occupancy shall be governed by the deed constituting such rights, and in default of them, by the following provisions. (Sp. Civ. C., sec. 526, 527).

**Usos del comercio observados generalmente en una plaza.** Commercial customs generally observed in each place.

**Usos y costumbres del comercio.** Usage of trade.

**Usos y prácticas.** Usages and practices. The parties are bound by any usage to which they have agreed and by any practices which they have established between themselves. (Unidroit, Prin., art. 1.8).

**Usual.** Usual, customary, habitual, routine, standard.

**Usuario.** User, consumer.

**Usucapión.** Statute of limitations, prescription.

**Usucapir.** To become an owner through the passage of time.

**Usufructo.** Usufruct. Usufruct is the right to enjoy a thing owned by another person and to receive all the products, utilities and advantages produced thereby, under the obligation of preserving its form and substance, unless the deed constituting such usufruct or the law otherwise decrees. (Sp. Civ. C., sec. 469).

**Usufructo, conteniendo créditos.** Usufruct containing credits. The usufructuary may personally claim the credits due which form a part of the usufruct, if he has given or gives the proper security. (Sp. Civ. C., sec. 506).

**Usufructo de cosas consumibles.** Usufruct of consumable things. If the things subject to the usufruct are consumables, the usufructuary becomes owner of them. He may consume, alienate, or encumber them as he sees fit. At the termination of the usufruct he is bound to pay to the naked owner either the value that the things had at the commencement of the usufruct or deliver to him things of the same quantity and quality. (Lou. Civ. C. art. 538 and note).

**Usufructo de cosas no consumibles.** Usufruct of nonconsumable things. If the things subject to the usufruct are nonconsumables, the usufructuary has the right to possess them and to derive the utility, profits, and advantages that they may produce, under the obligation of preserving their substance. (Lou. Civ. C. art. 539 and note).

**Usufructo, expropiación.** Usufruct, expropriation. If the thing in usufruct shall be expropriated for reasons of public utility, the owner shall be obliged, either to replace it with another thing of the same value, and having similar conditions, or to pay the usufructuary the legal interest on the amount of the indemnity during all the time the usufruct continues. (Sp. Civ. C., sec. 518).

**Usufructo, extinción.** Usufruct, extinction. Usufruct is extinguished: 1) By the death of the usufructuary. 2) By the expiration of the period for which it was established, or by the fulfillment of the resolutory condition expressed in the deed establishing the usufruct. 3) By merger of usufruct and ownership in the same party. (Sp. Civ. C., sec. 512, 513, 521).

**Usufructo, mal uso y abuso.** Usufruct, misuse and abuse. Usufruct is not extinguished by misuse of the thing in usufruct; but if the abuse causes considerable injury to the owner, the latter may demand that the things be delivered to him, binding himself to pay annually to the usufructuary the net proceeds of the same, after deducting the expenses and the compensation that may be assigned to him for its administration. (Sp. Civ. C., sec. 519).

**Usufructo, mejoras.** Usufruct, improvements. The usufructuary may make, on the property given in usufruct, whatever improvements he deems proper, either for a useful purpose or for pleasure, provided, he does not change its form or substance; but he shall have no right to be indemnified therefor. (Sp. Civ. C., sec. 487, 488).

**Usufructo paterno.** Parental usufruct. Parents have during marriage the enjoyment of the property of their children until their majority or emancipation. (Lou. Civ. C. art. 223).

**Usufructo, plazo.** Usufruct, time. The usufruct cannot be established in favor of a town, corporation or association for more than thirty years. (Sp. Civ. C., sec. 514, 515, 520).

**Usufructo, reparaciones.** Usufruct, repairs. The usufructuary shall be obliged to make the ordinary repairs necessary on things given in usufruct. (Sp. Civ. C., sec. 499, 501).

**Usufructo sobre cañaverales, cafetales, árboles o arbustos.** Usufruct on cane or coffee plantations, tree or shrubs. The usufructuary of cane or coffee plantations, or of any trees or shrubs, may make use of the dead trunks, or even of those cut off or torn off by accident, under the obligation of replacing them with others. (Sp. Civ. C., sec. 483, 484).

**Usufructo sobre cosas consumibles.** Usufruct on consumable things. When the usufruct includes property which cannot be used without being consumed, the usufructuary shall have the right to make use of them under the obligation of paying their appraised value on the expiration of the usufructo, if they were appraised when given to him. (Sp. Civ. C., sec. 482).

**Usufructo sobre cosas de gradual deterioro.** Usufruct on things that deteriorate gradually. When the usufruct includes things which, without being consumed, gradually deteriorate through use, the usufructuary shall have the right to make use thereof, in accordance with the purpose they are intended for, and shall not be obliged to return them at the termination of the usufruct. (Sp. Civ. C., sec. 481).

**Usufructo sobre ganado.** Usufruct on cattle. If the usufruct be established on cattle of any kind, the usufructuary shall be obliged to replace, with the young thereof, those that die during each year through natural causes or are missing by reason of the rapacity of beasts of prey. (Sp. Civ. C., sec. 498).

**Usufructo sobre parte de una cosa poseída en común.** Usufruct on part of a thing held in common. The usufructuary may set off any damage to the property with

the improvements he may have made thereon. (Sp. Civ. C., sec. 488).

**Usufructo sobre predios en que existen minas.** Usufruct on lands containing mines. The usufructuary on lands containing mines is not entitled to the proceeds of such mines unless they are expressly cede to him in the deed establishing the usufruct, or unless such usufruct be universal. (Sp. Civ. C., sec. 476, 478).

**Usufructo sobre renta o pensión.** Usufruct on a rent or allowance. When usufruct is established on the right to collect a rent or periodical allowance, whether in money or in fruits, or in interest on obligations or certificates payable to the bearer, each payment due shall be considered as proceeds or fruits of the said right. (Sp. Civ. C., sec. 475).

**Usufructo sobre un monte.** Usufruct on wood land. The usufructuary of wood land shall enjoy all the profits which the same may produce, according to the nature thereof. (Sp. Civ. C., sec. 485).

**Usufructo sobre una acción para recobrar un predio.** Usufruct on an action to recover a tenement. The usufructuary of an action to recover a tenement or real right, or any movable, has the right to enforce it and to oblige the owner of the action to assign him, for this purpose, his own power as owner, and to afford him whatever elements of evidence he may have. (Sp. Civ. C., sec. 486).

**Usufructo sobre una herencia.** Usufruct on an inheritance. If the usufruct be on the whole or any aliquot part of any inheritance, the usufructuary may advance the sums which may belong to the property in usufruct for the payment of the debts of the said inheritance, and shall have the right to demand their return from the owner, without interest, at the expiration of the usufruct. (Sp. Civ. C., sec. 509).

**Usufructo universal y sobre cosas particulares.** Universal usufruct and on individual things. If the usufruct be established on the whole of any patrimony, and if, at the time it is established, the owner has debts, it shall be understood that the usufructuary is only obliged to pay the debts contracted before such establishment or when the usufruct has been established to defraud the creditors. (Sp. Civ. C., sec. 505, 507).

**Usufructuador.** Usufructuary.

**Usufructuar.** To use and enjoy.

**Usufructuario.** Usufructuary. Person who uses and enjoys, beneficiary of a usufruct.

**Usufructuario, derechos.** Usufructuary's rights. The usufructuary shall have the right to all the natural, cultivated and civil fruits on the property in usufruct. (Sp. Civ. C., sec. 471, 474, 480).

**Usufructuario, oligaciones.** Usufructuary's obligations. The usufructuary, before entering on the enjoyment of any property, is obliged: 1) To make, after summoning the owner or his legitimate representative, an inventory of all the property, causing an appraisement of the furniture and a description of the condition of the immovables to be made. 2) To give security, binding himself to fulfill the obligations imposed on him by this Article. (Sp. Civ. C., sec. 490, 496, 510).

**Usura.** Usury, racketeering.

**Usurario.** Usurious, exorbitant, extortionate.

**Usurero.** Usurer, money lender.

**Usurpación.** Usurpation. Dislodgement of the rightful occupant of a house or land.

**Usurpación de un instrumento.** Conversion of instrument.

**Usurpador.** Usurper, intruder. Person who takes what is not hers.

**Usurpar.** To usurp. To unlawfully appropriate, seize, snatch, wrest.

**Utensilio.** Utensil, device, gadget, implement, tool.

**Uterino.** Uterine.

**Utilidad.** Utility. Earnings, gains, profit. Advantage, benefit, usefulness.

**Utilidades.** Earnings, proceeds, returns, revenue.

**Utopía.** Utopia.

**Uxoricida.** Person who murders his wife.

**Uxoricidio.** Murder of one's wife.

# V

**Vacación.** Holiday, vacation.

**Vacaciones.** Vacation. Workers are entitled to six vacation days after being employed for one year, and to two more days for each following year up to 12 days. As of the fifth year, the employee is entitled to 14 work days' vacation. (Mex. Labor Law).

**Vacante.** Vacant, empty, open. Vacancy.

**Vaciar.** To empty, remove.

**Vacío.** Train car.

**Vacío legal.** Legal gap.

**Vagancia.** Vagrancy, roving, roaming, wandering.

**Vago, vagabundo.** Vagrant, floater, roamer, rover, tramp, vagabond.

**Vaivén.** Movement in opposite ways, to and from, there and back.

**Vale.** Promissory note, voucher.

**Valedero.** Valid, acceptable, effective, proper, suitable, truthful, well grounded.

**Valer.** To cost, to be priced at, to go for.

**Valía.** Worth, benefit, merit, utility, worthiness.

**Validar.** To validate, authorize, certify, confirm, countersign, corroborate, ratify.

**Validez.** Validity, authenticity, acceptability, effectiveness, legality, power, properness.

**Válido.** Valid, authoritative, binding, lawful, licit, legitimate, mandatory, obligatory.

**Valioso.** Valuable, costly, esteemed, treasured.

**Valiza.** Beacon.

**Valor.** Value. Amount, appraisal, assessment, cost, price, worth. Merit, significance.

**Valor de mercado.** Market value. The market value of a property is the price that a purchaser would be willing to pay in a voluntary sale and that a vendor would be willing to accept, considering for said purpose the conditions of the property at the time of the appraisal and the most productive and beneficial use to which it could be devoted in the reasonably near future. (Basora Defillo v. Secretary of the Treasury, 88 PRR 1 (1963)).

**Valor mobiliario.** Chattel paper.

**Valor nominal.** Nominal value.

**Valor probatorio y credibilidad.** Weight and credibility.

**Valor recibido.** Valuable consideration.

**Valoración, valorización, valuación.** Appraisal, assessment, estimate, valuation.

**Valorador, valuador.** Appraiser, valuer.

**Valorar, valorizar, valuar.** To appraise, assess, estimate, evaluate, rank, rate, valuate.

**Valorativo.** Valuing.

**Valores.** Securities, bonds, negotiable instruments.

**Valuable.** Appraisable. Valuable.

**Vandalismo.** Vandalism.

**Vándalo.** Vandal, hooligan.

**Vaniloquio.** Useless and ungrounded oral argument.

**Vano.** Vain, purposeless, wasted.

**Varada, varamiento.** Stranding.

**Variación.** Variation, alteration, change, departure, difference, modification, variance.

**Varón.** Male, man.

**Vecinal.** Neighborly.

**Vecindad.** Vicinity, environs, neighborhood, residential area, surroundings.

**Vecino.** Neighbor. Close, kindred, related.

**Veda.** Ban, denial, prohibition, veto.

**Vedado.** Banned, out of bounds, prohibited.

**Vedar.** To ban, prohibit.

**Veedor.** Observer.

**Vehículo.** Vehicle.

**Vejación.** Mistreatment, humiliation.

**Vejar.** To abuse.

**Vejez.** Seniority, old age.

**Velar por el cumplimiento.** To make sure that compliance is being made.

**Velo corporativo.** Corporate veil.

**Velocidad.** Velocity, acceleration, rapidity, rate, speed.

**Venal.** Bribable, corrupt, dishonest, unprincipled, unscrupulous.

**Venalidad.** Venality, low ethical standards.

**Vencedor.** Winner, victorious party.

**Vencer.** To win. To conquer, defeat, vanquish. To become due through the passage of time.

**Vencido.** Losing party, loser. Due and owing.

**Vencimiento.** Maturity, expiration, expiry, lapse of time.

**Vencimiento del término.** Expiration of term, lapse of time.

**Vendaje.** Bandages.

**Vendedor.** Vendor, dealer, salesman, seller. Grantor, transferer.

**Vendedor ambulante.** Peddler.

**Vender.** To sell, alienate, convey, transfer.

**Vender a plazos.** To sell on time, by installments.

**Vender al fiado.** To sell on credit.

**Vendible.** Marketable, disposable, salable.

**Veneno.** Poison.

**Venia.** Authorization, license, permit, permission. Military salute.

**Venidero.** Ensuing, next, following.

**Venta.** Sale, alienation, conveyance.

**Venta a prueba.** Sale on approval.

**Venta contra documentos.** Documentary sale.

**Venta por precio alzado.** Sale for a fixed price.

**Ventilación.** Ventilation. Making public, bringing to the open.

**Ver.** To see.

**Veracidad.** Veracity, accuracy, exactitude, frankness, openness, sincerity, truthfulness, verity.

**Verbal.** Verbal, oral, said, spoken, voiced, unwritten, uttered. *Viva voce.*

**Verdadero.** Actual, real, truthful.

**Verdugo.** Executioner.

**Veredicto.** Verdict, adjudication, decision, determination, finding, judgment, sentence.

**Verificación.** Verification, accreditation, confirmation, corroboration, validation.

**Verificar.** To verify, attest, accredit, establish, support, sustain, validate.

**Verso.** Front side of a page.

**Vertiente.** Watershed.

**Vestigio.** Vestige, relic, remnant. Bit, indication, trace.

**Vetar.** To veto, ban, outlaw, prohibit, rule out.

**Veto.** Veto, ban, prohibition, opposition.

**Vía.** Road, approach, avenue, course, method, system.

**Vía de apremio.** Foreclosure proceedings.

**Vía oficial.** By official channels.

**Vía ordinaria.** Standard proceedings.

**Vía sumaria.** Summary proceedings.

**Viable.** Viable, feasible, possible. Able to survive.

**Viático.** Expenses incurred during traveling.

**Viajero.** Traveller, commuter, voyager, wonderer.

**Vicegobernador.** Lieutenant governor.

**Vicepresidente.** Vice president.

**Vicetesorero.** Deputy treasurer.

**Viciado.** Clouded, faulty, flawed, imperfect.

**Viciar.** To vitiate, annul, cloud, dilute, impair, invalidate, taint, weaken.

**Vicio.** Vice. Defect, flaw, imperfection. Debauchery, depravity, immorality, licentiousness.

**Vicio oculto.** Hidden vice. A defect in the operation of the gearshift of a motor vehicle which renders it practically useless constitutes a hidden vice which may be cause for rescission of the contract of sale by virtue of which the owner acquired it, especially since the purchaser—as in this case—was not an expert and, by reason of his occupation, it is presumed that he could not easily detect the defect stated. (Berrios v. Courtesy Motors of P. R., Inc., 91 PRR 428 (1964)).

**Vicio procesal.** Procedural error.

**Vicios de construcción**. Vices of Construction. Vices of construction—in a construction contract—means "defects of construction." (Pereira v. I.B.E.C., 95 PRR 28 (1967)).

**Vicios de la posesión.** Vices of possession. Possession that is violent, clandestine, discontinuous, or equivocal has no legal effect. (Lou. Civ. C. art. 3435).

**Vicios redhibitorios.** Redhibitory defects. Redhibitory defects, also known as hidden defects, are those hidden defects in a thing which may annul the sale of the same. (Ferrer v. General Motors Corp., 100 PRR 244 (1971)).

**Vicioso.** Person who succumbs to a vice.

**Víctima.** Victim, casualty.

**Victimología.** Victimology.

**Victorioso.** Victorious, triumphant, successful, winning.

**Vida.** Life, creation, existence, mankind, livelihood, living.

**Vida silvestre.** Wildlife.

**Vientre.** Abdomen, belly, stomach, womb.

**Vigencia.** Time of effectiveness.

**Vigente.** In force, applicable, operational.

**Vigilancia.** Surveillance, care, control, guidance, supervision.

**Vigilancia, quebrantamiento.** Surveillance, infringement. If surveillance measures are infringed, the court may extend the same, or substitute them for a commitment measure. (St. P.C. for LA, sec. 60).

**Vigilar, controlar, supervisar.** To superintend, control, oversee.

**Vigor.** Effectiveness, vigor, energy, force, might, strength.

**Vil.** Vile, base.

**Vilipendiar.** To denigrate, to attack verbally or in writing.

**Vinculación.** Link, contacts, ties.

**Vinculado.** Linked, related. Responding to the same interests.

**Vincular.** Affecting a particular relationship.

**Vínculo.** Bond, link, relationship.

**Vínculo doble.** Family relationship between siblings with both parents in common.

**Vindicación.** Vindication.

**Vindicar.** To vindicate.

**Vindicatorio.** Vindicatory, justified, vengeful.

**Viñeta.** Vignette, anecdote.

**Violación.** Rape, defilement. Violation, breach, contravention, disregard, encroach-ment, infraction, infringement, nonobservance, transgression, trespass.

**Violación de privacidad.** Intrusion upon seclusion.

**Violación de propiedad.** Trespass on land.

**Violador.** Rapist. Person who contravenes the law or breaches an obligation.

**Violar.** To rape, defile. To violate, breach, contravene.

**Violatorio.** Contravening, transgressional.

**Violencia.** Duress. Consent is vitiated when it has been obtained by duress of such a nature as to cause a reasonable fear of unjust and considerrable injury to a party's person, property or reputation. (Lou. Civ. C. art. 1959).
Violence, ferocity, force, might, power, strength.

**Violencia, intimidación.** Violence, intimidation. There is violence when, to extract the other party's consent, an irresistible force is used. There is intimidation when a rational and founded fear of suffering an imminent and serious injury is impressed on the other party, physically or materially, or in the person or assets of his/her spouse, ascendants or descendants. (Sp. Civ. C., sec. 1267).

**Violencia, intimidación por terceros.** Violence, intimidation by third parties. Violence or intimidation shall annul the obligation, even if employed by a third person, not intervening in the contract. (Sp. Civ. C., sec. 1268).

**Violentar.** To break open. To rape. To abuse.

**Viril.** Virile, manly, masculine.

**Virilidad.** Virility, manliness, masculity.

**Virreinatos.** Viceroyalties. A basic premise of Spanish colonial rule was the deep-seated suspicion that the king's distant representatives would misuse their authority unless closely watched. To guard against such abuses, an elaborate administrative system with overlapping grants of authority was designed. Until the 18th century, the New World colonies were divided into two viceroyalties, New Spain and Peru, each headed by a viceroy. (L & D in LA).

**Virtual.** Virtual, implied, indirect, practical, substantial.

**Virtud.** Virtue, value, worth. Reason why.

**Visa, visado.** Visa.

**Visación.** Acceptance, approval, signature, stamping.

**Visar.** To approve, sign, stamp.

**Visibilidad.** Visibility, clarity, predictability.

**Visible.** Visible, discernible, distinct, evident, manifest, patent, perceivable.

**Visita.** Visit, visitation right.

**Visitar.** To visit.

**Vista.** Hearing. Notification to the other party.

**Vista a puerta cerrada.** Closed hearing.

**Visto.** Seen, considered.

**Visto bueno.** Approval.

**Visto que.** Considering, taking into account.

**Vitalicio.** For life.

**Vituperable.** Appalling, intolerable, repulsive.

**Viuda.** Widow.

**Viudez.** Widowhood.

**Viudo.** Widower.

**Viva voz.** *Viva voce*, oral, spoken, unwritten.

**Viveros de árboles.** Tree nurseries.

**Vivir.** To live, inhabit. To cohabit.

**Vivo.** Alive.

**Vocación.** Vocation, aptitude, knack, talent.

**Vocal.** Vocal.

**Vocalía.** Board, voting, membership of a particular group.

**Voceador.** Crier, herald.

**Vocero.** Spokesman, representative.

**Voladura.** Damage caused by a bomb or explosion.

***Volenti non fit iniuria* (L).** The equivalent, in Roman law, of the theory of assumption of risk.

**Voluntad.** Will. The term will is defined as intention, disposition, or resolution to do a thing; want or desire to do a thing. (Ppl. v. Sanchez Lugo, 96 PRR 480).
Desire, inclination, wish.

**Voluntariamente.** Willfully.

**Voluntariedad.** Willfulness. A term of many meanings, precisely to cover a whole gamut of situations which in the last analysis are reduced to a qualification of mental or subjective status. (Ppl. v. Calzada, 93 PRR 783 (1966)).

**Voluntario.** Volunteer, amateur, unpaid. Voluntary.

**Volver.** To return, go back.

**Votación.** Voting, election, balloting.

**Votador.** Voter, suffragist.

**Votar.** To vote, to cast a vote, to elect.

**Voto.** Vote, ballot, poll suffrage. Right to vote.

**Voto acumulativo.** Cumulative voting.

**Voto cantado.** Vote expressed in a public way, not secretly.

**Voto de calidad.** Casting vote.

**Votó en sala y no pudo firmar.** Voted in chamber but was unable to sign. If, after an action has been decided by a court, one of the justices who voted at said decision should become unable to sign, the one who presided in the chamber shall do so for him, stating the name of the justice for whom he signs and placing thereafter the words: Voted in chamber, but was unable to sign. (Sp. L. Civ. P., sec. 365).

**Voz.** Voice, opinion, part, participation, role, say, vote.

**Voz cantante.** Person who expresses the majority opinion or who dominates a debate.

**Vuelta.** Return. Reversal, reversion. Reverse side of a page.

**Vulnerar.** To cause damage or injury. To overstep, trespass.

# W

**W.** This letter does not originally belong to the Spanish alphabet and is mainly used at the beginning of words taken from other languages.

**Warrant.** Deposit certificate that can be sold.

**Wat.** Watt.

# X

**Xenófilo.** Person who likes foreign cultures and foreigners.

**Xenófobo.** Person who dislikes foreign cultures and foreigners.

**Xenofobia.** Xenophobia, hatred of foreigners.

# Y

**Y/o.** And/or. The result of using in an insurance policy the copulative conjunction and the disjunctive conjunction or—policy issued to the Asociación Hípica de Puerto Rico and/or its individual members—is, as a matter of fact, the creation of three policies, insuring a) the Asociación as such; b) the Asociación and its members; and c) the members of the Asociación. (Barreras v. Santana, 87 D.P.R. 215 (1963)).

**Ya mencionado.** Already mentioned.

**Yacente.** Inheritance without any other claimant than the state.

**Yate.** Yacht.

**Yelmo.** Army or police helmet.

**Yerro.** Error, ambiguity, blunder, fault, miscalculation, mistake.

**Yugo.** Yoke, oppression.

# Z

**Zanjar.** To bridge, compromise, settle.

**Zanjar una disputa.** Solve a controversy.

**Zanjas, setos vivos o muertos.** Ditches, live or dead hedges.

**Zigzag.** Zigzag.

**Zona.** Zone, area, district, precinct.

**Zona franca.** Foreign-trade zone.

**Zona marítima-terrestre.** Maritime-terrestrial zone. Under the provisions of the Spanish Harbor Law of May 7, 1880, the maritime-terrestrial zone is described as the area which is washed by the sea in its ebb and flow and is extended to where the tide is perceptible, or the highest tidal waves in stormy weather when the tide is not perceptible. (Rubert Armstrong v. Commonwealth, 97 PRR 573 (1969)).

**Zozobrar.** To sink, shipwreck.

**Zurra.** Beating, assault.

**Zutano.** John Doe, way of naming an unknown person.

# English-Spanish

# A

**A.D.** Abreviación de era cristiana. *Anno Domini.*

**ADR.** Siglas de Alternative Dispute Resolution, medios alternativos de solucionar disputas. Técnicas tendientes a solucionar conflictos por medios no litigiosos como, por ejemplo, la mediación.

**A.K.A.** Alias. Conocido como. Abreviatura de *also known as.*

**A.M.** En horas de la mañana, antes del mediodía. Del latín *ante meridiem.*

**Abandon.** Abandonar, desamparar, dejar. Abdicar, ceder, renunciar. Desertar.

**Abandonee.** Parte que toma, o que recibe, alguna cosa abandonada.

**Abandonment.** Abandono, desamparo. Abdicación, cesión, renuncia, apatía, pasividad.

**Abatable.** Susceptible de abolición, anulación, suprimible, abatible.

**Abatable nuisance.** Restricción o molestia al goce de un derecho propietario, no permitida por la ley, pero que puede ser corregida. Por ejemplo, humo o ruido excesivo emanante de un inmueble que perjudica a un inmueble vecino.

**Abate.** Abolir, anular, caducar, expirar, perecer, suprimir, perder efecto, abatir.

**Abatement.** Abolición, anulación, supresión, pérdida de efecto, abatimiento.

**Abatement of action.** Terminación de un juicio, normalmente en razón de algún defecto procesal.

**Abator.** Parte que anula, suprime o reduce la efectividad de un derecho.

**Abbreviation.** Abreviación, abreviatura, compendio, digesto, extracto, resumen, síntesis, sumario.

**Abdicate.** Abdicar, abandonar, ceder, dimitir, renunciar, declinar, deponer.

**Abdication.** Abdicación, abandono, cesión, dimisión, renuncia, renunciamiento.

**Abdomen.** Abdomen, barriga, panza, vientre.

**Abduct.** Secuestrar, raptar. Apresar, esconder, ocultar.

**Abduction.** Rapto, secuestro. Apresamiento, ocultación.

**Abductor.** Secuestrador, raptor.

**Aberration.** Aberración, gran anormalidad.

**Abet.** Incitar, empujar, estimular, impulsar, instigar, persuadir, provocar.

**Abetment.** Incitación, estímulo, impulso, instigación, persuasión, provocación.

**Abettor.** Instigador, incitador, provocador, responsable indirecto, cómplice.

**Abeyance.** Pausa, alto, aplazamiento, cesación, cese, demora, receso, suspensión.

**Abeyant.** Aplazado, demorado, en receso, prorrogado, suspendido.

**Abhor.** Aborrecer, detestar.

**Abide by.** Acatar, cumplir, respetar, seguir.

**Ability.** Habilidad, capacidad.

**Abjuration.** Abjuración, abandono, apartamiento, deserción, renuncia, repudio, rescisión.

**Abjure.** Abjurar, abandonar, apartarse, desertar, renunciar, repudiar, rescindir.

**Able.** Capaz, apto, competente, diestro, hábil, idóneo.

**Abnegation.** Abnegación, altruismo, caridad, desprendimiento, renuncia, sacrificio.

**Abnormally dangerous activities.** Actividades de alto riesgo. Para determinar si una actividad es de alto riesgo, hay que considerar los siguientes factores: a) la existencia de un alto riesgo de que una persona, un tercero o los bienes muebles de la persona, sufran daño; b) probabilidad de que el daño sea grande; c) incapacidad de poder eliminar el riesgo mediante el ejercicio de un cuidado razonable. (Rstmnt, 2nd, Torts, sec. 520).

**Abode.** Hogar, domicilio, residencia.

**Abolish.** Abolir, anular, borrar, derogar, eliminar, extinguir, extirpar, prohibir, suprimir.

**Abolition.** Abolición, anulación, derogación, eliminación, extinción, extirpación, prohibición, supresión.

**Aboriginal title.** El derecho de propiedad que los indígenas tienen sobre las tierras que ocupan desde tiempo inmemorial.

**Abort.** Abortar, malparir, interrumpir, frustrar.

**Abortee.** Mujer que ha sufrido un aborto.

**Aborticide.** Aborticidio.

**Abortifacient.** Abortífero, medicamento que produce un aborto.

**Abortion.** Aborto, mal parto.

**Abortionist.** Abortista, abortero.

**About face.** Cambio de posicion súbito e inesperado.

**Above.** Arriba, sobre, supra.

**Aboveboard.** Honesto, verdadero, irreprochable.

**Abridge.** Abreviar, aligerar, compendiar, reducir, resumir, sintetizar.

**Abridgment.** Abreviación, compendio, digesto, resumen, síntesis.

**Abroad.** En un país extranjero.

**Abrogate.** Abrogar, anular, dejar de lado, rechazar, revocar.

**Abrogation.** Abrogación, abolición, anulación, destierro, erradicación, revocación.

**Abrogative.** Abrogatorio, anulatorio.

**Abscond.** Fugarse de una región, esconderse para evitar ser demandado o para escapar la competencia de un tribunal.

**Absence.** Ausencia.

**Absent.** Ausente, desaparecido, faltante, perdido.

**Absentee.** Ausente.

**Absentee voting.** Sistema de voto por correspondencia o ante un consulado para quien no puede votar en el lugar corriente.

**Absentism.** Ausentismo, no concurrencia al trabajo.

**Absolute.** Absoluto, concluyente, decisivo, definitivo, final total.

**Absolute deed.** Escritura de dominio pleno, sin ninguna restricción ni gravamen.

**Absolute liability.** Responsabilidad absoluta. Aquélla que existe sin que interese si ha mediado culpa o negligencia.

**Absolute nuisance.** Molestia producida al propietario de un fundo vecino y por la cual emerge responsabilidad sin que interese si ha mediado culpa o negligencia por parte del obligado.

**Absolute privilege.** Privilegio absoluto. Aquél que brinda inmunidad al autor de un acto que, de otra forma, sería responsable. Por ejemplo, derecho de que tienen los bomberos de entrar a una casa en llamas sin requerir autorización del dueño ni orden judicial.

**Absolution.** Absolución, amnistía, perdón.

**Absolutism.** Absolutismo.

**Absolutory.** Absolutorio.

**Absolve.** Absolver, amnistiar, dispensar, exculpar, eximir, liberar de culpa y cargo, sobreseer.

**Abstain.** Abstenerse de.

**Abstention.** Abstención, contención, freno, inhibición, privación, renuncia.

**Abstention doctrine.** Doctrina de la abstención, mediante la cual los tribunales federales ceden su competencia a los tribunales estatales para evitar inmiscuirse en cuestiones de administración interna. Por ejemplo, casos de derecho de familia.

**Abstinence.** Abstinencia, abstención, ayuno, castidad, moderación, privación, sobriedad.

**Abstract.** Abstracto, genérico, copia, resumen (s). Hacer abstracción (v).

**Abstract title.** Certificado de dominio. Documento emitido por el registro de la propiedad inmueble que resume datos esenciales al dominio, por ejemplo, anterior propietario, restricciones, gravámenes, etc.

**Abstraction.** Abstracción, idealización.

**Absurdity.** Absurdo, desatino, disparate, locura.

**Abulia.** Abulia, desgano, indiferencia, falta de energías, flojedad.

**Abuse.** Abuso, atropello, extralimitación, tropelía (s). Abusar, extralimitarse (v).

**Abuse of discretion.** Abuso de poderes discrecionales.

**Abuse of drugs.** Abuso de medicamentos o drogas.

**Abuse of power.** Abuso de poder.

**Abuse of process.** Temeridad y malicia, abuso de proceso. Aquella persona que utilice un proceso legal, ya sea criminal o civil, contra otro, para lograr un propósito para el cual no fue diseñado, será responsable a ese otro por el daño causado por el abuso del proceso. (Rstmnt, 2nd, Torts, sec. 682).

**Abusive.** Abusivo, excesivo.

**Abusive language.** Insultos, forma de hablar abusiva.

**Abut.** Colindar, tener un límite en común.

**Abuttal.** Límite, demarcación, frontera, lindero, línea divisoria.

**Abutter.** Propietario de una finca lindante, vecino.

**Abutting land.** Terreno limítrofe.

**Academia.** Conjunto de profesores o académicos.

**Academic.** Académico. Teórico.

**Academic question.** Pregunta meramente teórica e irrelevante de un punto de vista práctico.

**Accede.** Acceder, aceptar, consentir.

**Accelerated depreciation.** Depreciación acelerada. Método contable que amortiza el activo más rápidamente que otros.

**Acceleration clause.** Cláusula por la cual la mora provoca la exigibilidad del pago total.

**Accept.** Aceptar, admitir, aprobar, recibir.

**Acceptable.** Aceptable, bueno, correcto, suficiente.

**Acceptance.** Aceptación, admisión, allanamiento.

**Acceptance by silence or exercise of dominion.** Aceptación mediante silencio o acto de dominio. Cuando un ofrecido no contesta una oferta, su silencio o inacción operan como una aceptación sólo en los siguientes casos: a) cuando el ofrecido se beneficia de los servicios aun cuando tuvo oportunidad de rechazarlos y tiene motivos para creer que dichos servicios fueron ofrecidos con la expectativa de una compensación. b) cuando el oferente ha enunciado o ha dado motivos al ofrecido para creer que el consentimiento puede manifestarse mediante silencio e inacción; y que el ofrecido, al permanecer en silencio o inactivo, intenta aceptar la oferta. c) donde por negociaciones previas u otros actos, se considere razonable que el ofrecido notifique al oferente si no tiene la intención de aceptar. (Rstmnt, 2nd, Con., sec. 69).

**Acceptance for honor.** Aceptación por intervención.

**Acceptance of a draft.** Aceptación de un giro. La aceptación es el compromiso firmado del librado de honrar el giro a su presentación. Deberá constar por escrito en el giro y podrá consistir sólo de su firma. Será eficaz cuando se completa por la entrega o la notificación. (C.C.U. sec. 3-410, 3-412).

**Acceptance of an offer.** Aceptación de una oferta. La aceptación de una oferta es una manifestación de consentimiento a los términos o condiciones hechos por el requerido en forma solicitada por el oferente. (Rstmnt, 2nd, Con., sec. 50).

**Acceptance of goods.** Aceptación de mercancías. La aceptación de mercancías tiene lugar cuando el comprador: después de una oportunidad razonable para inspeccionar las mercancías hace saber al vendedor que las mercancías están de acuerdo con las especificaciones o que las aceptará o retendrá a pesar de no estar éstas de acuerdo con lo especificado. (C.C.U. sec. 2-606).

**Acceptance within a fixed period of time.** Aceptación dentro de un plazo fijo. El plazo de aceptación fijado por el oferente en un telegrama o en una carta, comenzará a correr desde el momento de la entrega del telegrama para su transmisión o desde la fecha indicada en la carta, o, si ésta no indica ninguna, desde la fecha que figure en el sobre. (Unidroit, Prin., art. 2.8).

**Acceptor.** Aceptante, aceptador, receptor.

**Acceptor for honor.** Interventor aceptante.

**Accessory.** Accesorio. Cómplice.

**Accessory after the fact.** Persona que brinda asistencia a un delincuente luego de la comisión de un delito, pero sin que medie acuerdo previo aunque sabiendo que el delito ha sido cometido. Encubrimiento.

**Accessory before the fact.** Persona que brinda asistencia para que otro cometa un delito futuro.

**Accessory building.** Edificio accesorio, anexo.

**Accessory contract.** Contrato accesorio.

**Accessory obligation.** Obligación accesoria.

**Accessory use.** Uso accesorio.

**Access.** Acceso, entrada, posibilidad de utilizar o de servirse de algo (s). Ingresar, acceder, especialmente a un sistema de ordenadora o computación (v).

**Accession.** Accesión.

**Accident.** Accidente, choque, tropiezo, siniestro.

**Accident prone.** Proclive a los accidentes.

**Accidental.** Accidental, circunstancial, fortuito.

**Accidental death.** Muerte causada por un accidente.

**Accommodated party.** Parte en cuyo favor se realizó cierta acción.

**Accommodation.** Ajuste, arreglo, servicio, alojamiento, hospedaje.

**Accommodation loan.** Préstamo gratuito, de favor.

**Accommodation maker.** Persona que firma un pagaré u otro documento a efectos de facilitar crédito a otro.

**Accommodation paper.** Instrumento de crédito suscrito por una persona para que otra pueda obtener crédito.

**Accommodation party.** Parte acomodante. Parte acomodante es aquélla que firma el instrumento en cualquier carácter con el propósito de prestar su nombre a otra parte contratante en el instrumento. (C.C.U. sec. 3-415).

**Accompany.** Acompañar, adjuntar.

**Accomplice.** Cómplice, coautor, colaborador, partícipe, secuaz.

**Accomplice liability.** Responsabilidad del cómplice, copartícipe o encubridor.

**Accomplishment.** Perfeccionamiento o cumplimiento de algo.

**Accord.** Acuerdo, alianza, convenio, pacto (s). Acordar, ceder (v).

**Accord and satisfaction.** Acuerdo en finiquito, transacción. Acuerdo en finiquito es un contrato bajo el cual el acreedor promete aceptar otro cumplimiento en satisfacción de la obligación. El cumplimiento de este acuerdo libera la obligación original. La obligación original queda suspendida hasta que se cumpla el acuerdo. (Rstmnt, 2nd, Con., sec. 281 (1)(2)).

**Accord executory.** Acuerdo que ha sido firmado por las partes, pero todavía pendiente de ejecución.

**Account.** Cuenta, cálculo, explicación (s). Responder (v).

**Account balance.** Saldo de una cuenta.

**Account debtor.** Deudor de la cuenta. Persona que está obligada en una cuenta, valor mobiliario, derecho contractual o intangibles en general. (C.C.U. sec. 9-105(a)).

**Account in trust.** Cuenta en fideicomiso.

**Account payable.** Obligaciones a pagar. Débito.

**Account receivable.** Obligaciones a cobrar. Crédito.

**Account rendered.** Cuenta presentada al deudor para su verificación y eventual pago.

**Account stated.** Cuenta convenida. Una cuenta convenida es una manifestación de consentimiento entre deudor y acreedor por una suma convenida como un cómputo preciso de la cantidad debida al acreedor. (Rstmnt, 2nd, Con., sec. 282).

**Accountability.** Responsabilidad.

**Accountable.** Responsable, culpable. Explicable, justificable.

**Accountant.** Contador, tenedor de libros.

**Accountant, certified public.** Contador público, debidamente licenciado para ofrecer servicios contables al público. Contador profesional.

**Accountant, chartered.** Contador (G.B.).

**Accounting.** Contabilidad, auditoría, teneduría de libros. Rendición de cuentas.

**Accounting period.** Período contable, normalmente coincide con el año natural.

**Accredit.** Acreditar. Establecer la autenticidad de algo. Reconocer como perteneciente a una categoría oficial.

**Accredited law school.** Escuela de derecho debidamente acreditada por las autoridades educacionales y cuyos graduados pueden presentarse a un examen para obtener una licencia profesional permitiéndoles ejercer como abogados.

**Accretion.** Acrecentamiento, acrecencia, avulsión, aumento, demasía, exceso.

**Accroach, encroach.** Irrumpir, ocupar, penetrar.

**Accrual.** Aumento, generación, multiplicación.

**Accrue.** Devengar, acumular, generar.

**Accrued.** Devengado, acumulado, vencido.

**Accrued dividend.** Dividendo devengado.

**Accrued expense.** Gasto incurrido.

**Accrued income.** Ganancia devengada.

**Accrued interest.** Intereses devengados.

**Accrued right, vested right.** Derecho adquirido.

**Accrued salary.** Sueldo devengado.

**Accumulated dividend.** Dividendo acumulado.

**Accumulated earnings tax.** Impuesto sobre ganancias obtenidas por una empresa pero todavía no distribuídas.

**Accumulated legacy.** Legado pendiente de distribución.

**Accumulated profit.** Ganancia acumulada.

**Accumulation trust.** Fideicomiso en el que deben acumularse por un período determinado los intereses o dividendos antes de ser distribuidos.

**Accumulative.** Acumulativo, retroactivo.

**Accumulative judgment.** Segunda sentencia dictada en contra de un individuo que queda suspendida hasta que la primera se cumpla.

**Accusation.** Acusación, denunciar, inculpación, querella, recriminación.

**Accusatory.** Acusatorio.

**Accusatory part.** Sección del auto de procesamiento, o de indiciamiento, en el que se especifican los cargos.

**Accusatory procedure.** Procedimiento acusatorio. Sistema procesal penal que acuerda mayor actividad a los particulares interesados, querellante y querellado. El sistema opuesto, con mayor intervención de la corte, se conoce como el procedimiento inquisitivo.

**Accuse.** Acusar, atacar, denunciar, delatar, imputar, procesar, querellar.

**Accused.** Acusado, inculpado, procesado, querellado, reo.

**Accuser.** Acusador, denunciante, ministerio público, querellante.

**Accustomed.** De costumbre, usual.

**Acid test.** Método o sistema contable para determinar la relación existente entre el activo y el pasivo.

**Acknowledge.** Reconocer, admitir.

**Acknowledged instrument.** Documento con una firma certificada por un notario u otra autoridad.

**Acknowledgement.** Admisión, constancia, corroboración, reconocimiento.

**Acknowledgement of debt.** Reconocimiento de una deuda.

**Acknowledgement of paternity.** Reconocimiento de paternidad.

**Acknowledgement of payment.** Carta de pago.

**Acquainted.** Familiarizado.

**Acquest.** Lo que se adquiere con dinero o servicios.

**Acquests, community of.** Sociedad de ganaciales, comunidad de bienes.

**Acquiesce.** Aceptar, asentir, conceder, consentir implícitamente.

**Acquiescence.** Aquiescencia, aprobación, asentimiento, conformidad en forma implícita o tácita.

**Acquiescence, estoppel by.** Preclusión del derecho a oponerse a algo tras haber expresado consentimiento, generalmente mediante silencio o inacción.

**Acquire.** Adquirir, lograr, obtener.

**Acquired.** Adquirido, inamovible.

**Acquired rights.** Derechos de los que se goza por haber sido adquiridos, por ejemplo, mediante una transacción comercial, una ley, etc.

**Acquisition.** Adquisición, compra.

**Acquisitive.** Adquisitivo.

**Acquit.** Absolver, amnistiar, exculpar, eximir, perdonar. Liberar de culpa y cargo, sobreseer.

**Acquitment.** Sentencia absolutoria.

**Acquittal.** Absolución, sobreseimiento.

**Acquittance.** Quita, condenación, liberación, remisión.

**Acquitted.** Absuelto, sobreseído.

**Acre.** Medida de tierra de 4.840 yardas cuadradas. Aproximadamente equivalente a 0,405 hectáreas.

**Acrimonious.** Cáustico, maligno.

**Act.** Acto, acción, evento, formalidad, hecho, ley escrita, decreto.

**Act, criminal.** Acto o conducta criminal.

**Act in concert.** Conducta realizada de común acuerdo entre dos o más personas. Actuar conjuntamente, de concierto.

**Act, legislative.** Ley formalmente emanada del Poder Legislativo.

**Act of bankruptcy.** Acción de un deudor insolvente susceptible de colocarlo en situación de quiebra fraudulenta y culposa. Por ejemplo, encubrimiento de bienes.

**Act of dominion.** Acto de dominio, aquél que excede medidas de administración o conservación.

**Act of God.** Fuerza mayor. El equivalente de la expresión inglesa *Act of God*—un suceso ocasionado exclusivamente por las fuerzas naturales y sin que medie intervención humana alguna—en el idioma español es, no "acto de Dios", sino fuerza mayor (*vis major*). (100 D.P.R. 106 (1971)).

**Act of grace.** Acto del gobierno por el cual se condonan ciertas penas.

**Act of parliament.** Ley formalmente emitida por el parlamento.

**Act of state.** Acto de estado o de gobierno. Acto del poder público en cumplimiento de sus atribuciones.

**Act of state doctrine.** Doctrina del acto de estado. Aquélla que impide juzgar en un país a un estado extranjero cuando los actos en cuestión sean manifestaciones oficiales del poder público.

**Act, private.** Acción o acto privado.

**Act, public.** Acción o acto realizado por funcionarios públicos en conjunción con sus tareas oficiales.

**Acting.** Interino, suplente, transitorio.

**Action.** Causa para entablar demanda. Actividad, conducta, hecho.

**Action for accounting.** Acción por rendición de cuentas.

**Action for money had and received.** Acción por la restitución de bienes y dinero.

**Action for negligence.** Juicio por negligencia. Queda sujeto a responsabilidad por negligencia quien invade algún derecho de otro individuo: 1) Si el derecho invadido es uno protegido contra una intrusión no-intencional; 2) Si la conducta del actor es negligente con relación a ese otro individuo, o una clase de personas a la cual pertenece ese individuo. (Restatement, Second, Torts, sec. 281).

**Action *in rem*.** Acción establecida para obtener control propietario sobre una cosa. La acción se establece directamente contra la cosa. La noción es más restringida que aquélla de acción in rem del sistema romanista.

**Action *quasi in rem*.** Acción personal, por ejemplo por el pago de una deuda, cuando la competencia del tribunal se basa en que cierto bien del deudor se halla dentro de la competencia territorial de tal tribunal.

**Action, real.** La acción que persigue recuperar bienes inmuebles. En el sistema del Derecho Común es mucho más restringida que las acciones reales de los sistemas romanistas.

**Action to quiet title.** Acción para resolver reclamaciones opuestas sobre propiedad inmueble. Acción mediante la cual el actor obliga al demandado a probar que el segundo tiene un mejor derecho sobre un inmueble.

**Actionable.** Accionable, con derecho a intervención judicial.

**Actionable fraud.** Fraude que contiene todos los elementos necesarios, por ejemplo dolo, para entablar demanda.

**Actionable misrepresentation.** Falsedad dolosa.

**Actionable nuisance.** Molestia, estorbo o restricción, de carácter ilegal, al goce de los derechos propietarios de otro y que puede ser remediado judicialmente.

**Actionable *per quod*.** Que sólo puede triunfar en un juicio al probar perjuicios específicos. Se aplica generalmente a las calumnia e injurias.

**Actionable *per se*.** Lo opuesto a per quod. No requiere prueba de perjuicios específicos. Por ejemplo, la imputación calumniosa de haber cometido un crimen.

**Actionable tort.** Cuasidelito que reune todas las condiciones para presentar una demanda judicial viable.

**Active.** Activo, diligente, energético.

**Active concealment.** Ocultamiento activo. Por oposición al pasivo, se realiza mediante declaraciones o acciones que son, a sabiendas, falsas.

**Active negligence.** Negligencia activa. Aquélla que denota un acto u omisión específico y que causa el daño en cuestión.

**Active trust.** Fideicomiso en el cual el administrador debe realizar ciertos actos. Se opone a la noción de fideicomiso pasivo.

**Activities dangerous to invitees.** Actividades peligrosas para invitados. El poseedor de un predio de terreno es responsable hacia sus invitados por el daño físico que éstos sufran como consecuencia de su falta de prudencia en las actividades que le son propias para la seguridad de éstos, si y sólo si, él sabe que no descubrirán el peligro y no podrán protegerse del mismo. (Rstmnt, 2nd, Torts, sec. 341A).

**Activities dangerous to known trespassers.** Actividades que resultan peligrosas a un transgresor conocido. El poseedor de un terreno que sabe o tiene motivos para creer que existe un transgresor que ha entrado a su predio, será responsable por los daños físicos causados al transgresor si no cumple con sus actividades en el inmueble con un cuidado razonable para la seguridad de dicho transgresor. (Rstmnt, 2nd, Torts, sec. 336).

**Activities dangerous to licensees.** Actividades peligrosas para licenciatarios. El poseedor de un predio de terreno es responsable ante sus concesionarios por los daños físicos que éstos sufran como consecuencia de su falta de prudencia en las actividades que le son propias, si, y sólo si: a) debe saber que éstos no descubrirán el peligro, y b) los concesionarios no conocen ni tienen motivos para conocer las actividades del poseedor ni el riesgo que envuelven. (Rstmnt, 2nd, Torts, sec. 341.)

**Acts under private signature.** Actos bajo firma privada. Documentos firmados por las partes, por ejemplo, un contrato.

**Actual.** Real, efectivo, verdadero.

**Actual authority.** Representación para actuar en favor de otro que ha sido expresamente conferida, por ejemplo, mediante un poder de representación.

**Actual cash value.** Precio de mercado, precio real.

**Actual cost.** Precio efectivamente pagado por algo en buena fe.

**Actual damages.** Daños y perjuicios efectivamente sufridos.

**Actual domicile.** Domicilio real de una persona.

**Actual eviction.** Lanzamiento llevado a cabo.

**Actual knowledge.** Conocimiento real.

**Actuary.** Actuario.

**Addict.** Adicto, normalmente respecto de narcóticos.

**Addictive drugs.** Drogas que causan adicción.

**Additional period for performance.** Plazo adicional para el cumplimiento. (1) En caso de incumplimiento, la parte agraviada podrá conceder a la otra un plazo adicional para que cumpla, y así se lo comunicará. (2) Durante el transcurso de ese plazo adicional, la parte agraviada podrá suspender el cumplimiento de sus propias obligaciones correlativas y reclamar daños y perjuicios, pero no podrá ejercitar ninguna otra acción. (Unidroit, Prin., art. 7.1.5).

**Additur.** Facultad del tribunal para modificar el monto indemnizatorio dictado por el jurado. El juez utiliza este poder, con acuerdo de la demandada, como condición para denegar un pedido de recomenzar el juicio.

**Address.** Domicilio, dirección (s). Dirigirse a alguien (v).

**Address for service.** Domicilio procesal.

**Address the court.** Dirigirse al tribunal.

**Addressee.** Destinatario de un documento, persona a la cual uno se dirige.

**Adduce.** Aducir, afirmar, alegar, argumentar, enunciar, declarar, informar, narrar, relatar.

**Adeem.** Revocar una manda testamentaria.

**Adeemed.** Situación en la que se halla un legado caduco.

**Ademption.** Caducidad de legado. Pérdida de un legado específico por no existir tal bien en el patrimonio del causante al momento de producirse el deceso.

**Adequate.** Adecuado, correcto, suficiente.

**Adequate assurance of due performance.** Garantía adecuada de cumplimiento. La parte que razonablemente crea que la otra incurrirá en un incumplimiento esencial, podrá exigir garantía adecuada de cumplimiento y, mientras tanto, podrá aplazar su propio cumplimiento. (Unidroit, Prin., art. 7.3.4).

**Adequate consideration.** Contraprestación razonable y adecuada.

**Adequate notice.** Notificación suficiente.

**Adhesion.** Adhesión

**Adhesion contract.** Contrato de adhesión. Aquél que puede aceptarse en pleno o rechazarse, pero no negociarse cláusula por cláusula.

**Adjacent.** Adyacente.

**Adjacent tenement.** Heredad confinante.

**Adjective.** Adjetivo.

**Adjective law.** Derecho adjetivo. Forma de referirse al derecho procesal y que se opone al derecho de fondo o sustantivo.

**Adjoining.** Colindante, limítrofe, próximo, vecino.

**Adjoining owner.** Propietario colindante.

**Adjourn.** Suspender, aplazar, diferir, levantar, posponer, prorrogar.

**Adjourned.** Suspendido, aplazado, diferido, prorrogado.

**Adjournment.** Suspensión, aplazamiento, dilación, postergación.

**Adjudge.** Adjudicar. Fallar, decidir, resolver. Ceder, otorgar, transferir.

**Adjudicate.** Adjudicar, decidir. Ceder, transferir.

**Adjudicated rights.** Derechos adjudicados. Bajo el efecto de cosa juzgada.

**Adjudicatee.** Adjudicatario, receptor.

**Adjudication.** Adjudicación, asignación.

**Adjudication in bankruptcy.** Declaración de quiebra.

**Adjudicative.** Adjudicativo.

**Adjudicator.** Adjudicador, juez, cedente.

**Adjudicature.** Adjudicación, decisión, transferencia.

**Adjunct.** Adjunto. Que acompaña algo considerado como principal.

**Adjuration.** Juramento, declaración solemne.

**Adjust.** Ajustar, componer, transar, arreglar, regular, dirimir, organizar.

**Adjusted gross income.** Ingreso o entradas brutas para fines impositivos.

**Adjuster.** Ajustador, encargado de determinar el monto y de negociar el pago de un reclamo, generalmente para una empresa de seguros.

**Adjustment.** Ajuste, arreglo, convenio, transacción.

**Adminicular.** Accesorio.

**Adminicular evidence.** Prueba corroborante.

**Adminiculate.** Corroborar, convalidar, ratificar.

**Administer.** Administrar, conceder, conferir, dispensar, gobernar, dirigir.

**Administer oaths.** Recibir juramentos.

**Administration.** Administración, manejo, gobierno, dirección de un grupo de personas, fondos.

**Administration expense.** Gastos de administración.

**Administrative.** Administrativo.

**Administrative acts.** Actos de administración, que no implican un cambio radical. Por ejemplo, pagar impuestos sobre una casa.

**Administrative agency.** Dependencia gubernamental encargada de tareas específicas.

**Administrative appeal.** Recurso administrativo.

**Administrative crime.** Delito administrativo.

**Administrative hearing.** Audiencia administrativa.

**Administrative interpretation.** Interpretación administrativa. Aquélla hecha por los órganos administrativos.

**Administrative law.** Derecho administrativo. El derecho administrativo se ocupa de los poderes y procedimientos de aquellas organismos estatales distintos de las legislaturas y los tribunales, cuyas normas y decisiones afectan a los intereses privados. El campos es relativamente joven y se halla aún en una etapa de rápido desarrollo. El énfasis está puesto fuertemente sobre los procedimientos y no incluye la ley substantiva creada por las agencias administrativas. (Intro al USA).

**Administrative law, content.** Derecho administrativo, contenido. El derecho administrativo es un compuesto de derecho constitucional, leyes, jurisprudencia, y resoluciones de las agencias. (Intro al USA).

**Administrative order.** Orden administrativa. Aquélla emitida por las autoridades administrativas dentro del área de su competencia.

**Administrative procedure.** Procedimiento administrativo.

**Administrative regulations.** Resoluciones administrativas. Los reglamentos y disposiciones de los organismos administrativos estaduales son de forma y objetivos semejantes a los de las agencias federales. Se ocupan de temas tales como el otorgamiento de licencias para el ejercicio de diversas actividades dentro del estado. (Intro al USA).

**Administrative tribunal.** Tribunal administrativo.

**Administratix.** Albacea, administradora.

**Administrator.** Administrador, albacea, curador, gerente, síndico.

**Admiral.** Almirante.

**Admiralty.** Almirantazgo.

**Admiralty court.** Tribunal de almirantazgo.

**Admiralty law.** Derecho marítimo.

**Admissibility.** Admisión, admisibilidad.

**Admissible.** Admisible, aceptable, adecuado, permisible, verosímil, creíble.

**Admissible evidence.** Medio de prueba admisible.

**Admission.** Admisión, confesión, asentimiento, ingreso, recepción.

**Admission against interest.** Manifestación hecha por una parte que perjudica su posición en el juicio pues tiende a corroborar lo que la contraparte sostiene.

**Admission by party opponent.** Admisión por la contraparte. Bajo ciertas condiciones este medio probatorio escapa a prohibición del testimonio por referencia (*hearsay*).

**Admission by silence.** Admisión mediante silencio. El hecho de no protestar ante la manifestación de alguien—cuando normalmente tal manifestación provocaría la protesta del interlocutor—puede interpretarse como una admisión de lo dicho.

**Admit.** Admitir, aceptar, asentir, confesar, reconocer, permitir, autorizar.

**Admitted to the bar.** Admitido, licenciado para ejercer el derecho.

**Admonish.** Amonestar, apercibir, prevenir.

**Admonition.** Admonición, amonestación, apercibimiento, aviso.

**Adolescence.** Adolescencia, juventud.

**Adopt.** Adoptar, amparar, proteger, aprobar, recoger, seguir.

**Adopter.** Adoptante.

**Adoption.** Adopción.

**Adoption by estoppel.** Adopción no formalizada legalmente pero reconocida en favor del adoptado. Ocurre cuando el adoptante promete llevar a cabo la adopción o actúa como si la adopción hubiese transcurrido.

**Adoption by reference.** Incorporación de lo dicho o escrito—por otros o en otra oportunidad—haciendo referencia a ello.

**Adult.** Adulto, mayor de edad.

**Adulterate.** Adulterar, falsificar, fraguar, rebajar.

**Adulteration.** Adulteración, desnaturalización, falsificación.

**Adulterator.** Adulterador, falsificador.

**Adulterer.** Adúltero, infiel, fornicador, falsificador.

**Adulteress.** Adúltera.

**Adulterine.** Adulterino.

**Adulterous.** Adúltero.

**Adultery.** Adulterio.

**Advance.** Adelanto, depósito, pago a cuenta, pronto, seña, avance, perfeccionamiento, progreso (s). Pagar un anticipo, progresar, proponer una idea (v).

**Advance payment.** Anticipo, pago anticipado.

**Advancement.** Anticipo irrevocable de herencia, avance, mejora, progreso.

**Advancement of a case.** Señalamiento anticipado.

**Advantage.** Ventaja, beneficio, ganancia, preeminencia, primacía, superioridad, supremacía.

**Adventitious.** Adventicio, accidental, casual.

**Adventure.** Aventura, empresa, lance, incertidumbre.

**Adventurer.** Aventurero.

**Adversary.** Adversario, antagonista, oponente, parte contraria.

**Adversary proceeding.** Proceso adversativo, contencioso.

**Adversary process.** Proceso adversativo. Cuando una investigación preliminar de un delito toma el cariz de acusatoria y se posa sobre un sospechoso en particular con miras a sacarle una confesión, cobra realidad el proceso adversativo de nuestro sistema de enjuiciamiento criminal, surgiendo la obligación de la policía u otra autoridad competente de advertirle al sospechoso de su derecho constitucional a permanecer en silencio y no incriminarse, y de su derecho cons-titucional a tener allí y entonces asistencia de abogado y el permitirle que la tenga. (Rivera Escute v. Jefe Penitenciaría, 92 D.P.R. 765 (1965)).

**Adverse.** Adverso, antagónico, contrapuesto, desfavorable, calamitoso, infortunado.

**Adverse party.** Parte contraria, adversa.

**Adverse possession.** Prescripción. Posesión adversa o adquisitiva.

**Adverse use.** Uso adverso. Aquél que, durante el tiempo necesario, conduciría a la prescripción.

**Adverse witness.** Testigo por la parte contraria.

**Advertisement.** Anuncio, aviso, espacio publicitario, reclamo, propaganda, publicidad.

**Advertiser.** Anunciador, patrocinador.

**Advertising.** Publicidad, comercialización, mercadeo, promoción, propaganda.

**Advice.** Aviso, advertencia, anuncio, citación, comunicación, confidencia, llamamiento, observación, participación, consejo, asesoramiento, dictamen, guía, orientación.

**Advise.** Avisar, advertir, citar, comunicar, aconsejar, asesorar, dictaminar, orientar.

**Advisedly.** Con conocimiento de causa, a propósito, concientemente, ex profeso, intencionalmente. Sabiamente tras estudio y reflexión.

**Advisement.** Proceso de análisis, estudio, reflexión.

**Adviser, advisor.** Asesor, abogado, consejero, consultor, letrado, licenciado.

**Advisory.** Consultivo, asesorativo, consulto.

**Advisory board.** Junta consultiva.

**Advisory committee.** Comité asesor.

**Advisory juridiction.** Tribunal consultivo, que emite opiniones que carecen de imperio.

**Advisory jury and trial by consent.** Jurado consultivo y juicio por consentimiento. En todos los pleitos no enjuiciables por jurado la corte a moción de parte o de su propia iniciativa podrá juzgar cualquier cuestión con un jurado consultivo, a excepción de pleitos contra los Estados Unidos. (R. Fed. P. Civ., sec. 39(c))

**Advisory opinion.** Opinión interpretativa de un tribunal sin que medie una contienda específica.

**Advocacy.** Abogacía, alegato, defensa, promoción.

**Advocate.** Abogado, consejero, jurisconsulto, jurista, letrado, licenciado, procurador, representante, togado (s). Abogar, alegar, defender, promover (v).

**Advocation.** Abogacía.

**Aerial.** Aéreo, desconectado, etéreo, intangible, remoto.

**Affair.** Asunto, caso, juicio, pleito.

**Affect.** Afectar. Establecer un gravamen. Destinar a un uso particular. Aparentar, disimular, fingir.

**Affected.** Afectado.

**Affecting commerce.** Atinente al comercio.

**Affiance.** Declaración, afirmación, enunciación, manifestación.

**Affiant.** Declarante, deponente, firmante, manifestante.

**Affidavit.** Declaración jurada.

**Affidavit of enquiry.** Declaración jurada que firma el actor, o su abogado, estableciendo que a pesar de diligentes esfuerzos no ha logrado averiguar el domicilio del demandado. Ello hace procedente la citación mediante publicación.

**Affidavit of merits.** Declaración jurada estableciendo que el demandado tiene defensas valederas.

**Affidavit of notice.** Declaración jurada en la que una parte establece que ha notificado debidamente a la otra parte sobre una audiencia.

**Affiliation.** Afiliación, asociación, dependencia, pertenencia, relación, unión, filiación.

**Affinity.** Afinidad. Forma de parentesco con la familia del cónyuge.

**Affirm.** Afirmar, afianzar, apoyar, asegurar, asentar, insistir, sostener.

**Affirmance.** Afirmación, apoyo, sostenimiento.

**Affirmant.** Afirmante, declarante, manifestante.

**Affirmation.** Afirmación, asentimiento, aserción, aseveración. Ratificación, robustecimiento.

**Affirmation in lieu of oath.** Afirmación en lugar de juramento. Cuando la ley requiera la toma de juramento, podrá aceptarse en lugar del mismo una afirmación solemne. (R. Fed. P. Civ., sec. 43(d)).

**Affirmative.** Afirmativo.

**Affirmative action.** Modo de integrar a los sectores minoritarios antes desfavorecidos, por ejemplo, mujeres y negros, prefiriéndolos para llenar vacantes de trabajo.

**Affirmative defenses.** Defensas de previo y especial pronunciamiento. Defensas afirmativas. Las partes respondientes al contestar alegaciones precedentes expondrán afirmativamente aceptación como finiquito, laudo y adjudicación, asunción de riesgo, negligencia contribuyente, exoneración por quiebra, coacción, impedimento, falta de causa, fraude común, ilegalidad, lesión por compañero de trabajo, incuria, autorización, pago, exoneración, cosa juzgada, fraude, prescripción extintiva, renuncia y cualquier otra materia constitutiva de excepción o de defensa afirmativa. (Reglas Fed. del Proc. Civ., sec. 8(c)).

**Affirmative proof.** Prueba afirmativa, que establece la verdad de lo que se alega.

**Affix.** Estampar, adherir, colocar, fijar, insertar, poner, sellar.

**Affliction.** Aflicción. Desmedro físico o pesadumbre de ánimo.

**Afforce.** Reforzar, mejorar, perfeccionar, robustecer.

**Affray.** Disputa, escaramuza, pelea, refriega, riña (s). Reyertar (v).

**Affreighter.** Fletador, consignador, despachante.

**Affront.** Afrenta, agravio, humillación, injuria, insulto, ofensa.

**Afloat.** Flotando, no sumergido.

**Aforementioned, aforenamed, aforesaid.** Mencionado anteriormente. Antedicho, referido arriba.

**Aforethought.** Deliberado, con premeditación, consciente, estudiando, ponderado.

**After.** Después, luego, más tarde, posteriormente, tras. Atrás de.

**After-acquired.** Adquirido con posterioridad a algo.

**After-born.** Póstumo, final, último, ulterior.

**After summoning.** Con citación.

**After the fact.** Con posterioridad a un hecho.

**Afterbirth.** Placenta y demás tejidos reproductivos que quedan inutilizados luego del nacimiento.

**Afternoon.** Tarde, oración.

**Afterthought.** Pensamiento al que se llega concientemente luego de un hecho.

**Against.** Contra.

**Against interest.** Contra el propio interés, en detrimento de uno mismo.

**Against the weight of the evidence.** Contra el peso de la prueba que ha sido presentada en un juicio. Una de las causales por la cual se puede apelar un fallo.

**Age.** Edad, época, tiempo.

**Age of consent.** Edad en la que puede prestarse consentimiento por uno mismo.

**Age of majority.** Mayoría de edad.

**Age of reason.** Edad por debajo de la cual un menor no puede ser imputado por un delito.

**Agency.** Mandato, representación. Mandato es la relación fiduciaria resultante de la manifestación del consentimiento de una persona hacia otra, en el sentido que la primera actuación en representación de la segunda y sujeta a su control, consintiendo

a ello la segunda parte. (Restatement, Second, Agency, sec. 1).
Dependencia, oficina.

**Agency, actual.** Mandato expreso.

**Agency by estoppel.** Mandato por preclusión o implícito. Aquel que la ley impone a quien permite que otro se comporte como mandatario del primero, resultando en que terceros crean de buena fe que efectivamente existe un mandato.

**Agency by operation of law.** Mandato impuesto por la ley.

**Agency coupled with an interest.** Situación en la que el mandatario posee además un interés personal en las transacciones que están a su cargo. En tales casos la muerte del mandante suele no terminar el mandato.

**Agency, general.** Mandato general.

**Agency, ostensible.** Mandato ostensible. Aquél que emerge de los hechos pero que no tiene fundamento legal. Por razones de equidad puede convertirse en un mandato implícito (*agency by estoppel*).

**Agenda.** Agenda, tema, orden del día.

**Agent.** Agente, apoderado, comisionista, gestor, mandatario, representante.

**Agent's loyalty.** Lealtad del mandatario. A menos que medie pacto en contrario, un mandatario está obligado a actuar solamente para beneficio de su mandante en todas las materias relacionadas con el contrato de agencia. (Rstmnt, 2nd, Agency, sec. 387).

**Aggravated.** Agravado, calificado.

**Aggravated assault.** Lesiones calificadas.

**Aggravated battery.** Acometimiento o agresión calificada.

**Aggravating.** Molesto, engorroso, intolerable, injurioso, ofensivo, agravante.

**Aggravation.** Agravante, calificación, molestia, injuria.

**Aggregate.** En total.

**Aggregate indebtedness.** Deuda total.

**Aggressor.** Agresor, acometedor, ofensor, provocador.

**Aggrieved.** Agraviado, damnificado, injuriado, ofendido, ultrajado.

**Aggrieved party.** Parte agraviada.

**Agitator.** Agitador, perturbador, revolucionario.

**Agnate.** Agnado, familiar, relacionado.

**Agnatic.** Agnático, con un origen de parentesco común.

**Agnation.** Agnación, vínculo de sangre o parentesco.

**Agrarian laws.** Leyes agrarias.

**Agrarian reform.** Reforma agraria.

**Agree.** Acordar, ajustar, aprobar, arreglar, avenir, concluir, concordar, determinar, establecer, pactar.

**Agreed.** Acordado, aprobado, arreglado, concluído, concordado, pactado.

**Agreed judgment.** Sentencia por acuerdo entre las partes. Aquélla a la que las partes consienten y cuyo texto ambas partes suscriben y someten al tribunal para ser firmada por el juez.

**Agreed payment for non-performance.** Indemnización por incumplimiento estipulada en el contrato. Cuando el contrato prevenga que la parte incumplidora pagará a la otra un monto determinado en razón de su incumplimiento, esta tiene derecho a cobrarla sin consideración al daño efectivamente sufrido. (Unidroit, Prin., art. 7.4.13).

**Agreed price.** Precio acordado.

**Agreed statement of appeal.** Memorial describiendo los hechos del caso en el que todas las partes concuerdan.

**Agreement.** Acuerdo. Acuerdo es la manifestación del mutuo consentimiento de dos o más personas. (Rstmnt, 2nd, Con., sec. 3).

**Agreement not to be performed within a year.** Acuerdo que no puede ejecutarse dentro de un año. Estos contratos deben realizarse por escrito para ser válidos.

**Agreement of rescission.** Acuerdo de rescisión. Acuerdo bajo el cual cada parte conviene en liberar a la otra de toda prestación o deber restante bajo un contrato existente. (Rstmnt, 2nd, Con., sec. 283 (1)).

**Agricultural insurance.** Seguro agrícola. "Seguro agrícola" incluye el seguro de edificaciones en fincas, maquinarias, equipo, animales, aves, plantaciones y cosechas pertenecientes a fincas, contra pérdidas o daños por cualquier causa, incluyendo pérdidas habidas durante la transportación y entrega de cosechas a puntos de embarque, pero sin incluir riesgos de transportación marítima, navegación o almacenaje comercial. (26 LPRA sec. 406).

**Agricultural lien.** Prenda flotante. Aquélla que se extiende a la cosecha cuando crece.

**Aid.** Asistencia, auxilio, ayuda, colaboración, concurso, cooperación, favor, patronición, refuerzo (s). Ayudar, prestar auxilio (v).

**Aid an escape.** Ayudar, a sabiendas, en la fuga de alguien que se encuentra legítimamente arrestado o detenido.

**Aid and abet.** Prestar auxilio o ayuda, generalmente en forma ilegal.

**Aide.** Asistente, colaborador.

**Aider and abettor.** Persona que participa en una acción delictuosa aunque no como autor principal. Por ejemplo, el instigador de un delito, el encubridor, etc.

**Ailment.** Enfermedad, indisposición, malestar generalizado.

**Air carrier.** Transportador aéreo. Compañía de transporte aéreo.

**Air charter.** Fletamento aéreo.

**Air Force.** Fuerza aérea. Aviación de guerra.

**Air law.** Derecho aeronáutico.

**Air piracy.** Piratería aérea.

**Air rights.** Derechos existentes respecto de la columna de aire que se eleva de una propiedad inmueble.

**Airbill.** Carta de porte aérea.

**Aircraft.** Avión, aeronave, aeroplano.

**Airline.** Línea aérea.

**Airmail.** Correo aéreo.

**Airport.** Aeropuerto.

**Airspace.** Espacio aéreo.

**Airworthiness.** Navegabilidad aérea.

**Akin.** Conectado, emparentado, relacionado.

**Alarm.** Alarma, alboroto, alerta, confusión, inquietud, nerviosismo, sobresalto, sorpresa.

**Alarmist.** Alarmista, descontrolado, mentiroso, pesimista.

**Alcoholism.** Alcoholismo, borrachera, embriaguez.

**Alderman.** Concejal, representante municipal, edil.

**Aleatory.** Aleatorio, azaroso, casual, contingente, incierto.

**Aleatory contract.** Contrato aleatorio.

**Alias.** Alias.

**Alias summons.** Segunda citación emitida en reemplazo de la primera, al haber ésta fracasado.

**Alias writ of execution.** Segundo mandamiento de ejecución firmado por el juez luego de haber fracasado el primero.

**Alibi.** Coartada. La prueba de coartada sólo constituye prueba que tiende a establecer que el acusado no cometió el delito que se le imputa al crear una duda en la mente del jurado con respecto a su culpabilidad. (Pueblo v. Moreau Pérez, 96 D.P.R. 60 (1968)).

**Alien.** Extranjero, ajeno, forastero, foráneo.

**Alien corporation.** Sociedad anónima, o empresa, creada en un país extranjero.

**Alien enemy.** Persona cuya ciudadanía corresponde a un país con el cual se está en guerra declarada.

**Alien friend.** Persona ciudadana de un país que se encuentra en situación de paz.

**Alienage.** Extranjería, condición de foráneo.

**Alienate.** Alienar, enajenar, transferir, vender.

**Alienate and encumber.** Enajenar y agravar.

**Alienation.** Enajenación, alienación, alienamiento, enajenamiento, locura.

**Alienation clause.** Cláusula de alienación. Aquélla que contractualmente brinda o prohibe el derecho de enajenar.

**Alienation of spouse's affection.** Incitación a la separación de un matrimonio. Una persona que a propósito desvía el afecto de un cónyuge por el otro cónyuge, será responsable por el daño causado a los intereses maritales legalmente protegidos de cualesquiera de los cónyuges. (Rstmnt, 2nd, Torts, sec. 683).

**Alienee.** Cesionario, adquirente, excepcionario de la propiedad transferida.

**Alienor.** Alienante, enajenante, transferente.

**Aligned parties.** Partes en un proceso que, sin ser litisconsortes, tienen intereses comunes.

**Alignment.** Alineamiento. Situación de encontrarse en un mismo plano o como parte de un sistema, estrategia, etc.

**Alimentary.** Alimentario, alimenticio.

**Alimony.** Alimentos entre cónyuges. Mientras el matrimonio subsiste, un cónyuge puede obtener una orden judicial de sostén que además esta protegida contra huida a través de la aprobación en todos los estados de la ley uniforme de reciprocidad en la protección de la manutención. (Intro al USA).

Alimentos, mantenimiento, manutención.

**Alimony in gross.** Alimentos pagados al cónyuge en una sola cuota.

**Alimony pendente lite.** También llamados *temporary alimony*, son los alimentos devengados o pagados al cónyuge mientras dura el juicio de divorcio.

**Aliquot.** Alícuota o cuota parte.

**Alive.** Vivo, viviente, agudo, enérgico, perspicaz.

**All.** Todo, todos, completo, total.

**All and singular.** El conjunto de todos los bienes y cada bien en particular. Expresión que indica que se trata de todo, sin excepción.

**All fours.** Expresión idiomática que significa que dos casos son prácticamente idénticos en cuanto a sus elementos relevantes. Esto normalmente implica que el segundo caso debería resolverse igual que el primero.

**Allegation.** Alegato, alegación, argumento, argumentación, defensa.

**Allegation of fact.** Alegato sobre hechos, opuesto al alegato sobre cuestiones de derecho.

**Allege.** Alegar, argumentar, interponer, oponer.

**Alleged.** Supuesto, alegado, interpuesto.

**Allegiance.** Lealtad, fidelidad, seguimiento.

**Alliance.** Alianza, casamiento, enlace, matrimonio, nupcias, acuerdo, asociación, coalición, confederación, convenio, liga, pacto, unión.

**Allision.** En derecho marítimo, cuando una nave embiste a otra.

**Allocation.** Alocación, cuota, distribución, parte, proporción, ración.

**Allocation of dividends.** Alocación o distribución de dividendos.

**Allocation of income.** Alocación o distribución de ganancias.

**Allocution.** Alocución. Denomínase alocución (*allocutus*) en el procedimiento criminal, la práctica del juez sentenciador—la cual tuvo su origen en el derecho consuetudinario ingles—de inquirir del convicto sobre las razones que pueda tener para que no se le dicte sentencia. (Pueblo v. Hernández, 94 D.P.R. 116 (1967)).

Discurso, ponencia.

**Allodium.** Inmueble del que se es propietario sin sumisión federal o de vasallaje.

**Allograph.** Escrito que no pertenece a su supuesto autor.

**Alloidal.** Libre de todo vínculo de sumisión federal o de vasallaje.

**Allonge.** Alargamiento. Papel que se agrega a un instrumento de crédito cuando los siguientes endosos requieren más lugar.

**Allot.** Asignar, conceder, dar, destinar, distribuir, repartir.

**Allotment.** Asignación, cupo, distribución, parte, reparto.

**Allottee.** Asignado, quien recibe parte de una distribución.

**Allow.** Acceder, admitir, ceder, conceder, consentir, habilitar, permitir, visar.

**Allowance.** Pensión o suma de dinero pagada regularmente. Bonificación, descuento. Admisión, autorización.

**Allurement.** Atractivo, lo que incita o lleva a realizar un acto determinado.

**Alluvion.** Aluvión.

**Ally.** Aliado, afiliado, amigo, asociado, colega, compañero, correligionario (s). Aliarse, afiliarse, asociarse, consolidar, juntar, unificar, unir (v).

**Almost.** Casi, a duras penas, apenas, cuasi.

**Alms.** Donaciones benéficas, beneficencia.

**Almshouse.** Hospicio, refugio de pobres.

**Alodial.** Ver *alloidal*.

**Alodium.** Ver *allodium*.

**Alter.** Alterar, cambiar.

**Alteration.** Alteración, cambio, modificación, falsificación, exaltación.

**Alteration of contract.** Alteración contractual. Cambio no establecido ni previsto en las cláusulas contractuales y que, según su gravedad, acuerda diversas acciones a la contraparte.

**Alteration of trust.** Alteración o cambio en las cláusulas de un fideicomiso realizados por el creador del mismo.

**Altercation.** Altercado, pelea verbal, riña.

**Altered.** Alterado, cambiado, modificado, trastrocado.

**Alternate.** Suplente, interino, sustituto, temporario. Alterado.

**Alternate jurors.** Jurados suplentes. La corte podrá disponer que no más de seis jurados sean convocados y electos para actuar como jurados suplentes en adición a los jurados ordinarios. (R. Fed. P. Civ., sec. 47(b)).

**Alternative.** Alternativa, elección, opción, posibilidad.

**Alternative contract.** Contrato alternativo, que permite varias prestaciones subsidiariamente.

**Alternative dispute resolution.** Ver *ADR*.

**Alternative obligation.** Aquélla que permite al obligado liberarse mediante el cumplimiento de una entre varias prestaciones, a su elección.

**Alternative pleading.** Alegato en subsidio.

**Amalgamation.** Amalgama, combinación, fusión, mezcla, unión.

**Ambassador.** Embajador, delegado, emisario, jefe de misión diplomática, nuncio, representante.

**Ambiguity.** Ambigüedad, confusión, incertidumbre, oscuridad.

**Ambiguous.** Ambiguo, ambivalente, bivalente, confuso, equívoco, incierto, oscuro, polivalente.

**Ambulance chaser.** Picapleitos.

**Ambulatory.** Itinerante, ambulante, ambulatorio, deambulatorio, móvil.

**Ambush.** Emboscada, celada, encerrona, encrucijada, engaño, estratagema, maniobra, trampa (s). Emboscar, atacar sorpresiva e inesperadamente (v).

**Amenable.** Culpable, responsable. Sujeto a jurisdicción. Accesible, aceptante, amistoso, flexible.

**Amendatory.** Referente a enmiendas.

**Amendment.** Reforma, alteración, cambio, corrección, enmienda.

**Amendment of judgment.** Cambio en los términos de una sentencia, por ejemplo, como consecuencia de un recurso de reposición.

**Amendment on court's own motion.** Cambio en parte de los documentos del procedimiento, dictado de oficio.

**Amendments to conform to the evidence.** Enmiendas para conformar las alegaciones. Cuando se sometieren a juicio con el consentimiento expreso o implícito de las partes cuestiones no suscitadas en las alegaciones, serán consideradas en todo respecto como si hubieren sido suscitadas en las alegaciones. (R. Fed. P. Civ., sec. 15(b)).

**Amendments to pleadings.** Enmiendas a las alegaciones. Las partes podrán enmendar sus alegaciones una vez como cuestión de rutina en cualquier momento antes de serles notificadas las alegaciones respondientes o, si sus alegaciones fueran de las que no admiten alegación respondiente y el pleito hubiera sido incluido en el calendario de juicios, podrán enmendarlas en cualquier momento dentro de los 20 días siguientes de haberles sido notificadas. (R. Fed. P. Civ., sec. 15(a)).

**Amends.** Resarcimiento, compensación, indemnización, reparación. Pago por daños y perjuicios.

**Amerce.** Imponer una multa o penalidad.

**Amercement.** Castigo, multa, penalidad, sanción.

**American rule.** Norma mediante la cual los costos de un juicio son por su orden.

**Amicable.** Amigable, amistoso, por mutuo acuerdo.

**Amicable action.** Acción presentada por las partes para que el tribunal se pronuncie en cuanto a derecho, mediando acuerdo en cuanto a los hechos.

**Amicable compounders.** Amigables componedores.

**Amicus curiae (L).** Amigo de la corte. Tercero que asesora al tribunal sobre un caso en particular.

**Amnesty.** Amnistía, absolución o perdón colectivo, moratoria.

**Amortization.** Amortización, depreciación, desgaste, pérdida de valor por el transcurso del tiempo, obsolencia, crédito impositivo.

**Amortize.** Amortizar, atenuar, disminuir el impacto.

**Amotion.** Remover a un funcionario del cargo que ocupa.

**Amount.** Monto, adición, agregado, cantidad, cifra, cuenta, cuota, magnitud, suma, tamaño, total, volumen (s). Alcanzar cierta proporción o volumen (v).

**Amount import.** Cuantía, cantidad, monto, suma.

**Ampliation.** Extensión del plazo, espera, prórroga.

**Analogous.** Análogo, equivalente, parecido, próximo, similar.

**Analogy.** Analogía, paralelismo, parecido, similitud.

**Analysis.** Análisis, comparación, cotejo, diagnóstico, dictamen, estudio, examen, observación.

**Analytical.** Analítico, agudo, concentrado, crítico, sistemático.

**Anarchist.** Anarquista.

**Anarchy.** Anarquía.

**Anathema.** Anatema.

**Anatocism.** Interés compuesto.

**Ancestor.** Antepasado, antecesor, ascendiente, predecesor, progenitor.

**Ancestral.** Ancestral.

**Ancestry.** Descendencia, linaje, prosapia.

**Anchorage.** Anclaje, derecho de entrar al puerto.

**Ancient.** Antiguo, pasado de moda, primigenio, primitivo, viejo.

**Ancient lights.** Servidumbre de vista adquirida por prescripción, normalmente tras 20 años.

**Ancient writing rule.** Regla mediante la cual un documento que ha existido por cierto tiempo—en algunos Estados de los Estados Unidos por 30 años—y que no presenta signos obvios de falsificación u otras anomalías, debe tenerse por auténtico.

**Ancillary.** Accesorio, auxiliar, complementario, satélite, secundario, subsidiario, subordinado.

**Ancillary administration.** Administración de bienes relictos que están ubicados fuera de la competencia territorial del tribunal interviniente.

**Ancillary jurisdiction.** Fuero de atracción. Competencia para decidir cuestiones conexas a una acción ya presentada.

**Ancillary proceeding.** Causa conexa. Proceso subordinado a otro.

**Angar.** Angaría, antiguo derecho a utilizar barcos mercantes enemigos para transportar tropas.

**Annex.** Anexo, apéndice, parte adicional (s). Anexar, consolidar, juntar, unir (v).

**Annexation.** Anexión, combinación, consolidación. Unión por la fuerza de un territorio a otro.

**Annotate.** Anotar, acotar, clarificar, comentar, explicar, glosar, interpretar.

**Annotation.** Anotación, acotación, clarificación, comentario, nota.

**Announce.** Anunciar. Acto por el cual el tribunal hace conocer el sentido de una decisión aunque todavía no se haya firmado la sentencia o auto correspondiente.

**Annoyance.** Molestia, fastidio.

**Annual.** Anual.

**Annual accounting period.** Año fiscal. Normalmente coincide con el año natural.

**Annual depreciation.** Amortización anual.

**Annually.** Anualmente.

**Annuitant.** Censualista.

**Annuity.** Canon, anualidad, jubilación, pensión, regalía, renta.

**Annuity, joint and survivorship.** Anualidad pagada conjuntamente a los beneficiarios, y enteramente a uno cuando el otro fallece.

**Annuity, life.** Anualidad vitalicia.

**Annuity policy.** Póliza de seguro mediante la cual, a partir de cierto momento—por ejemplo a los 60 años—el asegurado comienza a recibir una anualidad.

**Annul.** Anular, abolir, abrogar, cancelar, dejar sin efecto, rescindir, revocar.

**Annullability.** Anulabilidad.

**Annullable.** Anulable.

**Annulment.** Anulación, rescisión, revocación.

**Anoint.** Ungir, elegir, nombrar.

**Anomalous.** Anómalo, anormal, atípico, extraño, inusitado, inusual, irregular.

**Anonymous.** Anónimo.

**Answer.** Contestación de demanda, defensa, reconvención, réplica. Respuesta, solución (s). Contestar una demanda, presentar una defensa, reconvenir, replicar (v).

**Answer, frivolous.** Contestación de demanda realizada con temeridad y malicia, sin mérito alguno.

**Answer, irrelevant.** Contestación de demanda que no responde a los cargos presentados.

**Answer, sham.** Contestación de demanda que cumple con todos los requisitos formales, pero que resulta obviamente falsa.

**Answer, supplemental.** Contestación de demanda supletoria.

**Answerable.** Responsable, culpable.

**Antagonist.** Antagonista, adversario, contraparte, contrario, parte opuesta.

**Antecedent.** Anterior, antecedente, precedente, preexistente.

**Antecedent claim.** Crédito anterior, devengado con prioridad.

**Antecedent creditor.** Acreedor prioritario, aquél cuyo crédito surgió con anterioridad.

**Antecedent debt.** Deuda anterior.

**Antedate.** Antedata, fecha insertada con anterioridad a lo indicado (s). Antedatar (v).

**Antedated.** Antedatado.

**Antenuptial.** Antenupcial, prematrimonial, prenupcial.

**Antenuptial agreement.** Convención prenupcial, capitulaciones matrimoniales.

**Antenuptial gift.** Donación prenupcial.

**Anteriority.** Anterioridad, más temprano en el tiempo. Punto más avanzado o frontal.

**Anthropological.** Antropológico.

**Anthropometrical.** Antropométrico, referente a la medición y clasificación del cuerpo.

**Anti-dumping act.** Ley de lealtad comercial, que reprime la estrategia de vender bajo costo para desplazar a la competencia, quedando luego en situación monopólica.

**Anti-lapse statute.** Ley sobre derecho de representación. Mediante tal ley, las mandas realizadas a favor de un descendiente no fenecen al morir el beneficiario antes que el testador, sino que se transmiten a los descendientes del descendiente fallecido. (Texas Probate Code, sec. 68).

**Anticipation.** Anticipación, previsión. Con anterioridad a algo.

**Anticipatory breach.** Incumplimiento contractual anticipado. Situación por la cual la acción—o inacción—de una parte toma la aprestación a su cargo imposible antes del tiempo fijado para el cumplimiento. Por ejemplo, demoler la casa cuya venta se ha pactado.

**Anticipatory nonperformance.** Incumplimiento anticipado. Cualquiera de las partes podrá dar por terminado el contrato si con anterioridad a la fecha fijada para el cumplimiento se hace evidente que la otra parte incurrirá en un incumplimiento esencial. (Unidroit, Prin., art. 7.3.3).

**Anticipatory repudiation.** Repudio contractual anticipado, producido antes de la fecha establecida para el cumplimiento.

**Antitrust enforcement.** Ejecución de leyes antimonopólicas. El gobierno puede proceder contra las violaciones de tres maneras principales. Primero, por un procedimiento civil de *equity* iniciado por el Departamento de Justicia contra las violaciones de la *Sherman Act* o de la *Clayton Act*; segundo, por medio de una acción penal también iniciada por el Departamento de Justicia en el caso de un grupo más limitado de violaciones per se, sobre todo las contempladas en al *Sherman Act*; y tercero, por procedimientos administrativos iniciados por la Federal Trade Commission de acuerdo con la *Clayton Act* y a la *Federal Trade Commission Act*. (Intro al USA).

**Antitrust laws.** Leyes antimonopólicas, leyes de libre concurrencia.

**Antitrust legislation.** Leyes antimonopólicas. La primera y más importante fue la *Antitrust Act* (Ley antimonopólica), aprobado en 1890 durante el período de expansión industrial y concentración de poder económico que siguió a la Guerra Civil. Por ella se prohíben en términos generales las restricciones irrazonables al comercio, y su monopolio. La *Clayton Act* (Ley Clayton), de 1914, es un tanto más especifica. Con algunas excepciones, prohíbe: primero, los acuerdos de exclusividad, los llamados *tying arrangements* y similares restricciones sobre la distribución de mercancías; segundo, la discriminación o diferenciación de precios entre compradores, así como otras prácticas discriminatorias asociadas; y tercero, la adquisición por parte de una corporación de bienes o paquetes accionarios de otra, en tanto el efecto de cualquiera de estas acciones "sea disminuir sustancialmente la competencia o tener a crear un monopolio." (Intro al USA).

**Apartheid.** Apartheid, segregación racial, política relacionada con Sud Africa y basada en la supremacía de la raza blanca.

**Apostacy.** Renuncia total del Cristianismo al aceptar una religión falsa o ninguna religión.

**Apostille.** Apostilla. En la convención de la Haya sobre certificación de documentos públicos, la apostilla consiste en un certificado de autenticidad que se adhiere al final o al reverso del documento en cuestión.

**Apparatus.** Instrumento, aparato.

**Apparent.** Aparente. Claro, evidente, manifiesto, patente, visible, ostensible, supuesto.

**Apparent authority.** Autoridad aparente. Autoridad aparente es el poder para afectar las relaciones legales de una persona mediante transacciones con terceras personas, como presunto mandatario del primero, que surge de, y está de acuerdo con, las manifestaciones del primero a terceras personas. (Rstmnt, 2nd, Agency, sec. 8).

**Apparent danger.** Peligro aparente, que motiva actuar en defensa propia.

**Apparent defect.** Defecto aparente, obvio o manifiesto. Lo contrario de vicio oculto.

**Apparent heir.** Heredero aparente. Aquél cuyo derecho sólo se condiciona a sobrevivir al causante.

**Appeal.** Apelación. Después del juicio, una de las partes puede apelar la sentencia, aduciendo errores del juez de primera instancia. Esta parte recibe el nombre de apelante, *petitioner* o *plaintiff*—; la contraria, la demandada en apelación, respondent or *defendant*—. Durante la apelación, la ejecución de la sentencia es suspendida para lo que el petitioner deposita una caución. (Intro al USA).

Apelación, alzada, objeción, protesta, queja, recurso (s). Apelar, recurrir (v).

**Appeal bond.** Caución o depósito en garantía para poder apelar un auto.

**Appeal *in forma pauperis*.** Beneficio concedido a un indigente, que le permite apelar sin prestar caución. Beneficio de litigar sin gastos.

**Appealable.** Fallo no firme, sujeto a apelación.

**Appealable for review and for stay of proceedings.** Apelable en ambos efectos.

**Appear.** Comparecer en juicio, constituirse en parte, actuar, participar, ser parte, participación. Aparecer, parecer.

**Appearance.** Comparecencia en juicio, actuación, participación.

**Appearance by attorney.** Comparecencia por medio de representante letrado.

**Appearance, initial.** Auto de procesamiento, indiciamiento. Etapa procesal en casos criminales en la que se da a conocer al reo el delito imputado así como los derechos que le competen, por ejemplo, el de asistencia letrada.

**Appearance, notice of.** Acto procesal mediante el cual el demandado hace conocer que interviene formalmente en el proceso.

**Appearer.** Compareciente, actuante, peticionante, recurrente, solicitante.

**Appellant.** Apelante, agraviado, quejoso, recurrente.

**Appellate court.** Corte de apelaciones, tribunal de alzada.

**Appellate jurisdiction.** Competencia que le cabe al tribunal de alzada para supervisar las decisiones de tribunales inferiores.

**Appellate procedure.** Procedimiento de apelación. El tribunal de apelaciones no lleva a cabo un nuevo proceso con jurado y testigos. Su conocimientos del caso se basa exclusivamente en las actas taquigráficas del proceso de primera instancia, que contienen los pretendidos errores del juez. Tiene a su disposición, además, escritos presentados por las partes en apoyo de sus puntos de vista. (Intro al USA).

**Appellee.** Parte contra la cual se interpone apelación.

**Appendant.** Accesorio, anexado, añadido, secundario, subordinado, subsidiario.

**Appendix.** Apéndice, anexo.

**Appertain.** Pertenecer, competir, concernir.

**Applicable law in absence of an effective choice.** Derecho aplicable en ausencia de una elección efectiva. En ausencia de una elección efectiva del derecho aplicable por las partes, los contactos a tomarse en cuenta para determinar el derecho aplicable a un asunto incluyen: a) el lugar donde se celebró el contrato; b) el lugar donde se negoció el contrato; c) el lugar de ejecución del contrato; d) la localización del objeto del contrato; e) el domicilio, residencia, nacionalidad, lugar de incorporación, y lugar de negocios de las partes. (Rstmnt, 2nd, Conflict, sec. 188(2)).

**Applicable law to torts.** Derecho aplicable a cuasidelitos. Los derechos y responsabilidades de las partes respecto a los cuasidelitos se determinan por la ley local del Estado que—en lo referente a ese asunto—tenga la relación más significativa a la ocurrencia del suceso y a las partes. (Rstmnt, 2nd, Conflict, sec. 145).

**Applicant.** Solicitante, apelante, aspirante, demandante, peticionante, recurrente, requirente, suplicante.

**Application.** Solicitud, demanda, petición, súplica.

**Application for public permission.** Solicitud de autorización pública. Cuando la ley de un Estado exija una autorización pública que afecte la validez del contrato o su cumplimiento, sin que la ley o las circunstancias del caso indiquen algo distinto: si sólo una de las partes tiene su establecimiento en tal Estado, ella deberá tomar las medidas necesarias para obtener dicha autorización. (Unidroit, Prin., art. 6.1.14).

**Application form.** Formulario, forma, solicitud.

**Apply.** Acudir, recurrir.

**Appoint.** Elegir, encomendar, seleccionar. Nombrar, designar, discernir, nominar.

**Appointee.** Persona designada para realizar algo. Por ejemplo, un embajador designado por el poder ejecutivo. Se contrapone a la situación en la cual alguien es elegido por voto popular.

**Appointer, appointor.** Persona que designa a otro.

**Appointment.** Selección y nombramiento para desempeñar un cargo. Cargo, empleo, posición. Entrevista, cita.

**Apportion.** Aporcionar, alocar, distribuir, dividir, repartir.

**Apportioned liability.** Responsabilidad alocada o distribuida específicamente entre un grupo de co-obligados.

**Apportioned rent.** Alquiler alocado o distribuido específicamente entre los colocatarios respectivos.

**Apportionment.** Reparto.

**Appraisable.** Valuable, tasable.

**Appraisal, appraisement.** Valuación, avalúo, estimación, tasación. Cálculo del valor o precio.

**Appraise.** Valuar, estimar el precio, evaluar, tasar.

**Appraiser.** Tasador, evaluador, justipreciador, perito tasador.

**Appreciable.** Aquello que se puede categorizar en forma definida, por ejemplo, en cuanto a su valor económico, número de unidades, peso, etc.

**Appreciate.** Apreciar, estimar. Tener conciencia de algo en el sentido de comprender su significado, extensión, etc.

**Appreciation in value.** Apreciación en el valor, encarecimiento.

**Apprehend.** Aprehender. Tener conciencia de algo, comprender, internalizar, percibir. Arrestar, aprisionar, capturar, detener.

**Apprehension.** Aprehensión. Conciencia, conocimiento, entendimiento.
    Arresto, aprisionamiento, captura, temor, miedo.

**Apprentice.** Aprendiz, artesano, asistente, ayudante, estudiante. Persona que aprende un arte u oficio trabajando para alguien con mayor experiencia. Pasante.

**Apprenticeship.** Aprendizaje, conocimiento, estudio, perfeccionamiento.

**Appriorism.** Apriorismo, anterioridad.

**Approach.** Enfoque, ángulo, cariz, espíritu, política, preconcepto, aproximamiento (s).

Enfocar, concebir, tomar una posición determinada, acercarse, aproximarse (v).

**Approach, right of.** Derecho que le cabe a una nave de acercarse a otra para proceder a inspeccionar a la primera.

**Appropriate.** Apropiado, acorde, adecuado, armonioso, conveniente, oportuno (s). Apropiarse, adueñarse, adjudicarse, apoderarse, atribuirse, incautarse, tomar para sí (v).

**Appropriation.** Apropiación. Apoderamiento, incautación, usurpación. Partida de dinero o de bienes específicos para atender necesidades determinadas.

**Appropriation of name or likeness.** Apropiación de nombre o parecido físico. Una persona que se apropie para su uso o beneficio, del nombre o parecido o semejanza de otro, será responsable ante ese otro por una invasión a su privacidad. (Rstmnt, 2nd, Torts, sec. 652 C).

**Appropriator.** Parte que se apropia, como sin derecho, de alguna cosa.

**Approval.** Aprobación, aceptación, aquiescencia, beneplácito, complacencia, consentimiento.

**Approval sale.** Venta a gusto, que sólo se perfecciona al manifestarse la conformidad del adquiriente con el objeto en cuestión.

**Approve.** Aprobar, aceptar, asentir, consentir, ratificar, sancionar.

**Appurtenance.** Parte anexa a un cuerpo principal. Añadido o apéndice secundario.

**Appurtenant.** Perteneciente a algo más importante. Accesorio, agregado, dependiente, subordinado.

**Aprioristic.** Apriorístico, antecedente, anterior, inicial, preliminar.

**Aqueduct.** Acueducto.

**Arable lands.** Tierras labrantías.

**Arbiter.** Árbitro, arbitrador, amigable componedor, componedor, intercesor, mediador, perito.

**Arbitrable.** Arbitrable, capaz de ser derimido arbitrariamente.

**Arbitrage.** Especulación mediante la compra y venta de valores en mercados bursátiles.

**Arbitrager.** Persona que compra y vende valores profesionalmente.

**Arbitral.** Perteneciente al arbitraje.

**Arbitrariness.** Arbitrariedad, atropello, exorbitancia, ilegalidad, injusticia, parcialidad, autoritarismo, despotismo, tiranía.

**Arbitrary.** Arbitrario, abusivo, exorbitante, injusto, ilegal, autoritario, despótico, tirano.

**Arbitrate.** Arbitrar, armonizar, arreglar, intercede, mediar, reconciliar. Somete a arbitraje. Laudar, decidir arbitrariamente.

**Arbitration.** Arbitraje. Proceso arbitral, armonización, arreglo, buenos oficios, intercesión, mediación. Laudo, fallo o dictamen arbitral.

**Arbitration board.** Junta de arbitraje.

**Arbitration clause.** Cláusula arbitral, o de arbitraje.

**Arbitrator.** Árbitro, componedor, dictaminador, intercesor, juez, mediador, perito, regulador.

**Archenemy.** Archienemigo, enemigo acérrimo.

**Archives.** Archivos, fichero, registro.

**Archivist.** Archivista, archivador.

**Area.** Área, región, territorio, zona, tema o conjunto de temas, esfera.

**Argue.** Argüir, alegar, altercar, contradecir, objetar, refutar, replicar.

**Arguendo.** Como argumento, objetando hipotéticamente.

**Argument.** Argumento, disputa, desacuerdo, desaveniencia, discusión, línea de defensa o de ataque, razón lógica de lo que se sustenta.

**Argument by counsel.** Alegato hecho por el abogado.

**Argument, oral.** Alegato oral.

**Argument to the jury.** Alegato al jurado.

**Argumentative.** Argumentativo, cuestionador, litigioso, peleador.

**Argumentative question.** Modo ilegal de presentar preguntas a un testigo, pues condiciona la respuesta. Por ejemplo, "¿cuándo dejó de pegarle a su esposa?" sugiere que alguna vez el sujeto comenzó a pegarle.

**Arise.** Aparecer, derivar, emerger, ocurrir, originar, provenir.

**Arising out and in the course of employment.** Con motivo y en ocasión del trabajo.

Tal situación toma aplicables las leyes laborales de protección al trabajador, tipicamente compensándolo por un accidente sufrido.

**Aristocracy.** Aristocracia, nobleza, gobierno o liderato de la nobleza.

**Aristocrat.** Aristócrata, noble, sangre azul.

**Aristocratic.** Aristocrático, elitista, noble, privilegio.

**Arm's length litigation.** Juicio en el cual cada parte trata de derrotar a la otra, sin ningún tipo de connivencia.

**Arm's length transaction.** Transacción en la cual cada parte trata de sacar el mejor partido posible y vela sólo por sus propios intereses.

**Armament.** Armamento, armas, arsenal.

**Armed forces.** Fuerzas armadas, ejército, marina y aviación, militares, soldados, tropas. F.F.A.A.

**Armed robbery.** Robo a mano armada, robo con armas.

**Armistice.** Armisticio, cese o cesación de hostilidades, convenio, pacto, tregua.

**Armory.** Polvorín, sala de armas.

**Arms.** Armas, armamento.

**Army.** Ejército, fuerza armada.

**Arraignment.** Auto de procesamiento.
Lectura de la acusación. La lectura de la acusación se efectuará en corte abierta y consistirá en leerle al acusado el indicia miento del gran jurado o la acusación del fiscal o en explicarle el contenido del cargo y se le requerirá para que alegue con relación a la misma. Se le dará una copia del indiciamiento o de la acusación antes de que se le requiera que alegue. (Regla 10, Reglas Fed. de Proc. Crim.).

**Arrangement.** Arreglo, acuerdo, pacto, transacción.

**Array.** Miembros potenciales del jurado (s). Poner en orden, agrupar, clasificar, sistematizar (v).

**Arrearage, arrears, (in).** Mora, atraso, impaga aunque vencida.

**Arrest.** Arresto, detención, captura, aprisionamiento, custodia, encarcelamiento, reclusión (s). Arrestar, capturar, detener (v).

**Arrest, consequences.** Arresto, consecuencias. En el primer acto oficial de la mayor parte de los casos penales es el arresto por parte de oficio de policía de la persona sospechosa de haber comitido el delito. El sospechosos debe ser llevado ante un funcionario judicial denominado magistrado sin innecesarias demoras, quien conducirá el examen preliminar. Esta es una audiencia pública informal destinada a determinar si la evidencia justifica la detención. (Intro al USA).

**Arrest judgment.** Abstención de sentencia. La corte a moción de un acusado, podrá abstenerse de dictar sentencia si el indiciamiento o la acusación no imputan delito o si la corte no tuviere jurisdicción sobre el delito imputado. (Regla 34, Reglas Fed. de Proc. Crim.).

**Arrest record.** Acta de arresto. Prontuario policial.

**Arrest warrant.** Orden de arresto. Si apareciera de la denuncia, o de uno o más afidavits presentados con la misma, que existe causa probable para creer que se ha cometido un delito y que el acusado lo cometió, se expedirá una orden de arresto de dicho acusado dirigida a cualquier funcionario autorizado por la ley para ejecutarla. (Regla 4(a) y (c), Reglas Fed. de Proc. Crim.).

**Arrestable.** Pasible de arresto.

**Arrogation.** Apoderamiento o apropiación indebida, usurpación.

**Arsenal.** Arsenal, polvorín. Depósito de armas y municiones.

**Arsenic.** Arsénico, veneno.

**Arson.** Incendio intencional y malicioso.

**Arson clause.** Cláusula en contratos de seguro mediante la cual un incendio provocado por el asegurado mismo no es compensable.

**Arsonist.** Incendiario, pirómano.

**Art, term of.** Expresión técnica que conlleva un significado especial.

**Article.** Artículo, cláusula, ítem, parte, párrafo, porción, punto, sección.

**Articled clerk.** Pasante, aprendiz de abogado en un bufete (G.B.).

**Articles of agreement.** Minuta o memorandum sobre los puntos acordados, típicamente tras una negociación.

**Articles of amendment.** Acta modificatoria del contrato social original o procedente.

**Articles of incorporation.** Estatutos, carta orgánica, contrato social, estatutos de constitución de una sociedad.

**Artificial.** Artificial, fabricado, falso, incómodo, inverosímil, irreal, no natural, sintético.

**Artificial insemination.** Inseminación artificial.

**Artificial person.** Persona de existencia jurídica.

**Artificial respiration.** Respiración artificial, primeros auxilios, respiración boca a boca, vida latente.

**Artillery.** Artillería.

**Artisan.** Artesano.

**Artisan's lien.** Prenda con retención en favor del trabajador.

**As.** Como.

**As from.** Desde una fecha posterior.

**As is.** En el estado en que se encuentra, sin garantía.

**As of.** Desde una fecha anterior.

**As soon as practicable.** Tan pronto como sea razonablemente posible.

**Ascendancy, ascendance.** Dominio, poder, superioridad, ascendencia.

**Ascendants.** Ascendiente.

**Ascertain.** Cerciorarse, averiguar, informarse, verificar.

**Ascribe (to).** Suscribir, atribuir, patrocinar, pertenecer, promover, relacionar.

**Ask.** Pedir, requerir, solicitar.

**Asking price.** Precio inicialmente requerido por el vendedor.

**Aspersions.** Manifestaciones desfavorables y maliciosas.

**Asphyxia.** Asfixia, ahogo, estrangulación. Cese o dificultad respiratoria.

**Asportation.** Remoción de un objeto. Uno de los elementos del hurto.

**Assailant.** Agresor, acometedor, asaltante, atacante, hostigador.

**Assassin.** Asesino, criminal.

**Assassinate.** Asesinar, matar a un ser humano ilegalmente, a sabiendas y sin justificación.

**Assassination.** Asesinato, crimen.

**Assault.** Acometimiento, agresión, asalto.

**Assault and battery.** Lesiones. Contacto físico no permitido por la ley ni consentido por la víctima.

**Assault with a deadly weapon.** Agresión a mano armada.

**Assault with intent to commit rape.** Agresión con la intención de cometer una violación.

**Assault with intent to commit murder.** Agresión con la intención de cometer un homicidio.

**Assault with intent to commit manslaughter.** Agresión con medios idóneos para causar la muerte.

**Assembly.** Asamblea, convención, grupo de gente en una actividad común, parlamento, reunión.

**Assembly, right of.** Derecho de asamblea o de reunión.

**Assent.** Asentimiento, aprobación, beneplácito, consentimiento (s). Asentir, afirmar, aprobar, expresar acuerdo y conformidad (v).

**Assent, express.** Consentimiento expreso.

**Assent, mutual.** Consentimiento mutuo o recíproco.

**Assert.** Afirmar, aseverar, decir, manifestar como cierto. Hacer valer un derecho o condición, presionar.

**Assertion.** Aserción, aseveración, afirmación, declaración categórica, deposición.

**Assertory, assertive.** Afirmativo, decidido, decisorio, firme, sin vacilación.

**Assess.** Calcular el valor, evaluar. Imponer un cargo o impuesto, gravar.

**Assessable.** Tasable, valuable. Sujeto a impuestos, gravámenes o contribuciones.

**Assessed.** Tasado, valuado. Gravado con un impuesto o cargo.

**Assessment.** Tasación, valuación, impuesto, carga, cargo, contribución, tasa.

**Assessor.** Funcionario que determinó el valor imponible de un bien.

**Asset.** Componente del activo, bien, crédito, ventaja, ayuda, beneficio.

**Assets.** Haber, activo, conjunto de bienes y créditos, patrimonio.

**Assets, accrued.** Bienes devengados.

**Assets, current.** Activo de una empresa o individuo. Contablemente se opone a obligaciones a pagar.

**Assets, fixed.** Activo fijo, inmuebles.

**Assets, frozen.** Activo indisponible. Bienes que no se pueden enajenar, por ejemplo, sujetos a un embargo preventivo.

**Assets, intangible.** Bienes inmateriales, por ejemplo, valor llave.

**Assets, liquid.** Bienes susceptibles de ser liquidados rápidamente. Caja, bancos, valores al cobro.

**Assets, net.** Bienes netos, aquéllos que sobrepasan el nivel de obligaciones o el pasivo.

**Asseveration.** Aseveración, afirmación formal y categórica, certificación, ratificación, testimonio.

**Assign.** Beneficiario de una transferencia de bienes, cesionario. Transferir, ceder, afectar, alocar, aplicar, indicar el uso debido (v).

**Assignability.** Cesibilidad, transferibilidad.

**Assignable.** Cesible, enajenable, transferible.

**Assignee.** Cesionario, persona que recibe la propiedad de bienes o derechos.

**Assignment.** Asignación, transferencia de bienes o derechos. Alocación, aporcionamiento, división, distribución, prorrateo.

**Assignment of account.** Cesión de crédito. Transferencia a otra persona del derecho a cobrar sobre una cuenta.

**Assignment of cases for trial.** Señalamiento de casos para el juicio.

**Assignment of error.** Exposición de errores.

**Assignment of future rights.** Cesión de derechos futuros. Excepto si se dispone lo contrario por ley, la cesión de un derecho al pago que se espera surja de una relación existente de trabajo, o alguna otra relación de negocio, tendrá la misma efectividad de un derecho existente. (Rstmnt, 2nd, Con., sec. 321).

**Assignment of income.** Cesión de ingresos. Normalmente se usa la expresión para connotar una transacción tendiente a pagar menos impuestos. Tales derechos cedidos y los réditos del caso no serían imponibles.

**Assignment of rights.** Cesión de derechos. La cesión de un derecho es una manifestación hecha por el cedente, de la intención de transferir dicho derecho, por virtud de la cual el derecho que tiene el cedente sobre el cumplimiento por parte del obligado se extingue en todo o en parte y el cesionario adquiere derecho sobre dicho cumplimiento. (Rstmnt, 2nd, Con., sec. 317).

**Assignment of wages.** Cesión de sueldo.

**Assignor.** Cedente, enajenante, persona que transfiere la propiedad de bienes o derechos.

**Assigns.** Sucesores, derechohabientes.

**Assist.** Asistir, amparar, auxiliar, ayudar, cooperar. Contribuir económicamente.

**Assistance.** Asistencia, amparo, auxilio, ayuda, concurso, cooperación.

**Assistance of counsel.** Patrocinio letrado. Derecho a la defensa concedido por la constitución de USA en causas criminales. Tal derecho fue introducido por la sexta enmienda constitucional (*Sixth Amendment*).

**Assistant.** Asistente, adjunto, asociado, auxiliar, ayudante, lugarteniente, mano derecha.

**Assize.** Antiguo tribunal inglés.

**Associate.** Asociado. Abogado que todavía no es socio de un despacho jurídico. Coautor, cómplice.

**Associate justice.** Conjuez. Juez que no preside el tribunal.

**Association.** Asociación, colegio, compañía, conjunto, empresa, relación existente entre personas o ideas, rasgos comunes.

**Association of brokers.** Colegio de corredores.

**Assortment.** Conglomerado, conjunto, grupo, selección.

**Assume.** Conjeturar, asumir, tomar conciencia, suponer, imaginar, tomar a cargo o por cuenta propia.

**Assumed.** Supuesto, asumido, ficto, fingido, imaginado, imaginario.

**Assumed facts.** Hechos no probados, hipotéticos.

**Assumed name.** Alias, nombre artístico, nombre de guerra, seudónimo, sobrenombre.

**Assumpsit.** Promesa, acuerdo o pacto. Acción por incumplimiento contractual.

**Assumption.** Asunción, suposición, tesis, supuesto, toma a cargo, toma de control.

**Assumption clause.** Cláusula en una escritura hipotecaria indicando que la hipoteca no puede transferirse sin el consentimiento escrito del acreedor.

**Assumption of indebtedness.** Acto por el cual una persona se responsabiliza por las deudas de otra.

**Assumption of risk.** Asunción del riesgo. Un demandante que voluntariamente asumió el riesgo del sufrir dado como consecuencia de la conducta negligente o temeraria del demandado, no podrá recobrar de éste por tal daño. (Restatement, Second, Torts, sec. 496 A).

**Assurance.** Garantía de pago, ya sea real o personal.

**Assure.** Asegurar, certificar, garantizar, ratificar, reconfortar.

**Asylum.** Asilo, albergue, orfanato, protección, refugio.

**At any time prior to.** En cualquier momento antes de.

**At arm's length.** En oposición abierta y franca. Sin convivencia ni acuerdos encubiertos.

**At bar, case.** Caso de marras, en cuestión, pendiente ante el tribunal.

**At issue.** En cuestión. Punto sobre el cual se centra una contienda.

**At the courthouse door.** Literalmente en la puerta del tribunal. Se usa la expresión como "en los estrados del juzgado" para notificaciones automáticas o en situaciones de rebeldía. En el derecho americano tales notificaciones se colocan en un lugar específico, donde pueden ser consultadas por el público.

**At the expense of.** A costa de.

**At the foot, at the end.** Al pie, al calce, al final.

**At the head.** Al frente, al tope.

**Atavism.** Atavismo, adorno, decoración, embellecimiento.

**Atheist.** Ateo.

**Attributing.** Atributivo, atribuyente.

**Atrocious.** Atroz, aberrante, bárbaro, cruel, desmedido, gravísimo, horrible, inhumano, truculento.

**Atrocity.** Atrocidad, aberración, barbaridad, crueldad, enormidad, exceso, salvajada, ultraje.

**Attach.** Embargar, capturar, afectar, secuestrar, trabar embargo, anotar la litis, atar, abrochar, anexar, adjuntar, incluir.

**Attachable.** Embargable, afectable, disponible, gravable, secuestrable.

**Attaching party.** Parte embargante.

**Attachment.** Embargo, apropiación, arresto, comiso, confiscación, incautación, retención, usurpación. Anexación, agregado, anexo, unión. Afecto, amistad, ligamen, vínculo.

**Attachment bond.** Caución suficiente prestada para sustituir y liberar un embargo.

**Attachment jurisdiction.** Competencia para embargar. Un tribunal tiene competencia para embargar propiedad localizada dentro del estado mediante secuestro o comiso de la propiedad, o algún otro procedimiento similar, en una acción de reclamación contra el dueño de la propiedad si: 1) El tribunal pudiese apropiadamente ejercer su jurisdicción para adjudicar la reclamación; o 2) La acción tiene como propósito hacer cumplir una sentencia dictada en contra del dueño de la propiedad; o 3) La acción es complementaria y consistente con otros procedimientos relacionados a la reclamación; o 4) El ejercicio de jurisdicción es uno razonable. (Rstmnt, 2nd, Judg., sec. 8).

**Attachment of persons.** Orden de arresto sobre una persona incursa en desacato al tribunal.

**Attainder.** Pérdida de derechos civiles impuesta a los condenados a muerte, a los traidores.

**Attainder, bill of.** Ley especial dictada contra un individuo, o grupo de individuos, imponiendo graves castigos en violación del debido proceso. Ley persecutoria.

**Attempt.** Tentativa. Una persona es culpable de una tentativa para cometer un delito si, al actuar con la especie de culpabilidad que de otra manera se requiere para la comisión del delito, él:

A propósito incurre en conducta que constituiría el delito si las circunstancias concurrentes fueran como él las creyó. (Cód. Pen. Mod., § 5.01 (1)).

Tentativa, ensayo, intento (s). Intentar (v).

**Attend.** Asistir, amparar, auxiliar, ayudar, cooperar.

**Attendance.** Comparecencia, asistencia, presencia.

**Attest.** Atestiguar, afirmar, atestar, autenticar, certificar, corroborar, declarar, deponer, endosar, evidenciar, refundar, probar.

**Attestation.** Testimonio, afirmación, certificación, corroboración, declaración, deposición, endoso, evidencia, prueba.

**Attestation clause.** Parte de una declaración jurada donde consta que el documento ha cumplido con todas las formalidades de la ley. Típicamente se halla tal cláusula al final de un testamento.

**Attestation of a will.** Parte final de un testamento, donde los testigos declaran sobre la forma en que el testamento fue firmado.

**Attested.** Atestiguado, corroborado, probado.

**Attesting.** Testificante, deponente.

**Attesting witness.** Testigo que certifica sobre las formalidades transcurridas en la firma de un documento.

**Attestor.** Testigo, deponente.

**Attorney.** Abogado. No existe una división de los abogados según función. La distinción entre *barristers* y *solicitors* existente en Inglaterra no arraigó en los Estados Unidos; no existe una especialidad que posea el derecho exclusivo o especial de presentarse ante los tribunales, ni una que se dedique a la redacción de instrumentos legales. Las incumbencias del abogado americano incluyen el patrocinio letrado, el asesoramiento y la redacción de documentos jurídicos. Además, lo que puede llamarse "práctica del Derecho" es de su incumbencia exclusiva y está vedado a los demás. (Intro al USA).

**Attorney at law.** Abogado, agente, apoderado, consejero, defensor, intercesor, jurista, jurisconsulto, licenciado, mandatario, procurador, togado, representante.

**Attorney-client privilege.** Secreto profesional por el cual el abogado no puede ser compelido a brindar información que le fue suministrada por su cliente, o de la que se enteró representando a tal cliente.

**Attorney, corporate.** Abogado de empresa. De cada veinte abogados, dos están empleados por empresas privadas, tales como corporaciones industriales, compañías de seguros, o bancos. En general, ocupan funciones de asesores dentro del departamento jurídico de la firma. (Intro al USA).

**Attorney fees.** Honorarios judiciales. Costos u honorarios del abogado.

**Attorney general.** Procurador general, fiscal general, ministro de justicia.

**Attorney in fact.** Apoderado, no necesariamente abogado, para realizar actos ordinarios. Mandatario, administrador, delegado, encargado, representante.

**Attorney of record.** Abogado que interviene en el juicio.

**Attorney, power of.** Mandato por escrito.

**Attorney, state.** Abogado del estado. Una evolución similar ha tenido lugar en la administración; hoy dos de cada veinte abogados son funcionarios nacionales, estaduales, de condado o municipales. No se tienen en cuenta, aquí, los que están en la esfera judicial. Muchos de ellos son abogados recién recibidos para los que los salarios estatales resultan suficientemente atractivas en esta etapa de su carrera y están interesados en el entrenamiento que puedan conseguir de esta manera, para luego utilizarlo en el ejercicio privado. (Intro al USA).

**Attractive nuisance.** Peligro atrayente. Doctrina que responsabiliza al propietario de un inmueble por los daños que puedan sufrir los niños atraídos a jugar por tal inmueble.

**Attribute.** Característica, calidad, condición, cualidad, rasgo, rasgo típico (s). Atribuir, acreditar, achacar, asignar, cargar, endilgar, imponer, imputar (v).

**Attribution.** Atribución, acreditación, asignación, cargo, endilgamiento, imposición, imputación, inculpación, nexo causal.

**Auction.** Subasta, licitación, puja, remate, venta al mejor postor, subasta, venta judicial (s). Rematar (v).

**Auctioneer.** Rematador, subastador.

**Audience.** Audiencia concedida por alguien de gran importancia. En términos forenses se utiliza la palabra "hearing."

**Audit.** Inspección o verificación contable (s). Inspeccionar un sistema de contabilidad, comprobar gastos, etc. (v).

**Auditor.** Auditor, contador, contador público, experto contable, revisor de cuentas.

**Austere.** Austero, económico, frugal, retraído, sobrio.

**Austerity.** Austeridad, ahorro, economía, dureza, ascetismo, estrechez.

**Austerity policity.** Política de austeridad, restricción del gasto público.

**Authentic.** Auténtico, autorizado, cierto, fidedigno, genuino, indubitable, legalizado, legítimo, real, verdadero.

**Authentic manner.** Forma fehaciente.

**Authenticate.** Autenticar, certificar, corroborar, legalizar, visar.

**Authentication.** Autenticación, certificación, legalización.

**Authentication or identification of evidence.** Autenticación o identificación de evidencia. El requisito de autenticación o identificación como condición previa a la admisibilidad se satisface con evidencia suficiente para sostener una determinación de que la materia en cuestión es lo que el proponente pretende. (Regla 901, R. Fed. Evid.).

**Authenticity.** Autenticidad, certeza, condición de verdadero.

**Author.** Autor, creador, inventor (s). Escribir, crear, inventar (v).

**Authorities.** La autoridad, la administración, el gobierno.

**Authority.** Autoridad. Autoridad es el poder del mandatario para afectar las relaciones legales del mandante mediante actos realizados de acuerdo a las manifestaciones de consentimientos hechos por el mandante al mandatario. (Rstmnt, 2nd, Agency, sec. 7).

Poder para actuar, fuente legal, poder, convencimiento, dominio, influencia.

**Authority, actual.** Con facultades reales, efectivamente recibidas.

**Authority, apparent.** Facultades aparentes, aunque no reales.

**Authority by estoppel.** Facultades derivadas de la falta de oposición por quien, al enterarse que eran ejercidas, no protestó si razonablemente era de esperar que protestase en caso de desacuerdo.

**Authority, express.** Facultades expresas.

**Authority, general.** Facultades genéricas, poder general.

**Authority, implied.** Facultades implícitas.

**Authority, incidental.** Facultades incidentales.

**Authorization.** Autorización, aprobación, consentimiento, licencia, permiso, venia.

**Authorize.** Autorizar, acreditar, aprobar, consentir, permitir.

**Auto theft.** Hurto de automóviles.

**Autobiographical.** Autobiográfico.

**Autobiography.** Autobiografía, memorias.

**Autocracy.** Autocracia.

**Autocrat.** Autócrata, déspota, tirano.

**Autocratic.** Autocrático.

**Autograph.** Autógrafo, firma, inicial.

**Automatically.** Automáticamente, reflejamente, sin meditar ni pensar.

**Automobile guest statute.** Ley que contempla la responsabilidad del conductor, en caso de un choque, respecto de los acompañantes que sufren daños.

**Autonomous.** Autónomo, autárquico, independiente, libre, soberano.

**Autonomy.** Autonomía, autarquía, autogobierno, independencia, libertad, soberanía.

**Autopsy.** Autopsia, examen post mortem.

**Auxiliary.** Auxiliar, de emergencia, secundario, subsidiario.

**Available.** Disponible, a mano, abierto, expedito, utilizable.

**Aval.** Aval, endoso, contrafirma, garantía.

**Aver.** Alegar, decir, manifestar.

**Average.** Promedio, común, equidistante, mediano, medio, mediocre, estándard, término medio.

**Average man test.** Examen del hombre ordinario. Sistema para determinar si un jurado propuesto está tan vinculado al caso como para resultar parcial.

**Averages, law of.** Ley de los grandes números, cálculos de probabilidades, estadísticas.

**Averment.** Alegación, alegato, afirmación, aseveración, declaración, manifestación, ponencia.

**Aviation.** Aviación, aeronavegación.

**Aviator.** Aviador, piloto.

**Avoid.** Evitar. Esquivar, sustraerse. Cancelar, anular, invalidar un acto.

**Avoidable consequences.** Consecuencias evitables. Por ejemplo, perjuicios que pueden ser minimizados por actos de una de las partes.

**Avoidance.** Acto de evitar, escapar a las consecuencias, anular, bloquear, cancelar.

**Avow.** Admitir, asentir, confesar, reconocer.

**Avowal.** Admisión, confesión, reconocimiento.

**Avowant.** Parte que admite o confiesa.

**Avulsion.** Avulsión.

**Award.** Laudo arbitral. Dar, asignar, atribuir, disponer, distribuir (v).

**Awarder.** Árbitro, adjudicador, corte, juez, tribunal.

**Axiom.** Axioma.

**Axiomatic.** Axiomático.

**Axis.** Eje. En sentido figurado, coalición, aliniamiento de intereses.

# B

**B.C.** Antes de Cristo.

**Bachelor.** Bachiller. El estudiante norteamericano termina habitualmente la escuela secundaria (*high school*), etapa final del sistema escolar público gratuito, a la edad de 17 ó 18 años. Puede, entonces, intentar ingresar a una universidad o a un *college* (que pueden ser privados o estaduales) para comenzar una educación general (*college education*) que conduce a un título de *Bachelor* al cabo de cuatro años. (Intro al USA). El derecho es carrera de post-grado en los Estados Unidos. Para comenzar a estudiarlo hace falta contar con un título previo.

Soltero, célibe, con capacidad nupcial.

**Bachelor of laws.** Bachiller en leyes, graduado en derecho, abogado diplomado. LL.B.

**Back.** Atrás, anterior, detrás, tras.

**Back pay.** Salario devengado y no pagado o pagado tardíamente.

**Back rent.** Alquiler atrasado, en mora.

**Backward.** Retrógrado, incivilizado, primitivo. Retardado, débil mental. Retraído, tímido, timorato.

**Bad.** Malo, dañino, dañoso, defectuoso, equivocado, incorrecto.

**Bad check.** Cheque sin provisión de fondos.

**Bad conduct.** Mala conducta.

**Bad debt.** Deuda incobrable.

**Bad faith.** Mala fe.

**Badge.** Insignia, chapa, distintivo. Rasgo identificatorio.

**Bail.** Fianza, afianzamiento, caución, cautela, garantía (s). Dar fianza, afianzar, garantizar (v).

**Bail bond.** Fianza para obtener excarcelación.

**Bailable.** Sujeto a fianza, susceptible de caución. Excarcelable.

**Bailee.** Asignatario, comodatario, depositario, locatario, recipiente. Parte que recibe un objeto que debe custodiar y restituir oportunamente.

**Bailiff.** Oficial de un tribunal. Ujier. Depositario judicial o legal.

**Bailment.** Contrato de depósito. Acuerdo por el cual un objeto se recibió por quien no es su dueño, con cargo de devolverlo posteriormente.

**Bailor.** Depositante. Persona que entrega a otra un objeto para su custodia y eventual devolución.

**Bait and switch.** Técnica mercantil para atraer clientes, ofreciéndoles algunas mercaderías a bajo precio para que compren otra más caras.

**Balance.** Remanente, excedente, saldo, sobrante. Saldo deudor de una cuenta. Aplomo, equilibrio, solvencia moral (s). Equilibrar, especialmente los activos y pasivos contables (v).

**Balance due.** Saldo vencido.

**Balance sheet.** Balance.

**Bale.** Fardo.

**Ballast.** Balastro, contrapeso, lastre, peso.

**Ballistics.** Balística. Estudio sistematizado, de aplicación forense, sobre amas de fuego y balas.

**Balloon note.** Instrumento de deuda que se paga por cuotas. Las primeras cuotas representan mayoritariamente, o únicamente, el pago de los intereses. Las últimas cuotas representan mayoritariamente, o únicamente, el pago del cuerpo de la deuda.

**Ballot.** Papeleta, boleta, voto, comicios, elección, sufragio, voz (s). Votar, elegir, sufragar (v).

**Ballotage.** Sistema electoral que impone una segunda rueda si en la primera no se obtiene una proporción mayoritaria mínima preestablecida.

**Balloting.** Voto, sufragio, votación.

**Band.** Banda, bando, barra, cuadrilla, grupo, pandilla.

**Bandage.** Vendas, vendaje.

**Bandit.** Bandido, atracador, bandolero, fascineroso, ladrón, malhechor, salteador.

**Banditism.** Bandidaje, bandalaje, bandolerismo, criminalidad, delincuencia.

**Banditry.** Bandidaje, bandalaje, bandolerismo, criminalidad, delincuencia.

**Banishment.** Exilio, deportación, destierro, ostracismo. Prohibición, interdicción.

**Bank.** Banco. Se entiende por "Banco" una corporación doméstica con suficiente capital, autorizada por la ley para recibir depósitos en efectivo o valores, abrir créditos y cuentas corrientes y de ahorros, hacer préstamos, descontar giros, pagarés y otra clase de valores negociables, comprar y vender giros, traficar en oro y plata y en general en toda clase de negocios bancarios. (7 LPRA sec. 3).

Bancar, apuntalar financieramente, operar con cierto banco (v).

**Bank deposits and collections, uniform commercial code.** Cobranzas y depósitos bancarios, código de comercio uniforme. El Artículo 4 se ocupa de esta rama. Tales transacciones han alcanzado cifras enormes. Se estima que en toda la nación los bancos manipulan efectos bancarios en un número que oscila entre 25 y 50 millones en cada día laborable. (C.C.U., Prefacio).

**Banker.** Banquero.

**Banking.** Banca. Actividades bancarias o financieras.

**Bankrupt.** Quebrado, concursado, fallido, insolvente.

**Bankruptcy.** Bancarrota, concurso de acreedores, falencia, insolvencia, quiebra. Desastre, colapso, desmoronamiento, ruina.

**Bankruptcy assets.** Masa de la quiebra.

**Baptism.** Bautismo, bautizo, denominación.

**Baptismal record.** Fe de bautismo.

**Bar.** Colegio de abogados. La reglamentación del ejercicio de la profesión de abogado es responsabilidad de los estados, cada uno de los cuales establece los requisitos que un abogado debe cumplir para poder ejercer en su jurisdicción. (Intro al USA).

Colegio de abogados, abogacía (s). Eludir, prohibir, impedir, obstaculizar (v).

**Bar and merger.** Cosa juzgada.

**Bar Association.** Colegio de abogados, barra.

**Bare.** Desnudo, limitado, restringido, (s). Descubrir, comunicar, revelar (v).

**Bare owner.** Nudo propietario. Persona que retiene la titularidad del inmueble, pero ha cedido el uso y goce.

**Bare ownership.** Nuda propiedad. Propiedad despojada de su uso y goce, restando sólo la facultad de alienar.

**Bargain.** Negociación. Una negociación consiste de un intercambio de promesas, o el intercambio de una promesa a cambio de una actuación, ejecución o cumpliendo, o para intercambio de actuaciones, ejecuciones o cumplimientos. (Rstmnt, 2nd, Con., sec. 3).

Acuerdo, consenso, contrato, pacto. ocasión, transacción ventajosa (s). Regatear, discutir el precio, negociar (v).

**Bargainee.** Parte adquirente.

**Bargainor.** Parte transferente.

**Barrack.** Cuartel.

**Barratry.** Chicanería, promoción de pleitos innecesarios, temeridad y malicia procesal.

**Barren.** Estéril, desértico, improductivo.

**Barrier.** Barrera, barricada, impedimento, obstáculo, parapeto, traba.

**Barring.** Excluyendo, dejando de lado. Prescripción, caducidad.

**Barrister, barrister-at-law (G.B.).** Abogado en el sistema inglés que se especializa en litigación.

**Base year.** Año básico o de base.

**Based upon.** Basado en.

**Bases of judicial jurisdiction over individuals.** Bases jurisdiccionales sobre individuos. Un estado tiene poder para ejercitar jurisdicción judicial sobre un individuo apoyándose en una o más de las siguientes bases: a) presencia física, b) domicilio, c) residencia, d) nacionalidad o ciudadanía, e) consentimiento, f) comparecencia judicial, g) llevar a cabo negocios en el estado, h) un acto realizado en el estado, i) causar un efecto en el estado por un acto realizado en cualquier otra lugar, j) propiedad, uso o posesión de una cosa en el estado, k) otras relaciones con el estado que hacen razonable el ejercicio de la jurisdicción judicial (Rstmnt, 2nd, Conflict, sec. 27).

**Basic.** Básico. esencial, principal, sustancia. Elemental, simple.

**Bastard.** Bastardo. Hijo extramatrimonial, ilegítimo o natural. Adulterado, espurio, desnaturalizado, falso, falsificado.

**Bastardy.** Bastardía, condición de bastardo.

**Battered wife.** Mujer que ha sufrido malos tratos por parte de su marido.

**Battery, harmful contact.** Agresión, contacto dañoso. Un persona será responsable ante otra persona por agresión si: a) actúa con la intención de causar un contacto físico dañoso u ofensivo en esa otra persona, o un tercero; o hay una inminente aprehensión de que tal contacto ocurrirá y, b) ocurre un contacto dañoso contra esa otra persona, ya sea en forma directa o indirecta. (Rstmnt, 2nd, Torts, sec. 13).

**Battery, offensive contact.** Agresión, contacto ofensivo. Una persona será responsable ante otra persona por agresión si: a) actúa con la intención de causar un contacto físico dañoso u ofensivo en esa otra persona, o un tercero; o hay una inminente aprehensión de que tal contacto ocurrirá y, b) ocurre un contacto dañoso contra esa otra persona, ya sea en forma directa o indirecta. (Rstmnt, 2nd, Torts, sec. 13).

**Battle of forms.** Conflicto entre formularios. Cuando ambas partes utilizan cláusulas estándar y llegan a un acuerdo excepto en cuanto a dichas cláusulas, el contrato se entenderá celebrado en base a lo acordado y a lo dispuesto en aquellas cláusulas estándar que sean sustancialmente comunes, a menos que una de las partes hubiera indicado claramente con antelación, o que luego y sin demora le comunique a la otra, que no tiene el propósito de quedar obligada por dicho contrato. (Unidroit, Prin., art. 2.22).

**Bawdy house.** Casa de tolerancia, prostíbulo.

**Be it enacted.** Decrétase.

**Be it resolved.** Se resuelve.

**Beacon.** Baliza, guía.

**Bear.** Generar, crear, ganar, producir. Sostener, mantener. Tolerar.

**Bear arms.** Portar armas.

**Bearer.** Portador, depositario, recipiente, tenedor.

**Bearing the risk of mistake.** Asunción del riesgo de error. Una parte asume el riesgo de un error cuando: a) el riego se le ha

señalado, por acuerdo de las parte, o b) él está conciente al momento en que se celebra el contrato, de que sólo tiene un conocimiento limitado con respecto a los hechos con los que se relaciona el error, pero creyó que su conocimiento limitado era suficiente, o c) el riesgo le ha sido asignado a él por la corte con el fundamento de que es razonable hacerlo en tales circunstancias. (Rstmnt, 2nd, Con., sec. 154).

**Become effective, binding.** Surtir efecto.

**Before.** Antes, anterior, anteriormente, ante.

**Before me.** Ante mí, en mi presencia.

**Behoove.** Concernir.

**Being duly sworn.** Habiendo prestado debido juramento.

**Belief.** Creencia, certeza, certidumbre, conjetura, convencimiento, convicción, credo, doctrina, dogma, juicio, parecer, religión, secta, suposición.

**Belligerancy.** Beligerancia, batalla, belicosidad, combate, guerra, hostilidades, lucha, ofensiva, operaciones.

**Belligerent.** Beligerante, combatiente, guerrero, militante, soldado. Antagónico, belicoso, hostil, inamistoso.

**Bench.** Magistratura, corte, poder judicial, tribunal. Banco.

**Bench trial.** Juicio realizado sin un jurado, en el que el juez decide tanto cuestiones de hecho como de derecho.

**Bench warrant.** Orden de arresto emitida por el juez durante una audiencia.

**Beneficial.** Beneficioso, benéfico, favorable, ganancioso, lucrativo, provechoso, útil.

**Beneficial interest.** Interés o derecho económico. Derecho que en equidad tiene el beneficiario de un *trust*.

**Beneficial use.** Facultad de gozar de la propiedad de una cosa, pero no de venderla, aunque el propietario legal sea otra persona.

**Beneficiary.** Beneficiario. Cesionario de un derecho. Recipiente de dinero o de algún objeto.

**Benefit.** Beneficio, ganancia, ventaja, rendimiento, utilidad (s). Beneficiarse, sacar provecho, acordar una ventaja o favor (v).

**Benevolent.** Benevolente, caritativo, desinteresado, gratis.

**Bequeath.** Legar, donar o hacer una manda testamentaria de un bien mueble.

**Bequeather.** Legador, donante, testador.

**Bequest.** Legado, donación o manda testamentaria.

**Best.** Mejor de todos, lo mejor (s). Sobrepasar, derrotar, mejorar (v).

**Best evidence rule.** Necesidad del original. Para probar el contenido de un escrito, grabación o fotografía, se requerirá el original del escrito, grabación o fotografía, a menos que otra cosa se disponga en estas reglas o por ley del Congreso. (Reglas 1002, 1003, R. Fed. Evid.).

**Best of my knowledge and belief, to the.** Según mi leal saber y entender.

**Bet.** Apuesta (s). Apostar (v).

**Betrayal.** Traición, delación, deslealtad, engaño, falsedad, falsía, infidencia, infidelidad, maquinación.

**Betrothal.** Compromiso para casarse. Se trata normalmente de una situación social que no genera una situación jurídica distinta.

**Betterment.** Mejora, adelanto, avance, enaltecimiento, mejoramiento, mejoría, perfeccionamiento.

**Beyond.** Más allá, allende, por sobre, sobre, ulterior.

**Beyond a reasonable doubt standard.** Mas allá de una duda razonable. Es el grado de convicción que debe alcanzarse para lograr una condena penal.

**Bias.** Parcialidad, inclinación, interés, predisposición, prejuicio, propensidad, subjetividad.

**Bicameral.** Bicameral. Cámara de representantes y senado.

**Bid.** Oferta, ofrecimiento, licitación, precio sugerido, proposición, propuesta de precio, puja (s). Hacer una propuesta de precio durante una licitación, pujar (v).

**Bidder.** Oferente, postar en una licitación.

**Bidding.** Licitación. Propuesta o conjunto de propuestas.

**Big.** Amplio, considerable, enorme, desarrollado, grande, inmenso, sustancial.

**Bigamist.** Bígamo.

**Bigamy.** Bigamia. Situación en la cual a sabiendas una persona contrae matrimonio sin haberse disuelto un matrimonio anterior.

**Bilateral.** Bilateral, que requiere un mínimo de dos partes. Consensual, mutuo, recíproco.

**Bilateral act.** Acto bilateral, consensual.

**Bill.** Proyecto de ley, propuesta legislativa. Cuenta, factura (s). Facturar, cargar, mandar una cuenta, debitar (v).

**Bill of attainder.** Ley de proscripción. Un estatuto de proscripción (bill of attainder)—estatuto que niega el derecho a un juicio en que las personas afectadas puedan obtener una adjudicación de sus derechos— es una forma que utilizaba el poder soberano para castigar a una persona designada por su nombre o a miembros determinables de un grupo de personas. (Pueblo v. Figueroa Pérez, 96 D.P.R. 6 (1968)).

**Bill of exchange.** Letra de cambio.

**Bill of lading.** Carta de porte. "Carta de porte" o "conocimiento de embarque" significa un documento que evidencia el recibo de mercancías para su embarque expedido por una persona dedicada al negocio de transportación o embarque de mercancías e incluye un conocimiento aéreo. (C.C.U. sec. 1-201 (6)).

**Bill of Rights.** Carta de derechos civiles. El Bill of Rights, formado por las primeras diez enmiendas ratificadas en 1791, asegura los derechos del individuo frente al gobierno federal. De aun mayor significación son las garantías con la Constitución federal protege al individuo frente a los estados. Su frente principal es la Decimocuarta Enmienda, la más importante de las tres enmiendas a la Constitución que se adoptaron después de la Guerra Civil, y que originalmente estuvieron destinadas a abolir la esclavitud y asegurar la libertad de los negros. Sus cláusulas principales disponen que ningún estado podrá "privar a ninguna persona la igual protección de las leyes dentro se su jurisdicción." (Intro al USA).

**Bills in a set.** Letra en diversos ejemplares.

**Bimetalism.** Bimetalismo, patrón monetario de oro y de plata.

**Bind.** Obligar, comprometer, constreñir, forzar, imponer ligar.

**Binder.** Resguardo provisional. El resguardo provisional se utiliza para hacer obligatorio el seguro temporalmente, pendiente de expedición de la póliza. Podrá ser oral o escrito. (26 LPRA sec. 1121).

**Binding.** Obligatorio, compulsivo, forzoso, oponible, vinculante.

**Binding character of contract.** Efecto vinculante del contrato. Todo contrato celebrado válidamente es vinculante para las partes. (Unidroit, Prin., art. 1.3).

**Binding authority.** Fuente jurídica formal, de obligatoria aplicación.

**Binnacle book.** Cuaderno de bitácora.

**Birth.** Nacimiento, comienzo, inicio, origen.

**Birth certificate.** Partida de nacimiento, acta de nacimiento, fe de bautismo.

**Birth control.** Control de la natalidad.

**Birth delivery.** Parto, dar a luz, nacimiento.

**Birthday.** Cumpleaños, fecha de nacimiento.

**Birthplace.** Lugar de nacimiento.

**Black acre.** Nombre ficticio que se le da a una propiedad inmueble cuando se quiere explicar o enseñar un punto jurídico. Así también se habla de *white acre*, *green acre*, etc.

**Black letter law.** Es el derecho expresado en forma clara y convincente en materiales estatutarios, así como leyes, reglamentos, decretos, etc.

**Black list.** Lista negra, boicot, discriminación (s). Boicotear (v).

**Black list to prevent employment.** Lista negra para negar empleo. Cualquier persona, firma, corporación, o patrono, agente, o encargado que por motivo de opiniones políticas, induzca en cualquier forma, o notifique a cualquier otra firma, corporación o patrono a que a uno o más trabajadores no se les dé trabajo y que sean anotados en cualquier forma con el propósito de no darles trabajos o prevenir que lo obtengan en cualquier localidad, será culpable del delito menos grave. (29 LPRA sec. 134).

**Black market.** Mercado negro.

**Blackjack.** Cachiporra, clava, garrote, palo, porro.

**Blackmail.** Chantaje, amenaza, exacción, extorsión, intimidación (s). Chantajear (v).

**Blackmailer.** Chantajista, extorsionista.

**Blame.** Culpa, responsabilidad. Censura, condena, desaprobación, reproche (s). Censurar, culpar, responsabilizar (v).

**Blank.** Formulario, forma, modelo. Vacío, en blanco, incompleto.

**Blanket disability.** Incapacidad general.

**Blasphemy.** Blasfemia, agravio, grosería, juramento, irreverencia, maldición, ofensa, reniego.

**Blemish.** Arruinar, ensuciar, estropear, manchar, mancillar, perjudicar.

**Blind.** Ciego, no vidente.

**Blockade.** Bloqueo, asedio, cordón (s). Bloquear, asediar, acordonar (v).

**Blocking statute.** Ley promulgada en un país para combatir, neutralizar o compensar por los efectos extra territoriales de una ley extranjera.

**Bloodshed.** Derramamiento de sangre, hecho sangriento, crueldad, muerte, violencia.

**Blot.** Tachadura, tachón, borrón.

**Blue-chip stocks.** Acciones de empresas fuertes y prestigiosas. Este tipo de acciones, que normalmente cotizan en bolsa, se consideran una inversión segura.

**Blue-sky laws.** Regulación administrativa de comercialización de títulos-valores.

**Board.** Comité, directorio, junta, plenario, pleno, reunión. Gastos por alimentos o comidas (s). Abordar, subir a bordo de una nave o vehículo (v).

**Board and lodging.** Comida y habitación.

**Board of directors.** Junta de directores, junta directiva.

**Board of receivers.** Consejo de incautación.

**Bodily heir.** Herederos de sangre, descendientes.

**Body.** Cuerpo, asociación, ente, entidad, organización, organismo, órgano. Cadáver.

**Bogus.** Falso, espurio, falsificado, imitado.

**Boilerplate.** Cláusulas, normalmente de un contrato, repetitivas y que han sido incorporadas a un nuevo documento, copiadas de otra parte. El término es despectivo y sugiere que tales clausulas no son muy importantes.

**Bomb scare.** Medidas de seguridad puestas en marcha ante la posible presencia de una bomba activada.

**Bona fide purchaser.** Adquirente de buena fe.

**Bond.** Vínculo, ligamen, ligamento, ligazón, unión. Título, bono, efecto de comercio, título-valor, valores. Caución, fianza, garantía (s). Afianzar, caucionar, garantizar (v).

**Bondage.** Estado de esclavitud o de servidumbre.

**Bonded.** Asegurado, con fianza, garantizado.

**Bonded warehouses.** Almacenes de adeudo. Los locales destinados para almacenes de adeudo serán construídos en el sitio, en la forma y del material que el Secretario prescribiere. (14 LPRA sec. 6058/63).

**Bonding company.** Empresa que extiende garantías en forma profesional.

**Bondsman.** Persona que aparece como garante.

**Bonus.** Bonificación, aguinaldo, bono, descuento, premio, reintegro.

**Book.** Libro, cuaderno, libreta, tomo, volumen. Sección, capítulo, parte (s). Registrar un arresto (v).

**Book value.** Valor histórico, nominal. Valor original, registrado en los libros contables.

**Bookkeeper.** Tenedor de libros, contable, contador.

**Booklet.** Libro pequeño, folletín, folleto, librejo, libreta, librito.

**Booty.** Botín, despojo, botín de guerra, presa.

**Border.** Frontera, confín, división, linde, límite, perímetro (s). Estar en posición limítrofe o muy vecina (v).

**Bordering.** Vecino, adjunto, adosado, adyacente, anexo, limítrofe, próximo, yuxtapuesto.

**Borrow.** Tomar prestado. Tomar como propio.

**Borrower.** Deudor, persona que toma prestado.

**Bound.** Obligado, compelido, constreñido, requerido por ley. Ligado, atado.

**Boundary.** Límite, frontera, hito, linde, línea divisoria, perímetro.

**Bounty.** Bono, bonificación, premio, prima, recompensa.

**Boycott.** Boicot, exclusión, lista negra.

**Brain.** Cerebro, intelecto, inteligencia, sesos, sustancia gris.

**Brain wash.** Lavado de cerebro, influencia ejercida en la voluntad de un individuo (s). Convencer totalmente a alguien (v).

**Brand.** Marca comercial, designación industrial. Insignia, logo, seña, señal (s). Categorizar derogativamente a una persona. Marcar (v).

**Branded.** Marcado (para animales). Categorizado, clasificado de antemano. Dícese de alguien a quien se le atribuyen anticipadamente ciertas cualidades, generalmente negativas.

**Brawl.** Pelea, alboroto, conmoción, disputa, refriega, reyerta.

**Breach.** Rompimiento, incumplimiento, contravención, infracción, inobservancia, rompimiento, transgresión, quebrantamiento, violación (s). Incumplir, contravenir, romper, trasgredir, quebrantar, violar (v).

**Breach of contract.** Incumplimiento contractual. Cuando el cumplimiento de una obligación bajo un contrato se torna exigible, lo que no se cumpla es incumplimiento (Rstmnt, 2nd, Con., sec. 235(2)).

**Breach of peace.** Disturbio de la tranquilidad pública. El disturbio de la tranquilidad es una ofensa pública cometida mediante violencia, o un acto que cause o pueda causar un disturbio inmediato del orden público. (Rstmnt, 2nd, Torts, sec. 116).

**Breach of warranty.** Violación de una garantía.

**Bread winner.** Sostén de familia. Persona que gana su propio sustento.

**Break.** Ruptura, desavenencia, discordia, disolución, pelea, quebrantamiento, quiebra, rompimiento, separación (s). Romper, disolver, pelear, quebrar, separar (v).

**Break open.** Abrir a viva fuerza.

**Breakage.** Proporción pequeña de la carga que normalmente se pierde sin que medie culpa ni negligencia del transportista. Merma.

**Breakdown.** Desbaratamiento, accidente, avería, caída, daño, desquiciamiento, percance.

**Breathalyzer.** Aparato en el que se expira para medir el contenido de alcool en una persona.

**Brethren.** Estilo antiguo de mencionar a los integrantes de una organización en particular como, por ejemplo, una congregación religiosa, un tribunal colegiado, etc.

**Bribe.** Soborno cohecho, corrupción (s). Sobornar, cohechar, corromper (v).

**Briber.** Sobornador.

**Bribery.** Soborno, cohecho, corrupción.

**Brief.** Escrito, alegato, argumento (s). Breve, conciso, sumario. Informar, poner al corriente (v).

**Bridge loan.** Préstamo financiero por un período corto, normalmente para atender a una necesidad urgente.

**Brigand.** Salteador, bandido, bandolero, fascineroso, malhechor, matrero.

**Brigandage.** Bandidaje, bandalaje, bandolerismo, criminalidad, delincuencia.

**Bring an action.** Entablar acción, enjuiciar, encausar, llevar a los tribunales.

**Bring suit.** Demandar, accionar, ejecutar, encartar, encausar, enjuiciar, presentar demanda, querellar.

**Broker.** Corredor, agente, intermediario.

**Brokerage.** Corretaje, intermediación.

**Brook.** Arroyo.

**Brothel.** Burdel, casa de prostitución, casa de tolerancia, lupanar, mancebía, prostíbulo.

**Brother.** Hermano.

**Brother-in-law.** Hermano político, cuñado.

**Buccaneer.** Bucanero, corsario, filibustero, pirata.

**Budget.** Presupuesto, estimación de gastos. v. presupuesto.

**Building.** Edificio, construcción, edificación, inmueble.

**Bulk reinsurance.** Reasegurado en masa.

**Bulk sales.** Ventas a granel. El Código de Comercio Uniforme, en su Artículo 6, se ocupa de las ventas a granel para evitar el fraude a los acreedores. La mayoría de los Estados tienen actualmente leyes sobre esta materia, pero hay muchas variantes de unas a otras y el Código Uniforme ha seleccionado la mejor de cada una para uniformarlas del modo más práctico.

Este Artículo busca simplificar y uniformar las bulk sales laws en los Estados que adopten esta Ley. (C.C.U., Prefacio).

**Bulk transfers.** Cesiones a granel. "Cesión a granel" será cualquier cesión a granel y no en el curso ordinario de los negocios del cedente de la mayor parte de materiales, suministros, mercancías u otro inventario. La cesión de una parte importante del equipo de dicha empresa será una cesión a granel si se hiciere en conexión con una cesión a granel de inventario, pero no en otra forma. Las empresas serán aquéllas cuyo negocio principal fuere la venta de mercancías en existencia, incluyendo aquellas que manufacturen lo que venden. (C.C.U. secs. 6-102, 6-103).

**Bull market.** Mercado de valores en alza. Se opone a bear market, que es un mercado menos vigoroso.

**Bullet.** Bala, cápsula, munición, proyectil.

**Bulletproof.** Blindado, a prueba de balas.

**Bulletin.** Boletín, anuncio, comunicado, información, informe, panfleto, parte, participación.

**Burden of proof.** Peso de la prueba, carga de la prueba, onus probandi.

**Bureau.** Oficina, agencia, departamento, dirección, ente, entidad, negociado, repartición.

**Burglar.** Ladrón, atracador, bandido, bandolero, caco, expoleador, hurtador, rapaz.

**Burglary.** Robo agravado, típicamente con fractura o escalamiento y durante la noche.

**Burial.** Entierro, funeral, inhumación, sepulcro, sepultura, últimos ritos.

**Bury.** Enterrar, inhumar, sepultar. Ocultar, esconder.

**Business.** Negocio, asunto, ocupación, transacción.

**Business enterprises.** Empresas comerciales. Las empresas comerciales están organizadas casi invariablemente de acuerdo al Derecho estadual, y las corporaciones se han considerado históricamente como basadas en derechos otorgados por los estados. (Intro al USA).

**Business law.** Derecho comercial. Para el abogado practicante la práctica del derecho puede ser *comercial* en la medida en que se ocupe de todos los aspectos del comercio, inclusive los impuestos, pero con el advenimiento del Código Comercial Uniforme el término *comercial* ha adquirido una significación más restringida. Se consideran incluidos los temas de: venta de bienes, documentos negociables (en especial pagarés, letras de cambio y cheques), depósitos y recaudaciones bancarios, títulos de crédito, títulos de propiedad (en especial conocimientos de embarque y recibos de almacenamiento), títulos de inversión (en especial acciones y bonos), y operaciones garantizadas (inclusive cesiones de deudas). (Intro al USA).

**Businessman.** Persona de negocios, comerciante.

**Buy.** Comprar, adquirir. Adueñarse, apropiar.

**Buyer.** Comprador, adquirente.

**Buyer in ordinary course of business.** Comprador en el curso ordinario del negocio. Significa una persona, que de buena fe y sin conocimiento de que la venta hecha a él es en violación de los derechos de propiedad o derechos garantizados de un tercero en las mercancías compradas en el curso ordinario de una persona dedicada al negocio de venta mercancías de esa clase, pero no incluye a los prestamistas. (C.C.U. sec. 120(9)).

**Bylaws.** Estatutos, reglamentos. Los estatutos iniciales de la corporación podrán adoptarse por los incorporadores. La facultad para hacer, alterar o derogar posteriormente los estatutos corresponde a los accionistas. No obstante, la corporación podrá, en su certificado de incorporación, conferir tal facultad a los directores. (14 LPRA sec. 1109).

# C

**C. & F. (cost & freight).** C. y F. El término C. & F. o C.F. significa que el precio de esa manera incluye costo y flete al destino señalado. Savo pacto en contrario el término C. & F. o su equivalente tiene el mismo efecto e impone en el vendedor las mismas obligaciones y riesgos que el término C.I.F., excepto la obligación referente al seguro. (C.C. U. sec. 320(1) (2)(4)). Ver *C.F.R.*

**C.F.R. (cost and freight).** Significa que el vendedor ha de pagar los gastos y el flete necesarios para hacer llegar la mercancía al puerto de destino convenido, si bien el riesgo de pérdida o daño de la mercancía, así como cualquier gasto adicional debido a acontecimientos ocurridos después del momento en que la mercancía haya sido entregada a bordo del buque, se transfiere del vendedor al comprador cuando la mercancía traspasa la borda del buque en el puerto de embarque. (Incoterms). Ver *C. & F.*

**C.I.F. (cost, insurance, freight).** C.I.F. El término C.I.F. significa que el precio incluye en una suma alzada el costo de las mercancías y el seguro y flete al destino señalado.

Bajo el término C.I.F. salvo pacto en contrario el comprador hará el pago contra la oferta formal de los documentos requeridos y el vendedor no podrá ofrecer formalmente ni el comprador podrá demandar la entrega de las mercancías en sustitución de los documentos. (C.C.U. sec. 2-320).

*Cost, Insurance, and Freight* significa que el vendedor tiene las mismas obligaciones que bajo CFR, si bien, además, ha de conseguir seguro marítimo de cobertura de los riesgos del comprador de pérdida o daño de la mercancía durante el transporte. El vendedor contrata el seguro y paga la prima correspondiente. (Incoterms).

**C.I.P. (carriage and insurance paid to).** Significa que el vendedor tiene las mismas obligaciones que bajo CPT, con el añadido de que ha de conseguir un seguro para la carga contra el riesgo, que soporta el comprador, de pérdida o daño de la mercancía durante el transporte. El vendedor contrata el seguro y paga la correspondiente prima. (Incoterms).

**C.P.T. (carriage paid to).** Significa que el vendedor paga el flete del transporte de la mercancía hasta el destino mencionado. El riesgo de pérdida o daño de la mercancía, así como cualquier gasto adicional debido a acontecimientos que ocurran después del momento en que la mercancía haya sido entregada al transportista, se transfiere del vendedor al comprador cuando la mercancía ha sido entregada a la custodia del transportista. (Incoterms).

**Cabinet.** Gabinete. Junta consultiva, directorio. Ministerio, cartera, consejo, gobierno.

**Cable.** Cable. Telegrama, fax, telex. Cadena.

**Cadaveric.** Cadavérico, mortecino.

**Cadet.** Cadete, infante, menor.

**Caducary.** Caducante.

**Caducity.** Caducidad, falta de acción, inoponibilidad.

**Calendar.** Calendario. Lista de casos para ser sustanciados. Almanaque, agenda. Orden del día.

**Calendar call.** Llamado a las partes para que se presenten a las audiencias fijadas para ese día. Lista de casos pendientes de adjudicación.

**Calendar quarter.** Trimestre natural.

**Calendar year.** Año natural.

**Call.** Llamar. Citar, emplazar, ordenar la comparecencia. Atraer, convidar, invitar. Designar, apellidar, denominar, nombrar, titular. Evocar, invocar. Gritar, anunciar, proclamar (v). Llamada. Citación. Invitación. Denominación. Evocación. Proclamación (s).

**Call loan.** Préstamo, generalmente a corto plazo, cuya devolución puede exigirse en cualquier momento.

**Call money.** Dinero invertido por un período breve.

**Call option.** Opción de compra.

**Call to order.** Llamar al orden. Requerir la atención de alguien o de un grupo de gente.

**Call to the bar.** Momento en que una persona se colegia como abogado y puede ejercer la profesión.

**Callable.** Rescatable, redimible. Condición de valores que pueden ser rescatados por la sociedad emisora.

**Calligrapher.** Calígrafo, perito calígrafo.

**Calligraphic.** Caligráfico, relativo a la escritura.

**Calligraphy.** Caligrafía, escritura. Modo particular de escribir.

**Calumniate.** Calumniar, acusar falsamente, agraviar, denigrar, deshonrar, difamar, mentir.

**Calumniation.** Ver *calumny.*

**Calumniator.** Calumniador, calumniante.

**Calumnious.** Calumnioso, calumniante, difamatorio.

**Calumny.** Calumnia, acusación falsa, agravio infundado. Difamación. Atribución peyorativa o deshonrosa, sobre otra persona, hecha pública sabiendo que es falsa.

**Calvo doctrine.** Doctrina que establece la no ingerencia de un Estado en los asuntos de otro y por la cual los inversores extranjeros no pueden solicitar el apoyo de su país.

**Camera.** Cámara, despacho del juez.

**Camp.** Campo, campamento militar.

**Cancel.** Cancelar, abolir, abrogar, acabar, anular, borrar, derogar, extinguir, liquidar, pagar, terminar, revocar, rescindir.

**Cancelable.** Cancelable, abrogable, derogable, revocable.

**Cancellation.** Cancelación, abolición, abrogación, anulación, extinción, fin, liquidación, pago, terminación, revocación, rescisión.

**Cannon shot.** Principio antiguo según el cual el mar territorial se extendía por la superficie cubierta por un tiro de cañón desde la costa.

**Canon.** Regla, código, decreto, dictado, edicto, guía, medida, ordenanza, pauta, precepto.

**Canon law.** Derecho canónico, derecho eclesiástico.

**Canvasser.** Persona que trabaja en escrutinios electorales ya sea contando y recontando votos, ya sea apoyando la elección de un partido determinado.

**Capability.** Capacidad, aptitud, calificaciones, competencia, condiciones, destreza, disposición, habilidad, idoneidad, facultades, poder, talento.

**Capable.** Capaz, apto, calificado, capacitado, competente, diestro, hábil, idóneo, talentoso. Disponiendo de las facultades legales necesarias.

**Capacity.** Capacidad. Aptitud, condiciones, facultades, talento. Cabida, contenencia, contenido.

**Capacity to contract.** Capacidad para contratar. Una persona que carezca de capacidad legal no puede obligarse contractualmente, ni tan siquiera en aquellos contratos que sean anulables. (Rstmnt, 2nd, Con., sec. 12).

**Capacity to sue or be sued.** Capacidad para demandar o ser demandado. La capacidad de una persona, salvo la que actúa en su capacidad representativa, para demandar y ser demandada se determinará por la ley de su domicilio. (R. Fed. P. Civ., sec. 17(b)).

**Capehart project.** Proyecto Capehart. El término proyecto Capehart significa un contrato de construcción de viviendas en tierras pertenecientes a, o arrendadas por Estados Unidos para proveer residencias adecuadas al personal militar. (Tropicari MFG. Corp. v. The Coite Somers Co., 96 D.P.R. 145 (1968)).

**Capital.** Capital. Bienes y derechos, patrimonio, recursos líquidos. Disponibilidades. Dinero, efectivo, fondos. Metrópolis, ciudad principal, sede de gobierno. Básico, importante, sustancial. Lo más elevado.

**Capital gains or losses.** Ganancias de capital o pérdidas.

**Capital offense.** Delito que acarrea la pena de muerte, o la pena más alta.

**Capital punishment.** Pena capital.

**Capitalization.** Capitalización, aumento del capital. Uso de un evento o circunstancia para provecho propio.

**Capitalize.** Capitalizar.

**Capitation.** Capitación, impuesto per cápita, por cada individuo.

**Capitulation**. Capitulación. Acuerdo, ajuste, arreglo, contrato, pacto. Abandono, abdicación, cesión, entrega, rendición.

**Captain.** Capitán, jefe.

**Caption.** Sumario y párrafo introductorio de un escrito. Título, encabezamiento, leyenda.

**Captors.** Apresadores.

**Capture.** Captura. Aprehensión, apresamiento, arresto, detención. Botín, despojo, presa, tesoro, trofeo (s). Capturar, aprehender, tomar (v).

**Carbon copy.** Copia carbónica, fotocopia.

**Card.** Tarjeta. Utilizado como verbo significa verificar en un documento de identidad que su titular sea mayor de edad.

**Card holder.** Titular de una tarjeta de crédito o de otro documento.

**Cardinal.** Cardinal, esencial, predominante, vital. Cardenal.

**Cardozo, Benjamin.** Benjamin Nathan Cardozo (1870–1938) ejerció la profesión en la ciudad de Nueva York después de terminar sus estudios en el Columbia College y en el Columbia School of Laws, y fue juez y más tarde presidente de la Corte de Apelaciones de New York, y fue designado juez asociado de la Corte Suprema de los Estados Unidos en 1932, para ocupar el puesto que Holmes había dejado vacante. Su obra más conocida es una serie de conferencias bajo el título de The Nature of the Judical Process (1921). (Intro al USA).

**Care.** Cuidado. Asistencia, atención, diligencia, respecto, solicitud (s). Cuidar, atender, ayudar, custodiar, interesarse, proteger, resguardar (v).

**Career.** Carrera, ocupación, profesión, trabajo, vocación.

**Careless.** Descuidado, abandonado, confiado, despreocupado, indiferente, indolente, negligente.

**Carelessness.** Descuido, despreocupación, indiferencia, negligencia.

**Caretaker.** Guardián, cuidador.

**Carnal.** De la carne, carnal. Erótico, libidinoso, sexual.

**Carriage.** Carro, coche, compartimiento, vagón. Transportación, acarreo, desplazamiento de mercaderías, envío.

**Carrier.** Transportador, acarreador, porteador, cargador. Empresa transportista.

**Carry.** Cargar, aparejar, conllevar, llevar, resultar.

**Carry back.** Facultad de imputar la pérdida sufrida en un año fiscal a años anteriores.

**Carry over.** Facultad de imputar la pérdida sufrida en un año fiscal a años posteriores.

**Carte blanche.** Del francés, significa dar autoridad ilimitada a una persona.

**Cartel.** Cartel. Organización monopólica entre productores o comerciantes destinada a manipular los precios de plaza.

**Case.** Caso. Acción judicial, causa, demanda, expediente, litigio, procedimiento, proceso, querella. Ejemplo, hipótesis, instancia.

**Case at bar.** Caso de marras, en la especie.

**Case dismissed.** No ha lugar, se rechaza la demanda. Desestimación del recurso.

**Case law.** Precedente judicial. Por varias razones la doctrina del procedente no ha gozado en los Estados Unidos de la autoridad absoluta que parece haber alcanzado en Inglaterra. La enorme cantidad de fallos, que establecen precedentes diferentes en distintas jurisdicciones tienden a disminuir la autoridad de las decisiones individuales. La rapidez del cambio social ha debilitado a menudo la aplicabilidad de precedentes a casos posteriores surgidos después de que las condiciones económicas y sociales se han alterado. Aun si la doctrina del precedente, aunque aplicada con menos rigidez que en Inglaterra, todavía esta firmemente arraigada en los Estados Unidos. (Intro al USA).

Jurisprudencia, casos, decisiones, precedentes. Derecho decisional, derecho común, *common law.*

**Case of first impression.** Caso que no se ha presentado antes. *Res nova.*

**Case ready to be set for hearing.** Caso listo para señalamiento.

**Case reports.** Colecciones de jurisprudencia. El diluvio de fallos sólo es manejable gracias a la existencia de dos sistemas bien organizados, uno de digestos y otro de citas. El American Digest System es el digesto más utilizado; está coordinado con el National Reporter System y comprende los fallos de las Cortes de apelaciones desde 1658 hasta la actualidad. (Intro al USA).

**Casebook.** Tipo de libro usado en escuelas de derecho del *common law* donde se reproducen sentencias literalmente, acompañadas de breves comentarios o de preguntas específicas.

**Cases, cite.** Cita de casos. En virtud de la doctrina del precedente, tiene importancia para la compresión del Derecho norteamericano tener cierta conocimiento sobre la forma de presentación de los informes de los fallos de los tribunales. La jurisprudencia se encuentra fundamentalmente en las decisiones de las Cortes de apelaciones, ya que, salvo en el caso de la justicia federal y unos pocos estados, los fallos de los tribunales de primera instancia no se publican. (Intro al USA).

**Cases, computer search.** Casos, búsqueda por computadora. En la actualidad la información ha contribuido a ahorrar tiempo y a evitar omisiones en la ubicación de jurisprudencia. Se dispone de dos sistemas computacionales, Lexis y Westlaw. Ellos permiten al usuario recuperar la mayor parte de los fallos federales y estaduales de las ultimas son décadas y algunos más antiguos. (Intro al USA).

**Cash.** Dinero, circulante, efectivo, metálico, moneda, plata. Caja, numerario (s). Cobrar un cheque u otro documento (v).

**Cash basis system.** Sistema de recibo y pagado. En el sistema de recibo y pagado el agricultor incluye las partidas de ingresos cuando recibe dinero efectivo a su equivalente y deduce los gastos cuando éstos son satisfechos en efectivo a su equivalente. (Ramos Hermanos v. Srio de Hacienda, 89 D.P.R. 552 (1963)).

**Cash book.** Libro caja, libro de caja.

**Cash flow.** Efectivo, flujo de caja.

**Cash transactions.** Operaciones al contado.

**Cash value.** Valor en efectivo.

**Cashier.** Cajero.

**Cassation.** Casación de un fallo. Revocación de una sentencia y devolución al tribunal de origen para la redacción de un nuevo fallo.

**Cast.** Arrojar, echar, emitir (v). Molde, matriz (s).

**Casting vote.** Voto de calidad, voto que rompe una situación de empate, decisorio.

**Castrate.** Castrar, emascular.

**Casual.** Casual. Espontáneo, fortuito, no planeado. Informal, improvisado, superficial.

**Casual employment**. Empleo casual, accidental temporario.

**Casualty.** Accidente, desgracia, siniestro. Muerte o herida seria producida en un accidente o acción bélica.

**Casualty insurance.** Seguro contra accidentes. "Seguro contra accidentes" incluye el seguro de vehículos, y además es: Seguro de responsabilidad. Seguro contra responsabilidad legal por muerte, lesión o incapacidad de un ser humano, o por daños a la propiedad; y suministro de beneficios médicos, de hospital, quirúrgicos, funerales o individuos lesionados, independientemente de la responsabilidad legal del asegurado, cuando ha sido emitido como protección incidental al seguro de responsabilidad, o complementario de éste. (26 LPRA Sec. 803).

**Catalogue.** Catálogo, clasificación, lista, listado, repertorio (s). Catalogar, clasificar, inventariar (v).

**Catastrophe.** Catástrofe, calamidad, desastre, desgracia, infortunio.

**Catch.** Botín, caza, pesca, sorprende (s). Aprehender, apresar, capturar, secuestrar (v).

**Catchline.** Apostilla.

**Category.** Categoría, clase, clasificación, departamento, división.

**Cattle.** Ganado, semovientes.

**Cattle lifter.** Cuatrero, ladrón de ganado.

**Cattle lifting.** Abigeato, cuatrerismo.

**Cattle livestock**. Ganado, semovientes.

**Caucus.** Reunión de un subgrupo político. Asamblea, comité, consejo, convención.

**Causal.** Causal, nexo de conexión entre dos eventos.

**Causation, legal cause.** Causalidad. Para que un actor negligente sea sujeto a responsabilidad por el daño causado a otra persona, es necesario probar no solo que la conducta del actor es negligente con relación a otra persona, pero además que la negligencia del acto es la causa legal del daño del otro individuo. (Rstmnt, 2nd, Torts, sec. 430, 431).

**Cause.** Causa. Fuente, finalidad, origen. Caso judicial, acción, litigio (s). Causar, originar, provocar (v).

**Cause the seal affixed.** Hacer estampar el sello.

**Caution.** Cautela, circunspección, precaución, prudencia (s). Advertir, aconsejar, apercibir, avisar (v).

**Cautionary.** Cautelar, precautorio, preventivo.

**Cautionary instruction.** Parte de las instrucciones al jurado en la que el juez determina ciertos aspectos restrictivos de la prueba presentada. Por ejemplo, que de tal prueba el jurado sólo puede inferir que el reo estaba presente en el lugar de los hechos, pero no su intención de cometer un delito.

**Caveat.** Advertencia, reserva.

**Cease.** Cesar, abandonar, acabar, ceder, cejar, dejar, dimitir, finalizar, interrumpir, terminar.

**Cease and desist.** Dejar de hacer algo, obligación de no hacer, normalmente impuesta por orden judicial.

**Cede.** Ceder. Acceder, aceptar, amainar, aplacarse, avenirse, capitular, cesar, claudicar, consentir, flaquear, rendirse, renunciar. Transferir, enajenar, entregar, traspasar.

**Ceiling.** Tope máximo, control, extremo, límite, restricción.

**Celebration of marriage.** Celebración de matrimonio.

**Cell.** Celda, prisión, célula, calabozo,

**Cemetery.** Cementerio, camposanto, necrópolis.

**Censor.** Censor (s). Censurar, borrar, suprimir (v).

**Censure.** Condena, desaprobación o rechazo oficial (s). Condenar o desaprobar oficialmente (v).

**Census.** Censo, recuento del número de habitantes.

**Center.** Centro. Equidistancia, medio, mitad. Parte central o esencial (s). Centrar, apuntar, concentrar (v).

**Central.** Central. Céntrico, en el medio, equidistante de los extremos. Más importante, básico, esencial, sustancial.

**Ceremonial.** Ceremonial, formal, pomposo, ritual.

**Certain.** Cierto, absoluto, certero, claro, confiado, definido, exacto, preciso, seguro.

**Certainty.** Certeza, certidumbre, certitud, convicción, predictibilidad.

**Certainty of harm.** Certeza del daño. Es resarcible solamente el daño que pueda determinarse con un grado razonable de certeza, aún cuando sea futuro. (Unidroit, Prin., art. 7.4.3).

**Certificate.** Certificado, certificación, constatación, deposición, diploma, documento, evidencia escrita, prueba testimonial.

**Certificate of amendment.** Constancia oficial de la modificación de los estatutos de una sociedad.

**Certificate of deposit.** Certificado de depósito.

**Certificate of good conduct.** Certificado de buena conducta.

**Certificate of incorporation.** Certificado de incorporación. Deberá consignarse en el certificado de incorporación: El nombre de la corporación, nombre que deberá zcontener uno de los términos siguientes: corporación, corp. o Inc., o palabras o abreviaturas de similar significación en otros idiomas (siempre que se escriban en letras o caracteres romances o ingleses); y que será de naturaleza tal que pueda distinguírsele en los registros del Departamento de Estado de los nombres de otras corporaciones organizadas o autorizadas a hacer negocios en el país con arreglo a las leyes del Estado. (14 LPRA sec. 1102).

**Certified check.** Cheque certificado.

**Certified public accountant, CPA.** Contador público.

**Certified security.** Valor. Un "valor" es un documento que es expedido al portador o nominativamente; y es del tipo que corrientemente se cotiza en bolsa o mercados de valores o es corrientemente admitido en cualquier área en que se emitiere o negociare como un medio de inversión; y es uno de una clase o series o que por sus términos es divisible en una clase o serie de documentos; y evidencia una acción, participación u otro interés en una propiedad o una empresa o evidencia una obligación del emisor. (C.C.U. sec. 8-102(1)(a)).

**Certified signature.** Firma certificada o legalizada.

**Certify.** Certificar, acreditar, afianzar, afirmar, atestar, autentificar, confirmar, corroborar, deponer, documentar, legalizar, legitimar, ratificar, testimoniar.

**Certiorari.** Procedimiento de apelación mediante el cual el tribunal de alzada requiere copia de las actuaciones para determinar si intervendrá en la causa o no. (Ver: *writ of certiorari.*)

**Cessation.** Cesación, alto, aplazamiento, cese, detención, interrupción, parada, paro, pausa, suspensión, tregua.

**Cession.** Cesión, entrega, transferencia, traspaso, venta.

**Cesspool.** Letrina, baño, cloaca, excusado, pozo negro.

**Cestui que trust, trustent.** Beneficiario de un *trust* o fideicomiso.

**Chain.** Cadena, ciclo, secuencia, serie, sucesión (s). Encadenar, restringir, sujetar (v).

**Chain of custody.** Determinación de las personas bajo cuya custodia ha quedad sucesivamente la prueba.

**Chain of title.** Lista o sucesión de personas que han sido los dueños anteriores de una cosa, normalmente de inmuebles.

**Chair.** Sillón, sitial del director o presidente. Presidencia, dirección.

**Chairman.** Presidente, director.

**Chairperson.** Presidente/a, director/a.

**Chairwoman.** Presidenta, directora.

**Challenge.** Desafío, reto. Recusación de un juez. Tacha de un testigo. Impugnación de un resultado (s). Contradecir, cuestionar, impugnar, recusar, tachar oponerse, rebatir, refutar (v).

**Challengeable.** Cuestionable, atacable, impugnable, incierto, recusable.

**Chamber.** Cámara judicial o legislativa, despacho, sala.

**Chamber of commerce.** Cámara de comercio.

**Champertor.** Persona que compra un juicio en trámite.

**Champerty.** Contrato ilegal por el cual un extraño al litigio paga todos los gastos judiciales y en caso de ganar, recibe una proporción de lo que la sentencia acuerde.

**Chance.** Azar, accidente, casualidad, destino, suerte (s). Arriesgar, intentar (v).

**Chancellery.** Cancillería, oficio de primer ministro. Ministerio de asuntos exteriores.

**Chancellor.** Canciller. Juez de una corte de equidad. Primer ministro. Presidente de una universidad.

**Chancery.** Equidad. Sistema inglés de cortes paralelas que decidian basadas no en la estricta ley pero en la equidad y justicia de cada caso. Sistema opuesto al de las cortes reales.

**Change.** Cambio, alteración, reforma, transformación, variación (s). Cambiar, alterar, reformar (v).

**Change of remedy.** Cambio de pretensión. La parte agraviada que habiendo requerido el cumplimiento de una obligación no dineraria, no la obtenga dentro del término fijado para ello o, en su defecto, dentro de un término razonable, podrá recurrir a cualquier otra pretensión. (Unidroit, Prin., art. 7.2.5).

**Changed conditions as grounds to modify a judgment.** Cambio de circunstancias como razón para modificar una sentencia. Sujeto a algunas limitaciones, se puede ignorar o modificar una sentencia si: 1) Dicha sentencia es modificable por disposición propia o por derecho aplicable, y la ocurrencia de algunos eventos, subsiguiente al momento de dictar sentencia, garantiza la modificación que se pretende; o 2) Ha ocurrido un cambio de tal magnitud en las circunstancias que seria injusto permitir que la sentencia continúe vigente. (Rstmnt, 2nd, Judg., sec. 73).

**Chantage.** Chantaje, exacción ilegal, extorsión. Amenaza.

**Chapter.** Capítulo, división, sección. Filial de una organización no comercial.

**Character.** Carácter, condición, índole, naturaleza. Humor, genio, personalidad, temple. Entereza, firmeza, voluntad.

**Character evidence.** Evidencia de carácter. Evidencia del carácter de una persona o de un rasgo de su carácter no será admisible para el propósito de probar que actuó de acuerdo con el mismo en una ocasión, determinada, excepto: Evidencia de un rasgo pertinente de su carácter ofrecida por un acusado, o por el fiscal para refutarla; Evidencia de un rasgo pertinente del carácter de la víctima de un delito ofrecida por un acusado, o por el fiscal para refutarla, o evidencia del carácter pacifico de la víctima ofrecida por el fiscal en un caso de homicidio para refutar evidencia de que la víctima fue el primer agresor. (Regla 404, R. Fed. Evid.).

**Character evidence, means of proof.** Evidencia de carácter, medios de prueba. En todos los casos en que sea admisible evidencia de carácter o de un rasgo del carácter de una persona, podrá presentarse la prueba mediante testimonio en cuanto a la reputación o mediante testimonio en la forma de opinión. (Regla 405, R. Fed. Evid.).

**Character witness.** Persona que atestigua sobre el tipo de personalidad de una de las partes. Por ejemplo, si es o no violento.

**Characterization.** Clasificación o calificación. La clasificación e interpretación de los conceptos y términos del conflicto de leyes se determinan de acuerdo a la ley del foro. (Rstmnt, 2nd, Conflict, sec. 7).

**Charge.** Cargo. Encargo, deber, imposición, obligación. Afectación de un bien, carga, gravamen. Acusación, crítica, denuncia. Costo, precio (s). Cargar, acusar, encargar, imponer, comprar a crédito (v).

**Chargeable.** Cargable, atribuible, imputable, responsable. Atacable.

**Charges.** Cargo, costo, precio.

**Charging.** Atribuyente, atacante.

**Charging order.** Mandamiento de ejecución, ejecución de bienes.

**Charitable.** Caritativo, benéfico, filantrópico.

**Charitable contribution.** Donación benéfica.

**Charitable deduction.** Deducción impositiva resultante de una donación benéfica.

**Charitable institution.** Institución benéfica.

**Charity.** Caridad, beneficencia, filantropía.

**Charter.** Acta de constitución societaria. Documento constitucional, Carta de porte. Fletamento (s). Fletar, enviar. Planear el curso de algún evento.

**Charterer.** Fletador o fletante. Persona que envía mercaderías.

**Chastisement.** Castigo, corrección, medida disciplinaria, plena.

**Chattel dangerous for intended use.** Bien mueble peligroso para su uso específico. Quien supla, directamente o a través de un tercero, un bien mueble a ser utilizado según los propósitos del negocio del suplidor, será responsable ante quienes han en definitiva recibido el bien mueble o ante quienes están en peligro por su uso, por el daño físico ocasionado por el uso de dicho bien: si el suplidor no ha ejercido un cuidado razonable para que el bien sea seguro al utilizarse según su propósito. (Rstmnt, 2nd, Torts, sec. 392).

**Chattel mortgage.** Gravamen sobre bienes muebles. Prenda, privilegio.

**Chattel paper.** Valor mobiliario. Valor mobiliario significa uno o varios escritos que representan una obligación monetaria y un interés garantizado o arrendamiento sobre mercancías específicas. (C.C.U. sec. 9-105(b)).

**Chattels.** Bienes muebles.

**Cheat.** Engañar, defraudar, estafar. Cometer dolo.

**Check, cheque (G.B.).** Cheque (s). Comprobar, determinar, inspeccionar, revisar. Contener, jaquear, neutralizar (v).

**Checks and balances.** En política, el sistema por el cual los tres poderes del estado—legislativo, judicial y ejecutivo—se controlan los unos a los otros impidiendo que el poder se concentre en unos pocos.

**Chief.** Jefe, cabecilla, cabeza, capitán, director. Principal, dominante, más importante.

**Chief justice.** Presidente de la Corte Suprema. Para el cargo de Presidente de las Cortes Supremas estaduales se utiliza habitualmente el mismo método que para los demás cargos, pero hay estados en que la presidencia es ejercida por los jueces de la corte en forma rotativa, o por antigüedad, o por voto de los mismos jueces. (Intro al USA).

**Child.** Niño/a, hijo/a, infante.

**Child abuse.** Malos tratos, incluyendo sevicia sexual, realizada contra niños.

**Child support.** Alimento para hijos menores.

**Chilling effect.** Paralización de un tipo de conducta, que se estima legítima, por temor a ser comprendido bajo una ley punitiva de otra conducta similar o cercana.

**Choate.** Completo, perfeccionado.

**Choate lien doctrine.** Doctrina del gravamen privado que se halla perfeccionado. Para que ello ocurra deben darse tres requisitos: Primero: que se establezca la propiedad sujeta al gravamen; Segundo: la identidad del dueño del gravamen debe ser cierta y definida; Tercero: el gravamen debe ser por una cantidad exacta, que ha sido definitivamente fijada. La determinacio sobre si el gravamen se encuentra perfeccionado o no es una cuestión federal. (Morales Lebrón).

**Choice.** Elección, alternativa, decisión, opción, preferencia, selección.

**Choice of jurisdiction.** Elección de jurisdicción.

**Choice of law.** Elección del derecho aplicable. Los Estados particulares son competentes para decidir cuáles serán las normas de derecho internacional privado aplicables. Correlativamente, tales reglas pueden variar de un Estado al otro. Como en el caso de la competencia, aun un tribunal federal tiene que aplicar los principios de derecho internacional privado del Estado particular donde está situada la corte. Por ejemplo, un Tribunal Federal situado en Miami está obligado a aplicar las normas de conflicto de leyes formuladas por el derecho del Estado de Florida. (Carl).

**Choice of law, principles.** Elección del derecho, principios. Una corte, sin perjuicio de restricciones constitucionales, seguirá las leyes de su propio Estado en materia de derecho aplicable.

En ausencia de tales leyes, los factores relevantes para la elección del derecho aplicable incluyen: a) las necesidades de los sistemas interestatales e internacionales, b) las políticas públicas relevantes del foro, c) las políticas públicas relevantes de otros Estados interesados y los intereses relativos

de esos estados en la determinación del asunto particular, d) la protección de expectativas justificadas, e) las políticas públicas básicas que fundamentan el campo del derecho en particular, f) certeza, predecibilidad y uniformidad del resultado, y g) facilidad en la determinación y aplicación de la ley a ser aplicada. (Rstmnt, 2nd, Conflict, sec. 6).

**Chose.** Cosa mueble.

**Christian.** Cristiano.

**Christian name.** Nombre de pila, primer nombre.

**Church.** Iglesia, clero, religión.

**Circuit.** Circuito, departamento judicial. Areas mayores en las que se divide la competencia territorial federal en USA.

**Circuit court.** Tribunal federal con competencia en un circuito determinado.

**Circular.** Circular. Nota, carta, memorándum, instrucción.

**Circumstance.** Circunstancia, evento, ocasión.

**Circumstantial.** Circunstancial, casual, indirecto, fortuito, por implicancia.

**Circumstancial evidence.** Prueba circunstancial o indirecta.

**Citation.** Citación, apercibimiento, cédula, cita, emplazamiento, mandamiento, orden de comparecencia. Referencia, mención, nota.

**Cite.** Citar. Ordenar la comparecencia a juicio, emplazar. Mencionar a la doctrina o a casos en un escrito.

**Citizen.** Ciudadano, domiciliario, habitante, local, nacional, natural, vecino, paisano, residente.

**Citizen's arrest.** Arresto civil.

**Citizenship.** Ciudadanía, nacionalidad. Condición de súbdito de un país.

**City.** Ciudad, metrópolis, municipalidad, municipio, urbanización.

**Civil.** Civil. A veces también se utiliza en Estados Unidos el término *civil* como contrapuesto a *penal*. No es habitual en los Estados Unidos hablar de *derecho civil* para referirse a la materia de un código civil, y en contraposición, por ejemplo, a derecho comercial. (Intro al USA).

Referente al sistema de derecho continental o romano. Perteneciente al derecho doméstico de los ciudadanos y excluyendo áreas especializadas como el derecho criminal, administrativo, etc.

**Civil defense volunteers corps.** Cuerpo de voluntarios de defensa civil.

**Civil docket.** Registro de pleitos y procedimientos civiles. El secretario llevará un libro conocido como "registro de pleitos y procedimientos civiles" (*civil docket*) y anotará en el mismo todo pleito civil. A los pleitos se les asignarán números de radicación consecutivos. (R. Fed. P. Civ., sec. 79(a)).

**Civil judgments and orders.** Sentencias y órdenes civiles. El secretario llevará una copia exacta de cada sentencia final u orden apelable, u orden que afecte el título a o gravamen sobre bienes muebles o inmuebles y cualquier otra orden que la corte disponga que se ejecute. (R. Fed. P. Civ., sec. 79(b)).

**Civil law.** Sistema jurídico basado en el derecho romano antiguo o clásico, como el que prima en América Latina y en Europa Occidental. Rama del derecho que regula vida privada o doméstica de los individuos, por oposición a ramas más especializadas como el derecho administrativo o penal.

**Civil liability.** Responsabilidad civil. El objetivo esencial del derecho de daños es compensatorio y, si bien a veces se otorgan compensaciones punitivas, su función es distinta de la del derecho penal. Por el contrario, el derecho penal es eminentemente punitivo; las víctimas no obtienen compensación en los procedimientos penales. (Intro al USA).

**Civil liability, state.** Responsabilidad civil del estado. Una de las leyes federales mas importantes es la *Federal Torts Claims Act* (Ley de responsabilidad civil del Estado por daños) de 1946, por el cual el estado federal (con ciertas excepciones) ha renunciado a su inmunidad absoluta respecto de los delitos y cuasidelitos de sus empleados, de modo que hoy es posible obtener reparaciones a través de una acción contra los Estados Unidos ante los tribunales federales (pero sin jurado) en las mismas circunstancias en que

un particular seria responsable. (Intro al USA).

**Civil partnership.** Sociedad civil.

**Civil rights.** Derechos civiles o políticos.

**Civil servant.** Funcionario público, empleado estatal, burócrata.

**Civil suit.** Pleito civil.

**Civilian.** Ciudadano, civil. Relacionado con el sistema de derecho romano.

**Claim.** Demanda. Acción judicial, aserción, derecho, exordio, petición, pretensión, querella, reclamación, reclamo, solicitud (s). Demandar, accionar, acertar, desear, encausar, exigir, pretender, proclamar, querellar (v).

**Claim damages.** Demandar por daños y perjuicios.

**Claim for relief.** Solicitud de remedio. Las alegaciones que expusieren solicitudes de remedio, ya fueren demandas originales, reconvenciones, demandas contra coparte o demandas contra tercero, contendrán una relación sucinta y sencilla de los fundamentos de la jurisdicción de la corte, a menos que la corte ya tuviera jurisdicción y la reclamación no necesitare nuevos fundamentos para la misma. (Reglas Fed. del Proc. Civ., sec. 8(a)).

**Claimable.** Accionable, reclamable, que puede ser solicitado por vía judicial.

**Claimant.** Actuar, accionante, demandante, querellante, reclamante, requirente, solicitante.

**Claimant plaintiff.** Reclamante, actor, demandante, denunciante.

**Claims adjustor.** Ajustador de seguros. "Ajustador" es la persona que, por compensación como contratista independiente o como empleado de un contratista independiente, o por honorarios, comisión o sueldo, investiga y negocia el ajuste de reclamaciones que surjan de contratos de seguros exclusivamente a nombre del asegurador o del asegurado. Un abogado postulante que ajuste pérdidas de seguros de tiempo en tiempo incidentalmente al ejercicio de su profesión, o un comisario de averías, no se considera "ajustador" para los fines de este capítulo. Un abogado que en representación de un asegurador ajuste pérdidas tendrá que poseer una licencia de ajustador independiente. (26 LPRA sec. 905).

**Claims court.** Tribunales de menor cuantía. En muchas ciudades existen tribunales secundarios (*claims court*), que tiene jurisdicción sobre la mayor parte de las cuestiones civiles que involucren sumas de mil dólares o menos, y utilizan procedimientos informales en los que los costos son mínimos y no se necesita un abogado. (Intro al USA).

**Clandestine.** Clandestino, anónimo, discreto, encubierto, furtivo, oculto, secreto, subrepticio.

**Class action.** Pleito de clase, acción colectiva. Uno o más miembros de una clase podrán demandar o ser demandados como partes representantes a nombre de todos únicamente si 1) la clase fuera tan numerosa que la acumulación de todos los miembros resultará impracticable, 2) existieran cuestiones de derecho o de hecho comunes a la clase, 3) las reclamaciones o defensas de las partes representantes fueran reclamaciones o defensas típicas de la clase, y 4) las partes representantes protegieren justa y adecuadamente los intereses de la clase. (R. Fed. P. Civ., sec. 23(a)).

**Class action, dismissal or compromise.** Pleito de clase, desistimiento o transacción. Un pleito de clase no podrá ser desistido o transado sin la aprobación de la corte, y se dará aviso del desistimiento o transacción propuestos a todos los miembros de la clase en la forma que dispusiera la corte. (R. Fed. P. Civ., sec. 23(e)).

**Class action, orders in conduct.** Pleito de clase, órdenes en la tramitación. En la tramitación de los pleitos a que esta regla fuere aplicable, la corte podrá dictar las órdenes pertinentes: para determinar el curso de los procedimientos o prescribir las medidas para evitar repeticiones o complicaciones indebidas en la presentación de evidencia o alegatos. (Reglas Fed. del Proc. Civ., sec. 23(d)).

**Class actions maintainable.** Pleitos de clase sostenibles. Un pleito podrá sostenerse como pleito de clase si se cumpliesen los requisitos generales, y en adición: la tramitación por separado de pleitos por o contra miembros individuales de la clase pudiera crear un riesgo de a) adjudicaciones inconsistentes o distintas con respecto a miembros individuales de la clase, que establecerían normas incompatibles de conducta para la parte que se opone a la clase, o b) adjudicaciones con respecto a miembros individuales de al clase que como cuestión práctica dispondrían de los intereses de los otros miembros no partes en las adjudicaciones o sustancialmente perjudicarían o dificultarían su capacidad para proteger sus intereses. (R. Fed. P. Civ., sec. 23(b)).

**Class gift.** Donación o legado que se realiza en favor de una clase de personas.

**Classification.** Clasificación, catalogación, orden, ordenamiento, sistematización.

**Classified.** Clasificado, secreto, restringido.

**Clause.** Cláusula, acápite, apartado, artículo, disposición, estipulación, formula, párrafo, parte, sección.

**Clean.** Limpio, claro, diáfano, honesto, libre, libre de gravámenes, libre de restricciones, puro, transparente (s). Limpiar, depurar, mejorar (v).

**Clean bill of lading.** Carta de porte sin ninguna limitación específica.

**Clean hands.** Literalmente significa manos limpias. Expresión usada para indicar uno de los requisitos en los que se basa, históricamente, el sistema de equidad (*equity*) del *common law*. Si el actor no ha obrado rectamente, si no tiene "manos limpias," los tribunales de equidad desestimaban su demanda.

**Clear.** Claro, entendible, inteligible, libre de gravámenes o de restricciones, transparente (s). Depurar, purificar, limpiar, remover trabas, embargos y demás gravámenes (v).

**Clear and present danger doctrine.** Teoría del peligro inminente. Se utiliza en derecho penal como justificativo, o eximente, de una conducta que de otra forma sería criminal. Para que ello ocurra es necesario que el individuo se sienta amenazado por un riesgo percibido como actual y claro.

**Clear title.** Título de propiedad donde no se percibe ninguna restricción. Por ejemplo, sin embargos ni inhibiciones.

**Clearance.** Permiso de salida de una nave. Aprobación, autorización, visto bueno.

**Clearance sale.** Liquidación de saldos.

**Clearing bank.** Banco de compensación.

**Clemency.** Clemencia, amnistía, condonación, indulgencia, misericordia, perdón, remisión.

**Clergyman.** Sacerdote, cura, fraile, ministro.

**Clerical error.** Error tipográfico, error material.

**Clerical staff.** Personal administrativo.

**Clerk.** Secretario, actuario, escribano. Empleado judicial, oficinista, personal administrativo. v. trabajar como empleado en un bufete, especialmente mientras se llevan a cabo estudios universitarios de derecho.

**Clerk of chamber.** Escribano de cámara.

**Client.** Cliente, consumidor.

**Clientele.** Clientela.

**Close.** Cerrado, confidencial, impenetrable, reservado, secreto. Cerrar, bloquear, cesar, detener, restringir, terminar (v).

**Closed hearing.** Vista a puerta cerrada. Haciendo salvedad del derecho a vista en corte abierta en procedimientos por desacato, la corte ordenará que la vista de asuntos que afecten el procedimiento ante el gran jurado se celebre a puerta cerrada en cuanto fuera necesario para evitar la revelación de cuestiones tratadas ante el mismo. (Regla 6(e)(5), Reglas Fed. de Proc. Crim.).

**Closed season.** Período de veda.

**Closing.** Cierre, firma de una escritura traslativa de dominio.

**Closing argument.** Informe final. Después de practicada toda la prueba el fiscal dará comienzo a los informes. Se permitirá que la defensa conteste a continuación. Después se permitirá que el fiscal refute. (Regla 29.1, Reglas Fed. de Proc. Crim.).

**Closure.** Cierre, clausura, conclusión, fin, término.

**Cloture.** Cierre de debates legislativos para proceder a una votación.

**Clouded title.** Literalmente, título envuelto en una nube. Expresion opuesta a *clear title*. Significa que la persona en cuestión no goza del dominio irrestricto de la cosa, o que sus derechos estan en duda.

Título viciado, imperfecto, susceptible de ataque o impugnación.

**Club.** Club, asociación, lugar de reunión, garrote, cachiporra, palo (s). Golpear con un palo o garrote (v).

**Clue.** Indicio, huella, pista, rastro.

**Co-sign.** Firmar conjuntamente.

**Coaccused.** Coacusado/a, coencartado/a, coencausado/a, conquerellado/a.

**Coadministrator.** Coadministrador.

**Coagent.** Coagente.

**Coalition.** Coalición, agrupación, amalgama, asociación, fusión, liga, unión.

**Coast.** Costa, borde del mar o río, playa. Costera, navegar cerca de la costa.

**Coasting.** Cabotaje.

**Coastwise trade.** Comercio de cabotaje.

**Coat of arms.** Escudo de armas.

**Cocaine.** Cocaína.

**Cochairman, cochairperson, cochairwoman.** Copresidente/a.

**Cock fight.** Riña de gallos.

**Cocreditor.** Coacreedor, acreedor conjunto.

**Codastral.** Codastral.

**Code.** Código, colección o recopilación orgánica de leyes y otras normas obligatorias.

**Codebtor.** Codeudor, coobligado. Garante, fianza.

**Codefendant.** Codemandado, co-acusado, coencausado, coencartado, coprocesado, coquerellado.

**Codicil.** Codicilo, adición a un testamento ya finalizado.

**Codification.** Codificación, recopilación orgánica y sistemática de leyes y demás normas obligatorias.

**Codify.** Codificar, compilar, recopilar el derecho. Promulgar un código.

**Codirector.** Codirector.

**Coefficient.** Coeficiente, grado, proporción, resultado.

**Coerce.** Obligar.

**Coercible.** Coercible, accionable, constreñible, sujeto a ser impuesto por la fuerza pública del estado.

**Coercion.** Coerción, coacción, ejecución forzada, imposición, intimidación.

**Coercive.** Coercitivo, coactivo, forzoso, impuesto, obligatorio.

**Coexecutor.** Coalbacea.

**Cogent.** Convincente, autoritario, coherente, concluyente, creíble, persuasivo.

**Cognates.** Emparentados por el lado materno.

**Cognition.** Cognición, conciencia, conocimiento, entendimiento, esclarecimiento, percepción, sabiduría.

**Cognitive.** Cognitivo, relacionado al aprendizaje, conocimiento y entendimiento lógico.

**Cognizable.** Conocible, sujeto a la competencia, actual o potencial, de un tribunal.

**Cognizance.** Conocimiento, avocación, asunción de la competencia por parte de un tribunal.

**Coguarantor.** Cogarante, cofiador.

**Cohabilitation.** Cohabitación, vida en común de una pareja estando o no casados.

**Cohabit.** Cohabitar.

**Coheir.** Coheredero.

**Coin.** Moneda, dinero, efectivo (s). Emitir moneda, metálica o en billete. Inventar y poner en circulación una palabra, frase o concepto (v).

**Coin money.** Acuñar moneda.

**Coinage.** Emisión de moneda metálica. Moneda metálica emitida y en circulación.

**Coinheritance.** Herencia conjunta, derechos hereditarios en común.

**Coinheritor, coheir.** Coheredero.

**Coinsurance.** Coseguro, reaseguro.

**Coinsurer.** Coasegurador.

**Coitus, coition.** Coito, acceso carnal, cópula, penetración, relación sexual.

**Cold blood, in.** En sangre fría, con premeditación y a sabiendas.

**Colegatee.** Colegatario.

**Colessee.** Coarrendatario, coinquilino.

**Colessor.** Coarrendador, copropietario.

**Colitigant.** Colitigante, coparte, coactor, codemandado, litis consorte.

**Collaborator.** Colaborador, ayudante, colega, cotrabajador.

**Collapse.** Desmoronamiento, derrota, quiebra.

**Collapsible.** Desmoronable, peligroso, precario, provisorio. De fácil desmantelación y remoción.

**Collate.** Encuadernar, fijar, pegar. Constatar, comparar.

**Collateral.** Colateral. "Colateral" significa la propiedad gravada con un interés garantizado e incluye cuentas, derechos contractuales y valores mobiliarios que hubiesen sido vendidos. (C.C.U. sec. 9-105(c)). Medida de garantía por una deuda, así como la fianza o hipoteca.

**Collateral estoppel.** Impedimento colateral. Cosa juzgada por afinidad. Preclusión o inoponibilidad de una sentencia por haber mediado una decisión judicial previa e incompatible en un procedimiento distinto. Se requiere que la decisión obstaculizante haya sido litigada por las partes y que resulte esencial para la segunda causa.

**Collateral estoppel by judgment.** Impedimento colateral por sentencia. La doctrina de impedimento colateral por sentencia impide que se litigue en un pleito cualquier cuestión de hecho—y a veces de derecho—realmente litigada y adjudicada en un pleito anterior entre las mismas partes aunque sobre una causa de acción distinta de la litigada y adjudicada en el pleito anterior. (Riera v. Piza, 85 D.P.R. 268 (1962)).

**Collateral impediment.** Impedimento colateral. Principio que impide que se litigue en un pleito cualquier cuestion de hecho, y a veces de derecho, realmente litigada y adjudicada en un pleito anterior entre las mismas partes aunque sobre una causa de accion distinta de la litigada y adjudicada en el pleito anterior. (Morales Lebrón).

**Collateral negligence.** Negligencia colateral. En la determinación de la responsabilidad en daños de un patrono por los actos torticeros de un contratista independiente, el término negligencia collateral—que exime al patrono de responsabilidad—significa la forma impropia o inadecuada en que se ejecuta la obra o el trabajo contratado por el patrono y que crea un riesgo de daños que dicho patrono no podía razonablemente prever, si la gestión encomendada se realizaba en la manera usual y corriente. (Bonet

v. Municipio de Barceloneta, 87 D.P.R. 81 (1963)).

**Collect.** Coleccionar, cobrar, percibir fondos, recaudar o recibir dinero, recobrar. Llamada telefónica o envío de mercaderías con cargos revertidos, pagados por el recipiente.

**Collectibility.** Situación de deudas donde cabe acción judicial y cuyo deudor es solvente. Cobrabilidad.

**Collectible.** Cobrable, recobrable, reembolsable.

**Collection.** Colección. Cobro, cobranza, recaudación, reclamo y percepción de una deuda.

**Collection by constraint.** Cobro mediante procedimiento de apremio.

**Collective.** Colectivo, común, comunal, grupal, societario.

**Collective bargaining.** Proceso mediante el cual se llega a una convención colectiva de trabajo.

**Collective bargaining agreement.** Convenio colectivo de trabajo.

**Collectivism.** Colectivismo, comunismo.

**Collector.** Coleccionista. Cobrador, colector, recaudador, perceptor. Agencia de cobranzas. Acopiador, recopilador.

**Collegatary.** Colegatario.

**Collision.** Colisión, abordaje, choque, confrontación. Contradicción entre dos sistemas jurídicos o leyes cuando ambos son inicialmente aplicables al mismo caso.

**Collusion.** Colusión, arreglo encubierto, confabulación, conspiración, estratagema, pacto secreto.

**Collusive.** Colusorio, oculto, secreto, solapado.

**Colonial.** Colonial, imperialista, metropolitano.

**Colony.** Colonia, enclave, posesión, protectorado, territorio.

**Color.** Color, coloramiento, tintura, pigmentación. Que presenta la apariencia de algo, vg. de legalidad, pero sin serlo realmente (s). Pintar, colorar, describir una situación inyectando apreciaciones personales, no siempre ciertas, y bajo apariencia de objetividad (v).

**Color of law.** Apariencia de legalidad, impresión errónea, pero convincente, de la oficialidad de un acto. Ejemplo, fuerza policial que por lucro personal allana un inmueble y decomisa varios objetos.

**Color of title.** Justo título. Título de propiedad que en apariencia es perfecto pero que adolece de un defecto intrínseco.

**Colors.** Colores, bandera, insignia, pabellón.

**Comaker.** Cofirmante de un título de crédito. Coautor.

**Combat.** Combate, conflicto armado, guerra, pelea (s). Combatir, hostigar, oponerse (v).

**Combination.** Combinación, asociación, grupo, mezcla, unión.

**Comity.** Cortesía. Unica razón por la cual originalmente, el derecho extranjero, o el internacional, era aplicado por los tribunales de otro Estado. Tolerancia, concesión graciosa, favor. Paralelamente, razón original por la cual, dentro de USA, tribunales de un Estado aplicaban el derecho de otro Estado.

**Command.** Comando, mandato, mando. Control, autoridad, dominio. Estructura jerárquica (s). Comandar, mandar, ordenar (v).

**Commandeer.** Requisar, confiscar, expropiar. tomar algo de un particular para uso inmediato y urgente del estado, sin que medie proceso legal o formal previo, y contra la voluntad del despojado. Ejemplo, requisar un vehículo para dar alcance a delincuentes peligrosos.

**Commander.** Comandante, capitán.

**Commander in chief.** Comandante en jefe.

**Commando.** Comando, grupo guerrillero de ataque, pelotón especial.

**Commencement.** Comienzo, iniciación, principio.

**Commentator.** Comentador, comentarista, glosador, jurista que describe la ley en publicaciones, tratadista.

**Commerce.** Comercio, actividad comercial, interrelación, ocupación profesional de los comerciantes, relaciones comerciales u otras, tráfico, transacción.

**Commercial clause.** Cláusula comercial de la Constitución. Para asegurar la libertad del mercado interno nacional, los redactores de la Constitución otorgaron al Congreso el poder de "regular el comercio con las naciones extranjeras, y entre los diversos estados, y con las tribus indígenas." (Intro al USA).

**Commercial code.** Código de comercio, código comercial.

**Commercial custom generally observed in each place.** Usos del comercio observados generalmente en una plaza.

**Commercial employee.** Dependiente de comercio.

**Commercial law.** Derecho comercial, legislación mercantil.

**Commercial paper, interpretation of ambiguous terms.** Documento comercial, interpretación de términos ambiguos. Las siguientes reglas se aplicarán a todo instrumento: a) Cuando exista duda de si el instrumento es un giro o un pagaré, el tenedor podrá considerarlo como cualquiera de los dos. Un giro librado contra el librador, tendrá la eficacia de un pagaré. b) Los términos escritos a mano predominan sobre los mecanografiados e impresos, y los mecanografiados predominan sobre los impresos. c) Las palabras prevalecen sobre los guarismos y cuando las palabras fueren ambiguas prevalecerán los guarismos. (C.C.U. sec. 3-118).

**Commercial paper, uniform commercial code.** Documentos comerciales, código de comercio uniforme. El Artículo 3 que trata de los instrumentos negociables se titula "Documento comercial." Básicamente condensa la antigua ley y suprime preceptos en desuso. No amplía su radio de acción. (C.C.U., Prefacio).

**Commercialize.** Comercializar, poner en el mercado, vender. Usar para fines mezquinos o poco nobles. Explotar, utilizar, sacar provecho.

**Comminatory.** Conminatorio, improrrogable. Sujeto a sanciones en caso de incumplimiento. Admonitorio.

**Commingling.** Combinación o mezcla de fondos pertenecientes a dos personas o a dos cuentas distintas.

**Commissary.** Comisario encargado, oficial.

**Commission.** Comisión. Directorio, junta, grupo ejecutivo. Porcentaje o proporción aplicable a ventas y demás transacciones realizadas. Encargo, cometido, mandato, recado. Acción o realización de un acto. Comisionar, asignar, encargar, encomendar, instruir, mandar.

**Commissioner.** Comisionado. Persona a la cabeza de una repartición pública, ejemplo, el jefe de policía. Administrador, encargado, gerente.

**Commit.** Cometer, llevar a cabo, perpetrar, realizar. Encarcelar, recluir. Encomendar a alguien a un asilo de ancianos o a un manicomio.

**Commitment.** Orden de arresto o de confinamiento a un asilo o manicomio. Promesa, compromiso, obligación.

**Committed.** Dedicado, comprometido, jugado. En prisión o en un asilo o manicomio.

**Committee.** Comité, comisión, dirección, grupo ejecutivo, junta.

**Committee of creditors.** Junta de acreedores.

**Commodity.** Artículo, mercadería, mercancía. Inventario, producto.

**Commodity exchange.** Bolsa de comercio, lonja, mercado.

**Commodity option.** Opción para comprar determinados bienes muebles o mercaderías.

**Common.** Común. Colectivo, comunal, conjunto, grupal, societario. Corriente, ordinario.

**Common capital.** Haber social, capital.

**Common funds.** Masa común.

**Common good.** Bien común bienestar general.

**Common knowledge.** De público y notorio, generalmente conocido.

**Common law.** Derecho común. El juez no sólo aplica la ley, sino que a su vez constituye la mejor fuente de creación del Derecho. Según la doctrina de "*stare decisis*," una sentencia judicial tiene, dentro su territorio, la validez de una ley, en tanto y en cuanto ella no haya sido revocada (*overruled*) por una sentencia posterior. Una sentencia del Tribunal Supremo del Estado de California obliga a las cortes en California; pero no es obligatoria afuera de su territorio. Por ejemplo, tal sentencia no tiene fuerza ni validez de ley ante las cortes del Estado de Nueva York. El abogado norteamericano suele usarlo en tres sentidos. El primero se refiere al derecho establecido por los tribunales (*case law*). El segundo uso de la expresión *common law* se refiere a las reglas que aplican los tribunales de *common law*, en contraposición a los tribunales especiales de *equity* o de *admiralty*. El tercer sentido es el que se usa cuando se habla de los Estados Unidos como un país de *common law*, cuyo Derecho se basa en el Derecho inglés, en contraposición a los países de derecho civil, cuyo derecho se origina en el Derecho romano. (Intro al USA).

**Common-law marriage.** Matrimonio de hecho.

**Commonwealth**. Organización política actual del anterior imperio británico.

**Commonwealth of Puerto Rico.** Estado Libre Asociado de Puerto Rico.

**Commorientes.** Comurientes. Personas que efectivamente mueren simultáneamente o cuya muerte simultánea la ley presume.

**Communicate.** Comunicar, avisar, expresar, hablar, hacer conocer, notificar.

**Communication.** Comunicación, acuerdo, intercambio. Mensaje, carta, fax.

**Communist.** Comunista, colectivista, estatista, marxista, socialista.

**Commuter.** Pasajero que se desplaza entre su casa y el trabajo.

**Comparative fault.** Culpa concurrente. Según la doctrina de la culpa concurrente, aun si el demandado ha sido negligente, puede no considerarselo responsable si demuestra que la negligencia del actor contribuyo al daño. (Intro al USA).

**Comparative law.** Derecho comparado.

**Compartamentalization.** División o clasificación por grupos o temas y tratados individualmente.

**Compel.** Compeler.

**Competent.** Competente, apto, capaz, capacitado, hábil.

**Competitive.** Competitivo, efectivo, viable. Dentro del precio de mercado.

**Compilation.** Compilación, recopilación, digesto.

**Complaint.** Denuncia. La denuncia es una exposición por escrito de los hechos esenciales que constituyen el delito imputado. Se otorgará bajo juramento ante un magistrado. (Regla 3, Reglas Fed. de Proc. Crim.).

**Complaisance**. Complacencia, buena disposición, pasividad, predisposición, tolerancia.

**Complement.** Complemento, adición, suplemento (s). Completar, añadir, suplementar (v).

**Complex.** Sistema formado por varias unidades (s). Complejo, complicado, difícil, engorroso.

**Compliance.** Cumplimiento, conformidad, ejecución, realización.

**Complicity.** Complicidad. Una persona será legalmente responsable de la conducta de otra cuando:

a) Actuando con la forma de culpabilidad que sería suficiente para la comisión de la ofensa, incita a otra persona inocente o irresponsable a incurrir en tal conducta; o,

b) Es legalmente responsable por la conducta de otra persona por disposición de este Código u otro estatuto que defina la ofensa; o

c) Es cómplice de alguna otra persona en la comisión de una ofensa. (Cód. Pen. Mod., § 2.06 (2)).

**Complimentary.** Cortés, de cortesía, elogioso, gratis.

**Composite.** Combinación, composición, algo formado con varias o muchas unidades más pequeñas.

**Composition and respite.** Quita y espera.

**Compound.** Transigir, llegar a un acuerdo o entendimiento. Agravar o complicar.

**Comprise.** Incluir, comprender.

**Comprised.** Comprendido, incluído.

**Compromise.** Comprometer, arreglar, transigir, transar.

**Compulsory.** Obligatorio, coactivo, forzoso, necesario.

**Compulsory counterclaim.** Reconvención compulsoria. Las alegaciones incluirán por via de reconvención cualquier reclamación que tuviere la parte que la formula al momento de notificarla, contra cualquier parte adversa, si surgiere del evento o serie de eventos a que se contrae la reclamación de la parte adversa y no requiriere para su adjudicación la presencia de terceros sobre quienes la corte no pudiere adquirir jurisdicción. (Reglas Fed. del Proc. Civ., sec. 13(a)).

**Compulsory joinder.** Litisconsorcio necesario.

**Computation of time.** Cómputo del tiempo.

**Concealed property.** Bienes ocultos.

**Concealment.** Ocultamiento. Una acción intencional o un acto que se entiende que podría impedirle a otra persona conocer un hecho, es equivalente a una afirmación de que el hecho no existe. (Rstmnt, 2nd, Con., sec. 160).

**Concentration camp.** Campo de concentración.

**Conception.** Concepción, preñez, embarazo, procreación. Idea, creencia, opinión.

**Concern.** Interés, preocupación. Establecimiento comercial, tienda (s). Preocuparse por algo, referirse a algo (v).

**Concessionaire.** Concesionario.

**Conciliation.** Conciliación.

**Conciliator.** Conciliador.

**Conclusive.** Concluyente, que no se puede rebatir ni discutir.

**Concourse.** Reunión de personas con fines comunes, asamblea. Vía de circulación.

**Concubinage.** Concubinato, mancebamiento.

**Concubine.** Concubina/o.

**Concurrent jurisdiction.** Jurisdicción concurrente. Tanto los tribunales estaduales como los federales con competentes, lo que significa que la parte actora puede elegir en cual de ellos iniciar la acción. Los casos de *diversity jurisdiction*, y muchos casos de *federal question* son ejemplos de esto. (Intro al USA).

**Condemnation.** Expropiación, venta forzosa.

**Condemnation of property.** Expropiación forzosa. La demanda contendrá una exposición breve y sencilla de la autoridad para la expropiación, el uso para el cual se expropia la propiedad, una descripción de la propiedad suficiente para su identificación, los derechos a adquirirse. Si un demandado no tuviere objeción o defensa que interponer a la expropiación forzosa de su propiedad, podrá notificar un aviso de comparecencia designando la propiedad en la que alegare tener derecho. Subsiguientemente recibirá notificación de todos los procedimientos que afecten dicha propiedad. (R. Fed. P. Civ. sec. 71A(c)(2); (e)).

**Condition.** Condición. Una condición es un evento, de ocurrencia incierta, el cual debe suceder, a menos que su no ocurrencia sea excusada, antes que tenga luego el cumplimiento de un contrato. (Rstmnt, 2nd, Con., sec. 224).

**Condition precedent.** Condición suspensiva.

**Condition subsequent.** Condición resolutoria.

**Conditional plea.** Alegación condicional. Con aprobación de la corte y el consentimiento del gobierno, el acusado podrá hacer una alegación condicional de culpable o *nolo contendere*, reservándose por escrito el derecho de poder revisar en apelación de la sentencia la determinación adversa de cualquier moción específica hecha antes del juicio. (Regla 11(a)(2), Reglas Fed. de Proc. Crim.).

**Conduct.** Conducta, actitud, interrelación, comportamiento (s). Conducir, dirigir, llevar a cabo, realizar (v).

**Conduct within scope of employment.** Acto cometido en ocasión del trabajo. Para considerar en ocasión del trabajo, la conducta de un empleado debe ser de la misma naturaleza genérica que la autorizada, o incidental a tal conducta autorizada. (Rstmnt, 2nd, Agency, sec. 229).

**Confederate.** Cómplice, corresponsable, secuaz.

**Confer.** Conferir, dar, otorgar. Conferenciar, intercambiar opiniones.

**Confederation.** Confederación, unión de Estados. Pacto de alianza.

**Confess.** Confesar, admitir la comisión de un delito.

**Confession.** Confesión, admisión.

**Confession judgment.** Sentencia por admisión.

**Confidence.** Confianza, creencia, dependencia. Aplomo, seguridad. Confidencia, secreto.

**Confinement as protective force.** Uso del confinamiento como fuerza defensiva. La justificación concedida por esta Sección se extiende al uso de confinamiento como fuerza defensiva sólo si el autor toma todas las medidas razonables para finalizar el confinamiento tan pronto sepa que puede hacerlo con seguridad para la propiedad, a menos que la persona confinada haya sido arrestada por la imputación de un delito. (Cód. Pen. Mod., § 3.06 (4)).

**Confirm.** Confirmar, corroborar, constatar, establecer, probar, ratificar.

**Confirmation.** Confirmación. No habrá lugar a la anulación del contrato si la parte facultada para darlo por anulado lo confirma de una manera expresa o tácita una vez que ha comenzado a correr el plazo para comunicar la anulación. (Unidroit, Prin., art. 3.12).

**Confirming bank.** Banco que confirma. Es un banco que se compromete tanto a que el mismo honrará un crédito expedido antes por otro banco o a que dicho crédito será honrado por el dador o por un tercer banco. (C.C.U. sec. 5-103).

**Conflict of authority.** Conflicto de autoridades o de jurisdicciones.

**Conflict of interest.** Conflicto de intereses.

**Conflict of laws.** Derecho internacional privado. La materia conocida en los Estados Unidos como conflicto de leyes, que corresponde a lo que en otros países se denomina derecho internacional privado, comprende los problemas de competencia, al aplicación de los fallo de tribunales extranjeros y la elección del derecho. (Intro al USA).
Conflicto de leyes.

**Conflicting evidence.** Prueba contradictoria.

**Conformed copy.** Copia de un documento autenticada por autoridad judicial.

**Confrontation.** Confrontación, careo, repreguntas. Comparación, cotejo. Ataque, conflicto, guerra.

**Congress.** Congreso. La leyes federales son aprobadas por el Congreso de los Estados Unidos, que es una legislativa bicameral consistente en una cámara baja, la Cámara de Representantes (*House of Representatives*), y una cámara alta, el Senado. (Intro al USA).

**Conjugal.** Conyugal, perteneciente al matrimonio.

**Conjugal duty.** Deberes conyugales.

**Conjugal rights.** Derechos conyugales.

**Connection.** Conexión, contacto, enlace, nexo relación, unión, vínculo.

**Connivance.** Connivencia, puesta de acuerdo para realizar algo ilegal o turbio.

**Conquest.** Conquista.

**Consanguinity.** Consanguinidad, de la misma sangre, de descendencia común.

**Conscientious objector.** Objetor de conciencia, persona que por sus convicciones religiosas o morales se niega a portar armas y, en algunos casos, a vestir uniforme militar.

**Conscription.** Servicio militar obligatorio. Conscripción.

**Consent.** Consentimiento. El consentimiento de la víctima a conducta que constituya delito o al resultado de ella será una defensa si tal consentimiento contrarresta algún elemento del delito o impide infligir el daño o mal que el estatuto busca prevenir. (Cód. Pen. Mod., § 2.11 (1)).
Consentimiento. Implica la voluntariedad de la parte afectada, para que un acto o la violación de un derecho se efectúe. (Rstmnt, 2nd, Torts, sec. 10 A). Aquiescencia, aceptación, anuencia, asentimiento, conformidad (s). Consentir (v).

**Consent for a tort.** Consentimiento a un cuasidelito. Alguien que de una manera efectiva preste consentimiento a la conducta de otro, destinada a perjudicar los intereses del primero, no puede radicar una acción por responsabilidad extracontractual reclamando que dicha conducta le afectó o le causó un daño. (Rstmnt, 2nd, Torts, sec. 892 A).

**Consequential damages.** Resarcimiento por daños sufridos indirectamente.

**Consider.** Considerar, meditar, reflexionar una cosa con atención.

**Consideration.** Contraprestación contractual. Aparte del requisito de documento escrito, por lo general un contrato no s por lo general ejecutable en lo Estados Unidos si no incluye una contraprestación. La contraprestación es alguna cosa (por ejemplo: una promesa o documento) que el promitente ha negociado y recibe a cambio de su promesa. (Intro al USA).

Causa, contraprestación. 1) Para que exista causa, debe negociarse para ésta un cumplimiento o una promesa. 2) Se negocia un cumplimiento o una promesa en respuesta si el promitente original las proyecta a cambio de otra promesa, y se da al tenedor de la promesa, a cambio de esta última. (Rstmnt, 2nd, Con., sec. 71).

**Consideration, adequacy.** Contraprestación, valor. Si se cumple con el requisito de causa, no se requerirá: a) una ganancia, ventaja o beneficio al prominente; ni una pérdida, desventaja o detrimento al tenedor de una promesa; b) una equivalencia en las prestaciones; o c) una "mutualidad en las obligaciones." (Rstmnt, 2nd, Con., sec. 79).

**Consideration of a commercial paper.** Causa de un documento comercial. La ausencia o falta de causa será una defensa contra cualquier persona que no tenga los derechos de un tenedor legítimo, excepto que no será necesaria causa a un instrumento u obligación dado en pago o como garantía de una obligación anterior de cualquier clase. (C.C.U. sec. 3-408).

**Consignee.** Consignatario.

**Consignment.** Consignación.

**Consolidation.** Consolidación. Cuando pleitos que impliquen cuestiones comunes de derecho y de hecho estuviesen ante la corte, ésta podrá ordenar una vista o un juicio conjuntos de cualesquiera o de todas las cuestiones en controversia en los mismos; podrá ordenar la consolidación de todos ellos y podrá dictar las órdenes en relación con los procedimientos de los mismos que tiendan a evitar gastos o demoras innecesarios. (R. Fed. P. Civ., sec. 42(a)).

**Consolidation of defenses in motion.** Consolidación de defensas por moción. La parte que presentare una moción a tenor con esta regla podrá unirle cualesquiera

otras mociones que en la misma se disponen y a las cuales tuviere derecho en esa oportunidad. (R. Fed. P. Civ., sec. 12 (g)).

**Consortium.** El derecho y los beneficios de la compañía, afecto y presencia del cónyuge. Incluye elementos físicos como el placer sexual, intangibles como el amor abstracto, así como los beneficios económicos resultantes de un matrimonio.

**Conspicuous.** Evidente. Un término o cláusula es evidente cuando está escrito de tal modo que una persona razonable contra quien éste ha de operar debe notarlo. Un letrero impreso en mayúsculas (como: CONOCIMIENTO DE EMBARQUE NO NEGOCIABLE) es evidente. (C.C.U. sec. 1201(10)).

**Conspiracy.** Conspiración. En términos generales una conspiración es un acuerdo, convenio o pacto entre dos o más personas para realizar un acto ilegal empleando medios legales o ilegales, esto es, es una sociedad con fines criminales. (Pueblo v. Velez Rivera, 93 D.P.R. 649 (1966)).

**Constable.** Agente de policía (UK).

**Constitution, federal.** Constitución federal. La Constitución es, en sus propias palabras, la Ley suprema del País y a ella están supeditadas todas las demás normas legales; la Corte Suprema de los Estados Unidos es, por supuesto, arbitro final de todas las disputas sobre constitucionalidad. (Intro al USA).

**Constitution, state.** Constitución estatal. La Constitución de un estado esta supeditada a la legislación federal válida pero es la máxima autoridad dentro del estado. (Intro al USA).

**Constitutional law.** Derecho constitucional. El estudio del derecho constitucional, en el sentido que se da al término en los Estados Unidos, es más que nada el estudio de las decisiones de la Corte Suprema de los Estados Unidos.

**Constitution federal, interpretation.** Constitución federal, interpretación. Esto incluye algunas cuestiones de interpretación constitucional que la Corte se ha rehusado a zanjar por opinar que son *cuestiones políticas*, que deben ser resueltas por el poder legislativo o el ejecutivo, y por lo tanto no posibles de revisión judicial. (Intro al USA).

**Constitutional review.** Revisión constitucional. Una de las limitaciones cardinales al poder de revisión de la constitucionalidad de la legislación federal y estadual consiste en que la Corte solo toma decisiones sobre una controversia que hay llegado a la situación procesal correspondiente, en la que los resultados tengan consecuencias inmediatas para las partes, y no emite opiniones en función asesora ni lleva adelante procesos no controvertidos. (Intro al USA).

**Construction.** Construcción, edificio, obra. Interpretación de un documento o de una ley o norma.

**Constructive.** Ficto. Lenguaje que se usa, no en forma literal pero en sentido lato.

**Constructive malice.** El dolo que la ley imputa bajo ciertas circunstancias, aunque no pueda probarse por las reglas generales.

**Constructive trust.** Un *trust* que la ley impone, normalmente como medio de proteger a la parte afectada. Por ejemplo, quien con abuso de confianza se apropiase de un bien, podría ser considerado legalmente como *trustee* de la cosa. Con ello se le reclamarían los deberes que el *trustee* debe cumplir.

**Constructive receipts doctrine.** Doctrina de recibos implícitos. La doctrina de recibos implícitos dispone que, no empece el hecho de que un contribuyente se acoja al método de recibido y pagado, si al finalizar cualquier año contributivo se le tenia a éste separado y a su entera disposición determinado ingreso, sin restricción o limitación alguna en cuanto al modo o tiempo en que pueda hacerlo efectivo, tal utilidad debe, en ese año, ser declarada como ingreso y no en aquél en que al contribuyente le plazca hacerla efectiva. (Ramos v. Srio. de Hacienda, 93 D.P.R. 233 (1966)).

**Contemnor.** Contumaz, rebelde, parte en desacato

**Contempt of court.** Desacato al tribunal. En el *common law* se trata de una sanción mucho mas amenazante y real que en paises civilistas.

**Contested.** Controvertido, conflictivo, disputado.

**Contiguous.** Contiguo, vecino, adyacente.

**Continental law.** Derecho utilizado en Europa continental, derecho sel sistema romano.

**Continental shelf.** Plataforma continental.

**Contingency.** Contingencia.

**Contingency fee.** Honorarios bajo pacto de cuota litis.

**Contingent estate.** Es un derecho real, en el sentido del *common law*, de propiedad, que depende de que ocurra o no un hecho en particular. Podría equipararse, aunque no exactamente, a un derecho propietario sujeto a una condición suspensiva.

**Continuance.** Prórroga, aplazamiento.

**Continuing jurisdiction.** Bajo la competencia continuada de un mismo tribunal para el caso que se presenten nuevos reclamos entre las mismas partes.

**Continuing legal education.** Formación jurídica permanente. Un fenómeno de aparición reciente es la intensificación de la formación jurídica permanente de los abogados. Pionero en este campo ha sido el *Practicing Law Institute*, que es una organización educativa sin fines de lucro. Desde 1947 el *American Law Institute* (Instituto de los Profesionales del Derecho) y la *American Bar Association*, vienen colaborando a través de una comisión conjunta que supervisa los programas de enseñanza jurídica de admisión a cargos en toda la nación. (Intro al USA).

**Continuity.** Continuidad.

***Contra proferente* rule.** Interpretación *contra proferente*. Si las cláusulas de un contrato dictadas por una de las partes no son claras, se preferirá la interpretación que perjudique a dicha parte. (Unidroit, Prin., 4.6).

**Contraband.** Contrabando. Objetos de posesión ilegal o clandestina.

**Contract.** Contrato. Se puede definir un contrato como una promesa, cuyo incumplimiento es castigado por la ley, aunque la palabra "Contrato" puede usarse también para referirse al acuerdo de las partes o al documento firmado por ellos. (Intro al USA).

Un contrato consiste de una promesa o una serie de promesas. En caso de que haya un incumplimiento, la ley concede una acción. Su ejecución se considera un deber. (Rstmnt, 2nd, Con., sec. 1).

**Contract against public policy.** Contrato contra el orden público. Una promesa u otro término de un acuerdo no se puede hacer cumplir en términos de política pública si la legislación estipula que no se puede ejecutar, o si la política publica en contra del cumplimiento de tales términos se contrapone claramente—en virtud de las circunstancias—al interés en su ejecución. (Rstmnt, 2nd, Con., sec. 178(1), 178(3)).

**Contract for an indefinite period.** Contrato por tiempo indefinido. Cualquiera de las partes podrá dar por terminado un contrato de tiempo indefinido, comunicándoselo a la otra con una anticipación razonable. (Unidroit, Prin., art. 5.8).

**Contract formation.** Formación del contrato. Todo contrato podrá celebrarse mediante la aceptación de una oferta o por la conducta de las partes que sea suficiente para demostrar la existencia de un acuerdo. (Unidroit, Prin., art. 2.1).

**Contract law.** Derecho contractual. El derecho de contratos se ocupa principalmente de la ejecución de las obligaciones contractuales. La responsabilidad contractual puede basarse en un consentimiento en forma de promesa o bien implícita de los actos de las partes. (Intro al USA).

**Contract law, topics.** Derecho contractual, temas. El derecho contractual de la capacidad de la partes, las formalidades, propuesta y aceptación, contraparte, error y falsa representación, coacción e inconciencia, inaplicabilidad por motivos de orden público, interpretación, ejecución y condiciones de ejecución, liberación, derechos de cesionarios y beneficiarios contractuales, y compensaciones. (Intro al USA).

**Contract not to sue.** Contrato de no demandar. Un contrato de no demandar, es un contrato bajo el cual el tenedor de una obligación promete no demandar nunca al obligado o tercera persona para exigir una prestación o no hacerlo durante un tiempo limitado. (Rstmnt, 2nd, Con., sec. 285(1)(2)).

**Contract with terms deliberately left open.** Contrato con estipulaciones dejadas deliberadamente pendientes. Si las partes han tenido el propósito de celebrar un contrato, el hecho de que intencionalmente hayan dejado algún punto sujeto a negociaciones ulteriores, o a su determinación por un tercero, no impedirá la celebración del contrato. (Unidroit, Prin., art. 2.14).

**Contracting party.** Contratante, parte contrayente.

**Contracting under standard terms.** Contratación con cláusulas estándar. Cuando una o ambas partes utilicen cláusulas estándar para celebrar un contrato, se aplicarán las normas generales que se refieren a la formación del contrato. (Unidroit, Prin., art. 2.19).

**Contractor.** Contratista, empresario.

**Contracts under seal.** Contratos bajo sello. En la Inglaterra medieval, debido en parte al analfabetismo, los documentos eran autenticados comúnmente con sellos sin mediar firma. Para aquel tiempo el sellar un instrumento era una formalidad impresionante y consistía de la adhesión de cera con una impresión; un instrumento sellado estaba inmune a cualquier ataque en las cortes de derecho común (*Common Law*), aunque éstas sí concedían compensación en casos de fraude, pago anterior y similares.

Una promesa escrita está sellada si el promitente adhiere o imprime un sello en el documento o adopta un sello que ya está puesto. (Rstmnt, 2nd, Con., sec. 97 y nota).

**Contractual choice of law.** Elección contractual de la ley del estado. La ley del Estado, escogida por las partes para regir sus derechos y obligaciones contractuales, será aplicada si el asunto particular pudo resolverse por las partes mediante una provisión explícita en el acuerdo concerniente. En ausencia de una indicación contraria de intención, la referencia será la ley local del Estado de la jurisdicción escogida. (Rstmnt, 2nd, Conflict, sec. 187).

**Contractual damages.** Daños contractuales. Todo incumplimiento otorga a la parte agraviada el derecho a ser indemnizada por daños y perjuicios, ya sea exclusivamente o en concurrencia con otras pretensiones, a menos que el incumplimiento fuere excusable. (Unidroit, Prin., art. 7.4.1).

**Contractual gap.** Omisión, laguna contractual. Cuando las partes en una negociación suficientemente definida para llegar a ser un contrato no han acordado un término esencial a la determinación de sus derechos y deberes, la corte provee entonces un término razonable, tomando en consideración las circunstancias. (Rstmnt, 2nd, Con., sec. 204).

**Contractual interpretation.** Interpretación contractual. Las palabras y otras conductas se interpretan a la luz de la totalidad de las circunstancias. Si el propósito principal de las partes es discernible, se le otorga gran valor. Un escrito se interpreta globalmente. Todos los escritos que son parte de una misma transacción se interpretan en conjunto. (Rstmnt, 2nd, Con., sec. 202).

**Contractual remedies.** Acciones contractuales. Las acciones judiciales disponibles para la protección de intereses en expectativa, confiabilidad o restitución incluyen una sentencia u orden judicial: adjudicando una suma de dinero adeudada bajo un contrato o como daños. (Rstmnt, 2nd, Con., sec. 345).

**Contrary to morality.** Contrario a las buenas costumbres.

**Contributing tortfeasors.** Co-autores de un cuasidelito. Cada una de dos o más personas cuya conducta torticera—constitutiva de responsabilidad extracontractual—sea la causa legal de un daño único e indivisible, responderá a la parte afectada por el daño completo. (Rstmnt, 2nd, Torts, sec. 875).

**Contribution among tortfeasors.** Responsabilidad entre co-autores de un cuasidelito. Cuando dos o más personas incurren en responsabilidad extracontractual a una misma persona por un mismo daño, existe el derecho de contribución entre los causantes del daño, incluso en casos en que aún no se haya recibido indemnización de todos o alguno de ellos. (Rstmnt, 2nd, Torts, sec. 886 A).

**Contributory negligence.** Negligencia contribuyente. La negligencia contribuyente es una conducta del demandante que cae por debajo de las normas que debería obedecer

para su propia seguridad, constituye esto una causa contribuyente junto con la negligencia del demandado en el surgimiento del daño. (Rstmnt, 2nd, Torts, sec. 463).

**Contributory negligence as bar to action.** Negligencia contribuyente como obstáculo a la demanda. Con excepción de la situación en que el demandado tiene la última oportunidad expedida, la negligencia contribuyente del demandante impide poder recobrar del demandado, cuya conducta de otro modo lo haría responsable ante el demandante por el daño causado. (Rstmnt, 2nd, Torts, sec. 467).

**Contributory negligence, types.** Negligencia contribuyente, tipos. La negligencia contribuyente del demandante puede ocurrir como consecuencia de: una exposición intencional e irrazonable de si mismos al peligro creado por la negligencia del demandado; peligro del cual el demandante tiene conocimiento o tiene motivos razonables para conocer. (Rstmnt, 2nd, Torts, sec. 466).

**Controller.** Contralor, inspector.

**Controversy.** Controversia, disputa.

**Contumacy.** Rebeldía, contumacia.

**Convenience.** Conveniencia.

**Convention.** Convención, pacto, tratado internacional.

**Conventional.** Convencional. Normal u ordinario.

**Conversion.** Conversión, apropiación ilícita. Conversión es un ejercicio intencional de dominio o control sobre un bien mueble que interfiere gravemente con el derecho de otro de ejercer su control, donde al actor se le requiere el pago total del valor del bien. (Rstmnt, 2nd, Torts, sec. 222).

La conversión, como elemento necesario del delito de abuso de confianza, es la apropiación fraudulenta de bienes ajenos para uso propio, aclarándose que la frase "apropiarse para su uso propio" no quiere decir necesariamente, en su propio beneficio personal. (Pueblo v. Bonilla Lugo, 91 D.P.R. 449 (1964)).

**Conversion of instrument.** Usurpación de un instrumento comercial. Se considera usurpado un instrumento cuando un librado a quien se le ha entregado éste para aceptación se niega a devolverlo cuando se le demanda. (C.C.U. sec. 419).

**Conveyance of ownership.** Título traslativo de dominio.

**Convict.** Convicto, reo, persona condenada por un tribunal penal.

**Conviction.** Convicción, acto por el cual un tribunal penal condena al acusado.

**Conviction of lesser offense.** Convicción por delito inferior. El acusado podrá ser declarado culpable de cualquier delito necesariamente incluido en el delito imputado o de tentativa de cometer, bien el delito o un delito necesariamente incluido en el mismo si tal tentativa constituyera delito. (Regla 30(c), Reglas Fed. de Proc. Crim.).

**Cooling period.** Período de enfriamiento. La norma para determinar la aplicabilidad de la doctrina sobre el período de enfriamiento—la cual da margen para reducir el delito de asesinato a homicidio a base de súbita pendencia o arrebato de cólera—debe ser el período de tiempo que necesitaría una persona ordinaria y razonable situada en circunstancias similares al acusado y no el período de tiempo que necesitaba el acusado para calmarse o enfriarse. (Pueblo v. Roman Marrero, 96 D.P.R. 796 (1968)).

Período de enfriamiento, plazo para recapacitar. Por ejemplo, los sesenta días que, en el derecho de Texas, debe permanecer la acción de divorcio paralizada para dar a los cónyuges la oportunidad de reconciliarse.

**Cooperation between the parties.** Cooperación entre las partes. Una parte debe cooperar con la otra cuando quiera que dicha cooperación pueda ser razonablemente esperada para el cumplimiento de las obligaciones de esta última. (Unidroit, Prin., art. 5.3).

**Co-owner.** Condómino.

**Copy.** Copia, ejemplar.

**Copyright.** Derechos de autor. Derecho de propiedad intelectual.

***Coram nobis* (L).** Literalmente "ante nosotros" o "en nuestra presencia." Es un recurso de reposición interpuesto cuando se estima que el fallo adolece de algún error de hecho. Se contrapone la expresión a coram vobis, o sea un recurso—como el de apela-

ción— interpuesto ante un tribunal distinto del sentenciante.

**Corollary.** Corolario.

**Coroner.** Médico forense (UK).

**Corporal punishment.** Castigo corporal. Pena física, por ejemplo, azotes.

**Corporate.** Corporativo, empresarial, perteneciente a una sociedad comercial.

**Corporate duty.** Fidelidad empresarial. Los directivos de una sociedad anónima. Tienen un deber de fidelidad hacia los accionistas, de actuar en beneficio de la corporación y no el propio, y pueden ser considerados responsables de incumplimiento de este deber en perjuicio de los intereses de los accionistas o aun de un grupo minoritario de ellos. (Intro al USA).

**Corporate stock.** Acciones corporativas de una sociedad anónima. Toda corporación podrá emitir una o más clase de acciones del capital corporativo, o una o más series de acciones en cualquiera de las clases. (14 LPRA 1639).

**Corporate tax.** Impuesto sobre las sociedades comerciales.

**Corporation.** Sociedad anónima, S.A., sociedad por acciones. Empresa, compañía. Corporación.

**Corporations.** Sociedades anónimas. La mayor parte de los estados tiene una ley única para todas las corporaciones de negocios, independiente de su tamaño o de la forma en que este distribuido su paquete accionario. Sin embargo, las variaciones de estructura son grandes, y uno de los problemas actuales del derecho de corporaciones es como tener en cuenta las diferencias entre la corporación grande con acciones accesible al público (public corporation), y la corporación pequeña cuyas acciones son mantenidas en pocas manos (close corporation). (Intro al USA).

**Corporations, management.** Sociedades anónimas, dirección. Aunque el poder de hacer cambios organizativos fundamentales, tales como fusiones de empresas, disolución, enmiendas a los estatutos, etc., queda en los manos de los accionistas en su carácter de propietarios de la corporación; la dirección de la empresa era confiada a un cuerpo separado, el directorio (*board of directors*). (Intro al USA).

**Correct an error.** Salvar un error.

**Correction of sentence for changed conditions.** Reducción de sentencia por cambio de circunstancias. La corte a moción del gobierno dentro del año de su pronunciamiento podrá reducir la sentencia para que refleje la cooperación por parte del acusado en la investigación o el procesamiento de otra persona que hubiere cometido un delito. (Regla 35(b), Reglas Fed. de Proc. Crim.).

**Correlate.** Correlacionar.

**Correspond.** Corresponde.

**Corroborate.** Corroborar, confirmar.

**Corroborative.** Corroborante.

**Cost of collection.** Gastos de cobranza.

**Costs.** Costas. A excepción del caso en que hubiere disposiciones expresas al efecto en una ley de los Estados Unidos o en estas reglas, las costas excepto honorarios serán concedidas como cuestión de rutina a la parte vencedora, a menos que la corte dispusiera otra cosa; pero las costas contra los Estados Unidos, sus funcionarios y agencias se pondrán tasar las costas con un día de aviso. (R. Fed. P. Civ., sec. 54(d)).

**Costs of performance.** Gastos del pago. Cada parte debe asumir los gastos derivados del cumplimiento de sus obligaciones. (Unidroit, Prin., art. 6.1.11).

**Council.** Consejo, asamblea, junta.

**Councilor.** Consejero, abogado, asesor, consultor, letrado.

**Counsel.** Abogado, consejero, asesor. Representar jurídicamente, aconsejar, asesorar.

**Counsellor.** Consultor, asesor, abogado.

**Count.** Peticiones o acusaciones específicas que contiene la demanda.

**Counter offer.** Contraoferta. Una contra oferta es una oferta hecha por el requisito a su oferente sobre la misma materia de la oferta original, proponiendo un negocio sustituto, distinto del propuesto en la oferta original. (Rstmnt, 2nd, Con., sec. 39).
Contraofertar (v).

**Counterclaim.** Reconvención (s). Reconvenir (v).

**Counterclaim exceeding opposing claim.** Reconvención en exceso de la demanda. Las reconvenciones podrán aminorar o no o derrotar o no las pretensiones de la parte adversa. Las mismas podrán solicitar un remedio en exceso de la cantidad o de distinta naturaleza del solicitado en las alegaciones de la parte adversa. (Regla Fed. del Proc. Civ., sec. 13(c)).

**Counterclaim maturing or acquired after pleading.** Reconvención por alegación suplementaria. Una reclamación que deviniere exigible o fuere adquirida por el peticionario después de haber notificado sus alegaciones podrá ser deducida como reconvención mediante alegación suplementaria, con permiso de la corte. (Reglas Fed. del Proc. Civ., sec. 13(e)).

**Counterclaim not interposed.** Reconvención no interpuesta. En casos en que el demandado pueda radicar una acción a manera de reconvención, y no lo hace, no por ésto perderá su derecho a radicar una acción basada en la misma reclamación. (Rstmnt, 2nd, Judg., sec. 22).

**Countersign.** Refrendar, visar, corroborar.

**Countersignature.** Refrendata, segunda firma.

**Course of dealing.** Conducta anterior. La conducta anterior es una secuencia de conducta previa entre las partes en un acuerdo que establece razonablemente una base común de entendimiento para interpretar sus expresiones y otra conducta. (Rstmnt, 2nd, Con., sec. 223).

**Course of dealing and usage of trade.** Curso de negocio y uso de comercio. Un curso de negocio es una secuencia de conducta previa entre las partes en una transacción específica que se considera que establece una base común de entendimiento para interpretar sus expresiones y conducta. (C.C.U. sec. 1-205).

**Court.** Corte, tribunal.

**Court approval.** Autorización judicial.

**Court below.** Tribunal inferior.

**Court decision.** Decisión judicial, auto, fallo, resolución, sentencia.

**Court of appeals for the circuit.** Cámara de apelaciones del circuito. Las apelaciones de los fallos de un tribunal de distrito son llevados, por lo común, al tribunal de apelaciones del circuito correspondiente a ese distrito, aunque en circunstancias poco frecuentes la apelación puede ir directamente a la Corte Suprema. Hay doce circuitos, once de los cuales abarcan agrupamientos geográficos de estados y comprenden varios distritos; el duodécimo corresponde al distrito de Columbia. (Intro al USA).

**Covenant.** Contrato, pacto (s). Contratar, convenir (v).

**Cover.** Cubrirse. Después de un incumplimiento, el comprador podrá "cubrirse" haciendo de buena fe y sin demora irrazonable cualquier compra razonable de o contrato de compra de mercancías en sustitución de aquellas que debía recibir del vendedor. (C.C.U. sec. 2-712).

**Coverage.** Cobertura.

**Credibility.** Credibilidad.

**Credit.** Crédito (s). Acreditar (v).

**Credit union.** Asociación, cooperativa de ahorro y crédito. "Cooperativa de Ahorro y Crédito" una sociedad cooperativa organizada de acuerdo con este Capítulo, con el doble propósito de estimular el ahorro entre sus asociados y de brindarles crédito a tipos de interés razonables, para afrontar necesidades personales y para negocios lícitos. (7 LPRA sec. 1102).

**Creditor.** Acreedor.

**Creditors' meetings.** Junta de acreedores.

**Creditors' schedule.** Relación de acreedores.

**Crime, punishment.** Delito, pena. La diferencias más notables entre estados son las diferencias en la severidad del tratamiento de diversos crímenes y en el tipo de sentencias. En muchos estados se hace en uso profuso de alternativas a la prisión, tales como libertad bajo palabra; libertad condicionada, libertad vigilada, multas, etc. En otros estado, sin embargo, la respuesta común aun en el caso de crímenes menores como ratería o posesión de drogas es la sentencia de encarcelamiento. (Intro al USA).

**Criminal.** Criminal, ilegal, reprimido penalmente.

**Criminal contempt.** Desacato criminal. El desacato podrá castigarse sumariamente si el juez certifica que vio u oyó la conducta constitutiva del desacato y que fue cometido en presencia de la corte. La resolución que se dicte expondrá los hechos y será firmada por el juez, con constancia en autos. (Regla 42, Reglas Fed. de Proc. Crim.).

**Criminal conversation with a spouse.** Adulterio con cónyuge ajeno. Una persona que sostenga relaciones sexuales con uno de los cónyuges, será responsable al otro cónyuge por el daño causado a sus intereses maritales legalmente protegidos. (Restatment, Second, Torts, sec. 685).

**Criminal forfeiture.** Decomiso penal. No podrá dictarse sentencia de decomiso en una causa criminal a menos que en el indiciamiento del gran jurado la acusación del fiscal indique la extensión del interés o propiedad sujeto a decomiso. (Regla 7(C)(2), Reglas Fed. de Proc. Crim.).

**Criminal law.** Derecho penal. Cada estado tiene sus propias leyes penales que definen, tanto, los delitos mayores como los menores, así como numerosas infracciones secundarias. (Intro al USA).

**Criminal proceeding.** Procedimiento penal. El procedimiento penal en los Estados Unidos tiene en lo esencial características de acusación y no de instrucción; es decir, el papel principal recae sobre el fiscal y no sobre el juez. El juzgamiento de causas penales refleja la naturaleza contradictoria del proceso judicial y la confianza en la capacidad del jurado legal. (Intro al USA).

**Criminology.** Criminología. Estudio de las circunstancias que promueven el crimen y de las formas de controlarlo.

**Cross-claim against co-party.** Demanda contra coparte. En las alegaciones se podrá plantear por via de demanda contra coparte cualquier reclamación de una parte contra una coparte que surgiere del evento o eventos a que se contrae el pleito original o una reconvención contra el mismo o relacionada con cualquier propiedad que fuere objeto del pleito original. (Reglas Fed. del Proc. Civ., sec. 13(g)).

**Cross-examination.** Contrainterrogatorio. El contrainterrogatorio deberá limitarse a la materia objeto del examen directo y a las materias que afectan la credibilidad del testigo. (Regla 611(b), R. Fed. Evid.).

**Cross reference.** Contrarreferencia.

**Crown.** Corona. En Inglaterra se usa también como sinónimo de Estado.

**Cruel and unusual punishment.** Castigo cruel e inusitado.

**Cumulative.** Acumulativo.

**Cumulative voting.** Voto acumulativo. El certificado de corporación podrá prescribir que en todas las elecciones de directores cada accionista tendrá derecho a emitir un número de votos igual a los que tendría derecho a emitir de no haber disposición en cuanto al voto acumulativo, multiplicado tal número de votos por el número de directores a elegirse. (14 LPRA sec. 1704).

**Curator.** Curador ejemplar.

**Cure by nonperforming party.** Purga del incumplimiento. La parte incumplidora podrá, a su costo, purgar cualquier incumplimiento, siempre y cuando dicha parte comunique sin demora injustificada su intención de purgar su incumplimiento, indicando la manera en que intenta purgarlo y el término dentro del cual se llevará a cabo dicha purga. (Unidroit, Prin., art. 7.1.4).

**Curfew.** Toque de queda. Impedimento de circular libremente a partir de cierta hora.

**Currency not expressed.** Moneda que no ha sido especificada. Si el contrato no señala una determinada moneda en la que se deba pagar la obligación, el pago se hará en la moneda del lugar donde debe efectuarse el pago. (Unidroit, Prin., art. 6.1.10).

**Currency of payment.** Moneda de pago. Si una obligación de dinero se expresa en moneda diferente de la del lugar del pago, este podrá hacerse en la moneda de dicho lugar, a menos que dicha moneda no fuere libremente convertibile. (Unidroit, Prin., art. 6.1.9).

**Custody.** Custodia, guarda, tenencia.

**Custom.** Costumbre, uso, tradición.

**Customer's right to stop payment.** Derecho del cliente de detener el pago. Todo cliente podrá mediante orden a su banco, detener el pago de cualquier efecto pagadero a su cuenta, pero la orden deberá recibirse a tal tiempo y de tal manera que le conceda al banco una oportunidad razonable para actuar antes de que hubiere tomado cualquier acción con respecto al efecto. (C.C.U. sec. 4-403).

**Cypres.** Doctrina que permite la interpretación de un testamento o de otro documento jurídico por un tribunal.

# D

**D.A.** *District Attorney*, el Fiscal. En el derecho estadounidense el Fiscal tiene el monopolio de la acción penal, por lo que los particulares no pueden ejercerla.

**D.A.F. (delivered at frontier).** Significa que el vendedor ha cumplido su obligación de entrega cuando ha entregado la mercancía, despachada en aduana para la exportación, en el punto y lugar convenidos de la frontera, pero antes de la aduana fronteriza del país colindante. (Incoterms).

**D.C.** *District of Columbia*, Capital Federal de los Estados Unidos.

**D.D.P. (delivered duty paid).** Significa que el vendedor ha cumplido su obligación de entregar la mercancía cuando ha sido puesta a disposición en el lugar convenido del país de importación. (Incoterms).

**D.D.U. (delivered duty unpaid).** Significa que el vendedor ha cumplido su obligación de entregar la mercancía cuando ha sido puesta a disposición en el lugar convenido del país de importación. (Incoterms).

**D.E.A.** *Drug Enforcement Adminstration*, entidad federal encargada de combatir el consumo ilegal de drogas.

**D.E.Q. (delivered *ex quay* [duty paid]).** Significa que el vendedor ha cumplido su obligación de entrega cuando ha puesto la mercancía a disposición del comprador sobre el muelle (desembarcadero), en el puerto de destino convenido, despachada en aduana para la importación. (Incoterms).

**D.E.S. (delivered ex ship).** Significa que el vendedor ha cumplido su obligación de entrega cuando ha puesto la mercancía a disposición del comprador a bordo del buque, en el puerto de destino convenido, sin despacharla en aduana para la importación. (Incoterms).

**D.J.** *Doctor Juris*, denominación dada por algunas facultades de derecho estadounidenses al diploma de abogado. No es un diploma de doctorado.

**DNA.** ADN. Composición química y biológica propia de cada individuo.

**D.W.I.** *Driving while intoxicated*, conducir un vehículo en estado de embriaguez.

**Dactylography.** Dactilografía.

**Damages.** Indemnización, resarcimiento. "Indemnización" o "resarcimiento" significa la suma de dinero otorgada a una persona afectada o dañada por la acción u omisión de otra, que a su vez conlleva responsabilidad extracontractual. (Rstmnt, 2nd, Torts, sec. 902).

Indemnización. Es aquella suma de dinero otorgada o concedida a una persona que ha sufrido un daño por un acto torticero de otro. (Rstmnt, 2nd, Torts, sec. 12).

Daños y perjuicios. Independientemente de que el contrato sea o no dado por anulado, la parte que conoció o tenía que haber conocido la causal de anulación habrá de resarcir a la otra, de modo de colocarla en la misma situación en que se encontraría de no haber celebrado el contrato. (Unidroit, Prin., art. 3.18).

**Damages based on reliance.** Indemnización basada en justas expectativas. Como una alternativa a la medida de daños en un indemnización genérica, la parte afectada tiene derecho a indemnización a base de su derecho de confiabilidad, excluyendo los gastos incurridos en la preparación para o durante el cumplimiento, menos cualquier pérdida que la parte incumplidora pueda probar que la parte afectada habría sufrido con certeza razonable en caso de que el contrato hubiera sido cumplido. (Rstmnt, 2nd, Con., sec. 349).

**Damages, compensatory.** Indemnización compensatoria. Indemnización compensatoria es la indemnización o resarcimiento otorgado a una persona como compensación o restitución por daños sufridos. (Rstmnt, 2nd, Torts, sec. 903).

**Damages for nonpecuniary harm.** Indemnización por pérdidas no pecuniarias. Indemnización compensativa que puede ser recibida sin establecer prueba de pérdida pecuniaria a tales efectos incluye compensación a) por daño corporal, y b) por sufrimientos y daños emocionales. (Rstmnt, 2nd, Torts, sec. 905).

**Damages for partial breach.** Indemnización por incumplimiento parcial. Una reclamación de daños por incumplimiento parcial es una basada solamente en parte de los derechos restantes del perjudicado al cumplimiento. (Rstmnt, 2nd, Con., sec. 236(2)).

**Damages for past, present and prospective harm.** Indemnización por pérdidas pasadas, presentes y futuras. Alguna persona afectada por el acto de otro que conlleva responsabilidad extracontractual, tiene derecho a que el otro lo indemnice por todas las pérdidas pasadas, presentes y futuras resultantes como consecuencia legal del acto torticero. (Rstmnt, 2nd, Torts, sec. 910).

**Damages for pecuniary harm.** Indemnización por pérdidas pecuniarias. Indemnización compensativa que no será otorgada sin el previo establecimiento de pérdidas pecuniarias incluye compensación por a) daño a la propiedad b) daño a la capacidad para generar ingresos, y c) el surgimiento de deudas. (Rstmnt, 2nd, Torts, sec. 906).

**Damages for total breach.** Indemnización por incumplimiento total. Una reclamación de daños por incumplimiento total es una por daños basados en todos los derechos que la parte perjudicada tenía al cumplimiento. (Rstmnt, 2nd, Con., sec. 236(1)).

**Damages, general.** Indemnización genérica. Indemnización genérica es la indemnización o resarcimiento compensatorio recibido por un daño tan frecuentemente resultante de una acción que conlleva responsabilidad extracontractual y la que a su vez constituye la base de la acción incoada, que normalmente se anticipa o presume la existencia de daños los cuales no tienen que ser alegados para ser probados. (Rstmnt, 2nd, Torts, sec. 904).

**Damages, nominal.** Indemnización nominal. Indemnización nominal es una suma de dinero trivial que se otorga a un litigante que ha establecido una causa de acción pero que no ha establecido que tiene derecho a in-demnización compensatoria. (Rstmnt, 2nd, Torts, sec. 907).

**Damages, payment and assessment.** Indemnización, pago y estimación. La indemnización se pagará en forma global. No obstante, cuando la naturaleza del daño lo justifique, podrá pagarse a plazos. (Unidroit, Prin., arts. 7.4.11 y 7.4.12).

**Damages, punitive.** Indemnización punitiva. Indemnización punitoria, a diferencia de la indemnización compensatoria o nominal, es la indemnización que se otorga en contra de una persona a modo de castigo, ya por una conducta en extremo chocante u ofensiva, ya para desalentar a la persona u otras personas de observar conducta similar en el futuro. (Rstmnt, 2nd, Torts, sec. 908).

**Damages, special.** Indemnización específica. Indemnización específica es la indemnización o resarcimiento compensatorio recibido por un daño distinto a uno por el cual se otorga indemnización general. (Rstmnt, 2nd, Torts, sec. 904 (2)).

***Damnum absque injuria* (L).** Pérdida o daño que no genera una acción legal por reparación o resarcimiento.

**Danger.** Peligro.

**Dangerous.** Peligroso.

**Dangerous chattel.** Objeto peligroso.

**Dangerous driving.** Conducción de un vehículo en forma imprudente, negligente o peligrosa.

**Dangerous weapon.** Arma peligrosa.

**Data.** Datos.

**Date.** Fecha, fechar.

**Day in court.** Día en corte, oportunidad para defenderse.

**Day to show cause.** Día establecido para comparecer a una audiencia y hacer valer los derechos, prueba o argumentos que uno estime tener.

***De minimis* (L).** Algo mínimo, trivial o insignificante.

***De minimis* infractions.** De infracciones mínimas. El tribunal podrá desestimar une acusación si, teniendo en cuenta la naturaleza de la conducta gravada con el hecho de ser un delito y la naturaleza de las circunstancias presentes, encuentra que la conducta del acusado: Estaba dentro de lo usualmente autorizado o tolerado, a no ser que sea expresamente contradicho por la persona cuyo interés haya sido infringido y no sea inconsistente con el propósito del estatuto que define el delito. (Cód. Pen. Mod., § 2.12).

**De novo (L).** Nuevamente.

**Dead.** Muerto, fallecido.

**Deadline.** Plazo, término, vencimiento.

**Deadlock.** Situación de empate, o de imposibilidad de llegar a un acuerdo, en un jurado u otro tipo de cuerpo colegiado.

**Deadlocked jury.** Jurado que no puede llegar a una decisión por no ponerse de acuerdo.

**Deadly.** Mortal, fatal.

**Deadly force.** Fuerza mortal. Significa fuerza la cual el autor usa con el propósito de causar, o que sabe que crea un riesgo substancial de causar muerte o serio daño corporal. Por ejemplo: Disparar a propósito un arma de fuego en la dirección de otra persona o hacia un vehículo en el cual se cree que está otra persona constituye fuerza mortal. (Cód. Pen. Mod., § 3.11 (2)).

Acto suficientemene violento como para causar la muerte de una persona. Por ejemplo, un golpe de puño normalmente no lo sería, pero un disparo de arma de fuego sí.

**Deadly weapon.** Arma capaz de producir la muerte.

**Deaf.** Sordo.

**Deaf and dumb.** Sordomudo.

**Deal.** Negocio, acuerdo. Comerciar, dedicarse a comprar, vender o desempeñarse como intermediario.

**Dealer.** Comerciante.

**Dean.** Decano.

**Death.** Defunción, deceso, fallecimiento.

**Death certificate.** Certificado de defunción.

**Death duty.** Impuesto a la herencia, impuesto sucesorio.

**Death penalty.** Pena de muerte. En USA la práctica más corriente es suministrarla con una inyección (*lethal injection*).

**Deathbed declaration.** Declaración *in extremis*, hecha por una persona al borde de la muerte.

**Debate.** Debate, discusión (s). Debatir, discutir (v).

**Debentures, bonds.** Obligaciones, debentures.

**Debt financing.** Financiación de pasivos o deudas.

**Debt in severalty.** Deuda mancomunada.

**Decedent.** Causante de una sucesión. De cujus.

**Decedent's estate.** Patrimonio sucesorio, bienes relictos.

**Deceit.** Engaño, maquinación fraudulenta.

**Deceitful.** Engañoso.

**Deceptive.** Engañoso, falso.

**Deceptive practices.** Prácticas desleales.

**Decipher.** Descifrar.

**Decision.** Decisión.

**Decision of appeal.** Decisión de alzada. La decisión en sí se toma por voto mayoritario y se enuncia a continuación de los fundamentos. Ella puede consistir en confirmar, anular, o modificar la decisión de la instancia inferior, y puede contener directivas para la continuación del proceso en el tribunal inferior. (Intro al USA). [Ver: *Opinion.*]

**Declarant.** Declarante, deponente, testigo que presta testimonio.

**Declaration of dividends.** Declaración de dividendos. Los dividendos podrán pagarse en efectivo, en bienes o en acciones del capital corporativo, a la par cuando las acciones tengan valor a la par y cuando no lo tengan, al precio que fije la junta de directores. (14 LPRA sec. 1520).

**Declaratory judgment.** Sentencia meramente declarativa. Una sentencia válida, final y firme dictada en una acción que pretendía la declaración o adjudicación de derechos u otras relaciones legales entre las partes tiene carácter concluyente entre las partes en una acción subsiguiente entre ellos con respecto a las cuestiones ventiladas y de acuerdo con las reglas de impedimento de controversias ("*issue preclusion*"), con respecto a cualesquiera controversias propiamente litigadas entre ellos y resueltas en la acción (Rstmnt, 2nd, Judg., sec. 33).

**Declaratory statute.** Ley meramente aclaratoria.

**Decoy.** Señuelo o trampa para atraer a una persona determinada.

**Decree.** Decreto, sentencia (s). Decretar, sentenciar (v).

**Decriminalization.** Tornar una actividad, antes delictuosa, en algo legal.

**Deductible.** Deducible, que puede descontarse de algo.

**Deduction.** Deducción.

**Deed.** Escritura, título de propiedad sobre un inmueble (s). Otorgar mediante escritura (v).

**Deem.** Considerar, pensar.

**Deep pocket.** Literalmente, bolsillo profundo. Significa adinerado.

**Deface.** Desfigurar, tornar ilegible o irreconocible.

**Defalcation.** Desfalco, estafa, malversación.

**Defamation actionable *per se.*** Difamación que no requiere prueba de perjuicio. Una persona que falsamente publique material difamatorio de otro, de tal forma que haga de la publicación una de carácter libelosa, será responsable ante el otro, aunque no haya ocurrido daño a causa de dicha publicación. (Rstmnt, 2nd, Torts, sec. 569).

**Defamation defense, attorney's privilege.** Defensa contra difamación, privilegio del abogado. Un abogado goza del privilegio absoluto de publicar material difamatorio relacionado con otra persona en comunicaciones preliminares a un proceso judicial propuesto, o en la institución donde se esté efectuando o en el curso de y como parte de, un proceso judicial donde esté participando como defensor, si guarda alguna relación con dicho proceso. (Rstmnt, 2nd, Torts, sec. 586).

**Defamation defense, spousal privilege.** Defensa contra difamación, privilegio conyugal. El esposo o la esposa goza del privilegio absoluto de transmitir a su cónyuge material difamatorio concerniente a un tercero. (Rstmnt, 2nd, Torts, sec. 592).

**Defamation defense, truth.** Defensa contra difamación, veracidad. Una persona que publique una manifestación difamatoria de un hecho, no sería sujeto a responsabilidad por difamación si la declaración es cierta. (Rstmnt, 2nd, Torts, sec. 581 A).

**Defamation of a group or class.** Difamación de un grupo o clase de personas. Una persona que publique material difamatorio relacionado con un grupo o una clase de personas, será responsable ante un miembro individual de tal grupo o clase: sólo si el grupo o clase es tan reducido que puede entenderse que el material se refiere a un sólo miembro, las circunstancias en que se publica razonablemente llevan a concluir que hay una particular referencia a un miembro. (Rstmnt, 2nd, Torts, sec. 564 A).

**Defamation of a private person.** Difamación de personas privadas. Una persona que publique una manifestación falsa y difamatoria relacionada con una persona privada, o relacionada con un oficial público o una figura pública respecto a un asunto puramente privado que o afecta su conducta o aptitud al desempeñar su cargo, será sujeto a responsabilidad, si, y sólo si, a) esa persona sabe que la declaración es falsa y difama a otro, b) actúa con menosprecio temerario sobre ese asunto, o c) actúa negligentemente al no verificarlo. (Rstmnt, 2nd, Torts, sec. 580 B).

**Defamation of corporations.** Difamación de empresas. Una persona que publique material difamatorio relacionado con una corporación, será responsable ante ésta si la corporación es una con fines de lucro y tiende a perjudicarla en sus negocios o a disuadir a los demás de negociar con ésta, si es una corporación sin fines de lucro, pero depende de la ayuda financiera del público, y el material tiende a interferir con sus actividades perjudicando la estimación que le tiene dicho público. (Rstmnt, 2nd, Torts, sec. 561).

**Defamation of deceased persons.** Difamación de personas fallecidas. Una persona que publique material difamatorio relacionado con una persona ya fallecida, no será responsable ante el patrimonio de esa persona, sus descendientes o familiares. (Rstmnt, 2nd, Torts, sec. 560).

**Defamation of public official or public figure.** Difamación de un funcionario o de una figura pública. Una persona que publique una manifestación falsa y difamatoria relacionada con un oficial público o una figura pública respecto a su conducta, o aptitud al desempeñar su cargo, será, sujeta a responsabilidad, si, y sólo si: a) esa persona sabe que la declaración es falsa y que difama a otra persona, o b) actúa conforme a un menosprecio temerario sobre esta materia. (Rstmnt, 2nd, Torts, sec. 580 A).

**Defamatory communications.** Comunicaciones difamatorias. Una comunicación o manifestación es difamatoria si tiende a afectar la reputación de una persona para minimizar o reducir la estimación de la comunidad hacia ésta, o para disuadir a terceras personas de asociarse o relacionarse con esta persona. (Rstmnt, 2nd, Torts, sec. 559).

**Defaulting witness.** Testigo en rebeldía.

**Default, against the United States.** Rebeldía, contra los Estados Unidos. No se dictará sentencia alguna en rebeldía contra Estados Unidos o contra funcionarios o agencias del mismo a menos que el reclamante pruebe su reclamación o derecho mediante evidencia a satisfacción de la corte. (R. Fed. P. Civ., sec. 55(e)).

**Default, entry.** Rebeldía, anotación. Cuando una parte contra quien se hubiere solicitado sentencia para conceder un remedio afirmativo dejare de alegar o de otro modo defenderse a tenor con lo dispuesto en estas reglas y dicho hecho se hiciere constar mediante afidávit o de otra manera, el secretario anotará su rebeldía. (Reglas Fed. del Proc. Civ., sec. 55(a)).

**Default, setting aside.** Rebeldía, dejada sin efecto. La corte, por causa justificada, podrá dejar sin efecto una anotación de rebeldía y, si se hubiera dictado sentencia en rebeldía, podrá igualmente dejarla sin efecto en casos de error, inadvertencia, negligencia excusable, descubrimiento de nueva evidencia, fraude, etc. (R. Fed. P. Civ., sec. 55(c)).

**Defeasance.** Documento o condición que revoca un derecho anterior, normalmente un derecho real.

**Defeasible.** Derrotable. Se utiliza para indicar que un derecho real (*interest*) esta sujeto a una condición capaz de suprimirlo o disminuirlo.

**Defect.** Defecto o vicio. Pasarse al bando adversario.

**Defendant.** Demandado, acusado, procesado, reo.

**Defendant's prior record.** Antecedentes del acusado. A solicitud del acusado, el gobierno le suministrará copia de sus antecedentes penales, si hubiere lagunas, que estuvieran en posesión o bajo la custodia o control del gobierno, cuya existencia el fiscal conoce, o que mediante el ejercicio de debida diligencia pudiera conocer. (Regla 16(a)(1)(B), Reglas Fed. de Proc. Crim.).

**Defense attorney.** Abogado defensor. Abogado que defiende a empresas cuando son demandadas por particulares.

**Defense in law or fact.** Defensa de derecho o de hecho. Toda defensa, de derecho o de hecho, contra una solicitud de remedio en cualquier alegación, ya sea demanda, reconvención, demanda contra coparte o demanda contra tercero, se expondrá en la alegación respondiente a las mismas, si ésta fuere requerida, pero, a opción del peticionario, las siguiente defensas podrán hacerse mediante moción: 1) falta de jurisdicción sobre la materia, 2) falta de jurisdicción sobre la persona, 3) incompetencia. (R. Fed. P. Civ., sec. 12(b)).

**Defense of alibi.** Defensa de coartada. A requerimiento por escrito del fiscal con indicación de la hora, la fecha y el lugar en que el alegado delito fue cometido, el acusado le notificará dentro del término de diez días o en otra fecha que la corte dispusiera, aviso por escrito de su intención de presentar la defensa de coartada. (Regla 12.1(a), Reglas Fed. de Proc. Crim.).

**Defense of insanity.** Defensa de locura. Si el acusado intentara fundarse en la defensa de locura en la fecha del alegado delito, tendrá que, dentro del término dispuesto para la radicación de mociones antes del juicio o en fecha posterior que la corte ordenara, notificar por escrito al fiscal tal intención y presentar copia de la notificación al secretario. (Regla 12.2(a), Reglas Fed. de Proc. Crim.).

**Defense of possession by force.** Defensa de la posesión por la fuerza. Un actor tiene el privilegio de utilizar una fuerza razonable, no con la intención de causar la muerte o daño físico, pero sí para prevenir o terminar con la intrusión de otro individuo en sus propiedades muebles e inmuebles. (Rstmnt, 2nd, Torts, sec. 77).

**Defenses and denials.** Defensas y negaciones. Las partes expondrán en términos sucintos y sencillos sus defensas contra cada reclamación interpuesta y admitirán o negarán las aseveraciones en que descansare la parte contraria. (Regla Fed. de Proc. Civ., sec. 8(b)(d)).

**Deficiency.** Deficiencia, déficit, faltante, insuficiencia.

**Definite time to pay a commercial paper.** Fecha determinada para pagar un documento comercial. Un instrumento será pagadero a una fecha determinada si según sus términos es pagadero en o antes de una fecha señalada o en un plazo fijo después de una fecha señalada. (C.C.U. sec. 3-109).

**Degree.** Grado, nivel, rango, título.

**Delegate.** Delegado o representante.

**Delegation of duty.** Transferencia de obligaciones. Transferencia del cumplimiento de obligaciones: El obligado puede transferir adecuadamente el cumplimiento de su obligación a otro, a menos que en dicha transferencia sea contraria a política pública o a los términos de su promesa. (Rstmnt, 2nd, Con., sec. 318).

**Delete.** Suprimir, borrar, cancelar, tachar, testar.

**Delinquency.** Delincuencia. Morosidad.

**Delinquent.** Atrasado, moroso, impago.

**Delivery.** Entrega, cesión, expedición, libranza, reparto.

**Delivery "ex-ship."** Entrega "ex-barco." Salvo pacto en contrario el término para entregas de mercancía "ex-barco" (que significa desde el buque de carga) o lenguaje equivalente no estará restringido a un buque determinado y requerirá la entrega desde un buque que ha llegado al lugar del puerto señalado para su destino donde mercancías de esa clase usualmente se descargan. (C.C.U. sec. 322).

**Demand.** Exigir, demandar.

**Demand liabilities.** Obligaciones pagaderas a la vista. Se entiende por "obligaciones pagaderas a la vista" todas aquéllas que un banco esté obligado a pagar dentro de un plazo no mayor de tres días. (7 LPRA sec. 3).

**Demandable.** Exigible.

**Demeanor.** Apariencia física, comportamiento, forma de caminar o de presentarse ante otros.

**Democracy.** Democracia.

**Demonstrative evidence.** Toda la prueba que no es testimonial.

**Demonstrative legacy.** Donación testamentaria por una suma de dinero, a ser satisfecha de un fondo cierto o de una propiedad en particular.

**Demur.** Excepción planteada contra una acción y basada en una cuestión de puro derecho.

**Demurrer.** Excepción previa.

**Denial.** Negación, rechazo.

**Dependent.** Dependiente, persona que depende de otra, como los niños de sus padres.

**Dependent relative revocation.** Revocación relativa dependiente. Doctrina del *common law* que cancela una revocación testamentaria causada por un error de hecho o de derecho.

**Depletion.** Agotamiento.

**Deponent.** Deponenete, declarante, dicente.

**Deposit certificate.** Certificado de depósito. Se entiende por "certificado de depósito" aquel depósito que haya sido evidenciado por recibo o acuerdo escrito, en el que conste el término por el cual se ha hecho tal depósito y que además tendrá que ser presentado al banco para su cobro. (7 LPRA sec. 3).

**Deposit in court.** Depósito en la corte. En todo pleito en que cualquier parte del remedio solicitado sea una sentencia para el pago de una suma de dinero o la disposición de una suma de dinero o la disposición de cualquier otra cosa que pudiera entregarse, cualquier parte, previa notificación a cada una de las otras y, con permiso de la corte, podrá depositar en la corte la totalidad o cualquier parte de dicha suma o cosa. (R. Fed. P. Civ., sec. 67).

**Deposition.** Deposition es una declaración de testigo bajo juramento, recibida en la forma de pregunta y respuesta, dándole oportunidad al contrario de estar presente y repreguntar (*cross-examine*), todo ello registrado y transcrito estenográficamente ante un funcionario autorizado para dar fe (el estenógrafo de Corte es también notario público).

La mayor ventaja que tiene una *oral depositions* sobre otros métodos de *discovery* es su flexibilidad al probar al testigo, requeriéndole respuestas inmediatas a preguntas orales permitiéndole al interrogador presentar sus preguntas al tiempo que progresa el testimonio, a la luz de las contestaciones que se le van dando.

La gran desventaja de la *oral deposition* es su costo.

**Deposition before action.** Deposición antes del pleito. Cualquier persona que desheare perpetuar su propio testimonio o el de otra persona en relación con cualquier asunto del cual pueda entender cualquier corte de los Estados Unidos, deberá presentar una petición jurada en la corte de distrito de los Estados Unidos en el distrito de la residencia de cualquier presunta parte adversa. (R. Fed. P. Civ., sec. 27(a)(1)).

**Deposition by telephone.** Deposición por teléfono. Las partes podrán estipular por escrito o la corte podrá a moción del parte ordenar que se tome deposición por teléfono. (Reglas Fed. del Proc. Civ., sec. 320(b)(7)).

**Deposition in foreign countries.** Deposiciones en países extranjeros. En un país extranjero, podrán tomarse deposiciones 1) previa notificación, ante una persona autorizada para tomar juramentos en el lugar en que se lleve a cabo el interrogatorio, ya sea por la ley del lugar o por la ley de los Estados Unidos, o 2) ante una persona comisionada por la corte y la persona así comisionada tendrá facultad a virtud de su comisión para tomar los juramentos necesarios y tomar testimonios, o 3) a tenor con un suplicatorio. (Regals Fed. de Proc. Civ., sec. 28(b)).

**Deputy.** Auxiliar, representante, adjunto, delegado, suplente.

**Derelict.** Abandonado.

**Derivative action.** Acción en representación de la sociedad. Aunque un accionista no puede entablar una acción en su propio nombre para defender los derechos de la corporación, puede en cambio, con algunas limitaciones, iniciar los que se conoce como

un juicio derivativo (en *equity*) en nombre de la corporación si los directivos han omitido indebidamente defender un derecho de la corporación afectado por personas pertenecientes o no a ella. (Intro al USA).

**Derivatory actions by shareholders.** Pleitos por accionistas, acción derivada. En todo pleito entablado por uno o más accionistas o miembros para reclamar derechos de una corporación o de una asociación no incorporada, que dicha corporación o asociación no hubiera reclamado debiendo haberlo hecho, la demanda será jurada y deberá alegar 1) que el demandante era accionista o miembro en la fecha del acto en virtud del cual demanda o que su participación o subsiguiente calidad de miembro le fue trasmitida por ministerio de la ley, y 2) que el pleito no es colusorio, para conferir a una corte de los Estados Unidos la jurisdicción que no tendría de otro modo. (R. Fed. P. Civ., sec. 23.1).

Este tipo de acción, típica del derecho americano, es desconocido en España y en la mayoría de los paises latinoamericanos.

**Derogation.** Derogación.

**Derogatory clause.** Cláusula testamentaria que invalida mandas anteriores.

**Descendant.** Descendiente.

**Designation of heirs.** Declaración de herederos.

**Desire.** Deseo. Desear.

**Detainer.** Interferencia ilegítima contra un derecho posesorio o contra la libertad personal.

**Detention.** Detención, retención de una persona en contra de su voluntad.

**Deter.** Realizar un acto disuasivo.

**Deterioration.** Deterioro, degradación, arruinamiento, menoscabo.

**Determined and demandable.** Líquido y exigible.

**Determination of kind of duty involved.** Criterios para determinar el tipo de obligación. Para determinar en qué medida la obligación de una de las partes implica una obligación de medios o de resultado, se tendrá en cuenta, entre otros criterios, los siguientes: (a) la manera en que la obligación se expresa en el contrato; (b) el precio y demás elementos del contrato. (Unidroit, Prin., art. 5.5).

**Determination of quality of performance.** Determinación de la calidad de la prestación. Cuando la calidad de la prestación no ha sido precisada ni puede ser determinada en base al contrato, la prestación debe ser de una calidad razonable y en ningún caso inferior a la calidad mediana, según las circunstancias. (Unidroit, Prin., art. 5.6).

**Detinue.** Acción para recuperar la posesión de bienes muebles.

**Detriment.** Perjuicio, detrimento, lesión, menoscabo, pérdida.

**Detour.** Desvío. Dar un rodeo.

**Detournement.** Estafa, desfalco, malversación.

**Detraction.** Remover bienes de una herencia para transferirlos a otra persona.

**Detrimental reliance.** Acto de tomar en cuenta los dichos de otra persona y actuar consecuentemente, gastando tiempo y/o dinero y/o esfuerzos en ello.

**Devaluation.** Devaluación.

**Developing country.** País en vías de desarrollo.

**Devise.** Manda testamentaria. Legado.

**Devisee.** Legatario.

**Devisor.** Testador.

**Devolution.** Transmisión de derechos.

**Dictate.** Dictar, ordenar.

**Dictator.** Dictador.

**Dictum.** Parte de una sentencia judicial que se expresa en términos generales y que no contiene la parte obligatoria del fallo. La expresión opuesta es *ratio decidendi*.

**Die intestate.** Morir intestado.

**Die without issue.** Morir sin descendencia.

**Dilatory.** Dilatorio.

**Diligence.** Diligencia.

**Diligent.** Diligente.

**Diminished responsibility.** Responsabilidad reducida.

**Diplomacy.** Diplomacia.

**Diplomat.** Diplomático, que desempeña un cargo diplomático.

**Diplomatic.** Diplomático.

**Diplomatic immunity.** Inmunidad diplomática.

**Diplomatic relations.** Relaciones diplomáticas.

**Direct and cross-examination.** Preguntas y repreguntas. El primer testigo de la parte actora es llamado al estrado para ser interrogado por el abogado del demandante (*direct examination*), previo a lo cual debe prestar juramento de atenerse a la verdad. A continuación el abogado del demandado interroga al testigo (*cross-examination*) con el objeto de establecer hechos adicionales o inconsistencias, o para poner en tela de juicio la veracidad del testigo. (Intro al USA).

**Dirty hands.** Literalmente, manos sucias. Significa la persona que ha realizado actos deshonestos o desleales y que, por ello, la ley no le brinda protección. Se contrapone el término a la expresión clean hands, manos limpias.

**Disability.** Incapacidad.

**Disability insurance.** Seguro de incapacidad física. "Seguro de incapacidad física" es el seguro contra daños corporales, incapacidad, o muerte por accidente o medios accidentales, o los gastos ocasionados con tal motivo; seguro contra incapacidad o los gastos ocasionados por enfermedad y cualquier otro seguro perteneciente a este ramo. (26 LPRA sec. 403).

**Disable.** Inhabilitar, descalificar, incapacitar.

**Disaffirm.** Rectificar, negar, desmentir.

**Disagreement.** Desacuerdo.

**Disallow.** Desautorizar.

**Disbar.** Echar del colegio de abogados. Privar a alguien de la facultad de ejercer la abogacía.

**Disbursement.** Desembolso, gasto.

**Discharge a duty.** Ejercer un cargo.

**Discharge of defendant.** Exoneración del acusado. Si de la prueba apareciera que no hay causa probable para creer que se ha cometido un delito o que el acusado lo cometió, el magistrado federal sobreseerá la denuncia y exonerará al acusado. (Regla 5.1 (b), Reglas Fed. de Proc. Crim.).

**Discharge of judgment against one of several co-obligors.** Satisfacción de una sentencia contra uno de varios obligados.

Cuando se ha dictado sentencia en contra de una de varias personas, cada una de las cuales es responsable por la pérdida reclamada en una acción sobre la cual se dictó la sentencia: La satisfacción de la sentencia mediante pago, el descargo de la misma, un pacto para su no ejecución, o cualquier otro convenio que termine en todo o en parte la obligación que impone en el deudor la sentencia, no libera a las otras personas de la responsabilidad por la pérdida. (Rstmnt, 2nd, Judg., sec. 50).

**Disclaim.** Negar responsabilidad.

**Disclosure.** Revelación, dar a conocer.

**Disclosed principal.** Mandante manifiesto. Si al momento de una transacción realizada por un mandatario, la otra parte (en la relación mandante-mandatario) tiene conocimiento de que el mandatario trabaja para un mandante y conoce la identidad del mandante, dicho mandante es un mandante manifiesto. (Rstmnt, 2nd, Agency, sec. 4(1)).

**Discontinuance.** Cesantía, despido.

**Discovery.** Descubrimiento. Las partes podrán hacer descubrimientos mediante uno o más de los métodos siguientes: deposiciones mediante examen oral o preguntas por escrito; interrogatorios por escrito; producción de documentos u objetos o autorización para entrar en terreno u otras propiedades, para inspeccionar y otros fines; exámenes físicos y mentales, y solicitudes de admisión. (R. Fed. P. Civ., sec. 26(a)).

**Discovery conference.** Conferencia de descubrimiento. En cualquier momento después de iniciado un pleito la corte podrá disponer que los abogados de las partes comparezcan ante la misma para una conferencia sobre la cuestión del descubrimiento. (R. Fed. P. Civ., sec. 26).

**Discovery, scope and limits.** Descubrimiento alcance y límites. Las partes podrán hacer descubrimiento en relación con cualquier materia no privilegiada que fuere pertinente al asunto objeto del pleito pendiente, ya estuviere relacionada con la reclamación o la defensa de la parte que solicita el descubrimiento o con la reclamación o defensa de cualquier otra parte. (Reglas de Proc. Civ., sec. 26(b)(1)).

**Discrimination.** Discrimen, discriminación.

**Discrimination by employer.** Discrimen (discriminación) por el patrono. Todo patrono que despida, suspenda o discrimine contra un empleado suyo en relación a su sueldo, salario, jornal o compensación, términos, categorías, condiciones o privilegios de su trabajo, o que deje de emplear o rehuse emplear o reemplear a una persona, o limite o clasifique sus empleados en cualquier forma que tienda a privar a una persona de oportunidades de empleo o que afecten sus status como empleado, por razón de edad, según ésta se define más adelante, raza, color, sexo, origen social o nacional, condición social, ideas políticas o religiosas del empleado o solicitante de empleo, incurrirá en responsabilidad civil. (29 LPRA sec. 146).

**Discrimination by labor union.** Discriminación por organización obrera. Toda organización obrera que limite, divida o clasifique su matrícula en tal forma que prive o tienda a privar a cualquier o cualesquiera de sus miembros, o a cualesquiera o cualesquiera personas que aspiren o tengan derecho a ingresar en dicha matrícula, de oportunidades de empleo por razón de edad, raza, color, religión, sexo, origen social o nacional, credo político, condición social, incurrirá en responsabilidad civil. (29 LPRA sec. 147).

**Dishonor.** Falta de pago.

**Dishonor of a commercial paper.** Deshonor de un documento comercial. Se considerará que no se ha hecho honor a un instrumento cuando: a) se hace debidamente una presentación necesaria u opcional dentro del tiempo fijado o en el caso de cobranzas bancarias el instrumento se devuelve oportunamente antes del término improrrogable de media noche; o b) la presentación no sea obligatoria y el instrumento no sea debidamente aceptado o pagado. (C.C.U. sec. 3-507).

**Dismissal.** Despido, cesantía. No ha lugar a una demanda.

**Dismissal by attorney for government.** Sobreseimiento por el fiscal. El Secretario de Justicia o el fiscal de los Estados Unidos podrá, con permiso de la corte, radicar una solicitud de sobreseimiento del indiciamiento por el gran jurado o de la acusación por el fiscal o de una denuncia, y el proceso quedara entonces terminado. (Regla 48(a), Reglas Fed. de Proc. Crim.).

**Dismissal by court.** Sobreseimiento por la corte. Si hubiera demora innecesaria en la presentación de los cargos al gran jurado o en la formulación de una acusación contra el acusado que hubiere sido detenido para responder ante la corte de distrito, o si hubiera demora innecesaria en presentar al acusado a juicio, la corte podrá sobreseer el indiciamiento por el gran jurado o la acusación por el fiscal o la denuncia. (Regla 48(b), Reglas Fed. de Proc. Crim.).

**Dismissal shall be without prejudice.** Desistimiento será sin perjuicio. El término "desistimiento será sin perjuicio" significa que aquél que solicita el desistimiento de su acción conserva el derecho a entablar una nueva acción. (De la Matta v. Carreras, 92 D.P.R. 85 (1965)).

**Dismissal without notice.** Despido sin previo aviso.

**Disobedience.** Desobediencia.

**Disparaging statement.** Manifestación de descrédito o menosprecio. Una manifestación es de descrédito o menosprecio si se hace para crear duda sobre la calidad de un predio de terreno, bienes muebles o cosas intangibles pertenecientes a otros o sobre la existencia o extensión de su derecho sobre éstos y, a) el que la publica tiene la intención de que dicha declaración cree duda o b) el entendimiento del recipiente de que ocasiona duda, es razonable. (Rstmnt, 2nd, Torts, sec. 629).

**Dispossess.** Desposeer, desalojar, desahuciar, lanzar.

**Dispossession.** Desahucio, desalojo, desposesión, lanzamiento.

**Dispute.** Impugnar, disputar, recusar, objetar.

**Disseminate.** Diseminar, divulgar, esparcir.

**Dissolution.** Disolución.

**Distribution.** Distribución.

**District Attorney.** Ver *D.A.*

**District court.** Corte de distrito.

**District courts.** Tribunales de distrito. Los tribunales de distrito son federales y tienen competencia general en primera instancia en cuestiones civiles, penales, y de derecho marítimo. (Intro al USA).

**District judge.** Juez de distrito.

**Ditches, live or dead hedges.** Zanjas, setos vivos o muertos.

**Diversity.** Diversidad. Término usado en casos estatales cuando una de las partes se domicilia en un Estado distinto del foro.

**Diversity jurisdiction.** Jurisdicción federal basada en el hecho que las partes son de estados o de naciones diferentes.

**Dividing wall.** Pared divisora.

**Divorce.** Divorcio. Las más moderadas de las nuevas leyes permiten el divorcio por consentimiento mutuo, como en New York, donde se ha agregado como casual el haber vivido separados durante dos años. Las más extremas admiten el divorcio a pedido de una de las partes (como ocurre en California, donde basta que un cónyuge demuestre "diferencias irreconciliables que causaron la ruptura irremediable del matrimonio"). (Intro al USA).

**Divorce, jurisdiction.** Divorcio, competencia. La Corte Suprema de los Estados Unidos he determinado que el domicilio de cualquiera de los cónyuges por separado es suficiente como argumento jurisdiccional para que la cláusula de plena fe y crédito pueda aplicarse a la sentencia de divorcio. (Intro al USA).

**Dock.** Muelle.

**Docket.** Rótulo, carátula. Lista de casos con audiencia prevista en un día determinado (s). Incluir en la lista de casos (v).

**Dockyard.** Astillero.

**Doctor-patient privilege.** Privilegio que tiene el paciente para que su médico no divulge sus datos personales.

**Doctrine *in solido*.** Doctrina de in sólido. La doctrina de in sólido—que tiene sus raíces en el derecho común—establece que cuando en una acusación penal se hace una relación general de la declaración que contiene los hechos falsos que dan lugar a una acusación, y no se separan o particularizan dichos hechos, es necesario probar la falsedad de todo lo alegadamente falso. (Pueblo v. Ortiz Colon 85 D.P.R. 160 (1962)).

**Document of title.** Documento de resguado. Incluye conocimiento de embarque, conocimiento de almacén, recibo de muelle, resguardo de almacén u orden para la entrega de las mercancías, y también cualquier otro documento que en el curso regular de negocios o financiamientos se considera como prueba suficiente de que la persona en posesión del documento tiene derecho a recibir, retener y disponer del documento de resguardo, un documento debe dar a entender que se ha expedido por o está dirigido a un depositario con la intención de que cubra las mercancías en posesión del depositario las cuales están identificadas o son porciones fungibles de una masa identificada. (C.C.U. sec. 1201(15)).

**Doing business.** Realizar actos de comercio. Es una de las bases de competencia usadas en USA.

**Domestic International Sales Corporation, DISC.** Tipo de empresa que realiza transacciones internacionales y que goza por ello de ciertos beneficios fiscales.

**Domestic law.** Derecho interno, por oposición al derecho internacional o al derecho extranjero.

**Domestic relations.** Ver *Family law.*

**Domestic servant.** Criado doméstico.

**Domicil(e).** Domicilio. Domicilio es el lugar, usualmente el hogar de una persona, al cual las reglas de conflicto de leyes confieren a veces una importancia determinante debido a la identificación de la persona con ese lugar. Toda persona tiene un domicilio en todo momento y, por lo menos para el mismo propósito, ninguna tiene más de un domicilio a la vez. (Rstmnt, 2nd, Conflict, sec. 11, 13).

**Domicil(e) of choice.** Domicilio de elección. El domicilio de elección puede ser adquirido por una persona que sea legalmente capaz de cambiar su domicilio. Además de la capacidad legal para adquirir un domicilio de elección se requiere: a) presencia y b) estado mental. (Rstmnt, 2nd, Conflict, sec. 15).

**Domicil(e) of origin.** Domicilio de origen. Domicilio de origen es el domicilio que una persona tuvo al nacer. El domicilio de un hijo legítimo de nacimiento es el domicilio de sus padres en ese momento. (Rstmnt, 2nd, Conflict, sec. 14).

**Dominant and servient tenements.** Predios, dominantes y sirvientes.

**Done in duplicate.** Hecho por duplicado.

**Donee.** Donatario.

**Donor.** Donante, donador.

**Dormant.** Durmiente, un derecho o privilegio que no se ejerce.

**Double jeopardy.** Doble exposición por el mismo delito. La causal sobre doble exposición no es contra el ser castigado dos veces, sino contra el ser dos veces puesto en riesgo. (Pueblo v. Lozano Diaz, 88 D.P.R. 834 (1963)).

**Double wages.** Paga doble.

**Doubt.** Duda, incertidumbre.

**Dower.** Derecho de habitación que beneficia a la viuda.

**Down payment.** Pago adelantado, depósito.

**Dowry.** Dote.

**Draft.** Proyecto, borrador.

**Draft, bill of exchange.** Giro, letra de cambio, libranza, envío de dinero.

**Drain.** Acequia. Drenar.

**Draw a juror.** Seleccionar un jurado.

**Drawee.** Librado.

**Drawer.** Librador.

**Drop charges.** Desistir, abandonar, renunciar, retractar una querella o denuncia.

**Drunkard, drunk.** Ebrio, borracho, embriagado, intoxicado.

**Dual purpose rule.** Dualidad de propósitos, regla de. Denomínase regla sobre dualidad de propósitos en viajes emprendidos por empleados la fórmula usada para determinar si es compensable un accidente del trabajo que le ocurre a un empleado mientras éste realiza un viaje. (Sucn. Pérez Puerta v. Comisión Industrial, 94 D.P.R. 557 (1967)).

**Dubious.** Dudoso, cuestionable, discutible, incierto, sospechoso.

**Due.** Debido, vencido y pendiente de pago.

**Due process, fourteenth and fifth amendment.** Debido proceso, enmienda XIV y v. Ninguna persona será obligada a responder por delito capital o infamante, sino en virtud de denuncia o acusación por un gran jurado, salvo en los casos que ocurran en las fuerzas de mar y tierra, o en la milicia, cuando se hallen en servicio activo en tiempos de guerra o de peligro público; ni podrá nadie ser sometido por el mismo delito dos veces a un juicio que pueda ocasionarle la pérdida de la vida o la integridad corporal; ni será compelido en ningún caso criminal a declarar contra sí mismo, ni será privado de su vida, de su libertad o de su propiedad, sin el debido procedimiento de ley; ni se podrá tomar propiedad privada para uso público, sin justa compensación... ni ningún estado privará a persona alguna de su vida, de su libertad o de su propiedad, sin el debido procedimiento de ley, ni negará a nadie, dentro de su jurisdicción, la igual protección de las leyes. (Constitución de USA, enmienda V y XIV, sec. 1).

**Dues.** Cuotas que se pagan por pertenecer a una asociación.

**Dumb.** Mudo.

**Dummy.** Testaferro, intermediario fingido, prestanombre.

**Duplicity.** Duplicado.

**Duress.** Coacción. Será defensa afirmativa para el autor que haya incurrido en la conducta imputada constitutiva de delito, el que haya sido forzada a tal por el uso o la amenaza de fuerza ilegal contra su persona o la de otro, tal que una persona de razonable firmeza en su situación hubiese sido incapaz de resistir. (Cód. Pen. Mod., § 2.09).

**Duress by physical compulsion.** Violencia física. Si una conducta que aparenta ser una manifestación de consentimiento de una parte, que no tiene la intención de comprometerse por tal conducta, y es compelida físicamente a hacer dicha manifestación, tal conducta no es efectiva como una manifestación de consentimiento. (Rstmnt, 2nd, Con., sec. 174).

**Duress by threats.** Violencia mediante amenazas. Si la manifestación de consentimiento de una parte es inducida por una amenaza impropia efectuada por otra parte de modo que no deja alternativa razonable a la víctima, el contrato es anulable por la víctima. (Rstmnt, 2nd, Con., sec. 175).

**Duties.** Derechos, carga, impuesto, tributo.

**Duty.** Deber.

**Duty not to obstruct compliance with judgment.** Deber de no obstruir el cumplimiento de una sentencia. Una persona a quien las reglas de cosa juzgada no le prohiben litigar una acción o reclamación resuelta mediante sentencia podría, no obstante, tener el deber de no obstruir el cumplimiento de una sentencia. (Rstmnt, 2nd, Judg., sec. 63).

**Duty of confidentiality.** Deber de confidencialidad. Si una de las partes proporciona información confidencial durante el curso de las negociaciones, la otra tiene el deber de no revelarla ni utilizarla injustificadamente en provecho propio, independientemente de que luego se celebre un contrato. (Unidroit, Prin., art. 2.16).

**Duty to achieve a specific result and duty of best efforts.** Obligación de resultados y obligación de medios. En la medida en que la obligación de una de las partes implique el deber de alcanzar un resultado específico, dicha parte estará obligada a obtener dicho resultado. (Unidroit, Prin., art. 5.4).

**Duty to act for protection of others.** Deber de actuar para proteger a otros. El hecho de que un actor reconozca o deba reconocer que un acto suyo es necesario para ayudar o proteger a otra persona, no le impone el deber de ejecutar tal acto. (Rstmnt, 2nd, Torts, sec. 314).

**Duty to control conduct of third persons.** Deber de controlar la conducta de terceros. No existe el deber de controlar la conducta de un tercero para evitar que éste cause daño corporal a otro a menos que exista una relación especial entre el actor y el tercero, la cual le impone el deber al actor de controlar la conducta del tercero. (Rstmnt, 2nd, Torts, sec. 315).

**Dwelling.** Domicilio. Significa cualquier edificio o estructura, aunque sea móvil o temporal, o una porción de ésta, que en ese momento es el hogar del autor o lugar de alojamiento. (Cód. Pen. Mod., § 3.11 (3)).

**Dysfunctional.** Que funciona de forma totalmente inadecuada.

# E

**E.C.** Abreviación de European Community, Comunidad Europea.

**E.X.W. (ex works).** Significa que el vendedor ha cumplido su obligación de entrega cuando ha puesto la mercancía, en su establecimiento (p.e., fábrica, taller, almacén, etc.), a disposición del comprador. En especial, no es responsable ni de cargar la mercancía en el vehículo proporcionado por el comprador, ni de despacharla de aduana para la exportación, salvo acuerdo en otro sentido. (Incoterms).

**Earlier performance.** Cumplimiento anticipado. El acreedor podrá rechazar el cumplimiento anticipado de la obligación, a menos que carezca de interés legítimo para hacerlo. (Unidroit, Prin., art. 6.1.5).

**Earned.** Devengado, ganado.

**Earnest money.** Seña, pago a cuenta de precio.

**Earning capacity.** Capacidad remunerativa.

**Earnings.** Ingresos, entradas, ganancias, sueldo, salario.

**Easement.** Servidumbre.

**Economic tort.** Responsabilidad civil por haber cometido irregularidades de índole económica.

**Effective date.** Fecha de vigencia.

**Effective date of final judgment.** Fecha efectiva de una sentencia definitiva. Para propósitos de cosa juzgada, la fecha efectiva de una sentencia definitiva es la fecha en que se dictó, sin importar la fecha en que comenzó la acción que la motivó o la acción que propiciara su ejecución. (Rstmnt, 2nd, Judg., sec. 14).

**Effects of personal judgments.** Efecto de sentencias sobre las personas. Cuando una sentencia sobre una persona es válida, final y firme, será concluyente entre las partes, excepto cuando se interponga algún recurso de apelación revisión, en la medida siguiente: 1) Si la sentencia es a favor del demandante, la reclamación se extinguirá por vía de la sentencia, sin perjuicio de que surja una nueva causa de acción basada en la sentencia; 2) Si la sentencia es a favor del demandado, la reclamación se extinguirá, y la sentencia impedirá una acción subsiguiente basada en la misma reclamación. (Rstmnt, 2nd, Judg., sec. 17).

**Eighteenth Amendment.** Décimo octava enmienda constitucional estadounidense que principalmente introduce restricciones a la venta de bebidas alcohólicas.

**Ejectment.** Lanzamiento, desahucio, evicción, expulsión.

**Election.** Elección, escogencia.

**Election among remedies.** Elección entre acciones contractuales. Si alguna parte tiene más de una acción contractual a su disposición, el escoger alguna(s) mediante la radicación de demanda no conllevará la renuncia de la(s) otra(s) a menos que dichas acciones sean inconsistentes y que la otra parte se vea significativamente afectada al confiar en la manifestación previa. (Rstmnt, 2nd, Con., sec. 378).

**Electrocution.** Una de las formas en que se aplica la pena de muerte en USA, por electrocución.

**Eleventh Amendment.** Onceava enmienda a la Constitución de USA. Establece que los estados de USA gozan de inmunidad procesal respecto de los particulares que sólo pueden atraerlos a juicio con el consentimiento de tales estados.

**Eligible.** Elegible, idoneo para desempeñar un cargo.

**Eligibility.** Eligibilidad.

**Emancipated minor.** Menor emancipado.

**Embargo.** Prohibición de comerciar con empresas de cierta nación (s). Prohibir el comercio con empresas de cierta nación (v).

**Embezzlement** Defraudación, estafa.

**Embezzler.** Estafador, desfalcador.

**Emergency powers.** Suma del poder público. Poderes extraordinarios que son permitidos en caso de emergencia.

**Eminent domain.** Dominio eminente del estado.

**Emissary.** Emisario, representante, nuncio.

**Emotional distress.** Angustia mental. Aquella persona que por su conducta extrema, violenta u ofensiva, intencionalmente o en forma temeraria causa una angustia mental severa en otra persona, será responsable por tal angustia mental, y si ocurre daño físico como resultado de esa conducta, también incurrirá en responsabilidad. (Rstmnt, 2nd, Torts, sec. 46).

**Emotional distress intended.** Angustias mentales intencionales. Será responsable quien intencional e irrazonáblemente someta a otro individuo a angustias mentales, cuando debió reconocer que esto ocasionaría una enfermedad o daño físico: a) aun cuando el actor no tenia la intención de infligir daño, y b) irrespectivamente de que el acto estaba dirigido hacia otro individuo o un tercero. (Rstmnt, 2nd, Torts, sec. 312).

**Emotional distress unintended.** Angustias mentales no intencionales. Quien en forma no intencional causa a otro individuo angustias mentales, será responsable por la enfermedad o daño físico que sufra ese individuo si: a) debió saber que su conducta conllevaba un riesgo irrazonable de causar tal angustia, de otro modo que no sea por el conocimiento del daño o riesgo por una tercera persona; y b) de los hechos conocidos por el, debió saber que tal angustia produciría enfermedad o daño físico. (Rstmnt, 2nd, Torts, sec. 313).

**Emotional disturbance.** Daño emocional. No se indeminizará por concepto de daño emocional a menos que el incumplimiento también cause daño físico, o el contrato o el incumplimiento sean de naturaleza tal que un daño emocional serio resulte como consecuencia probable. (Rstmnt, 2nd, Con., sec. 353).

**Emphyteuticary.** Enfiteuta.

**Employee.** Empleado, dependiente, factor.

**Employer.** Patrono, patrón, empleador, dueño, empresario.

**Employment.** Empleo, cargo, locación de servicios, ocupación, posición.

**Empower.** Otorgar facultades suficientes para realizar algo.

**Empty nester.** Persona cuyos hijos han formado sus hogares independientes.

**En banc.** Sesión plenaria de un tribunal o cuerpo colegiado.

**Enabling clause.** Cláusula que autoriza la realización de algun acto.

**Enact.** Acción de aprobar una ley.

**Enacting clause.** Cláusula que promulga una ley.

**Encourage.** Fomentar, ayudar, facilitar, promover.

**Encroach.** Tomar el lugar de algo o de alguien en forma ilegal o injusta. Usurpar.

**Encumber.** Gravar, afectar, endeudar, inscribir.

**Encumbrance.** Restricción al dominio. Por ejemplo, un embargo o una hipoteca.

**Endorse.** Endosar.

**Endow.** Dotar. Realizar una donación a un escuela, hospital, etc.

**Endowment.** Donación realizada a una entidad, normalmente con fines benéficos.

**Enforce his rights.** Hacer valer sus derechos.

**Enforceability.** Ejecutoriedad, fuerza ejecutoria, imperio.

**Enforcement of foreign judgments.** Ejecución de sentencias extranjeras. Según la cláusula de plena fe y crédito, el tribunal de un estado debe reconocer una sentencia valida y definitiva de un tribunal de otro estado. La cláusula también se aplica cuando uno de los dos tribunales es estadual y el otro federal. El requisito de plena fe y crédito solo alcanza a los fallos de tribunales norteamericanos; los tribunales extranjeros son aplicables solo en virtud del principio de cortesía, sin obligatoriedad. De todos modos, los tribunales norteamericanos han aplicado con liberalidad también los fallos extranjeros. (Intro al USA). (Carl).

**Enforcement of judgments.** Ejecución de sentencias. El procedimiento para ejecutar sentencias para el pago de dinero será mediante mandamiento de ejecución, a menos que la corte dispusiera otra cosa. El trámite de ejecución, en procedimientos suplementarios para y en auxilio de una sentencia. (R. Fed. P. Civ., sec. 69(a)).

**Engage in occupation.** Ejercer un oficio.

**English Constitution.** Constitución inglesa. Se trata de una Constitución dispersa o no escrita en un documento único y que incluye usos, costumbres y decisiones judiciales.

**Enjoin.** Ordenar se abstenga.

**Enjoy.** Gozar, disfrutar.

**Enjoyment.** Uso, goce y disfrute ya sea de un derecho o de una cosa.

**Enlargement, civil cases.** Prórroga, casos civiles. Cuando por estas reglas o por una notificación dada a tenor con las mismas o por una orden de la corte se requiere o permitiere la realización de un acto en o dentro de un plazo especificado, la corte podrá, por causa justificada, en cualquier momento y a su discreción ordenar la prórroga del término si se le presentare una solicitud para ello antes de la expiración del término originalmente prescrito. (R. Fed. P. Civ., Sec. 6(b)).

**Enlargement, criminal cases.** Prórroga, casos penales. Cuando se requiera o permita ejecutar un acto en fecha o dentro de término especificado, la corte podrá, por causa justificada, en cualquier momento a su discreción ordenar la prórroga del término si se presentar una solicitud para ello antes de la expiración del término originalmente prescrito. (Regla 45(b), Reglas Fed. de Proc. Crim.).

**Enmity.** Enemistad, hostilidad.

**Enrichment.** Enriquecimiento.

**Enroll.** Inscribir(se), matricular(se).

**Ensuing.** Venidero, siguiente.

**Enter a judgment.** Dictar sentencia.

**Enterprise.** Empresa.

**Entrapment.** Entrampamiento. Un oficial del orden público o persona que actué en co-operación con tal oficial comete un etrampamiento si con el propósito de obtener evidencia en la comisión de un delito, induce o ayuda a otra persona a incurrir en conducta constitutiva de tal delito. (Cód. Pen. Mod., § 2.13 (1)).

**Entrusting.** Encomienda. "Encomienda" incluye cualquier entrega y cualquier consentimiento de retención de posesión a pesar de cualquier condición expresa de las partes para la entrega o consentimiento y a pesar de que la obtención de la encomienda o la disposición de las mercaderías por el poseedor se considere como robo o hurto bajo la ley penal. (C.C.U. sec. 2-403 (3)).

**Entry.** Asiento, anotación, entrada, inscripción, registro.

**Entry of judgment.** Registro de sentencias. Después del veredicto general del jurado, o después de una decisión de la corte ordenando que una parte recobre solamente una suma determinada o costas o que se deniegue todo el remedio. (R. Fed. P. Civ., sec. 58(1)).

**Environment.** Calidad ambiental, medio ambiente.

**Environmental impact statement.** Declaración de impacto ambiental.

**Epidemic.** Epidemia.

**Epileptic seizure.** Ataque epiléptico.

**Equal protection.** Garantía constitucional de igual protección bajo la ley. Ver *Fourteenth Amendment.*

**Equitable estoppel.** Teoría que impone consecuencias adversas a quien, ante los hechos, debería de haber protestado en su oportunidad y omitió hacerlo.

**Equitable servitude.** Restricción al dominio en forma de servidumbre y acordado por un tribunal en base a razones de equidad.

**Equity.** Equidad. La equidad es una rectificación de la ley en la parte en que ésta es deficiente por su carácter general. (Silva v. Comisión Industrial, 91 D.P.R. 891 (1965)). Parte ya pagada de una deuda.

**Equivalency.** Equivalencia.

**Equivalent.** Equivalente.

**Erasure.** Raspadura, borradura, borrón, tachón, corrección.

**Erasure of record.** Acto por el cual el Estado destruye los antecedentes penales que alguien pueda tener. A partir de ese momento tales antecedentes no pueden considerase.

**Error.** Yerro, equivocación, error.

**Error in expression or transmission.** Error en la expresión o en la transmisión. Una equivocación en la expresión o en la transmisión de una declaración será considerada como un error de la parte de quien emanó dicha declaración. (Unidroit, Prin., art. 3.6).

**Error of/in fact.** Error de hecho.

**Error of/in law.** Error de derecho.

**Errors and omissions excepted.** Salvo error u omisión.

**Escape clause.** Cláusula de escape normalmente prevista en un contrato para defenderse de o para contrarrestar situaciones adversas.

**Escheat.** Reversión de un patrimonio al estado por causa de herencia vacante.

**Escrow holder.** Depositario. Un depositario no es un mandatario como tal de ninguna de las partes en una transacción hasta que ocurra un evento que dé por terminada la relación de depositario. (Rstmnt, 2nd, Agency, sec. 14D).

**Escrow, in.** En depósito, para ser pagado a un tercero al cumplirse ciertas condiciones.

**Esq.** Abrebiación de *Esquire*, título que se le da a los abogados, así como el de Licenciado o Doctor en América Latina.

**Establishment clause.** Cláusula de la Constitución americana (Primera Enmienda) que garantiza la libertad de culto: "El Congreso no promulgará ninguna ley estableciendo una religion oficial, ni prohibiendo el libre ejercicio de culto..."

**Estate.** Acervo hereditario, patrimonio, propiedad inmueble.

**Estate subject to an annuity.** Finca asensuada.

**Estopped to deny.** Impedido de negar.

**Estoppel by judgment.** Impedimento colateral por sentencia. Bajo esta doctrina la sentencia anterior es concluyente solamente en cuanto a aquellas materias que de hecho se suscitaron y verdaderamente o por necesidad se litigaron y adjudicaron, pero no es concluyente en cuanto a aquellas materias que pudieron ser pero que no fueron litigadas y adjudicadas en la acción anterior. (Morales Lebrón).

**European Community.** Comunidad Europea.

**Euthanasia.** Eutanasia.

**Evacuation.** Evacuación.

**Evidence.** Prueba. La teoría de la prueba se ocupa de temas tales como las pruebas judiciales, la competencia de los testigos, la interrogación de los mismos, al admisión o exclusión de evidencia, los privilegios, la carga de la prueba y las presunciones. (Intro al USA).
Probanza, evidencia.

**Evidence against.** Hacer fe contra.

**Evidence, civil and criminal standard.** Prueba, sede civil y penal. La persuasión del jurado "por una preponderancia de la evidencia" en los casos civiles o "mas allá de toda duda razonable" en los casos penales. (Intro al USA).

**Evidence, erroneous decision.** Evidencia, decisión errónea. El error no servirá de base contra una decisión que admite o excluye evidencia a menos que un derecho sustancial de la parte resulte perjudicado. (Regla 103(a), R. Fed. Evid.).

**Evidence heard by jury.** Evidencia audible por el jurado. En casos ante jurado, los procedimientos se conducirán, en cuanto sea factible, de manera de evitar que evidencia inadmisible sea sugerida al jurado por cualesquiera medios, tales como haciendo declaraciones sobre ofertas de prueba o haciendo preguntas audibles por el jurado. (Regla 103(c), 104(c), R. Fed. Evid.).

**Evidence, illegality.** Prueba, ilegalidad. Como cuestión de derecho constitucional, la Corte Suprema ha dictaminado que las pruebas obtenidas por medio de registros abusivos o de confesiones arrancadas por la fuerza no son inadmisibles tanto en los tribunales federales como los estaduales. (Intro al USA).

**Evidence of compromise and offers to compromise.** Evidencia de transacciones y oferta para transar. Evidencia de 1) provisión, oferta o promesa de proveer, o 2) aceptación, oferta o promesa de aceptar remuneración para transar o tratar de transar una reclamación litigada en cuanto a validez o cuantía, no será admisible para probar responsabilidad o falta de validez de la reclamación o su cuantía. (Regla 408, R. Fed. Evid.).

**Evidence of habit or routine practice.** Evidencia de hábito o costumbre. Evidencia del hábito de una persona o de la costumbre en una organización, ya sea corroborada o no y con independencia de la presencia de testigos oculares, será pertinente para probar que la conducta de la persona u organización en una ocasión especifica fue de conformidad con dicho hábito o costumbre. (Regla 406, R. Fed. Evid.).

**Evidence of liability insurance.** Evidencia de seguro de responsabilidad. Evidencia de que una persona estaba o no estaba asegurada contra responsabilidad no será admisible a los efectos de si actuó negligentemente o en otra forma culpablemente. (Regla 411, R. Fed. Evid.).

**Evidence of payment for medical and similar expenses.** Evidencia de pago de gastos médicos y similares. Evidencia de proveer, ofrecer o prometer pagar gastos médicos, hospitalarios y similares ocasionados por lesiones no será admisible para probar responsabilidad por las lesiones. (Regla 409, R. Fed. Evid.).

**Evidence of subsequent remedial measures.** Evidencia de medidas de reparación posteriores. Cuando después de un evento, se toman medidas que, de haberse tomado anteriormente, hubieran tendido a hacer menos probable su ocurrencia, evidencia de las medidas posteriores no será admisible para probar negligencia o conducta culpable en relación con el evento. (Regla 407, R. Fed. Evid.).

**Evidence, scope.** Prueba, alcances. De forma acorde con la naturaleza contenciones de los procedimientos, son las partes (y no el juez) quiere tiene la iniciativa tanto en cuando a establecer las pruebas como a controlar su admisión. Sólo ellas son responsables de que la evidencia sea presentada. (Intro al USA).

**Exceptions.** Excepciones.

**Exceptions, objections.** Excepciones, objeciones. Las excepciones formales a la decisiones u órdenes de la corte serán innecesarias; pero para todos aquellos fines para los cuales hasta ahora necesaria una excepción será suficiente que la parte, al tiempo de dictarse o solicitarse la decisión u orden de la corte, haga saber a la corte las medidas que interesa que tome o su objeción a la actuación de dicha corte y sus motivos para la misma. (R. Fed. P. Civ., sec. 46).

**Exchange.** Permuta, cambio, canje, trueque.

**Excise tax.** Impuesto a las compras de bienes y servicios.

**Excuse from default.** Justificación de la rebeldía. Se puede evitar una sentencia por rebeldía si: 1) La ausencia fue resultado de negligencia excusable; 2) El solicitante del remedio actuó con diligencia razonable al indagar que se había dictado sentencia y con la prontitud debida al procurar un remedio y la solicitud fue hecha dentro del término permitido para ello y al amparo del estatuto o regla aplicable. (Rstmnt, 2nd, Judg., sec. 67).

**Exclusionary rule.** Principio que excluye el uso de prueba obtenida ilegalmente.

**Execute.** Ejecutar.

**Executive council.** Consejo ejecutivo.

**Executive director.** Director ejecutivo.

**Executive orders.** Decretos. El Presidente tiene facultades limitadas de formar decretos (*executive orders*) que suelen tener carácter legislativo. (Intro al USA).

**Executive privilege.** Fuero personal del que goza el Poder Ejecutivo, normalmente el presidente del país o altos funcionarios, para no tener que dar cuenta de ciertos actos.

**Executor.** Albacea, administrador de una sucesión.

**Executorship.** Albaceazgo.

**Executrix.** Albacea o administradora de una sucesión.

**Exemplary damages.** Costas por temeridad y malicia, daños punitorios.

**Exemption clauses.** Cláusulas de exoneración. No podrá invocarse una cláusula que limite o excluya la responsabilidad por incumplimiento, o que le permita a una parte ejecutar una prestación de una manera sustancialmente diferente de lo que la otra podía esperar razonablemente, siempre que ello fuere manifiestamente desleal en función de la finalidad del contrato. (Unidroit, Prin., art. 7.1.6).

**Exhaustion of remedies.** Agotamiento de recursos procesales o administrativos.

**Exhibit.** Exhibir. Apéndice adjuntado a un escrito judicial o a un contrato. Prueba documental o de otro tipo.

**Exempt.** Exonerar, absolver, disculpar, liberar, perdonar.

**Exoneration of liens.** Exoneración de gravámenes. Doctrina mediante la cual los gravámenes sobre legados testamentarios son pagados con dinero del acervo, siempre que el gravamen haya obligado personalmente al causante. (Currie v. Scott, 187 S.W.2d 551 (Tex. 1945)).

**Expatriation.** Expatriación.

**Expectations of privacy constitutionally justifiable.** Expectativa de privacidad constitucionalmente justificable. En el área de registros y allanamientos, desígnase como expectaciones de privacidad constitucionalmente justificables aquellas expectaciones que serían protegidas por la Cuarta Enmienda de la Constitución de los Estados Unidos en ausencia de una orden de allanamiento. (Pueblo v. Bogard, 100 D.P.R. 565 (1971)).

**Expenses for luxury or pleasure.** Gastos de lujo y recreo.

**Expert testimony.** Testimonio pericial. Cuando el conocimiento científico, técnico o de otra especialización sea de ayuda al juzgador de los hechos para entender la evidencia o determinar un hecho en controversia, un testigo capacitado como perito por su conocimiento, habilidad, experiencia, entrenamiento o educación declarará en relación con ello en forma de opinión o de otra manera. (Regla 702, R. Fed. Evid.).

**Expert testimony, bases of opinion.** Testimonio pericial, fundamentos. Los hechos y datos relativos al caso en particular sobre los cuales el perito habrá de basar su opinion o inferencia podrán ser los percibidos por él mismo o dándosele a conocer durante o antes de la vista. (Regla 703, R. Fed. Evid.).

**Experts, appointment.** Peritos, nombramiento. La corte podrá por iniciativa propia o a moción de cualquier parte dictar una orden para mostrar causa por la que no deba ser nombrado un perito y podrá requerir de las partes que sometan candidatos. (Regla 706, R. Fed. Evid.).

**Expiration of term.** Vencimiento del término.

**Export.** Exportación (s). Exportar (v).

**Express assumption of risk.** Asunción expresa del riesgo. Un demandante, quien por medio de un contrato o expresamente haya acordado o aceptado el riesgo de sufrir un daño como resultado de una conducta negligente o temeraria de parte del demandado, no podrá recobrar por tal daño, a menos que el contrato o acuerdo sea inválido por ser contrario al orden público. (Rstmnt, 2nd, Torts, sec. 496 B).

**Express repeal.** Derogación expresa.

***Expressio unius est exclusio alterius* (L).** Norma de interpretacion. Establece que la enumeracion que la ley hace de ciertos elementos implicitamente descalifica a elementos similares que podrian haber sido incluidos por el legislador, de haberlo este querido pero que, al haber sido dejados fuera, no se les puede aplicar el texto de la ley.

**Extenuating circumstances.** Circunstancias atenuantes.

**Extinguishment.** Extinsión, fenecimiento.

**Extort.** Obtener alguna cosa en forma ilegítima. Extorsionar.

**Extra hours.** Horas extra. Son horas extra de trabajo las horas que un empleado trabaja para su patrono en exceso de ocho horas durante cualquier período de 24 horas consecutivas. (29 LPRA sec. 273).

**Extradition.** Extradición.

**Extraordinary circumstances.** Circunstancias extraordinarias.

**Extraterritorial.** Extraterritorial.

**Extrinsic evidence.** Prueba extrínseca.

**Eyewitness.** Testigo ocular.

# F

**F.A.A.** *Federal Aviation Administration*, la autoridad federal de USA que regula cuestiones de aviación.

**F.A.S. (free alongside).** Libre al lado. Salvo pacto en contrario el término F.A.S. del buque que significa "libre al lado" (*free alongside*) en un puerto determinado, aunque se emplee solamente en conexión con el precio establecido, es un término de entrega bajo el cual el vendedor deberá: de su cuenta y riesgo entregar las mercancías al lado del buque en la forma usual en ese puerto o en un muelle designado y provisto por el comprador; y obtener y ofrecer formalmente un recibo por las mercancías a cambio del cual el portador estará obligado a expedir una carta de porte. (C.C.U. Sec. 319(2)(3)(4)).

*Free Alongside Ship* significa que el vendedor cumple su obligación de entrega cuando la mercancía ha sido colocada al costado del buque, sobre el muelle o en barcazas, en el puerto de embarque convenido. (Incoterms).

**F.B.I.** *Federal Bureau of Investigation.* Agencia federal de USA destinada a prevenir y a investigar delitos federales.

**F.C.A. (free carrier).** Significa que el vendedor ha cumplido su obligación de entregar la mercancía cuando la ha puesto, despachada de aduana para la exportación, a cargo del transportista nombrado por el comprador, en el lugar o punto fijado. Si el comprador no ha indicado ningún punto específico, el vendedor puede escoger dentro del lugar o punto fijado. (Incoterms).

**F.O.B. (free on board).** Libre a bordo. *Free on Board* significa que el vendedor cumple con su obligación de entrega cuando la mercancía ha sobrepasado la borda del buque en el puerto de embarque convenido. Esto significa que el comprador ha de soportar todos los gastos y riesgos de pérdida o daño de la mercancía a partir de aquel punto. (Incoterms).

**Fabricate.** Urdir, inventar algo que no es cierto.

**Fabricated evidence.** Prueba falsificada.

**Face.** Cara, lado, superficie.

**Face of record.** La totalidad de actuaciones en una causa judicial.

**Face value.** Valor nominal, precio indicado en el objeto mismo. Expresión que se opone a *market value* o valor de mercado.

**Facial disfigurement.** Desfiguramiento del rostro.

**Fact.** Hecho, acto, circunstancia, evento. Suele oponerse a la palabra *law* (derecho).

**Fact, conclusion of.** Conclusión de hecho.

**Fact-finder.** Jurado, aquél que determina cuestiones de hecho.

**Factor.** Factor, intermediario comercial encargado de vender a comisión.

**Fact, mistake of.** Error de hecho.

**Factoring.** Contrato por el cual una empresa financiera adquiere las cuentas a cobrar de otra, pagando por ello y asumiendo los riesgos y los beneficios de las cobranzas resultantes.

**Facts of independent significance.** Hechos de significado independiente. Doctrina por la cual hechos realizados por el causante afectan la disposición de bienes en su testamento. Por ejemplo, vendiendo una casa que ha sido legada a un descendiente.

**Factual evidence.** Prueba de los hechos.

**Faculty.** Facultades, poder para realizar algún acto. Profesores de una universidad.

**Fail.** Fracasar, fallar, incumplir, dejar de hacer algo a lo cual se está obligado.

**Failure.** Fracaso. Incumplimiento.

**Failure of consideration.** Inexistencia de objeto o causa contractual.

**Failure to appear.** Incomparecencia.

**Failure to comply with licensing requirement.** Falta de autorización laboral o administrativa. Si a una parte se le prohíbe actuar por no haber cumplido con un requisito de licencia o registro, una promesa en consideración de llevar a cabo tal acto o su promesa de hacerlo no es ejecutable por razón de política pública si: a) el requisito tiene un propósito regulador, y; b. el interés en la ejecución de la promesa está claramente contrapesado por la política pública subyacente al requisito. (Rstmnt, 2nd, Con., sec. 181).

**Failure to give assurances.** Falta de asegurar el cumplimiento. Cuando haya bases razonables para creer que la actuación del obligado dará lugar a un incumplimiento que de por sí otorgará al acreedor una reclamación de daños por incumplimiento total, el acreedor puede requerir el afianzamiento de la obligación. (Rstmnt, 2nd, Con., sec. 251).

**Fair and proper.** Justo y adecuado.

**Fair comment.** Comentario adecuado, defensa en un juicio por difamación.

**Fair hearing.** Audiencia que satisface los requisitos de debido proceso.

**Fair, honest, neutral, unbiased.** Imparcial, equitativo, justo, neutral.

**Fair market value.** Precio que normalmente se pagaría en el mercado.

**Fair use.** Uso adecuado.

**Fairs, markets, and ships.** Ferias, mercados y tiendas.

**Faith.** Fe.

**Fallacious.** Falaz.

**Fallacy.** Falacia.

**False arrest.** Arresto o detención ilegal, aunque sea realizado por la policía.

**False entry.** Registro erróneo, v.g. en un libro de comercio.

**False imprisonment.** Aprisionamiento indebido. Un actor estará sujeto a responsabilidad ante otro individuo por aprisionamiento indebido si sus actos tienen la intención de confinar a ese otro individuo o a una tercera persona, dentro de unos límites fijados por el propio actor. (Rstmnt, 2nd, Torts, sec. 35).

**False return.** Citación judicial falsamente diligenciada, v.g. en la que en realidad no se ha citado al demandado.

**Falsehood.** Falsedad.

**Falsify.** Falsificar moneda, documentos, etc.

**Family allowance.** Asignación familiar.

**Family head.** Cabeza de familia.

**Family law.** Derecho de familia. El derecho de familia (o de relaciones domésticas, como a veces se las denomina) se ocupe de las relaciones entre cónyuges y entre padres y hijos, juntos con los derechos y obligaciones que derivan de estas relaciones por ley o por contrato, y con el estado jurídico de las personas casadas y de sus hijos. (Intro al USA).

**Fault.** Culpa, falta, negligencia, responsabilidad.

**Faulty.** Defectuoso, con errores o vicios.

**Faulty possession.** Posesión viciosa.

**Federal common law.** La jurisprudencia de los tribunales federales que no ha sido modificada por leyes estatales.

**Federal exclusive jurisdiction.** Competencia federal exclusiva. Hay casos en que el Congreso ha otorgado competencia exclusiva a los tribunales federales. Los caos en que se aplican leyes penales federales, los regidos por las leyes de derechos de autor o de patentes, los procesos por quiebras, y ciertos casos de derecho marítimo, no pueden ser llevados ante un tribunal estadual. (Intro al USA).

**Federal judge.** Juez federal. Los jueces federales son designados por el Presidente con el acuerdo del Senado. (Intro al USA).

**Federal jurisdiction.** Competencia federal. La jurisdicción penal de los tribunales de distrito, en la que se apoya una minoría importante de los casos, incluye todos los delitos contra la ley federal. La mayor parte de las cuestiones civiles pertenece a uno de los siguientes tipos; en primer lugar, los casos en los que el estado federal es parte; en segundo lugar, los casos en que las partes son particulares y están involucradas leyes federales (*federal question*); y tercer lugar, los casos en que las partes son ciudadanos de diferente estados (*diversity jurisdiction*). (Intro al USA).

**Federal law reporting.** Repertorios de derecho federal. La disposiciones y reglamentos de los organismos federales y los decretos del ejecutivo federal se publican al ser promulgados en el *Federal Registrar*, de aparición diaria; aquéllos que son generales, permanentes y están en vigencia se publican en colección y ordenados sistemáticamente en el *Code of Federal Regulations*. (Intro al USA).

**Federal rules of appellate procedure.** Reglas federales de procedimiento de apelación. En USA la apelación es una especialidad que cuenta con un cuerpo de normas propio.

**Federal rules of civil procedure.** Reglas federales de procedimiento civil.

**Federal rules of evidence.** Reglas federales de evidencia. A diferencia de los códigos latinoamericanos, en USA la prueba tiene su propio código.

**Federal system of the U.S.A.** Sistema Federal de U.S.A. No se puede entender el sistema de derecho de los E.E.U.U. sin comprender su sistema federal, el cual es verdaderamente particular en el mundo. Para muchos fines es posible imaginar a los Estados Unidos como si fueran cincuenta naciones soberanas. Por razones históricas, gran parte del poder de elaboración de las leyes permanece en manos de cada Estado individualmente constituido, como Nueva York o Florida. (Carl).

Ver *enforcement of foreign judgments, choice of law* y *jurisdiction*.

**Federal tax.** Impuestos federales. El grueso de la recaudaciones federales proviene del impuesto a los réditos (*income tax*), que constituye cerca de la mitad del total. (Intro al USA).

**Fee, attorney's.** Honorarios de abogado, costas de un juicio.

**Fee, finder's.** Comisión pagada a quien obtiene al comprador o vendedor deseado.

**Fee simple absolute.** Dominio perfecto o pleno.

**Fee simple conditional.** Dominio pleno sujeto a condición resolutoria.

**Fee simple defeasible.** Dominio pleno que puede terminar debido al suceso de un evento.

**Fee tail.** Dominio transferido a una persona y a sus descendientes (*heirs of his body*).

**Fees.** Honorarios, honorario, emolumento.

**Fees, contingent.** Pacto de cuota lítis. Porcentaje sobre lo recaudado en el juicio que queda para el abogado en pago de honorarios.

**Fellow servant.** Co-empleado. Co-empleados son empleados trabajando para el mismo empleador en la misma empresa u oficio, y tan relacionados en su labor que, debido a la proximidad o alguna otra causa, si uno de ellos es negligente, existe un riesgo especial de peligro para el otro. (Rstmnt, 2nd, Agency, sec. 475).

**Fellow servant rule.** Regla del co-empleado. Un empleado no responderá a empleados o subempleados quienes, mientras desempeñan las funciones de su cargo o alguna otra función relacionada, resulten lesionados debido a las negligencias de un coempleado durante la realización de actos no constitutivos de una violación de las funciones noasignables del empleado, excepto si dichos empleados fueron coaccionados o engañados para que trabajaran, eran muy jóvenes para entender los riesgos o fueron empleados en violación a alguna ley. (Rstmnt, 2nd, Agency, sec. 474).

**Felon.** Delincuente, felón.

**Felonious.** Con intención de cometer el delito de que se trata.

**Felonious assault.** Agresión intencional.

**Felonious homicide.** Homicidio sin atenuante o justificación.

**Felony.** Delito. Denominación genérica para los delitos más serios que llevan pena de muerte o superior a un año de prisión. Se opone el término a los delitos más leves llamados *misdemeanors*.

**Felony murder rule.** Principio que imputa las consecuencias del homicidio a la muerte producida inintencionalmente durante la comisión de un delito.

**Fence.** Cerca que indica los límites de una propiedad. En derecho penal, reducidor o persona que vende objetos robados sabiendo que lo son.

**Fictitious.** Ficticio, apócrifo, falso, supuesto.

**Fiduciary.** Fiduciario.

**Field artillery.** Artillería de campaña.

**Field hands.** Empleados de labranza, peones.

**Fifteenth Amendment.** Quinceava enmienda constitucional, de 1870, y que acuerda el sufragio universal.

**Fifth Amendment.** Quinta enmienda constitucional. La Quinta Enmienda dispone que

"Ninguna persona...está obligado a testificar contra sí misma en un caso penal..." y hay disposiciones analogías en muchas Constituciones estaduales. (Intro al USA).

**Fighting words.** Palabras utilizadas para presentar una idea y, como tales, gozan de la protección de libre expresión aunque inciten a cierta actividad política como marchas, manifestaciones, etc.

**File.** Carpeta, caso, prontuario (s). Archivar, registrar (v).

**File a motion.** Presentar un escrito al tribunal.

**File an appeal.** Apelar formalmente.

**Filed.** Archivado.

**Filing.** Radicación. Todos los escritos posteriores a la demanda que deban ser notificados a las partes se presentarán en la corte antes de su notificación o dentro de un término razonable después de la misma. (R. Fed. P. Civ., sec. 5(d); 6(a)).
Registro o presentación de documentos.

**Final judgment.** Sentencia firme.

**Final pretrial conference.** Última conferencia con antelación al juicio. Las conferencias finales con antelación al juicio se celebrarán lo más cerca de la fecha del juicio que fuere razonable dentro de las circunstancias. Los participantes de cualesquiera de dichas conferencias formularán un plan para el juicio, que incluirá un programa para facilitar la admisión de evidencias. (R. Fed. P. Civ., sec. 16(d)).

**Final state court conviction.** Fallo estatal final condenatorio. Se entiende por un fallo estatal final—a los fines de la aplicación retroactiva de la doctrina constitucional establecida en *Escobedo v. Illinois*, 378 U.S. 478—aquel caso en que se ha dictado sentencia condenatoria, la disponibilidad de una apelación se ha agotado y el término para solicitar certiorari estaba ya vencido a la fecha en que se resolvió el caso de Escobedo. (Rivera Escute v. Jefe Penitenciaría, 92 D.PR. 765 (1965)).

**Finance.** Finanzas, economía, hacienda (s). Financiar, proveer capital (v).

**Finance charges.** Interés, costo del financiamiento.

**Financial.** Financiero, relativo al dinero.

**Financial statement.** Balance, resultado financiero.

**Financial worth.** Valor neto.

**Financial year.** Año contable.

**Financing agency.** Agencia de financiamiento. Significa un banco, compañía de financiamiento u otra persona que en el curso ordinario de los negocios hace anticipos sobre mercancías o documentos de resguardo o que por arreglo con el comprador o el vendedor interviene en el curso ordinario para hacer pagos o cobros vencidos o reclamados bajo un contrato de venta, como al comprar o pagar el giro del vendedor o al hacer anticipos contra él o al tomarlo simplemente al cobro sin tener en cuenta si documentos de resguardo lo acompañan. (C.C.U. sec. 2-104(2)).

**Find.** Encontrar, hallar. Decidir judicialmente en un sentido o en otro.

**Finder.** Quien debe determinar cuestiones de hecho en un proceso, normalmente al jurado.

**Finder of fact.** Ver *fact-finder*.

**Finder of law.** Tribunal aquél encargado de decidir el derecho.

**Finding of fact.** Conclusión de hecho.

**Finding of law.** Conclusión de derecho.

**Findings by the court.** Determinaciones de hechos por la corte. En todos los pleitos juzgados a tenor con los hechos sin jurado o con jurado consultivo, la corte determinará los hechos específicamente y expondrá por separado sus conclusiones de derecho al respecto de los mismos. (R. Fed. P. Civ., sec. 52(a)(b)).

**Fine.** Multa (s). Multar (v).

**Fingerprint.** Impresiones digitales, huellas dactiloscópicas (s). Tomar impresiones digitales (v).

**Firm.** Empresa, casa comercial.

**Firm offer.** Oferta firme.

**Firm rooting.** Afincamiento.

**First Amendment.** Primera enmienda a la constitución de U.S. que garantiza derechos de libertad de palabra, culto, expresión, asamblea y petición a las autoridades.

**First and second lift.** Primera y segunda leva.

**Firstborn.** Primogénito.

**First degree murder.** Homicidio agravado, con premeditación o alevosía.

**First in first out, FIFO.** Norma contable que asume que lo que ingresa en primer término es también lo que sale antes, por ejemplo referido a las mercancías en existencia.

**First mortgage.** Hipoteca en primer grado.

**First offender.** Reo sin antecedentes penales.

**Fix.** Situación difícil (s). Fijar (v).

**Fixture.** Inmueble por accesion.

**Fixtures doctrine.** Accesión. Lo accesorio sigue a lo principal.

**Flag.** Pabellón, bandera.

**Floating.** Flotante, sin asignación específica.

**Floating charge.** Cargo flotante.

**Floating debt.** Deuda flotante.

**Flout.** Incumplir.

**Folioed and stamped books.** Libros foliados y sellados.

**Followers.** Seguidores, secuaces.

**Foolscap.** Hoja de papel o folio tamaño oficio.

**For value.** A título oneroso.

**Forbearance.** Abstención unilateral y voluntaria a hacer algo, o a invocar un derecho.

**Force.** Fuerza física, violencia.

**Force, deadly.** Force majeure. Fuerza mayor, acto de Dios, caso fortuito.

*Force majeure.* Fuerza mayor. El incumplimiento de una de las partes es excusable si dicha parte prueba que se debió a un impedimento ajeno a su control y que no cabía razonablemente esperar al tiempo de celebrarse el contrato, o que hubiese evitado o superado tal impedimento o sus consecuencias. (Unidroit, Prin., art. 7.1.7).

**Forced heir.** Heredero forzoso. Típicamente no existe esta institución en el *common law.*

**Forced labor.** Trabajo forzado.

**Forced sale.** Expropiación, subasta judicial.

**Forcible entry.** Usurpación de domicilio, violación de propiedad.

**Forcible entry and detainer.** Juicio de evicción o lanzamiento.

**Forcible taking of chattels.** Posesión sobre muebles por la fuerza. El uso de una fuerza razonable en contra de otra persona para el recobro de bienes es privilegiado si esa persona ha poseído al actor en forma torticera, sin haber reclamado un derecho; o si reclamando un derecho ha actuado mediante la fuerza, coacción o fraude. (Rstmnt, 2nd, Torts, sec. 101).

**Foreclose.** Presentación de un juicio hipotecario. Cerrar o impedir una oportunidad.

**Foreclosed property.** Propiedad ejecutada.

**Foregoing.** Anterior.

**Foreign bank.** Banco extranjero. Se entiende por "banco extranjero" una corporación organizada con el propósito de dedicarse a negocios bancarios bajo las leyes de otro territorio o Estado o de un país extranjero, que mantenga un banco y haga negocios en el lugar de su incorporación y que haya sido autorizado para operar en el país. (7 LPRA sec. 3).

**Foreign exchange.** Cambio de dinero extranjero.

**Foreign law, determination.** Ley extranjera, determinación. Toda parte que intentare levantar una controversia en relación con la ley de una nación extranjera lo notificará en sus alegaciones o mediante otra notificación razonable por escrito. (R. Fed. P. Civ., sec. 44.1).

**Foreman.** Capataz, presidente del jurado.

**Foreseeability.** Previsibilidad.

**Foreseeability of harm.** Previsibilidad del daño. La parte incumplidora es responsable solamente del daño previsto o que razonablemente debió prever al tiempo de la celebración del contrato como consecuencia probable de su incumplimiento. (Unidroit, Prin., art. 7.4.4).

**Forfeiture.** Pérdida, comiso, confiscación, decomiso.

**Forgery.** Falsificación.

**Formal contracts.** Los siguientes tipos de contratos están sujetos en algunos aspectos a reglas especiales que dependen de sus características formales y difieren de aquellos que regulan los contratos en general: a) contratos bajo sello, b) admisiones judiciales sobre sumas adeudadas, c) instrumentos y documentos negociables, d) cartas de crédito. (Rstmnt, 2nd, Con., sec. 6).

**Forms of judgment.** Proyectos de sentencia. Los abogados no someterán proyectos de sentencia salvo por instrucción de la corte y tales instrucciones no se darán como cuestión de rutina. (R. Fed. P. Civ., sec. 58(2)).

**Fort.** Fuerte.

**Forthwith.** Inmediatamente.

**Fortuitous event.** Caso fortuito, accidente imprevisible.

***Forum non conveniens* (L).** Teoría del tribunal inconveniente. Son varias las razones por la cuales el forum non conveniens viola el derecho latinoamericano y, por lo tanto, no puede generar competencia. Estas razones son tan poderosas que al juez latinoamericano le basta con enunciar sólo algunas -constitucionales, procesales, una ley especial- antes de concluir que el caso debe rechazarse. Adviértase, en primer lugar, el funcionamiento gobal de esta doctrina: El juez extranjero es plenamente competente y carece de todo motivo personal (e.g. parentezco, grado de amistad, etc.) para declinar el caso. Sin embargo decide, contra la voluntad del actor, que existe otro tribunal—con competencia concurrente—más conveniente y envía allí al actor a radicar una nueva demanda. Cuando el tribunal "mas conveniente" se encuentra en el extranjero, el juez original no envía rogatorio alguno ni solicita de otra forma la anuencia de las autoridades del país extranjero. Simplemente ordena al actor radicar una nueva demanda en otro país. Es frecuente que el juez original imponga ciertas condiciones—por ejemplo que la demanda sea presentada dentro de los 30 dias, que las demandadas no puedan oponer ciertas excepciones—v.g. prescripción liberatoria—que para retornar al juzgado original es necesario un fallo de incompetencia de la Corte Suprema del segundo país, etc. Bajo este sistema, los actores latinoamericanos deben replantear su demanda en su país de origen, produciéndose las siguientes particularidades:

a) El juez original sigue manteniendo una competencia subyacente y es normal que las partes se dirijan a él, de tanto en tanto, para quejarse de lo que la otra parte hace u omite en el segundo tribunal, para pedirle reconsideración de un auto anterior, etc.

b) Los actores quedan amordazados, sin poder decirle al juez del segundo país que están allí contra su voluntad o que ellos creen que tal juez debería declararse incompetente.

c) Cuando los actores vuelven al tribunal original con una declaración de incompetencia del segundo tribunal, lo normal es que la demandada se oponga y solicite al primer tribunal que considere la declinatoria del segundo tribunal como "indebida," "abusiva," "producto de mala fe procesal," etc. Que un juez extranjero competente decida unilateralmente endilgarle el trabajo a su colega latinoamericano implica que se comporte como tribunal de alzada. No es menos ofensivo que un juez extranjero disponga, también unilateralmente, la comisión de actos procesales en Latinoamérica, imponiendo condiciones, plazos, etc. (Comité Jurídico Interamericano de la OEA, Propuesta para una Convención Interamericana sobre los Efectos y Tratamiento de la Teoría del Tribunal Inconveniente, Rio de Janeiro, 1999, p. 2).

**Forum shopping.** Estrategia de buscar el tribunal más conveniente para radicar una demanda. Muchas veces se emplea esta expresión en sentido derogatorio implicando que la elección de tal tribunal, si bien no es ilegal es cuando menos abusiva.

**Forward.** Remitir, dirigir, enviar, mandar.

**Foster brother.** Hermano de crianza.

**Foundation.** Fundación.

**Foundling.** Expósito.

**Fourteenth Amendment.** Catorceava enmienda constitucional, de 1868. Prohíbe que los estados restrinjan los privilegios de los ciudadanos a los que garantiza igualdad en la protección jurídica de sus derechos, privilegios e inmunidades.

**Fourth Amendment.** Cuarta enmienda constitucional. Protege la inviolabilidad del domicilio contra búsquedas y allanamientos irrazonables.

**Frame.** Marco, puntos de referencia (s). Incriminar falsamente a alguien (v).

**Franchise.** Franquicia, autorización especial concedida por el gobierno y de la que no gozan los demás (s). Otorgar una franquicia o concesión (v).

**Fraud.** Dolo. Cualquiera de las partes puede dar por anulado un contrato cuando fue inducida a celebrarlo mediante maniobras dolosas de la otra parte, incluyendo palabras o prácticas, o cuando dicha parte omitió revelar información que debería haber sido revelada conforme a criterios comerciales razonables de lealtad negocial. (Unidroit, Prin., art. 3.8).

Fraude, defraudación.

**Fraud, constructive.** Fraude implícito. Aquél que la ley asume aunque el perpetrador haya carecido de intención fraudulenta.

**Fraud, extrinsic.** Fraude procesal tendiente a evitar que la contraparte pueda defenderse adecuadamente.

**Fraud in the inducement.** Tipo de dolo consistente en obtener un consentimiento aparentemente válido, pero merced a haber proporcionado información errónea a sabiendas.

**Fraud upon the court.** Fraude al tribunal. Bajo las disposiciones de las Reglas de Procedimiento Civil, se entiende por fraude al tribunal aquellos tipos de fraude cuyo efecto o cuya intención es mancillar al tribunal como tal, o que es fraude perpetrado por oficiales del tribunal, de tal forma que la maquinaria judicial no puede ejercer como de costumbre su imparcial labor de juzgar los casos que se le presentan para adjudicación. (Municipio de Coamo v. Tribunal Superior, 99 D.P.R. 932 (1970)).

**Fraudulent.** Fraudulento, doloso, ilegal.

**Fraudulent misrepresentation.** Dolo fraudulento. El dolo se considera fraudulento si el que incurre en tal acto intenta que su afirmación induzca a otra parte a manifestar su consentimiento y el que incurre en tal acto: a) conoce o tiene motivos para creer que la afirmación no concuerde con los derechos, b) no tiene confianza ninguna en la certeza de su afirmación, c) conoce que su afirmación carece de base. (Rstmnt, 2nd, Con., sec. 162(1)).

Falsa representación fraudulenta. Una persona que fraudulentamente hace una falsa representación de hecho, opinión, intención, o de la ley; con el propósito de inducir a otro a actuar o evitar que actúe, de conformidad, será responsable al otro individuo al engañarlo, por la pérdida económica causada, por su confianza en esa falsa representación. (Rstmnt, 2nd, Torts, sec. 525, 537).

**Free.** Libre, gratuito. Liberar (v).

**Free enterprise.** Libre empresa, economía de mercado.

**Free and clear.** Sin gravamen alguno.

**Free of charges.** Libre de gastos.

**Freedom.** Libertad.

**Freedom of contract.** Libertad de contratación. Las partes tienen libertad para celebrar un contrato y determinar su contenido. (Unidroit, Prin., art. 1.1).

**Freedom of expression.** Libertad de palabra.

**Freedom of Information Act (F.O.I.A.).** Ley federal que obliga a agencias gubernamentales a entregar copia de documentos públicos a quienes las pidan.

**Freedom of press.** Libertad de prensa.

**Freedom of religion.** Libertad de culto.

**Freedom of speech, First Amendment.** Libertad de palabra o prensa, primera enmienda. El Congreso no aprobará ninguna ley con respecto al establecimiento de religión alguna, o que prohiba el libre ejercicio de la misma o que corte la libertad de palabra o de prensa; o el derecho del pueblo a reunirse pacíficamente y a solicitar del Gobierno la reparación de agravios. (Constitución de USA, primera enmienda).

**Freehold.** Derecho de propiedad plena que dura, al menos, por la vida del propietario.

**Freightage.** Fletamento, cargamento, flete, porte.

**Frivolous litigation.** Temeridad y malicia procesal.

**Fruit of the poisonous tree doctrine.** Literalmente, doctrina del arbol de frutos envenenados. Se usa para indicar que la prueba obtenida ilegalmente por el estado en un proceso penal no puede ser admitida en el caso, aunque pruebe sin lugar a duda alguna la culpabilidad del reo. Se aplica, por ejemplo, a la prueba obtenida en un domicilio sin orden de allanamiento, a las confesiones forzadas, etc.

**Fruits and crops.** Frutos y cosechas.

**Frustration of contract.** Teoría del cambio de circunstancias que permite la resción contractual basada en la excesiva onerosidad, o imposibilidad, sobreviniente.

**Frustration of purpose.** Teoría que permite la resción contractual por la pérdida o el gran cambio del objeto perseguido por el contrato.

**Full.** Completo, pleno, suficiente.

**Full age.** Mayoría de edad.

**Full answer.** Respuesta completa.

**Full authority.** Poder amplio suficiente.

**Full compensation.** Pago integral. La parte agraviada tiene derecho a la reparación integral del daño derivado del incumplimiento. La indemnización comprende toda pérdida sufrida y cualquier ganancia de la que se haya visto privada, tomando en consideración cualquier ganancia que la parte agra-

viada hubiera obtenido al evitar gastos o daños. (Unidroit, Prin., art. 7.4.2).

**Full disclosure.** Revelación total de la información pertinente.

**Full faith and credit.** Entera fe y crédito. Se dará entera fe y crédito en cada Estado a los actos públicos, documentos y procedimientos judiciales de los otros Estados (Constitución de USA, art. IV, sec. 1).

**Full hearing.** Audiencia en la que puedan ejercerse todas las garantías procesales como el derecho de información, de defensa, etc.

**Full name.** Nombre completo.

**Full payment.** Pago total.

**Full proof.** Plena prueba.

**Fungible.** Fungible. Respecto a mercancías o valores significa mercancía o valores de los cuales cualquier unidad es, por naturaleza o por uso de comercio, el equivalente de otra unidad semejante. (C.C.U. sec. 1201 (17)).

**Future earnings.** Ganancias futuras.

**Futures contract.** Operación a término.

# G

**G.A.A.P.** Principios contables generalmente aceptados (*generally accepted accounting principles*).

**G.A.T.T.** *General Agreement on Tariffs and Trade.*

**Gag order.** Orden que imparte el juez impidiendo a las partes, abogados, etc. hacer comentarios públicos—y a veces privados —informando sobre la marcha del juicio.

**Gain.** Beneficio, ganancia, utilidad. Realizar una ganancia, salir ganando.

**Gainful occupation.** Ingreso en forma estable derivado del trabajo.

**Gallows.** Cadalso, horca, patíbulo.

**Gambler.** El que apuesta por dinero, jugador profesional, tahur.

**Gambling debts.** Deudas de juego.

**Game laws.** Leyes aplicables a la caza de animales.

**Game preserve.** Heredad de caza, coto de caza.

**Gaol.** Carcel, celda, prisión.

**Gaoler.** Carcelero.

**Gap.** Laguna, algo no previsto en la ley o en un contrato.

**Garnish.** Embargar.

**Garnishee.** Persona contra la cual se ha trabado embargo.

**Garnishment.** Embargo de bienes muebles. Consiste en una citación que se hace a una persona para que comparezca, en una causa en que no es parte, a fin de que informe y explique al tribunal ciertos puntos referentes a dicha causa; ese término se usa ahora generalmente para indicar el procedimiento en virtud del cual se embargan dineros o bienes que pertenecen a un demandado y que se encuentran en poder de una tercera persona. (Morales Lebrón).

**Gas chamber.** Cámara de gas.

**Gavel.** Pequeño martillo de madera, usado por los jueces para indicar que una audiencia comienza, termina y para imponer silencio.

**Gavel to gavel.** De principio al fin.

**Gazette.** Gaceta.

**Gender discrimination.** Discriminación sexual.

**General agent.** Mandatario general. Un mandatario general es un mandatario autorizado para realizar una serie de transacciones que conlleva la continuidad de un servicio. (Rstmnt, 2nd, Agency, sec. 3(1)).

**General appearance.** La primera presentación ante un tribunal, realizada en calidad de parte demandada, sin opone una excepción de incompetencia.

**General assembly.** Asamblea general.

**General assignment for the benefit of creditors.** Puesta del patrimonio de una persona a la disposición de sus acreedores para que de la venta de tales bienes cobren sus créditos.

**General average.** En derecho marítimo, avería común.

**General conditions of sale.** Condiciones generales de venta.

**General damages.** Indemnización genérica. Sujeto a algunas limitaciones, la parte afectada tiene derecho a indemnización a base de su expectativa o interés según medido por a) la pérdida experimentada como consecuencia de que la otra parte incumpla total o parcialmente, más b) cualquier otra pérdida, ya incidental, ya consecuente, causada por el incumplimiento, menos c) cualquier costo o alguna pérdida que la parte incumplida evite o se ahorre al incumplir. (Rstmnt, 2nd, Con., sec. 347).

**General jurisdiction.** Competencia general.

**General meeting.** Asamblea general.

**General partner.** Socio colectivo, activo, gestor, solidario.

**General principles of law.** Principios generales del derecho.

**General power of attorney.** Poder general.

**General rule.** Regla general.

**General verdict.** Veredicto general. La corte podrá someter al jurado, junto con los modelos pertinentes para un veredicto general, interrogatorios por escrito sobre una o más controversias de hecho, la decisión de las cuales haya de ser necesaria para un veredicto. (R. Fed. P. Civ., sec. 49(b)).

**General warranty.** Garantía general.

**Gentleman's agreement.** Acuerdo entre caballeros.

**Germane.** Afín, similar, conexo, que se rige por las mismas reglas.

**Gerrymander.** Táctica de dividir distritos electorales en forma tal de asegurar el triunfo de ciertos candidatos.

**Gift.** Regalo, donación, obsequio.

**Gimmick.** Truco, estratagema, jugarreta.

**Gist.** La parte más importante de un argumento o de un tema.

**Give and bequeath.** Donar por acto entre vivos o de última voluntad.

**Give bail.** Prestar fianza, dar fianza, afianzar.

**Give evidence.** Presentar prueba.

**Give good and sufficient security.** Prestar buena y suficiente fianza.

**Give warning.** Dar aviso.

**Given under my hand and seal of office.** Dado bajo mi firma y sello oficial.

**Globalization.** Globalización.

**Glossary.** Glosario.

**Going and coming rule.** Regla de ir y venir del trabajo. A los fines de determinar la compensabilidad de un accidente bajo las disposiciones de la Ley de Compensaciones por Accidentes del Trabajo, la doctrina conocida como la regla de ir y venir del trabajo es aquélla que sostiene que los accidentes del trabajo ocurridos mientras un obrero va de su casa al trabajo y del trabajo a su casa, no son compensables. (Gallart Admor. v. Comisión Industrial, 87 D.P.R. 17 (1962)).

**Going concern.** Negocio que está funcionando.

**Going public.** Cotización de las acciones de una empresa, por primera vez, en el mercado de valores.

**Gold clause.** Cláusula oro.

**Golden handshake.** Indemnización pagada a un alto ejecutivo cuando se retira.

**Golden parachute.** Pagos y otros incentivos económicos brindados a un alto ejecutivo que se retira, normalmente cuando la empresa pasa a manos de otro grupo de personas.

**Go-slow.** Trabajo a tristeza, trabajo de brazos caídos.

**Good cause.** Causa suficiente.

**Good faith and fair dealing.** Lealtad contractual. Todo contrato impone sobre cada parte un debe de buena fe y trato justo en su cumplimiento y ejecución. (Rstmnt, 2nd, Con., sec. 205).

Buena fe y lealtad negocial. (1) Las partes debe actuar con buena fe y lealtad negocial en el comercio internacional. (2) Las partes no podrán excluír ni restringir la aplicación de este deber. (Unidroit, Prin., art. 1.7).

**Good Samaritan doctrine.** Teoría del buen samaritano. Es una defensa oponible por el demandado que en el hecho desencadenante del juicio actuó tratando de socorrer a otro.

**Goods.** Mercancías. Significa toda cosa (incluyendo mercancías especialmente manufacturadas) que sean movibles al momento de identificación con el contrato de venta y que no sea el dinero en el cual el precio será pagado, valores de inversión y derechos de acción. "Mercancías" también incluye las crías no nacidas de animales, las cosechas en crecimiento y otras cosas identificadas unidas a bienes raíces. Las mercancías deben de existir y ser identificadas antes que cualquier interés en ellas pueda existir. (C.C.U. sec. 2-105(1)(2)(3)(4)).

**Goodwill.** Valor llave, plusvalía.

**Government.** Gobierno.

**Governmental immunity.** Inmunidad estatal.

**Governmental interest doctrine.** Doctrina del interés estatal. Aquélla que toma en cuenta la conveniencia del foro como factor importante para resolver un caso de conflicto de leyes.

**Governor.** Gobernador.

**Grace period.** Período de gracia.

**Graft.** Cohecho, soborno (s). Corromper, sobornar (v).

**Grand jury.** Gran jurado. La corte ordenará que se convoque uno o más de un gran jurado siempre que lo requiera el interés publico. (Regla 6(a), Regla Fed. de Proc. Crim.).

**Grand jury, petit jury.** En algunos estados la composición del *grand jury* puede llegar a 23 miembros, en comparación con los 12 del petit jury. Tiene la facultad de ordenar la presentación de testigos, y es por ello que el fiscal puede preferir el procedimiento del *indictment* en vez de la *information*. (Intro al USA).

**Grand larceny.** Hurto por valor superior a cierta suma, por ejemplo cien dólares, la que varía segun las leyes de cada estado.

**Grandfather clause.** Sistema que permite que lo que ya funcionaba legalmente bajo una nueva ley sea tolerado durante la vigencia de una ley posterior más estricta. Es tan sólo un aspecto del principio de irrectroactividad.

**Grant.** Concesión, beca (s). Conceder (v).

**Grantee.** Persona que recibe algo en propiedad. Beneficiario.

**Grantor.** Persona que transfiere algo a otra. Cesionista, otorgante.

**Gratuitous.** Gratuito.

**Green belt.** Cinturón ecológico.

**Grievance.** Queja, agravio, perjuicio, protesta.

**Gross disparity.** Desproporción excesiva. Cualquiera de las partes puede dar por anulado un contrato o caulquiera de sus disposiciones si al momento de su celebración, éste o alguna de sus cláusulas le otorga a la otra parte una ventaja excesiva. (Unidroit, Prin., art. 3.10).

**Gross negligence.** Culpa grave.

**Ground damage from aircraft.** Daño terrestre producido desde aeronaves. Si se ocasiona daño a un predio de terreno, a personas o a bienes muebles que estén en tierra firme, como resultado del ascenso, descenso o vuelo de una aeronave, o por la expulsión o caída de un objeto de la misma el operador de dicha aeronave será responsable por el daño, aun cuando haya ejercido sumo cuidado para prevenirlo. (Rstmnt, 2nd, Torts, sec. 520 A).

**Grounding.** Encalladura.

**Groundless.** Sin mérito.

**Grounds.** Bases, por ejemplo bases jurisdiccionales.

**Guarantee.** Ver *guaranty*.

**Guarantee clause.** Cláusula de garantia.

**Guaranty.** Garantía. Una promesa hecha para garantizar el cumplimiento de una obligación contractual es vinculante si la promesa se hace en forma escrita y es firmada por el promisor y establece una causa significativa. (Rstmnt, 2nd, Con., sec. 88).

**Guardian.** Guardian, tutor, curador.

**Guardianship.** Tutela, custodia, curaduría.

**Guerrilla.** Guerilla, guerrillero.

**Guest statute.** Ley que determina la responsabilidad de un conductor por los accidentes de ruta en los que se lesione o muera su pasajero.

**Guilty.** Culpable.

**Gun Control.** Legislación que controla el uso y la posesión de armas de fuego.

# H

**Habeas corpus.** Orden judicial para que se haga comparecer a un detenido delante del tribunal, a fin de tomarle declaración y apreciar si la detención es debida o no.

**Habit.** Hábito, costumbre, adicción.

**Habitability.** Habitabilidad.

**Habitual drunkard.** Ebrio habitual.

**Half brother.** Medio hermano, hermanastro.

**Half sister.** Medio hermana, hermanastra.

**Halfway house.** Institución para la rehabilitación de los ex-presidiarios y para su reinserción social.

**Hallucinogenic drug.** Droga alucinógena.

**Hammer sale.** Subasta, remate.

**Hand and seal.** Firma y sello.

**Handcuffs.** Esposas, cadenas.

**Handicapped.** Que sufre una discapacidad, física y/o mental.

**Handling.** Manipulación, tramitación.

**Handwriting.** Letra manuscrita.

**Hang.** Ahorcar.

**Hangman.** Verdugo.

**Harassment.** Acosamiento, ostigamiento.

**Harboring.** Protegiendo, brindando refugio.

**Hard labor.** Trabajos forzados.

**Hardship.** Excesiva onerosidad. Se presenta un caso de "excesiva onerosidad" (*hardship*) cuando ocurren sucesos que alteran fundamentalmente el equilibrio del contrato, ya sea por el incremento en el costo de la prestación a cargo de una de las partes, o bien por una disminución del valor de la ejecución de la prestación a cargo de la otra, y, además, cuando dichos sucesos ocurren o son conocidos por la parte en desventaja luego de la celebración del contrato. (Unidroit, Prin., 6.2.2).

**Hardship, effects.** Excesiva onerosidad, efectos. En caso de "excesiva onerosidad" (*hardship*), la parte en desventaja puede solicitar la renegociación del contrato. Tal solicitud deberá formularla sin demora injustificada, con indicación de los fundamentos en los que se basa. (Unidroit, Prin., art. 6.2.3).

**Harm.** Daño. Es una pérdida o detrimento que sufre una persona resultante de cualquier causa. (Restatement, Second, Torts, sec. 7(2)).

**Harm caused by tort against other spouse.** Daño por cuasidelito causado al cónyuge. Aquella persona que mediante su conducta torticera sea responsable ante un cónyuge por el daño corporal causado, también será responsable al otro cónyuge por la pérdida de la compañía y los servicios del primer cónyuge, incluyendo el menoscabo a la capacidad sexual y por los gastos incurridos por el segundo cónyuge para proveer servicios médicos. (Rstmnt, 2nd, Torts, sec. 693(1)).

**Harm due in part to the aggrieved party.** Daño imputable parcialmente a la parte agraviada. Cuando el daño se deba en parte a un acto u omisión de la parte agraviada o a otro evento cuyo riesgo ella asumió, el monto de la indemnización se reducirá en la medida en que tales factores hayan contribuído al daño, tomando en consideración la conducta de cada una de las partes. (Unidroit, Prin., art. 7.4.7).

**Harmless error.** Error no perjudicial. Ningún error ya fuera en la admisión o exclusión de evidencia y ningún error o defecto en cualquier decisión u orden o en cualquier cosa hecha o admitida por la corte o por cualesquiera de las partes será motivo para la concesión de un nuevo juicio o para anular un veredicto o para dejar sin efecto, modificar o de otro modo alterar una sentencia u orden, a menos que la negativa para dicha actuación pareciere a la corte ser incongruente con la justicia sustancial. (R. Fed. P. Civ., sec. 61.).

**Hauling and transportation.** Arrimo y arrastre.

**Hazard.** Riesgo, peligro.

**Hazardous goods.** Mercaderías excesivamente peligrosas.

**He who seeks equity must do equity.** Quien solicita equidad debe haberla dispensado. Es una forma de expresar la teoría de las manos limpias. Significa que el tribunal no brinda amparo a quienes se han comportado con falta de equidad.

**Headed paper.** Papel con membrete.

**Hear a case.** Avocarse el conocimiento de un caso.

**Hearing.** Audiencia, sesión, vista.

**Hearsay.** Prueba de referencia. Prueba de referencia es una declaración, aparte de la hecha por el declarante al testificar en el juicio o vista, que se ofrece en evidencia para probar la verdad de la materia aseverada. Prueba de referencia no será admisible. (Regla 801(c), 802, Reglas de Fed. de Evidencia).

**Hearsay exceptions.** Excepciones a la prueba de referencia. 1) Percepción contemporánea 2) Declaración por excitación 3) Condición mental, emocional o física entonces existente 4) Declaraciones para propósitos de diagnóstico o tratamiento médico 5) Escrito para refrescar memoria 6) Récords de actividad conducida con regularidad. (Reglas 803, R. Fed. Evid.).

**Hearsay rule.** Testimonio referido. Una consecuencia particular de la institución del jurado es que, además de excluirse la evidencia irrelevante, también existen reglas que excluye evidencias relevantes si se considera que, siendo su valor escaso, hay riesgo considerable de que sean sobrevaluadas por el jurado. (Intro al USA).

**Heat of passion.** Emoción violenta.

**Heatstroke.** Tabardillo.

**Heir.** Heredero.

**Heir apparent.** Heredero aparente.

**Heiress.** Heredera.

**Heirs and assigns.** Herederos y sucesores.

**Heist.** Robo a mano armada.

**Henceforth.** De ahora en adelante.

**Heraldry.** Heráldica.

**Hereby.** Por la presente.

**Hereditary.** Hereditario.

**Hereinafter.** De ahora en más, a partir de ahora.

**Hereof.** De lo cual.

**Heresy.** Herejía.

**Hereto.** De ésto, a ésto.

**Herewith.** Con la presente, se adjunta con ésto.

**Heritge.** Herencia. Patrimonio común.

**Hermeneutics.** Hermenéutica, principios de interpretación.

**Hidden defect.** Defecto o vicio oculto.

**High contracting parties.** Altas partes contratantes.

**High seas.** Alta mar.

**High treason.** Alta traición.

**Highest bidder.** Postor más alto.

**Highest degree of care.** El nivel de cuidado más elevado.

**Highway robbery.** Asalto en carreteras.

**Hijacking.** Secuestro de aeronaves y otros medios de transporte. Piratería aerea.

**Hire.** Alquilar un bien mueble. Emplear a alguien.

**Hire purchase.** Locación con opción de compra.

**Hit and run accident.** Accidente automovilístico en el que un conductor huye con su vehículo.

**Hit man.** Asesino profesional.

**Hitherto.** Hasta ahora.

**Hoarder.** Acaparador.

**Hold.** Tener, poseer. Celebrar una reunión. Afirmar o mantener una opinión.

**Hold harmless agreement.** Acuerdo por el cual una parte promete a otra que la indemnizará en forma tal que, si el hecho temido se cumple, la primera quede en igual posición económica que si tal hecho no hubiese tenido lugar.

**Holder.** Tenedor.

**Holder in due course.** Tenedor legítimo. Un tenedor legítimo es un tenedor que toma el instrumento a) por causa onerosa; y b) de buena fe; y c) sin aviso de que está vencido o de que no se ha hecho honor o de cualquier defensa o reclamación contra éste de parte de cualquier persona. (C.C.U. sec. 3-302, 3-205).

**Holder not in due course.** Tenedor que no es de buena fe.

**Holding and dictum.** *Ratio decidendi* y *obiter dictum*. El *holding* es la regla de Derecho necesaria para resolver el caso. Cualquier otra cosa que hayan afirmado los jueces pero que fuese innecesaria para su decisión constituye el *dictum*. (Intro al USA).

**Holding company.** Empresa controlante.

**Holdup.** Asalto.

**Holiday.** Feriado, licencia, vacaciones.

**Holmes, Oliver.** Oliver Wendell Holmes (1841-1935), graduado del Harvard College y la Harvard Law School, practicó leyes en Boston. Fue durante un breve período profesor de leyes en Harvard, y luego, durante veinte años, fue, primero juez de la Corte Suprema de Justicia de Massachuttes y luego, Presidente de la misma. En 1902 fue nombrado juez asociado de la Corte Suprema de los Estados Unidos, donde la calidad de sus opiniones en disidencia le valieron el título de "Gran Disidente." Renunció por motivos de salud en 1932. Su trabajo más famoso es *The Common Law* (1881), basado en una serie de conferencias. (Intro al USA).

**Holograph.** Hológrafo, ológrafo.

**Holographic will.** Testamento ológrafo.

**Home.** Hogar, casa, vivienda. Hogar es el lugar donde una persona vive y es el centro de su vida doméstica, social y civil. (Rstmnt, 2nd, Conflict, sec. 12).

**Home rule.** Principio que favorece la autonomía de las autoridades municipales en materias respecto de las cuales la autoridad central no tiene un interés directo ni superior.

**Home worker.** Trabajador a domicilio. Toda persona que se ocupe en un domicilio en la manufactura de artículos o materiales para un patrono, un representante contratista o un subcontratista. (29 LPRA sec. 373(e)).

**Homestead.** Bien de familia, hogar seguro.

**Homework.** Trabajo a domicilio.

**Homicide.** Homicidio.

**Homosexuality.** Homosexualidad.

**Honorarium.** Honorarios.

**Honorary consul.** Consul honorario.

**Hornbook.** Libro básico para aprender materias de derecho.

**Hostage.** Rehén.

**Hostel keeper.** Mesonero.

**Hostile.** Hostil.

**Hostile witness.** Testigo adverso.

**Hot pursuit.** Persecución de un delincuente inmediatamente después de cometido el delito.

**House of representatives.** Cámara de representantes, Cámara de Diputados.

**House arrest.** Arresto domiciliario.

**Housewife.** Ama de casa.

**Hull of the vessel.** Casco del buque.

**Hung jury.** Jurado que no puede reunir los suficientes votos en un sentido para pronunciarse válidamente.

**Hunger strike.** Huelga de hambre.

**Husband.** Marido, cónyuge, esposo.

**Husbandry.** Labranza.

# I

**I.D.** Documento de identidad.

**I.O.U.** *I owe you.* Reconocimiento escrito de una deuda.

**I have hereunto set my hand.** Firmo la presente.

**Ignorance or mistake.** Ignorancia o error. Ignorancia o error como cuestión de hecho o derecho será defensa si la ignorancia o error contrarrestan propósito, conocimiento, creencia, temeridad o negligencia necesarias para establecer uno de los elementos de delitos. (Cód. Pen. Mod., § 2.04 (1)).

**Illegal.** Ilegítimo, ilegal, prohibido.

**Illegal origin.** Procedencia ilegítima.

**Illicit.** Ilícito, ilegal.

**Illiteracy.** Analfabetismo.

**Illiterate.** Analfabeto.

**Illness.** Enfermedad.

**Immaterial.** Inmaterial.

**Immigrant.** Inmigrante.

**Immigration.** Inmigración.

**Imminent danger.** Peligro inminente.

**Imminent peril.** Peligro inminente.

**Immoral.** Inmoral.

**Immovable property.** Propiedad inmueble.

**Immune from prosecution.** Que no puede ser demandado.

**Immunity.** Inmunidad.

**Impair.** Atentar.

**Impairment of recouse or of collateral.** Menoscabo del derecho a reclamar o de colateral. El tenedor liberará a cualquiera parte responsable en el instrumento hasta donde sin el consentimiento de ella el tenedor sin expresar reserva de derecho libera o pacta no demandar a cualquier persona contra quien la parte según conocimiento del tenedor, tiene derecho a reclamar o pacta suspender el derecho de hacer cumplir con respecto a dicha persona el instrumento o la colateral o de otro modo libera a dicha persona, excepto que la falta o demora al efectuar cualquiera presentación, protesto o aviso de que no se ha hecho honor con respecto a cualquiera de dichas personas no liberará a parte alguna para quien la presentación, protesto o aviso de que no se ha hecho honor es eficaz o innecesario. (C.C.U. sec. 3-606).

**Impanel a juror.** Elegir un jurado.

**Impartial.** Imparcial.

**Impeachment.** Juicio político. Acción criminal ejercida contra un funcionario ante un tribunal distinto de los ordinarios.

**Impleader.** Acto de atraer al proceso al un tercero como demandado.

**Implicate.** Implicar, comprometer.

**Implied assumption of risk.** Asunción implícita del riesgo. El demandante que entiende cabalmente el riesgo del daño que puede sufrir tanto en su persona como en sus cosas como consecuencia de la conducta del demandado o por la condición en que se encuentran las tierras o los bienes muebles del demandado; y voluntariamente entra o permanece o permite que sus cosas entren o permanezcan dentro del área de riesgo, bajo circunstancias que manifiestan su aceptación, no podrá reivindicarse por el daño que sufra. (Rstmnt, 2nd, Torts, sec. 496 (c)).

**Implied by law.** Lo que la ley presume o infiere.

**Implied consent.** Consentimiento tácito o implícito.

**Implied contract.** Contrato inferido por la ley. Para todos los efectos prácticos es como un contrato expresamente firmado por las partes.

**Implied easement.** Servidumbre legal, presumida por la ley.

**Implied obligations.** Obligaciones implícitas. Las obligaciones implícitas emanan de: (a) la naturaleza y finalidad del contrato; (b) las prácticas establecidas entre las partes y los usos; (c) la buena fe y la lealtad negocial; (d) el sentido común. (Unidroit, Prin., art. 5.2).

**Implied renewal.** Tácita reconducción.

**Implied repeal.** Derogación tácita.

**Implied warranty.** Garantía implícita. Según esta doctrina, toda persona tiene conocimiento de las cualidades buenas o malas de las cosas que fabrica en el ejercicio de su arte, oficio o negocio. (Morales Lebrón).

**Import.** Importación (s). Importar (v).

**Import duty.** Tasa de importación.

**Impossibility.** Imposibilidad.

**Impostor.** Impostor.

**Impotency.** Impotencia

**Impound.** Confiscar, depositar bienes por orden judicial.

**Imprison.** Recluir, poner en prisión.

**Imprisonment.** Encarcelamiento.

**Improper.** Impropio, indecente, incorrecto.

**Improper threat.** Amenaza indebida. Una amenaza es impropia si: a) se amenaza con cometer un crimen o un daño o la amenaza por sí sola sería un crimen o un cuasidelito si resultara en la obtención de propiedad. b) lo que se amenaza es un enjuiciamiento criminal. c) lo que se amenaza es el uso del proceso civil y la amenaza se hace de mala fe. d) la amenaza es el incumplimiento del deber de buena fe y trato justo en un contrato con la otra parte amenazada. (Rstmnt, 2nd, Con., sec. 176).

**Improper use.** Uso impropio.

**Improvement.** Mejora, mejoramiento, reparación, perfeccionamiento.

**Impunity.** Impunidad.

**Imputation of payments.** Imputación de pagos. El deudor de varias obligaciones de dinero a favor del mismo acreedor puede indicar al momento de pagar a cuál de ellas se imputará su pago. Empero, el pago ha de imputarse en primer lugar a cualquier gasto, luego a los intereses vencidos y finalmente al pago del capital. (Unidroit, Prin., art. 6.1.12).

**Imputed.** Imputado.

**In being.** Existente.

**In blank.** En blanco.

**In camera inspection.** Diligencia probatoria dirigida por el juez, no en la sala de audiencias pero en su oficina, con exclusión del público y del jurado. Se usa, por ejemplo, si el juez quiere interrogar a un menor de edad protegiéndolo de la publicidad. La mayoría de las veces se usa este procedimiento para que el juez decida si una prueba específica puede ser mencionada o presentada al jurado.

**In cash.** En efectivo, en especie.

**In contemplation of death.** En consideración de la muerte de alguien.

**In effect.** En vigor, vigente.

**In faith whereof.** En fe de lo cual.

**In forma pauperis (L).** Con beneficio de pobreza, beneficio de litigar sin gastos.

**In his (her) own name.** A nombre propio.

**In pari delicto (L).** Con el mismo grado de criminalidad o de falta. Por ejemplo, los copartícipes en una acción criminal.

**In pari materia (L).** Pertenecientes a la misma materia o con un objetivo común. Se usa la frase hablando de la interpretación armónica de dos textos legales.

**In testimony whereof.** En testimonio de lo cual.

**In writing.** Por escrito.

**Inadmissibility of pleas, plea discussions and related statements.** Inadmisibilidad de alegaciones, discusiones de alegaciones y declaraciones relacionadas. Excepto cuando otra cosa se disponga en esta regla, evidencia de lo siguiente, en cualquier procedimiento civil o criminal, no será admisible contra el acusado que hizo la alegación o participó en las discusiones de la alegación: 1) alegación de culpabilidad posteriormente retirada; 2) alegación de nolo contendere. (Reglas 410, R. Fed. Evid.).

**Inalienable rights.** Derechos inalienables.

**Inapplicable.** Inaplicable.

**Inavertence.** Inadvertencia, descuido.

**Incapable.** Incapaz, no susceptible, insusceptible.

**Incapacity.** Inhabilidad, discapacidad, incapacidad, incompetencia.

**Incest.** Incesto.

**Inchoate.** Comenzado pero no terminado. Imperfecto.

**Inchoate lien.** El embargo u otra medida precautoria, que surge de una sentencia estando tal sentencia sujeta a apelación u a otro ataque. Si tal sentencia cae, el embargo o la medida precautoria siguen la misma suerte.

**Incident.** Incidente.

**Incite.** Incitar.

**Income.** Rédito, ingreso de dinero.

**Incompetent.** Incompetente, deficiente.

**Inconsistency.** Incongruencia, contradicción, contrasentido.

**Inconsistent.** Inconsistente.

**Incontestable.** Incontestable.

**Incopatibilidad.** Incompatibilidad.

**Incorporate.** Incorporar. Crear una sociedad anónima.

**Incorporation by reference.** Incorporación de un texto en otro pero solamente por referencia, es decir, sin hacer una transcripción literal.

**Incriminate.** Incriminar.

**Inculpate.** Inculpar.

**Incur.** Incurrir.

**Indebtedness.** Deuda, adeudado.

**Indecency.** Indecencia.

**Indefeasible.** Que no puede ser derrotado.

**Indemnification.** Indemnificación, reparación.

**Indenture.** Escritura sobre un derecho inmobiliario. El término indenture significa una escritura en la que dos o más personas se conceden derecho mutuamente o se obligan reciprocamente o convienen ambas cosas y en su sentido más amplio implica una transacción (*conveyance*).

**Independent contractor.** Contratista independiente. Un contratista independiente es la persona quien contrata con otra para que haga algo por él, pero que no está controlada ni sujeta a que el otro tenga derecho de controlar su conducta física (la del contratista independiente) durante la realización de la encomienda o empresa. (Rstmnt, 2nd, Agency, sec. 2(3)).

**Indices, calendars.** Índices, calendarios. Se llevará por el secretario, bajo la supervisión de la corte, índices adecuados del registro de pleitos y procedimientos y de todas las sentencias y órdenes civiles. (R. Fed. P. Civ., sec. 79(c)).

**Indictable.** Que puede ser acusado penalmente.

**Indictment.** Indiciamiento. Todo delito que pueda ser sancionado con la pena de muerte requiere indiciamiento por el gran jurado. Todo delito que pueda ser sancionado con la pena de reclusión por un término que exceda de un año o trabajos forzados requiere indiciamiento por el gran jurado, pero en caso de renuncia a ese derecho podrá ser procesado mediante indiciamiento del gran jurado, o acusación del fiscal. (Regla 7(a)(c), Reglas Fed. de Proc. Crim.).

**Indictment, finding and return.** Indiciamiento, determinación y formulación. El indiciamiento podrá determinarse únicamente con la concurrencia de 12 o más jurados. El indiciamiento se presentaré por el gran jurado a un magistrado federal en corte abierta. (Regla 6, Reglas Fed. Proc. Crim.).

**Indictment, information.** Acusación fiscal. La acusación formal, que tiene la función de informar al acusado de los cargos, puede tener la forma de *indictment* o *information*, según los estados. (Intro al USA).

**Individual.** Individuo. Individual.

**Indorsee.** Endosatario.

**Indorsement.** Endoso.

**Indorsement especial and in blank.** Endoso especial y en blanco. Un endoso especial especificará la persona a quien o a cuya orden ha de pagarse el instrumento.

Un instrumento pagadero a la orden y endosado en blanco se convertirá en pagadero al portador y podrá negociarse por la simple entrega hasta que sea especialmente endosado. (C.C.U. sec. 3-204).

**Indorser.** Endosante.

**Indubitable.** Indubitable.

**Industrial accident.** Accidente laboral.

**Industrial and commercial securities.** Valores industriales y mercantiles.

**Industrial design.** Diseño industrial.

**Industrial espionage.** Espionaje industrial.

**Infamous.** Infame.

**Infamy.** Infamia.

**Infant.** Menor, niño.

**Infant mortality.** Mortalidad infantil.

**Infanticide.** Infanticidio.

**Inference.** Inferencia. A los efectos de la Ley de Evidencia, inferencia es la deducción que de los hechos probados hace en su discernimiento el juez o jurado, sin que al efecto medie mandato expreso de la ley. (Pueblo v. Picó Vidal, 99 D.P.R. 708 (1970)).

**Infidelity.** Infidelidad.

**Inflation.** Inflación.

**Information and belief.** En su leal saber y entender.

**Infraction.** Infracción.

**Infringement.** Infringimiento, violación, incumplimiento.

**Ingratitude.** Ingratitud, indignidad.

**Ingress and egress.** Entrada y salida.

**Inhabitant.** Habitante, ciudadano.

**Inherent.** Inherente.

**Inherent agency power.** Poder de mandato inherente. Poder de mandato inherente es el término usado en el restatement de este tema para indicar el poder de un mandatario que se deriva no de autoridad, autoridad aparente ni impedimento, sino solamente de la relación de mandato que existe para la protección de personas afectadas por, o en negociaciones con un empleado u otro mandatario. (Rstmnt, 2nd, Agency, sec. 8A).

**Inheritance.** Herencia.

**Injunction.** Interdicto prohibitorio.

**Injunctive relief.** Protección otorgada por el tribunal basada en poderes de equidad.

**Injurious falsehood.** Falsedad injuriosa. Una persona que publique una declaración falsa que perjudique los intereses de otro, será responsable por la pérdida económica que sufra ese otro si la intención de la publicación de esa declaración es ocasionar daño al otro en cuanto a sus intereses con valor pecuniario o reconoce o debería reconocer que tal actuación produciría ese resultado. (Rstmnt, 2nd, Torts, sec. 623 A).

**Injury (tort).** Daño, perjuicio. Es la invasión de un derecho legalmente protegido. (Rstmnt, 2nd, Torts, sec. 7(1)).

**Injustice.** Injusticia.

**Inland.** Del país.

**Inmate.** Confinado, prisionero, preso, presidiario.

**Innkeeper.** Fondista.

**Innocent.** Inocente.

**Innocent purchaser.** Comprador de buena fe.

**Inns of Court.** En Inglaterra, las cuatro asociaciones profesionales de abogados: *Gray*, *Lincoln*, *Inner Temple* y *Middle Temple*.

**Innuendo.** Insinuación, inuendo.

**Inoperative.** Sin efecto, inoperante.

**Insane.** Loco, demente, insano.

**Insanity.** Insania, demencia, locura.

**Insanity defense.** Defensa de demencia.

**Insert.** Insert, fijar.

**Insider trading.** Es el acto, penal y civilmente castigado, de quienes en razón de su trabajo tienen información confidencial sobre maniobras empresariales a cumplirse que afectan el valor de las acciones respectivas. Consiste la figura en utilizar tal información en provecho propio o de terceros, por ejemplo, comprando las acciones destinadas a subir y/o vendiendo aquellas destinadas a bajar.

**Insolvency.** Insolvencia, quiebra.

**Insolvent.** Insolvente. Es "insolvente" una persona si ha dejado de pagar sus deudas en el curso ordinario de negocio o no puede pagarlas cuando se hacen exigibles o si es insolvente a tenor con la ley federal de quiebra. (C.C.U. sec. 1201(23)).

**Installment contract.** Contrato de entregas parciales. Un "contrato de entrega parcial" es uno que requiere o autoriza la entrega de mercancías en lotes por separado para que sean aceptados separadamente, aunque el contrato contenga una cláusula "cada entrega es un contrato por separado" o su equivalente. (C.C.U. sec. 2-612).

**Instructions to the jury.** Instrucciones al jurado. El juez instruye al jurado sobre la forma en la cual deben decidir las preguntas que finalmente se les someten. Antes de presentar sus alegatos finales, ambas partes pueden proponer al juez las instrucciones que consideran que deben impartirse al jurado y el juez les comunica las que tiene intención de impartir, a fin de que puedan tenerlas en cuenta en sus alegatos. (R. Fed. P. Civ., sec. 51).

**Instrumentality.** Instrumentalidad, conducto.

**Instruments of crime.** Instrumentos de delito. Una persona comete un delito menos grave si posee algún "instrumento de delito" con el propósito de emplearlo criminalmente. "Instrumento de delito" significa cualquier cosa especialmente hecha o adaptada para uso criminal. (Cód. Pen. Mod., § 5.06 (1)).

**Insular.** Insular.

**Insurable interest.** Interés asegurable.

**Insurance.** Seguro. "Seguro" es el contrato mediante el cual una persona se obliga a indemnizar a otra o a pagarle o a proveerle un beneficio específico o determinable al producirse un suceso incierto previsto en el mismo. El término seguro incluye reaseguro. (26 LPRA sec. 102).

**Insurance contract, point of contact doctrine.** Contrato de seguro, doctrina del centro de gravedad. Doctrina que sostiene que un contrato de seguros se rige por la ley del Estado que tiene más contacto con la cosa objeto del contrato y no las leyes del Estado en que dicho contrato se solicitó, se firmó, y se pagó la prima correspondiente al primer año de vigencia de dicho contrato. (Maryland Cas'y Co. v. San Juan Racing Assoc., Inc., 83 D.P.R. 559 (1961)).

**Insurance vending machine.** Máquinas vendedoras de seguros.

**Insure effectiveness of a judgment.** Asegurar la efectividad de una sentencia.

**Insured.** Asegurado.

**Insurer.** Asegurador.

**Intangible property.** Propiedad intangible.

**Intangibles.** Valores intangibles.

**Integrated agreement.** Contrato integrado. Un contrato integrado es uno en forma escrita, que constituye la expresión final de uno o más términos del contrato. (Restatement, Second, Contract, sec. 209(1)).

**Intelligible.** Inteligible.

**Intended beneficiary.** Beneficiario directo. A menos que se pacte lo contrario, el beneficiario de una promesa será un beneficiario directo, si el reconocimiento de su derecho al cumplimiento se considera apropiado para lograr la intención de las partes.

**Intendment.** Espíritu, propósito.

**Intent.** Intención. Circunstancias en la que el actor desea causar las consecuencias de su acto o tiene la creencia de que ciertamente ocurrirían esas consecuencias de su acto. (Rstmnt, 2nd, Torts, sec. 8).

**Intent to kill a fellow creature.** Intención de ocasionar la muerte de un semejante. Manifiéstase la intención de ocasionar la muerte de un semejante en un caso de asesinato, a través de uno de los dos siguientes elementos, cualquiera de los cuales es suficiente para determinar la existencia de malicia premeditada, a saber: a) la intención específica de matar, considerada como equivalente al deseo y propósito directo, explícito y definido de matar, o sea, precisamente formulado con el objetivo directo de matar; o, b) con la intención de realizar un acto o de producir grave daño corporal cuya consecuencia probable sea la muerte de una persona. (Pueblo v. Mendez, 74:913, seguido, Pueblo v. Reyes Lara, 100 D.P.R. 676 (1971)).

**Intention of the parties.** Intención de las partes. (1) El contrato debe interpretarse conforme a la intención común de las partes. (2) Si dicha intención no puede establecerse, el contrato se interpretará conforme al sentido que le habrían dado personas sensatas de la misma condición que las partes, colocadas en las mismas circunstancias. (Unidroit, Prin., art. 4.1).

**Intentional torts.** Cuasidelitos intencionales. Los delitos intencionales que causan daños a las personas o a los bienes incluyen los delitos clásicos que previenen, con pocos cambios, del derecho inglés: agresión, vías de derecho, usurpación de bienes, detención arbitraria e intrusión. (Intro al USA).

**Intentionally preventing assistance.** Ayuda impedida intencionalmente. Aquella persona que intencionalmente impida que un tercero brinde ayuda, necesaria para prevenir que otro sufra daño corporal, será responsable por el daño físico sufrido por éste. (Rstmnt, 2nd, Torts, sec. 326).

**Interchange.** Intercambio.

**Intercurrent accident.** Accidente intercurrente. A los fines de la Ley de Compensaciones por Accidentes del Trabajo, un accidente intercurrente significa una lesión subsiguiente de un obrero, sea ésta una agravación de otra anterior o una lesión distinta. Dicho accidente intercurrente es compensable bajo las disposiciones de dicho estatuto. (Admor, F.S.E. v. Comisión Industrial, 100 D.P.R. 363 (1971)).

**Interest as damages.** Indemnización con intereses. Si el incumplimiento consiste en el no pagar una suma de dinero definida o realizar algún cumplimiento con un valor monetario fijo o calculable, se podrá reclamar intereses desde el momento pactado para el cumplimiento sobre la cantidad adeudada menos todas las deducciones a las cuales la parte incumplidora tenga derecho. (Rstmnt, 2nd, Con., sec. 354).

**Interest for failure to pay money.** Intereses por incumplimiento de obligaciones dinerarias. Si el deudor no paga una suma de dinero cuando corresponde, el acreedor tiene derecho a cobrar intereses sobre dicha suma durante el tiempo que transcurre entre el vencimiento de la obligación hasta el momento del pago, sea o no excusable la falta de pago. (Unidroit, Prin., art. 7.4.9).

**Interest on damages.** Intereses sobre el monto de la indemnización. A menos que se convenga otra cosa, los intereses sobre el monto de la indemnización correspondiente al incumplimiento de obligaciones no dinerarias comenzarán a devengarse desde el momento del incumplimiento. (Unidroit, Prin., art. 7.4.10).

**Interest on delay.** Intereses de mora, moratorios.

**Interest on interest.** Intereses compuestos.

**Interference by the other party.** Interferencia de la otra parte. Ninguna de las partes podrá valerse del incumplimiento de la otra cuando dicho incumplimiento fue causado por actos u omisiones suyas o por cualquier otro evento cuyo riesgo ella asumió. (Unidroit, Prin., art. 7.1.2).

**Interference with inheritance or gift.** Interferencia con herencia o donación. Alguien quien intencionalmente e impropiamente interfiera con el cumplimiento de un contrato (excepto un contrato matrimonial) entre otro y una tercera persona, impidiendo que el otro cumpla con el contrato

u ocasionando que el cumplimiento resulte más costoso u oneroso, será responsable al otro por la pérdida pecuniaria que resulte. (Rstmnt, 2nd, Torts, sec. 766 A).

**Interference with performance of contract by third person** Interferencia con cumplimiento contractual por un tercero. Alguien quien intencional e impropiamente interfiera con el cumplimiento de un contrato (excepto un contrato matrimonial) entre otro y una tercera persona, induciendo a dicha tercera persona a que no cumpla con el contrato, será responsable al otro por la pérdida pecuniaria resultante como consecuencia de que la tercera persona no cumpliera con el contrato. (Rstmnt, 2nd, Torts, sec. 766).

**Interference with prospective contractual relation.** Interferencia con relación contractual prospectiva. Alguien quien intencional e impropiamente interfiera con la relación contractual prospectiva de otro (excepto un contrato matrimonial) está sujeto a responder al otro por el daño pecuniario resultante de la pérdida de los beneficios de la relación contractual, consista dicha interferencia de que se induzca o cause que una tercera persona no entre o no continúe en la relación contractual prospectiva. (Rstmnt, 2nd, Torts, sec. 766B).

**Interlineations.** Interpolación, entre líneas, interlineado.

**Interlocking control.** Control entrelazado.

**Interlocutory.** Interlocutorio.

**Internal-Revenue Stamp.** Sello de rentas.

**Interpleader.** Procedimiento para obligar a reclamantes adversos a litigar entre sí. Todas las personas que tuvieran reclamaciones contra el demandante podrán ser acumuladas como demandadas y ser requeridas para que litiguen entre sí cuando sus reclamaciones fueren de tal naturaleza que el demandante quedare o pudiere quedar expuesto a una responsabilidad doble o múltiple. (Reglas Fed. del Proc. Civ., sec. 22(1)).

**Interpretation.** Interpretación, explicación.

**Interpretation of statements and other conduct.** Interpretación de declaraciones y otras conductas. Las declaraciones y demás conducta de cada una de las partes se interpretarán conforme a su intención, siempre que la otra la haya conocido o no la haya podido ignorar. (Unidroit, Prin., art. 4.2).

**Interpreter, compensation.** Intérprete, compensación. La corte podrá nombrar intérpretes de su propia selección y podrá fijar su compensación razonable. La compensación será pagada de los fondos provistos por ley o por una o más partes según lo dispusiera la corte o podrá imponerse en última instancia como costas, a discreción de la corte. (R. Fed. P. Civ., sec. 43).

**Interrogation.** Interrogatorio. La corte ejercitará un control razonable sobre el modo y el orden del interrogatorio de los testigos y la presentación de evidencia a fin de 1) hacer el interrogatorio y la presentación efectivos para el esclarecimiento de la verdad, 2) evitar el consumo innecesario de tiempo, y 3) proteger a los testigos contra hostigamiento o situación embarazosa excesiva. (Regla 611(a), R. Fed. Evid.).

**Interrogatories to parties.** Interrogatorios a las partes. Cualquier parte podrá notificar a cualquiera otra parte interrogatorios por escrito para ser contestados por la parte notificada o, si la parte notificada fuere una corporación pública o privada o una sociedad o asociación o agencia gubernamental, por cualquier funcionario o agente, quien suministrará la información que estuviere disponible para la parte. (Reglas Fed. del Proc. Civ., sec. 33(a)).

**Interstate commerce.** Comercio interestatal.

**Intervening cause.** Causa interveniente.

**Intervenor.** Parte interveniente.

**Intervention of right.** Intervención como cuestión de derecho. Mediante la oportuna solicitud se permitirá a cualquier persona intervenir en un pleito: 1) cuando una ley de los Estados Unidos confiera un derecho incondicional a intervenir; 2) cuando el solicitante reclame un derecho en relación con los bienes o acto objetos del pleito y se encuentre en tal situación que la adjudicación del pleito pudiera como cuestión práctica perjudicar o dificultar su capacidad para proteger tal derecho, a menos que el derecho del peticionario estuviera adecuadamente representado por las partes apersonadas. (R. Fed. P. Civ., sec. 24(a)).

**Intestacy.** Situación en la que se encuentra quien no hubiese redactado un testamento válido. Ab intestato.

**Intimidation.** Intimidación, coacción, coerción, compelimiento.

**Intoxicating.** Embriagante, intoxicante.

**Intruder.** Intruso.

**Intrusion upon seclusion.** Violación de privacidad. Una persona que intencionalmente se interponga o se inmiscuya, ya sea físicamente o de cualquier otra forma en la soledad o aislamiento de otro o en sus asuntos privados, será sujeto a responsabilidad por una invasión a la privacidad de ese otro, si la intrusión resulta altamente ofensiva a una persona razonable. (Rstmnt, 2nd, Torts, sec. 652 B).

**Inure.** Beneficiar.

**Invalid judgment.** Sentencia inválida. Una sentencia dictada en un estado y usada como base para una reclamación o defensa para una acción subsiguiente en otro Estado, puede ser atacada en el transcurso de la acción subsiguiente, alegando que dicha sentencia se dictó en incumplimiento con los requisitos que exigen que el tribunal sentenciador tenga jurisdicción territorial, jurisdicción sobre la cosa en controversia, y que ejerza dicha jurisdición notificando adecuadamente a las partes. (Rstmnt, 2nd, Judg., sec. 81).

**Invalidity.** Invalidez.

**Invasion of privacy.** Ataque a la privacidad, a la vida privada.

**Investiture.** Investidura.

**Investment.** Inversión de dinero, bienes o trabajo.

**Investment securities.** Valores de inversión. El tercer desprendimiento de la *Negotiable Instruments Law* se refiere a los valores corporativos que forman el Artículo 8 del Código de Comercio Uniforme. La consideración que reciben se aparta de la vieja ley al permitir el traspaso y negociación de valores corporativos sin poner las trabas y restricciones legales que para su negociación existían bajo la *Negotiable Instruments Law*. Las nuevas disposiciones retienen el derecho del comprador de buena fe por valor o causa onerosa de adquirir sin sujeción a las posibles reclamaciones contra su cedente. (C.C.U., Prefacio).

**Investor.** Inversor.

**Inviolable.** Inviolable, inmune.

**Invitee.** Invitado. El concepto del invitado abarca tanto al invitado público como a un visitante de negocios. (Rstmnt, 2nd, Torts, sec. 332).

**Invoice or manifest of the cargo.** Conocimiento o guía de la carga.

**Involuntary dismissal.** Desestimación involuntaria. Por dejar el demandante de proseguir el pleito o de cumplir con estas reglas o cualquier orden de la corte, un demandado podrá pedir mediante moción que se desestime el pleito o cualquier reclamación contra el mismo. (R. Fed. P. Civ., sec. 41(b)).

**Involuntary manslaughter.** Homicidio involuntario. Comete el delito de homicidio involuntario aquél que dé muerte ilegal a un ser humano sin que medie malicia, cuando ocurre al realizarse un acto legal que no constituyere delito grave; o al realizarse un acto legal que pudiera ocasionar muerte en forma ilegal, o sin la debida prudencia o circunspección. (Pueblo v. Matos Pretto, 93 D.P.R. 113 (1966)).

**Irrecoverable.** Imposible de recuperar.

**Irrefutable.** Irrefutable.

**Irregular notice.** Notificación defectuosa. Si se ha efectuado notificación real sobre la pendencia de una acción, las irregularidades en el contenido o procedimiento con que se efectuó dicha notificación no anularán su efecto ni la convertirán en defectuosa o inadecuada. (Rstmnt, 2nd, Judg., sec. 3).

**Irregularity.** Irregularidad.

**Irresponsible.** Irresponsable.

**Irrevocable.** Irrevocable.

**Irrevocable offer.** Oferta irrevocable. La regla tradicional en los Estados Unidos es que el oferente puede retirar la oferta en cualquier momento anterior a que sea aceptada; una promesa de no retirar la oferta no se considera efectiva si no media contraprestación. (Intro al USA). [Ver: *consideration.*]

**IRS, Internal Revenue Service.** Dirección Recaudadora de Impuestos. La responsabilidad primaria en la administración de las leyes encabezado por el *Commissioner of Internal Revenue* (Comisionado de Recaudaciones Internas) bajo la supervisión de la Secretaría del Tesoro. (Intro al USA).

**Issue.** Cuestión, tema, emisión de documentos (s). Expedir, emitir, enviar, mandar, remitir (v).

**Issue preclusion.** Preclusión de una cuestión. Cuando mediante sentencia válida, final y firme se resuelve una controversia de hecho o de derecho que fue litigada apropiadamente y la resolución de la controversia fuere esencial para la sentencia, la resolución de dicha sentencia será concluyente en una acción posterior entre las partes, ya sea por la misma reclamación o por una diferente. (Restatement, Second, Judgments, sec. 27). Principio e impedimento de controversias.

**Issuer.** Emisor.

**Issuance.** Expedición, emisión.

**Item.** Item, número o concepto dentro de una lista.

**Itemized statement of the account.** Detalle de las partidas de la cuenta.

**Itinerant worker.** Trabajador itinerante.

# J

**J.D.** *Juris Doctor*. Título otorgado a los estudiantes que se reciben de abogados en facultades de derecho estadounidenses. Se trata de un título de abogado solamente, no de un doctorado. El título no faculta a ejercer el derecho, para lo cual debe aprobarse un largo y complicado examen llamado el *bar exam*.

**Jactitation.** Jactancia. Se aplica típicamente al que dice ser cónyuge de cierta persona o heredero de otra, sin que sea ello cierto.

**Jail.** Cárcel, prisión, calabozo (s). Mandar a la cárcel, aprisionar, recluir (v).

**Jailer.** Carcelero, celador.

**Jailhouse lawyer.** Preso en una carcel que entiende de cuestiones jurídicas aplicables a sus compañeros de reclusión, a quienes aconseja.

**Jane Doe.** Nombre de mujer ficticio, fulana de tal, NN. Ver *John Doe*.

**Jaundice.** Ictericia.

**Jaywalker.** Peatón que cruza una calle en forma ilegal, por el medio en vez de hacerlo por las esquinas.

**Jeopardize.** Comprometer, arriesgar, exponer, poner en peligro.

**Jeopardy.** Riesgo, peligro.

**Jettison.** Alijo, echazón (s). Alijar, echar mercancías al mar para salvar el resto de la carga.

**Job.** Empleo, trabajo, tarea.

**John Doe.** Nombre de varón ficticio, fulano de tal, NN. Ver *Jane Doe*.

**Join.** Acumular.

**Joinder.** Acumulación de acciones o de partes.

**Joinder of additional parties.** Inclusión de partes adicionales. Podrá hacerse parte de una reconvención o demanda contra coparte a personas que no fueren partes en el pleito original. (Reglas Fed. de Proc. Civ., sec. 13(h)).

**Joinder of claims.** Acumulación de reclamaciones. Toda parte que expusiere una reclamación de remedio como demanda original, reconvención, demanda contra coparte o demanda contra tercero, podrá acumular, como reclamaciones independientes o alternativas, cuantas reclamaciones de ley, de equidad o marítimas tuviera contra la parte adversa. (R. Fed. P. Civ., sec. 18(a)).

**Joinder of defendants.** Acumulación de acusados. Dos o más acusados podrán ser incluidos en el mismo indiciamiento o acusación si se les imputare haber participado en el mismo acto u operación o en la misma serie de actos u operaciones que constituyan un delito o delitos. (Regla 8(b), Reglas Fed. de Proc. Crim.).

**Joinder of offenses.** Acumulación de delitos. Dos o más delitos podrán imputarse en el mismo indiciamiento o acusación en cargos separados para cada delito, si dichos delitos imputados, ya fueran delitos graves o delitos menos graves o ambos, son de la misma o similar naturaleza o están basados en el mismo acto u operación o en dos o más actos u operaciones relacionados entre sí o que constituyen partes de un designio o plan común. (Regla 8(a), Reglas Fed. de Proc. Crim.).

**Joint.** Conjunto, solidario.

**Joint and several obligation.** Obligación mancomunada.

**Joint creditor.** Acreedor solidario.

**Joint debtor.** Deudor solidario, codeudor.

**Joint liability.** Responsabilidad solidaria.

**Joint resolution.** Resolución conjunta.

**Joint tortfeasor.** Coparticipante en la comisión de un cuasidelito.

**Joint venture.** Empresa común. Cuando concurren los siguientes hechos: a) aportación (*contribution*) de dinero, propiedad, tiempo o destreza en un empeño común (*common undertaking*); b) un interés propietario conjunto y un manejo mutuo del negocio; c) participación en las ganancias, aparte de cualquier retribución recibida en concepto de sueldo, y aunque no haya participación en las pérdidas. (Suárez Fuentes v. Srio. de Hacienda, 85 D.P.R. 388 (1962)).

**Journeyman.** Bracero.

**Judge.** Juez. Los jueces provienen del foro prácticante mucho más a menudo que de la docencia o de la función pública. No hay en los Estados Unidos una carrera judicial como en otros países; no hay ninguna ruta trazada para el abogado recién recibido que aspira a llegar a juez. (Intro al USA).

Juez, magistrado (s). Sentenciar, fallar, decidir (v).

**Judge, election.** Juez, elección. Los jueces estaduales habitualmente son electos, en la mayor parte de los casos por voto popular, en otros por la legislatura del estado. (Intro al USA).

**Judgment.** Sentencia. "Sentencia," incluirá resoluciones y cualesquiera órdenes que puedan apelarse. La sentencia no contendrá relación de alegaciones, informes de comisionados o autos de procedimientos anteriores.

**Judgment based on mistake.** Sentencia basada en error. Sujeto a algunas limitaciones se puede evitar una sentencia dictada en una acción contenciosa si dicha sentencia fue el resultado de un error de derecho o de hecho. (Rstmnt, 2nd, Judg., sec. 71).

**Judgment based upon another one that is subsequently reversed.** Sentencia basada en otra que luego es anulada. Una sentencia basada en otra que se dictó previamente no se anulará automáticamente por razón de que la sentencia previa fue revocada en apelación de alguna otra manera anulada. (Rstmnt, 2nd, Judg., sec. 16).

**Judgment book.** Libro de sentencias, registro de sentencias.

**Judgment by confession.** Sentencia por confesión. Desígnase como sentencia por confesión el procedimiento sumario por convenio consagrado por el *Common Law* y autorizado por nuestro código procesal, mediante el cual una parte confiesa que adeuda a otra determinada cantidad y acepta que un tribunal le dicte sentencia en su contra, sin más. (E.L.A. v. Isla Verde Inv. Corp., 98 D.P.R. 255 (1970)).

**Judgment by default.** Sentencia en rebeldía. Una sentencia en rebeldía no será distinta en especie ni excederá la cuantía de lo pedido en la demanda. (R. Fed. P. Civ., sec. 54(c)).

**Judgment determining interests in things.** Sentencia que determina derechos reales. Cuando se dicta sentencia válida, final y firme en una acción basada solamente en jurisdicción para adjudicar los intereses sobre una cosa: La sentencia tendrá carácter concluyente con respecto a los intereses sobre la cosa en cuanto a todas las personas si ése es el propósito de la sentencia (tradicionalmente descrito como in rem), o en cuanto a las partes en la acción, si ése es el propósito de la sentencia tradicionalmente descrito como quasi in rem. (Rstmnt, 2nd, Judg., sec. 30).

**Judgment for defendant, rule of bar.** Sentencia para el demandado, preclusión de la acción. Una sentencia válida, final y firme, dictada a favor de la persona del demandado, prohibe al demandante radicar cualquier otra acción basada en la misma reclamación. (Rstmnt, 2nd, Judg., sec. 19).

**Judgment for plaintiff, merger rule.** Sentencia para el demandante, consolidación de la acción. Cuando se dicta sentencia válida, final y firme a favor de un demandante: El demandante no podrá subsiguientemente sostener su reclamación original, ni parte de la misma, en ningún tipo de acción, con excepción de acciones basadas en la sentencia. (Rstmnt, 2nd Judg., sec. 18).

**Judgment for specific acts.** Sentencia para ejecutar actos específicos. Si una sentencia ordenara a una parte que otorgue un traspaso de terreno o que entregue escrituras u otros documentos o que ejecute cualquier otro acto específico y la parte dejara de cumplir dentro del plazo especificado, la corte podrá ordenar que se ejecute el acto a expensas de la parte desobediente por cualquier otra parte nombrada por la corte, y cuando se ejecutare el acto éste tendrá el mismo efecto que si hubiera sido ejecutado por la parte obligada. (R. Fed. P. Civ., sec. 70).

**Judgment *non obstante veredicto*, directed judgment.** La parte perdedora puede presentar una moción de sentencia a pesar del veredicto (*non obstante veredicto*) que permite al juez dictar sentencia a su favor, yendo al fondo de la cuestión, cuando antes no tuvo éxito en una moción de veredicto dirigido en su favor. (Intro al USA).

**Judgment roll.** Legajo de la sentencia.

**Judicial.** Judicial.

**Judicial action.** Acción judicial, causa, litigio, pleito.

**Judicial notice.** Conocimiento judicial. Un hecho del cual podrá tomarse conocimiento judicial habrá de ser uno que no esté sujeto a una controversia razonable porque sea generalmente conocido dentro de la jurisdicción territorial de la corte. (Regla 201(b)(c),(d), R. Fed. Evid.).

**Judicial notice, instructing the jury.** Conocimiento judicial, instrucciones al jurado. En una acción o procedimiento civil, la corte instruirá al jurado para que acepte como concluyente cualquier hecho del que se tomó conocimiento judicial. (Regla 201(g), R. Fed. Evid.).

**Judicial officer.** Funcionario judicial.

**Judicial orders.** Diligencias.

**Judicial penalty.** Pena judicial. La orden de un tribunal de ejecutar la prestación puede agregar la prevención de que si la parte no cumple, pagará una pena. (Unidroit, Prin., art. 7.2.4).

**Judicial process.** Diligencias judiciales.

**Judicial review.** Control judicial. La revisión judicial, tal como el término es usado en el derecho constitucional norteamericano, se refiere al poder de un tribunal de decidir sobre la constitucionalidad de la legislación, y de negar vigencia a aquella legislación que decida que es inválida por motivos constitucionales. (Intro al USA).

**Judiciary, judicature.** Poder judicial. Judicatura.

**Juridical.** Jurídico.

**Juridical person.** Persona de existencia moral, persona jurídica.

**Jurisdiction.** Competencia judicial, jurisdicción. En los Estados Unidos, existen tres métodos básicos para asegurar la competencia. Existe la competencia in personam y la competencia in rem; estos términos significan prácticamente lo mismo en el derecho norteamericano que en el derecho civil Napoleónico. Una tercera base de la com-petencia se está desarrollando en los Estados Unidos; ella es la *quasi in rem*. No existe nada comparado a la competencia *quasi in rem* en la mayoría de los otros países. (Carl).

**Jurisdiction, doing business in state.** Jurisdicción, actos de negociación en el territorio. Un Estado tiene el poder de ejercer su jurisdicción sobre una corporación extranjera que haya hecho o causado un acto, respecto al cual pueda surgir una causa de acción por daños y perjuicios. (Rstmnt, 2nd, Conflict, sec. 49(1)).

**Jurisdiction *in personam*.** Competencia sobre la persona. Existen cinco alternativas de base para la competencia *in personam* en los Estados Unidos. Ellas son: 1) domicilio o residencia del demandado en el Estado, 2) consentimiento, 3) comparecencia, 4) presencia física del demandado y entrega de la notificación o citación en ese Estado y 5) realización de ciertos actos en el estado, como los de llevar a cabo negocios o realizar contratos. Si cualquiera de estas alternativas pueden ser satisfechas, entonces la corte tiene competencia personal. (Carl).

**Jurisdiction over litigants concerning related claims.** Jurisdicción sobre litigantes respecto de acciones conexas. Un tribunal podrá ejercer jurisdicción sobre una persona que sea parte en una acción pendiente en ése o en cualquier otro tribunal del mismo estado cuando la reclamación objeto de la acción surja como producto de la transacción objeto de la acción pendiente, o sea otra acción que en el ejercicio de la justicia pueda ser ventilada simultánea o concurrentemente. (Rstmnt, 2nd, Judg., sec. 9).

**Jurisdiction, physical presence and notification.** Competencia, presencia física y notificación. El método más común utilizado en los Estados Unidos para obtener competencia es sencillamente encontrar al demandado en el Estado y entregar la notificación y la demanda a él. En la jurisprudencia norteamericana este acto tiene un doble propósito: 1) le otorga la competencia a la corte y 2) le informa al demandado sobre la demanda. Debido a lo frecuente de este método, los expertos norteamericanos en materia legal tienden a combinar "competencia" y "notificación" en una sola idea, en vez de separarla en dos problemas diferentes. (Carl).

**Jurisdictional grounds.** Bases de competencia. Si el procedimiento seguido para notificar y para dar una oportunidad de defensa no cumple con los criterios de razonabilidad y de equidad y justicia que la Corte Suprema ha fijado para el cumplimiento de la cláusula, la sentencia es inválida. (Intro al USA).

**Juror.** Miembro del jurado.

**Jury.** Jurado. Sus miembros son elegidos por azar entre un conjunto de ciudadanos respetable y representativos de la comunidad que ha sido convocado a estos efectos. Los jurados de *common law* eran doce, pero ahora en muchos estados el número es menor (seis como mínimo). (Intro al USA).

**Jury trial.** Juicio por jurado. El derecho a juicio por jurado declarado por la Enmienda Séptima de la Constitución o conferido por una ley de los Estados Unidos se preservará inviolado para las partes. (Regla Fed. de Proc. Civ., sec. 38(a)(b)).

***Jus tertii* (L).** Derechos de un tercero.

**Just.** Justo, equitativo.

**Just cause.** Justa causa.

**Just cause for discharge.** Justa causa para el despido. Se entenderá por justa causa para el despido de un empleado de un establecimiento: a) que el obrero siga un patrón de conducta impropia o desordenada. b) la actitud del empleado de no rendir su trabajo en forma eficiente o de hacerlo tardía y negligentemente o en violación de las normas de calidad del producto que se produce o maneja por el establecimiento. (29 LPRA sec. 185(b)).

**Justice.** Justicia. Juez.

**Justiciable.** Controversia que puede ser objeto de una acción judicial.

**Justifiable.** Justificado, justificable.

**Juvenile.** Juvenil.

# K

**K.B.** Ver *King's Bench.*

**K.C.** Ver *King's Counsel.*

**Kangaroo court.** Tribunal parcial que conduce el proceso como una mera formalidad y que ya tiene decidido el caso de antemano.

**Keelage.** Derechos de amarre de una nave.

**Keep.** Continuar con una acción o acto, guardar, llevar, mantener, retener.

**Keep books.** Mantener los papeles y documentos en orden, llevar la contabilidad, realizar anotaciones sistemáticas y descriptivas en una actividad comercial.

**Keep the peace.** Mantener el orden.

**Key.** Llave, clave, muelle.

**Keyage.** Derecho de amarre, derecho de carga y descarga (mar).

**Kickback.** Especie de comisión pagada a un funcionario público o a alguien que trabaja para el comprador a fin de realizar la transacción. Normalmente una conducta ilegal.

**Kidnapping.** Secuestro, rapto.

**Kill.** Matar, asesinar.

**Killer.** Homicida, asesino.

**Kin, kindred.** Pariente, emparentado, relacionado por vínculo de sangre.

**Kind, in.** En especie.

**King.** Rey, majestad, monarca, soberano.

**King can do no wrong.** Literalmente, el Soberano no puede hacer nada mal o nada ilegal. Se utiliza la expresión para denotar aquellos sistemas en los que las acciones contra el Estado por actos ilícitos se encuentran prohibidas o severamente restringidas.

**King regent.** Rey regente.

**King's Bench.** Tribunal superior del sistema judicial inglés.

**King's Counsel.** Cuerpo colegiado de abogados que asesora a la Corona. En tiempos en que gobierna una reina, la institución se llama *Queen's Counsel*, o Q.C. Los abogados pertenecientes a este grupo colocan ya sea K.C. o Q.C., según el caso, detrás de sus nombres, junto con sus calificaciones profesionales.

**Kiting.** Usar cheques cuando el respectivo depósito todavía no ha sido acreditado, especulando con que sí lo esté al momento de la presentación.

**Kleptomania.** Cleptomanía.

**Knight.** Orden nobiliaria, caballero.

**Knock and announce rule.** Obligación de la fuerza pública de anunciar su arribo y la razón del mismo antes de ingresar a una morada.

**Know all men by these presents.** Sépase por la presente. Forma antigua de comenzar un documento dando a entender su carácter público.

**Knowingly.** A sabiendas, concientemente.

**Knowledge.** Conocimiento sobre algún asunto.

**Knowledge and belief.** Leal saber y entender.

**Knowledge and notice.** Conocimiento y notificación. Una persona tiene notificación de un hecho si la persona conoce del hecho, tiene razón para conocer del hecho, debería conocer del hecho o ha sido notificada del mismo. (Rstmnt, 2nd, Agency, sec. 9(1)).

**Known.** Sabido, conocido.

**Known heirs.** Herederos conocidos.

**Known to me.** De mi conocimiento.

# L

**L.C.** Ver *Lord Chancellor.*

**LL.B., J.D., LL.M., J.S.D.** A pesar del carácter de postgrado de los estudios, la mayor parte de las escuelas de leyes otorgaba el título de *Bachelor of Laws* (LL.B.) en lugar de un doctorado hasta 1970 aproximadamente, en que se comenzó a reemplazar por el *Juris Doctor* (J.D.). Algunas instituciones ofrecen además los títulos de *Master of Laws* (LL.M.) y *Doctor of the Science of Law* (J.S.D. o S.J.D.), que requieren estudios adicionales. (Intro al USA).

**LL.D.** *Doctor of Laws*, título de Doctor en Derecho otorgado por univesidades inglesas y estadounidenses.

**LTD.** Iniciales de *limited*, denotando un tipo específico de sociedad comercial.

**Labor.** Trabajo, actividad laboral (s). Trabajar (v).

**Labor accident.** Accidente de trabajo.

**Labor contract.** Contrato de trabajo. "Contrato de trabajo" significa todo convenio verbal o escrito mediante el cual se obliga el empleado a ejecutar una obra, realizar una labor o prestar un servicio para el patrono por un salario o cualquier otra retribución pecuniaria. (29 LPRA).

**Labor dispute.** Disputa obrera, de trabajo. El término disputa obrera incluye cualquier controversia relativa a término o condiciones de empleo o relativa a la asociación o representación de personas al negociar, fijar, mantener, cambiar o tratar de llegar a un acuerdo sobre términos o condiciones de empleo, aunque las partes se encuentren o no en la relación inmediata de patrono y empleado. (29 LPRA sec. 109(c)).

**Labor, in.** Etapa final del proceso de dar a luz.

**Labor law, branches.** Derecho laboral, ramas. La primera rama se ocupe del bienestar de los trabajadores como individuos. Esta rama incluye las leyes estaduales que instituyen compensaciones por accidente de trabajo, las que establecen normas sobre honorarios y salarios, las que prohíben el trabajo infantil insalubre, o las que proscriben la discriminación por motivos raciales, religiosos o de nacionalidad. (Intro al USA).

**Labor law, definition.** Derecho laboral, definición. El derecho laboral, en su sentido más amplio, es aquel que afecta a los trabajadores en virtud de su relación con un empleador, que en los Estrados Unidos es de ordinario privado. (Intro al USA).

**Labor-management controversy.** Controversia obrero patronal.

**Labor union.** Uniones, sindicatos.

**Laborer.** Asalariado, trabajador, obrero.

**Laches.** Defensa de incuria. Para que esta defensa prospere la dilación en el ejercicio de un derecho debe haber causado algún daño al demandado. Se trata de una defensa basada en razones de equidad. (Morales Lebrón).

**Lack.** Carencia de, falta de.

**Lack of evidence.** Falta de prueba.

**Lack of inventory.** Falta de existencia.

**Lack of jurisdiction.** Incompetencia.

**Lame duck.** Funcionario cuyo mandato está próximo a expirar y que no puede ser reelecto o ha perdido la reelección.

**Land.** Tierras.

**Landlord.** Arrendador de un inmueble.

**Lapse.** Lapso, fenecimiento, caducidad (s). Caducar, fenecer (v).

**Lapsing of an action.** Caducidad o perención de instancia.

**Larceny.** Hurto.

**Last clear chance.** Teoría de la última oportunidad. Aquélla que da por sentado la existencia de una situación peligrosa creada por la negligencia tanto del demandante como del demandado, pero supone que hubo un momento después de ocurrir tal negligencia en que el demandado podía, y el demandante no podía, mediante el uso de los medios disponibles, evitar el accidente. (Morales Lebrón).

**Last clear chance, helpless plaintiff.** Última oportunidad efectiva, demandante imposibilitado. Un demandante que negligentemente se ha sometido a un riesgo de sufrir daño como consecuencia de la negligencia subsiguiente del demandado, puede recobrar por el daño si inmediatamente antes de sufrir tal daño: el demandante estaba imposibilitado de poder evitarlo mediante el ejercicio de un cuidado razonable. (Restatemente, Second, Torts, sec. 479).

**Late acceptance.** Delay in transmission. Aceptación tardía. Demora en la transmisión. No obstante, la aceptación tardía producirá efectos si el oferente informa inmediatamente de ello al destinatario o le envía una comunicación en tal sentido. (Unidroit, Prin., art. 2.9).

**Laudemio.** Laudemio.

**Laughing heir statute.** Ley que establece un límite de parentesco mínimo para la sucesión intestada.

**Law.** Ley, derecho. La palabra *law* se usa en inglés, tanto, para referirse a la suma de todas las normas legales (por lo tanto, equivalente a las siguientes de otros idiomas: *ius, droit, diritto, Recht, derecho*) como a la norma expresa establecida por una autoridad legislativa (*lex, loi, legge, Gesetz, ley*). (Intro al USA).

Abogacía, carrera de abogado.

**Law and equity.** Derecho y equidad. La historia de esta distinción comienza con el sistema jurídico que se desarrollo con posterioridad a la conquista de Inglaterra por los normandos. Un litigante que deseaba que su demanda fuese vista en los tribunales reales y no en los locales debía comprar en la oficina del *chancellor* un *writ* u orden real acorde con la demanda, que ordenaba la presentación del demandado ante el tribunal. (Intro al USA).

**Law clerk.** Oficial jurídico. Empleado en un bufete de abogados.

**Law of the case.** Ley del caso. Es un principio bien sentado que las cuestiones discutidas y resueltas en una apelación constituyen la ley del caso (*law of the case*), y no pueden ser objeto de nueva argu-

mentación en una segunda apelación interpuesta en el mismo caso. (Morales Lebrón).

**Law office.** Bufete, estudio, despacho jurídico, oficina de abogados.

**Law-office failure.** Error cometido por un despacho jurídico en la tramitación de un pleito.

**Law professor.** Profesor de derecho. En los Estados Unidos los profesores de leyes, como los jueces, no necesitan cumplir un período como aprendices antes de ser nombrados y muy a menudo provienen directamente del ejercicio activo de la profesión. (Intro al USA).

**Law reviews.** Revistas jurídicas. Las más prestigiosas son las publicaciones universitarias; hoy existe más de doscientas. (Intro al USA).

**Law, study.** Derecho, estudio. Durante los tres años de entrenamiento profesional intensivo, el estudiante es sometido al método de enseñanza peculiarmente norteamericano conocido como *case method* (método de análisis de casos). (Intro al USA).

**Lawful.** Lícito, legal.

**Lawless.** Ilícito, ilegal.

**Laws, federal.** Leyes federales. Además de enumerar ciertas facultades legislativas especificas del Congreso, la Constitución le otorga la atribución de "hacer todas las leyes que sean necesario y apropiadas para el ejercicio" de aquellos poderes que son otorgados expresamente a cualquier departamento o división de la administración federal. (Intro al USA).

**Laws, state.** Leyes estatales. Las leyes aprobadas por las legislaturas estaduales, aunque supeditadas a la legislación federal valida y a las Constituciones estaduales, son de importancia fundamental en las numerosas áreas del Derecho que han quedado en la esfera estadual. De acuerdo con la Décima Enmienda de la Constitucion, "los poderes no delegados a los Estados Unidos por la Constitución, y que ella no prohíbe a los estados, quedan reservados a los respectivos estados o al pueblo." (Intro al USA).

**Lay off.** Cesantía.

**Lay witness.** Testigo que no depone como experto o perito en alguna materia.

**Layman.** Seglar, lego, secular.

**Lead to error.** Inducir a error.

**Leading case.** Caso que determina el derecho y, como tal, seguido por los jueces. Caso guía.

**Leading question.** Pregunta sugestiva o capciosa. De ordinario no se permitirán preguntas sugestivas en el contrainterrogatorio. Cuando una parte llame a un testigo hostil, a una parte adversa o a un testigo identificado con una parte adversa, el interrogatorio podrá hacerse mediante preguntas sugestivas. (Regla 611(c), Reglas Fed. en Evidencia).

**Lease.** Arrendamiento, aparcería, arriendo, alquiler, locación.

**Lease for partnership of arable lands.** Aparcería de tierras de labor.

**Leasehold.** Propiedad sujeta a locación.

**Leaseholder.** Arrendatario.

**Leases, uniform commercial code.** Locación , código de comercio uniforme. El nuevo Artículo 2A—agregado en 1987— representa un acontecimiento importante en el derecho comercial al referirse a un tipo de transacción comercial, el alquiler de propiedad personal, que ha existido desde hace mucho. (C.C.U., Prefacio).

**Leave.** Permiso, autorización, licencia, permiso.

**Leaving no blank space.** Sin blancos.

**Lecturer.** Profesor universitario. Conferencista.

**Legacy.** Legado.

**Legal.** Legal, lícito.

**Legal aid.** Defensoría de pobres. Uno de lo objetivos de muchas de las asociaciones de abogados es el de poner los servicios jurídicos al alcance de más personas, en especial de las de menos recursos. (Intro al USA).
Patrocinio jurídico gratuito a indigentes.

**Legal impossibility.** Imposibilidad legal. Si el cumplimiento de un deber se hace imposible por tener que cumplir con una norma u orden gubernamental doméstica o extranjera, tal norma u orden es un evento cuya no-ocurrencia es un presupuesto básico sobre el cual se hizo el contrato. (Rstmnt, 2nd, Con., sec. 264).

**Legal opinion.** Opinión legal emitida por un funcionario dentro del area de su competencia o por un experto en la materia.

**Legal owner.** Dueño directo.

**Legal reserve.** Reserva legal. Se entiende por "reserva legal" la cantidad mínima que todo banco sujeto estará obligado a tener siempre disponible. (7 LPRA sec. 3).

**Legal tender.** Curso legal, moneda de curso forzoso.

**Legalistic.** Forma de expresar que una cuestión jurídica es excesivamente técnica o innecesariamente complicada.

**Legatee.** Legatario.

**Legator.** Testador.

**Legislative.** Legislativo.

**Legislative immunity.** Inmunidad parlamentaria.

**Legislative power.** Poder legislativo. Congreso.

**Legislature.** Congreso, Asamblea Nacional, Parlamento.

**Legitimacy.** Legitimidad.

**Legitimate.** Legítimo.

**Lend.** Prestar, otorgar.

**Lender.** Prestamista.

**Lender on bottomry.** Prestador a la gruesa.

**Lending rate.** Porcentual de interés al que se realiza un préstamo.

**Lessee.** Arrendatario, inquilino, locatario.

**Lessor.** Arrendador, arrendante, locador.

**Let.** Arrendar o alquilar un bien inmueble.

**Lethal injection.** Inyección con la que se ejecuta la pena de muerte.

**Letter of advice of international sight draft.** Carta de aviso de giro internacional a la vista. Una "carta de aviso" es la comunicación del librador al librado de que el giro descrito ha sido librado. (C.C.U. sec. 3-701).

**Letter of intent.** Carta de intención. Documento que describe cual es la intención de las partes para facilitar la prueba que eventualmente se pudiese necesitar. Generalmente no es un instrumento obligatorio como lo es un contrato.

**Letter of marque.** Patente de corso.

**Letters of credit, uniform commercial code.** Cartas de crédito, código de comercio uniforme.

Salvo pacto en contrario el término "carta de crédito" o "crédito bancario" en un contrato de venta significa un crédito irrevocable expedido por una agencia de financiamiento de buena reputación y, cuando el embarque sea para ultramar, por una agencia de buena reputación internacional. La falta del comprador de entregar oportunamente una carta de crédito convenida será una violación al contrato de venta. (C.C.U. sec. 325).

**Letters rogatory.** Exhorto, carta rogatoria.

**Letters testamentary.** Cartas testamentarias. Declaratoria de herederos cuando no hay un testamento.

**Leverage.** El control que se ejerce con una parte menor del capital, o de una inversión, sobre el resto.

**Levy.** Embargo, exacción, incautación, gravamen (s). Gravar con un impuesto o cargo (v).

**Lex fori (L).** Ley del foro o del tribunal. Ley local.

**Liability.** Pasivo, deudas. Responsabilidad, culpa, culpabilidad.

**Liability of independent contractor's employer.** Responsabilidad del empleador de un contratista independiente. Con ciertas excepciones el que emplea un contratista independiente no será responsable por los daños corporales causados a otro individuo por un acto u omisión del contratista a quienes le sirvan a éste. (Rstmnt, 2nd, Torts, sec. 409).

**Liability of supplier of dangerous chattel.** Responsabilidad del proveedor de cosa mueble peligrosa. Quien supla, directamente o a través de un tercero, un bien mueble a otro individuo, será responsable ante las personas quienes se espera que utilicen el bien mueble con el consentimiento de ese otro individuo o ante quienes peligran por su uso, por los daños físicos que se ocasione por el uso de dicho bien mueble. (Rstmnt, 2nd, Torts, sec. 388).

**Liability of vendor of land for undisclosed danger.** Responsabilidad del vendedor de tierras por peligro no revelado. 1) Un vendedor de tierras que oculta u omite comunicar a su comprador cualquier condición, ya sea natural o artificial, que envuelva un riesgo irrazonable a las personas que ocupen un terreno, será responsable ante el comprador y las demás personas con el consentimiento del comprador o subcomprador por los daños corporales causados por dicha condición, después que el comprador haya tomado posesión. (Rstmnt, 2nd, Torts, sec. 353).

**Liaison.** Enlace, unión.

**Libel.** Libelo, calumnia, difamación (s). Difamar, injuriar (v). El libelo consiste de una publicación de material difamatorio, ya sea mediante palabras escritas o impresas, contenidas en un documento o cualquier otra forma de comunicación que tenga las mismas cualidades potencialmente dañinas de las palabras escritas o impresas. (Rstmnt, 2nd, Torts, sec. 568(1)).

**Libel per quod.** Libelo *per quod.* Los elementos esenciales de la modalidad del libelo denominada libelo per quod son la malicia y los daños provenientes de los alegados errores de la publicación, elementos que no se probaron en este caso. (Sanfiorenzo Acosta v. El Mundo, Inc. 87 D.P.R. 281 (1963)).

**Libelous.** Difamatorio, injurioso.

**Liberty.** Libertad.

**Liberty of conscience.** Libertad de conciencia.

**License.** Licencia, permiso, autorización (s). Licenciar (v).

**License to use a patent.** Licencia para usar una patente. Constituye una mera licencia para usar una patente cualquier cesión o traspaso de ésta que no sea: a) la cesión, venta o traspaso de la patente completa; b) la cesión, venta o traspaso de parte de la patente; y c) la cesión, venta o traspaso de la patente para hacer, vender o usar el producto o proceso patentado dentro de un área específica de los Estados Unidos. (González Chemical v. Srio. de Hacienda, 86 D.P.R. 72 (1962)).

**Licensee.** Licenciatario, concesionario, permisionario, autorizado. Un concesionario es aquella persona a quien se le ha concedido el privilegio de entrar o permanecer en un predio de terreno mediante el consentimiento del poseedor. (Rstmnt, 2nd, Torts, sec. 330).

**Lie.** Mentir. Mentira. Corresponder o resultar apropiado (en el caso de una acción jurídica).

**Lien.** Anotación de la litis. Embargo. Nexo. Restricción al dominio, gravamen.

**Lien creditor.** Acreedor con gravamen. Un "acreedor con gravamen" (Lien creditor) significa un acreedor que hubiere adquirido un gravamen sobre propiedad afectada por embargo, gravamen o cosa similar e incluye a un cesionario para beneficio de acreedores desde la fecha de la cesión, y a un *trustee* de quiebra desde la fecha de la radicación de la petición o a un administrador en equidad (*receiver in equity*) desde la fecha del nombramiento. Salvo que todos los acreedores representados tuviesen conocimiento del interés garantizado de tal representante. (C.C.U. sec. 9-301(3)).

**Lieutenant.** Teniente, lugar teniente, representante.

**Life estate.** Derechos propietarios (en el sentido del *common law*, no del derecho romanista) que una persona tiene en forma vitalicia.

**Life expectancy.** Expectativa de vida.

**Life imprisonment.** Cadena perpetua.

**Life insurance.** Seguro de vida. "Seguro de vida" es el seguro sobre vidas humanas o seguro correspondiente a las mismas o relacionadas con éstas. Para los fines de este título el negocio de seguros de vida incluye la concesión de rentas anuales y beneficios dotales, beneficios adicionales en caso de muerte o mutilación por accidente o medios accidentales, beneficios adicionales en caso de incapacidad total o permanente del asegurado, métodos opcionales para la liquidación de réditos. (26 LPRA sec. 402).

**Life member.** Miembro o socio vitalicio.

**Life peerage.** Título nobiliario vitalicio.

**Life sentence.** Cadena perpetua.

**Limited admissibility.** Admisibilidad limitada. Cuando determinada evidencia sea admisible en cuanto a una parte o para un propósito, pero inadmisible en cuanto a otra parte, o se admite para otro propósito, la corte, previa solicitud, limitará la evidencia

a su alcance apropiado e instruirá al jurado de conformidad. (Regla 105, R. Fed. Evid.).

**Limited jurisdiction.** Competencia limitada, por ejemplo sobre los bienes existentes dentro de la competencia territorial del juzgado. La competencia limitada sobre ciertos bienes no necesariamente acarrea competencia sobre la persona del demandado.

**Lineup.** Rueda de sospechosos.

**Linguistic discrepancies.** Discrepancias idiomáticas. En caso de discrepancia entre varias versiones idiomáticas del mismo contrato, todas con la misma jerarquía, se preferirá la interpretación acorde con la versión en el idioma en el cual el contrato fue redactado originalmente. (Unidroit, Prin., art. 4.7).

**Lion's share.** Porción leonina.

**Liquid assets.** Dinero o bienes de venta inmediata.

**Liquidate.** Liquidar, pagar.

**Liquidated damages.** Cláusula penal. La indemnización a ser recibida por razón de incumplimiento por cualquiera de las partes podrá ser acordada en el contrato sólo si constituye una cantidad razonable a la luz de la pérdida anticipada o real causada por el incumplimiento y de la dificultad de probar la pérdida. Por razones de orden publico no se harán cumplir cláusulas penales que impongan indemnizaciones excesivas e irrazonables como penalidad. (Rstmnt, 2nd, Con., sec. 356(1)).

**Liquidity.** Liquidez.

***Lis pendens* (L).** Excepción de litis pendencia.

**Listed securities.** Valores que se cotizan en bolsa.

**Literary property.** Propiedad literaria.

**Litigant.** Litigante, parte en un juicio.

**Litigator.** Abogado especializado en tramitar juicios. Procesalista.

**Litigious.** Litigioso.

**Littering.** Arrojar basura en forma ilegal.

**Littoral.** Litoral.

**Live together as husband and wife.** Vivir juntos, como marido y mujer.

**Livelihood.** Trabajo con el cual uno se gana la vida.

**Living trust.** Fideicomiso activo o constituído para suplantar un testamento y para evitar las complicaciones e incertidumbres de un proceso sucesorio.

**Living will.** Disposición testamentaria que comienza a tener vigencia durante la vida del testador. Normalmente incluye instrucciones que el paciente o su representante da a un médico o al hospital sobre si desea o no que lo mantengan viviendo artificialmente.

**Loan for fixed time.** Préstamo con vencimiento fijo.

**Loan secured by collateral.** Préstamo con garantía.

**Lobby.** Grupo de presión para obtener una legislación determinad (s). Tratar de influir sobre los legisladores (v).

**Lockout.** Lockout, cierre forzoso.

**Log book.** Libro diario de navegación.

**Lodge a complaint.** Presentar un reclamo o una queja.

**Lodger.** Inquilino, pensionista, locatario.

**Lodging house.** Casa de pensión.

**Lodgings.** Cuarto o cuartos arrendados como vivienda.

**Long-arm statute.** Ley que atribuye competencia judicial a un Estado cuando ciertos actos, o sus efectos, tienen lugar en tal Estado, aunque el demandado se domicilie en otra parte.

**Longhand.** Escrito de puño y letra.

**Longshoreman.** Estibador.

**Loophole.** Parte de una ley en la que, por imprevisión de legislador, se permite la realización de actos que, de haber sido mejor redactada tal ley, se hubiesen prohibido o se hubiesen penado.

**Lord Chancellor.** Persona en la cúspide del poder judicial inglés.

**Lord Chief Justice.** El juez de mayor jerarquía en materia penal del sistema judicial inglés.

**Losing party.** Parte vencida, derrotada, perdidosa.

**Loss.** Pérdida, daño.

**Loss of the right to avoid.** Adaptación del contrato en caso de error. Si una de las partes se encuentra facultada para dar por anulado el contrato por causa de error, pero la otra parte declara quererlo ejecutar o cumple el contrato tal como lo previó la parte facultada para darlo por anulado, el contrato se considerará celebrado en dichos términos. (Unidroit, Prin., art. 3.13).

**Losses and damages.** Daños y perjuicios.

**Lost, destroyed or stolen instruments.** Instrumentos perdidos, destruidos o robados. El dueño de un instrumento que se ha perdido por destrucción, robo o de cualquier otra forma, podrá iniciar una acción a su nombre y cobrar de cualquier parte obligada en el instrumento mediante la debida prueba de su condición de dueño, de los hechos que le impiden exhibir el instrumento y de los términos de éste. (C.C.U. sec. 3-804).

**Lost or destroyed stock certificates.** Certificados de acciones extraviados o destruidos. Toda corporación organizada podrá expedir un nuevo certificado de acciones del capital en sustitución de cualquier certificado de éstas anteriormente emitido y alegadamente extraviado o destruido. (14 LPRA sec. 1516).

**Lottery.** Lotería.

**Lower tenement.** Predio inferior.

**Loyalty oath.** Juramento de fidelidad.

**Lucid interval.** Intervalo lúcido.

**Lucrative title.** A título oneroso.

**Lump sum.** Suma global.

**Lynch.** Linchar.

# M

**M.D.** *Medical Doctor*, médico, doctor en medicina.

**Machination.** Maquinación, preparación de un ardid o treta con intención aviesa.

**Made.** Hecho, fabricado, manufacturado, realizado.

**Made known.** Literalmente. hecho saber. Conocimiento oficial que la ley infiere, por ejemplo, que el demandado conoce los términos de la demanda luego de haber sido legalmente notificado.

**Madman.** Insano, loco.

**Madness.** Locura, demencia.

**Magazine.** Almacén.

**Magistrate.** Magistrado, juez.

**Magistrates, pretrial dispositive matters.** Magistrados cuestiones dispositivas antes del juicio. Un magistrado designado sin consentimiento de las partes para ver una cuestión antes del juicio dispositiva de una reclamación o defensa de una parte o la solicitud de un recluso objetando las condiciones del confinamiento tramitará inmediatamente los procedimientos que fueren necesarios. (Reglas Fed. Pro. Civ., sec. 72(b)).

**Magistrates pretrial, nondispositive matters.** Magistrados cuestiones no dispositivas antes del juicio. El magistrado a quien se le asignare para su vista y determinación una cuestión antes del juicio no dispositiva de la reclamación o defensa de una parte, inmediatamente tramitará los procedimientos que fueren requeridos y cuando fuere pertinente registrará en los autos una orden escrita exponiendo la disposición del asunto. (Reglas Fed. Proc. Civ., sec. 72(a)).

**Magistrates, trial by consent.** Magistrados, juicio por consentimiento. Cuando fuere especialmente designado para actuar a tenor con la ley local o una orden de la corte de distrito y cuando todas las partes lo consintieren, un magistrado podrá tramitar cualesquiera y todos los procedimientos incluso juicios con jurado o sin jurado, en un caso civil.

**Magna Charta.** Carta Magna.

**Magnuson-Moss Warranty Act.** Ley federal, 15 U.S.C.A., sección 2301 y siguientes, que establece la obligación de presentar la garantía acordada a productos de consumo en forma escrita y claramente visible.

**Maiden.** Señorita, mujer soltera, virgen.

**Mail box.** Buzón.

**Mail-box rule.** Doctrina por la cual el contrato por correspondencia se perfecciona al depositarse en el correo la aceptación de la oferta.

**Mail contract.** Contrato por correspondencia.

**Mail fraud.** Fraude realizado mediante el uso del servicio de correos.

**Maim, disfigure or disable a member of the human body.** Mutilar, desfigurar o inutilizar un miembro del cuerpo humano —a los fines del delito de mutilación—es lesionar dicho miembro de modo tal que no pueda usarse, no ya sólo en el combate, sino para todos los fines ordinarios, corrientes y prácticos de la vida. Dicha inutilización ha de ser de carácter permanente según se entendía en el derecho común. (Pueblo v. Rios Rivera, 88 D.P.R. 165 (1963)).

**Main office.** Oficina principal. Sede.

**Maintenance.** Alimentos, mantenimiento, sostén económico.

**Majesty.** Majestad, soberano.

**Major.** Mayor, grave, importante. Recibirse con un grado académico (v).

**Majority.** Mayoría, mayoría de edad.

**Majority opinion.** Opinión de la mayoría, voz cantante.

**Majority rule.** Gobierno de la mayoría.

**Make a claim.** Realizar una petición o un reclamo.

**Make a contract.** Firmar un contrato.

**Make a deal.** Acordar un negocio.

**Make a living.** Trabajar de, ganarse la vida con.

**Make a loss.** Tener una pérdida.

**Make a payment.** Realizar un pago.

**Make a profit.** Realizar una ganancia.

**Make a statement.** Emitir una declaración.

**Make an objection.** Objetar.

**Make whole.** Compensar, indemnizar.

**Maker.** Otorgante.

**Making a port in distress.** Arribada forzosa.

**Male.** Varón, hombre, macho.

**Malfeasance.** Acto doloso o criminal encaminado a causar un daño y que carece de justificativo.

**Malice.** Malicia.

**Malice aforethought.** Malicia premeditada.

**Malicious prosecution.** Temeridad y malicia, abuso de proceso penal. Una persona privada que inicie o procure la institución de un proceso criminal contra otro que no es culpable del delito imputado, será responsable ante ese otro por una acusación maliciosa.(Rstmnt, 2nd, Torts, sec. 653).

**Malign.** Hablar mal de alguien injustificadamente, calumniar, difamar.

**Maligner.** Persona que finge una incapacidad, especialmente para no trabajar.

**Malpractice.** Mal desempeño profesional que causa un daño al cliente o paciente quien puede demandar al profesional.

**Maltreatment.** Malos servicios profesionales brindados por un médico a su paciente. Malos tratos.

**Man.** Hombre, persona, humanidad.

**Man of straw.** Testaferro, prestanombre, hombre de paja.

**Manacles.** Esposas, grillos, cadenas.

**Manager.** Gestor, administrador, encargado, ejecutivo, gerente.

**Managing partner.** Socio gerente.

**Mandamus.** Orden judicial dirigida a un funcionario público—incluso a un juez de menor rango—o a una persona jurídica, disponiendo que se cumpla o que cese un acto en particular. Normalmente se usa como recurso de apelación para obtener la revisión de una sentencia interlocutoria. Mandamiento, oficio.

**Mandate of the Supreme Court.** Mandato de la Corte Suprema. Un mandato del Tribunal Supremo es el medio oficial de que se vale dicho Tribunal para comunicar al tribunal de instancia la disposición que ha hecho de la sentencia objeto de revisión y de ordenarle el cumplimiento con los términos de la actuación del Tribunal Supremo. (Pueblo v. Tribunal de Distrito, 97 D.P.R. 241 (1969)).

**Mandatory.** Obligatorio, exigido por la ley.

**Mandatory rules.** Normas imperativas. Ninguno de estos Principios tendrá por efecto restringir la aplicación de normas imperativas, sean ellas de origen nacional, internacional o supranacional, que resulten aplicables conforme a las normas pertinentes de derecho internacional privado. (Unidroit, Prin., art. 1.4).

**Maneuver.** Maniobra.

**Mangrover.** Manglar.

**Manhood.** Hombría, mayoría de edad.

**Manic.** Maníaco.

**Manifest.** Manifiesto, patente.

**Manifestation of assent.** Manifestación de consentimiento. La manifestación de mutuo consentimiento para un intercambio requiere que cada parte haga una promesa o realice una conducta. La manifestación del consentimiento puede hacerse total o parcialmente, ya sea en forma oral o escrita, o a través de otros actos o de una abstención de actuar. (Rstmnt, 2nd, Con., sec. 18, 19).

**Manipulation.** Manipulación.

**Mankind.** Humanidad.

**Manslaughter.** Homicidio simple. El homicidio cometido sin malicia y en el calor de la pasión, mediando provocación adecuada de la víctima, se consideró *manslaughter* en el *common law*. La distinción con murder (homicidio deliberado) radica en la provocación causante del estado pasional. Solamente algunos actos se consideran suficientemente provocativos al respecto: la agresión del ofendido, la tentativa de detener ilegalmente al reo, la riña provocada con propósito de matar, el sorprender a la mujer en adulterio. (T. B. Stuchiner).

**Manual delivery.** Entrega manual.

**Manufacture.** Manufactura (s). Manufacturar (v).

**Maraud.** Merodear, saquear.

**_Marbury v. Madison._** En este caso de 1803, la Corte Suprema se rehusó a convalidar una sección de una ley federal, sobre la base de que el Congreso al aprobarla se había excedido de los poderes otorgados por la Constitución. Por esta decisión quedó establecido firmemente que la legislación federal estaba sujeta a la revisión judicial por parte de los tribunales federales. (Intro al USA).

**Mareva injunction.** En Inglaterra, medida preventiva trabada contra los bienes de demandados extranjeros en casos de incumplimiento contractual.

**Margin.** Margen, diferencia, dinero que se entrega para la compra de acciones sin pagar la suma total.

**Marine and transportation insurance.** Seguro contra siniestros marítimos y de transportación. Esto es el seguro contra pérdida o daños sufridos por buques, embarcaciones, aeronaves, coches, automóviles y vehículos de todas clases, así como toda clase de géneros, flete, cargas, mercancías, efectos, desembolsos, y cualquier otra clase de propiedad e interés en la misma, con respecto a cualquier y todos los riesgos de guerra sobre cualesquiera mares u otras aguas o bajo éstos, en tierra o en el aire, o mientras fueren armados, embalados, puestos en cajas, empacados, compresados, o similarmente preparados para embarque, o mientras espera reembarque, o durante cualquier retraso, almacenaje, trasbordo, o reembarque incidental al mismo, incluyendo riesgos marítimos del constructor y todo riesgo de bienes muebles flotantes, pertenecientes a dichos riesgos o peligros o en relación con los mismos. (26 LPRA sec. 405).

**Mariner's lien.** Derecho de pago preferencial de la tripulación de una nave.

**Marital.** Marital, relativo a los cónyuges.

**Marital agreement.** Convención o contrato nupcial.

**Marital deduction.** Deducción marital, aquélla autorizada por leyes impositivas que grava con menores impuestos las donaciones entre cónyuges.

**Marital privilege.** Inmunidad procesal que autoriza a no prestar declaraciones contra el cónyuge. Usase también para denotar los derecho, v.g. económicos, que derivan del matrimonio.

**Maritime court.** Tribunal de almirantazgo, tribunal marítimo.

**Maritime law.** Derecho marítimo.

**Mark.** Marca, señal. Marcar, señalar.

**Mark down.** Reducir el precio.

**Mark up.** Aumentar el precio.

**Market.** Mercado, plaza (s). Vender o poner en venta (v).

**Market, open.** Mercado no controlado por el Estado, en el cual la oferta y la demanda actúan libremente.

**Market price.** Valor comercial, precio de mercado.

**Marketable.** Con mercado, que puede venderse fácilmente.

**Marketable title.** Dominio sin restricciones, título perfecto.

**Marriage.** Matrimonio, casamiento. El matrimonio es en los Estados Unidos fundamentalmente en relación creada por mutuo consentimiento de los cónyuges. Todos los estados tienen leyes que prevén la emisión de licencias de matrimonio; algunos requieren una ceremonia formal durante la cual se afirme solemnemente el consentimiento frente a un representante del clero o un funcionario público. (Intro al USA).

**Marriage certificate.** Partida de Matrimonio.

**Marriage, Informal.** También llamado _common law marriage_, aquél que la ley acuerda sin formalidades públicas, matrimonio consensual.

**Marriage license.** Documento que autoriza la celebración oficial de un matrimonio una vez que todas las formalidades son satisfechas.

**Marriage settlement.** Convención o contrato nupcial.

**Marsh.** Marisma.

**Marshall.** Alguacil, funcionario a cargo de cada distrito judicial encargado de hacer cumplir las órdenes de los tribunales federales (s). Dirigir (v).

**Marshall, John.** John Marshall (1755-1835) fue el cuarto Presidente de la Corte Suprema de los Estados Unidos, desde 1801 hasta 1835. (Intro al USA).

**Martial law.** Ley marcial.

**Master.** Patrón, empleador. Un patrono empleador es un mandante quien emplea a un mandatario para realizar un servicio relacionado con los asuntos del primero y quien controla o tiene el derecho de controlar la conducta física del mandatario durante la realización del servicio. (Rstmnt, 2nd, Agency, sec. 2(1)).

**Master and servant.** Patrón y empleado.

**Master of vessel.** Patrón de buque.

**Masters.** Comisionados. La corte ante la cual estuviere pendiente cualquier pleito podrá nombrar un comisionado para el mismo. Tal como se usa en estas reglas la palabra "comisionados" incluirá árbitros, auditores, examinadores y asesores. (R. Fed. P. Civ., sec. 53(a)(b)(c)).

**Mate.** Subcomandante de un barco mercante (s). Generar cría entre animales (v).

**Material breach.** Incumplimiento substancial. Al determinar si el incumplimiento es substancial, las siguientes circunstancias son significativas: a) hasta qué punto se privará a la parte perjudicada del beneficio que razonablemente esperó; b) hasta qué punto la parte perjudicada puede ser compensada adecuadamente por la parte de ese beneficio del cual se le privará. (Rstmnt, 2nd, Con., sec. 241).

**Material misrepresentation.** Dolo sustancial. El dolo es sustancial si es capaz de inducir a una persona razonable a manifestar su consentimiento, o si el que incurre en un acto doloso conoce que tal acto será capaz de inducir a la otra parte a expresar consentimiento. (Rstmnt, 2nd, Con., sec. 162(2)).

**Materialman's lien.** Derecho de pago preferencial en favor de quien ha suministrado los materiales.

**Maternity.** Maternidad.

**Matrimonial.** Matrimonial.

**Matrimony.** Matrimonio, casamiento.

**Matron.** Mujer casada o de cierta edad. Administradora de un hospital.

**Matter of fact.** Cuestión de hecho.

**Matter of law.** Cuestión de derecho.

**Maturity.** Vencimiento, expiración, fin de plazo.

**Mayhem.** Mutilación. Se comete el delito de mutilación cuando se priva a un ser humano de un miembro de sus cuerpo o se mutila, desfigura o inutiliza dicho miembro. (Pueblo v. Ríos Rivera, 88 D.P.R. 165 (1963)).

**Mayor.** Alcalde, intendente.

**McNaghten test.** La medida o test usado en la mayor parte de los Estados para determinar la capacidad de la persona para entender la criminalidad de un acto, se basa en el criterio de si tal persona puede distinguir entre lo justo o injusto. (Stuchiner).

**Means of proof.** Medio de prueba.

**Measure of damages.** Determinación de daños.

**Mechanic's Lien.** Gravamen por labor de operarios. Siempre que un obrero o empleado trabajare en la construcción, ampliación, conservación o reparación de cualquier obra, casa o edificio, el importe total de los salarios que devengare por razón de su trabajo constituirá un gravamen sobre dicha propiedad. (29 LPRA sec. 186).

**Mechanical means.** Medio mecánico.

**Mediation.** Mediación, también conocido como alternative dispute resolution o ADR.

**Medicaid.** Asistencia médica gratuita o subvencionada por el Estado.

**Member of cabinet.** Secretario de despacho, miembro de gabinete, ministro.

**Memorandum.** Nota, apunte, memorándum.

**Memorandum of agreement.** Minuta del convenio.

***Mens rea* (L).** Intención de cometer un delito. Mentalidad delictuosa.

**Mental anguish.** Angustia mental.

**Mental cruelty.** Crueldad mental.

**Mental disease.** Enfermedad mental. Ninguna persona quien como resultado de enfermedad o defecto mental carezca de capacidad suficiente para comprender los procedimientos en su contra o para ayudar a su propia defensa será enjuiciada, convicta o sentenciada por la comisión de una ofensa, mientras dure tal incapacidad. (Cód. Pen. Mod., § 4.04).

**Merchandise.** Mercancía, mercadería, efectos.

**Merchant.** Mercader, comerciante, vendedor al por menor.

**Merchantable.** De calidad comercializable, de mercado.

**Merciless.** Cruel, sin clemencia.

**Mercy.** Gracia, clemencia.

**Mercy killing.** Acto de matar por piedad, eutanasia.

**Mere.** Mero.

**Merger.** Fusión.

**Merger clauses.** Cláusulas de restricción probatoria. Todo contrato que contenga una cláusula indicativa de que lo allí escrito cubre completamente lo acordado, no puede ser contradicho o complementado mediante prueba de declaraciones o de acuerdos anteriores. No obstante, tales declaraciones o acuerdos podrán utilizarse para interpretar lo escrito. (Unidroit, Prin., art. 2.17).

**Meritorious defense.** Defensa efectiva, capaz de convencer al tribunal.

**Merits.** Mérito, razones sustantivas—no procesales—por las que se gana o pierde un pleito. v.g. *To win on the merits*, ganar por razones sustantivas.

**Mesne process.** Auto interlocutorio.

**Metes and bounds.** Mojones y límites de una propiedad.

**Middleman.** Intermediario.

**Midwife.** Partera.

**Milestone.** Hito, mojón, deslinde.

**Military.** Militar.

**Military court.** Tribunal marcial o militar.

**Military law.** Ley militar.

**Military orders.** Ordenes militares. Será una defensa afirmativa que el autor, que haya incurrido en la conducta imputada y constitutiva de delito, no hace más que ejecutar una orden de su superior en las fuerzas armadas la cual desconoce que sea ilegal. (Cód. Pen. Mod., § 2.10).

**Militia.** Milicia.

**Miller Act.** Ley Miller. Desígnase como la Ley Miller el estatuto federal de carácter general que requiere la prestación de fianzas en todo contrato para la construcción, reparación o alteración de un edificio u obra pública federal. (Casablanca v. Tribunal Superior, 100 D.P.R. 204 (1971)).

**Mind.** Mente, mentalidad, estado de conciencia (s). Preocuparse por algo, tener algo en cuenta (v).

**Mineral.** Mineral, relativo a minas.

**Mineral deed.** Escritura que transfiere derechos sobre el subsuelo.

**Mineral lease.** Arriendo minero, contrato de exploración y explotación minera.

**Mineral right.** Derechos mineros, derechos de subsuelo.

**Minimum wage.** Salario mínimo, paga mínima.

**Ministry.** Ministerio.

**Minor.** Menor. Area de concentración menor en estudios universitarios.

**Minority.** Minoría.

**Misadventure.** Accidente, catástrofe, infortunio.

**Misapplication.** Aplicación indebida.

**Misappropiate.** Malversar fondos, apoderación indebida, delito o cuasidelito contra la propiedad ajena usada en provecho propio.

**Miscarriage.** Aborto.

**Miscegenation.** Mezcla de razas, matrimonio interracial.

**Mischief.** Daño, agravio. Travesura.

**Misconduct.** Mala conducta.

**Misdemeanor.** El *common law* divide a los delitos en *felonies* (los más graves) y *misdemeanors* (los menos graves). Los *misdemeanors* se definen por exclusión, diciendo que son todos aquellos delitos que no constituyen *felonies*. Como regla general, son misdemeanors los delitos que no llevan pena de muerte ni de reclusión.

**Misfeasance.** Infracción, contravención, falta, quebrantamiento.

**Misjoinder and nonjoinder parties.** Acumulación indebida o no acumulación de partes. La indebida acumulación de partes no será motivo para desestimar un pleito. Podrán eliminarse o adicionarse partes por orden de la corte o a moción de cualquier parte o a su propia iniciativa en cualquier estado del pleito y bajo las condiciones que estimare justas. (R. Fed. P. Civ., sec. 21).

**Misleading.** Engañoso, que confunde, que conduce a un resultado falso o equivocado a sabiendas.

**Misprision.** Acto de rebelión o de insubordinación, negligencia por parte de funcionarios públicos.

**Misprision of felony.** Tener conocimiento de la comisión de un delito grave (*felony*) y no dar parte a las autoridades.

**Misrepresentation.** Dolo civil. El dolo civil es una afirmación que no concuerda con los hechos. (Rstmnt, 2nd, Con., sec. 159).

**Mistake.** Error. El error consiste en una concepción equivocada sobre los hechos o sobre el derecho, la cual debió existir al tiempo de la celebración del contrato. (Unidroit, Prin., art. 3.4).

Un error es una creencia que no concuerda con los hechos. (Rstmnt, 2nd, Con., sec. 151). Confundir (v).

**Mistake by both parties.** Error de ambas partes. Cuando ambas partes incurren en un error al momento de realizar el contrato en torno a un supuesto básico del mismo y este error tiene un efecto material en el intercambio de las prestaciones, el contrato es anulable por la parte adversamente afectada a menos que haya el riesgo del error. (Rstmnt, 2nd, Con., sec. 152).

**Mistake by only one part.** Error de una sola parte. Cuando una sola parte comete un error en cuanto a un supuesto básico del contrato y este error tiene un efecto material sobre el intercambio de las prestaciones acordada que le resulta adverso, el contrato es anulable por esta parte si no ha asumido el riesgo del error.(Rstmnt, 2nd, Con., sec. 153).

**Mistress.** Ama de casa, amante, maestra.

**Mistrial.** Anulación de un proceso debido a un vicio procesal con el consiguiente resultado de tener que comenzar otro nuevamente.

**Mitigating circumstances.** Circunstancias atenuantes, atenuante.

**Mitigation of damages.** Medidas tomadas para mitigar los daños y evitar que se generen pérdidas mayores de las necesarias. Normalmente es el acreedor de la obligación incumplida quien está en posición—y también obligado por ley—a atenuar las pérdidas que le cause el incumplimiento contractual de su contraparte.

**Mixed.** Mezclado, combinado.

**Mixed laws.** Leyes que a la vez se refieren a las personas y a los objetos.

**Mixed marriage.** Matrimonio interracial.

**Mixed nuisance.** Acción que es simultáneamente por molestia pública y por molestia particular.

**Mob.** Muchedumbre descontrolada que comete desórdenes. Término aplicado informalmente a una organización delictiva, sinónimo de mafia.

**Mock trial.** Juicio fingido. Se usa en los casos muy importantes para probar la fuerza de convicción que tienen los argumentos a favor y en contra.

Juicio determinado de antemano pero que continúa aparentando imparcialidad.

**Mode of acceptance.** Modo de aceptación. Constituirá una aceptación toda declaración o cualquier otro acto del destinatario que indique su asentimiento a una oferta. Ni el silencio ni la conducta omisiva, por sí solos, implican una aceptación. (Unidroit, Prin., art. 2.6).

**Model Penal Code.** Cód. Pen. Mod. El más importante de los adelantos introducidos por el Cód. Pen. Mod. es el análisis de los criterios de culpabilidad. Se definen cuatro tipos de culpabilidad: intencionalidad, conocimiento, imprudencia, y negligencia. (Intro al USA).

**Model Penal Code, special part.** Código Penal Modelo, parte especial. Como ejemplo de la parte especial del Cód. Pen. Mod. podemos citar la sección referida al homicidio. Distingue tres categorías de homicidio: asesinato, homicidio impremeditado y homicidio por negligencia. (Intro al USA).

**Modified acceptance.** Aceptación disconforme. La respuesta a una oferta hecha en términos de aceptación, pero con adiciones, limitaciones u otras modificaciones, se considerará como un rechazo de la oferta y constituirá una contraoferta. (Unidroit, Prin., art. 2.11).

**Modus operandi (L).** Modo de operar.

**Moiety.** Mitad hereditaria.

**Money.** Dinero. Cualquier medio de intercambio autorizado por un gobierno nacional o extranjero como parte de su moneda circulante. (C.C.U. SEC. 1201 (24)).

**Money judgment.** Sentencia que obliga al pago de una suma de dinero.

**Money order.** Orden de pago.

**Moonshine.** Fabricación ilegal y privada de bebidas alcohólicas.

**Mooring.** Anclaje, atraque de una embarcación.

**Moot.** Cuestión que no se halla resuelta por la ley o por la jurisprudencia.

**Moot court.** Tribunal simulado, utilizado en escuelas de derecho con fines educativos.

**Moot question.** Cuestión irrelevante o de importancia tan sólo académica.

**Moral.** Moral, relacionado con la ética.

**Moral consideration.** Contraprestación sin valor comercial, sino sólo simbólica.

**Moral obligation.** Obligación moral.

**Moral turpitude.** Seria contravención de las obligaciones morales y éticas.

**Moratorium.** Moratoria.

**Morgue.** Morgue.

**Mortgage.** Hipoteca.

**Mortgagee.** Hipotecario.

**Mortgagor.** Deudor hipotecario.

**Mother country.** Metrópolis.

**Motion and order.** Petición y ordenanza. Una moción es una solicitud de que el tribunal tome cierta decisión, en este caso una ordenanza de rechazo del caso. Todas las decisiones judiciales que no sean un fallo que resuelve el caso, toman al forma de ordenanzas. (Intro al USA).

**Motion before submission to jury.** Moción antes de someterse el caso al jurado. Las mociones para que se ordene un veredicto quedan abolidas y en su lugar se usarán las mociones para fallo absolutorio. (Regla 29(a), Reglas Fed. de Proc. Crim.).

**Motion day.** Día para mociones. A menos que las condiciones locales lo hicieran impracticable, cada corte de distrito establecerá fechas y lugares ordinarios, a intervalos suficientemente frecuentes para el pronto despacho de asuntos, en los cuales podrán verse y decidirse mociones que requieran notificación y vista. (R. Fed. P. Civ., sec. 78).

**Motion docket.** Libro de mociones.

**Motion for a more definite statement.** Moción para solicitar una exposición más definida. Si las alegaciones contra las cuáles se permitan alegaciones respondientes fueren tan vagas o ambiguas que nos sería razonable exigirle a cualquiera de las partes formular una alegación respondiente, éstas podrán solicitar mediante moción una exposición más definida antes de presentar sus alegaciones respondientes. (R. Fed. P. Civ., sec. 12(e)).

**Motion for directed verdict.** Moción para veredicto ordenado por la corte. Toda moción para veredicto ordenado por la corte especificará los fundamentos del mismo. La orden de la corte por la cual se declare con lugar una moción para veredicto ordenado por la corte surtirá efecto sin asentimiento alguno del jurado. (R. Fed. P. Civ., sec. 50(a)).

**Motion for judgment notwithstanding the verdict.** Moción para sentencia no obstante el veredicto. Nunca después de 10 días siguientes al registro de la sentencia, la parte que hubiere solicitado mediante moción el veredicto ordenado por la corte podrá solicitar que el veredicto y cualquier sentencia dictada a tenor con el mismo sean dejados sin efecto o que se dicte sentencia de acuerdo con su moción para veredicto ordenado por la corte. (R. Fed. P. Civ., sec. 50(b)).

**Motion for judgment on the pleadings.** Moción para que se dicte sentencia por las alegaciones. Después de concluída la fase de alegaciones, pero dentro de un plazo que no demore el juicio, cualquier parte podrá solicitar que se le pronuncie sentencia por las alegaciones. (Reglas Fede. de Proc. Civ., sec. 12(c)).

**Motion for order compelling discovery.** Moción para obligar al descubrimiento. Una parte, con razonable notificación a las otras partes y a todas las personas afectadas, podrá solicitar una orden que obligue al descubrimiento. (R. Fed. P. Civ., sec. 37(a)).

**Motion to alter or amend a judgment.** Moción para modificar o enmendar la sentencia. Las mociones para modificar o enmendar la sentencia tendrán que ser notificadas a más tardar 10 días después del registro de la sentencia. (R. Fed. P. Civ. sec. 59(e)).

**Motion to strike.** Moción eliminatoria. A moción de parte antes de contestar a una alegación o, si estas reglas no permitieren una alegación respondiente, a moción de parte presentada dentro de los 20 días siguientes a la notificación a la misma de dicha alegación, o a iniciativa de la propia corte en cualquier momento, ésta podrá ordenar que se elimine de cualquier alegación cualquier defensa insuficiente o cualquier materia redundante, superflua, impertinente o escandalosa. (R. Fed. P. Civ., sec. 12(f)).

**Motions and other papers.** Mociones y otros escritos. Las solicitudes a la corte para que expida órdenes se harán mediante mociones por escrito, a menos que fueren hechas durante una vista o juicio, en las cuales se especificarán en detalle los fundamentos de las mismas, y se consignará el remedio u orden que se interesa. El requisito de que sean por escrito quedará cumplido si las mociones se hicieren constar en la notificación escrita para la vista sobre las mismas. (R. Fed. P. Civ, sec 7(b)(1)).

**Motive.** Motivo, intención, móvil para cometer un acto o para abstenerse del mismo.

**Mourning.** Luto, duelo.

**Movant.** Peticionante.

**Moving expenses.** Gastos de mudanza.

**Moving party.** Parte solicitante.

**Municipal law.** Legislación comunal. Las normas municipales, habitualmente llamadas ordenanzas, tienen por lo común solo interés local. También puede haber organismos administrativos locales que promulgan reglamentaciones. (Intro al USA).

**Municipality.** Municipio.

**Muniment of title.** Título hereditario que se obtiene mediante el testamento, su homologación (*probate*) y un inventario detallando los bienes heredados.

**Murder.** Homicidio deliberado, por oposición al homicidio simple (*manslaughter*). Se trata de un homicidio calificado. Se caracteriza como la muerte ilícita producida con malicia deliberada. Esta malicia puede ser expresa o implícita, bien—en este último caso—por existir propósito de causar lesiones o por cometer un acto cuyo resultado natural sería la muerte o por cometer el homicidio durante la ejecución de otro delito grave (*felony*). (Stuchiner).

**Mutiny.** Motín, rebelión contra autoridades militares o navales.

**Mutual.** Mutuo, recíproco.

**Mutual agreement.** Consentimiento recíproco.

**Mutual consideration.** Contraprestación recíproca.

**Mutual fund.** Grupo de inversión.

**Mutual mistake.** Error recíproco.

**Mutual wills.** Testamentos recíprocos o conjuntos.

# N

**NASA.** *National Aeronautics and Space Administration.* Agencia estadounidense responsible por la conquista y la investigación espacial.

**NASD.** *National Association of Securities Dealers.* Asociación de corredores de bolsa.

**N.Y.S.E.** *New York Stock Exchange.* Mercado de valores de Nueva York.

**Naked promise.** Promesa unilateral o gratuita.

**Name.** Nombre. Nombre y apellido (s). Nombrar (v).

**Named insured.** Persona designada como el asegurado en la póliza.

**Narcotic.** Narcótico.

**Narrative evidence.** Prueba en la que el deponente se expresa con libertad—en forma narrada—sobre los hechos que dice conocer.

**Nation.** Nación, país.

**National.** Nacional.

**National origin.** Origen nacional.

**Nationality.** Nacionalidad.

**Nationalization.** Nacionalización.

**Native.** Nativo.

**Native inhabitants.** Habitantes naturales.

**Native speaker.** Persona que habla un idioma como lengua materna.

**Natural death.** Muerte natural.

**Natural law.** Derecho natural.

**Natural obligation.** Obligación natural, basada en la equidad.

**Natural resources.** Recursos naturales.

**Naturalization.** Naturalización. Adquisición de nacionalidad para quien no es nativo del Estado en cuestión.

**Naval law.** Almirantazgo. Derecho marítimo.

**Navigable.** Navegable.

**Navigable waters.** Rios y mares navegables.

**Navigate.** Navegar.

**Navigation.** Navegación.

**Navigation certificate.** Patente de navegación.

**Navy.** Marina.

**Necessaries.** En derecho de familia, aquellos gastos básicos que pueden ser cobrados a otros miembros de la familia.

**Needy.** Indigente, sumamente pobre, menesteroso.

**Neglect.** Descuido, negligencia, falta de atención debida.

**Neglected child.** Niño abandonado o sujeto a males tratos, lo que justifica un cambio en la guarda o en la patria potestad.

**Negligence.** Negligencia, culpa, descuido, imprudencia, indolencia.

**Negligence claim.** Demanda por negligencia. Un ejemplo de demanda por negligencia se encuentra en el formulario 9 de las *Federal Rules of Civil Procedure*: 1) Fundamentación de competencia. 2) El 1 de junio de 1936, en una vía pública de Boston (Massachusetts), llamada Boylston Street, el demandado condujo con negligencia un vehículo automotor lanzándolo contra el querellante que cruzaba en esos momentos la mencionada arteria. 3) La caída consecuente le provoco la rotura de una pierna y otras heridas, le impidió continuar con sus actividades, le causo grave sufrimiento corporal y mental, y lo obligo a gastos por atención médica y internación que ascendieron a 1000 dólares. Por todo lo cual el querellante reclama una reparación de 10000 dólares más las costas. Con el sistema del *fact pleading* la demanda habría sido más detallada y contendría mayor cantidad de parágrafos. (Intro al USA).

**Negligent conduct (tort).** Conducta negligente (cuasidelito). La conducta negligente puede darse: a) mediante un acto donde el actor debió reconocer que existía un riesgo irrazonable de causar la invasión de un derecho de otro individuo, o b) por no ejecutar un acto que era necesario para proteger o asistir a otro individuo, cuando era deber del actor el así hacerlo. (Restatement, Second Torts, sec. 284).

**Negligent performance of services.** Negligencia en la prestación de servicios. Aquella persona que, gratuitamente o por remuneración, rinde servicios que estima necesarios para la protección de otra persona o sus pertenencias, será responsable a esa otra persona por el daño sufrido cuando no ejerza el debido cuidado en sus funciones. (Restatement, Second, Torts, sec. 323).

**Negligent tort.** Cuasidelito por negligencia. Negligencia es una conducta que no cae dentro de las normas establecidas por ley, para así proteger a los demás contra el riesgo de sufrir daño. (Restatement, Second, Torts, sec. 282).

**Negligently preventing assistance.** Ayuda impedida negligentemente. Aquella persona que sabe, o tiene motivos para creer que un tercero está asistiendo o está en la disposición de asistir a otro individuo para prevenir que éste sufra daño corporal, e impida u obstaculice dicha ayuda en forma negligente, será responsable por los daños físicos causados a ese otro individuo por la falta de la ayuda ofrecida por el tercero. (Rstmnt, 2nd, Torts, sec. 327).

**Negotiability.** Negociabilidad.

**Negotiable instrument.** Documento negociable, valor, efecto de comercio.

**Negotiated plea.** En derecho penal, acusación entrada de común acuerdo entre el fiscal y el acusado.

**Negotiations in bad faith.** Negociaciones con mala fe. Cada cual es libre de entrar en negociaciones y no incurre en responsabilidad en el evento de que las negociaciones no culminen en un acuerdo. (Unidroit, Prin., art. 2.15).

**Net.** Neto.

**Net income.** Ingresos netos.

**Net worth.** Patrimonio. Valor del activo una vez deducido el pasivo.

**Neutrality.** Neutralidad.

**New trial.** Nuevo juicio. La corte, a moción del acusado, podrá concederle nuevo juicio si lo requiriere el interés de la justicia. (Regla 33, Reglas Fed. de Proc. Crim.).

**Next of kin.** Paciente más cercano.

**No arrival, no sale.** No arribo no venta. Bajo el término "no arribo, no venta" o términos de significado parecido, salvo pacto en contrario:—el vendedor embarcará debidamente las mercancías conformes y si éstas llegaren por cualquier medio las ofrecerá formalmente a su arribo, pero no asumirá la obligación de que las mercancías llegarán salvo que él hubiere causado el no arribo. (C.C.U. sec. 2-324).

**No-fault liability.** Responsabilidad sin culpa. La responsabilidad sin culpa—excepción a la básica relación causal culpa-daño-responsabilidad es también denominada responsabilidad absoluta y responsabilidad objetiva. (Rivera v. Caribbean Home Const. Corp., 100 D.P.R. 106 (1971)).

**No par value stock.** Acciones sin valor a la par. De tiempo en tiempo, podrá emitirse por la corporación acciones del capital corporativo que no tengan valor a la par, sean éstas comunes, preferidas o especiales, al precio de venta que de tiempo en tiempo fije la junta de directores, a menos que en el certificado de incorporación se haya reservado a los accionistas la facultad para fijar el precio. (14 LPRA sec. 1503).

**No-par stock.** Acciones sin valor par.

***Nolle prosequi* (L).** Declaración formal del fiscal en el sentido que la acción penal no será continuada en el caso de marras. También se aplica la expresión a acciones civiles, pero no tan frecuentemente.

***Nolo contendere* plea (L).** Alegación de *nolo contendere*. Un acusado podrá hacer alegación de *nolo contendere* únicamente con consentimiento de la corte. Dicha alegación será aceptada por la corte únicamente después de debida consideración de los puntos de vista de las partes y del interés público en la administración efectiva de la justicia. (Regla 11(b)(d), Reglas Fed. de Proc. Crim.).

**Nominal.** Nominal.

**Nominal damages.** Indemnización simbólica.

**Nominal shares.** Acciones nominativas.

**Non-delegable duties of master.** Deberes no delegables del empleador. Las palabras "deber no delegable" no implican que sean deberes cuya obligación no pueda ser cumplida nombrando a otros para que las realicen. Esas palabras describen deberes cuyo cumplimiento puede ser propiamente delegado a otra persona, pero sujeto a la condición de que surgirá responsabilidad si la persona a quien se delega el cumplimiento actúa impropiamente. (Rstmnt, 2nd, Agency, Introductory note to Title C, Ch. 14. sec. 492).

**Non-disclosure.** No revelación. La no revelación de un hecho conocido por una persona es equivalente a una afirmación de que ese hecho no existe sólo en los casos siguientes cuando esta persona conoce que la revelación del hecho es necesaria para evitar que una afirmación previa se considere como dolo civil, fraudulento, o material. (Rstmnt, 2nd, Con., sec. 161).

***Non obstante veredicto* (L).** Se aplica esta frase al fallo que el juez emite contradiciendo lo que el jurado ha decidido.

**Nonprofit association.** Asociación con fines no pecuniarios, o sin fines de lucro.

**Non qualified.** Inhábil.

**Noncompliance.** Incumplimiento, inobservancia, quebrantamiento, rompimiento.

**Nonfeasance.** Omisión de realizar un acto obligatorio.

**Nonmember.** No socio.

**Nonnegotiable.** No negociable.

**Nonpayment.** Falta de paro, mora.

**Nonperformance.** Incumplimiento. Incumplimiento es la falta de ejecución por una de las partes de cualquiera de sus obligaciones contractuales, e incluye tanto el cumplimiento defectuoso como el cumplimiento tardío. (Unidroit, Prin., art. 7.1.1).
Falta de cumplimiento, mora.

**Nonprivileged matter.** Materia no privilegiada.

**Nonprobate assets.** Bienes que se transfieren automáticamente por causa de muerte, sin intervencion judicial. Tales son: seguros de vida, co-propiedad con derechos para el co-propietario sobrevivinte y fideicomisos que continúan luego de fallecido el creador de los mismos.

**Notary public.** Notario público, escribano. En el sistema estadounidense el notario no es un profesional de carrera. Para ser notario sólo hace falta ser mayor de edad, no tener condenas penales y pagar un modesto arancel. Los notarios estadounidenses no llevan protocolo. (Intro al USA).

**Notation credit.** Anotación de crédito. "Crédito anotable" será aquél que especifica que cualquier persona que comprase o pagare giros librados o demandas de pago hechas bajo éste deberá anotar el importe del giro o demanda en la carta o aviso de crédito. (C.C.U. sec. 5-108).

**Notation on margin.** Anotación marginal.

**Note.** Nota, pagaré (s). Anotar, darse cuenta (v).

**Notice.** Comunicación. (1) Cuando sea necesaria una comunicación, ésta se hará por cualquier medio apropiado según las circunstancias. (2) La comunicación surtirá efectos efectos cuando llegue a la persona a quien vaya dirigida. (Unidroit, Prin., art. 1.9).

**Notice of orders or judgments.** Notificación de órdenes o sentencias. Inmediatamente después del archivo de una orden o sentencia el secretario diligenciará notificación de archivo por correo a cada una de las partes no rebeldes por falta de comparecencia, y anotará el envío por correo en el registro de actuaciones. (R. Fed. P. Civ., sec. 77(d)).

**Notice, to be on notice.** Conocimiento, tener conocimiento. Una persona tiene "aviso" o "conocimiento" de un hecho cuando a) tiene conocimiento real de éste; o b) ha recibido un aviso o notificación de éste; o c) de todos los hechos y circunstancias que le son conocidos en la fecha en cuestión tiene razón de saber que éste existe. (C.C.U. sec. 1201 (25)-(27)).

**Notification.** Notificación. Una persona es notificada por otra de un hecho si la última: a) le informa del hecho por medios adecuados o acordados, o de otros hechos de los cuales razonablemente se puede o podría inferir conocimiento; o b) realiza un acto el cual, bajo las reglas aplicables a la transacción, tiene el mismo efecto en la relación legal de las partes que el adquirir conocimiento o inferir la adquisición del mismo. (Rstmnt, 2nd, Agency, sec. 9(2), (3)).

**Notwithstanding.** Aun cuando, sin perjuicio de.

**Novation.** Novación. La novación es un contrato sustituto que incluye como parte a quien no era ni el deudor ni el acreedor de la obligación original. (Rstmnt, 2nd, Con., sec. 280).

**Now, therefore, be it resolved.** Por lo tanto, resuélvase.

**Nuisance.** Perturbación, disturbio, turbación.

**Null and void.** Nulo y sin valor.

**Nullity.** Nulidad.

**Nuncupative will.** Testamento abierto.

# O

**O.A.S.** *Organization of American States*; OEA, Organización de Estados Americanos.

**O.S.H.A.** *Occupational Safety and Health Administration*. Agencia federal que contrala cuestiones de higiene y de seguridad laboral.

**Oath.** Juramento prestado con todas las fomalidades de ley.

**Oath of allegiance.** Juramento de lealtad, v.g. a la bandera.

**Oath of office.** Juramento que prestan los funcionarios al ser puestos en posesión de sus cargos.

**Obedience.** Obediencia.

**Obedience, due.** Obediencia debida.

**Obedience to military orders.** Obediencia a órdenes militares. Un miembro de las fuerzas armadas de los Estados Unidos o de cualesquiera de los Estados está facultado para infligir daño o de cualquier modo invadir algún derecho ajeno, si tal invasión es razonablemente necesaria para ejecutar un mandato emitido por un superior, si tal mandato: a) es legal, o b) el actor cree que es legal y tal mandato no es manifiestamente ilegal, de modo que cualquier hombre razonable pueda reconocer su ilegalidad. (Rstmnt, 2nd, Torts, sec. 146).

**Obiter dicta** (L). Son las consideraciones expresadas en el fallo que no son estrictamente esenciales para llegar al resultado. Se podría decir que son las consideraciones generales. Ver *ratio decidendi*.

**Object.** Objeto (s). Oponerse (v). En derecho procesal, oponerse a una petición de la contraparte o a la admisión de alguna medida probatoria.

**Objection.** Objeción. Frase que emplea un abogado para oponerse a algo validado por el abogado adverso durante una audiencia. También se usa esta palabra en mociones por escrito.

**Objectionable.** Objetable, discutible.

**Objector.** Persona que objeta, protesta o disiente.

**Obligate.** Obligar, imponer una obligación.

**Obligation to protect others.** Obligación de proteger a otros. 1) Un porteador público tiene el deber para con sus pasajeros de tomar una acción razonable: a) para protegerlos de un riesgo irrazonable de sufrir daño corporal, y b) darles los primeros auxilios cuando sepa o tiene motivos para creer que los pasajeros están enfermos o heridos y de cuidarlos hasta tanto dejarlos al cuidado de otros. 2) Un hospedero tiene un deber similar para con sus huéspedes. 3) El poseedor de un terreno abierto al público, tiene un deber similar hacia el público que entre al terreno mediante invitación suya. (Rstmnt, 2nd, Torts, sec. 314A).

**Obligee.** Acreedor de una obligación.

**Obligor.** Deudor de una obligación.

**Obliterate.** Eliminar, borrar.

**Oblivion.** Olvido, perdón.

**Obscene.** Obsceno, lascivo.

**Obscenity.** Obscenidad.

**Obsolescence.** Obsolescencia, vetustez, deuso.

**Obsolete.** Obsoleto, caído en desuso.

**Obstruct.** Obstruir.

**Obstructing an officer.** Impidiendo o restringiendo la labor de un funcionario público.

**Obstructing justice.** Entorpecimiento de la justicia, acción encaminada a desviar el curso natural de un proceso judicial con intención de influir en el resultado, todo ello mediante actos aviesos e ilegales.

**Obstruction.** Obstrucción, presentación de una oposición o resistencia indebidas.

**Occasion.** Ocasión, evento, circunstancia (s). Ocasionar, originar (v).

**Occupancy.** Ocupación, tenencia o posesión de un inmueble.

**Occupant.** Ocupante, persona que detenta la posesión o tenencia.

**Occupation.** Ocupación, tenencia, posesión, trabajo, medio por el cual se gana uno la vida, profesión.

**Occupational disease.** Enfermedad ocupacional, profesional, de trabajo.

**Occupational hazard.** Riesgo de la profesión.

**Occupational safety and health standard.** Norma de seguridad y salud ocupacional. Aquélla que requiere condiciones, o la adopción o uso de una o más prácticas, medios, métodos, operaciones, procesos, artefacto, salvaguardias o equipo de protección personal, razonablemente necesarios o apropiados para proveer empleos y sitios de empleos seguros y saludables. (29 LPRA sec. 361b(h)).

**Occupier.** Ver *occupant.*

**Occupy.** Ocupar, emplear para un trabajo, estar en posesión de un inmueble.

**Occur.** Ocurrir, acontecer.

**Ocean.** Océano, mar abierto, aguas marítimas internacionales.

**Ocean floor.** Suelo marítimo.

**Odd lot.** Número de acciones que no es múltiplo de diez como es lo usual y que, por lo tanto, causa dificultades en su comercialización.

**Of counsel.** Abogado asesor de un bufete, pero que no participa en el desarrollo cotidiano del mismo. Abogado consultor.

**Of course.** Por derecho, que corresponde inalienablemente, sin que la contraparte pueda oponerse validamente.

**Of its own motion.** Por propia iniciativa.

**Off the record.** Evento que no queda registrado en ninguna parte.

**Offender.** Perpetrador de un délito o de un cuasidelito.

**Offense.** Ofensa.

Delito, crimen, infracción, violación de una norma jurídica, especialmente penal. En Derecho anglo-americano se conserva la voz *offence* para designar genericamente el delito o infracción penal, clasificándose éste con arreglo a criterios de gravedad y de enjuiciamiento: a) *Indictable offences,* las más graves; y b) *non indictable offences,* todas las demás. (T. B. Stuchiner).

**Offer.** Oferta. Toda propuesta de celebrar un contrato constituye una oferta, si es suficientemente precisa e indica la intención del oferente de quedar vinculado en caso de aceptación. (Unidroit, Prin., art. 2.2).

Una oferta es la manifestación de la voluntad de iniciar un negocio, hecha con el fin de indicar a otra persona que su consentimiento a tal negocio es solicitado y lo concluirá. (Restatement, Second, Contracts, sec. 24).

Ofrecer (v).

**Offer in (to) evidence.** Ofrecimiento de prueba.

**Offer of judgment.** Oferta de sentencia. En cualquier momento antes de los 10 días precedentes al comienzo del juicio, la parte demandada podrá notificar a la parte contraria una oferta para consentir que se dicte sentencia en su contra por la cantidad de dinero o bienes o los efectos especificados en su oferta, con las costas devengadas hasta ese momento. (R. Fed. P. Civ., sec. 68).

**Offer of proof.** Oferta de prueba.

**Offer to compromise.** Oferta de transacción.

**Offeree.** Ofrecido. Sujeto pasivo de una oferta.

**Offeror.** Oferente. Sujeto activo de una oferta.

**Office.** Escritorio, agencia, despacho, estudio, gabinete, oficina.

**Official of the chamber.** Oficial de sala.

**Officious manager.** Gestor oficioso.

**Offset.** Compensación, reconvención (s). Interponer la defensa de compensación, reconvenir (v).

**Offshore banking.** Servicios bancarios que son prestados desde otro país.

**Offshore company.** Sociedad comercial constituída y que funciona en el extranjero.

**Offspring.** Descendencia directa, hijos.

**Olograph testament.** Testamento ológrafo.

**Omitted counterclaim.** Reconvención omitida. Cuando los peticionarios dejaren de formular reconvenciones por descuido, inadvertencia o negligencia excusable, o cuando lo requiera la justicia, podrán, con la venia de la corte, formularlas mediante enmienda. (Regla Fed. de Proc. Civ., sec. 13(f)).

**Omnibus clause.** Cláusula omnibus. En una póliza de seguros, denomínase omnibus clause la cláusula de dicho contrato que define el término "asegurado." (Velez v. García Commercial, 100 D.P.R. 645 (1971)).

**On behalf of.** En representación de.

**On business.** Por razón de oficio, durante o en ocasión del trabajo.

**On demand.** A petición. Requerido, solicitado.

**On file.** Archivado, que consta en autos.

**On motion.** A instancia de parte.

**On or about.** En o aproximadamente tal fecha.

**Onerous title.** Título oneroso, lo contrario de gratuito.

**Open account.** Cuenta corriente.

**Open court and orders in chamber.** Corte abierta y órdenes en cámara. Todos los juicios sobre los méritos se celebrarán en corte abierta siempre que fuere conveniente, en una sala del Tribunal. Todos los demás procedimientos o actuaciones podrán ejecutarse o llevarse a cabo por el juez en cámara. (Regla Fed. de Proc. Civ., sec. 77(b)).

**Open price term.** Cláusula sobre precio abierto. Las partes si así lo desean pueden llevar a cabo el contrato de venta aunque el precio no se hubiera acordado. En tal caso el precio será uno razonable a la fecha de la entrega. (C.C.U. sec. 2-305).

**Open seas.** Mar abierto, alta mar.

**Open season.** Temporada de caza.

**Operation of law, by.** Automáticamente, *ipso jure.*

**Opinion.** Fundamentos del fallo. Los fundamentos pueden tener una extensión de una a veinte páginas, pero lo más común es que oscilen en torno a las cinco páginas. Aunque los fundamentos son opinión del tribunal, en general están redactados por uno de los jueces, cuyo nombre figura al comienzo. Este juez habitualmente resume los hechos y la historia procesal del caso, y desarrolla una exposición detallada y completa de las razones de la decisión tomada, citando leyes, precedentes y otras autoridades. (Intro al USA). [Ver: *decision on appeal.*]
Opinión, dictamen, creencia.

**Opinion on ultimate issue.** Opinión sobre cuestión última. El testimonio en forma de opinión o inferencia que fuere admisible no será objetable por el hecho de que incluya una cuestión última a ser decidida por el juzgador de los hechos. (Regla 704, R. Fed. Evid.).

**Opinion testimony by lay witness.** Testimonio de opinión por testigos no peritos. Si el testigo no estuviere declarando como perito, su declaración en forma de opiniones o inferencias se limitará a aquellas opiniones o inferencias que estén a) racionalmente basadas en la percepción del testigo y b) que ayuden al claro entendimiento de su declaración o a la determinación de un hecho en controversia. (Regla 701, R. Fed. Evid.).

**Opposition.** Oposición, confrontación, resistencia.

**Oppression.** Opresión, abuso de autoridad pública.

**Option contracts.** Contratos de opción. Un contrato de opción es una promesa que reune los requisitos para la formación de un contrato y limita la potestad del promisor para revocar su oferta. (Rstmnt, 2nd, Con., sec. 25).

**Option to accelerate at will.** Opción para anticipar a discreción. Un término disponiendo que una parte o su causahabiente en derecho pueda anticipar el pago o cumplimiento o requerir colateral o colateral adicional "a discreción" o "cuando ésta se siente insegura" o en palabras de significado similar se interpretará como que tendrá poder para hacerlo sólo si de buena fe cree que la perspectiva de pago o cumplimiento está en peligro. El peso de probar la falta de buena fe recae en la parte contra quien el poder se ha ejercitado. (C.C.U. sec. 1-208).

**Optional.** Potestativo, facultativo, optativo.

**Oral agreement.** Acuerdo oral, verbal.

**Oral evidence.** Prueba oral, no escrita.

**Ordained priest and other ministers of the gospel.** Sacerdotes y otros ministros del evangelio.

**Ordeal.** Ordalía.

**Order.** Orden, decreto, instrucción, mandamiento, providencia (s). Ordenar, mandar (v).

**Order, agreed.** Sentencia consentida y propuesta al tribunal por ambas partes.

**Order for proceeding.** Providencia de sustanciación.

**Order, interlocutory.** Sentencia interlocutoria.

**Order, money.** Giro de dinero, orden de pago.

**Order of performance.** Secuencia en el cumplimiento. En la medida de lo posible, las partes cumplirán simultáneamente sus obligaciones, a menos que las circunstancias indiquen otro modo de cumplimiento. (Unidroit, Prin., art. 6.1.4).

**Order of the Coif.** Distinción académica para estudiantes en escuelas de derecho.

**Order, restraining.** Interdicto, orden judicial de no interferir con los derechos de la otra parte.

**Order to show cause.** Orden judicial para indicar la razón de un acto.

**Orders by clerk.** Ordenes por el secretario. Todas las mociones y solicitudes en secretaría para la expedición de mandamientos intermedios y mandamientos definitivos para hacer cumplir y ejecutar sentencias, para anotar rebeldías o dictar sentencias en rebeldía y para otros procedimientos que no requieran permiso u orden de la corte serán otorgadas usualmente por el secretario; pero su actuación podrá ser suspendida, alterada o dejada sin efecto por la corte por causa justificada. (R. Fed. P. Civ. sec. 77(c)).

**Ordinance.** Ordenanza, decreto, orden.

**Ordinary course of business.** Curso ordinario de los negocios.

**Ordinary negligence.** Culpa simple.

**Organic act.** Ley del congreso otorgando poderes políticos sobre cierto territorio.

**Organic law.** Constitución, carta orgánica, ley fundamental.

**Original jurisdiction.** Competencia original.

**Orphan.** Huérfano, sin progenitores vivos.

**Ostensible.** Ostensible, aparente.

**Other.** Otro distinto, diferente de, por añadidura a lo que ya se tiene.

**Ounce.** Onza, unidad de peso doce veces menor que una libra (*pound*).

**Ouster.** Juicio de lanzamiento, evicción.

**Ouster of jurisdiction.** Pérdida de la competencia judicial inicial, v.g. si las partes firman una cláusula arbitral.

**Out.** Fuera, afuera, fuera de.

**Out of court.** Fuera del tribunal o fuera del control directo del juez.

**Out of wedlock.** Extramatrimonial, fuera del matrimonio.

**Outbid.** Desplazar a un rival mediante una postura más alta en un remate, o menor en una licitación.

**Outgo.** Gastos.

**Outlaw.** Históricamente un muerto civil. Bandido, fugitivo, proscripto (s). Proscribir, prohibir (v).

**Outright.** Irrestricto, directo, completo.

**Outstanding.** Sobresaliente, pendiente de pago.

**Outstanding debt.** Deuda impaga.

**Over.** Sobre, por sobre, más que.

**Overbreadth doctrine.** Teoría que invalida una ley si es susceptible de ser aplicada para punir a individuos que ejercen el derecho constitucional de libertad de palabra o de otros derechos constitucionalmente protegidos.

**Overcharge.** Parte de un precio que sobrepasa lo normal, sobreprecio (s). Cobrar de más (v).

**Overdraft.** Giro en descubierto.

**Overdraw.** Girar en descubierto.

**Overdue.** Algo cuyo plazo de realización, v.g. pago, ya ha vencido hace algún tiempo.

**Overextension.** Esfuerzo extraordinario.

**Overflow.** Exceso de algo v.g. *overflow capital*, exceso de capital.

**Overflowed lands.** Tierras inundadas.

**Overhead.** Gastos necesarios para operar, costos administrativos, v.g. alquiler del local, sueldo de empleados, etc.

**Overload.** Sobrecarga (s). Sobrecargar (v).

**Overrule.** Desestimar, denegar, rechazar, rehusar.

**Overseas.** En el extranjero.

**Overtime.** Tiempo extra, trabajo adicional.

**Overthrow.** Derrocar, por ejemplo, un gobierno.

**Overturn.** Anular.

**Overt act.** Acto ulterior. Un acto ulterior (*overt act*)—cuando es necesario alegarlo y probarlo para establecer el delito de conspiración—es algo aparte e independiente de la conspiración; es un acto realizado para llevar a cabo el convenio. (Pueblo v. Vélez Rivera, 93 D.P.R. 649 (1966)).

**Owe.** Deber dinero u otra prestación.

**Own.** Poseer en propiedad, ser dueño de algo.

**Owner.** Dueño, propietario.

**Owner in common.** Comunero.

**Ownership.** Propiedad, derecho de propiedad.

**Oyez.** Expresión arcaica inglesa, de origen francés, que significa "oid" y es usada por el ujier para anunciar que se acerca el magistrado y el comienzo de las audiencias del día.

**Ozone layer.** Capa de ozono.

# P

**P.A.** Abreviatura de Asociación Profesional (*Professional Association*).

**PIN.** Número de identificación personal (*personal identification number*).

**P.M.** Pasado el medio día. Entre el medio día y la media noche.

**P.O.D.** Abreviatura de "*pay on delivery*," pago contra entrega.

**Package.** Bulto, paquete, lote.

**Pact.** Pacto, acuerdo, arreglo, contrato convenio.

**Paid.** Pagado.

**Pain and suffering.** Dolor y sufrimineto. Una de las categorias por las cuales se puede reclamar indemnización.

**Palimony.** Pensión pagada a la persona con quien uno ha convivido pero sin que haya mediado un matrimonio formal. La expresión viene de "*alimony*," alimentos y de "*pal*" que significa amigo/a.

**Panel.** Miembros del jurado.

**Paper.** Papel, documento, periódico.

**Paper money.** Papel moneda, billetes.

**Paper work.** Burocracia, documentación.

**Par.** A la par, paridad.

**Paragraph.** Párrafo.

**Paralegal.** Asistente jurídico.

**Pardon.** Perdón, absolución, amnistía, gracia, indulto, remisión (s). Perdonar, indultar (v).

**Parent.** Progenitor, padre o madre.

**Parent company.** Sociedad matríz.

**Parental rights.** Patria potestad.

***Pari passu* (L).** Sin privilegios ni preferencia, normalmente aplicable a acciones y otros títulos de crédito.

**Parliament.** Congreso.

**Parliamentary privilege.** Inmunidad parlamentaria.

**Parol evidence rule.** Primacía de un contrato completo y posterior sobre otros acuerdos. Un contrato integrado vinculante descarta contratos previos en la medida en que éstos sean inconsistentes con el primero. Un con-

trato integrado completamente vinculante descarta contratos previos en la medida en que éstos estén dentro de su alcance. (Rstmnt, 2nd, Con., sec. 213).

**Parole, on.** En libertad condicional.

**Parolee.** Persona en libertad condicional.

**Parricide.** Parricidio.

**Partial avoidance.** Anulación parcial. Si la causal de anulación afecta sólo algunas cláusulas del contrato, el efecto de la anulación se limitará a dichas cláusulas, a menos que, en consideración de las circunstancias, no sea razonable conservar la validez del resto del contrato. (Unidroit, Prin., art. 3.16).

**Partial performance.** Cumplimiento parcial. El acreedor podrá rechazar la oferta de un cumplimiento parcial que se le haga en la oportunidad en que deba cumplirse la obligación, independientemente de si el deudor garantiza o no el cumplimiento del resto de la obligación, a menos que el acreedor carezca de interés legítimo para el rechazo. (Unidroit, Prin., art. 6.1.3).

**Partially disclosed principal.** Mandante parcialmente manifiesto. Si una de las partes en una transacción tiene conocimiento de que el mandatario está o podría estar trabajando para un mandante, pero no conoce la identidad de dicho mandante, el mandante para quien el mandatario trabaja se conoce como un mandante parcialmente manifiesto. (Rstmnt, 2nd, Agency, sec. 4(2)).

**Participant-informer.** Confidente-participe. Un "confidente-partícipe" (*participant-informer*) es una persona que participa, que toma parte en la transacción delictiva y luego ofrece información a las autoridades sobre el delito cometido. (Pueblo v. López Rivera, 91 D.P.R. 693 (1965)).

**Parties aligned on the same side.** Partes con un interés similar. Partes en un pleito entre ellos y un tercero, partes que de las alegaciones resulta que no son adversarios entre ellos, están obligados por, y tienen derecho a los beneficios del principio de impedimento de controversias ("*issue preclusion*"), con respecto a controversias que se litiguen completa y justamente entre ellos siendo adversarios y que resulten esenciales a la sentencia que se dicta. (Rstmnt, 2nd, Judg., sec. 38).

**Parties to an action.** Partes en un pleito. Cualquier persona nombrada como parte en un pleito y sujeta a la jurisdicción del tribunal, se considera como una parte en el pleito. (Rstmnt, 2nd, Judg., sec. 34).

**Partly paid shares.** Acciones parcialmente pagadas. Toda corporación podrá emitir la totalidad o cualquier parte de sus acciones como acciones parcialmente pagadas y obligadas por el balance del precio que haya de pagarse por ella. (14 LPRA sec. 1507).

**Partner.** Socio, asociado, miembro.

**Partner in a law firm.** Socio de un bufete jurídico. Hoy en día se pueden encontrar en muchas ciudades firmas jurídicas con más de cien abogados, de los que algunos son socios, y muchos más son empleados de la firma. Si bien cada cliente trata por lo común con un único socio, hay socios que se especializan en ciertos campos como impuestos, corporaciones, leyes antimonopólicas, régimen inmobiliario, o litigios. (Intro al USA).

**Partnership.** Sociedad colectiva, asociación.

**Partnership agreement.** Contrato social, acta constitutiva de una sociedad colectiva o de una sociedad de responsabilidad limitada.

**Partnership assets.** Bienes pertenecientes a una sociedad.

**Partnership debt.** Deuda perteneciente a una sociedad.

**Partnership property.** Activo de una sociedad.

**Party.** Parte en un juicio o en un contrato. Partido.

**Party appearing in different capacities.** Parte que comparece en otro carácter. Una parte comparece en su carácter individual a menos que, cuando se le nombró parte o mediante otra manifestación, resulta evidente que comparece en otro carácter. (Rstmnt, 2nd, Judg., sec. 36).

**Party wall.** Medianera, pared divisora.

**Pass legislation.** Promulgar una ley.

**Passage of a law.** Aprobación de una ley.

**Passage of bills.** Aprobación de proyectos de legislación.

**Passing of title.** Traspaso de título. El título sobre mercancías no podrá adquirirse bajo un contrato de venta antes de la identificación de éstas al contrato y, salvo pacto expreso en contrario, el comprador adquirirá mediante la identificación de éstas una propiedad especial del vendedor del título (propiedad) en mercancías embarcadas o entregadas al comprador está limitada en sus efectos legales a una reserva de un interés garantizado. (C.C.U. sec. 2-401).

**Passing off.** Imitación y/o falsificación de un producto, una patente, etc.

**Passion.** Pasión, emoción violenta.

**Passive.** Pasivo.

**Passive assets.** Activo intangible.

**Passive debt.** Deuda que no devenga intereses.

**Passive use.** Uso permisivo.

**Passport.** Pasaporte.

**Past due.** Inpago, exigible, en mora.

**Pasturage in common.** Comunidad de pastos.

**Patent.** Patente, patente de invencion (s). Patentar, registrar una patente (v).

**Patent ambiguity.** Ambiguedad manifiesta.

**Patent attorney.** Abogado especializado en derecho de patentes.

**Patent defect.** Defecto evidente.

**Patent infringement.** Violación de derechos conferidos por una patente.

**Patent license.** Licencia para explotar una patente.

**Patent suit.** Juicio por violación de un derecho de patente.

**Patentable.** Patentable.

**Patentee.** Beneficiario de una patente.

**Patentee pooling.** Acuerdo para intercambiar patentes con otros miembros de un grupo.

**Paternity.** Paternidad.

**Paternity test.** Examen médico para determinar la paternidad.

**Patient-physician privilege.** Privilegio que tienen los médicos para no revelar datos de sus pacientes a no ser que éstos brinden su consentimiento.

**Patricide.** Parricidio.

**Patrimony.** Patrimonio.

**Patrol.** Patrulla (s). Patrullar (v).

**Patron.** Persona que brinda apoyo a una causa. Cliente de un establecimiento comercial.

**Patronage.** Patrocinio, representación legal.

**Pattern.** Tipo de conducta que se repite y que es predecible.

**Pauper.** Indigente, pobre, sin recursos financieros.

**Pawn.** Empeñar objetos para recibir un préstamo de dinero. Peón.

**Pawn shop.** Casa de empeño, montepío.

**Pay.** Pago (s). Pagar (v).

**Payback.** Reembolsar, devolver dinero.

**Payday.** Día de pago.

**Payable on demand.** Pagadero a la vista.

**Payable to bearer.** Pagadero al portador. Un instrumento será pagadero al portador cuando por sus términos es pagadero a a) el portador o a la orden del portador; o b) una persona específica o al portador; o c) "efectivo" o a la orden de "efectivo," o cualquiera otra indicación que no signifique que se designa un tomador determinado. (C.C.U. sec. 3-111).

**Payable to order.** Pagadero a la orden. Un instrumento será pagadero a la orden cuando de acuerdo a sus términos es pagadero a la orden o a los causahabientes de cualquier persona especificada en él con razonable certeza, o a ella o a su orden, o cuando esté evidentemente designado en el texto como "a cambio" o cosa semejante y nombra un tomador. (C.C.U. sec. 3-110).

**Payee.** Tomador.

**Payer for honor.** Interventor en el pago.

**Payment by check or other instruments.** Pago con cheque u otro instrumento. El pago puede efectuarse en cualquier forma utilizada en el curso ordinario de los negocios en el lugar del pago. (Unidroit, Prin., art. 6.1.7).

**Payment by funds transfer.** Pago mediante transferencia de fondos. El pago podrá efectuarse mediante una transferencia a cualquier institución financiera en la que el acreedor haya hecho saber que mantiene una cuenta, a menos que hubiera indicado una cuenta específicamente para ello. (Unidroit, Prin., art. 6.1.8).

**Payment for honor.** Intervención en el pago.

**Payment in due course.** Pago a su debido tiempo.

**Payroll.** Nómina de pago, lista de pago.

**Peace official.** Oficial encargado de mantener la tranquilidad pública.

**Peaceable assembly.** Reunión pacífica.

**Peculation.** Peculado, malversación de fondos.

**Peddler.** Vendedor ambulante. "Vendedores ambulantes" son aquellos empleados que se dedican a la venta, ofrecimiento para la venta, solicitud, colección o distribución de cualquier artículo, producto o mercancía o material publicitario, en la calle, en cualquier sitio público o de casa en casa, sin que el patrono ejerza control sobre sus horas de trabajo para realizar tales actividades fuera del establecimiento del patrono. (29 LPRA sec. 288).

**Pedigree.** Linaje, descendencia, genealogía, prosapia.

**Pedophilia.** Pedofilia.

**Peer.** Par del reino, con título de nobleza.

**Penal.** Penal, criminal.

**Penal action.** Acción penal.

**Penal clause.** Claúsula penal.

**Penal code.** Código penal, código criminal.

**Penalty.** Penalidad, sanción.

**Penalty clause.** Cláusula penal.

**Pendent jurisdiction.** Teoría que permite a un tribunal federal la adjudicación de una cuestion estatal si las partes estan ante el tribunal federal por una cuestión propiamente federal.

**Pending.** Pendiente.

**Peninsular.** Peninsular.

**Penitentiary.** Penitenciario, cárcel.

**Pension.** Pensión, jubilación, renta, retiro (s). Acordar la jubilación (v).

***Per curiam* (L).** Por el tribunal. Expresión que indica que la sentencia fue redactada por todo el tribunal, en oposición a aquélla redactada por un juez en particular. También se usa para indicar que la sentencia le pertenece al presidente del tribunal. Finalmente, se usa cuando sólo se anuncia el sentido en el que se falla pero sin expresión de motivos.

**Per day.** Por día, a diario, diariamente.

***Per diem* (L).** Dietas, emolumento, dotación.

***Per stirpes*.** Por estirpes.

**Per week.** Por semana, semanalmente.

**Peremptory.** Perentorio.

**Peremptory challenges.** Recusaciones perentorias del jurado. Si el delito imputado fuera sancionable con la pena de muerte, cada parte tendrá derecho a 20 recusaciones perentorias. Si el delito imputado fuera sancionable con la pena de reclusión por más de un año, el gobierno tendrá derecho a 6 recusaciones perentorias y el acusado o acusados conjuntamente a 10 recusaciones perentorias. (Regla 24(b), Reglas Fed. de Proc. Crim.).

**Peremptory challenge.** Impugnación sin causa a un miembro del jurado.

**Performance.** Prestación, cumplimiento.

**Performance at one time.** Cumplimiento único. Cuando el cumplimiento de cada parte se da bajo un intercambio de promesas, y la totalidad del cumplimiento de una parte se puede efectuar en un mismo momento, en tal momento torna exigible, a menos que el lenguaje o las circunstancias indiquen lo contrario. (Rstmnt, 2nd, Con., sec. 233(1)).

**Performance at one time or in installments.** Cumplimiento instantáneo o en etapas. En los casos de contratos con término, o dentro de un plazo razonable, el deudor debe cumplir sus obligaciones instantáneamente, siempre que tal cumplimiento sea susceptible de cumplimiento instantáneo y que las circunstancias no indiquen otro modo de cumplimiento. (Unidroit, art. 6.1.2).

**Performance bond.** Garantía que prestan, normalmente empresas constructoras, sobre lo adecuado de los trabajos que realizan.

**Performance in installments.** Cumplimiento en cuotas. Cuando sólo se ha efectuado una porción del cumplimiento de una de las partes contratantes al momento de su vencimiento; si el cumplimiento de la otra parte puede ser distinguido o prorroteado de modo que haya una porción equiparable que pueda ser rendida en ese momento, se entenderá que tal porción está vencida también, a menos que el lenguaje o las circunstancias indiquen lo contrario. (Rstmnt, 2nd, Con., sec. 233(2)).

**Performance, initial impossibility.** Cumplimiento, imposibilidad inicial. No afectará la validez del contrato el mero hecho de que al momento de su celebración no sea posible la ejecución de la obligación contraída. (Unidroit, Prin., art. 3.3).

**Performance of monetary obligation.** Cumplimiento de obligación dineraria. Si el deudor no cumple con una obligación dineraria, el acreedor podrá exigir su pago. (Unidroit, art. 7.2.1).

**Performance of non-monetary obligation.** Cumplimiento de obligaciónes no-dinerarias. Si el deudor no cumple con una obligación distinta de la de pagar una suma de dinero, el acreedor puede exigir su cumplimiento, a menos que: (a) el cumplimiento sea jurídica o físicamente imposible; (b) el cumplimiento o, en su caso, la ejecución forzada, sea excesivamente gravoso y oneroso. (Unidroit, Prin., art. 7.2.2).

**Performance or acceptance under reservation of rights.** Cumplimiento o aceptación bajo reserva de derechos. Una parte que con reserva explícita de derechos realiza o promete realizar o consiente cumplir en la forma demandada u ofrecida por la otra parte no perjudica por ello los derechos reservados. Palabras tales como "sin perjuicio", o "bajo protesta" o semejantes son suficientes. (C.C.U. sec. 1-207).

**Period.** Plazo, término, fecha, duración.

**Periodicity.** Periodicidad.

**Perjury.** Perjurio, delito de falso testimonio.

**Permission.** Permiso, autorización, licencia.

**Permission neither granted nor refused.** Autorización que no ha sido otorgada ni denegada. Cualquiera de las partes puede dar por terminado el contrato si pese a que la parte obligada a obtener la autorización tomó todas las medidas requeridas al efecto, la autorización no es otorgada ni rechazada dentro del plazo convenido, o, en el caso de no haberse fijado plazo alguno, dentro de un plazo prudencial a partir de la celebración del contrato. (Unidroit, Prin., art. 6.1.16).

**Permission refused.** Autorización denegada. La denegación de una autorización indispensable para la validez del contrato comporta la nulidad del mismo. Si la denegación únicamente involucra la validez de alguna o algunas de las cláusulas del contrato, tan sólo estas serán nulas, siempre y cuando, teniendo en cuenta las circunstancias, resulte razonable conservar el resto del contrato. (Unidroit, Prin., art. 6.1.17).

**Permissive counterclaim.** Reconvención permisible. Las alegaciones podrán incluir por vía de reconvención contra parte adversa cualquier reclamación que no surgiere del evento o serie de eventos a que se contrae la reclamación de la parte adversa. (Regla Fed. de Proc. Civ., sec. 13(b)).

**Permissive intervention.** Intervención permisible. Mediante la oportuna solicitud se podrá permitir a cualquier persona intervenir en un pleito: 1) cuando una ley de los Estados Unidos confiera un derecho incondicional a intervenir; o 2) cuando la demanda o la defensa del solicitante y el pleito principal impliquen una cuestión de derecho o de hecho en común. (R. Fed. P. Civ., sec. 24(b)).

**Permissive joinder.** Litisconsorcio facultativo.

**Permit.** Permiso, autorización (s). Permitir (v).

**Perpetrator.** Perpetrador, autor de un delito u otra acción ilegal.

**Perpetuating testimony.** Testimonio obtenido anticipadamente, v.g. antes.

**Perpetuity.** Perpetuidad.

**Perquisites.** Ventajas, económicas y de otra índole, que vienen aparejados con cierto cargo, v.g. seguro médico para el resto de las familia.

**Person in the position of a seller.** Persona con carácter de vendedor. Una "persona con carácter de vendedor" incluye con respecto al comitente a un comisionista que ha pagado o que es responsable por el precio de las mercancías a nombre de su comitente o cualquier persona que de otra manera tenga un interés garantizado u otro derecho en mercancías similar a ése del vendedor. (C.C.U. sec. 2-707).

**Person represented by a party.** Persona representada por una parte. Una persona que no es parte en un pleito, pero que está representada por una parte, está obligada por, y tiene derecho a, los beneficios de la sentencia que se dicte, como si dicha persona fuera parte. (Rstmnt, 2nd, Judg., sec. 41).

**Personal action.** Acción personal.

**Personal bond.** Caución personal.

**Personal effects.** Efectos personales.

**Personal expenses.** Gastos particulares.

**Personal property.** Bienes muebles.

**Personal surety.** Garantía personal.

**Personalty.** Bienes muebles.

**Petit jury.** Jurado ordinario. Se distingue así del *grand jury*.

**Petition.** Solicitud, demanda, petición, súplica.

**Petitioner.** Parte actora, solicitante, requirente, apelante.

**Pettifogger.** Picapleitos, chicanero.

**Petty.** Pequeño, menor, secundario.

**Petty cash.** Caja chica.

**Petty larceny.** Hurto. Hurto menor.

**Petty misdemeanor.** Delito menor. Un delito es menos grave si así está designado en este Código o en otro estatuto que se promulgue posteriormente. (Cód. Pen. Mod., § 1.04 (3)).

**Petty offense.** Delito menor, normalmente redimible con multa.

**Petty officer.** Suboficial de marina.

**Phone-tapping.** Escucha telefónica.

**Physical.** Físico, atinente al cuerpo.

**Physical disabilty.** Discapacitación física. Incapacidad física.

**Physical force.** Fuerza física.

**Physical necessity.** Necesidad imprescindible.

**Physical violence.** Violencia física.

**Physician.** Médico, doctor.

**Picket.** Piquete (s). Congregarse frente a un establecimiento para ejecer presión, o no dejar pasar a quienes quieren ingresar (v).

**Picklock.** Ganzúa.

**Pickpocket.** Pungista, carterista.

**Piecework.** Trabajo por pieza.

**Piercing the corporate veil.** Perforando el velo corporativo. Realidad empresarial. Teoría que castiga los abusos de una empresa privandola de ciertos beneficios que, de otra manera la brindaría el derecho societario. Típicamente la sanción consiste en imponer responsabilidad solidaria a los dirigentes responsables del abuso.

**Pignorate.** Pignorar, ofrecer en prenda o hipoteca.

**Pilfer.** Hurtar en pequeñas cantidades.

**Pilfering.** Robo hormiga, robo en pequeñas cantidades.

**Pillage.** Pillaje, saqueo (s). Pillar, saquear (v).

**Pillory.** Picota, instrumento de tortura.

**Pilot.** Piloto, práctico (s). Pilotear (v).

**Pimp.** Proxeneta.

**Pioneer patent.** Patente primaria o básica.

**Piracy.** Piratería.

**Place of performance.** Lugar de cumplimiento. En caso de que el contrato no determine el lugar de cumplimiento, ni este pueda determinarse con base a aquél, el deudor habrá de cumplir: (a) en el establecimiento del acreedor cuando se trate de obligaciones de dinero; (b) en su propio establecimiento, cuando se trate de cualquier otra obligación. (Unidroit, Prin., art. 6.1.6).

**Place of prosecution.** Lugar del proceso. Salvo que la ley o estas reglas permitieren otra cosa, el proceso tendrá lugar en el distrito en que se cometió el delito. La corte fijará el lugar para el juicio dentro del distrito con debida consideración de la conveniencia del acusado y los testigos y la rápida administración de justicia. (Regla 18, Reglas Fed. de Proc. Crim.).

**Place upon interest.** Colocar a interés.

**Placing a person in false light.** Crear una falsa impresión sobre alguien. Una persona que le dé publicidad a un asunto concer-

niente a otro, creando una falsa impresión de éste, será sujeto a responsabilidad por una invasión a la privacidad de ese otro, si: a) la falsa impresión o imagen creada resulta altamente ofensiva a una persona razonable, y b) el actor tenía conocimiento de, o actuó con menosprecio temerario con relación a la falsedad del asunto publicado y la falsa impresión creada. (Rstmnt, 2nd, Torts, sec. 652 E).

**Plain error.** Error evidente. Errores o defectos obvios que afecten derechos sustanciales podrán ser advertidos aunque no se hubiera llamado la atención de la corte sobre los mismos. (Regla 52(b), Reglas de Proc. Crim.).

**Plainclothes man.** Policía secreto, policía vestido de civil.

**Plaintiff.** Actor, accionante, demandante, persona que interpone una demanda.

**Plea.** Alegación, alegato. Todo acusado podrá hacer alegación de no culpable, culpable o *nolo contendere*. Si el acusado se negase a alegar o si una corporación acusada dejare de comparecer, la corte registrará alegación de no culpable. (Regla 11(a)(12), Reglas Fed. de Proc. Crim.). Alegar (v).

**Plea bargaining, acceptance.** Alegación preacordada, aceptación. Si la corte aceptara la alegación preacordada informará al acusado que la disposición correspondiente sobre la misma será incorporada al fallo y la sentencia. No obstante la aceptación de la alegación de culpable, la corte no dictará sentencia basada en dicha alegación sin hacer las investigaciones que la convenzan de que existe una verdadera base para la alegación. (Regla 11(e)(3), (f) Reglas Fed. de Proc. Crim.).

**Plea bargaining, plea agreement.** Alegación preacordada, acuerdo sobre la alegación. El fiscal y el abogado defensor, o el acusado cuando estuviera actuando por sí mismo, podrán celebrar discusiones con vista a llegar a un acuerdo acerca de que si el acusado hiciere alegación de culpable o nolo contendere por el delito imputado o un delito menor o relacionado, el fiscal hará cualquiera de los siguientes: a) solicitar el sobreseimiento de otros cargos; o b) recomendar, o convenir no oponerse a la solicitud del acusado de una sentencia específica bajo el entendimiento de que tal recomendación o solicitud no obligará a la corte; o c) convenir que una sentencia específica constituye la disposición pertinente de la causa.

La corte no participará en ninguna de dichas discusiones. (Regla 11(e)(1), Reglas Fed. de Proc. Crim.).

**Plea bargaining, rejection.** Alegación preacordada, rechazo. Si la corte rechazare la alegación preacordada, con constancia en el récord, lo informará así a las partes, advertirá al acusado personalmente en corte abierta o, por causa justificada, en cámara, que la corte no viene obligada por el acuerdo sobre alegación, concederá al acusado la oportunidad para retirar entonces su alegación. (Regla 11(e)(4), Reglas Fed. de Proc. Crim.).

**Plea withdrawal.** Retiro de alegación. Si antes de dictarse la sentencia se radicare una moción para retirar una alegación de culpable o nolo contendere, la corte podrá permitir que se retire dicha alegación, previa demostración por el acusado de que existe razón adecuada y justa para ello. (Regla 32(d), Reglas Fed. de Proc. Crim.).

**Plead.** Alegar, rogar.

**Plead guilty/not guilty.** Declararse culpable/no culpable.

**Pleading.** Escrito. En los Estados Unidos el término *pleading*, se utiliza en el procedimiento civil solamente para estos documentos que se presentan antes del juicio, y no incluye la argumentación que hace el abogado durante el juicio. (Intro al USA).

**Pleadings.** Alegaciones. Habrá demandas y contestaciones, réplicas o reconvenciones así denominadas; contestaciones a demandas contra coparte, si las contestaciones contuvieran tales demandas; demandas contra tercero, si las personas que originalmente no fueron partes fueren emplazadas, y contestaciones de tercero, si se diligenciaren tales demandas. (R. Fed. P. Civ., sec. 7(a)).

**Pleadings, content.** Alegaciones, contenido. Las aseveraciones en una alegación serán sencillas, concisas y directas. No se requerirán fórmulas técnicas para las alegaciones o mociones. Las partes podrán formular dos o más partes exposiciones de una reclamación o defensa, alternativa o hipotéticamente, ya fuere en una reclamación o defensa o en reclamaciones o defensas separadas cuando se hicieren dos o más exposiciones en la alternativa y una de ellas, si se hiciere independientemente, fuere suficiente, la alegación no se considerará insuficiente por insuficiencia de una o más de las exposiciones alternativas. (R. Fed. P. Civ. sec, 8(e)(f)).

**Pleadings, form.** Alegaciones, forma. Toda alegación tendrá un encabezamiento en el que se consignará el nombre de la corte, el título del pleito, el número de radicación y la denominación. En las demandas el título del pleito incluirá los nombres de todas las partes, pero en las otras alegaciones será suficiente exponer el nombre del primer litigante de cada parte con una referencia apropiada a las otras partes. (R. Fed. P. Civ., sec. 10).

**Pleadings, signature.** Alegaciones, firma. Todas las alegaciones, mociones y escritos de otra clase de partes representadas por abogado serán firmados por lo menos por un abogado de autos en su propio nombre, expresándose su dirección. Las partes no representadas por abogado firmarán sus alegaciones, mociones o escritos de otra clase y expresarán su dirección. (R. Fed. P. Civ., sec. 11).

**Plebiscite.** Plebiscito.

**Pledge.** Pignoración, caución, prenda (s). Prendar, pignorar (v).

**Pledgee.** Acreedor prendario.

**Pledgor.** Deudor prendario.

**Plenary powers.** Poderes plenos.

**Plenipotentiary.** Plenipotenciario.

**Plot.** Complot, conjura, parcela de tierra (s). Complotar, tramar, urdir (v).

**Plunderage (Mar.).** Hurto de mercadería cargada en una nave.

**Plurality.** Pluralidad.

**Poach.** Cazar en forma clandestina.

**Point blank.** A quemarropa.

**Point of order.** Moción de orden.

**Poison.** Veneno (s). Envenenar (v).

**Police.** Policía, fuerza pública (s). Ejercer vigilancia o control (v).

**Police court.** Tribunal de faltas, tribunal municipal.

**Police custody.** Custodia policial. El concepto custodia policíaca—a los efectos de la doctrina elaborada en *Escobedo v. Illinois*, 378 U.S. 478 (1964), y *Miranda v. Arizona*, 384 U.S. 436 (1966)—, se define para incluir no sólo la detención en el cuartel del sospechoso, sino también cualquier otra detención—aunque no sea por la comisión del delito de que se le sospecha y por el cual posteriormente se procesa—incluyendo la detención en el propio hogar del acusado, al interrogársele mientras éste se encuentra incomunicado. (Pueblo v. Tribunal Superior, 97 D.P.R. 199 (1969)).

**Police power.** Poder de policía.

**Police record.** Antecedentes policiales.

**Police state.** Estado autoritario y despótico.

**Policy.** Política, línea de conducta establecida oficialmente. Póliza.

**Poligamy.** Poligamia.

**Political question.** Cuestión política que escapa a las atribuciones del tribunal y queda reservada a la discreción de los gobernantes.

**Poll of jury.** Preguntas al jurado. Cuando el jurado hubiere rendido un veredicto y antes de que éste fuere registrado, el jurado será escrutado a solicitud de cualquier parte o a instancias de la propia corte. Si como resultado del escrutinio se demuestra que no hay una concurrencia unánime, se podrá ordenar al jurado que se retire para deliberaciones adicionales o podrá ser disuelto. (Regla 30(d), Reglas Fed. de Proc. Crim.).

**Polygraph.** Detector de mentiras.

**Pornographic.** Pornográfico.

**Port of call.** Puerto de escala.

**Port of destination.** Puerto de destino.

**Port of distress.** Puerto al que se llega por una emergencia.

**Portfolio.** Conjunto de acciones y demás títulos en cartera.

**Positive.** Positivo, explícito, escrito.

**Positive evidence.** Prueba directa.

**Positive law.** Derecho positivo.

**Possess.** Poseer.

**Possession.** Posesión. Bienes.

**Possession, actual.** Posesión material.

**Possession, adverse.** Prescripción, posesión adversa.

**Possession, constructive.** Posesión ficta.

**Possession is nine-tenths of the law.** Literalmente: la posesión equivale a las nueve décimas del derecho. Frase que destaca el gran valor práctico de detentar la posesión material cuando se reclama la propiedad de la cosa.

**Possession, open.** Posesión pública y notoria.

**Post nuptial agreement.** Pacto nupcial celebrado luego del matrimonio.

**Post office.** Correo.

**Posthumous.** Póstumo.

**Postpone.** Postpone, aplazar, relegar.

**Postponement.** Aplazamiento.

**Poverty.** Pobreza, falta de recursos económicos.

**Power.** Poder, facultades, mandato. Un poder es la habilidad de parte de una persona para producir un cambio en una relación legal dada, realizando o dejando de realizar un acto en particular. (Rstmnt, 2nd, Agency, sec. 6).
Atribuciones, atributos, autoridad.

**Power coupled with an interest.** Mandato unido a un derecho que el mandatario ya disponía sobre la cosa.

**Power of attorney.** Mandato, poder de representación, poder general.

**Power of attorney, irrevocable.** Mandato o poder irrevocable.

**Practice law.** Ejercer como abogado, ejercer el derecho.

**Prayer.** Súplica, petición, solicitud.

**Precarious.** Precario, meramente tolerado, que puede ser revocado en cualquier momento.

**Precedent, mandatory.** Precedente obligatorio. La jurisprudencia imperativa, a la que si se aplica la doctrina del precedente, incluye las decisiones de tribunales más altos de la misma jurisdicción y las del mismo tribunal. (Intro al USA).

**Precedent, persuasive.** Precedente persuasivo. La jurisprudencia suele dividirse en *persuasiva* e *imperativa*. Ejemplo de jurisprudencia persuasiva son las decisiones de los tribunales de otras jurisdicciones o de tribunales del mismo nivel en la misma jurisdicción, tales como otros tribunales de apelación del mismo estado u otros tribunales de apelación federales. El grado de persuasividad de la decisión dependerá en gran medida de la solidez del razonamiento que la fundamenta y de la aparente corrección del resultado. (Intro al USA).

**Precedent.** Precedente, antecedente.

**Precept.** Precepto, norma.

**Precinct.** Distrito administrativo, normalmente policial.

**Precious metals, either coined or in bullion.** Metales preciosos, amonedados o en pasta.

**Preclude.** Precluir, bloquear, dejar sin efecto, impedir.

**Precondition.** Condición previa.

**Predisposition.** Predisposición, propensidad.

**Pre-existent.** Preexistente.

**Pre-emption.** Teoría que acuerda prioridad al derecho federal por tratarse de temas en los que la nación tiene un interés claro y fuerte.

**Preface.** Prefacio, introducción (s). Hacer una introducción (v).

**Preference of credits.** Prelación de créditos.

**Preferred creditiors.** Acreedores privilegiados.

**Pregnancy.** Embarazo, preñez, gravidez.

**Prejudicial error.** Error procesal que conlleva una desventaja tan grande a la parte que sufre sus consecuencias que justifica la anulación del proceso y el comienzo de uno nuevo.

**Preliminary.** Preliminar, anterior.

**Preliminary hearing.** Audiencia tendiente a determinar si puede o no dictarsele auto de procesamiento al reo.

**Preliminary injunction.** Interdicto preliminar, sujeto a las resultas de la causa.

**Premeditated design.** Propósito premeditado. A los efectos de una acusación por asesinato en segundo grado los términos "con intención legal, alevosía, voluntaria, ilegal e intencionalmente"—"*willfully, wrongfully, unlawfully, intentionally, and*

*feloniously*"—tiene un significado similar al termino *propósito premeditado* usado en el estatuto. (Pueblo v. Reyes Lara, 100 D.P.R. 676 (1971)).

**Pre-emption.** Teoría que acuerda prioridad al derecho federal por tratarse de temas en los que la nación tiene un interés claro y fuerte.

**Preparatory proceedings.** Diligencias preliminares.

**Preponderance of the evidence.** Preponderancia de evidencia. Tal término no significa la mera superioridad numérica de testigos, sino el peso, crédito y valor de la totalidad de la evidencia aportada por cada una de las partes. Si, sin embargo, los testigos son de igual honradez, candor, inteligencia y verdad, y están igualmente corroborados en otros extremos de sus declaraciones e igualmente libres de interés en el pleito, entonces el mayor número determina la preponderancia. (Morales Lebrón).

**Presentment for payment.** Presentación al pago. La presentación es una demanda de aceptación o de pago hecha al deudor, aceptante, librado u otro obligado al pago por el tenedor o a su nombre. La presentación podrá hacerse: a) por correo, en cuyo caso la fecha de presentación se determina por la fecha del recibo del correo; o b) a través de una cámara de compensación; o c) en el lugar de aceptación o pago especificado en el instrumento y si no hubiere ninguno en el lugar de negocio o residencia de la persona que debe aceptar o pagar. (C.C.U. sec. 3-504).

**Presentment of "on arrival" draft.** Presentación de giros "a su recibo." Cuando un giro o las instrucciones pertinentes requieren la presentación "a su recibo," "cuando las mercancías se reciban" o cosa similar, el banco colector no estará obligado a presentarlo hasta que a su juicio transcurriere un tiempo razonable para el arribo de las mercancías. (C.C.U. sec. 4-502).

**Preservation.** Conservación.

**Preservation expenses.** Gastos de conservación.

**Preserve.** Conservar, retener.

**Preserve and enforce.** Mantener y asegurar.

**Preserve secrecy.** Guardar secreto.

**Presumed intent.** Intención presunta.

**Presumption.** Presunción, conjetura, indicio, probabilidad.

**Presumption of death.** Presunción de muerte.

**Presumptions in civil proceedings.** Presunciones en acciones civiles. En todos los procedimientos y acciones civiles, a menos que otra cosa se disponga por ley del Congreso o por estas reglas, una presunción impondrá a la parte contra la cual se establece el peso de producir evidencia para rebatir o destruir la presunción, pero no trasladará a tal parte el peso de la prueba en el sentido del riesgo de no persuadir al juzgador, que permanecerá durante todo el juicio sobre la parte a la cual le fue impuesto originalmente. (Regla 301, R. Fed. Evid.).

**Presumptive heir.** Heredero presunto.

**Pretermitted child statute.** Ley sobre hijos nacidos luego de haber testado los padres. Mediante esta ley se reconocen a tales hijos —aun adoptivos—derechos sucesorios *ab intestato* aunque no figuren en el testamento. (Texas Probate Code, sec. 67).

**Pretermitted spouse.** Cónyuge que contrae matrimonio con posterioridad al testamento del otro cónyuge.

**Pretrial conference, civil.** Conferencia con antelación al juicio. En todo pleito la corte podrá a su discreción ordenar a los abogados de las partes y a las partes no representadas por abogado que comparezcan ante la misma para una o varias conferencias con antelación al juicio con los siguientes propósitos: 1) acelerar la resolución del pleito; 2) establecer un control inicial y continuo sobre el caso de manera que no se prolongue por falta de dirección; 3) desalentar cualesquiera actuaciones inútiles anteriores al juicio; 4) mejorar la calidad del juicio por medio de una preparación más cabal; y 5) facilitar la transacción del caso. (R. Fed. P. Civ., sec. 16(a)).

**Pretrial conference, criminal.** Conferencia con antelación al juicio. En cualquier momento después de la presentación del indiciamiento o la acusación la corte, a moción de cualquier parte o a su propia iniciativa, podrá ordenar una o más conferencias para discutir las cuestiones que puedan procurar un juicio justo y rápido. A la conclusión de toda conferencia la corte preparará y registrará un memorándum sobre las materias acordadas en la misma. (Regla 17.1, Reglas Fed. de Proc. Crim.).

**Pretrial conference, scheduling and planning.** Conferencia con antelación al juicio. El juez, o el magistrado autorizado por regla de la corte deberá dictar orden aprobando un programa que limite los términos: 1) para acumular otras partes y enmendar las alegaciones; 2) para presentar mociones y celebrar vistas sobre las mismas; y 3) para concluir el descubrimiento. El programa también podrá incluir: 4) la fecha o fechas para conferencias con antelación al juicio, conferencia final con antelación al juicio, y el juicio; y 5) cualesquiera otros asuntos pertinentes a las circunstancias del caso. (Regla Fed. del Proc. Civ., sec. 16(b)).

**Pretrial conference, scope.** Conferencia con antelación. Los participantes del cualquier conferencia a tenor con esta regla podrán discutir y tomar medidas con respecto a: 1) la formulación y simplificación de los hechos controvertidos, incluso la eliminación de reclamaciones o defensas frívolas; 2) la necesidad o deseabilidad de enmiendas a las alegaciones; 3) la posibilidad de obtener admisiones de hechos y documentos que evitarán pruebas innecesarias, estipulaciones con respecto a la autenticidad de documentos y decisiones por anticipado de la corte sobre la admisibilidad de evidencia; 4) evitar pruebas innecesarias y evidencia acumulativa. (R. Fed. P. Civ., sec. 16(c)).

**Pretrial discovery.** Para el jurista del *common law*, el *pretrial discovery* es un sistema probatorio anterior al juicio, pero normalmente posterior al intercambio de *pleadings* y siempre relacionado con el litigio que se está intentando. Pero también puede darse el caso de que las partes ya sea para preparar su demanda o temerosas de que la hubiere, lleven a cabo procedimientos probatorios.

**Pretrial motions.** Mociones antes del juicio. Cualquier defensa, objeción o solicitud susceptible de una determinación sin pronunciamiento en los méritos podrá presentarse antes del juicio mediante moción. Las mociones podrán ser por escrito u orales a discreción del juez. (Regla 12(b), Reglas Fed. de Proc. Crim.).

**Pretrial order.** Orden dictada luego de la conferencia con antelación al juicio. Después de cualquier conferencia celebrada a tenor con esta regla, se dictará una orden en que se expondrá todo lo acordado. (R. Fed. P. Civ., sec. 16(e)).

**Prevail.** Predominar, prevalecer.

**Prevailing party.** Litigante victorioso.

**Prevaricate.** Prevaricar, ofrecer pruebas falsas para ocultar la verdad de los hechos.

**Prevent.** Impedir, evitar, estorbar, obstaculizar, prevenir, trabar.

**Preventive detention.** Arresto preventivo.

**Price determination.** Determinación del precio. Si el contrato no fija el precio ni prevé su determinación, a falta de cualquiera indicación en contrario, se entenderá que las partes se remitieron al precio generalmente cobrado por tales prestaciones al momento de celebrarse el contrato, en circunstancias semejantes dentro del respectivo ramo comercial. De no poder establecerse el precio de esta manera, se entenderá que las partes se remitieron a un precio razonable. (Unidroit, Prin., art. 5.7).

**Price fixing.** Puesta de acuerdo con la competencia para controlar los precios.

**Primage.** Capa.

**Primogeniture.** Primogenitura.

**Principal.** Comitente, mandante.

**Principal, mandator.** Mandante, comitente, poderdante, principal.

**Prior law.** Ley anterior.

**Priority.** Prioridad, precedencia, preferencia, prelación.

**Prison.** Prisión, cárcel, penitenciaría.

**Prisoner of war.** Prisionero de guerra.

**Private.** Privado, individual, íntimo. soldado.

**Private (letter) ruling.** Dictamen de la autoridad impositiva emitido a petición del interesado directo y para evacuar una consulta formulada por él mismo.

**Private act.** Ley especial que se dirije a un individuo, o pequeño grupo de individuos, solamente.

**Private foundation.** Institución benéfica privada, fundación privada.

**Private funds.** Fondos particulares.

**Private international law.** Derecho internacional privado, conflicto de leyes.

**Private law.** Derecho privado, por oposición al derecho público.

**Private nuisance.** Molestia privada. Una molestia privada es la invasión o transgresión no-física del interés de una persona en el uso y disfrute privado de la tierra. (Rstmnt, 2nd, Torts, sec. 821 D).

**Private offering.** Oferta de venta de acciones en una sociedad anónima hecha, no al público en general, pero a un grupo reducido de personas con las que se tiene una relación especial. La expresión se opone a *public offering* u oferta pública.

**Private police.** Policía o fuerza de seguridad privada.

**Private property.** Propiedad privada, fuera del dominio público.

**Privateer.** Corsario, pirata, filibustero.

**Privilege.** Privilegio. Denota el hecho de que una conducta que bajo circunstancias ordinarias conllevaría la imposición de responsabilidad al actor, bajo circunstancias particulares no se le impone tal responsabilidad. (Rstmnt, 2nd, Torts, sec. 10).

Alguien que de otra manera incurrirá en responsabilidad extracontractual no responderá por daños causados si actúa al amparo, y dentro de los límites, de un privilegio propio, o de un privilegio de otra persona que le fue debidamente asignado. (Rstmnt, 2nd, Torts, sec. 890).

**Privilege ancillary to duty of protection.** Privilegio derivado del deber de protección. Quien tiene a su cargo proteger a un tercero, sus bienes muebles e inmuebles, contra los actos de otro individuo, goza del privilegio de utilizar la fuerza o coerción contra ese individuo siempre que: a) sea razonable con relación al daño a infligirse, b) razonablemente necesario en vista del deber de protección. (Rstmnt, 2nd, Torts, sec. 156).

**Privilege to discipline children.** Privilegio para disciplinar a los niños. El padre o madre están facultados o gozan del privilegio de ejercer una fuerza razonable o imponer una detención razonable sobre sus hijos, para su control, entrenamiento o educación. (Rstmnt, 2nd, Torts, sec. 147).

**Privileged.** Que goza de un privilegio, v.g. *privileged information* la información cuya revelación no puede ser ordenada por un tribunal como lo sería el secreto profesional de los abogados.

**Privileges and immunities.** Privilegios e inmunidades. Los ciudadanos de cada Estado disfrutarán de todos los privilegios e inmunidades de los ciudadanos de otros Estados. (Constitución de USA, art. IV, sec. 2).

**Privity.** Relación entre dos personas que las coloca en una situación jurídica determinada. Se usa la expresión para contrastar la suerte que, en forma distinta, corren quienes son solamente terceros o terceros interesados.

***Pro hac vice* (L).** Se llama así la petición que hace un abogado al tribunal requiriendo autorización para intervenir a pesar de no estar matriculado en tal jurisdicción.

**Probable cause.** Causa probable. Si los hechos aparentes que se desprenden de una declaración jurada ofrecida como base para la expedición de una orden autorizando un registro son de tal naturaleza que una persona prudente y razonable pudiera creer que se ha cometido la ofensa imputada, hay causa probable que justifica la expedición de dicha orden. (Pueblo v. Tribunal Superior, 91 D.P.R. 19 (1964)).

**Probable cause finding.** Determinación de causa probable. Si de la prueba apareciere que existe causa probable para creer que se ha cometido un delito y que el acusado lo cometió, el magistrado federal lo detendrá inmediatamente para que responda ante la corte de distrito. (Regla 5.1(a), Reglas Fed. de Proc. Crim.).

**Probate.** Sucesorio, juicio sucesorio.

**Probation.** Libertad bajo fianza, libertad condicional.

**Probe.** Investigación. Investigar.

**Procedural.** Procesal.

**Procedural code.** Código de procedimiento.

**Procedural law.** Derecho procesal.

**Procedural law, US system.** Sistema estadounidense de procedimiento civil. El procedimiento civil norteamericano—aunque también su derecho substantivo—es una técnica para resolver específicas controversias legales. Funciona dentro de un sistema extremadamente práctico y dirigido a los hechos y es necesariamente muy flexible y complejo. Como las reglas del procedimiento están escritas a menudo en un lenguaje amplio y sólo ponen límites modestos a las facultades del tribunal o a su creatividad, el juez norteamericano tiene una discreción considerable en sus decisiones. Además, dicho juez también tiene un control intenso sobre el procedimiento, las partes, los abogados y los terceros.

El Poder Judicial norteamericano tiene un amplio papel social y político. Los jueces con frecuencia crean una política pública importante y por medio de precedentes regulan aspectos sociales con las sentencias privadas litigiosas. Aunque el juez juega un papel central en el sistema legal norteamericano, los efectos de un sistema de jurado deben también ser considerados para entender sus técnicas procesales.

El procedimiento civil norteamericano evolucionó con el sistema de jurado, el cual necesariamente interfiere por ser un elemento no profesional en la administración de justicia y en consecuencia en un cierto grado no es predecible, a menudo en los casos de altas compensaciones por daños. La audiencia final con el jurado también exige una extensa preparación previa para evitar la sorpresa y la dilación en la audiencia. La división estructural del procedimiento entre la fase previa a la audiencia y ésta (*trial*) permitió el desarrollo del sistema previo de apertura de pruebas (*discovery*) el que, a su vez, determinó que fueran flexibles las reglas de las peticiones. Al mismo tiempo, un *discovery* generoso permite una aplicación estricta de las reglas para terminar el caso. El *discovery* ha jugado un papel predominante en los procedimientos legales estadounidenses. Sin embargo, el *discovery* tiene doble filo: facilita encontrar la verdad, pero también puede resultar una carga y un procedimiento caro en casos complejos. El derecho substantivo provee altas compensaciones a través del pago de daños morales, daños como castigo (*punitive damages*) y otras compensaciones que no se otorgan usualmente en los sistemas de derecho civil. Estos factores, entre otros, explican en parte la litigiocidad norteamericana.

Los abogados norteamericanos están muy bien pagados, generalmente por hora y/o con una proporción alta del monto del éxito. Altos honorarios a los abogados, al lado de altas compensaciones al jurado, pactos de quota litis y la regla general norteamericana que prohibe no cobrarlos (con importantes excepciones en la ley en litigios de interés público) ha provocado el surgimiento de una "barra empresarial." Esta práctica aumenta el acceso a la justicia para algunos tipos de reclamaciones, pero también genera problemas éticos y estimula más litigios, pues los actores no necesitan gastar los costos asociados con el procedimiento para lograr hacer una gran recuperación.

Las audiencias finales pueden ser dramáticas, pero la realidad es que en la mayoría de los casos hay un arreglo. La estimación de la prueba en las acciones civiles es "la preponderancia de la evidencia," lo que hace comparativamente más fácil para los actores satisfacer la carga de la prueba que en los sistemas de derecho civil. Desde un punto de vista comparado, el sistema en su conjunto está notablemente orientado a favorecer al demandante.

Finalmente, la cultura política norteamericana ha apoyado fuertemente, como una forma positiva de regular la sociedad y cambiar el status quo, este tipo de litigio. Esta perspectiva contribuye a un clima legal flexible sin las dilaciones legislativas, pero la amenaza de una responsabilidad puede conducir a una exagerada vigilancia de actividades útiles socialmente. (Antonio Gidi).

**Proceedings.** Procedimiento, acción, actuaciones.

**Proceedings against sureties.** Procedimiento contra fiadores. Cada fiador se someterá a la jurisdicción de la corte e irrevocablemente nombrará al secretario de la corte como su agente a quien le podrán ser notificados todos los escritos que afectasen su responsabilidad en la fianza o garantía. Su responsabilidad podrá hacerse efectiva mediante moción sin necesidad de un pleito independiente. (R. Fed. P. Civ., sec. 65.1).

**Proceedings to avoid litigation.** Actos para evitar un proceso, v.g. intentos de conciliación.

**Proceedings to declare heirship.** Declaratoria de herederos.

**Proceeds.** Beneficios, recaudación, frutos, ganancia, rédito, utilidad.

**Process.** Proceso.

**Process, due.** Debido processo.

**Process in behalf of and against persons not parties.** Procedimiento a favor y en contra de personas que no fueren parte. Cuando se dictare una orden a favor de una persona que no fuere parte en el pleito, ésta podrá exigir el cumplimiento de la orden por el mismo procedimiento como si fuera parte; y cuando el cumplimiento de una orden pudiere ser exigido legalmente contra una persona que no fuere parte, ésta estará sujeta al mismo procedimiento para hacer cumplir la orden como si fuera parte. (R. Fed. P. Civ., sec. 71).

**Process of posting.** Proceso de anotación. El "proceso de anotación" significa el procedimiento usual seguido por un banco pagador para efectuar el pago de un efecto y registrarlo incluyendo uno o más de los siguientes u otros pasos según lo determine el banco: —verificación de cualquier forma; —confirmación de que existen suficientes fondos disponibles;—ponerle "pagado" u otro cuño;—anotar un cargo o asiento a la cuenta del cliente; —corregir o anular un asiento o acción errónea con respecto al efecto. (C.C.U. sec. 4-109).

**Process server.** Notificador de órdenes judiciales que trabaja en forma privada.

**Proclaim.** Publicar, proclamar.

**Proclamation.** Proclama.

**Prodigal.** Pródigo.

**Produce exchange.** Lonja, bolsa de comercio.

**Production of documents and things.** Producción de documentos y objetos. Cualquier parte podrá notificar a cualquier otra una solicitud para producir y permitir a la parte que presentare la solicitud, o a alguien en su nombre, inspeccionar y copiar cualquier documento determinado (incluso escritos, dibujos, gráficos, diagramas, fotografías, discos o grabaciones fonográficos y otras compilaciones de datos de los que el demandado pudiera obtener información).

**Products liability.** Responsabilidad objetiva por defecto de las mercaderías o servicios que se producen o que se comercian.

**Profession.** Profesión, arte u oficio.

**Promise.** Promesa. Promesa es la manifestación de una intención de actuar o de abstenerse de actuar en forma determinada, hecha de modo que justifique en el tenedor de la promesa la creencia de que se ha hecho un compromiso. Una promesa puede ser hecha tanto en forma oral como escrita o puede inferirse total o parcialmente de la conducta. (Rstmnt, 2nd, Con., sec. 2(1), 4). Prometer (v).

**Promise in restraint of marriage.** Promesa contra la libertad de matrimonio. Una promesa no se puede ejecutar en términos de política pública si atenta irrazonablemente contra la libertad de matrimonio. (Rstmnt, 2nd, Con., sec. 189).

**Promissory.** Promisorio, que contiene una promesa.

**Promissory estoppel.** Principio jurídico sobre la imposibilidad de no honrar una promesa que ha sido tomada seriamente por otra perona.

**Promissory note.** Pagaré, vale.

**Promotion.** Ascenso.

**Proof.** Pueba, evidencia.

**Proof of harm by current price.** Determinación del daño por referencia a precio corriente. Si la parte agraviada que dio por terminado el contrato no efectuó una operación sucedánea, pero la prestación contractual tiene un precio corriente, dicha parte podrá recuperar la diferencia entre el precio del contrato y el precio corriente al tiempo de la terminación del contrato, así como el resarcimiento de cualquier daño adicional. (Unidroit, Prin., art. 7.4.6).

**Proof of harm in case of replacement transaction.** Prueba del daño en caso de una operación sucedánea. La parte agraviada que dió por terminado el contrato y efectuó una operación sucedánea dentro del término y de una manera razonables, podrá recobrar la diferencia entre el precio del con-

trato y el precio de la operación sucedánea, así como el resarcimiento de otro daño adicional. (Unidroit, Prin., art. 7.4.5).

**Proof of negligence.** Prueba de negligencia. En una acción por negligencia, el demandante tiene la carga de probar hechos que demuestren la existencia de un deber legal de parte del demandado, de acuerdo a la norma establecida en protección del demandante. (Rstmnt, 2nd, Torts, sec. 328A).

**Proof of official records, domestic.** Prueba de récords oficiales, nacionales. Los récords oficiales llevados en Estados Unidos, o en cualquier Estado, distrito, comunidad, territorio o posesión insular del mismo, cuando fueren admisibles para cualquier propósito, podrán probarse mediante publicación oficial de los mismos mediante copia autenticada por un funcionario que tuviere la custodia legal del récord, o por su delegado, y acompañada de una certificación de que dicho funcionario tiene la custodia. (R. Fed. P. Civ., sec. 44(a)(1).

**Proof of official records, lack of record.** Prueba de récords oficiales, falta de récord. Una declaración por escrito en el sentido de que después de una búsqueda diligente no pudo encontrarse que existiera un récord o inscripción de un tenor especificado en los registros señalados por la declaración, será admisible como evidencia de que los registros no contienen tal récord o inscripción. (R. Fed. P. Civ., sec. 44(b)).

**Proof of official records, foreign.** Prueba de récords oficiales, extranjeros. Los récords oficiales extranjeros, o una inscripción en los mismos, cuando fueren admisibles para cualquier propósito, podrán aprobarse mediante publicación oficial de los mismos o mediante su copia, autenticada por una persona autorizada para ello, y acompañada por una certificación definitiva al respecto de la autencidad de la firma y del cargo oficial (i) de la persona que auténtica, o (ii) de cualquier funcionario extranjero cuya certificación de la autencidad de la firma y del cargo oficial se refiera a la autencidad o fuera parte de una cadena de certificaciones de autenticidad de la firma y del cargo oficial relacionados con la autenticación. (R. Fed. P. Civ., sec. 44(a)(2)).

**Proper.** Apropiado, correcto, acertado.

**Property insurance.** Seguro de propiedad. "Seguro de propiedad" es el seguro de toda clase de bienes raíces o muebles, e interés sobre los mismos, contra pérdida o daños por cualquier riesgo o causa, y contra pérdida como consecuencia de tales pérdidas o daños, que no sea una responsabilidad legal no contractual por tales pérdidas o daños. Seguro de propiedad también incluirá seguros misceláneos, con excepción de protección de seguro de responsabilidad que pueda incluirse en la misma. (26 LPRA sec. 404).

**Property law.** Derechos reales. El complejo sistema de propiedad que caracterizaba el derecho de tierras inglés en la época de la Revolución fue adoptado casi en su totalidad en los Estados Unidos. En primer lugar se distinguen los derechos que restringen la facultad de otros al uso de la tierra (por ejemplo: servidumbres y privilegios) de los que conferir derecho real de posesión. Estos últimos se subdividen en *possesory estates* que confieren un derecho de posesión en el presente, y *future estates*, cuyo tenedor se convertirá o podrá convertirse en poseedor en el futuro. (Intro al USA).

**Proprietary.** Propietario.

**Proprietary article.** Mercadería sobre la cual se tiene algún derecho adicional como ser, marcario, de exclusividad, etc.

**Proprietary interest.** Derechos propietarios, derechos reales o personales sobre la cosa.

**Proprietary right.** Derecho de propiedad.

**Prosecute.** Comenzar y continuar una acción judicial.

**Prosecuting witness.** Denunciante en un proceso penal.

**Prosecution.** Acción penal. El término "*prosecution*" se ha definido como el medio adoptado para traer a un supuesto criminal a la justicia y castigarlo, siguiendo el debido curso de la ley, e incluye una serie de procedimientos desde el momento en que se hace la acusación formal al jurarse un mandamiento, la presentación de una acusación por el gran jurado (*indictment*) o por el fiscal (*information*), el juicio y la sentencia final. (Pueblo v. Vélez López, 83 D.P.R. 486 (1961)).

**Prosecutor.** Fiscal, agente fiscal.

**Protective order.** Orden protectora. A moción de parte o de la persona de quien se solicita el descubrimiento, y por justa causa justificada, la corte ante al cual el pleito estuviere pendiente o alternativamente, en materias relacionadas con una deposición, la corte del distrito en que se tome la deposición, podrá dictar cualquier orden que se requiera en justicia para proteger a las partes o personas contra hostigamiento, perturbación, opresión o carga o gastos indebidos. (R. Fed. P. Civ., sec. 26(c)).

**Protest.** Protesto. Un protesto es un certificado de que no se ha hecho honor a un instrumento hecho bajo la dirección y sello de un cónsul o vicecónsul de los Estados Unidos o de un notario público o de otra persona autorizada para certificar que no se ha hecho honor a tenor con las leyes del lugar en donde ocurre el deshonor. Podrá hacerse después que dicha persona se considere satisfactoriamente informada. El protesto deberá describir al instrumento y certificar que se hizo debida presentación a la razón por la cual es innecesaria y que no se ha hecho honor al instrumento por falta de aceptación o de pago. (C.C.U. sec. 3-509).

Protesta (s). Protestar (v).

**Protest for nonpayment.** Protesto por falta de pago.

**Protocol.** Protocolo, matrícula, registro.

**Provision.** Precepto, artículo, disposición, dispositivo, orden.

**Provisions and munitions of war.** Municiones de boca y guerra.

**Proviso.** Bajo la condición de.

**Provocation of the accused of murder by the deceased.** Provocación al acusado de asesinato por el occiso. Para reducir el delito de asesinato a homicidio voluntario, la provocación del acusado de asesinato por el occiso tiene que ser aquélla de naturaleza tal que haga perder el dominio de sí mismo a un hombre de temperamento corriente obligándolo a actuar por el impulso producido por notable provocación, sin la debida reflexión y sin formar un determinado propósito (Pueblo v. Saltari, 100 D.P.R. 703 (1971)).

**Proximate cause.** Causa desencadenante.

**Proxy.** Delegación de poderes o facultades.

**Puberty.** Pubertad.

**Public.** Público, conjunto de personas que, colectivamente, gozan de ciertos derechos (s). El conjunto de habitantes de una nacion o de una jurisdiccion. Público, que pertenece al Estado, que pertenece a todos.

**Public and private law.** Derecho público y privado. La división del Derecho sustantivo en derecho público y derecho privado es frecuente, aunque su utilidad es menos evidente que la de la distinción entre sustancia y procedimiento. Como ha afirmado la Corte Suprema de los Estados Unidos, "Es a menudo conveniente caracterizar una demanda en particular como apoyada en derechos públicos o privados, y sin duda esta clasificación de cómodo, es valida para ciertos fines. Pero por lo común la importancia real y las consecuencias jurídicas de ambos términos dependerá del contexto y de la naturaleza de los intereses en virtud de los cuales se los invoca". Como no existen tribunales que se ocupen de temas de derecho público hay pocas ocasiones en que la distinción tenga importancia práctica. (Intro al USA).

**Public auction.** Subasta pública, remate.

**Public contract.** Contrato público, realizado con fondos públicos.

**Public corporation.** Entidad de derecho público, v.g. una empresa estatal o una circunscripcion municipal.

**Public documents.** Documentos públicos.

**Public domain.** Dominio público.

**Public easement.** Servidumbre de uso público.

**Public holidays.** Días feriados, de fiesta.

**Public interest.** Interés público.

**Public international law.** Derecho internacional público.

**Public lands.** Terrenos fiscales.

**Public law.** Derecho público.

**Public notice.** Aviso al público en general.

**Public nuisance.** Molestia pública. Una molestia pública es la interferencia irrazonable con un derecho común del público en general. (Rstmnt, 2nd, Torts, sec. 821 B).

**Public office.** Cargo oficial, puesto electivo.

**Public official.** Funcionario o empleado público, de cierto rango, con facultades para realizar actos que sobrepasan la mera administracion o trámite.

**Public policy.** Interés estatal. Política perseguida por el estado.

**Public record.** Documento público que puede ser consultado por cualquier persona y que ha sido creado por disposición de la ley.

**Public safety.** Seguridad pública.

**Public servant.** Empleado estatal.

**Public use.** Uso público.

**Publicity.** Publicidad, propaganda.

**Publicity given to private life.** Publicación de evento privado. Una persona que le dé publicidad a algún asunto concerniente a la vida privada de otro, será sujeta a responsabilidad ante el otro por una invasión a su privacidad si el asunto publicado: a) es de tal naturaleza que resulte altamente ofensivo a una persona razonable, y b) no constituye un interés o una injusticia legítima del público. (Rstmnt, 2nd, Torts, sec. 652 D).

**Punish.** Castigar, penalizar.

**Punitive damages.** Indemnización punitiva. No se recibirá indemnización punitiva por incumplimiento de contrato a menos que la conducta constitutiva del incumplimiento sea también un daño que conlleva la responsabilidad civil extracontractual por el cual se pueda recibir indemnización punitiva. (Rstmnt, 2nd, Con., sec. 355).

**Purpose.** Propósito, ánimo, fin, finalidad, intención.

**Pursuant to.** Con arreglo a, acordemente con.

**Put on notice.** Apercibir.

**Putative.** Putativo.

**Pyromania.** Piromanía.

# Q

**Q.B.** *Queen's Bench*, o *Queen's Bench Division*, tribunal ingles, llamado también *King's Bench*, o K.B., si el monarca es un rey.

**Qualification.** Cualidad, calidad, calificación, facultad.

**Quantum meruit (L).** Acción jurídica residual que se usa a falta de otra teoria aplicable al caso. Literalmente significa "cuanto merece". Por ejemplo, el actor ha realizado trabajos para el demandado basándose en un contrato. Suponiendo que el contrato adolece de serios defectos y no puede sustentar una acción, el actor puede apoyar su demanda en la teoria de *quantum meruit*.

**Quarantine.** Cuarentena.

**Quare clausum fregit (L).** Por lo que penetró en un lugar cerrado. Expresión usada en la acción por violación a la propiedad (*trespass*). Suele hallarse también bajo forma abreviada como *qu. cl. fr.*, o *q.c.f.*

**Quarter.** Trimestre, cuarto (s). Desmembrar (v).

**Quash.** Revocar un fallo.

**Quasipublic.** Cuasipúblico.

**Question.** Preguntar (s). Poner en duda, cuestionar (v).

**Question of fact.** Cuestión de hecho.

**Question of law.** Cuestión de derecho.

**Questionary.** Cuestionario.

**Questionnaire.** Cuestionario.

**Qui tam action (L).** Tipo de acción entablada por un individuo en favor propio y también del Estado.

**Quiet enjoyment.** Goce pacífico.

**Quiet title.** Acción de jactancia. Forma de causar efecto de cosa juzgada sobre derechos propietarios demandando a quien pretende mejores derechos, con lo que se lo obliga a probar un mejor derecho o, contrariamente, a no cuestionar nunca más el derecho que alega el actor.

**Quitclaim deed.** Instrumento de venta de un inmueble que no acuerda al comprador recurso alguno contra el vendedor. Por ejemplo, con esta modalidad el vendedor no responde por vicio redhibitorio alguno ni tampoco si no resulta ser el verdadero dueño.

**Quo warranto (L).** ¿Con qué derecho? ¿Con qué autoridad? Procedimiento que se seguía contra la persona que había usurpado un derecho o una atribución propia del rey. Es un procedimiento, o acción, que le compete al Estado en su función protectora de los derechos de los ciudadanos.

**Quorum.** Quórum.

**Quotation.** Cotización.

# R

**R.I.C.O.** *Racketeer Influenced and Corrupt Organizations Act.* Ley para combater los delitos económicos perpetrados en forma organizada.

**Race.** Raza. Carrera. Correr.

**Racist.** Racista.

**Racket.** Acción sistemática ilegal, que puede ser más o menos grave según el caso.

**Raid.** Redada. Lanzar una redada.

**Rain water.** Aguas pluviales.

**Rainmaker.** Abogado que consigue los clientes en un bufete jurídico, ya sea por su buen trabajo jurídico, ya sea por sus buenas relaciones públicas.

**Raise a defense.** Oponer una defensa.

**Raise capital.** Solicitar y obtener contribuciones de capital, v.g. mediante la oferta pública de acciones.

**Ransom.** Rescate. Rescatar.

**Rape.** Violación.

**Rapist.** Violador.

**Rate.** Rango, tipo de cambio de moneda extranjera. Tasa de interés (s). Evaluar (v).

**Rate of discount.** Tipo de descuento.

**Ratification.** Ratificación.

**Ratio decidendi (L).** Razón para decidir. Es el motivo expreso y directo por el cual el juez fallo de la forma en que lo hizo. Ver *obiter dicta.*

**Ravishment.** Violación o abuso sexual.

**Ready for trial.** Listo para todas las etapas del juicio.

**Real estate.** Bien raíz, inmueble, tierras.

**Real party in interest.** Parte interesada propiamente dicha. Todo pleito se tramitará a nombre de la parte realmente interesada. (R. Fed. P. Civ., sec. 17(a)).

**Reapportionment.** Cambio en la estructura de distritos electorales como consecuencia de una suba o baja en la población. Obedece al imperativo de igualdad de representación establecido por el Artículo 1, numeral 2 de la Constitución americana.

**Reasonable man standard.** La conducta que es dable esperar de una persona razonable.

**Reasonable time, reasonably.** Tiempo razonable, oportunamente. Siempre que esta ley requiera hacer alguna cosa dentro de un término razonable, cualquier término que no fuere manifiestamente irrazonable podrá pactarse. (C.C.U. sec. 1204).

**Reasonably believes.** Cree razonablemente. Es la creencia del actor de que existe un hecho particular o una combinación de hechos, y que las circunstancias que éste conoce o debe conocer, son de tal naturaleza, que llevan a un hombre razonable a sostener tal creencia o convencimiento. (Rstmnt, 2nd, Torts, sec. 11).

**Recall.** Devolución solicitada por el fabricante o por el vendedor de un producto por haberse descubierto que es peligroso o que está fallado. Solicitar la devolución de algo. Recordar.

**Recapture.** Represamiento.

**Receipt.** Recibo.

**Receiver.** Síndico. Persona que recibe algo oficialmente en nombre de otra.

**Recess.** Receso, intervalo, recreo.

**Reciprocal wills.** Testamentos recíprocos.

**Reciprocally.** Reciprocar, mutuamente.

**Reciprocity.** Reciprocidad.

**Recission.** Recisión.

**Recital.** Relato, relación, considerandos.

**Recited.** Relatado.

**Receivership.** Sindicatura.

**Reckless disregard of safety.** Inobservancia temeraria de la seguridad. La conducta de un actor se considera inobservancia temeraria de la seguridad de los demás si ejecuta un acto o si intencionalmente incurre en una omisión con relación a un deber que tiene frente a otro individuo, cuando sabe o tiene motivos fundados para creer, como lo haría un hombre razonable, que no sólo su conducta crea un riesgo irrazonable de que otro individuo sufra daño corporal, sino también que tal riesgo es sustancialmente mayor que el creado por una conducta negligente. (Rstmnt, 2nd, Torts, sec. 500).

**Recklessness.** Imprudencia, temeridad.

**Reclaimed land.** Terreno saneado, terreno ganado a las aguas.

**Recognition of foreign nation judgments.** Reconocimiento de sentencia extranjera. Una sentencia válida emitida en una nación extranjera, luego de un juicio válido con un procedimiento equitativo, será reconocido en los Estados Unidos. Ello será así en lo concerniente a las partes involucradas en forma inmediata y a la causa de acción. (Rstmnt, 2nd, Conflict, sec. 98).

**Record.** Actuaciones, expediente judicial, prueba escrita, actas (s). Anotar, inscribir, registrar (v).

**Record of attachment.** Anotación de embargo.

**Record on appeal.** Expediente de apelación.

**Recording.** Protocolización.

**Recording clerk.** Escríbano de actuaciones.

**Records and files.** Autos, legajos.

**Recourse.** Recurso.

**Recover.** Recuperar, cobrar, obtener.

**Recurrence.** Recurrencia.

**Red tape.** Burocracia, papeleo.

**Redemption.** Redención, desempeño, rescate.

**Redemption of a mortgage.** Cancelación de una hipoteca.

**Redhibitory vice.** Vicio redhibitorio, vicio oculto.

**Redress.** Reparar, compensar, indemnificar, resarcir.

**Reduction.** Disminución, rebaja, reducción.

**Reduction and extension.** Quita y espera.

**Reduction of harm.** Atenuación del daño. La parte incumplidora no es responsable del daño sufrido por la parte agraviada en cuanto éste podía haberlo reducido adoptando medidas razonables que no adoptó. (Unidroit, Prin., art. 7.4.8).

**Redundant.** Redundante, innecesario.

**Referee.** Arbitro. Arbitrar.

**Referendum.** Referendum.

**Reformatory.** Reformatorio.

**Refugee.** Refugiado.

**Refund.** Reembolso. Reembolsar.

**Refusal.** Denegación, negación, negativa, rechazo, rechazamiento.

**Refutation.** Refutación.

**Regency.** Regencia.

**Regent.** Regente.

**Regicide.** Regicidio.

**Register.** Registro. Caja registradora. Registrar.

**Register a title.** Registrar un título.

**Register a trademark.** Registrar una marca.

**Registration.** Registro, inscripción, matriculación.

**Registrar.** Registrador.

**Registration number.** Matrícula, inscripción, registro, matriculación.

**Regular hours.** Horas regulares. Son horas regulares de trabajo ocho horas durante cualquier período de 24 horas consecutivas y 40 horas durante cualquier semana. (20 LPRA sec. 272).

**Reimburse.** Reembolsar, devolver, reintegrar.

**Reinstate.** Restituir, rehabilitar.

**Reinstatement.** Reinstalación, rehabilitación, reposición, restablecimiento.

**Reinsurance.** Reaseguro.

**Rejection of offer.** Rechazo de la oferta. La oferta se extingue cuando la comunicación de su rechazo llega al oferente. (Unidroit, Prin., art. 2.5).

**Rejoinder.** Dúplica, réplica.

**Related.** Relacionado.

**Related company.** Empresa vinculada.

**Relation.** Relación. Vínculo familiar.

**Release.** Liberación. Documento escrito, indicando que una prestación debida al otorgante es liberada inmediatamente, o al cumplimiento de una condición. (Rstmnt, 2nd, Con., sec. 284(1)).

**Relevant circumstances.** Circunstancias relevantes. Deberán tomarse en consideración todas las circunstancias, incluso: (a) las negociaciones previas entre las partes; (b) las prácticas que ellas hayan establecido entre sí; (c) la conducta observada por las partes luego de celebrarse el contrato; (d) la naturaleza y finalidad del contrato. (Unidroit, Prin., art. 4.3).

**Relevant evidence.** Evidencia pertinente. Evidencia pertinente significa aquélla que tiende a hacer la existencia de cualquier hecho que es de importancia para la decisión de la acción más probable o menos probable de lo que sería sin la evidencia. (Regla 401, 402, R. Fed. Evid.).

**Relevant evidence excluded.** Evidencia pertinente excluída. Aunque pertinente, la evidencia podrá ser excluída si su valor probatorio pesa sustancialmente menos que el peligro de causar un perjuicio indebido, confusión de los hechos, desorientación del jurado, o por consideraciones de demoras indebidas, pérdida de tiempo o innecesaria presentación o prueba acumulativa. (Regla 403, R. Fed. Evid.).

**Relevant mistake.** Error relevante. Cualquiera de las partes podrá dar por anulado un contrato, basándose en error, solamente si al momento de su celebración el error fue de tal magnitud que una persona razonable y colocada en la misma situación, no habría contratado o lo habría hecho en términos sustancialmente diferentes en caso de haber conocido la realidad de las cosas. (Unidroit, Prin., art. 3.5).

**Reliance.** Conducta seguida en contemplación de lo expresado por la otra parte.

**Relief from a judgment in the course of a subsequent action.** Ataque contra una sentencia durante una acción subsiguiente. Si una alegación o defensa dentro de una acción subsiguiente están basadas en una sentencia previa, se puede atacar dicha sentencia presentando las alegaciones y prueba apropiadas en la acción subsiguiente si el solicitante no tiene disponibles otros medios para atacar la sentencia, o si se favorece la administración conveniente de la justicia decidiendo sobre la cuestión del remedio en la acción subsiguiente o posterior. (Rstmnt, 2nd, Judg., sec. 80).

**Relief from judgment by independent action.** Ataque contra una sentencia mediante acción independiente. Si no resulta conveniente atacar una sentencia mediante petición en la acción original, dicha sentencia se puede atacar mediante una acción que tenga como efecto dejar de hacer cumplir la sentencia, declarar la sentencia inefectiva, o

algún otro remedio similar. (Rstmnt, 2nd, Judg., sec. 79).

**Relief from judgment by motion.** Ataque contra una sentencia mediante petición. Si se desea atacar una sentencia, deberá hacerse mediante una petición a tales fines ante el tribunal que dictó sentencia, a menos que se pueda obtener algún remedio más completo, conveniente o apropiado mediante otro procedimiento. (Rstmnt, 2nd, Judg., sec. 78).

**Relinquish.** Renunciar, abandonar, abdicar, dejar, dimitir.

**Relocation.** Reubicación, reinstalación.

**Reluctant.** Reacio, sin entusiasmo, desganadamente.

**Remainder.** Lo que resta de los derechos reales luego de haberse dispuesto específicamente sobre algunos. Remanente.

**Remainder of related writings or recorded statements.** Resto de escrito o declaraciones. Cuando un escrito o declaración grabada o parte de los mismos sean sometidos como evidencia por una parte, una parte contraria podrá requerirla en ese momento para que someta cualquier otra parte u otro escrito u otra declaración que en justicia deban ser considerados coetáneamente con los mismos. (Regla 106, R. Fed. Evid.).

**Remand.** Devolver un caso al tribunal inferior para que éste dicte una nueva sentencia concordante con la opinión expresada por el tribunal de alzada.

**Remedies for nonperformance.** Derechos y acciones por incumplimiento. La parte equivocada no puede dar por anulado el contrato invocando error, si los hechos en los que basa su pretensión le otorgan o le podrían haber otorgado derechos y acciones por incumplimiento del contrato. (Unidroit, Prin., art. 3.7).

**Remedy.** Remedio legal.

**Remission.** Remisión, quita, renuncia, perdón.

*Remittitur* **(L).** Si el juez juzga que las reparaciones acordadas por el jurado son irrazonablemente altas, puede disminuirlas por medio de un procedimiento denominado *remittitur* y disponer un nuevo juicio si las partes no aceptan la modificación. (Introduciónal Sistema Legal de USA).

**Remittitur damna (L).** Declaración del actor en el sentido de haber recibido pago de parte de la indemnización que la sentencia le ha acordado.

**Remote.** Remoto, lejano.

**Removal.** Destitución, cesantía, eliminación, remoción, despido.

**Removal of actions.** Traslado de pleitos.

**Remuneration.** Remuneración, compensación, paga, recompensa.

**Render.** Entregar, producer.

**Renew.** Renovar, extender, prorrogar.

**Renewable resources.** Recursos renovables.

**Rental, rent.** Renta, alquiler, arriendo (s). Arrendar (v).

**Renunciation.** Renuncia, abandono.

**Renvoi.** Reenvío. Un foro aplica la ley local del otro Estado cuando se rige por su propia regla de conflicto de leyes para aplicar la ley del otro Estado. (Rstmnt, 2nd, Conflict, sec. 8).

**Reorganization.** Reorganización.

**Repair and replacement of defective performance.** Reparación y reemplazo de cumplimiento defectuoso. El derecho de exigir el cumplimiento incluye, cuando haya lugar a ello, el derecho de exigir la reparación, el reemplazo u otra purga del cumplimiento defectuoso. (Unidroit, Prin., art. 7.2.3).

**Repairs.** Reparaciones.

**Repatriation.** Repatriación.

**Repayment.** Devolución de dinero, reintegro.

**Repeal by implication.** Derogación tácita.

**Repeal of laws.** Derogación de leyes.

**Repealing clause.** Cláusula derogatoria.

**Repeat offender.** Reo con antecedentes penales, recidivista.

**Replead.** Alegar nuevamente.

**Replevin.** Acción para recobrar propiedad mueble.

**Replication.** Réplica.

**Reply.** Respuesta. Réplica.

**Report.** Informe, reporte, información oral o escrita. Informar.

**Reportedly.** Supuestamente, según se ha informado.

**Repossess.** Recuperar la posesión.

**Represent.** Representar.

**Representation.** Representación.

**Representation in criminal cases.** Representación en casos penales. El acusado esta representado de ordinario por un abogado. Un abogado particular puede aceptar o negarse a hacerse cargo de un caso independientemente de su opinión acerca de la inocencia del acusado. (Intro al USA).

**Representative.** Representante, diputado.

**Reprieve.** Suspensión de una pena o de un castigo.

**Reprimand.** Reprimenda. Reprender.

**Reprisal.** Represalia, retaliación, retorsión.

**Repudiation.** Repudio, repudiación. El repudio es una declaración del obligado al tenedor de una obligación, indicando que el obligado cometerá incumplimiento. Ello dará al tenedor de una obligación una reclamación de daños por incumplimiento total. (Rstmnt, 2nd, Con., sec. 250).

**Reputable.** De buena reputación.

**Request.** Solicitud. Solicitar.

**Request for admissions.** Solicitud de confesión o de admission. Pliego para absolver posiciones.

**Requisition.** Requerimiento, solicitud. Requerir, tomar algo para su uso público en tiempo de emergencia.

**Requirement.** Requisito, exigencia.

**Res gestae (L).** Literalmente, cosas hechas. Se usa para justificar la excepción que admite el testimonio por referencia. Se trata de algo dicho en un estado de exaltación, por ejemplo inmediatamente luego de un accidente. Lo espontaneo de tal declaración, bajo circunstancias trágicas, le daría valor probatorio mayor, exceptuandose de la prohibición del testimonio referido.

**Res ipsa loquitur (L).** La cosa habla por sí misma. Podrá inferirse que el daño sufrido por el demandante es causado por la negligencia del demandado cuando: a) el acto o evento es uno que de ordinario no ocurre en ausencia de negligencia; b) la defensa de causas interventoras, como la conducta del propio demandante y terceras personas, no pueden sostenerse con la evidencia presentada; y c) la alegada negligencia está dentro del ámbito del deber del demandado hacia el demandante. (Rstmnt, 2nd, Torts, sec. 328 D).

**Res judicata (L).** Cosa juzgada. Las reglas de *res judicata* se aplican sólo cuando un tribunal dicta sentencia que adviene final y firme. No obstante, para propósitos de evitar confusión, "sentencia final y firme" incluye cualquier adjudicación previa de alguna controversia en otra acción que demuestra ser lo suficientemente firme como para tener efectos concluyentes. (Restatement, Second, Judgments, sec. 13).

**Resale.** Reventa.

**Rescind.** Rescindir.

**Rescission.** Rescición.

**Rescissory.** Rescisorio.

**Research.** Investigación. Investigar.

**Reserve fund.** Fondo de reserva. Se entiende por "fondo de reserva" un fondo formado o aumentado bien por derrame entre los accionistas, y por el total de las primas obtenidas en la venta de acciones, bien por transferencias de los beneficios líquidos o de los beneficios sin distribuir del banco, cuyo fondo no podrá utilizarse para enjugar las pérdidas de operación del banco mientras haya algún saldo disponible en la cuenta de beneficios sin distribuir, ni tampoco podrá utilizarse para el pago de dividendos si tal pago reduce el fondo de reserva a menos del diez por ciento (10%) del total de los depósitos, o al total del capital del banco, cualquiera que sea mayor. (7 LPRA sec. 3).

**Residence.** Residencia.

**Residual value.** Valor residual.

**Residuary estate.** Remanente de los bienes.

**Resolution.** Decreto, acordada, auto, bando, edicto, resolución.

**Resort.** Recurso, instancia. Interponer un recurso o un argumento.

**Respondeat superior (L).** Se usa esta expresión en el area de responsabilidad extracontractual. Significa que los subordinados generan responsabilidad civil, dentro del area de sus funciones, hacia sus superiores.

Por ejemplo, si choca el conductor de un medio de transporte, no sólo puede el mismo quedar obligado personalmente a reparar los danos, pero tambien queda obligada la empresa para la cual trabaja tal conductor. Literalmente significa "responde el superior."

**Respondent.** Demandado, parte contra la cual se apela.

**Responsibility.** Responsabilidad.

**Responsible.** Responsable.

**Rest the case.** Conclusión del alegato final.

**Restatement of the Law.** Este documento abarca aquellos campos del Derecho en que la jurisprudencia predominada y la aplicación de leyes estaduales divergentes es mínima: el mandato, conflicto de leyes, contratos, fallos, propiedad, restitución de bienes, hechos ilícitos y fideicomisos. El *Restatement* en cada uno de estos campos fue elaborado por uno o mas "redactores," profesores de leyes eminentes que fueron asistidos por un grupo de asesores en el que se contaban profesores, abogados practicantes y jueces. (Carl).

**Restitution.** Restituciones. Cualquiera de las partes puede reclamar a la otra a la terminación del contrato la restitución de todo lo que haya entregado en razón de dicho contrato, siempre y cuando restituya concurrentemente lo que recibió. De no ser posible o apropiada la restitución en especie, se proverá una compensación en dinero, siempre que sea razonable. (Unidroit, Prin., art. 7.3.6).

**Restrain.** Restringir, contener, limitar, prohibir.

**Restraining order.** Interdicto de realizar ciertos actos. Por ejemplo, de aproximarse al cónyuge que radicó demanda de divorcio, de enajenar ciertos bienes, etc.

**Restraint of trade.** Atentado contra la libertad de comercio. Una promesa no se puede ejecutar en términos de política pública si atenta contra la libertad de comercio en forma irrazonable. (Rstmnt, 2nd, Con., sec. 186).

**Restraint on alienation.** Prohibición a la que el vendedor sujeta al comprador de un inmueble de no venderlo durante cierto período o de cierta forma.

**Restrictive covenant.** Acuerdo que restringe una libertad, v.g. la de trabajar para la competencia.

**Restrictive endorsement.** Endoso restrictivo. Un endoso es restrictivo ya a) sea condicional; o b) tenga la intención de prohibir el traspaso posterior del instrumento; o c) incluya las palabras "para cobrar," "para depositar," "páguese a cualquier banco," o términos similares que indiquen el propósito de depósito o cobranza; o d) exprese de otro modo que es para el beneficio o uso del endosante o de otra persona. (C.C.U. sec. 205, 3-206).

**Retail.** Minoreo. Vender al por menor.

**Retain.** Retener.

**Retainer fee.** Pago anticipado de honorarios de abogado.

**Retire.** Jubilarse, retirarse.

**Retired worker.** Trabajador jubilado, pensionado.

**Retirement system.** Sistema de retiro.

**Retorsion.** Retorsión.

**Retract.** Retractar, revocar, retirar.

**Retractable.** Retractable, anulable.

**Retraction.** Retracción, rectificación.

**Retribution.** Retribución, castigo.

**Retroactive effect.** Efecto retroactivo.

**Retroactive effect of avoidance.** Efecto retroactivo de la anulación. (1) La anulación tendrá efectos retroactivos. (2) La anulación del contrato habilita a cada parte para pedir la restitución de lo entregado conforme al contrato o a las cláusulas que sean anuladas, siempre que proceda concurrentemente a restituír lo recibido conforme al contrato o a dichas cláusulas. (Unidroit, Prin., art. 3.17).

**Return.** Prueba del diligenciamiento. La persona que diligencie el emplazamiento presentará sin demora en la corte la prueba de tal diligenciamiento, y, a más tardar, dentro del plazo durante el cual la persona emplazada habrá de responder al emplazamiento. (R. Fed. P. Civ., sec. 4(g)).

Planilla (s). Devolver, retornar, volver (v).

**Revaluation.** Revalúo, revaluación.

**Reveal.** Revelar, dar a conocer, divulgar, descubrir, exponer.

**Revenue.** Entrada de dinero o bienes, ingreso.

**Reverse discrimination.** Discriminación realizada contra un miembro de la raza dominante o mayoritaria.

**Reversion.** Reversión, vuelta.

**Reverter.** Reversión de derechos reales al enajenante.

**Revival of debt.** Deuda revivida.

**Revocation of acceptance in whole or in part.** Revocación total o parcial de aceptación. El comprador podrá revocar su aceptación de un lote o unidad comercial cuya no-conformidad sustancialmente menoscababa el valor de éste o ésta en su perjuicio si ya ha aceptado:—en el supuesto razonable de que la no-conformidad fuese subsanada y no la ha sido oportunamente; o—sin descubrir dicha no-conformidad si su aceptación estuvo razonablemente inducida por la dificultad del descubrimiento antes de la aceptación o por las afirmaciones del vendedor. (C.C.U. sec. 2-608).

**Revocation of offer.** Revocación de la oferta. Cualquier oferta puede ser revocada hasta que el contrato se celebre, si la comunicación de su revocación llega al destinatario antes de que éste haya enviado la aceptación. (Unidroit, Prin., art. 2.4).

**Rider.** Anexo, documento adicional.

**Rigging.** Aparejo.

**Right.** Derecho, prerrogativa, potestad. Correcto.

**Right of survivorship.** Copropiedad con derechos de propiedad absoluta para el copropietario sobreviviente.

**Right of preemption.** Derecho de tanteo.

**Right of way.** Sevidumbre de paso.

**Right to adequate assurance of performance.** Derecho a adecuada garantía de cumplimiento. Se configura al contrato de venta imponer una obligación en cada una de las partes de que la probabilidad de la otra parte de recibir el cumplimiento adecuado no se perjudicará. Cuando surjan motivos razonables de inseguridad con respecto al cumplimiento de cualquiera de las partes la otra podrá demandar por escrito la garantía adecuada del cumplimiento debido y hasta que reciba tal seguridad podrá, si fuere comercialmente razonable, suspender cualquier cumplimiento por el cual no haya recibido la contraprestación acordada. (C.C.U. sec. 2-609).

**Right to assign counsel.** Derecho a designar abogado. Todo acusado imposibilitado de obtener abogado tendrá derecho a que se le designe abogado que lo represente en todos los trámites del proceso desde su comparecencia inicial ante el magistrado federal o la corte hasta la apelación, a menos que renunciare al derecho a tal designación. (Regla 44(a), Reglas Fed. de Proc. Crim.).

**Right to legal counsel.** Derecho a asistencia jurídica. A partir del caso *Gideon v. Wainwright*, 372 U.S. 335 (1963), la Corte Suprema de los Estados Unidos ha sostenido que los acusados indigentes (salvo en el caso de delitos menores) tienen derecho a un defensor de acuerdo a la Constitución tanto en el ámbito de los tribunales federales como en el de los estaduales, y el estado está obligado a proveerlo. (Intro al USA).

**Rightful.** Justo, legal.

**Riparian land.** Tierra ribereña. El término "tierra ribereña" se refiere a un pedazo de tierra que constituye la orilla de una vía de agua o lago, sea o no parte del lecho o fondo de la vía de agua o lago. (Rstmnt, 2nd, Torts, sec. 843).

**Riparian nations.** Naciones riparias, Estados con una frontera fluvial común.

**Ripeness.** Estado de desarrollo en el que se haya una cuestión litigiosa que hace oportuna la intervención del tribunal de alzada. Normalmente la apelación en Estados Unidos se acuerda a medida que se vayan atacando las diversas resoluciones interlocutorias, pero el tribunal superior interviene una sola vez al final.

**Risk of loss in the absence of breach.** Riesgo de pérdida en ausencia de infracción. Cuando el contrato requiere o autoriza al vendedor a embarcar las mercancías por medio de un porteador:—si no se requiere de él que las entregue en un lugar determinado, el riesgo de pérdida pasará al comprador cuando las mercancías sean entregadas debidamente al porteador aunque el embarque sea bajo reserva; pero—si no se requiere que la entregue en un lugar de destino determinado y las mercancías fueren allí formalmente ofrecidas mientras estuvieren en posesión del porteador; el riesgo de pérdida pasará al comprador cuando las mercancías fueren ofrecidas allí en tal forma que permita al comprador recibir la entrega. (C.C.U. sec. 2-509; 2-510).

**Rite.** Rito, formalidad.

**River bed.** Cauce.

**Roadstead.** Ensenada.

**Robbery.** Robo, asalto.

**Rogatory letter.** Carta rogatoria, exhorto.

**Roll.** Lista, legajo, documento.

**Roman law.** Derecho romano, tradición jurídica romana o continental.

**Roster.** Registro, lista.

**Royalty.** Regalía, canon. Realeza.

**Rule.** Regla, norma a seguir (s). Gobernar, mandar (v).

**Rule of proximity.** Proximidad, regla de la. La regla de proximidad—la que extiende la aplicabilidad de la regla en la propiedad del patrono—hace compensable bajo la Ley de Compensaciones por Accidentes del Trabajo las lesiones sufridas por un obrero en un accidente que le ocurrió en la proximidad de la propiedad del patrono, cuando la ruta a seguir por el obrero lesionado es la única disponible o una conveniente, que expone a dicho obrero a riesgos especiales, como por ejemplo, un cruce de ferrocarril. (Valentín Nadal v. Comisión Industrial, 94 D.P.R. 659 (1967)).

**Ruling.** Decisión o sentencia interlocutoria.

**Running water.** Aguas vivas.

**Rural and town property.** Fincas rústicas y urbanas.

# S

**Sabotage.** Sabotaje (s). Sabotear (v).

**Sack.** Saquear. Despedir del trabajo.

**Sacrilege.** Sacrilegio.

**Sadism.** Sadismo.

**Safe.** Seguro, a salvo. Caja fuerte.

**Safe box.** Caja fuerte.

**Safety.** Seguridad.

**Safety at sea.** Seguridad en el mar.

**Safety violation.** Violación de normas de seguridad.

**Salable.** Vendible.

**Salary.** Salario, sueldo.

**Sale for a fixed price.** Venta por precio alzado.

**Sale on approval.** Venta a prueba. Salvo pacto en contrario, si el comprador puede devolver las mercancías aunque éstas estén de acuerdo con el contrato, la transacción será una "venta a prueba" si las mercancías se entregan principalmente para su uso, las mercancías recibidas a prueba no estarán sujetas a reclamaciones de los acreedores del comprador hasta que sean aceptadas. (C.C.U. sec. 2-326).

**Sale or return.** Venta o devolución. Salvo pacto en contrario, si el comprador puede devolver las mercancías aunque éstas estén de acuerdo con el contrato, la transacción será: una "venta o devolución" si las mercancías se entregan principalmente para reventa. Excepto lo dispuesto subsiguientemente, estarán sujetas a reclamaciones de los acreedores del comprador, las mercancías recibidas a venta o devolución mientras se encuentren en posesión del comprador. (C.C.U. sec. 2-326).

**Sale to spouse of habit-forming drug.** Venta a un cónyuge de drogas adictivas. Una persona que ilegalmente venda o supla a un cónyuge una droga adictiva, a sabiendas de que su uso causará daño a cualesquiera de los intereses maritales legalmente protegidos del otro cónyuge, será sujeto a responsabilidad por el daño causado por la droga a aquellos intereses, a menos que el otro cónyuge consienta a la adquisición o uso de esa droga. (Rstmnt, 2nd, Torts, sec. 696).

**Sales, uniform commercial code.** Ventas, código de comercio uniforme. Con respecto a la *Uniform Sales Act* y la *Negotiable Instruments Law* el Artículo 2 del Código Uniforme simplemente pone al día esta materia adiciona algunas nuevas reglas de importancia que se extrajeron de casos prácticos y usos de comercio. La modificación principal es eliminar el énfasis en el traspaso del título o dominio, aunque contiene reglas para el traspaso, remedios para las partes contratantes y detalla los riesgos entre ellas mediante reglas especiales basadas en general en la manera en que se verifican las operaciones. (C.C.U., Prefacio).

**Salvage.** Salvamento. Salvar, rescatar, recuperar.

**Sanction.** Sanción (s). Sancionar (v).

**Sanctuary.** Santuario.

**Satisfaction of judgment.** Cumplimiento de sentencia.

**Save.** Ahorrar. Salvar.

**Saving clause.** Cláusula de salvedad.

**Savings account.** Cuentas de ahorro. Se entiende por "cuenta de ahorro" aquéllas en que, de acuerdo con el Reglamento del Banco, éste tiene la facultad de exigir al depositante que antes de efectuar cualquier retiro de fondos de dicha cuenta, avise al banco a tal efecto con más de treinta (30) días de antelación. (7 LPRA sec. 3).

**Scarcity.** Escasez, desabastecimiento.

**Schedule.** Apéndice, programa, horario, lista. Establecer una entrevista, programar algún evento en el tiempo.

**Scheme.** Plan. Planear.

**Schism.** Cisma.

**Schizophrenia.** Esquizofrenia.

**Schmutz formula.** Fórmula Schmutz. En el campo de expropiación forzosa desígnase como fórmula Schmutz aquella formula desarrollada para determinar la compensación a ser pagada a un arrendatario de un inmueble parcialmente expropiado. (E.L.A. v. Sociedad Protectora, 100 D.P.R. 844 (1971)).

**Scholarship.** Saber científico. Beca.

***Scienter* (L).** Con conocimiento de lo que se hace.

***Scire facias* (L).** Autos para mostrar causa.

**Scope.** Ambito, alcance.

**Scope of coverage.** En el derecho de seguros, el campor de cobertura.

**Scope of employment.** En ocasión del trabajo. La conducta de un empleado se considera en ocasión del trabajo si: a) es del tipo de actividad para la que fue contratado; b) ocurre sustancialmente dentro del tiempo y del área autorizados; c) se realiza, por lo menos en parte, con el propósito de servir al patrón; d) si el empleado utiliza la fuerza contra otra persona, tal uso de fuerza no resulta inesperado para el patrono. (Rstmnt, 2nd, Agency, sec. 228).

**Scorn.** Gran desprecio. Despreciar, tener una muy baja opinión.

**Scrivener.** Escritor, escriba. Persona encargada de redactar documentos.

**Scrutiny.** Escrutinio. Estudio profundo.

**Sea.** Mar.

**Sea carrier.** Empresa de transporte marino.

**Seabed.** Lecho maritime, plataforma marítima.

**Seal.** Un sello es una manifestación en forma tangible y convencional de la intención de que un documento sea sellado. Un sello puede tomar la forma de un pedazo de cera, una oblea u otra sustancia adhesiva al documento o una impresión hecha en el documento. (Rstmnt, 2nd, Con., sec. 96).
Sellar (v). Sello. Estampilla, lacre, timbre (s).

**Seal of the court.** Sello del juzgado.

**Sealed indictment.** Indiciamiento sellado. El magistrado federal ante quien se presente un indiciamiento de gran jurado podrá ordenar que el mismo se mantenga en secreto hasta que el acusado se encuentre detenido o hubiera sido puesto en libertad pendiente juicio. Entonces el secretario sellará el indiciamiento del gran jurado, y nadie podrá revelar su contenido salvo cuando fuera necesario para la expedición y ejecución de una orden de arresto o citación. (Regla 6(e)(94), Reglas Fe. de Proc. Crim.).

**Sealed records.** Récords sellados. Los récords, órdenes y citaciones relacionados con el procedimiento ante el gran jurado se mantendrán bajo sellos por todo el tiempo que fuera necesario para evitar la revelación de los asuntos tratados ante el mismo. (Regla 6(e)(6), Reglas Fed. de Proc. Crim.).

**Seaman.** Marinero, marino.

**Search.** Búsqueda, registro (s). Buscar, registrar (v).

**Search and seizure.** Registros e incautaciones. Podrá expedirse una orden a tenor de esta regla para registrar e incautarse de cualesquiera 1) bienes que constituyan evidencia de la comisión de un delito; o 2) contrabando, los frutos del crimen, o casas poseídas de cualquier modo ilegalmente. (Regla 41(b), Regla Federal de Procedimiento Criminal).

**Search warrant.** Orden de allanamiento o registro. Denomínase orden del allanamiento o registro un mandamiento firmado por un magistrado, ordenando buscar y ocupar determinada propiedad mueble, mandamiento en el cual se nombrarán o describirán con particularidad la persona o el lugar a ser registrado y las cosas a ocuparse. (Pueblo v. Costoso Caballero, 100 D.P.R. 147 (1971)).

**Seasonable.** En tiempo util.

**Seat of government.** Asiento o sede de gobierno.

**Secondary authority.** Fuentes secundarias. La expresión "fuentes de autoridad secundaria" se aplica a los tratados, las revistas jurídicas, las enciclopedias y todo otro documento auxiliar que contribuya a determinar o interpretar las "fuentes de autoridad primaria" tales como las leyes o la jurisprudencia. (Intro al USA).

**Secretary.** Secretaria/o.

**Secretary of the treasury.** Secretario de hacienda, ministro de economía.

**Secured party.** Parte contratante garantizada. "Parte contratante garantizada" (*Secured* *party*) significa un prestamista, vendedor u otra persona en cuyo favor se constituye un interés garantizado, incluyendo una persona a quien hubiesen sido cedidas cuentas, derechos contractuales o valores mobiliarios. (C.C.U. sec. 9-105(i)).

**Secured transactions, uniform commercial code.** Intereses garantizados, código uniforme de comercio. El más original e importante de los Artículos del Código Uniforme es el 9 que trata de las transacciones garantizadas. Comprende las cesiones de cuentas, derechos contractuales y valores mobiliarios y una gran variedad de transacciones en las que las deudas quedan garantizadas con bienes muebles, tangibles e intangibles. (C.C.U., Prefacio).

**Securities.** Acciones, títulos, valores.

**Security interest.** Interés garantizado. "Interés garantizado" significa un derecho en bienes muebles o muebles adheridos a un inmueble que garantiza el pago o cumplimiento de una obligación. La retención o reserva del título por un vendedor de mercancías a pesar del embarque o entrega al comprador se limita en su efecto a una reserva de "interés garantizado." El término también incluye cualquier derecho de un comprador de cuentas, valores mobiliarios o derechos contractuales. No es un interés garantizado el interés especial en la propiedad de un comprador de mercancías en la identificación de tales mercancías a un contrato de venta. (C.C.U. sec. 1201 (37)).

**Sedicious speech.** Arenga o discurso sedicioso.

**Sedition.** Sedición.

**Seduce.** Seducir.

**Seduction.** Seducción.

**Seize.** Apresar, embargar, tomar para sí, apropiarse.

**Seizure of person or property.** Detención de personas o embargo de bienes. Al inicio o durante el curso de un pleito, todos los remedios para la detención de una persona o el embargo de bienes con el objeto de asegurar la efectividad de la sentencia que en definitiva habrá de dictarse en el pleito estarán accequibles. (Reglas Fed. de Pro. Civ., sec. 64).

**Self-authentication.** Autenticación prima facie. Son prima facie auténticos los siguientes: 1) Documentos públicos nacionales bajo sello 2) Documentos públicos nacionales no bajo sello 3) Documentos públicos extranjeros 4) Copias certificadas de récords públicos 5) Publicaciones oficiales 6) Periódicos y revistas 7) Inscripciones comerciales y similares 8) Documentos reconocidos 9) Instrumentos comerciales y otros documentos 10) Presunciones a tenor con leyes del congreso. (Regla 902, R. Fed. Evid.).

**Self-defense by force.** Auto defensa mediante fuerza. Un actor tiene el privilegio de usar una fuerza razonable, no con la intención de causar la muerte o daño físico, pero sí para defenderse contra un contacto dañino u ofensivo, o de cualquier otro daño físico que él razonablemente crea que otro individuo intencionalmente le va a causar. (Rstmnt, 2nd, Torts, sec. 63).

**Self-incrimination.** Autoincriminación. El hecho de prestar declaración, ya sea el acusado o cualquier otro testigo, no funcionará como una renuncia al derecho contra la autoincriminación mientras sean interrogados respecto de materias relacionadas únicamente con la credibilidad. (Regla 608(b), R. Fed. Evid.).

**Self-serving.** En beneficio propio.

**Self-dealing.** Negocios personales realizados por un miembro del directorio o funcionario con la misma empresa.

**Sell on credit.** Vender al fiado.

**Sell on time.** Vender a plazos.

**Senate.** Senado.

**Senator.** Senador.

**Send.** Enviar. "Enviar" en conexión con un escrito o aviso significa echar en el correo o entregar para su remisión por cualquier otro medio usual de comunicación con franqueo o costo de remisión provisto y debidamente dirigido y en el caso de un instrumento a una dirección especificada en éste o pactada de cualquier otra manera, o si no hubiere ninguna a cualquier dirección razonable bajo las circunstancias. (C.C.U. sec. 1201 (38)).

**Sentence.** Sentencia, fallo (s). Sentenciar, condenar (v).

**Separate trials.** Juicios por separado. La corte, por razones de conveniencia o para evitar perjuicios, o cuando los juicios por separado condujeren al aceleramiento y economía, podrá ordenar juicio por separado para cualquier reclamación, demanda contra coparte, reconvención o demanda contra tercero. (R. Fed. P. Civ., sec. 42(b)).

**Separation of powers.** Separación de poderes.

**Sequestered jury.** Jurado que permanece secuestrado, por orden el juez, hasta que llegue a un fallo.

**Sergeant-at arms.** Macero.

**Servant.** Empleado dependiente. Un empleado o dependiente es un mandatario empleado por un patrón para realizar un servicio relacionado con los asuntos del primero cuya conducta física en la realización de dicho servicio es controlada, o está sujeta al derecho a ser controlada por el patrón. (Rstmnt, 2nd, Agency, sec. 3(1)).

**Service in a foreign country.** Emplazamiento en país extranjero. Cuando la ley federal o estatal mencionada en el inciso (e) de esta regla autorizare el emplazamiento de una parte no residente del Estado o que se encontrare fuera de aquél en que funcione la corte de distrito, será suficiente que el diligenciamiento del emplazamiento y de la demanda se haga a) en forma prescrita por la ley del país extranjero para el emplazamiento en dicho país en un pleito ante cualesquiera de sus cortes de jurisdicción general; o b) según lo que dispusiere la autoridad extranjera en respuesta a una carta rogatoria, cuando el emplazamiento en cualesquiera de dichos casos tuviere el propósito razonable de realizar una citación eficaz. (R. Fed. P. Civ., sec. 4(h)(i)(1)).

**Service of pleadings and other papers.** Notificación de alegaciones y otros escritos. Necesidad. Excepto cuando estas reglas dispusieren otra cosa, toda orden que de acuerdo con sus términos deba ser notificada, toda alegación subsiguiente a la demanda original a menos que la corte ordenara otra cosa debido al gran número de demandados, todo escrito relacionado con descubrimiento de prueba que deba ser notificado a una parte a menos que la corte

ordenara otra cosa, toda moción por escrito, a no ser que pueda ser vista ex parte y todo aviso por escrito, comparecencia, demanda, oferta de sentencia, designación de autos en apelación y escritos similares, deberán ser notificados a cada una de las partes. (R. Fed. P. Civ., sec. 5(a)(b)).

**Service of process.** Notificación de la demanda.

**Servient estate.** Fundo sirviente.

**Servitude.** Servidumbre. Esclavitud.

**Session.** Sesión.

**Setoff.** Compensación.

**Settle.** Transigir, lograr un acuerdo extrajudicial o judicial.

**Settlement.** Convenio, transacción.

**Settler.** Colono, aparcero.

**Sever.** Separar.

**Severable.** Divisible.

**Several debtor.** Deudor solidario.

**Several liability.** Responsabilidad solidaria.

**Severance of charges or defendants.** Separación de cargos o de acusados.

**Sexual harassment.** Hostigamiento sexual.

**Shadow jury.** Jurado privado, pagado por uno de los abogados, para detectar las posibles reacciones del jurado verdadero.

**Share.** Acción, Título, valor, parte que a uno le toca (s). Compartir (v).

**Sharecropper.** Aparcero.

**Sheriff.** Oficial del juzgado. Agente de policía.

**Sheriff's sale.** Remate judicial.

**Ship.** Nave, embarcación.

**Shipment.** Remesa, carga, embarque, envío.

**Shipment by seller.** Embarque por el vendedor. Cuando el vendedor estuviere obligado o autorizado a enviar las mercancías al comprador y el contrato no lo obliga a entregarlas en un lugar determinado, entonces, salvo pacto en contrario, deberá poner las mercancías en posesión de un porteador y contratar su transportación en forma razonable teniendo en cuenta la naturaleza de las mercancías y otras circunstancias del caso. (C.C.U. sec. 2-504).

**Shipper.** Cargador.

**Shore.** Costa. Prestar ayuda.

**Shortage.** Escasez, desabastecimiento.

**Show cause.** Demostrar razones suficientes para que el tribunal falle en un sentido determinado.

**Shyster.** Abogado deshonesto, picapleitos.

**Siblings of full blood.** Hermanos de doble vínculo.

**Siblings on the maternal side.** Hermanos uterinos, medios hermanos.

**Siblings on the paternal side.** Hermanos consanguíneos, medios hermanos.

**Sick leave.** Licencia por enfermedad.

**Sick pay.** Remuneración recibida durante una licencia por enfermedad.

**Sight, at.** A la vista.

**Sighting land.** Recalada.

**Signature by procuration.** Firma por poder.

**Signature of a commercial paper.** Firma de un documento comercial. Nadie será responsable de un instrumento salvo que su firma aparezca en él. Se firma un instrumento mediante el empleo de cualquier nombre, inclusive cualquier razón social o nombre ficticio en un instrumento, o por cualquier palabra o marca empleada en sustitución de una firma escrita. Toda firma será un endoso, salvo que el instrumento claramente indique que se firmó con carácter distinto. (C.C.U. sec. 3-401/04).

**Silent partner.** Socio comanditario.

**Single interest endorsement.** Endoso "*single interest*." En el campo de seguros desígnase como un endoso "*single interest*"—en una póliza de las denominadas de riesgos combinados de automóviles—aquel endoso mediante el cual, de ocurrir una pérdida, el endosatario—acreedor hipotecario o prendatario, cesionario, etc.—tiene derecho a que se le satisfaga por la compañía de seguros hasta el balance insoluto de su crédito, correspondiendo al cedente o endosante cualquier remanente del valor del vehículo. (U.S. Casualty Co. v. P. R. & A. Ins. Co., 98 D.P.R. 489 (1970)).

**Sink.** Zozobrar, naufragar, hundirse.

**Slander.** Calumnia, denigración. La calumnia o denigración consiste en la publicación de material difamatorio, mediante palabras pronunciadas, gestos transitorios o cualquier otra forma de comunicación no escrita. (Rstmnt, 2nd, Torts, sec. 568(2)).

**Slanderous imputations affecting business, trade, profession or office.** Imputaciones calumniosas que afectan el negocio, industria, profesión o cargo. Una persona que publique una calumnia que atribuya a otro conducta, características, o una condición, que afecte adversamente su aptitud o capacidad para llevar a cabo su negocio, industria o profesión, o el cargo público o privado que desempeñe, ya sea en forma honoraria o por lucro, será responsable ante ese otro, aun sin probarse un daño específico. (Rstmnt, 2nd, Torts, sec. 573).

**Slanderous imputations of criminal conduct.** Imputaciones calumniosas de conducta criminal. Una persona que publique una calumnia, que imputa a otro conducta que constituya una ofensa criminal, será responsable a ese otro, sin tener que probarse un daño específico, si la ofensa imputada es de tal naturaleza, que si se cometiera en el lugar de la publicación: a) sería castigada con pena de reclusión en una institución estatal o federal, o b) es considerada por la opinión pública como una depravación moral. (Rstmnt, 2nd, Torts, sec. 571).

**Slanderous imputations of loathsome disease.** Imputaciones calumniosas de una enfermedad nauseabunda. Una persona que publique una calumnia que impute a otro, una enfermedad venérea u otra enfermedad nauseabunda y trasmisible, será sujeta a responsabilidad sin tener que probarse un daño específico. (Rstmnt, 2nd, Torts, sec. 572).

**Slanderous imputations of sexual misconduct.** Imputaciones calumniosas sobre la mala conducta sexual. Una persona que publique una calumnia que impute a otro una seria conducta irregular de naturaleza sexual, será responsable ante ese otro, aun sin probarse un daño específico. (Rstmnt, 2nd, Torts, sec. 574).

**Smuggler.** Contrabandista.

**Smuggling.** Contrabando.

**Sniper.** Francotirador.

**So help me God.** Forma solemne de terminar un juramento invocando la protección de Dios.

**Sodomy.** Acto sexual realizado por personas del mismo sexo o por una persona con un animal.

**Solicitation.** Incitación. Una persona es culpable de incitación para cometer un delito si con el propósito de promover o facilitar su comisión ordena, estimula, incita o pide a otra que incurra en conducta específica que constituiría ese delito o una tentativa de cometer ese delito, o establecería su complicidad en su comisión o tentativa. (Cód. Pen. Mod., § 5.02 (1)).

Procuración u ofrecimiento de un negocio.

**Solvency.** Solvencia.

**Son.** Hijo, niño.

**Sound discretion.** Prudente arbitrio.

**Sovereignty.** Soberanía.

**Special agent.** Mandatario especial. Un mandatario especial es un mandatario autorizado a realizar una transacción especifica o una serie de transacciones que no conlleva la continuidad de un servicio. (Rstmnt, 2nd, Agency, sec. 3(2)).

**Special appearance.** Comparecencia al solo efecto de alegar incompetencia. Un Estado no ejercerá su jurisdicción sobre un individuo que comparezca a la acción judicial, solamente con el propósito de objetar la jurisdicción sobre su persona. (Rstmnt, 2nd, Conflict, sec. 81).

**Special verdict.** Veredicto especial. La corte podrá requerir que el jurado rinda únicamente un veredicto especial en forma de determinación especial por escrito de cada una de las cuestiones en controversia. (R. Fed. P. Civ., sec. 49(a)).

**Specially preferred creditors.** Acreedores singularmente privilegiados.

**Specific performance.** Cumplimiento específico. El cumplimiento específico de una obligación contractual será impuesto (otorgado) a discreción del tribunal contra la parte que incumpla, o amenace con incumplir, el contrato. (Rstmnt, 2nd, Con., sec., 357(1)).

**Speedy and public trial.** Juicio rápido y público.

**Spend the night.** Pernoctar.

**Spouse.** Cónyuge, esposo/a.

**Springs.** Manantiales.

**Ss.** Viz., a saber.

**Standing.** Personeria para demandar o para ser demandado.

**Stare decisis (L).** Principio del *common law* que torna obligatorio el precedente judicial.

**State.** Estado o nación. Estado, físico o mental en el que alguien se halla. Expresar algo.

**State a claim.** Incoar una acción.

**State courts.** Tribunales estatales. En cada estado hay tribunales de competencia general, que reciben nombres tales como tribunales superiores, de distrito o de circuito, o *courts of common pleas*. Son presididos por un único juez, pudiendo haber o no jurado, y por lo general tienen competencia sobre todos los casos civiles o penales que no estén asignados a tribunales o divisiones especiales. (Intro al USA).

**State insurance fund.** Fondo de seguro del Estado.

**Statement.** Relación, declaración, enunciación, exposición.

**Statement of legislative intent.** Exposición de motivos.

**Statute of frauds.** Formalidad escrita. Ciertos tipos de contrato especificados son ejecutables sólo si están comprobados por un documento escrito. Los contratos más comunes regidos por estas leyes son los contratos para venta de bienes o de tierras, contratos de garantías y contratos con términos mayores de un año. (Rstmnt, 2nd, Con., sec. 110(1)).

**Statute of limitations.** Prescripción liberatoria.

**Statutory law.** Leyes escritas emanados del Congreso o de otra fuente legislativa.

**Stay.** Suspensión, aplazamiento, cese.

**Stay of execution, death.** Suspensión de ejecución, muerte. Se suspenderá una sentencia de pena de muerte si se interpusiere una apelación. (Regla 38(a), Reglas Fed. de Proc. Crim.).

**Stay of execution, imprisonment.** Suspensión de ejecución, reclusión. Se suspenderá una sentencia de pena de reclusión si se interpusiere una apelación y el acusado fuere puesto en libertad mientras se resuelva dicha apelación. (Regla 38(b), Reglas Fed. de Proc. Crim.).

**Stay of execution, probation.** Suspensión de ejecución, libertad a prueba. Toda sentencia que ponga al acusado en libertad a prueba podrá suspenderse si se interpusiere una apelación. Si la sentencia se suspendiere, la corte fijara los términos de la suspensión. (Regla 38(d), Reglas Fed. de Proc. Crim.).

**Stay of proceedings.** Suspensión de procedimientos.

**Steal.** Hurto, robo (s). Hurtar, robar (v).

**Stenographer.** Taquígrafo.

**Stenographic transcript.** Transcripción taquigráfica. Siempre que la declaración de un testigo en juicio o vista de la cual se hubieren tomado notas taquigráficas fuere admisible en evidencia en un juicio posterior, la misma podrá ser probada mediante su transcripción debidamente certificada por la persona que tomó notas de la declaración. (R. Fed. P. Civ., sec. 80(c)).

**Stipulation.** Estipulación.

**Stirpital share.** Porción por estirpe.

**Stock certificates.** Certificados de acciones. Todo tenedor de acciones en la corporación tendrá derecho a un certificado o certificados que representen el número de acciones que posea. (14 LPRA sec. 1508).

**Stock ledger.** Libro de registro de accionistas. El libro original del registro de acciones del capital, o el duplicado de tal libro, certificados por un oficial de la corporación como correctos, constituirán la única evidencia en cuanto a quiénes son los accionistas con derecho a examinar la relación requerida o a examinar los libros y las cuentas de la corporación; o a votar directamente o por poder en cualquiera de las elecciones a que se refiere tal sección. (14 LPRA sec. 1708).

**Stockholder.** Accionista.

**Stop and frisk.** Detención y cacheo.

**Stop, lock or slicegate.** Parada, o partidor.

**Stopping place.** Escala.

**Stores.** Pertrecho.

**Story, Joseph.** Joseph Story (1779-1845) fue nombrado en la Corte Suprema de los EE.UU. en 1811. En 1829, reteniendo su lugar en la Corte, comenzó a dictar cátedra de leyes en la Harvard Law School, donde reorganizó el currículum y revitalizó la escuela. Sus nueve comentarios se desarrollaron a partir de sus conferencias sobre temas que van de la Constitución hasta leyes incompatibles. (Intro al USA).

**Stowage.** Estiba, arrumaje.

**Stream.** Corriente.

**Street-risk doctrine.** Doctrina de los riesgos de la calle.

**Strict liability.** Resposabilidad absoluta u objetiva.

Responsabilidad objetiva, sin culpa. La persona que venda cualquier producto en unas condiciones defectuosas que constituyan un peligro irrazonable para el consumidor o su propiedad, será responsable por los daños físicos causados al consumidor último o su propiedad. (Rstmnt, 2nd, Torts, sec. 402A).

**Strict scrutiny.** Control constitucional estricto que deben pasar ciertas leyes que son sospechosas de infringir derechos constitucionales básicos.

**Strike.** Eliminación de ciertas mociones por orden del juez. Huelga laboral.

**Stub.** Talón.

**Stub book.** Talonario.

*Sua sponte* **(L).** De oficio.

**Subagent.** Submandatario. Un submandatario es la persona nombrada por un mandatario con la capacidad para hacer tal nombramiento, para realizar funciones respecto a las cuales el mandatario se comprometió con el mandante. El mandatario acuerda con el mandante que la responsabilidad principal sobre la conducta del submandatario recaerá en el mandatario. (Rstmnt, 2nd, Agency, sec. 5(1)).

**Subcontract.** Subcontrato. Subcontratar.

**Subject.** Sujeto, material, cuestión. Ciudadano, súbdito. Someter.

**Subject-matter jurisdiction.** Jurisdicción en razón de materia. El procedimiento de dictar sentencia contra una parte será apropiado sólo si el tribunal sentenciador tiene la autoridad para adjudicar el tipo de controversia objeto de la acción. (Rstmnt, 2nd, Judg., sec. 11).

**Sublease.** Subarriendo. Subarrendar.

**Sublessor.** Subarrendador.

**Sublet.** Subarrendar.

**Submission.** Sumisión.

**Submit.** Someter, entregar, proponer.

*Subpoena ad testificandum* **(L).** Citación para concurrir a testificar.

*Subpoena,* **contempt.** Citación, desacato. El incumplimiento sin excusa adecuada por cualquier persona de una citación notificándole podrá ser considerado como desacato a la corte que expidió la citación. (R. Fed. P. Civ., sec. 45).

*Subpoena duces tecum* **(L).** Para entender el contenido de esta expresión hace falta saber que las *depositions* son verdaderos testimonios pero administrados directamente por los abogados intervinientes, fuera de la presencia del tribunal. Cuando un abogado decide tomar la *deposition* de la parte adversa (en el proceso americano se puede ser testigo y parte a la vez) o de un tercero, puede requerir que el futuro deponente traiga consigo documentos o materiales relevantes. En tal caso el abogado requirente solicita—bajo apercibimiento de sanciones por desacato—la presencia del testigo con la obligacion que el mismo traiga consigo los documentos que el abogado describa en la citación.

*Subpoena,* **for attendance of witnesses.** Citación, para comparecencia de testigos. Toda citación será expedida por el secretario bajo el sello de la corte, expresará el nombre de la corte y el título del pleito, y requerirá a cada persona a quien fuere dirigida que comparezca a prestar declaración en la fecha y en el lugar especificados en la misma. (R. Fed. P. Civ., sec. 45(a)).

*Subpoena,* **for production of documentary evidence.** Citación, para producción de prueba documental. Las citaciones también podrán requerir a la persona a quien fuere dirigidas que produzca los libros, escritos, documentos o cosas tangibles señalados en la misma. (R. Fed. P. Civ., sec. 45(b)).

*Subpoena,* **service.** Citación, diligenciamiento. Cualquier citación podrá ser diligenciada por el marshal, por su delegado o por cualquiera otra persona que no sea parte en el pleito y no sea menor de 18 años de edad. (R. Fed. P. Civ., sec. 45(c)).

**Subservant.** Subempleado. Un subempleado es una persona nombrada por un empleado con la capacidad para hacer tal nombramiento, para realizar funciones respecto a las cuales el empleado se comprometió con el patrón, y sujeta al control de su conducta física tanto por el patrón como por el empleado. (Rstmnt, 2nd, Agency, sec. 5(2)).

**Subsidiary.** Subsidiario. Sucursal.

**Subsidy.** Subsidio, auxilio, ayuda, contribución, subvención.

**Substantive due process.** Derecho a gozar de la vida, la libertad y la propiedad sin restricciones arbitrarias.

**Substituted contract.** Contrato sustituto, novación. Un contrato sustituto es uno que se acepta por el acreedor en lugar de una obligación anterior del deudor. (Rstmnt, 2nd, Con., sec. 279).

**Substituted performance.** Cumplimiento sustituto. Cuando sin culpa de ninguna de las partes las facilidades para atraque, carga o descarga de mercancías fallan o una clase pactada de porteador no puede utilizarse o la forma de entrega acordada se hace imposible desde un punto de vista comercial, pero se dispone de una sustitución razonable, dicha sustitución deberá ser ofrecida formalmente y aceptada. Si la forma o medios pactados de pago fallan por causa de reglamentos domésticos o extranjeros, el vendedor podrá retener o detener la entrega a menos que el comprador provea un medio o manera de pago que comercialmente sea un equivalente sustancial. (Rstmnt, 2nd, Con., sec. 278(1)).

**Substitution in trust.** Sustitución fideicomisaria. Una disposición testamentaria en cuya virtud se encarga a un heredero que conserve y trasmita a un tercero el todo o parte de la herencia se denomina una sustitución fideicomisaria. (Díaz Lamoutte v. Luciano, 85 D.P.R. 834 (1962)).

**Substitution of parties.** Sustitución de partes.

**Substitution of parties, death.** Sustitución de partes, muerte. Si una parte falleciere y la reclamación no quedare por ello extinguida, la corte podrá ordenar la sustitución por las partes pertinentes. La solicitud de sustitución podrá ser hecha por cualquier parte o por los sucesores o representantes de la parte fallecida y, junto con el señalamiento para vista, será notificada a todas las partes en la forma dispuesta para el diligenciamiento de un emplazamiento, y podrán ser diligenciadas en cualquier distrito judicial. (R. Fed. P. Civ., sec. 25(a)(1)).

**Substitution of parties, incompetency.** Sustitución de partes, incapacidad. Si una parte se incapacitare, la corte a moción notificada a tenor con lo dispuesto en casos de sustitución de partes por muerte, podrá permitir que continúe el pleito por o contra su representante. (Regla Fed. de Proc. Civ., sec. 25(b)).

**Substitution of parties, transfer of interest.** Sustitución de partes, cesión del interés. En caso de cualquier cesión del interés, podrá continuarse el pleito por o contra la parte original, al menos que la corte a moción dispusiera que la persona a quien se transfiere el interés fuere sustituída en el pleito o acumulada a la parte original. (R. Fed. P. Civ., sec. 25(c)).

**Subtenant.** Subarrendatario.

**Succession.** Sucesión.

**Successor in interest.** Sucesor en derechos.

**Sudden emergency doctrine.** Doctrina de la emergencia súbita. La doctrina de la emergencia súbita (*sudden emergency or imminent peril*)—la cual exime a un demandado en un caso de daños y perjuicios de responsabilidad civil—enuncia que el hecho de que una persona se haya confrontado con una emergencia súbita, la cual no fue ocasionada por su culpa y la cual requirió acción rápida, es un factor a considerarse al determinar si el curso de acción tomado por esa persona fue razonable. (Banchs v. Colon, 89 D.P.R. 481 (1963)).

**Sue.** Demandar, entablar demanda, incoar una acción.

**Sufferance.** Tolerancia, aceptación, consentimiento.

**Suffering.** Sufrimiento.

**Suffrage.** Sufragio, voto.

**Suficient.** Suficiente, adecuado, bastante.

**Suit.** Juicio, pleito, fuerella.

**Sum certain.** Suma cierta. La suma pagadera se considerará cierta, aun cuando hubiere de pagarse a) con intereses señalados o a plazos señalados; o b) con diferentes tipos de interés señalados para antes y después del incumplimiento o a una fecha específica; o c) con tipo de descuento o recargo señalado si se paga antes o después de la fecha fijada para el pago. (C.C.U. sec. 3-106).

**Summary.** Resumen.

**Summary judgment, for claimant.** Sentencia sumaria, a favor del demandante. Toda parte que trate de obtener un remedio mediante demanda, reconvención o demanda contra coparte o de obtener una sentencia declaratoria podrá, en cualquier momento después del vencimiento de 20 días a partir del inicio del pleito o después de la notificación de una moción para sentencia sumaria por la parte contraria, radicar moción, con declaraciones juradas que la fundamenten o sin ellos, solicitando sentencia sumaria a su favor sobre la totalidad o cualquier parte de la reclamación. (R. Fed. P. Civ., sec. 56(a)).

**Summary judgment, for defendant.** Sentencia sumaria, a favor del demandado. Cualquier parte contra quien se hubiere formulado demanda, reconvención o demanda contra coparte o de sentencia declaratoria podrá, en cualquier momento, radicar moción, con declaraciones juradas que la fundamenten o sin ellos, solicitando sentencia sumaria a su favor sobre la totalidad o cualquier parte de la reclamación. (R. Fed. P. Civ., sec. 56(b)).

**Summation.** Alegato final dirigido al jurado.

**Summons, form.** Emplazamiento, forma. El emplazamiento será firmado por el secretario, llevará el sello de la corte, contendrá el nombre de la corte y los nombres de las partes, se dirigirá al demandado, especificará el nombre y la dirección del abogado del demandante, si lo hubiere o de lo contrario la dirección del demandante y el plazo dentro del cual estas reglas requieren que el demandado comparezca y se defienda y le apercibirá de que de no hacerlo así podrá dictarse sentencia en rebeldía en su contra concediendo el remedio solicitado en la demanda. (R. Fed. P. Civ., sec. 4(b)).

**Summons, issuance.** Emplazamiento, expedición. Presentada la demanda el secretario expedirá inmediatamente un emplazamiento y lo entregará al demandante o a su abogado quien será responsable de su rápido diligenciamiento junto con una copia de la demanda. A requerimiento del demandante se expedirán emplazamientos por separado o adicionales contra cualesquiera otros demandados. (R. Fed. P. Civ., sec. 4(a)).

**Summons, service.** Emplazamiento, diligenciamiento. Todo diligenciamiento, a excepción del de una citación o un emplazamiento con entrega de copia de la demanda, será realizado por un *marshall* de los Estados Unidos o un delegado del mismo, o por una persona especialmente nombrada para ese fin. (R. Fed. P. Civ., sec. 4(c)(1)(2)).

**Summons through the mail.** Emplazamiento por correo. Un emplazamiento con entrega de copia de la demanda podrá ser diligenciado: Mediante el envío por correo de una copia del emplazamiento y de la demanda (por correo de primera clase y porte pagado) a la persona a ser emplazada, junto con dos copias de un aviso y acuse de recibo y un sobre de vuelta de correo, porte pagado, dirigido al remitente. Si el acuse de recibo del emplazamiento hecho a tenor con el presente inciso de esta regla no fuera recibido por el remitente dentro de los 20 días siguientes a la fecha de envío por correo. (Regla Fed. de Proc. Civ., sec. 4(c)(2)(C), (C)(ii)).

**Summons upon an enterprise.** Emplazamiento a una empresa. A una corporación nacional o extranjera o a una sociedad u otra asociación no incorporada sujeta a ser demandada bajo un nombre común, mediante la entrega de una copia del emplazamiento y de la demanda a un funcionario, gerente o agente general, o a cualquier otro apoderado o persona autorizada por la ley para recibir emplazamientos y, en el caso de que fuere hecho a persona autorizada por ley para recibir el emplazamiento y la ley lo exigiere, remitiendo además por correo una copia al demandado. (R. Fed. P. Civ., sec. 4(d)(3)).

**Summons upon an individual.** Emplazamiento a un individuo. A una persona que no fuere menor de edad o incapacitado, entregándole personalmente copia del emplazamiento y de la demanda, o dejando copias de los mismos en su casa o lugar de residencia habitual con una persona de edad y discreción adecuadas que resida allí, o entregando una copia del emplazamiento y de la demanda a un apoderado o a una persona autorizada por ley para recibir emplazamiento. (Regla Fed. de Proc. Civ., sec. 4(d)(1)).

**Summons upon an infant or an incompetent person.** Emplazamiento a un menor o a un incapaz. A un menor de edad o persona incapacitada, mediante la notificación del emplazamiento con entrega de copia de la demanda en la forma dispuesta por la ley del Estado en que se hiciere el emplazamiento para el diligenciamiento de emplazamiento u otros procedimientos similares en relación con cualesquiera de dichos demandados en un pleito establecido en las cortes de jurisdicción general de dicho Estado. (R. Fed. P. Civ., sec. 4(d)(2)).

**Summons upon an officer or an agency of the United States.** Emplazamiento a un funcionario o agencia de los Estados Unidos. A un funcionario o agencia de los Estados Unidos, mediante el emplazamiento de los Estados Unidos y mediante el envío de una copia del emplazamiento y de la demanda por correo registrado o certificado a dicho funcionario o agencia. (Regla Fed. de Proc. Civ., sec. 4(d)(5)).

**Summons upon complaint.** Citación a base de denuncia. A solicitud del fiscal del gobierno podrá expedirse una citación en lugar de una orden de arresto. Si el acusado dejare de comparecer en respuesta a la citación, se expedirá una orden de arresto. (Regla 4(a), (c)(1), Reglas Fed. del Proc. Crim.).

**Summons upon the United States.** Emplazamiento a los Estados Unidos. A los Estados Unidos, mediante la entrega de una copia del emplazamiento y de la demanda al fiscal de los Estados Unidos para el distrito en que se interpusiere el pleito o a un fiscal auxiliar de los Estados Unidos o a un empleado de oficina designado por el fiscal de los Estados Unidos en un escrito presentado al secretario de la corte, y mediante el envío de una copia del emplazamiento y de la demanda por correo registrado o certificado al Secretario de Justicia de los Estados

Unidos en Washington, Distrito de Columbia y, además, en cualquier pleito en que se atacare la validez de una orden de un funcionario o agencia de los Estados Unidos que no fuere parte, remitiendo una copia del emplazamiento y de la demanda por correo registrado o certificado a tal funcionario o agencia. (Regla Fed. de Proc. Civ., sec. 4(d)(4)).

**Sundry.** Varios.

**Sunset law.** Ley mediante la cual las reparticiones estatales deben justificar la necesidad de su existencia de tiempo en tiempo frente al Congreso.

**Sunshine law.** Ley mediante la cual las actuaciones de una entidad estatal deben ser públicas y transparentes.

**Superintend.** Vigilar, controlar, supervisar.

**Superintendent.** Mayordomo, superintendente.

**Supersede.** Reemplazar.

**Supersedeas bond.** Fianza para auto de suspensión. Cuando se formalice una apelación el apelante mediante la prestación de fianza para auto de suspensión podrá obtener una suspensión. La suspensión surtirá efecto cuando la fianza para auto de suspensión sea aprobada por la corte. (R. Fed. P. Civ., sec. 62(d)).

**Supervening.** Sobreviniente.

**Supervening frustration.** Frustración sobreviniente. Celebrado un contrato, cuando el propósito principal de una parte queda frustrado sustancialmente sin su culpa, debido a un evento cuya no ocurrencia era un presupuesto básico sobre el cual se formó el contrato, tal parte queda liberado del resto de sus obligaciones a menos que el contrato o las circunstancias indiquen lo contrario. (Restatement, Second, Contracts, sec. 265).

**Supervening impracticability.** Imposibilidad sobreviniente. Cuando el cumplimiento de una parte se hace imposible sin su culpa, por la ocurrencia de un evento cuya no ocurrencia era un presupuesto básico del contrato, el cumplimiento queda liberado a menos que el contrato o las circunstancias indiquen lo contrario. (Rstmnt, 2nd, Con., sec. 261).

**Supplement.** Suplemento aditivo, adicional, extra.

**Supplementary source.** Fuente supletoria.

**Supplying an omitted term.** Integración del contrato. Cuando las partes no se hayan puesto de acuerdo acerca de una disposición importante para la determinación de sus derechos y obligaciones, se considerará integrada al contrato aquella disposición que resulte más apropiada a las circunstancias. (Unidroit, Prin., art. 4.8).

**Supremacy clause.** Cláusula de la Constitución de USA estableciendo la supremacía de la Constitución frente a otras fuentes jurídicas.

**Supreme Court.** Corte Suprema. La revisión de las decisiones de los tribunales de apelación está en manos de la Corte Suprema. El número de sus integrantes es fijado por el Congreso. Desde 1869 consta de nueve juices—un presidente (*chief justice*) y ocho jueces asociados—que actúan como cuerpo único, sin subdividirse. No es sólo el tribunal de ultima instancia del sistema federal, sino que además tiene en cierto grado, poderes de revisión sobre las decisiones de los tribunales estaduales. En ambos casos, sin embargo, es baja la proporción de los procesos que llegan a esta instancia de revisión. (Intro al USA).

**Supreme Court, appeal.** Corte Suprema, apelación. Se puede apelar una sentencia de un tribunal estadual de última instancia que establece que una ley estadual es valida, a pesar de haber sostenido una de las partes que esta en contradicción o con la ley federal; o que—aunque ésto es poco frecuente—juzga que no es valida una ley federal o un tratado. En situaciones excepcionales, también se puede apelar ante la Corte Suprema una decisión de un tribunal inferior. (Intro al USA).

**Supreme Court, original jurisdiction.** Corte Suprema, jurisdicción originaria. De acuerdo con la Constitucion, la Corte Suprema tiene jurisdicción de primera instancia para algunas clases de casos; los más usuales son las disputas entre estados o entre un estado y el tribunal federal. Tales juicios son presididos por un oficial de la Corte con el nombre de special master designado para el caso y cuyas conclusiones son elevadas a la Corte. Este tipo de casos es poco común. (Intro al USA).

**Supreme Court, scope.** Corte Suprema, ámbito. Una de las limitaciones más importantes a la actividad de la Corte, como también de los tribunales inferiores, es que su jurisdicción solo abarca *casos* y *controversias*. Es decir, que solo resuelve juicios entre litigantes que tengan intereses reales en juego en un asunto controvertido. No da opiniones de asesoramiento, ni siquiera sobre cuestiones constituciones, ni aun en el caso que sean requeridas por el Presidente o el Congreso. Otra restricción es que una *federal question* debe ser *sustancial* para que la Corte Suprema tenga jurisdicción en virtud de ella. En ningún caso la Corte revisa decisiones de tribunales estaduales referidas a cuestiones de Derecho estadual. Los tribunales estaduales son los arbitos finales del Derecho estadual, y sus decisiones en estas cuestiones son concluyentes. El Congreso ha establecido dos formas principales en que un caso puede llegar a la Corte Suprema para su revisión: la apelación y el *writ of certiorari*. (Intro al USA).

**Surcharge.** Recargo, aumento, sobretasa, suplemento.

**Sureties, justification.** Fiadores, justificación. Todo fiador, a excepción de una compañía de fianzas aprobada a tenor con lo dispuesto en la ley, justificará mediante afidávit, y podrá ser requerido a que describa en el mismo los bienes inmuebles que ofrece para garantía y los gravámenes sobre los mismos, el número y cuantía de otras garantías para fianzas suscritas por el mismo y que se encuentren en vigor, y todas sus demás obligaciones. No se aprobará fianza alguna a menos que conste que la garantía cumple con todos los requisitos. (Regla 46(d), Reglas Fed. de Proc. Crim.).

**Surety.** Fiador, caución, fianza, garante, garantía.

**Surety insurance.** Seguro de garantía. "Seguro de garantía" incluye: 1) Seguro de crédito como se define en la sec. 408(9) de este título. 2) Seguro de fidelidad que garantiza la probidad de personas que ocupan puestos públicos o privados de confianza. 3) Garantizar el cumplimiento de contratos y garantizar y otorgar fianzas, obligaciones y contratos de fianza. (26 LPRA sec. 409).

**Surname.** Apellido.

**Surplus.** Excedente, demasía, exceso, plus, sobrante, superávit.

**Surplusage rule.** Regla de lo excedente, mediante la cual el material impreso no indispensable para la validez de un testamento ológrafo no invalida tal testamento. (Maul v. Williams, 69 S.W.3d. 1107).

**Surprise.** Sorpresa.

**Surprising terms.** Estipulaciones sorpresivas. Carecerá de eficacia toda estipulación incorporada en cláusulas estándar cuyo contenido, redacción o presentación no fuere razonablemente previsible por la otra parte, salvo que dicha parte la acepte expresamente. (Unidroit, Prin., art. 2.20).

**Surrender.** Entregar, ceder, remitir, renunciar, suministrar, traspasar.

**Surveillance.** Vigilancia supervisación, guarda.

**Surviving.** Sobreviviente.

**Survivorship of action.** Causa de acción subsistirá.

**Suscribing.** Firmante, infrascrito, suscripto.

**Suspect classification.** Clasificación sospechosa.

**Suspensión of payment.** Suspensión de pagos.

**Suspicious.** Sospechoso.

**Sustain.** Sostener, mantener.

**Sustained.** Ha lugar. Expresión que usa el juez para indicar que una objeción hecha por un abogado es aceptada. Lo opuesto es *overruled* (no ha lugar).

**Swap.** Cambio. Intercambiar.

**Swear.** Jurar, prestar juramento. Maldecir.

**Swindle.** Estafa. Estafar.

**Swindler.** Estafador.

**Sworn declaration.** Declaración jurada.

**Syllabus.** Plan de curso, Lista de títulos o materias.

**System.** Sistema.

# T

**Table showing the correspondence.** Tabla de concordancia.

**Tacit.** Tácito.

**Tacking.** Consolidación de dos o más elementos del mismo género en uno solo. v.g. La suma de dos o más períodos posesorios, por distintos poseedores, para alcanzar el término requerido para obtener prescripción adquisitiva.

**Take.** Parte que a uno le toca (s). Incautar, apoderarse, confiscar, tomar, secuestrar (v).

**Take an inventory.** Inventariar, realizar un inventario.

**Take an oath.** Prestar juramento.

**Take bids.** Licitar, subastar, tomar ofertas.

**Take over.** Adquisición o control de una empresa (s). Adquirir o ganar control de una empresa (v).

**Taking.** Toma de posesión de bienes.

**Taking of testimony.** Declaraciones de testigos. En todos los juicios la declaración de los testigos se tomará oralmente en corte abierta, a menos que otra cosa estuviera dispuesta por una Ley del Congreso o por las Reglas Federales de Procedimiento Civil, las Reglas Federales de Evidencia u otras reglas adoptadas por la Corte Suprema. (R. Fed. P. Civ., sec. 43(a)).

**Tamper with evidence.** Destruir u ocultar pruebas.

**Tampering with a witness.** Influenciar indebidamente a los testigos.

**Tapping.** Acción de escuchar comunicaciones telefónicas en forma clandestina.

**Target.** Objetivo, meta, blanco, propósito de una acción o de una estrategia. Poner en la mira, apuntar.

**Tariff.** Arancel, derecho aduanero, tarifa, lista de precios.

**Tax.** Impuesto, tasa, contribución, tributo (s). Imponer un gravamen fiscal (v).

**Tax exemption.** Exención contributiva o impositiva.

**Taxpayer.** Sujeto contribuyente.

**Technical terms and phrases.** Palabras y frases técnicas.

**Temporary.** Temporero, temporario, provisorio.

**Temporary impracticability or frustration.** Imposibilidad o frustración temporera. La imposibilidad del cumplimiento o la frustración temporera del propósito sólo suspende las obligaciones del deudor mientras tal imposibilidad o frustración temporera subsista. (Rstmnt, 2nd, Con., sec. 269).

**Temporary restraining order.** Orden de entredicho provisional. Podrá concederse orden de entredicho provisional sin notificación escrita u oral a la parte contraria o a su abogado únicamente si apareciera claramente de hechos específicos justificados mediante afidávit o demanda jurada que se causarían perjuicios, pérdidas o daños inmediatos e irreparables al solicitante antes de que la parte contraria o su abogado pudiera ser oída en contra. (R. Fed. P. Civ., sec. 65(b)).

**Tenancy.** Tenencia.

**Tenancy at will.** Locación de un inmueble que puede ser rescindida en cualquier momento.

**Tenancy by the entirities.** Propiedad inmueble en co-propiedad, que sólo puede transmitirse con el consentimiento de los co-propietarios.

**Tenancy in common.** Condominio.

**Tenant.** Inquilino.

**Tendency.** Tendencia, proclividad, inclinación.

**Tender.** Licitación, propuesta (s). Entregar, ofrecer (v).

**Tender of payment.** Ofrecimiento de pago.

**Tender offer.** Oferta hecha por una sociedad a los accionistas de otra sociedad para comprarles sus acciones.

**Tenement.** Heredad, fundo, inmueble, bien raíz, finca, predio.

**Tenet.** Premisa.

**Tentative.** Tentativo, de prueba.

**Tenure.** Permanencia, inamovilidad, término (s). Ofrecer inamovildad en un cargo (v).

**Tenured faculty.** Profesores con inamovilidad.

**Term.** Término, plazo, período.

**Term of office.** Duración del cargo.

**Terminate.** Finiquitar, terminat, extinguir.

**Termination.** Terminación. La "terminación" tiene lugar cuando cualquiera de las partes de acuerdo con un poder creado mediante pacto o ley, termina el contrato de venta, de otro modo que no sea por el incumplimiento de éste. A su "terminación" todas las obligaciones que hubieren de ser cumplidas por ambas partes son canceladas, pero cualquier derecho basado en un incumplimiento o cumplimiento anterior subsiste. (C.C.U. sec. 2-106(3)).

**Termination of a job.** Cesantía, finalización de un empleo.

**Termination of contract.** Terminación del contrato. Cualquiera de las partes podrá dar por terminado el contrato cuando la falta de cumplimiento de una obligación por la otra constituya un incumplimiento esencial. (Unidroit, Prin., art. 7.3.1)

**Termination of contract, effects.** Terminación del contrato, effectos. La terminación del contrato releva a las partes hacia el futuro de la obligación de ejecutar y aceptar las prestaciones respectivas. (Unidroit, Prin., art. 7.3.5).

**Termination of power of acceptance.** Finalización del poder de aceptación. La facultad para aceptar una oferta puede terminar por: a) rechazo o contraoferta del requerido, o b) vencimiento del tiempo, o c) revocación por el oferente, o d) muerte o incapacidad del requerido u oferente. (Rstmnt, 2nd, Con., sec. 36).

**Territorial.** Territorial.

**Test.** Test, prueba, examen (s). Comprobar, examinar (v).

**Testament.** Testamento.

**Testator.** Testador.

**Testatrix.** Testadora.

**Testify.** Testificar, dar testimonio.

**Testimony.** Testimonio.

**Theft.** Hurto, robo, delito contra la propiedad.

**Theory of the case.** Teoría jurídica sobre la cual se basa la acción en un caso dado.

**Therein.** Allí incluído.

**Thereof.** De lo cual, de los cuales.

**Thereon.** Después.

**Thing bestowed.** Cosa donada.

**Third party.** Tercero.

**Third party liability.** Responsabilidad de terceros.

**Third party possessor.** Tercero poseedor.

**Third party practice.** Terceros procesales. En cualquier momento después de iniciado el pleito las partes demandadas como demandantes contra tercero, podrán obtener que se emplace con entrega de demanda a una persona que no fuere parte en el pleito y que le sea, o pueda serle, responsable por toda o parte de la reclamación del demandante. Cualquier parte podrá solicitar que se desestime la reclamación contra tercero o su separación para tramitar el juicio por separado. (R. Fed. P. Civ., sec. 14(a), (b)).

**Threat.** Amenaza, fuerza o intimidación. Cualquiera de las partes puede dar por anulado un contrato cuando fue inducida a celebrarlo mediante una amenaza injustificada de la otra parte, la cual, tomando en consideración las circunstancias del caso, fue tan inminente y grave que no le dejó otra alternativa razonable. (Unidroit, Prin., art. 3.9).

**Threaten.** Amenazar.

**Threatened strike.** Amenaza de huelga. Significa una situación en que una organización obrera comunica al patrono que en determinada fecha irá a la huelga, o una situación en que hay claros indicios de que ha habido una ruptura en la negociación colectiva y existe una amenaza de huelga patentemente evidenciada por actos concretos dirigidos o encauzados a dar comienzo a un movimiento huelgario. (29 LPRA sec. 91).

**Thus.** Así.

**Time of acceptance.** Cuándo produce efectos la aceptación. La oferta deberá ser aceptada dentro del plazo fijado por el oferente o, si no se hubiere fijado plazo, dentro del que sea razonable, teniendo en cuenta las circunstancias, que incluyen la velocidad de los medios de comunicación empleados por el oferente. Una oferta verbal tendrá que aceptarse inmediatamente, a menos que las circunstancias indiquen otra cosa. (Unidroit, Prin., art. 2.7).

**Time of performance.** Oportunidad de cumplimiento. Cada parte debe cumplir sus obligaciones: (a) en el momento estipulado en el contrato o determinable según éste; (b) en cualquier momento dentro del término estipulado en el contrato o determinable segun este, a menos que las circunstancias indiquen que a la otra parte le corresponde escoger el momento del cumplimiento; (c) en los demás casos, dentro de un plazo razonable luego de celebrado el contrato. (Unidroit, Prin., art. 6.1.1).

**Time of presentment of a commercial paper.** Fecha de presentación de un documento comercial. Salvo que se exprese una fecha distinta en el instrumento la fecha para cualquier presentación se determinará como sigue: a) cuando un instrumento sea pagadero en una fecha señalada o a un plazo fijo después de una fecha señalada cualquier presentación a la aceptación será en o antes de la fecha en que sea pagadero; b) cuando un instrumento sea pagadero a la vista deberá ser presentado para su aceptación o negociado dentro de un plazo razonable de tiempo después de las fechas o expedición cualquira de las dos que sea la última. (C.C.U. sec. 3-503).

**Tip.** Propina (s). Dar propina (v).

**Tippee.** Persona que recibe una información empresarial confidencial y que la usa para obtener una ganancia ilegal en la bolsa de valores.

**Tithe.** Impuesto o contribución equivalente a la décima parte de los ingresos de una persona.

**Title insurance.** Seguro de título. "Seguro de título" es el seguro de dueños de propiedad inmueble u otros que tengan interés o gravámenes o cargas sobre la misma, contra pérdida por gravamen, títulos defectuosos o invalidez o reclamación adversa al título y los servicios correspondientes. (26 L.R.A. sec. 410).

**Title of nobility.** Título de nobleza.

**Title search.** Estudio de títulos para detectar embargos y demás restricciones al dominio.

**To bearer.** Al portador.

**To have and to hold.** Fórmula sacramental medioeval que producía la transferencia de la propiedad inmueble. Hoy en día se sigue usando al oficiarse matrimonios. Quien oficia la ceremonia pregunta a un participante si acepta al otro como cónyuge *to have and to hold*.

**To order.** A la orden.

**Tolerate.** Tolerar.

**Toll.** Peaje. Dejar en suspenso.

**Tonnage.** Tonelaje.

**Top secret.** Alto secreto.

**Top security prison.** Prisión de alta seguridad.

**Tort immunity, husband and wife.** Inmunidad por cuasidelitos, marido y mujer. Un cónyuge no es inmune a incurrir en responsabilidad extracontractual frente al otro por virtud de la relación misma. (Rstmnt, 2nd, Torts, sec. 895 F).

**Tort immunity, parent and child.** Inmunidad por cuasidelitos, progenitor e hijo. Padres o hijos no serán inmunes a incurrir en responsabilidad extracontractual entre ellos sólo por razón de su relación familiar. La renuncia a inmunidad general por responsabilidad extracontractual no genera responsabilidad por un acto u omisión que, por virtud de la relación padre-hijo no esté privilegiado o exento de responsabilidad extracontractual. (Rstmnt, 2nd, Torts, sec. 895 G).

**Tort immunity, the United States.** Inmunidad por cuasidelitos, los Estados Unidos. Excepto en la medida en que los Estados Unidos presten consentimiento a ser demandados en acciones por responsabilidad extracontractual, tanto la nación como sus agentes son inmunes a responsabilidad. (Rstmnt, 2nd, Torts, sec. 895 A).

**Tort liability based on estoppel.** Responsabilidad extracontractual basada en "estoppel". Si una persona coacciona a otra para que ésta de hecho cometa un error con respecto al título o disposición de tierra, a sabiendas de que el segundo actuará de conformidad con el error y subsiguientemente el primero realiza o deja de realizar un acto que constituiría responsabilidad extracontractual si el engaño hubiese sido realidad y no eso, dado que el segundo confió a tal grado en el error cuando actuó y se afectó tanto al así hacerlo, que sería injusto no conceder una acción contra el primero por su acción u omisión al inducir al otro a error. (Rstmnt, 2nd, Torts, sec. 872).

**Tortfeasor.** Perpetrador de un cuasidelito.

**Tortious.** Cuasidelictivo, generador de responsabilidad civil.

**Tortious conduct.** Conducta cuasidelictiva, cuasidelito. La conducta cuasidelictiva la constituye aquel acto u omisión de tal naturaleza que conlleva responsabilidad de parte del actor. (Rstmnt, 2nd, Torts, sec. 6).

**Torts, classification.** Cuasidelitos, clasificación. La mayoría de los delitos y cuasidelitos puede agruparse en tres categorías según que la responsabilidad se base en la intencionalidad, al culpa o negligencia, o sea absoluta o estricta sin mediar intencionalidad ni negligencia. (Intro al USA).

**Township.** Ayuntamiento, municipalidad.

**Tract.** Parcela de tierra, lote, inmueble.

**Trade.** Comercio, ocupación, profesión (s). Comerciar, permutar (v).

**Trade law.** Derecho comercial.

**Trade union.** Gremio, sindicato laboral.

**Trade union membership.** Afiliación gremial. Está prohibido que se exija a un trabajador estar afiliado al sindicato para obtener un empleo (*closed shop*). Las leyes federales permiten en general que se le exija afiliarse después de ser contratado (*union shop*); pero en un grupo minoritario de estados existen leyes que lo prohíben (*right-to-work laws*), en virtud de leyes federales que disponen expresamente que una ley estadual más estricta prevalece sobre una ley federal en este aspecto. (Intro al USA).

**Trademark (TM).** Marca comercial, marca registrada (MR).

**Training.** Adiestramiento, aprendizaje, entrenamiento.

**Traitor.** Traidor.

**Transaction.** Transacción, negociación.

**Transaction.** Negocio, asunto, comercio, operación, transacción.

**Transactional attorney.** Abogado especializado en la negociación de contratos. Se opone el término a *trial attorney*, o abogado procesalista.

**Transactions on exchange.** Operaciones de bolsa.

**Transcript.** Copia de los autos, copia oficial de un certificado, v.g. de estudios o de una sentencia.

**Transfer of shares.** Traspaso de acciones. Podrá traspasarse el título de propiedad del certificado y de las acciones que éste representa, únicamente:—por entrega del certificado endosado en blanco, o a favor de persona determinada por el dueño de las acciones, según conste en el certificado que las representa;—por entrega del certificado y de documento aparte en que conste la cesión del certificado o un poder para vender, ceder o traspasar el certificado o las acciones que representa, documento que será firmado por el dueño de las acciones, según conste en el certificado que las representa, la sesión o el poder podrán ser en blanco o a favor de personas determinadas. (14 LPRA sec. 1601).

**Transferee.** Cesionario.

**Transferor.** Cedente, cesionista.

**Translation.** Traducción.

**Transmissible.** Trasmisible, contagioso.

**Transportation by river.** Transporte fluvial.

**Travel agent.** Agente viajero. "Agentes viajeros" significan aquellos empleados que ejercen las funciones de viajeros vendedores y cuya labor consiste en llevar a cabo transacciones de ventas de productos, servicio o de cualesquiera otros bienes tangibles e intangibles a nombre de un patrono, intervenga o no personalmente en la distribución o entrega del producto, servicios o bienes, incluyendo cualquier trabajo o servicio incidental o relacionado con la actividad principal de venta. (29 LPRA sec. 288).

**Treachery.** Traición.

**Treason.** Traición.

**Treasure trove.** Tesoro. Tesoro hallado.

**Treasury.** Tesorería, hacienda, tesorero.

**Treaties.** Tratados. Los tratados firmados por los Estados Unidos tienen igual jerarquía que las leyes federales, y están supeditadas solamente a la Constitución. En caso de conflicto entre un tratado y una ley tiene primacía el texto más reciente. Los tratados son firmados por el Presidente con el consentimiento del Senado por mayoría de dos tercios de los votos. Si es un tratado de aplicación automática, adquiere vigencia en cuanto es ratificado; si no, debe ser implementado por una ley federal. El Presidente tiene también las facultades limitadas de firmar acuerdos ejecutivos con países extranjeros sin aprobación del Congreso. Los tribunales han establecido que estos acuerdos, (que por otra parte han sido más numerosos que los tratados), tienen igual validez que estos. (Intro al USA).

**Treaty.** Tratado, acuerdo, convenio, pacto.

**Treble damages.** Triplicación del resarcimiento como medida ejemplar o punitoria.

**Tree nurseries.** Viveros de árboles.

**Trespass.** Perturbación, infringimiento, violación.

**Trespass by livestock.** Translimitación o transgresión de ganado. El poseedor de ganado que se ha introducido en un terreno perteneciente a otra persona, será responsable de tal intrusión aunque haya ejercido sumo cuidado de que no ocurriese dicha intrusión. (Restatement, Second, Torts, sec. 504).

**Trespass on land, abnormally dangerous activities.** Violación de propiedad, actividades de alto riesgo. Una persona que temeraria o negligentemente, o como resultado de una actividad particularmente peligrosa, entra en una propiedad poseída por otro u ocasiona que un tercero o alguna cosa entre en la propiedad; incurre en responsabilidad sólo si su presencia, la del tercero, o la de la cosa causa daño a la propiedad o a su poseedor; o causa daño a alguna cosa o una tercera persona a cuyo seguridad el poseedor tiene un derecho legalmente protegido. (Rstmnt, 2nd, Torts, sec. 165).

**Trespass on land, intentional intrusion.** Violación de propiedad, intrusión intencional. Incurrirá en responsabilidad por transgresión o translimitación, irrespectivamente de que cause daño a un derecho legalmente protegido de otro, si una persona intencionalmente: a) entre en la propiedad de otra persona, o causa que un tercero lo haga, b) permanece en esa propiedad, o c) no remueve alguna cosa de la propiedad, cuando tiene el deber de así hacerlo. (Restatemente, Second, Torts, sec. 158).

**Trespass to chattel.** Apoderamiento indebido de bienes muebles. La transgresión o translimitación de un bien mueble la comete quien intencionalmente: a) despoja a otro del bien mueble, o b) utiliza las cosas al entremezclarlas con un bien mueble que está bajo la posesión de otro. (Restamente, Second, Torts, 217).

**Trespasser.** Transgresor, violador de propiedad. Un transgresor o violador es aquella persona que entra o permanece en un predio de terreno cuya posesión pertenece a otra persona sin un privilegio que se lo permita y sin el consentimiento del poseedor. (Rstmnt, 2nd, Torts, sec. 329).

**Trial.** Juicio, juicio oral.

**Trial by the court.** Juicio por la corte. Las cuestiones para las cuales no se exija juicio por jurado serán enjuiciadas por la corte; sin embargo, no obstante la omisión de una parte de solicitar jurado en un pleito en el cual tal solicitud hubiera podido hacerse como cuestión de derecho, la corte a su discreción a virtud de moción, podrá ordenar un juicio por jurado de cualesquiera o todas las cuestiones. (Regla Fed. de Proc. Civ., sec. 39(b)).

**Tribunal.** Tribunal, corte.

**Trough.** Abrevadero.

**Trover and conversion.** Acción que el derecho angloamericano concede al titular de una cosa mueble cuando ha sido ilegalmente privado de su dominio o uso. El objetivo no es recuperar la posesión del mueble ni reivindicarlo, sino obligar al detentador ilegítimo a pagar su valor íntegro, aun en el caso de estar dispuesto a devolverlo. (Morales Lebrón).

**True and faithful record.** Registro fiel y exacto.

**Trust.** Fideicomiso. El fideicomiso es una institución de derecho angloamericano, desconocida en el sistema civilista. El fideicomiso es un mandato irrevocable a virtud del cual se transmiten determinados bienes a una persona llamada fiduciario para que disponga de ellos conforme lo ordene la que los tramite, llamada fideicomitente, a beneficio de este mismo o de un tercero llamado fideicomisario (*cestui que trust*). (31 LPRA sec. 2541).

**Trust, beginning.** Fideicomiso, comienzo. La vida legal de un fideicomiso comienza desde que el fiduciario acepta el mandato, con lo cual se hace irrevocable. (31 LPRA sec. 2556-57).

**Trust, *cestui que trust*, beneficiary.** Fideicomiso, fideicomisario. El fideicomisario puede ser persona natural o jurídica. En el caso de fideicomisos no pecuniarios, el fideicomisario puede ser una clase de personas indeterminadas, nacidas o por nacer. (31 LPRA sec. 2575-77).

**Trust company.** Compañía de fideicomisos. El término "compañía de fideicomisos," significa una corporación del país formada con el objetivo de tomar, aceptar y cumplir o ejecutar los fideicomisos que legalmente se le confíen, actuando, como fiduciaria en los casos prescritos por la ley, recibiendo depósitos de dinero y de otra propiedad mueble; así como emitiendo documentos por los mismos y prestando dinero con garantías reales o personales. (7 LPRA sec. 302).

**Trust, constituent, settlor.** Fideicomiso, fideicomitente. El fideicomitente puede designar uno o más sustitutos del fiduciario para que lo reemplacen en caso de incapacidad, destitución o muerte y puede encomendar al propio fiduciario o a un tercero el nombramiento de sustituto. (31 LPRA sec. 2563-65).

**Trust, duration.** Fideicomiso, duración. El fideicomiso puede ser particular o universal, puro o condicional, a día cierto, por tiempo determinado o durante la vida del fideicomitente, del fiduciario o del fideicomisario. Los fideicomisos para fines no pecuniarios podrán constituirse por tiempo indeterminado. Toda condición de la cual dependa la ejecución de un fideicomiso y cuyo cumplimiento tarda cada 30 años, contados desde la aceptación del cargo por el fiduciario se tendrá por prescrita. Esta disposición no será aplicables a los fideicomisos para fines no pecuniarios. (31 LPRA sec. 2546, 2548-54).

**Trust, end.** Fideicomisos, finalización. El fideicomiso se extingue: 1) Por cumplimiento de los fines para los cuales se constituyó; 2) Por imposibilidad de su cumplimiento; 3) Por falta absoluta de la condición dentro del término señalado; 4) Por renuncia del fideicomisario, siempre que no tenga sustitutos, o por su muerte; 5) Por destrucción de la cosa sobre la cual está constituido; 6) Por resolución del derecho del fideicomitente sobre los derechos fideicomitidos; 7) Por confusión del carácter del único fideicomisario con el del único fiduciario; 8) Por convenio expreso y personal de todas las partes. (31 LPRA sec. 2560, 2575).

**Trust indenture.** Documento que contiene las cláusulas que crean el fideicomiso.

**Trust, origin.** Fideicomiso, origen. EL concepto nació a partir de la operación siguiente: el propietario de un bien (*settlor*) lo entrega a otra persona (*trustee*) que lo custodiara en beneficio de tercero (*beneficiary*). Para que la operación tuviera éxito, fue necesario encontrar los medios para obligar al *trustee* a cumplir con las obligaciones que el *trust* le imponía. El sistema *equity*, al permitir acciones legales sobre los individuos, fue capaz de asegurar el cumplimiento de los derechos del *trust* por medio de penas como multa o prisión, sin dejar de reconocerle por ello un derecho de propiedad *legal*: al reconocer al beneficiario de derechos, en *equity* se genero la distinción entre propiedad *legal* y propiedad. (Intro al USA).

**Trust, removal of trustee.** Fideicomiso, remoción del fiduciario. Por orden del tribunal con jurisdicción competente se destituirá de su cargo al fiduciario:—Si sus intereses personales son incompatibles con los del fideicomisario;—Si malversa o fraudulenta o negligentemente administra los bienes fideicomitidos;—si se incapacita o inhabilita. (31 LPRA sec. 2574).

**Trust, set up.** Fideicomiso, constitución, creación. El fideicomiso puede constituirse por testamento, para que tenga efecto después de la muerte del fideicomitente, o por acto inter vivos. El fideicomiso inter vivos debe constituirse por escritura pública. Puede constituirse el fideicomiso sobre toda clase de bienes muebles e inmuebles, corporales o incorporales, presentes o futuros.

El fideicomiso constituido sobre bienes inmuebles debe constar en escritura pública, la cual habrá de inscribirse; y sólo perjudicará a terceros desde la fecha de su inscripción en un registro público. (31 LPRA sec. 2542-45, 2562).

**Trust, trustee.** Fideicomiso , fiduciario. El fiduciario puede ser persona natural o jurídica. Para un sólo fideicomiso puede haber uno o más fiduciarios. Y puede haber uno o más sustituto para un fiduciario de este título. El fiduciario y sus sustitutos, si son personales naturales, deberán tener todos los requisitos y condiciones que la ley exige a los tutores. (31 LPRA sec. 2566).

**Trust, trustee's rights and duties.** Fideicomiso, derechos y obligaciones del fiduciario. Todo fideicomiso se entiende remunerado. El fiduciario tendrá derecho a recibir y recibirá los mismos honorarios que la ley señala a los tutores salvo pacto en contrario. El fiduciario quedará encargado de la ejecución del fideicomiso desde el instante en que lo acepte y no será responsable de ninguna equivocación de criterio, de ningún error de ellos o de derecho, ni de ningún acto u omisión, a excepción de su propio descuido voluntario o negligencia manifiesta. (31 LPRA sec. 2558, 2569-73).

**Trustees or receivers for dissolved corporations.** Síndicos o administradores judiciales de corporaciones.

Los síndicos y administradores judiciales tendrán facultad para representar judicialmente a la corporación o actuar de otro modo con respecto a todos los pleitos que fueren necesarios o propios a los fines ante-

dichos; y tendrán asimismo facultades para nombrar agentes bajo sus órdenes, y para realizar todos los demás actos que la corporación realizaría si existiere, y que sean necesarios para la liquidación final de los asuntos corporativos pendientes. Podrán prorrogarse las facultades de los síndicos o administradores judiciales por el tiempo necesario y mediante las órdenes necesarias a juicio del Tribunal, para los fines antedichos. (14 LPRA sec. 2007).

**Try.** Intento, esfuerzo (s). Substanciar, conocer, juzgar, someter a la decisión de un tribunal y/o de un jurado (v).

**Try a case.** Completar un juicio hasta su etapa final.

**Tucker Act.** Por la *Tucker Act de 1887* (Ley Tucker) y sus enmiendas (una de las leyes federales más importantes en el tema) el gobierno de los Estados Unidos ha renunciado a su inmunidad total en la materia, consintiendo a litigar en los tribunales federales. (Intro al USA).

**Turn key operation.** Operación llave en mano.

**Tutor.** Tutor, curador (s). Servir como guía o maestro a alguien (v).

**Tying arrangement.** Venta ligada. Es el que involucra la venta o arriendo de un producto con la condición de que se compre conjuntamente un segundo producto. (Intro al USA).

**Tying of goods.** Acción monopolística consistente en forzar la venta de dos productos cuando el consumidor sólo quiere comprar uno.

# U

**Unabated.** Sin merma ni reducción de ninguna clase.

**Unaswerable.** Incontestable, irrefutable, que no admite réplica.

**Unappealable.** Inapelable, final.

**Unattached.** Libre de embargos.

**Unauthorized practice of law.** Ejercicio illegal de la profesión de abogado.

**Unavoidable accident.** Accidente inevitable. Circunstancia en la que el daño causado no es producido por un acto torticero de otra persona. (Rstmnt, 2nd, Torts, sec. 8).

**Uncertain damages.** Indemnización especulativa. No se podrá recibir indemnización por una pérdida mayor a la establecida con certeza razonable por la evidencia admitida. (Rstmnt, 2nd, Con., sec. 352).

**Uncertainty.** Incertidumbre. Unanimity. Unanimidad.

**Uncollectible.** Incobrable, irrecuperable.

**Uncollectible account.** Cuenta incobrable.

**Unconscionable contract.** Contrato leonino. Si un contrato o término es leonino al momento que se realiza el contrato, un tribunal puede rehusar ejecutar el contrato, o puede ejecutar el contrato, o puede ejecutar la parte restante del contrato sin el término leonino, o puede limitar la aplicación de cualquier término leonino para evitar así un resultado irrazonable. (Rstmnt, 2nd, Con., sec. 208).

**Unconstitutional.** Inconstitucional.

**Uncontested.** No contencioso. Procedimiento voluntario, v.g. una adopción o un divorcio cuando ambas partes estan de acuerdo.

**Undated.** Sin fecha.

**Under color of law.** Con abuso de función pública.

**Under seal.** Bajo sello. Formalidad contractual ya casi no usada. Originalmente esta formalidad daba fuerza legal a aquellos contratos que carecían de *consideration* o contraprestación.

**Under the surface.** Subsuelo, subterráneo.

**Under warning.** Apercibido.

**Under oath.** Bajo juramento solemne.

**Undertake.** Emprender.

**Undisbursed income.** Ingresos no distribuídos.

**Undisclosed dangerous condition known to lessor.** Condición peligrosa oculta conocida por el locador. El locador de un predio de terreno que oculte u omita alguna condición a su locatario ya fuese natural o artificial, que represente un riesgo irrazonable a las personas que ocupen el terreno; será responsable ante su locatario y los demás con el consentimiento del locatario o el sublocatario, por el daño corporal causado por la condición luego de que el locatario haya tomado posesión. (Rstmnt, 2nd, Torts, sec. 362).

**Undue.** Indebido, injustificado, sin razón de ser.

**Unduly.** Indebidamente.

**Unearned.** No devengado, no ganado.

**Undue influence.** Influencia indebida.

**Unencumbered.** Libre de gravamen, no comprometido, exento.

**Unenforceable contract.** Contrato no ejecutable. Contrato no ejecutable es aquél que al incumplirse no acuerda acción por daños ni por cumplimiento específico, pero al que se le asigna un deber de cumplimiento moral aunque no haya mediado ratificación. (Rstmnt, 2nd, Con., sec. 8).

**Unexecuted.** Sin cumplimentar, incumplido.

**Unfair.** Parcial, injusto.

**Unfair activities.** Actividades, injustas, prácticas desleales.

**Unfair labor practice by employer.** Práctica ilícita de trabajo por el patrono. 1) Será práctica ilícita de trabajo el que un patrono, actuando individualmente o concertadamente con otros intervenga, restrinja, ejerza coerción o intente intervenir, restringir o ejercer coerción con sus empleados en el ejercicio de los derechos garantizados por la ley. (29 LPRA sec. 69).

**Unfair labor practice by labor union.** Práctica ilícita de trabajo por una organización obrera. Será práctica ilícita de trabajo el que una organización obrera, actuando individualmente o concertadamente con otros viole los términos de un convenio colectivo, incluyendo un acuerdo en el que se comprometa a aceptar un laudo de arbitraje, esté o no dicho acuerdo incluido en los términos de un convenio colectivo. (29 LPRA sec. 69).

**Unfaithful spouse.** Cónyuge infiel.

**Uniform Commercial Code, general provisions.** Código de Comercio Uniforme, disposiciones generales. El Artículo 1 está totalmente dedicado a las disposiciones de carácter general y tal cosa es sin duda una contribución sustancial al Derecho mercantil. Estas son aplicables a todos los Artículos y establecen principios generales y reglas de interpretación. A propio tiempo este Artículo define 46 términos y expresiones legales con precisión y claridad en el lenguaje. El Código Uniforme probablemente ha ido más allá que cualquier legislación en el cuidado con que define y describe la terminología que emplea. (C.C.U., Prefacio).

**Uniform Commercial Code, U.C.C.** Código de Comercio Uniforme, C.C.U. La idea central del Código Uniforme es que el acto de comercio o transacción comercial es uno solo, a pesar de sus diversas facetas. Un sólo acto o transacción puede comprender un contrato de venta, un cheque, giro o letra por parte del precio y la aceptación de alguna forma de garantía por el precio aplazado. El cheque y el giro o letra pueden negociarse y finalmente pasar por uno o más bancos para su cobro. Si las mercancías son transportadas o almacenadas el objeto de la venta estará amparado por una carta de porte o conocimiento de embarque, o un resguardo de almacenes de depósitos o ambos. O tal vez la transacción pudo efectuarse en virtud de una carta de crédito nacional o extranjera. (C.C.U., Prefacio).

**Union.** Unión. Sindicato.

**Unitary action.** Fuero de atracción.

**United Nations Organization (UNO, UN).** Organización de Naciones Unidas (ONU, NU).

**United States Code.** Recopilación official de leyes federales de los Estados Unidos. Se abrevia como U.S.C.

**Unitelligible.** Ininteligible, confuso.

**Unknown owners.** Dueños desconocidos.

**Unlawful agreements.** Convenciones ilícitas.

**Unlawful detainer.** Desahucio, evicción, lanzamiento ilegal.

**Unlawful force.** Fuerza ilegal. Significa fuerza, incluyendo confinamiento, el cual es empleado sin el consentimiento de la persona contra la cual va dirigido y el empleo de lo cual constituye una ofensa. (Cód. Pen. Mod., § 3.11 (1)).

**Unnavigable.** No navegable.

**Unseemly criticism.** Crítica injuriosa.

**Unsound condition.** Situación precaria.

**Unworthiness.** Indignidad.

**Unworthy heir.** Heredero excluido por razón de indignidad.

**Upon notice.** Previa notificación.

**Upon the record and files.** Fundándose en los autos y legajos.

**Usage.** Uso, costumbre. Uso es la práctica habitual o costumbre. (Rstmnt, 2nd, Con., sec. 219).

**Usage of trade.** Usos y costumbres del comercio. El uso y costumbre del comercio es aquél que se observa con tal regularidad en un lugar, zona o comercio de modo que justifica la expectativa de que se observará con respecto a un acuerdo en particular. Puede incluir un sistema de reglas que se observan regularmente, aunque las reglas particulares cambien de tiempo en tiempo. (Rstmnt, 2nd, Con., sec. 222(1)).

**Usages and practices.** Usos y prácticas. Las partes quedarán obligadas por cualquier uso que hayan convenido y por cualquier práctica que hayan establecido entre ellas. (Unidroit, Prin., art. 1.8).

**Use of force to take possession of land.** Uso de la fuerza para toma posesión sobre inmuebles. El uso de la fuerza contra otro individuo para poder entrar en posesión de un inmueble no es de naturaleza privilegiada a menos que ese individuo haya despojado en forma torticera al acto o predecesor de su títulos: (i) sin haber reclamado un derecho, o (ii) si reclamando un derecho, ha utilizado la fuerza contra el actor, o mediante coacción o fraude, o irrumpiendo en la propiedad. (Rstmnt, 2nd, Torts, sec. 89).

**Usufructuary.** Usufructuario.

**Usurious.** Usurario.

**Usurp.** Usurpar.

**Usurper.** Usurpador.

**Usury.** Usura.

**Uterine.** Uterino.

**Utmost care.** Cuidado máximo.

**Utterance.** Exclamación, manifestación, declaración.

**Uxoricide.** Uxoricidio, asesinato de la esposa propia.

# V

**V.A.T.** I.V.A. Impuesto al valor agregado.

**Vacancy.** Vacante.

**Vacate.** Dejar sin efecto, anular, revocar.

**Vacation of judgment.** Anulación de la sentencia.

**Vacations.** Vacaciones, asueto, feria, feriado.

**Vagrancy.** Vagancia.

**Vagrant.** Vagabundo, vago.

**Vague.** Impreciso, confuso, vago.

**Vagueness.** Vaguedad.

**Valid.** Validez.

**Valid judgment requirements.** Sentencia válida, requisitos. Una sentencia es válida si: a) El Estado donde se emittió tiene jurisdicción para actuar en ese caso. b) se utiliza un método razonable de notificación, y se le provee a las personas afectadas de una oportunidad razonable para ser oídas. (Rstmnt, 2nd, Conflict, sec. 92).

**Valid judgment, requisites.** Sentencia válida, requisitos. Un tribunal tiene autoridad para dictar sentencia en una acción cuando dicho tribunal tiene jurisdicción en razón de materia sobre la cuestión en litiglo, y: 1) la parte contra la cual se dictará sentencia se ha sometido a la jurisdicción del tribunal, o 2) Se ha notificado adecuadamente a la parte contra la cual se dictará sentencia de la acción en su contra y el tribunal tiene jurisdicción territorial sobre la acción. (Rstmnt, 2nd, Judg., sec. 1).

**Validity.** Validez, efectividad.

**Valuable consideration.** Título lucrativo, oneroso.

**Value, for value.** Causa onerosa, a titulo oneroso. Valor o causa onerosa. Salvo lo dispuesto en contrario con respecto a instrumentos negociables y cobranzas bancarias una persona entrega valor a cambio de derecho si los adquiere a cambio de un compromiso obligatorio de extender crédito o para concesión de crédito inmediatamente disponible aunque no se gire contra él y aunque se pacte un nuevo cargo (*charge-back*) para el caso de dificultades en el cobro. (C.C.U. sec. 1201 (144)).

**Vandalism.** Vandalismo.

**Variance.** Incongruencia, contradicción, desacuerdo.

**Vassal.** Vasallo.

**Vassal states.** Estados vasallos.

**Vehicle insurance.** Seguro de vehículos. "Seguro de vehiculos" es el seguro contra péridida o los daños causados a un vehículo terrestre o aeronave o cualquier animal de tiro o de montura, o de propiedad mientras estuviere en los mismos o sobre los mismos, o cargándose en los mismos o descargándose de ellos, por cualquier riesgo o causa, y contra cualquier pérdida, gasto o responsabilidad por la pérdida, o los daños causados a personas o la propiedad, resultante de la posesión, conservación, o uso de cualquiera de dichos vehiculos, aeronaves o animales, o incidentales a los mismos. (26 LPRA sec. 407).

**Venal.** Venal, sobornable.

**Vendee.** Comprador.

**Vendor.** Vendedor, enajenante.

**Venire (L).** Comparecer ante el tribunal. Usado especialmente en la expresión *venire fascias*, u orden requiriendo la presencia de un jurado.

**Venire facias (L).** Orden emitida por el tribunal para que se convoque al jurado.

**Venue.** Competencia en razón de territorio.

**Verdict.** Veredicto. El veredicio puede ser genérico, decidiendo a favor de una de las partes y fijando una suma reparatoria; o puede requerirse que el jurado decida una serie de cuestiones de hecho específicas que el juez le plantea. En algunos lugares el veredictos se emite oralmente. En otros, el presidente del jurado firma un veredicto escrito que es leído en la audiencia, ante to cual el jurado da asentimiento en forma oral. (Intro al USA).

**Verdict, finding of the jury.** Veredicto, decisión del jurado.

**Verification.** Verificación. Autentificación de firma.

**Verified copy.** Copia con una firma que autentica su validez.

**Verified pleading.** Alegato con firma certificada.

**Vested right.** Derecho adquirido.

**Vesting of title.** Investidura de titulo. Si hubiera bienes inmuebles o muebles en el distrito, la corte en lugar de ordenar el traspaso de los mismos podrá dictar sentencia despojando del titulo a cualquier parte, traspasándolo a otras, y dicha sentencia tendrá el mismo efecto que un traspaso ejecutado en debida forma legal. (R. Fed. P. Civ., sec. 70).

**Veto.** Veto, oposición (s). Vetar (v).

**Violence.** Violencia.

**Visible means of support.** Manera de vivir conocida.

**Visitation rights.** Derechos de visita, normalmente aqullos acordados a los progenitores en juicios de divorcio.

**Viz.** A continuación.

**Void.** Nulo (s). Anular (v).

**Voir dire.** Selección de jurados. La corte podrá permitir a las partes o a sus abogados llevar a cabo el examen de los jurados en perspetiva o podrá ella misma llevarlo a cabo. En este último caso, la corte permitirá a las partes o a sus abogados complementar el examen mediante las investigaciones adicionales que considere pertinentes o podrá someter a los jurados en perspectiva las preguntas adicionales de las partes o de sus abogados que estimare pertinentes. (R. Fed. P. Civ., sec. 47(a)).

**Voluntary dismissal.** Desistimiento voluntario. Un pletto podrá ser desistido por el demandante sin orden de la corte mediante la presentación de un aviso de desistimiento en cualquier fecha antes de la notificación por la parte contraria de una contesiación o de una moción solicitando sentencia sumaria, cualquiera que ocurra primero. (R. Fed. P. Civ., sec. 41(a) (1)).

**Volunteer.** Voluntario. Ofrecerse como voluntario.

**Vote.** Voto, escrutinio (s). Votar, sufragar (v).

**Voting rights of stockholders.** Derecho al voto de los accionistas. Todo accionista tendrá, en cada junta de accionista y a menos que se disponga otra cosa en el certificado de incorporación, la facultad de emitir, personalmente o mediante apoderado, un 1) voto por cada acción del capital corporativo que posea, pero no podrá emitirse voto alguno por poder después del año de haberse otorgado el poder, a menos que en éste se disponga un plazo mayor. (14 LPRA sec. 1702).

**Voting trust.** Voto en fideicomiso. Un accionista o cualquier número de ellos podrá, mediante convenio escrito, depositar acciones de capital de emisión original o traspasar acciones de capital a cualquier persona o personas o corporación o corporaciones autorizadas para actuar en calidad de fiduciarios, con el fin de otorgar a tal persona o personas o corporación o corporactiones, que podrán ser designadas fiduciarias del voto, el derecho a votar que corresponda a las acciones por el tiempo (no más de diez (10) años), téminos y condiciones que se consignen en el convenio. (14 LPRA sec. 1706).

**Voucher.** Comprobante, recibo.

**Vulnerable.** Vulnerable.

# W

**Wager.** Apuesta. Cantidad u objeto que se apuesta. Apostar.

**Wages.** Sueldos.

**Waive.** Renunciar a un derecho.

**Waiver.** Renuncia a un derecho.

**Want of competence.** Falta de competencia. Un acto es negligente si se ejecuta sin la debida competencia o capacidad de parte del actor, cuando debió reconocer como hombre razonable, que tal capacidad o competencia era necesaria para evitar el riesgo de ocasionar daño a otro. (Rstmnt, 2nd, Torts, sec. 299).

**Want of prosecution.** Fenecimiento, abandono de una causa por la parte actora.

**Want of reasonable care.** Falta de cuidado razonable. Cuando el acto negligente se debe a que no se actuó con el debido cuidado, el cuidado que se le requiere al actor es aquél que observaría un hombre razonable en la misma posición, con su conocimiento y competencia, como un acto necesario para evitar el riesgo de ocasionar daño a otro. (Rstmnt, 2nd, Torts, sec. 298).

**Wantonness.** Ejecución conciente de un acto, u omission de realizar un acto, sabiendo que con ello se causa un daño o sin que a uno le importe si el daño se causa o no.

**War.** Guerra.

**Ward.** Pupilo, menor a cargo.

**Wardship.** Tutela, custodia.

**Warehouse.** Almacén, depósito.

**Warehouse receipts, Uniform Commercial Code.** Documentos de resguardo, Código de Comercio Uniforme. El Código Uniforme trata éstos en el Artículo 7, en el cual incorpora sin modificaciones esenciales de concepto las vigentes *Uniform Warehouse Receipts Act* y *Uniform Bills of Lading Act.* Este artículo constituye una refundición y revisión de la *Uniform Warehouse Receipts Act* y de la *Uniform Bills of Lading Act* y comprende todas las disposiciones de la *Uniform Sales Act* relativas a la negociación de documentos de resguardo. (C.C.U., Prefacio).

**Warning.** Advertencia, aviso.

**Warrant.** Documento o comprobante de constatación (s). Garantizar, asegurar (v).

**Warrant or summons upon indictment or information.** Orden de arresto o citación basada en indiciamiento o de acusación. A requerimiento del fiscal la corte expedirá orden de arresto para cada acusado nombrado en la acusación fundada en la existencia de causa probable bajo juramento, o en el indiciamiento a requerimiento del fiscal se podrá expedir una citación en lugar de orden de arresto. (Regla 9(a), Reglas Fed. de Proc. Crim.).

**Warranty.** Garantía.

**Waste.** Excedente, resaca.

**Watered stock.** Capital demasiado pequeño para la envergadura del objeto social. La consecuencia de esta situación es la posible responsabilidad personal y solidaria de los directivos de la empresa por las deudas sociales impagas.

**Wedlock.** Vínculo matrimonial.

**Weights and measures.** Pesas y medidas.

**Welfare.** Bienestar.

**Wharf.** Muelle.

**Wharton's rule.** Regla de Wharton. En relación con el delito de conspiración, la doctrina denominada *Wharton's Rule* establece que un acuerdo para cometer un delito que sólo puede ser realizado por la acción concertada de dos personas no constituye conspiración. (Pueblo v. Vélez Rivera, 93 D.P.R. 649 (1966)).

**White-collar crime.** Delito económico.

**Wild animal.** Animal salvaje. Un animal salvaje es uno que por costumbre no es dedicado al servicio del hombre. (Rstmnt, 2nd, Torts, sec. 506(1)).

**Whereas.** Visto lo cual.

**Wherefore premises considered.** En consideración de lo arriba expuesto. Lenguage formal con el que suele comenzarse el exordio o la súplica en un escrito.

**Wholesale.** Mayoreo, al por mayor.

**Wholly owned.** Bajo la propiedad y control total.

**Whore.** Prostituta.

**Widow.** Viuda.

**Wilfully.** Voluntariamente. A los fines del Código Penal, la palabra "*wilfully*" voluntariamente, aplicada a la intención con que se ejecuta un acto, o se incurre en una omisión, implica simplemente propósito o voluntad de cometer el acto o de incurrir en la comisión a que se refiere. (Pueblo v. Sánchez Lugo, 96 D.P.R. 491 (1968)).

**Win.** Victoria. Ganar.

**Wiretapping.** Intercepción de comunicaciones telefónicas.

**With malice aforethought.** Con premeditación.

**With notice.** Con previo aviso.

**With prejudice.** Con impedimento de plantear la misma acción nuevamente.

**Withdrawal of acceptance.** Retiro de la aceptación. La aceptación puede ser retirada siempre que la comunicación de su retiro llegue al oferente antes que la aceptación o simultáneamente con ella. (Unidroit, Prin., art. 2.10).

**Withdrawal of offer.** Retiro de la oferta. (1) La oferta surte efectos cuando le llega al destinatario. (2) Cualquier oferta, aun cuando sea irrevocable, puede ser retirada siempre que la comunicación de su retiro llegue al destinatario al mismo tiempo o antes que la oferta. (Unidroit, Prin., art. 2.3).

**Withholding performance.** Aplazamiento del cumplimiento. Cuando las partes han de cumplir simulatáneamente, cada cual puede aplazar el cumplimiento de su prestación hasta que la otra ofrezca cumplir. (Unidroit, art. 7.1.3).

**Without prejudice.** Con la facultad de intentar la misma acción nuevamente.

**Witness, calling and interrogation by court.** Testigo, llamada e interrogatorio por la corte. La corte podrá, a iniciativa propia o a petición de una parte, llamar testigos y todas las partes tendrán derecho a contrainterrogar a los testigos así llamados. (Regla 614, R. Fed. Evid.).

**Witness, conviction of a crime.** Testigo, convicción por un delito. A los fines de impugnar la credibilidad de un testigo, evidencia de que ha sido convicto de delito será admitida si ha sido obtenida del propio testigo o ha sido establecida mediante récord público durante el contrainterrogatorio. (Regla 609, R. Fed. Evid.).

**Witness, evidence of opinion and reputation.** Testigo, evidencia de opinión y reputación. La credibilidad de un testigo podrá ser impugnada o sostenida mediante evidencia en forma de opinión o reputación. (Regla 608(a), R. Fed. Evid.).

**Witness, exclusion.** Testigo, exclusión. A petición de una parte la corte ordenará la exclusion de testigos de manera que no puedan oir el testimonio de otros testigos y podrá dictar la orden por iniciativa propia. (Regla 615, R. Fed. Evid.).

**Witness, impeachment.** Testigo, impugnación. La credibilidad de un testigo podrá ser atacada por cualquier parte, inclusive la parte que lo llama. (Regla 607, R. Fed. Evid.).

**Witness, knowledge.** Testigo, conocimiento. Un testigo no podrá testificar sobre una materia a menos que se presente evidencia suficiente para sostener la determinación de que el mismo tiene conocimiento personal de la materia. (Regla 602, R. Fed. Evid.).

**Witness, oath or affirmation.** Testigo, juramento o afirmación. Antes de testificar, todo testigo será requerido para que declare que testificará la verdad, mediante juramento o afirmación prestados en forma ideada para despertar su conciencia y llevar a su mente su obligación de así hacerlo. (Regla 603, R. Fed. Evid.).

**Witness, religious belief or opinions.** Testigo, creencias u opiniones religiosas. Evidencia de creencias u opiniones de un testigo en materia de religión no será admisible a los fines de demostrar que por razón de su naturaleza su credibilidad está menoscabada o aumentada. (Regla 610, R. Fed. Evid.).

**Witness, specific instances of conduct.** Testigo, casos específicos de conducta. Casos específicos de conducta de un testigo, a los fines de impugnar o sostener su credibilidad, excepto convicción por delito cubierta por la Regla 609, (Ver *witness, conviction of a crime*) no podrá ser probada mediante evidencia extrínseca. Sin embargo, a discreción de la corte, y a los fines de probar veracidad o mendacidad, podrán investigarse en el contrainterrogatorio del testigo 1) respecto de su carácter en cuanto a veracidad o mendacidad, o 2) respecto del carácter en cuanto a veracidad o mendacidad de otro testigo respecto de cuyo carácter el testigo contrainterrogado haya declarado. (Regla 608(b), R. Fed. Evid.).

**Witnesses and expert witnesses.** Testigos y peritos. Los testigos *legos* deben (dentro de los límites de lo razonable) limitarse a enunciar *hechos*, o sea describir lo que observaron, y no dar *opiniones*. El jurado sacará sus propias conclusiones. Esta regla (que en los últimos años se ha hecho menos rígida) no se aplica a los expertos. (Intro al USA).

**Work.** Trabajo. Trabajar.

**Work product.** Teoría que proteje los documentos elaborados por el abogado de ser leídos, o de ser utilizados como prueba, por los abogados de la contraparte.

**Worker.** Trabajador, asalariado, obrero.

**Workmens' Compensation.** Ley de accidentes laborales. En la práctica se conoce también como *worker's comp*.

**Worthier title.** Teoría que acordaba un bien sucesorio al heredero más próximo entre dos herederos testamentarios cuando tal manda testamentaria era idéntica y no podía repartirse entre los dos beneficiarios. El heredero más próximo entre estos dos se reputaba con mejor derecho.

**Writ.** Auto, providencia, orden, mandamiento. Genéricamente, toda orden judicial.

**Writ of attachment.** Mandamiento de embargo.

**Writ of certiorari.** *Writ of certiorari.* En la mayor parte de los casos sólo se obtiene que la Corte revise un caso solo a través de un *writ of certiorari*, que es una orden emitida por la Corte Suprema, requiriendo del tribunal federal inferior o del tribunal estadual de ultima instancia que certifique y envíe el expediente del caso. En todos los casos el que se emita esta orden queda a discreción de la Corte. Puede acordarse ante la solicitud de una de las partes de cualquier caso que

este ante un tribunal federal de apelaciones. También puede emitirse para revisar la decisión de un tribunal estadual de ultima instancia cuando, por ejemplo, se ha impugnado una ley estadual en virtud de normas federales, o cuando se reclama un derecho asegurado por la Constitucion o por un ley federal. Pero el *certiorari* se otorga sólo por *razones especiales e importantes*, y no se considera tal el hecho de que la decisión de nivel inferior sea errónea. (Intro al USA).

**Writ of mandamus.** Orden emitida a un juez inferior, o a un funcionario ordenando que se proceda de un modo determinado.

**Writ of prohibition.** Orden de un tribunal de alzada prohibiendo al juez inferior a extender su competencia sobre un caso en particular a cuestiones que pertenecen a otro tribunal.

**Writing used to refresh memory.** Escrito para refrescar la memoria. Si un testigo utiliza un escrito para refrescar su memoria a fin de declarar, bien: 1) mientras esté declarando, o 2) antes de la declaración, si la corte en su discreción determina que es necesario en el interés de la justicia, una parte adversa tendrá derecho a que el escrito sea exhibido en la vista, a inspeccionarlo, a interrogar al testigo sobre el mismo y a presentar en evidencia aquellas porciones relacionadas con la declaración del testigo. (Regla 612, R. Fed. Evid.).

**Writings in confirmation.** Confirmación por escrito. Si un escrito que pretende constituírse en una confirmación del contrato fuere enviado dentro de un término razonable con posterioridad a su celebración y contiene estipulaciones adicionales o diferentes, estas pasarán a integrar el contrato, a menos que lo alteren sustancialmente o que el destinatario objete tal discrepancia sin demora injustificada. (Unidroit, Prin., art. 2.12).

**Written evidence.** Prueba documental, prueba escrita.

**Written law.** Derecho codificado, ley escrita.

**Written modification clauses.** Cláusulas que exigen que la modificación o extinción del contrato sea por escrito. Todo contrato escrito con cláusula que exija que toda modificación o extinción sea por escrito, no podrá ser modificado ni extinguido sino por ese medio. (Unidroit, Prin., art. 2.18).

**Wrong.** Cuasidelito, daño (s). Causar un daño (v).

**Wrongdoer.** Perpetrador de un delito civil o de un delito penal.

**Wronged party.** Parte que ha sufrido un daño.

**Wrongful act.** Acción ilegal.

**Wrongful civil proceedings.** Temeridad y malicia, abuso de proceso civil. Aquella persona que tome parte activa en la iniciación, continuación o incoación de procesos civiles contra otro, será responsable ante ese otro por un proceso civil dañoso si actúa sin mediar causa probable y con otro propósito que no es el de asegurar la justa adjudicación de la reclamación sobre la cual se basa el proceso. (Rstmnt, 2nd, Torts, sec. 674).

# X

**X-ray.** Rayo X, catódico o Roentgen (s). Radiografiar (v).

**Xenophobia.** Xenofobia, odio o antipatía hacia los extranjeros.

**Xmas.** Christmas. Navidad.

**Xylograph.** Grabado en madera.

**Xylographer.** Grabador en madera.

# Y

**Yea.** Expresión arcaica, todavía usada contemporaneamente para votar afirmativamente. Se usa particularmente para expresar un voto oral.

**Year of Our Lord.** Año del Señor.

**Yield.** Interés o rédito devengado por una inversión o por un cultivo (s). Producir, en el sentido económico (v).

**Yoke.** Yugo, opresión.

# Z

**Zeal.** Determinacion, esfuerzo, perseveración.

**Zealot.** Apasionado, exagerado, fanático, obsesivo.

**Zealous.** Activo, cuidadoso, diligente.

**Zone.** Zona, área, región.

**Zone, free trade.** Zona de libre comercio, aquélla que goza de ventajas aduaneras.

**Zoning laws.** Código de edificación. Conjunto de leyes y normas que regulan las características arquitectónicas de una zona determinada y, en especial, determinan en qué lugares pueden abrirse tiendas de acceso público.

# Table of Key Words

The following list is a guide to help the reader find a word or a concept when the reader does not have a precise idea of what he is looking for. The breakdown by subject matter allows the reader to focus in the area of interest, making it easier to find something helpful. This is just an alternative to the alphabetical search that a dictionary normally presupposes.

Only the words or expressions with an encyclopedic definition have been included. Also left out are entries so generic that they could not be placed under only one category. Consequently, the list is incomplete and many more words have been left out than have been included.

The bar (/) means that the words that follow are independent entries, but related to the word before the bar. The asterisk (*) shows that there are many entries that begin with the word(s) mentioned.

**Administrative Law (Derecho Administrativo)**
Derecho administrativo
Composición
Contencioso-
   administrativo

**Bankruptcy Law (Quiebras)**
Convenio del quebrado
Juicio universal o
   general
Quiebra*
Suspensión de pagos

**Business Law (Derecho Comercial)**
Acciones
Acto de comercio
Afianzamiento

Agentes*
Arbitraje*
Arbitro, nombramiento
Bancos*
Bolsa de comercio*
Cartas-órdenes de
   crédito
Cheques*
CIF
CIP
Comerciantes
Comisión*
Compañía(s)*
Compraventa*
Corporación,
   capacidad
Corredores de comercio
Costo en el punto de
   origen
CPT
Cuenta en participación

DAF
DDP
DDU
Derecho de los socios a
   examinar cuentas
DES
Documento negociable
Documento pagadero /
   a la orden / al
   portador
Endoso en blanco
EXW
FAS
FCA
Fiador solidario
Fianza*
FOB
Funcionarios que no
   pueden ejercer el
   comercio
Impedido

Inversión extranjera, tecnologia
Laudo no ejecutable
Letra de cambio*
Libranzas, vales y pagarés a la orden
Libro mayor
Libros comerciales*
Libros y contabilidad del comerciante
Maquiladora
Mediador
Nacionalidad*
Negociante en bienes raices, operador inmobiliario
Patente
Poder de representación*
Seguro industrial
Sistema de acumulación
Sociedad*
Valor de mercado

**Civil and Criminal Procedural Law (Derecho Procesal Civil y Penal)**
A quo
Acción*
Aclaración de sentencia
Acumulación
Admisión(es)
Amigable componedor
Amnistía
Antejuicio
Apelación*
Artículos de previo pronunciamiento

Asesores de jueces municipales
Auto de entrada y registro en domicilio particular
Auto inicial
Bajo libertad condicional
Beneficio de litigar sin gastos
Caducidad de instancia
Cédula de notificación
Citación
Comparecencia
Competencia*
Confesión*
Confiscación
Contestación*
Cooperación judicial
Correcciones disciplinarias
Cosa juzgada
Costas*
Cotejo de letras, de escritura
Declaración exculpatoria
Declinatoria
Defensa de pobres
Demanda*
Derecho a asistencia de abogado
Derecho de fondo y de forma
Derecho procesal internacional*
Desistimiento
Dictamen de peritos
Diligencia de reconocimiento
Diligenciamiento*

Dispensa de ser testigo
Documento privado / prueba / auténtico
Documento público, prueba
Duda razonable
Ejecutoria*
Ejecución de sentencias*
Ejercicio de acciones penales
Embargo
Emplazamiento
Escritos de conclusión
Evidencia circunstancial
Excepciones de previo y especial pronunciamiento
Excepciones dilatorias
Exhorto*
Extradición, Código Bustamante
*Forum non conveniens*
Generales de la ley
Guardián *ad litem*
Habilitación para comparecer en juicio
Hábito
Horas hábiles
Incidente
Incompetencia de oficio
Inferencia
Información sumaria
Informaciones para perpetuar memoria
Informe pericial
Inhibición*
Inhibitoria
Inspección ocular / personal del juez

Interdicción*
Interrogatorio bajo
custodia
Intervención adhesiva
Juicio de desahucio
Juicio ejecutivo
Juicio en rebeldía
Juicio ordinario
posterior
Juramento decisorio o
indecisorio
Jurisdicción*
Justicia gratuita
Laguna*
Lealtad y probidad
Litisconsorcio necesario
Litispendencia
Mala fe, dolo
Magistrado ponente
Mandamiento
Medidas preventivas*
Medios de prueba
Muerte del procesado
Multa penal*
Notificación*
Notificación de
demanda
Observancia de normas
procesales
Oficio
Parte*
Particular querellante
Pérdida de competencia
Perdón del ofendido
Perención
Plazos procesales
Policía judicial
Práctica profesional
prevaleciente en la
comunidad

Preguntas capciosas
Prescripción*
Presunción*
Primeras diligencias
Privilegio*
Procedimiento
criminal*
Procedimiento de
apremio
Procurador
Prórroga*
Prueba*
Publicidad de los
debates
Querella
Rebelde
Recibimiento a prueba
Reconocimiento*
Recurso*
Recusación*
Registro*
Renuncia*
Repartimiento de
negocios
Representacion de
indigentes
Resoluciones judiciales
Responsabilidad civil de
jueces y magistrados
Revisión judicial
Secuestro*
Sentencia*
Sobreseimiento*
Solución de disputas
Ss
Subasta*
Sumario
Sumisión*
Suplicatorio, exhorto,
carta-orden

Tachas de los testigos
Tasación de costas
Tercería / Terceros
Testigos*
Testimonio
Transacción
Votó en la sala y no
pudo firmar
Y/o

**Conflict of Laws
(Derecho
Internacional
Privado)**
Aplicación del derecho
extranjero
Arbitraje
Autonomia de la
voluntad, Venezuela
Código Bustamante
Competencia
internacional*
Conflicto entre
tribunales eclesiásticos
y seculares
Derecho aplicable
Derecho extranjero*
Derecho internacional
privado*
Derecho local,
aplicabilidad
Derecho penal,
aplicación territorial
Doctrina de los
contactos dominantes
Documentos extranjeros
Ejecución de sentencias
extranjeras
Ejecutoria
Exequatur

Exhorto internacional
Exhortos, Colombia
Jurisdicción extranjera
*Locus regit actum* (L),
  Argentina
No aplicabilidad del
  derecho extranjero
Prueba del derecho
  extranjero
Retroactividad de las
  leyes
Sentencias extranjeras*
Tratados de Montevideo

**Constitutional Law
(Derecho
Constitucional)**
Acción popular*
Amparo
Centralismo
Centralización ... del
  poder
Constitución
Constitucionalismo
Corte suprema*
Decreto-ley
Derechos
  constitucionales
Derechos individuales*
Estructura legal,
  México
Federalismo*
Garantías individuales
Habeas corpus
Igualdad
Libertad*
Ministerio del Interior
Régimen presidencial
Revisión judicial*
Sistema federal, México

**Contracts, Torts
(Obligaciones y
Contratos)**
Abuso de derecho
Aceptación*
Acto auténtico / bajo
  signo privado
Amenaza, fuerza o
  intimidación
Anulación parcial
Apariencia jurídica
Aplazamiento del
  cumplimiento
Apoderado constituido
Arredador y
  arrendatario
Atenuación del daño
Autorización*
Buena fe
Buena fe y lealtad
  procesal
Cambio de pretensión
Capacidad*
Caso fortuito*
Causa*
Causalidad
Censo, Código
  Bustamante
Certeza del daño
Circunstancias
  relevantes
Citación en garantía
Cláusulas*
Cobro de lo indebido
Comunicación
Confirmación*
Conflicto entre
  formularios
Confusión*
Consentimiento*

Conservación de
  artículos y bienes
Consignación en pago
Constitución en mora
Contratación con
  cláusulas estandard.
Contrato*
Contratos*
Cooperación entre las
  partes
Costumbre
Criterios para
  determinar el tipo de
  obligación
Cuasicontrato
Cuasicontratos, Chile
Cuasidelito
Cuasidelitos, Chile
Culpa*
Cumplimiento*
Custodia de una cosa
Dación en pago
Daño / daños*
Deber de
  confidencialidad
Defecto o vicios ocultos,
  jurídicos y de hecho
Delegación de
  cumplimiento
Demora en el pago del
  precio
Depositario
Depósito*
DEQ
Derecho de retracto
Derecho litigioso
Derechos y acciones por
  incumplimiento
Desproporción excesiva
Determinación*

Discrepancias
idiomáticas
Disolución contractual
Dolo
Donación*
Efecto retroactivo de la
anulación
Efecto vinculante del
contrato
Enriquecimiento
ilegítimo
Enriquecimiento
indebido, sin causa
Error*
Error sobre la causa
Estipulaciones
sorpresivas
Evicción en
saneamiento
Evitar el abuso de
derecho
Excesiva onerosidad*
Fondos suficientes
Fraude
Frutos*
Fuerza
Fuerza mayor
Garantía adecuada de
mantenimiento
Gestión de negocios
ajenos
Imposibilidad de
cumplimiento
Imprudente
Imputación de pago
Incumplimiento*
Indemnización*
Integración del
contrato
Intención de las partes

Intereses*
Interferencia de la otra
parte
Interpretación*
Juego y apuesta
Lesión*
Libertad de
contratación
Lucro cesante*
Lugar de cumplimiento
Mandato*
Modo de aceptación
Moneda*
Mora
Negociaciones con mala
fe
Negocio jurídico
disimulado
Normas imperativas
Novación*
Nulidad*
Obligación de resultados
y de medios
Obligación(es)*
Oferta*
Opción de compra
Oportunidad de
cumplimiento
Pago*
Pena judicial
Pérdida*
Permuta*
Persona interpuesta*
Plazo adicional para el
cumplimiento
Préstamo*
Preveer / Previsibilidad /
Previsión
Previsibilidad del daño
Principio de legalidad

Prueba del daño en caso
de una operación
sucedanea
Purga del
incumplimiento
Ratificación
Recepción de la
revocación, rechazo o
aceptación
Rechazo de la oferta
Reembolso de gastos
médicos
Remisión de deuda
Renta vitalicia
Renuncia*
Reparación integral
Rescisión
Responsabilidad*
Restituciones
Retiro de la aceptación /
oferta
Retracto*
Revocación*
Revocación de la
oferta
Saneamiento*
Secuencia en el
cumplimiento
Seña, anticipo
Simulación*
Solicitud de
autorización pública
Subrogación*
Tanteo y retracto
Tercero beneficiado
Terminación*
Tiempo de la aceptación
Todo daño debe
indemnizarse
Transacción

Transacciones
   fraudulentas
Transferencia de
   créditos no endosables
Transmisión de créditos
   y demás derechos
   incorporales
Usos y prácticas
Vicio oculto
Vicios*
Violencia
Violencia, intimidación*
Voluntad /
   voluntariedad

**Criminal Law
(Derecho Penal)**
Apropiación temporaria
Autor de un delito
Auxilio necesario o
   indispensable
Careo de testigos y
   procesados
Coacción
Códigos penales
Comiso de instrumentos
   delictivos
Cómplice
Comunicabilidad de
   circunstancias
Concurso*
Condena*
Conversión de sanciones
   penales
Convicto
Cuerpo del delito
Culpa*
Culpabilidad
Defensa propia
Delincuente*

Delito(s)*
Denuncia*
Depravación moral
Derecho de defensa
   penal
Derecho penal,
   aplicación*
Detención
Dolo
Entrada y registro
Entrampamiento
Error invencible
Error no punible
Error punible
Extradición
Fianza
Hacer funcionar un
   vehículo
Hecho falso
Imputabilidad*
Identificación del
   cuerpo
Indulto
Inhabilitación*
Inmoralidad
Internación
Intimación,
   quebrantamiento
Justificación*
Libertad*
Malicia*
Medidas de seguridad*
Muerte violenta
Negligencia criminal
Obediencia debida
Palo, garrote
Pena(s)*
Prevención de un mal
   mayor
Prisión*

Quiebra fraudulenta
Rehabilitación*
Reparación por
   delitos*
Tentativa
Vigilancia,
   quebrantamiento

**Environmental Law
(Derecho Ambiental)**
Agua*
Contaminante*
Desequilibrio ecológico
Emergencia ecológica
Equilibrio ecológico
Fauna silvestre
Flora silvestre
Legislación
Material peligroso
Residuos peligrosos
Sustancia*
Tierras mojadas

**Family Law (Derecho
de Familia)**
Acción negatoria de
   paternidad
Acta de defunción
Acuerdo pre-nupcial
Adopción*
Alimentos*
Ausencia
Ausente
Compañero/a de vida
Curador*
Deber de alimentos
Deberes filiales
División de bienes
   matrimoniales
Divorcio*

Donación matrimonial
Donaciones
   matrimoniales
Dote
Emancipación*
Estado civil,
   modificación
Fallecimiento,
   notificación
Familia
Gananciales
Guardián *ad litem*
Habilitación para
   comparecer en juicio
Hijos*
Impedimentos
   matrimoniales,
   extranjeros
Legitimación*
Legitimidad, presunción
Matrimonio*
Nacimiento, declaración
Nuevo matrimonio
Niño*
Parentesco*
Patria potestad
Pérdida de la patria
   potestad
Porción marital
Presunción de
   paternidad
Recién nacido
   abandonado
Reconocimiento de
   progenitura
Régimen de separación
   de bienes
Régimen matrimonial
Registro civil
Separación de bienes

Sociedad de ganancials
Tutela*
Tutor

**International Law
(Derecho
Internacional)**
Organización de Estados
   Americanos (OEA)
Derecho penal,
   aplicación territorial
Nacionalidad*

**Introduction to Law
(Introducción al
Derecho)**
Codificación / código
   comercial*
Código civil*
Código Civil, México
Códigos, México
Códigos procesales,
   México
Derecho civil, derecho
   romano
Derecho de fondo y de
   forma
Derogación de leyes
Derogación por revisión
Días hábiles
Disponiéndose
Doctrina, México
Domicilio*
Edificio
Escribano
Estudiantes de derecho
Formalismo
Fuentes de derecho
Interpretación de
   normas procesales

Juez de Registro Civil
Legalismo
Ley*
Mayoría de edad
Notario público
Paternalismo
Personalidad*
Personas*
Personas jurídicas*
Profesores de derecho
Programa de estudios
Publicación de casos,
   México
Publicación de leyes,
   México
Tácito

**Labor Law (Derecho
del Trabajo)**
Abandono de servicio
Accidente*
Aguinaldo
Ajustes por
   modernización
Aplicación de leyes
   laborales
Asociación sindical
   voluntaria
Códigos laborales
Condiciones de trabajo
Contrato*
Derecho colectivo*
Derecho laboral*
Derecho laboral federal
Derechos laborales
   mínimos
Descanso
Despido ilegal
Disputas de trabajo
Embarazo ...

Empleado permanente /
 probatorio
Empresa
En curso del empleo
En ocasión del trabajo,
 como consecuencia
 del empleo
Grupos empresarios
Horas extra
Huelga*
Incapacidad total
Intermediario
Invenciones de los
 trabajadores
Jornada*
Juicios civiles
Labor
Ley federal del trabajo
Locación de servicios
Medidas disciplinarias
Participación en las
 ganancias
Patrón*
Reglamento interior ...
Relación de trabajo
Renuncia*
Rescisión / causa
 justificada
Responsabilidad
 patronal
Riesgo*
Riesgos de trabajo
Salario
Seguridad*
Servicio doméstico
Sindicato*
Sirvientes domésticos
Supervisación laboral
Suspensión*
Terminación ...

Tiempo indeterminado
Trabajador*
Trabajadores, atención
 médica
Trabajo*
Vacaciones

## Legal History (Historia del Derecho)

Alfonso el Sabio
Burocracia colonial
Codificación visigótica
Codificaciones
 latinoamericanas
Consejo de Indias
Derecho colonial,
 compilaciones
Derecho español,
 orígenes
Derecho portugés,
 desarrollo
Derecho procesal,
 orígenes
Derecho romano,
 influencia
Fuero juzgo
Idealismo y religión
Leyes de Toro
Nueva Recopilación de
 las Leyes de España
Ordenamiento de
 Alcalá
Virreinatos

## Maritime Law (Derecho Marítimo)

Abordaje
Arribada forzosa
Avería*

Buques*
Echazón
Naufragio
Navegación a flote
 común o a tercio
Naves, nacionalidad
Préstamo a la gruesa o
 préstamo a riesgo
 marítimo
Recalar
Sobrecargos
Zona marítimo-terrestre

## Probate (Sucesiones)

Abintestato
Albacea(zgo)
Colación*
Curador*
Deducción
 hereditaria
Desheredación*
Disposición inoficiosa
Disposición
 testamentaria
Documento de la
 sucesión hereditaria,
 registro
Heredero y legatario
Herencia*
Indignidad*
Interpretación de
 testamentos
Juicio universal o
 general
Legado*
Legítima, porción
 legítima
Mandas y legados
Obligación
 hereditable

Partición hereditaria
Porción marital
Representación
  hereditaria
Revocación por
  testamento posterior
Sucesión*
Sucesor(es)*
Término de deliberación
Testamentaría
Testamento*
Tutela testamentaria

**Property Law
(Derechos Reales)**
A non domino
Accesión*
Aguas*
Aluvión
Anticresis
Apropiación por el
  gobierno
Asiento
Bienes*
Calificación de
  documentos
Censo*
Comodato*
Comunidad de bienes
Copropiedad
Cosa(s)*
Derecho de superficie
Derecho de uso
Derecho hipotecario
Deslinde y
  amojonamiento
División de la cosa
  común
Doble inmatriculación

Dominio público de la
  nación y dominio
  particular del estado
Edificios ruinosos y
  árboles que amenazan
  ruina
Enajenación de un
  inmueble
Error de concepto
Estado de buena fe
  civil
Expropiación
Habitación
Hipoteca*
Hipoteca y prenda
Inmatriculación por el
  estado
Inmuebles*
Inscripción*
Interdicto*
Juicio de desahucio
Marisma
Matrimonio*
Mejoras*
Mención
Muebles*
Negociante en bienes
  raices, operador
  inmobiliario
Nota marginal
Notario público
Obligación real*
Ocupación*
Patrimonio familiar
Porción marital
Poseedor de buena fe
Posesión*
Prenda
Prescripción*

Prescripción positiva
Presunción de
  propiedad sobre
  muebles
Privilegio*
Propiedad*
Quasi posesión
Rectificación de cabida
Régimen de separación
  de bienes
Régimen matrimonial
Registro*
Renuncia*
Reserva de prioridad
Segregación
Separación de bienes
Servidumbre*
Signo aparente
Sociedad de ganancials
Tercer hipotecario
Título(s)*
Tradición*
Uso*
Usufructo*
Vicios de la posesión

**Rural and Mining
Law (Derecho
Agrario y Minero)**
Beneficio, minería
Cartografía minera
Concesión minera
Derecho minero*
Derechos mineros
Ejido*
Exploración
Hacienda
Minería*
Unidad minera

# Tabla de Palabras Clave

La siguiente lista se brindan como simple guía para ayudar al lector a ubicar una palabra o concepto cuando no tenga idea precisa de lo que está buscando. Habiéndose dividido la lista por materia, puede el lector revisar las palabras bajo el título de su interés y encontrar algo que le ayude. Se trata simplemente de brindar una alternativa a la búsqueda alfabética que un diccionario normalmente presupone.

Solamente se han incluido palabras o expresiones con definiciones de tipo enciclopédico. También se han dejado fuera aquellas voces tan genéricas que no podían incluirse en sólo una de las clasificaciones. Por ello, la lista es incompleta y son muchas más las palabras no incorporadas a ella que las que se han incluído.

La barra (/) significa que las palabras que siguen forman entradas independientes, pero relacionadas con la primer palabra antes de la barra. El asterisco (*) indica que existen varias frases que comienzan con la palabra o palabras mencionadas.

## Derecho (Law)
Accredited law school
Attorney*
Bachelor
Bar
Boilerplate
Case*
Cases*
Chief justice
Civil law
Common law
Continuing legal
    education
Federal judge
Federal law reporting
Holding and dictum
Judge*

Law*
Law professor
Law reviews
Notary
Partner in a law firm
Precedent*
Public and private law
Restatement of the Law
Secondary authority

## Derecho Administrativo (Administrative Law)
Administrative law*
Administrative
    regulations
Capehart project

Executive orders
Federal tax
IRS, Internal Revenue
    Service
Municipal law
Zoning laws

## Derecho Comercial (Business Law)
Acceptance of a draft
Accommodation maker
    / paper / part
Account debtor / stated
Act of bankruptcy
Administrative law*
Administrative
    regulations

Antitrust legislation
Bank*
Bill of lading
Binder
Bonded warehouses
Bulk sales / transfers
Business enterprises
Business law
Buyer in ordinary
  course of business
Bylaws
C. & F.
C.I.F.
C.I.P.
C.P.T.
Cash basis system
Casualty insurance
Certificate of
  incorporation
Certified security
Chattel paper
Claims adjustor
Commercial paper*
Confirming bank
Conspicuous
Corporate duty
Corporate stock
Corporations*
Course of dealing and
  usage of trade
Cover
Credit union
Cumulative voting
Customer's right to stop
  payment
D.A.F.
D.D.P.
D.D.U.
D.E.Q.
D.E.S.

Declaration of
  dividends
Definite time to pay a
  commercial paper
Deposit certificate
Derivative action
Derivatory action by
  shareholders
Disability insurance
Dishonor of a
  commercial paper
Document of title
E.X.W.
Executive orders
F.A.S.
F.C.A.
F.O.B.
Federal tax
Financing agency
Foreign banks
Fungible
General agent
Goods
Guaranty
Holder in due course
Impairment of recourse
  or of collateral
Indorsement, especial
  and in blank
Insider trading
Insolvent
Insurance*
Investment securities
IRS, Internal Revenue
  Service
Letters of credit,
  Uniform Commercial
  Code
Lien creditor
Life insurance

Lost, destroyed or stolen
  instruments
Lost or destroyed stock
  certificates
Marine and
  transportation
  insurance
Municipal law
No arrival, no sale
No par value stock
Notation credit
Omnibus clause
Partially disclosed
  principal
Partly paid shares
Payable to bearer
Payable to order
Peddler
Person in the position of
  a seller
Piercing the corporate
  veil
Presentment*
Private offering
Property insurance
Protest
Reasonable time,
  reasonably
Reserve funds
Restrictive
  endorsement
Right to adequate
  assurances of
  performance
Risk of loss in the
  absence of breach
Sale*
Savings account
Secured party
Secured transactions

Security interest
Send
Shipment by seller
Signature of a
  commercial paper
Single interest
  endorsement
Special agent
Stock certificates
Stock ledger
Subagent
Sum certain
Surety insurance
Termination
Time of presentment
  of a commercial
  paper
Title insurance
Tying arrangement
Uniform Commercial
  Code*
Value, for value
Vehicle insurance
Voting rights of
  shareholders
Voting trust
Warehouse receipt
Zoning laws

**Derecho
Constitucional
(Constitutional Law)**
Bill of attainder
Bill of Rights
Commercial clause
Congress
Constitution*
Constitutional law /
  review
Due process

Expectations of privacy
  constitutionally
  justifiable
Fifth Amendment
Freedom of speech
Full faith and credit
Judicial review
*Marbury v. Madison*
Privileges and
  immunities
Right to legal counsel
Tucker Act

**Derecho Contractual
(Contract law)**
Acceptance by silence
Acceptance of an offer
Acceptance of goods
Acceptance within a
  fixed period of time
Accord and satisfaction
Act of God
Additional period for
  performance
Adequate assurance of
  due performance
Agency*
Agreed payment for
  non-performance
Agreement*
Alternative*
Anticipatory*
Anticipatory non-
  performance
Apparent authority
Application for public
  permission
Assignment*
Authority*
Bargain

Battle of forms
Bearing the risk of
  mistake
Binding character of a
  contract
Breach*
Capacity to contract
Certainty of harm
Change of remedy
Concealment
Condition
Confirmation
Consent
Consideration*
*Contra proferente* rule
Contract*
Contract law*
Contract(s)*
Contracting under
  standard terms
Contractual*
Cooperation between
  parties
Costs of performance
Counter-offer
Cure by non-performing
  party
Currency*
Damages*
Delegation of duty
Determination ... duty /
  quality of
  performance
Duress by physical
  compulsion
Duty of confidentiality
Duty to achieve a
  specific result and
  duty of best efforts
Earlier performance

483

Time of acceptance
Time of performance
Uncertain damages
Unconscionable contract
Usage of trade
Usages and practices
Withdrawal of offer /
    Acceptance
Withholding
    performance
Writings in
    confirmation
Written modification
    clauses

**Derecho de Familia
(Family Law)**
Adoption by estoppel
Alienation of spouse's
    affection
Alimony
Divorce*
Marital deduction
Marriage

**Derecho del Trabajo
(Labor Law)**
Arising out and in the
    course of employment
Black list to prevent
    employment
Collateral negligence
Conduct within scope of
    employment
Discrimination*
Dual purpose rule
Extra hours
Fellow servant*
Going and coming
    rule

Home worker
Independent contractor
Just cause for discharge
Labor contract
Labor dispute
Labor law*
Liability of independent
    contractor's employer
Master
Mechanic's lien
Miller Act
Non-delegable duties of
    master
Occupational safety and
    health standard
Rule of proximity
Scope of employment
Subservant
Threatened strike
Trade union
    membership
Travelling agent
Unfair labor practice*

**Derecho
Internacional
(International Law)**
Treaties

**Derecho
Internacional
Privado (Conflict of
Laws)**
Applicable law*
Characterization
Choice of law*
Conflict of laws
Contractual choice of
    law
Domicile(e)*

Enforcement of foreign
    judgments
Foreign law,
    determination
*Forum non conveniens*
Full faith and credit
Government interest
    doctrine
Home
Jurisdictional grounds
Recognition of foreign
    nation judgments
Renvoi
Service in a foreign
    country
Special appearance
Valid judgment
    requirements

**Derecho Penal
(Criminal Law)**
Accessory after the fact
Accessory before the
    fact
Accomplice / liability
Accusatory procedure
Attempt
Clear and present
    danger
Complicity
Confinement as
    protective force
Consent
Conspiracy
Cooling period
Correction of sentence
    for changed
    conditions
Crime, punishment
Criminal forfeiture

Criminal law
De minimis infractions
Deadly force
Double jeopardy
Duress
Dwelling
Entrapment
Felony
Ignorance or mistake
Instruments of crime
Intent to kill a fellow
creature
Involuntary
manslaughter
Kickback
Maim, disfigure or
disable a member of
the human body
Manslaughter
Mayhem
McNaghten rest
Mental disease
Military orders
Misdemeanor
Model Penal Code*
Murder
Offense
Overt act
Participant-informer
Petty misdemeanor
Police custody
Premeditated design
Prosecution
Provocation of the
accused of murder by
the deceased
Solicitation
Unlawful force
Wharton's rule
Wilfully

**Derecho Procesal,
Civil y Penal
(Procedural Law,
Civil and Criminal)**
Abstention doctrine
Abuse of process
Act of State
Action for negligence
Action in rem / quasi in
rem
Action to quiet title
Admissions*
Adversary process
Advisory jury and trial
by consent
Advisory opinion
Affidavit*
Affirmation in lieu of
oath
Affirmative action /
defenses
Agreed judgment /
statement of appeal
Allocution
Alternate jurors
Amendments*
Appeal
Appellate procedure
Argumentative
question
Arraignment
Arrest*
Attachment
Authentication or
identification of
evidence
Bases for judicial
jurisdiction over
individuals
Best evidence rule

Capacity to sue or be
sued
Changed conditions as
grounds to modify a
judgment
Character evidence
Choate lien doctrine
Civil and Criminal
Civil docket
Civil judgment and
orders
Claim for relief
Claims court
Class action*
Clean hands
Closed hearing
Closing argument
Collateral estoppel*
Collateral impediment
Complaint
Concurrent jurisdiction
Conditional plea
Consolidation*
Compulsory
counterclaim
Costs
Counterclaim*
Court of appeals for the
circuit
Criminal proceeding
Cross-claim against co-
party
Cross-examination
Default*
Defendant's prior record
Defense in law or in fact
Defense of alibi
Defense of insanity
Defenses and denials
Deposition*

Poll of jury
Pre-trial discovery
Preponderance of the
evidence
Presumptions in civil
proceedings
Pretrial conference*
Pretrial motions
Pretrial order
Probable cause*
Proceeding against
sureties
Process in behalf of and
against persons not
parties
Process of posting
Production of
documents and things
Proof*
Protective order
Real party in interest
Relevant evidence*
Relief from judgment*
Remainder of related
writings or recorded
statements
Remittitur
Representation in
criminal cases
Res judicata
Return
Right to assign counsel
Sealed indictment
Sealed records
Search and seizure
Search warrant
Seizure of person or
property
Self-authentication
Self-incrimination

Separate trials
Sequestered jury
Service of pleadings and
other papers
Special appearance
Special verdict
State courts
Stay of execution*
Stenographic transcript
Subject-matter
jurisdiction
Subpoena*
Substitution of parties*
Summary judgment*
Summons*
Supersedeas bond
Supreme court*
Sureties, justification
Taking of testimony
Temporary restraining
order
Third party practice
Trial by the court
Valid judgment
requisites
Verdict
Voir dire
Voluntary dismissal
Witness*
Witnesses and expert
witnesses
Writ*
Writing used to refresh
memory
Yeoman

**Derecho Sucesorio
(Probate Law)**
Abintestato
Exoneration of liens

Facts of independent
significance
Living will
Muniment of title
Nonprobate assets
Pretermitted*
Surplusage rule

**Derechos Reales
(Property Law)**
Passing of title
Possession*
Riparian land
Schmutz formula
Vesting of title

**Cuasidelitos (Torts)**
Abnormally dangerous
activities
Absolute liability
Activities dangerous to
invitees
Activities dangerous
to known
trespassers
Activities dangerous to
licensees
Appropriation of name
and likeness
Assault*
Assumption of risk
Battery*
Causation, legal cause
Chattel dangerous for
intended use
Civil liability
Comparative fault
Consent for a tort
Contributing
tortfeasors

Marshall, John
Story, Joseph

**Teoría Jurídica
(Legal Theory)**
Civil law
Common law

Equity
Federal system of the
USA
Law of the case
Notary public
Restatements
Trust*

Trustees or receivers for
dissolved corporations